W9-ADT-583
New York, N. Y. 10027

A SURVEY OF BUDDHISM

Bhikshu Sangharakshita
(Maha Sthavira)

WITHDRAWN

1980
Shambhala • Boulder
IN ASSOCIATION WITH
Windhorse • London

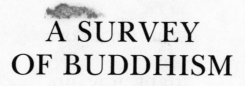

Burgess
BQ
4012
.S26
1980

TO
THE MEMORY OF

c 1

SHRI B. P. WADIA
('SHRAVAKA')
PHILOSOPHER AND PHILANTHROPIST

Shambhala Publications, Inc.
1123 Spruce Street
Boulder, Colorado 80302
IN ASSOCIATION WITH
Windhorse Publications
51 Roman Road
London E2 OHU, England

First Edition 1957
Second Edition 1959
Third Edition 1966
Fourth Edition 1976
Fifth Edition, totally reset and revised 1980

© 1957, 1980 Bhikshu Sangharakshita
All rights reserved

Distributed in the United States by Random House
and in Canada by Random House of Canada, Ltd.
Printed in the United States of America

LIBRARY OF CONGRESS CATALOGING IN PUBLICATION DATA
Sangharakshita, Bhikshu, 1925–
A survey of Buddhism.
Bibliography: p.
Includes index.
1. Buddhism I. Title.
BQ4012.S26 294.3 79-2149
ISBN 0-87773-168-3
ISBN 0-394-73732-6 (Random House)

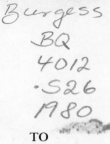

IW
1982 MAR 10

CONTENTS

PREFACE TO THE FIRST AMERICAN EDITION

The lectures on which this book is based were given at Bangalore, South India, in the summer of 1954, and published early in 1957. At that time I was living at Kalimpong, in the eastern Himalayas, where I had settled in 1950 after spending two years as a wandering ascetic and a year with my teacher in Benares. When I was invited to give the lectures I had been a Buddhist for thirteen years and a monk (i.e. *śrāmaṇera* and *bhikṣu*) for five. The giving of the lectures, and the subsequent preparation of them for publication in book form, gave me the opportunity of standing back and taking a look at the great spiritual tradition to which I had committed myself, and of trying to sum up, for my own benefit as much as for that of other people, what I had learned about Buddhism in the course of my thirteen years as a Buddhist and how, at the end of that time, I saw the Buddha's Teaching. It gave me the opportunity, in other words, of finding out what I really thought of Buddhism—what Buddhism really meant to me. The opportunity was all the more valuable in that the audience at my lectures consisted, for the most part, of Western-educated Indians who, while they were not Buddhists, nevertheless took a definite interest in what was for them part of the cultural and spiritual tradition of India, and who therefore heard what I had to say with sympathy and understanding but, at the same time, not uncritically.

In taking my look at Buddhism, I was concerned to do principally two things. I was concerned to see Buddhism in its full *breadth* and in its ultimate *depth,* that is to say, I was concerned (1) to see Buddhism as a whole and (2) to see it in its deeper interconnections both within itself and in relation to the spiritual life of the individual Buddhist. Since I was concerned to see Buddhism in its full breadth, I sought to give as comprehensive an account of it as I could, an account which would do justice to all its principal teachings and all its major historical forms, and it was for this very reason that both the lectures and the resultant book were entitled a "Survey" of Buddhism. A survey, however, does not consist in the enumeration of isolated and unconnected phenomena, however complete that enumeration may be. It was not enough, therefore, for me to do justice to all the principal teachings of Buddhism and all its major historical forms, in the comparatively superficial sense of describing them all one by one as though they existed on their own, separate from Buddhism as a whole. If I wanted really to do justice to them I had to show that they were all interconnected, which meant exploring their common basic principles, and show what bearing they had on the spiritual life of the individual, for the sake of which, after all, Buddhism had originally been promulgated. I was therefore concerned to see Buddhism not only in its full breadth but also in its depth. Indeed, I discovered that I could not see it in its breadth without seeing it in its depth. As I proceeded with my task, moreover, it dawned on me that many Western scholars of Buddhism, and even some Eastern Buddhist monks, were unable to see Buddhism either in its breadth or in its depth, and that the accounts they gave of it were therefore fragmentary, distorted, and often completely misleading. Not once, apparently, did some of them ever ask themselves: "Why did the Buddha (or Nāgārjuna, or Buddhaghosa) teach this particular doctrine? What bearing does it have on the spiritual life? How does it help the individual Buddhist actually to follow the spiritual Path?" Yet as I took my look at Buddhism, trying to see it in its breadth and in its depth, I found myself asking such questions again and again, for only in this way, I found, could I make sense—spiritual sense—of Buddhism. Without such questions freely asked, and faithfully answered, the Buddha's Teaching seemed only a sort of intellectual game, whether it was played by Western academics or 'scholarly' Eastern monks. Perhaps it was because I looked at Buddhism in the way I did, trying to see it in its breadth and its depth, and trying to relate it to the needs of the individual as he wrestled with the problems of existence. Perhaps it was because I took Buddhism *seriously*, that my "Survey," both when given as lectures and when published in book form, met with such an enthusiastic reception, and why during the twenty-one more years that have passed since its first appearance the demand for the book has steadily increased.

Be that as it may, twenty-one years *have* passed. I have had twenty-one more years in which to learn about Buddhism and reflect on what I learned, and it therefore seems appropriate that on the occasion of the appearance of this edition I should take a backward look over the intervening period and survey the "Survey." Reading it through from cover to cover for the first time in many years I find no reason to change my approach or method of treatment or to look at Buddhism in any other way than I did then. Indeed, since some of the major historical forms of Buddhism have become more easily accessible since I wrote, at least so far as Western Europe and North America are concerned, and since prominence is often given to what is distinctive in their doctrines and methods rather than to the fundamental principles and practices common to all Buddhist spiritual traditions, it becomes more necessary than ever that we should be concerned to see Buddhism in its full breadth and, therefore, in its ultimate depth. It becomes more necessary than ever that we should not mistake a particular historical manifestation of Buddhism for Buddhism and, thus, fail really to see Buddhism at all. For the same reason, it becomes more necessary than ever that we should see the Buddha's Teaching in terms of its bearing on the actual living of a life effectively committed to the Three Jewels instead of allowing ourselves either to be dazzled by the splendour of the "exotic" oriental cultural trappings arrayed in which the living body of the Dharma inevitably confronts our gaze, or to be distracted by considerations of a purely theoretical nature—or both. Indeed, if the living flame of spiritual aspiration is not to be completely smothered beneath the ever-growing accumulation of information "about" Buddhism now being heaped upon it from all sides, we shall have to insist that, if the flame is to be fed rather than smothered it must be kept supplied with fuel which it can actually *burn*—fuel with the help of which it can leap up in a great world-consuming blaze. This may well mean discriminating between what is essential and what is not essential—what is living and what is dead—in the extant Buddhist teachings and traditions much more rigorously than was done in the "Survey." It may well mean refusing to recognize as really Buddhism anything that cannot be directly related to the unique, ever-continuing act of going for refuge.

Though on looking back and surveying the "Survey" I find no reason to change my approach to Buddhism or my method of treatment, even in matters of detail, this is not to say that this work of twenty-one years ago does not have limitations. Most of these were due either to lack of space (the MS delivered to the publishers was in any case between five and six times longer than contracted for), or to my own lack of experience in certain areas of the enormous field the book covers. It was owing to lack of space that I could touch upon some of the most important teachings, for example, and some of the most prominent schools, only in the briefest manner, sometimes giving no more than an indication of the place they occupy within the general framework of the Doctrine or the process of the historical development of Buddhism. Some of these teachings or schools were dealt with more fully later on in other writings and lectures. The series of twelve "positive" nidanas, from Suffering (*dukkha*) to Knowledge of the Destruction of the Biases (*āsavakkhayañāṇa*), for instance, which between them exemplify the rationale of the "spiral" Path and, therefore, of the spiritual life itself, which I only enumerated in the "Survey" Chapter I, Section XIV, without going into detail, were dealt with at length in *The Three Jewels* (London, 1967) Part I, Chapter 13, "The Stages of the Path." Similarly, the Noble Eightfold Path (*āryāṣṭāṅga-mārgaḥ*), mentioned simply in passing in the "Survey," was the subject of a series of eight (tape-recorded) lectures delivered in London in 1968 in which I was concerned to make clear the distinction between the mundane and the transcendental Eightfold Path, particularly that between "Right Understanding" and "Perfect Vision." As with the teachings, so with the schools. Zen or Ch'an Buddhism, about which the "Survey" says little more than that it was paradoxical in character and connected with the Yogācāra School, was in 1965 the subject of five lectures subsequently brought out in book form as *The Essence of Zen* (London, 1973), while Tibetan Buddhism was the subject of a series of eight (tape-recorded) lectures delivered in London in 1965/6 and again in 1968. Aspects of the Bodhisattva Ideal not dealt with in the "Survey" Chapter IV were later discussed in *The Endlessly Fascinating Cry* (London, 1977), an Exploration of the *Bodhicaryavatara* of Santideva, the edited transcript of a seminar held in Norfolk in 1973. All these writings and lectures, besides many others, were not only based on, or grew naturally out of, the fundamental principles adumbrated in the "Survey," but also served to confirm the validity of the approach to Buddhism adopted in that work.

My lack of experience in certain areas of Buddhism, the other source of the "Survey's" limitations, was reflected principally in my comments on the New Burman Satipatthana Method and on the Nyingma School of Tibetan Buddhism. At the time of writing the "Survey" I was acquainted with the New Burman Satipatthana Method—which has since sought to limit the term Vipassana, or Vipassana Meditation, exclusively to its own techniques—only at second and third hand, and being glad to hear of the revival of any form of meditation in Theravada lands I therefore praised the new method unreservedly. Subsequent investigation revealed, however, that it was not without its dangers. As taught by some teachers, at least, and as practised by some pupils, it could lead to extreme nervous tension and to a schizoid state for which I coined the term "alienated awareness." On my return to England in 1964 I met twelve or fourteen people who were suffering from severe mental disturbance as a direct result of practising the so-called "Vipassana Meditation." Four or five others had had to be confined to mental hospitals. My remarks in Chapter I, Section XVII, should not, therefore, be taken as an unqualified endorsement of the New Burman Satipatthana Method. If I overestimated the New Burman Satipatthana Method, I underestimated the Nyingma or "Old Style" School of Tibetan Buddhism—and for much the same kind of reason. Until 1957 there were no Nyingma Lamas in Kalimpong. In the absence of personal contact with qualified representatives of the Nyingma School I had to gather what information I could from my Tibetan friends, and since most of them belonged to the Gelug School I tended to see the Nyingma School through Gelug eyes. Later on, eminent Nyingma Lamas having settled in the Kalimpong area, I had the good fortune to be initiated into the Nyingma tradition, and was thus able to study it at first hand. What is said about the Nyingma School in Chapter III, Section IX, is not incorrect (though Nyingma scholars might not agree that the earlier Tibetan translations of the Tantras were "imperfect"), but if I was to write about it now I would be able to do so from the inside, as it were, and would do greater justice to the profundity of its teachings and its tremendous spiritual vitality.

Though the "Survey" was widely reviewed on its first appearance, my lack of experience in two areas referred to went unnoticed, and among the favourable reviews and friendly letters that arrived at my hermitage in Kalimpong from many parts of the world there were only two criticisms. Both of these came from English Buddhists, one an adherent of Zen Buddhism, the other a universalist of the Guenon school with Tibetan Buddhist affiliations. The first took me to task in a review for my "dogmatism" in referring to the observance of celibacy as "that indispensable prerequisite to any form of higher spiritual life;" the other remonstrated with me by letter on the "harshness" of my strictures on monastic formalism within the modern Theravada. Whether their remarks were justified or not, both critics were singling out for comment matters of vital importance to the development of Western Buddhism. As I was to discover on my return to England, sex is a highly controversial—even highly emotive—subject, and though I would not disagree with my original statement about the importance of celibacy (i.e. chastity) in the higher spiritual life, the matter is perhaps not quite so straightforward as I then thought. By way of clarification I would therefore like to make the following points: (1) Abstention from sex does not, in itself, constitute spiritual progress; (2) Emotional dependence on one's sexual partner is a far greater hindrance to the spiritual life than the sexual relationship as such; (3) Even a "healthy" sexual impulse (i.e. one not associated with emotional dependence on one's sexual partner) pertains to a relatively lower level of consciousness and therefore tends to diminish in intensity as one becomes more firmly established in higher levels of consciousness. Monastic formalism proved to be a less controversial subject. Far from remonstrating with me on the "harshness" of my strictures, on the first appearance of the "Survey" some of the more thoughtful Theravādin bhikkhus not only welcomed the book but privately congratulated me on my outspokenness. "We dare not speak the truth about these matters," they said. "You are in a position to do so." Reading through these strictures twenty-one years later I find them milder than I had thought they were and, though severe enough, not unreasonably so. In the light of subsequent experience I am convinced that my criticisms of the modern Theravada were—and still are—not only fully justified but absolutely necessary, and I do not retract a word of what I wrote. I would only like to add that, far from being confined to the modern Theravada, the canker of formalism can sometimes be found in other forms of Buddhism too, not least in contemporary Zen.

In preparing this edition of the "Survey" for the press I have gone through the entire work with a view to making the extensive revisions which, I thought, would almost certainly be required. No changes of any significance have, in the event, been found necessary, and the text is substantially the same as that of previous editions—though I have taken the opportunity of making a number of minor improvements, as well as correcting a few mistakes that had crept into the printing of the fourth (1976) edition. The biggest difference between this and other editions of the "Survey" is the lengthy Introduction that has now been added. Written in 1964, on the eve of my departure from India, and not previously printed, it represents a higher degree of generality in the treatment of Buddhism than it was possible to attain in the "Survey" and gives as it were a bird's eye view of the whole subject. It also takes the historical dimension more into account than does the "Survey," the main emphasis of which is doctrinal and spiritual, and besides including a short biography of the Buddha and a summary of the canonical literature, gives a conspectus of the three main phases in the historical development of Buddhism, i.e. the Hīnayāna, the Mahāyāna, and the Vajrayāna. In preparing this edition I have also brought the Select Bibliography up to date, which I hope will make the work more useful to serious students.

SANGHARAKSHITA

Surlingham,
Norfolk.
December 27th 1978

NOTE ON TRANSLITERATION

On their first appearance in the text, Pali and Sanskrit technical terms and proper names are provided with their full equipment of diacritical marks. Later on, these are generally dropped, especially in the case of such words as may be expected to become part of the English language. A few words such as Nirvana, which have already been naturalized, appear without diacritical marks throughout.

PREFACE TO THE THIRD EDITION

Early in 1954 Shri B. P. Wadia and Shrimati Sophia Wadia invited me to deliver a series of lectures on Buddhism at the Indian Institute of World Culture, Bangalore. So great was the interest excited by these lectures, which I delivered in July of the same year, that Shri Wadia asked me to write them out for publication in book form, stipulating that the work should not exceed ninety printed pages. In October I therefore set to work, and despite two changes of abode in Kalimpong, where the greater part of the book was written, and preaching tours to Darjeeling and Bombay, where I also worked on it, by March 1955 I managed to produce a manuscript of about 200,000 words. This was, of course, five or six times what Shri Wadia had bargained for, but with characteristic magnanimity he uncomplainingly shouldered the heavy additional responsibility and in 1957, the year of the 2500th Buddha Jayanti, *A Survey of Buddhism* was published.

Shri Wadia's confidence that the book would be a success was fully justified. Indeed, the enthusiastic welcome which it received, from the scholar, the student of Comparative Religion and, not least, the English-reading Eastern Buddhist monk, far exceeded our expectations. One Theravadin Buddhist reviewer of Ceylon, a leading scholar, went so far as to hail the publication of the *Survey* as the principal event of the Buddha Jayanti Year. As the first edition was quickly exhausted, a second one was brought out in 1959. Now, with the demand for the book steadily growing, the publishers have decided not only to bring out another edition but also, most wisely, to print twice the number of copies.

Printing difficulties, while delaying production, have given me time to make a large number of minor corrections. Though more than a decade has passed since the *Survey* was written, and though my understanding of Buddhism has, I hope, deepened, on going through it again I have not found anything that I feel needs revision. The text is therefore substantially that of the previous editions. So far as the author and the publishers are concerned, the biggest difference between this edition and its predecessors is that it is being brought out without the benefit of the inspiring presence of its original sponsor. Shri B. P. Wadia died in 1958. This third edition of the *Survey* is therefore dedicated, as a small token of gratitude to his memory.

London
June 9th, 1966

SANGHARAKSHITA

INTRODUCTION

I. The Importance of Buddhism

"BUDDHISM, after all," declares a distinguished historian of Indian literature, "is and remains that production of the Indian mind, which is the most important in the history of the world."[1] Various grounds for such a judgment can be adduced. Although born on Indian soil, Buddhism is one of the three great world religions, with a following which, at the height of its influence, included between a third and a fourth part of the human race, and which even now is not negligible. Its founder, Gautama the Buddha, is universally recognized as the perfect embodiment of the ethical and spiritual ideals which He spent His life proclaiming. Indeed, it is the majestic figure of the Enlightened One, seated cross-legged in meditation, that confronts the Western mind as the image *par excellence* of the Wisdom of the East, and it is of Him we first think whenever this is mentioned. Buddhism is the greatest of the non-theistic faiths, and since both Christianity and Islam are forms of theism it is their sole representative among the world religions. Its influence upon other systems of belief has been profound. Hinduism, Confucianism, Shintō and Bön were all remodelled in its likeness, while through Neo-platonism and Sufism it exercized a remote but deeply spiritual-izing effect on at least two out of the three great Semitic mono-theisms. Besides being a carrier of culture and civilization for the whole of Asia, Buddhism affords the unique spectacle of a doctrine of salvation propagating itself on a hitherto unprece-dented scale entirely by peaceful means. In the course of its long history it has given the world, and continues to give, an ethics based on the ideal of absolute altruism, a psychology that ex-plores heights and depths of whose existence the modern professors of this branch of knowledge are beginning dimly to

---

[1] M. Winternitz, *A History of Indian Literature* (Calcutta, 1933), p. x.

be aware, and a philosophy that discloses perspectives the most awe-inspiring in human thought, while its literature and its art are among the supreme flowerings of the human spirit. Unlike the two other world religions, whose theologies and psychologies are Christianized or Islamized versions of either Plato or Aristotle, Buddhism evolved all these treasures largely from the depths of its own inner resources.

During the last century and a half Buddhism has received the increasingly respectful attention of Western students of comparative religion, as well as of psychologists, philosophers and lovers of art. In certain parts of the Western world a situation is fast developing in which, without some acquaintance with its basic teachings, one will be considered hardly educated. Proof of this remarkable growth of interest is to be found in the Spring and Autumn catalogues of leading publishers. Forty-two years ago de La Vallée Poussin could open an article with the remark, "An amazing number of popular and semi-popular books on Buddhism have been published during recent years."[1] This is truer than ever today. Hardly a month goes by without the appearance, in English alone, of some work, whether original treatise or translated Buddhist classic, that constitutes a permanent accession to our knowledge of the religion. Moreover, in some quarters there has been a significant change of attitude towards Buddhism. This change is reflected in the fact that Buddhism is no longer regarded as something to be studied by the professional orientalist but as a way of life for the spiritually committed individual—while societies devoted to the study of Buddhism are increasingly being replaced by spiritual communities committed to the actual practice of the Buddha's Teaching.

As exemplified by current expositions, there are a number of alternative approaches to Buddhism. In the first place there is the scientific *versus* the traditional approach, in the second the sectarian *versus* the synoptic. The scientific approach, which is of modern Western origin, is exemplified in the works of the great classical orientalists. As its assumptions differ fundamentally from those of Buddhism, and as it tends to accumulate facts rather than to illumine principles, it is not the best guide to a deeper understanding of the religion, much less still to its cor-

[1] *The Legacy of India* (Clarendon Press, Oxford, 1937), p. 162.

rect practice. This is still more the case with the pseudo-scientific approach. After examining Buddhism with a great parade of objectivity, the latter concludes by demonstrating its inferiority to some other brand of religious belief. The traditional approach is that of the Buddhist, who, whether learned or unlearned, takes refuge in The Three Jewels (*triratna*)—the Buddha, the Dharma, and the Sangha—in the serene confidence that They constitute the sole effective means of deliverance from suffering as well as to the attainment of Nirvana, Buddhahood, of the Triple Body (*trikāya*). Here, while other considerations are not ignored, the approach is predominantly pragmatic, Buddhism being intimately known from within through personal experience. The sectarian approach is limited rather than false. What is, in fact, only one part of the total Buddhist tradition, whether the Theravāda, the Jōdo Shin Shū, Zen, or any other, is presented as though it were the whole, all the remaining schools of Buddhism being either repudiated or ignored. This type of approach is represented by some of the tracts and pamphlets put out by Buddhist organizations. The synoptic approach recognizes the essential authenticity of the entire Buddhist tradition. Far from identifying Buddhism with any one of its forms, it assumes that "the doctrine of the Buddha, conceived in its full breadth, width, majesty and grandeur, comprises all those teachings which are linked to the original teaching by historical continuity, and which work out methods leading to the extinction of individuality by eliminating the belief in it."[1] This type of approach is exemplified in Conze's *Buddhism* (1951), from which the above quotation has been taken, as well as by the present writer's *The Three Jewels* (1967). In this Introduction, as well as in the following chapters of the book, we shall approach Buddhism in the spirit of traditional rather than of profane scholarship (though at the same time taking into account the results of modern research), and from the synoptic rather than from the sectarian point of view. We shall confine ourselves to major developments.

---

[1] E. Conze, *Buddhism, Its Essence and Development* (Cassirer, Oxford, 1963), p. 23.

II. The Unity of Buddhism

Like almost all productions of the Indian mind Buddhism is characterized by richness, profusion, amplitude and diversity. In the course of fifteen centuries of uninterrupted development on Indian soil its inherent spiritual vitality has found expression in a multitude of forms. Organizationally, it consists of an immense number of schools, all of which are branches of, or divisions within, the one Sangha, and all of which besides sharing in the common heritage have their own distinctive doctrines and practices, their own lineages of teachers, and their own literatures. Pluralistic Realism, Absolutism and Idealism all flourished in turn, each being regarded by men of the highest philosophical genius as the correct interpretation of Buddhist thought. Now Wisdom is recommended as the principal means to Deliverance, now Meditation, and now Faith and Devotion. One great spiritual movement proclaims emancipation of self alone as the goal of the religious life, another Supreme Enlightenment for the sake of all sentient beings. And so on and so on. These differences, amounting sometimes to logical contradictions, give to Buddhism an appearance not only of multifariousness but of confusion. Like a traveller lost in some enormous, architecturally complex Indian temple, the student tends to be so overwhelmed by the lavish abundance of the ornamentation as to be incapable of appreciating the simplicity and grandeur of the design. Since there is an almost complete absence of historical records, Chinese pilgrims and Tibetan historians being sometimes the sole available sources of information for crucial periods, he moreover finds himself alone in the temple at night—its immensities dimly lit by lamps that allow him, as he gropes his way round, no more than a glimpse of a column here and an archway there.

A clue through the labyrinth, a switch that, when turned on, will light up the whole edifice—in short a principle of unity that will enable us to see the schools as all "parts of one tremendous whole" which is Buddhism—does however exist. As we have explained in detail in Chapter II, "The unity of Buddhism consists in the fact that, through differences and divergencies of doctrine innumerable, all schools of Buddhism aim at Enlightenment, at reproducing the spiritual experience of the Buddha." This unity is not rational but transcendental. That is to say, the doctrinal and other differences between the schools are not resolved by being reduced on their own level one to another or all to a conceptual common denominator, but transcended by referring them to a factor which, being supra-logical, can be the common object of contradictory assertions. According to the *Prajñāpāramitā Sūtras*, indeed, recourse to paradoxes or propositions involving a logical oppugnancy, as when the Bodhisattva is urged to deliver sentient beings who do not exist,[1] is inevitable if justice is to be done to the non-conceptual nature of Reality and of the spiritual experience which has Reality for its "objective" counterpart. The specific differences between the schools are due to the fact that the latter approach the transcendental factor, Enlightenment or Nirvana, from opposite directions, or because, though approaching it from the same direction, one goes farther towards it than another. In other words the various schools tend to represent either different aspects of Buddhism or different stages of spiritual evolution within it.

This can be made clearer by a reference to the Five Spiritual Faculties (*pañcendriya*), a set of "cardinal virtues" figuring prominently in the early literature. The five are Faith (*śraddhā*), Vigour (*vīrya*), Mindfulness (*smṛti*), Concentration (*samādhi*) and Wisdom (*prajñā*). All these the disciple develops equally, counterbalancing, by means of Mindfulness, Faith and Wisdom, and Vigour and Concentration, in such a way as to attain a state of perfect psychological and spiritual equilibrium (*indriya-samatta*). Soṇa Kolivisa is rebuked for developing Vigour at the expense of Concentration. In a famous simile, the Buddha tells him that, just as a lute is unfit for playing when the strings are either too taut or too slack, so does too much output of vigour conduce to restlessness and too feeble a vigour to slothfulness. He should, therefore, determine on evenness of vigour.[2] Full development of the Five Spiritual Faculties makes one an Arahant.[3] After the Buddha's Parinirvāṇa, however, different schools tended to specialize, as it were, in one particular faculty and to approach Enlightenment from that "direction." Thus, for example, the

[1] E.g. *Vajracchedikā-prajñāpāramitā* 3.
[2] *Vinaya Piṭaka* I.182.
[3] *Saṁyutta-Nikāya* XLVIII.IV.II.ii.

Abhidharmikas and the Mādhyamikas developed Wisdom, the Yogācārins Concentration, the popular devotional movements Faith, and the esoteric Tantric traditions Vigour.[1] The Five Spiritual Faculties can also be cultivated one after another.[2] It is also possible, therefore, to regard them as representing so many successive stages of spiritual development. Explaining how those unworthy beings who are hard to tame are brought to subjugation, the Lord says in the *Hevajra Tantra*: "First there should be the public confession (*poṣadha*), then they should be taught the ten rules of virtuous conduct, then the *Vaibhaṣya* teachings and then the *Sautrāntika*, after that the *Yogācāra* and the *Mādhyamika*. Then when they know all *mantra*-method, they should start upon Hevajra."[3] Usually, however, when arranged according to the order of their spiritual progression the schools are subsumed under the three *yānas*, that is to say the Hīnayāna, the Mahāyāna, and the Vajrayāna, representing the three phases of the Buddha's personal teaching and the three stages of its historical development. By cultivating each *yāna* in turn, taking the earlier as the basis for the understanding and practise of the later, the disciple attains Supreme Enlightenment. The Triyāna system is, therefore, not just a philosophical synthesis, but the most practical possible expression of the Unity of Buddhism.

Inasmuch as all were regarded as aiming, in one way or another, at the same goal, it is not surprising that between the different schools of Buddhism there was a relationship of mutual respect and tolerance. This is not to say that doctrinal differences were not keenly felt and vigorously debated, or that sectarian feeling did not sometimes run high; but such differences were always settled peacefully, by means of discussion, no attempt ever being made to enforce conformity. Persecution, or "arguing by torture," was unknown. Neither was anyone ever consigned to hell by his opponent for holding unorthodox views. The Pudgalavādins, who believed in the real existence of the Person, were constantly refuted by other schools; but no one ever questioned their ability to gain Enlightenment. Such, in-

[1] For a detailed exposition see below, Chapter III.
[2] *Sikśā-samuccaya* 316.
[3] *Hevajra Tantra* II.viii.c.8, 9.

deed, was the harmony that prevailed, that monks of different schools sometimes occupied the same monastery, observing a common rule and sharing in the same corporate monastic life, but devoting themselves, in addition, each one to his own special studies and meditations.

III. The Buddha

From the traditional point of view Buddhism begins with going for refuge to The Three Jewels (*triratna*), the first of which is the Buddha. Although there is no longer any doubt about His historical existence, the exact dates of His Birth and Parinirvāṇa are still the subject of controversy. In all probability those given by the *Dīpavaṁsa* and the *Mahāvaṁsa* (excluding its continuation the *Cūlavaṁsa*, the dates of which are sixty years out), equivalent to 563-483 B.C., are not far wrong.

The events of His life are too well known to be recounted in detail. Born at Lumbinī, in the territory of the Śākya republic, of wealthy patrician stock, He went forth "from home into the homeless life" at the age of twenty-nine, attained Supreme Enlightenment at Buddha Gaya at the age of thirty-five, and passed away at Kuśinagara at the age of eighty. During His lifetime His Teaching spread throughout the kingdoms of Magadha and Kośala (corresponding to the modern Bihar and Uttar Pradesh), as well as in the circumjacent principalities and republics. From kings, merchant princes and orthodox brahmins, to outcastes, robbers and naked ascetics, His disciples were recruited from all classes of society, and included both men and women. Besides instructing an extensive circle of lay adherents, He trained a smaller, more select band of monks (and nuns) who constituted the Sangha proper and upon whom, after the Parinirvâṇa, the responsibility for carrying on His mission mainly devolved. His personality, as it emerges from the ancient records, was a unique combination of dignity and affability, wisdom and kindliness. Together with a majesty that awed and daunted kings, He possessed a tenderness that could stoop to comfort the bereaved and console the afflicted. His serenity was unshakeable, His self-confidence unfailing. Ever mindful and self-possessed, He faced opposition and hostility, even personal danger, with the calm and compassionate smile that has lingered down the ages.

In debate he was urbane and courteous, though not without a vein of irony, and almost invariably succeeded in winning over His opponent. Such was His success in this direction, that He was accused of enticing people by means of spells.

In addition to the "historical facts" of the Buddha's career, notice must be taken of the myths and legends from which, in the traditional biographies, these facts are inseparable. When Buddhism first came within the purview of Western learning it was generally assumed that myth and legend were synonymous with fiction and that, except as illustrations of primitive mentality, they were valueless. Since then we have begun to know better. Some incidents in the Buddha's biography, which appear as "legendary" within the materialistic framework of nineteenth-century science—such as those describing His exercize of supernormal powers—are now, with the expansion of that framework, seen to have been based, in all probability, on actual occurrences. Others apparently relate to a different order of reality and a different type of truth altogether, being poetic rather than scientific statements of psychological processes and spiritual experiences. Yet others are of the nature of illuminations struck out by the tremendous impact of the Buddha's personality on the minds of His disciples, and express the greatness of that personality subjectively in terms of the feelings of rapturous adoration which it evoked.

This introduces the great question of the alleged "deification" of the Buddha. According to some modern scholars the Buddha was a human teacher, and the devotion of His followers turned him into a god, or God. Based as it is on assumptions quite different from those of Buddhism, such an interpretation of an important doctrinal development must be rejected outright. Within the context of a non-theistic religion the concept of deification has no meaning. The Buddha claimed to be a fully enlightened human being, superior even to the gods, and as such He has invariably been regarded. Since He was already the highest being in the universe there remained no higher position to which He could subsequently be exalted. What really happened was that, the Buddha having realized the Truth, thereby becoming its embodiment and symbol, Reality came to be interpreted concretely in terms of Buddhahood and its attributes, as well as abstractly in terms of *śūnyatā, tathatā*, etc. At the same time the devotion with which the Buddha was worshipped was analogous to that which, in the theistic religions, is the prerogative of the Creator.

No deification of an originally "merely human" teacher ever having taken place, we must also dismiss as impertinent the several theories according to which the Buddha was in reality an ethical teacher like Socrates or Confucius, a rationalist, a humanist, a social reformer, and so on.

IV. The Dharma

The word Dharma probably has more meanings than any other term in the entire vocabulary of Buddhism. As the second of the three Refuges it has been variously translated as Law, Truth, Doctrine, Gospel, Teaching, Norm and True Idea, all of which express some aspect of its total significance. To the West it is known as Buddhism, and the question has often been asked whether it is a religion or a philosophy. The answer of course is that so long as religion is thought of in exclusively theistic terms and philosophy remains divorced from any kind of ethical and spiritual discipline, Buddhism is neither.

The general characteristics of the Dharma are summarized in an ancient stereotype formula which occurs repeatedly in the *sūtras* and which is still widely used for liturgical purposes. The Dharma is well taught; it belongs to the Lord, not to any other teacher; its results, when it is put into practise, are visible in this very life; it is timeless; it invites the enquirer to come and see personally what it is like; it is progressive, leading from lower to higher states of existence, and it is to be understood by the wise each one for himself.[1]

The specific doctrinal content of the Dharma consists of various doctrines or teachings. These represent neither speculative opinions nor generalizations from a limited range of spiritual experience, but are, ultimately, conceptual formulations of the nature of existence as seen by a fully Enlightened Being Who, out of compassion, makes known to humanity the truth that He has discovered. It is in this sense that Buddhism may be termed

[1] *Svākkhāto bhagavatā dhammo sandhiṭṭhiko akāliko ehipassiko opanayiko paccattaṃ veditabbo viññūhī.*

a revelation. According to the most ancient canonical accounts of a crucial episode, the truth, law or principle which the Buddha perceived at the time of His Enlightenment—in the perception of which, indeed, that Enlightenment consisted—and which, on account of its abstruseness, He was at first reluctant to disclose to a passion-ridden generation, was that of the "conditionally co-producedness" (*paṭicca-samuppanna*) of things. Conditioned Co-production is, therefore, the basic Buddhist doctrine, recognized and taught as such first by the Buddha and His immediate disciples and thereafter throughout the whole course of Buddhist history. Questioned by Śāriputra, then a non-Buddhist wanderer, only a few months after the Enlightenment, about his Master's teaching, the Arahant Aśvajīt replies in a resounding verse that has echoed down the centuries as the *credo* of Buddhism: "The Tathāgata has explained the origin of those things which proceed from a cause. Their cessation too He has explained. This is the doctrine of the great Śramaṇa."[1] Elsewhere the Buddha clearly equates Conditioned Co-production with the Dharma and both with Himself, saying: "He who sees Conditioned Co-production sees the Dharma; he who sees the Dharma sees the Buddha."[2]

As interpreted by the gifted early Buddhist nun Dhammadinnā, whose views were fully endorsed by the Buddha with the remark that He had nothing further to add to them, the doctrine of Conditioned Co-production represents an all-inclusive reality that admits of two different trends of things in the whole of existence. In one of them the reaction takes place in a progressive order between two counterparts or complements or between two things of the same genus, the succeeding factor augmenting the effect of the preceding one. The Saṁsāra or Round of Conditioned Existence represents the first trend. Herein, as depicted by the "Wheel of Life," sentient beings under the influence of craving, hatred and bewilderment revolve as gods, men, *asuras*, animals, *pretas* and denizens of hell in accordance with the law of karma and experience pleasure and pain. The

[1] See below, p. 84.

[2] *Yaḥ pratītyasamutpādaṁ paśyati sa dharmaṁ paśyati; yo dharmaṁ paśyati so buddhaṁ paśyati. Majjhima-Nikāya* I, 190-92. Ed. E. Conze, *Buddhist Texts Through the Ages* (Bruno Cassirer, Oxford, 1954), p. 65.

process is set forth briefly in the first and second of the Four Āryan Truths, the Truth of Suffering and the Truth of the Origin of Suffering, and at length in the full list of *nidānas* or links, which is often, though wrongly, regarded as exhausting the entire content of Conditioned Co-Production. Conditioned by spiritual ignorance (*āvidyā*) arise the karma-formations (*saṁskāra*); conditioned by the karma-formations arises consciousness (*vijñāna*); conditioned by consciousness arises name-and-form (*nāma-rūpa*); conditioned by name-and-form arise the six sense-fields (*ṣaḍāyatana*); conditioned by the six sense-fields arises contact (*sparśa*); conditioned by contact arises feeling (*vedanā*); conditioned by feeling arises thirst (*tṛṣṇā*); conditioned by thirst arises grasping (*upādāna*); conditioned by grasping arises becoming (*bhāva*); conditioned by becoming arises birth (*jāti*); and conditioned by birth arises decay-and-death (*jarā-maraṇa*), with sorrow, lamentation, pain, grief and despair. These twelve links are distributed over three lifetimes, the first two belonging to the past life, the middle eight to the present, and the last two to the future.

The Path to Deliverance and Nirvana together represent the second trend, Nirvana being not only a counter-process of cessation of the cyclic order of existence (i.e., the twelve links in reverse order) but the farthest discernible point of the progressive one. This process is set forth briefly in the third and fourth Āryan Truths, the Truth of the Cessation of Suffering (= Nirvana) and the Truth of the Way Leading to the Cessation of Suffering, as well as at length in another set of twelve links which is continuous with the first one in the same way that a spiral winds out of a circle. Conditioned by suffering (*duḥkha*—the 'decay-and-death' of the first list) arises faith (*śraddhā*); conditioned by faith arises delight (*pramodya*); conditioned by delight arises joy (*prīti*); conditioned by joy arises serenity (*praśrabdhi*); conditioned by serenity arises bliss (*sukha*); conditioned by bliss arises concentration (*samādhi*); conditioned by concentration arises knowledge and vision of things as they really are (*yathābhūta-jñānadarsana*); conditioned by knowledge and vision of things as they really are arises disgust (*nirvid, nirveda*); conditioned by disgust arises dispassion (*virāga*); conditioned by dispassion arises liberation (*vimukti*); and conditioned by liberation arises knowledge of the destruction of the intoxicants (*āsravakṣaya-jñāna*). The whole process can be experienced within a single lifetime. The Path is usually formulated, however, not in terms of the twelve "higher" links but in various other ways, such as the Three Trainings (*triśikṣā*), or Morality (*śīla*), Meditation (*samādhi*) and Wisdom (*prajñā*), the Āryan Eightfold Path, and the Six or Ten Pāramitās. Despite the fact that the connection of these formulations with the doctrine of Conditioned Co-production is often lost sight of, the fact that the Path is essentially a sequence of progressively higher mental and spiritual states, and that the practise of the Dharma consists above all in the cultivation of these states, is in all of them made sufficiently clear for practical purposes.

As the doctrine of Conditioned Co-production is not a theory of causation in the philosophical sense there is no question of whether, in the case of either the Round or the Path, the succeeding link is identical with the preceding one or different from it. The Buddhist position is simply that conditioned by, or in dependence on, A, there arises B. To say either that A and B are identical, or that they are different, is an extreme view, leading in one case to eternalism (*śāsvatavāda*) and in the other to nihilism (*ucchedavāda*). For Buddhism neither the category of being nor the category of non-being possesses ultimate validity. The Dharma is the Mean. As applied to the process of Conditioned Co-production this signifies that the one who is reborn and the one who died, and the one who gains Enlightenment and the one who followed the Path, are in reality neither the same nor different persons. Rebirth takes place but nobody is reborn; Nirvana is attained, but nobody attains it. Thus the doctrine of Conditioned Co-production involves that of *anātma* or no-self.

V. The Sangha

The last of the Three Refuges is the Sangha. In its primary sense this means the Ārya Sangha, or Assembly of the Elect, consisting of all those who have succeeded in traversing at least that stage of the Path whence retrogression into the Round for more than seven karma-resultant births is impossible. Such are the Stream-Entrants, the Once-Returners, the Non-Returners, the Arahants, and the Bodhisattvas.

Even as the Buddha is symbolized by the sacred icon and the Dharma by the handwritten or printed volumes of the Scriptures, so the Ārya Sangha is represented, for practical purposes, by the Bhikṣu-Sangha, or Order of Monks. This great institution, which, with the possible exception of its Jain counterpart, is the oldest religious order in the world, came into existence within a few months of the Buddha's Enlightenment. It consisted—and ideally still consists—of those of the Buddha's followers who, having renounced the household life, devote the whole of their time and all their energies to the realization of Nirvana. Like the Dharma, the Sangha passed through various stages of development. At first, during the earthly lifetime of the Founder, the Śākyaputra śramaṇas, as they were called, remained outwardly indistinguishable from the other religious fraternities of the time. What distinguished them was the special Dharma they professed. They, too, were of eleemosynary and eremitical habit, assembled twice a month on the full moon and new moon days, were of fixed residence during the Rains, and so on. The second period of development may have started before the Parinirvāṇa. It saw the compilation of a Rule of 150 articles known as the Prātimokṣa, the recitation of which replaced the original chanting of Dharma-stanzas at the fortnightly assemblies. Finally, the Sangha became cenobitical, whereupon the primitive undivided "Bhikṣu-sangha of the Four Quarters" split up into a number of virtually autonomous local communities, and the Prātimokṣa had to be supplemented by the Skandhakas or complete institutes of cenobitical monasticism. All these developments occurred within the space of about two centuries. Prātimokṣa and Skandhakas together constitute the Vinaya, a term originally connoting simply the practical or disciplinary aspect of the Dharma.

Parallel with the Bhikṣu-Sangha there developed the Bhikṣuṇī-Sangha, or Order of Nuns. But it seems the Buddha was reluctant to allow women to go forth into the homeless life, and in the history of Indian Buddhism, at least, it plays an insignificant part.

In a more general sense the Sangha comprizes the entire Buddhist community, sanctified and unsanctified, the professed religieux and the lay devotees, men and women. As such it is sometimes known as the Mahāsangha, or "Great Assembly." Lay devotees (*upāsakas* and *upāsikās*) are those who go for refuge to The Three Jewels, worship the relics of the Buddha, observe the

Five Precepts of ethical behaviour, and support the monks. Although as time went on the life of the monks diverged more and more sharply from that of the laity the fact that all alike went for refuge to the Buddha, the Dharma and the Sangha remained a common, potentially uniting, factor—a factor that, in the case of the Mahāyāna, was strengthened by the development of the Bodhisattva Ideal, which was an ideal equally for the monk and the layman, the nun and the laywoman.

The growth of cenobitical monasticism naturally encouraged the development, within the Sangha, of different regional traditions which, after being consolidated into distinct versions of the Dharma, eventually emerged as independent sects. Thus, a century or more after the Parinirvāṇa tensions arose between the monks of the East and the monks of the West, and the Mahāsanghikas, who were more sympathetic to the spiritual needs of the laity, seceded from the Sthaviravādins, who tended to interpret the Dharma in exclusively monastic terms. This was the first formal schism within the Sangha. During the century that followed the Sthaviravādins subdivided twice. First came the schism of the Pudgalavādins, who believed in the existence of the Person as a real absolute fact; then, that of the Sarvāstivādins, who asserted the real existence of the ultimate elements of experience (*dharma*) thoughout the three periods of time. In this way there had arisen, by the time of Aśoka, four independent monastic corporations, each with its own centres, its own ordination-lineage, its own orally transmitted version of the Dharma, its own distinctive tenets, and its own peculiarities of outward observance. Together with their respective subdivisions, the four make up the so-called "Eighteen Sects" (actually there were many more) of Early Buddhism.

In contradistinction to the Mahāyāna, the seeds of which were transmitted by the Mahāsanghikas and their offshoots, all the other sects, but especially the Sarvāstivādins, were retrospectively designated the Hīnayāna.

VI. The Oral Tradition

It is well known that the Buddha Himself wrote nothing. Spiritual influence and personal example apart, His Teaching was communicated entirely by oral means, through discourses to, and discussions with, His disciples and members of the public, as well as through inspired spontaneous utterance. While we do not definitely know what language He spoke, it would appear that He rejected the more "classical" Sanskrit in favour of the vernacular, especially the dialects of Kosala and Magadha. When two monks "of cultivated language and eloquent speech" complained that monks of various names, clan-names and races (or castes) were corrupting the Buddhavacana by repeating it in their own dialects, and asked for permission to put it into Vedic (*candaso āropema*), He firmly rejected their petition. " 'Deluded men!' " He exclaimed, " 'how can you say this? This will not lead to the conversion of the unconverted.' " And He delivered a discourse and commanded all the monks: " 'You are not to put the Buddhavacana into Vedic. Whoever does so shall be guilty of an offence. I authorize you, monks, to learn and teach the Buddhavacana each in his own dialect (*sakkāya niruttiya*).' "[1] In order to impress His Teaching upon the minds of His auditors, as well as to facilitate its dissemination, He moreover had recourse to the repetition of key words and phrases, the drawing up of numbered lists of terms, and other mnemonic devices.

All these facts are of far-reaching consequence. In the first place, the Dharma having been orally taught, there intervened between the Parinirvāṇa of the Buddha and the committing of His Teaching to writing a period of oral transmission lasting two or three centuries, in the case of some scriptures, and much longer in the case of others. Then the fact that the monks had been authorized to learn and teach the Buddhavacana in their own dialects meant that the Dharma was from the beginning extant in a number of linguistic forms so that, when finally it did come to be written down, this was done not in one language only but in many. Thus (it is said) the Canon of the Mahāsanghikas was in Prakrit, that of the Sthaviravādins in Paiśāci, that of the Pudgalavādins in Apabhramsa, and that of the Sarvāstivādins in Sanskrit. Hence when Buddhism spread outside India it came about that the Scriptures were translated into the languages of those countries, into Uighur, Chinese, Tibetan and so on. At no time, not even when Buddhism was confined to North-Eastern India, was there any one canonical language for all Buddhists.

[1] *Vinaya Piṭaka* ii.139.lff.

The attempts made by some writers to present Pāli as such are mistaken. The word *pāli*, meaning a line of the sacred text, is in fact not the name of a language at all, and the "Pāli" Canon of Ceylon is probably a Middle Indic recension of a version of the Tripiṭaka originating in Western India. The historical accident of its being the only Indian Canon to have survived complete in the original language should not cause us to overestimate its importance, much less still to regard its excellent but selective contents as the sole criterion of what is and what is not Buddhism. Finally, when the oral tradition was reduced to writing the mnemonic devices employed by the Buddha and His disciples for the transmission of the Dharma were responsible for giving the Scriptures as literary documents certain distinctive characteristics.

VII. The Canonical Literature

With the exception of the Pāli Canon, the actual writing down of which took place in Ceylon, and certain Mahāyāna *sūtras* that may have been composed in Central Asia or even in China, the canonical literature of Buddhism is of exclusively Indian provenance. Where, when and under what circumstances the thousands of individual texts of which it consists were first committed to writing is in most cases unknown. All that can be affirmed with certainty is that the canonical literature came into existence over a period of roughly a thousand years, from the first to the tenth century A.D., as a series of deposits from the oral tradition, the tendency apparently being for the more exoteric teachings to be committed to writing before the more esoteric ones. Even during the period of oral tradition the complete Buddhavacana was referred to as the Tripiṭaka, the three "baskets" or collections of the Buddha's words. These three are the Vinaya Piṭaka, the Sūtra Piṭaka and the Abhidharma Piṭaka. Together with the Tantras they make up the four chief divisions of the canonical writings.

The word *vinaya*, meaning "that which leads away from (evil)," stands for the practical or disciplinary aspect of Buddhism, and the Vinaya Piṭaka comprises the Collection of (Monastic) Discipline. In the form in which it is now extant it consists essentially of two parts, the Vinaya-vibhaṅga and the

Vinaya-vastu, together with historical and catechetical supplements. The Vinaya-vibhaṅga or "Exposition of the Vinaya" contains the Prātimokṣa-sūtra in 150 articles and its commentary the Sūtra-vibhaṅga, one work being embedded in the other. While the former embodies the various categories of rules binding upon members of the eremitical Sangha, the latter gives a word-for-word explanation of each rule and narrates the circumstances in which it came to be promulgated. The Vinaya-vastu contains the Skandhakas or "The Chapters," of which there are seventeen or more according to the individual recension. These comprize the complete institutes of cenobitical monasticism, and deal with such topics as Ordination, the Poṣadha or fortnightly meeting, the Rains Residence, Medicine and food, Robes, Dwellings and Schism. *Inter alia* the Vinaya Piṭaka records not only the regula of the monastic life but also, in the words of the pioneer scholar Csoma de Körös, "the manners, customs, opinions, knowledge, ignorance, superstition, hopes, and fears of a great part of Asia especially of India in former ages."[1] Together with the Sūtra Piṭaka it is our richest source of information on the civilization and culture, the history, geography, sociology and religion of India during the centuries immediately before and immediately after the advent of the Buddha. In the Buddhist world there are now extant seven complete recensions of this Collection, one in Pali and six from Sanskrit. These are essentially alternative arrangements of the same basic material and differ mainly in the extent to which non-monastic matter has been incorporated. The existence however of the *Mahāvastu Avadāna,* a bulky Vinaya work of the Lokottaravādins, a sub-sect of the Mahāsanghikas, which is not a disciplinary work at all but a life of the Buddha in which numerous legends have been inserted, suggests that the original nucleus of the Vinaya was a primitive Buddha-biography in which the monastic elements themselves were a later, though still very early, interpolation.

The *sūtra,* literally a thread, and hence by extension of meaning the "thread" of discourse connecting a number of topics, is perhaps the most important and characteristic of all Buddhist literary genres. It is essentially a religious discourse delivered by

---

[1] Quoted A. C. Banerjee, *Sarvāstivāda Literature* (Calcutta, 1957), p. 79.

the Buddha as it were *ex cathedra* to one or more disciples, whether members of the Sangha, lay people, Bodhisattvas, Śrāvakas, human beings, or gods. The Sūtra Piṭaka is thus the Collection of Discourses, and constitutes the principal source of our knowledge of the Dharma. Some discourses are either partly or wholly in dialogue form. Others are delivered not by the Buddha but by disciples speaking either with His approval or under His inspiration. Broadly speaking the *sūtras* belong to two groups, Hīnayāna and Mahāyāna, the latter being those discourses which, having been handed down among the Mahāsanghikas and their spiritual descendants, were not recognized as authentic by the followers of the Hīnayāna schools, though the converse was not the case. The Hīnayāna *sūtras* comprize four great collections known as Āgamas in Sanskrit and Nikāyas in Pāli. The Dīrghāgama (= Dīgha-Nikāya) or "Long" collection contains, as its name suggests, the lengthy discourses, thirty in number, while the Madhyamāgama (= Majjhima-Nikāya) or "Middle" collection contains those of medium length, of which there are about five times as many. These collections are the most important. The Saṁyuktāgama (= Saṁyutta-Nikāya) or "Grouped" collection contains some thousands of very short *sūtras* arranged subjectwise and the Ekottarāgama (= Aṅguttara-Nikāya) or "Numerical" collection a similar number of texts arranged according to the progressive numerical value of the terms and topics dealt with. Both collections draw partly on the first two Āgamas and partly from original, sometimes extremely ancient, sources. The Pāli Canon also contains a Khuddaka-Nikāya or "Minor" collection, consisting of works such as the *Dhammapada*, the *Thera-* and *Therī-gāthā* and the *Jātakas* which, in Sanskrit, are found either elsewhere in the Canon, mostly in the Vinaya Piṭaka, or outside it as independent quasi-canonical works. The Mahāyāna *sūtras* are distributed into six great collections, the first five of which represent natural divisions, while the last consists of independent miscellaneous works. First comes the group of Prajñāpāramitā or "Perfection of Wisdom" *sūtras*, of which there are more than thirty, ranging in length from some thousands of pages to a few lines. Their principal subject-matter is Śūnyatā or Voidness, and they have claim to be regarded as the profoundest spiritual documents known to mankind. The *Vajracchedikā*, popularly known as the

"Diamond Sutra," forms one of the shorter texts in this class. The Avataṁsaka or "Flower-Ornament" group consists principally of three enormous and complex discourses of that name, one of which, also known as the *Gaṇḍavyūha* or "World-Array" Sutra, describes the spiritual pilgrimage of the youth Sudhana, who in his search for Enlightenment visits more than fifty teachers. In a boldly imaginative manner it expounds the mutual interpenetration of all phenomena. The *Daśabhūmika Sūtra*, dealing with the ten stages of the Bodhisattva's career, also belongs to this group. The Ratnakūṭa and Mahāsaṁnipāta groups are both made up of much shorter *sūtras*, the former including such valuable and historically important works as the *Vimalakīrti-nirdeśa* or "Exposition of Vimalakīrti" and the longer *Sukhāvatī-vyūha* or "Array of the Happy Land." As its name suggests, the Nirvana or Parinirvāṇa group deals with the Buddha's last days and His final admonitions to His disciples. The sixth and last group, that of the miscellaneous independent works, includes some of the most important and influential of all Mahāyāna *sūtras*. Among them are the grandiose *Saddharma-puṇḍarīka* or "White Lotus of the Good Law," which presents in dramatic and parabolic form the main truths of the Mahāyāna, the *Laṅkāvatāra*, an unsystematic exposition of the doctrine of Mind-Only, and the shorter *Sukhāvatī-vyūha*, in which is taught salvation by faith in Amitābha, the Buddha of Infinite Light.

Abhidharma means "about Dharma," though traditionally the term was often interpreted as "higher Dharma" in the sense of a philosophically more exact exposition of the Teaching. The Abhidharma Piṭaka is a collection of highly scholastic treatises which annotate and explain the Āgama/Nikāya texts, define technical terms, arrange numerically classified doctrines in numerical order, give a systematic philosophical exposition of the teaching, and establish a consistent method of spiritual practise. Above all, they interpret the Dharma in terms of strict pluralistic realism and work out an elaborate philosophy of relations. Two different Abhidharma Piṭakas have come down to us, one compiled by the Theravādins and one by the Sarvāstivādins. Each contains seven treatises which, though covering similar ground in a similar manner, are really two independent sets of works. Among the Theravāda treatises the most important are the *Dhamma-saṅgaṇī* or "Enumeration of (Ultimate) Elements" and the gigantic *Paṭṭhāna* or "(Book of) Origination." The most important Sarvāstivāda work is the encyclopaedic *Jñāna-prasthāna* or "Establishment of Knowledge," which is known as the *kāya-śāstra* or "trunk treatise," the others being the *pada-śāstras* or "limbs." According to Theravāda tradition the Abhidharma Piṭaka is canonical inasmuch as, though the details are the work of disciples, the *mātṛkas* or "matrices of discourse" were laid down in advance by the Buddha. Sarvāstivādin tradition ascribes the treatises to individual authors. The philosophical writings of the great Mahāyāna sages, such as Nāgārjuna and Asaṅga, which stand in the same relation to the Mahāyāna *sūtras* as the Abhidharma treatises do to their Hīnayāna counterparts, are sometimes referred to as the Mahāyāna Abhidharma; but although immensely authoritative they were never collected into a Piṭaka.

The Tantras are the most highly esoteric of the canonical texts. The word itself, derived from a root meaning "to spread," is applied to a variety of treatises and affords no clue to the contents of these works. While resembling the *sūtras* in literary form, they differ from them in dealing with ritual and yoga rather than with ethics and philosophy and in being unintelligible without the traditional commentary. Moreover, the techniques they prescribe can be practised only when, through the rite of *abhiṣeka* or "aspersion," the requisite spiritual power has been transmitted to the disciple by a spiritual master in the succession. How many Tantras were originally published it is impossible to say. Standard editions of the Kanjur contain twenty-two huge xylograph volumes of these works, to which must be added twenty-five volumes of so-called Nyingma Tantras. Some Tantras exist in various degrees of expansion and contraction, each set of such recensions making up a complete Tantric Cycle, the publication of which is associated with the name of a particular Siddha or "Perfect One." Among the best known Tantras are the *Guhya-samāja* or "Esoteric Integration," the *Hevajra*, the *Śrīcakra-sambhāra* or "Binding Wheel," the *Māyā-jāla* or "Glorious Assembly," the *Vajra-bhairava* or "Fearful Adamantine One," and the *Kāla-cakra* or "Wheel of Time."

The greater part of this enormous literature is now available only in translation, the principal collections being the Imperial

Chinese Tripiṭaka and the Tibetan Kanjur or "Translated Word (of the Buddha)." In recent decades, however, a number of Sanskrit Buddhist texts, both canonical and non-canonical, have come to light in Gilgit (Pakistan) and been recovered from the sands of Central Asia. While the value of the Buddhist canonical literature will always be primarily spiritual, much of it provides, at the same time, a useful corrective to any view of the social, cultural and religious history of India derived exclusively from brahminical sources.

VIII. Phases of Development

From the Parinirvāṇa of the Buddha to the sack of Nālandā (*circ.* 1197 A.D.) Indian Buddhism passed through three great phases of development traditionally known as the Hīnayāna, the Mahāyāna and the Vajrayāna, each with its own characteristics and its own spiritual ideal. These phases were not mutually exclusive. The earlier *yānas*, besides continuing to exist as independent schools, were also incorporated in the later ones and regarded as constituting, with modifications, their indispensable theoretical and practical foundation.

The Hīnayāna, "Little Vehicle" or "Lower Way," is so called because it teaches the attainment of salvation for oneself alone. It is predominantly ethico-psychological in character and its spiritual ideal is embodied in the austere figure of the Arahant, a person in whom all craving is extinct, and who will no more be reborn. While mindfulness, self-control, equanimity, detachment and the rest of the ascetic virtues are regarded as indispensable, in the final analysis emancipation (*mokṣa*) is attained through insight into the transitory (*anitya*) and painful (*duḥkha*) nature of conditioned things, as well as into the non-selfhood (*nairātmyatā*) of all the elements of existence (*dharmas*), whether conditioned or unconditioned. This last consists in the realization that personality is illusory, and that far from being a substantial entity the so-called "I" is only the conventional label for a congeries of evanescent material and mental processes. At the price of complete withdrawal from all worldly concerns, emancipation, or Arahantship, is attainable in this very birth. The Hīnayāna therefore insists upon the necessity of the monastic life, with which, indeed, it tends to identify the spiritual life altogether. The laity simply observe the more elementary precepts, worship the relics of the Buddha, and support the monks, by which means merit (*puṇya*) is accumulated and rebirth in heaven assured. As for the difference between Buddha and Arahant, it is only a matter of relative priority and posteriority of attainment, and of relative extent of supernormal powers. The most widespread and influential Hīnayāna school was that of the Sarvāstivādins, who were greatly devoted to the study and propagation of the Abhidharma. They were, in fact, later also known as the Vaibhāṣikas, the Vibhāṣa being the gigantic commentary on the *Jñāna-prasthāna* which had been compiled by the leaders of the school in Kashmir during the first or second century A.D. The contents of the *Vibhāṣa* are systematized and explained in Vasubandhu's *Abhidharma-kośa* or "Treasury of the Abhidharma," a work which represents the culmination of Hīnayāna thought and has exercized enormous historical influence. The commentarial portion incorporates Sautrāntika views, thus not only bridging the gap between the Hīnayāna and the Mahāyāna but paving the way for Vasubandu's own "conversion" to the latter *yāna*.

The Mahāyāna, literally "Great Vehicle" or "Great Way," is so called because it teaches the salvation of all. Predominantly devotional-metaphysical in character, its ideal is the Bodhisattva, the heroic being who, practising the six or ten Perfections (*pāramitā*) throughout thousands of lives, aspires to the attainment of Buddahood for the sake of all sentient beings. Perspectives infinitely vaster than those of the Hīnayāna are here disclosed. At the same time the earlier vehicle is regarded not as wrong but only as inadequate, the provisional rather than the final teaching, given out by the Buddha to disciples of inferior calibre, whom a sudden revelation of the transcendent glories of the Mahāyāna might have stupefied rather than enlightened. Arahantship, far from being the highest achievement, is only a stage of the path; the true goal is Supreme Buddhahood. This is achieved not merely by piercing the gross veil of passions (*kleśāvaraṇa*) by insight into the non-selfhood of the person (*pudgala-nairātmya*) but, in addition, by piercing the subtle veil of cognizable objects (*jñeyāvaraṇa*) by the realization that the so-called ultimate elements of which, according to the Hīnayāna, the person consists, are only mental constructs and, therefore, themselves devoid of selfhood (*dharma-nairātmya*) and unreal. In this radical manner the Mahāyāna reduces all possible objects of experience, whether internal or external, to the Void (*śūnyatā*), which is not a state of non-existence or privation but, rather, the ineffable non-dual Reality which transcends all apparent oppositions, such as being and non-being, self and others, Saṁsāra and Nirvana. Expressed in more positive terms, all things exist in a state of suchness or thusness (*tathatā*) and, since this is one suchness, also in a state of sameness (*samatā*). On the mundane level, the Sangha/laity binary represents a socio-ecclesiastical rather than a spiritual division, all followers of the Buddha being united through their common devotion to the Bodhisattva ideal. Faith, as a means of attaining Enlightenment, ranks coordinate with Wisdom. The Buddha is regarded not only as an enlightened being but also as the embodiment of the Truth and Reality behind the universe. Besides being endowed with three Bodies (*trikāya*), the Dharmakāya or Body of Truth, the Sambhogakāya or Body of Reciprocal Enjoyment, and the Nirmāṅakāya or Created Body—corresponding to the absolute, the celestial and mundane planes of existence—He has various forms and attributes. These are different Buddhas and Bodhisattvas, such as Amitābha, the Buddha of Infinite Light, and Mañjuśrī, Avalokiteśvara and Vajrapāṇi, the Bodhisattvas of Wisdom, Compassion and Power respectively, around each of whom there centres a popular cult. In the field of philosophy the Mahāyāna is represented by the two great schools of the Mādhyamikas and the Yogācārins, the first founded (or rather systematized) by Nāgārjuna (*circ.* 150 A.D.) and the second by Asaṅga (*circ.* 400 A.D.) under the inspiration of the Bodhisattva Maitreya. Both are based primarily on the doctrine of *Śūnyatā* as taught in the Perfection of Wisdom *sūtras*; but there are important differences of approach which give to each their special character. The Mādhyamikas or followers of the Mean emphasize Wisdom, and their method is dialectical. They reduce mind and matter directly to Śūnyatā, the truth of which is revealed by exposing the self-contradictory nature of all statements about the Absolute. The Yogācārins or Practitioners of Yoga, on the other hand, stress Meditation, and their approach is intuitive. They reduce matter to mind and then mind to Śūnyatā, the truth of which dawns upon the purified consciousness in the depths of meditation. In later centuries the two teachings were sometimes regarded as constituting one continuous doctrinal system, wherein the Yogācāra represented the relative and the Mādhyamika the absolute truth.

The Vajrayāna, the "Diamond Vehicle" or "Adamantine Way," is so called because, like the irresistible *vajra*, meaning both thunderbolt and diamond, it immediately annihilates all obstacles to the attainment of Buddahood. It is predominantly yogic-magical in character, and its ideal is the Siddha, "a man who is so much in harmony with the cosmos that he is under no constraint whatsoever, and as a free agent is able to manipulate the cosmic forces both inside and outside himself."[1] Except that it aims at the realization of Śūnyatā not only mentally but also physically, the Vajrayāna differs from the Mahāyāna less in respect of doctrine than in its methods. Its goal is the transmutation of the body, speech and mind of the initiate into the Body, Speech and Mind of the Tathāgata, that is to say, into the Nirmāṇakāya, the Sambhogakāya and the Dharmakāya. In the case of the Lower Tantra this transmutation can take place in sixteen lives, and in that of the Higher Tantra in the space of one life. Such a tremendous acceleration of the normal rate of spiritual evolution requires not only the concentrated practise of various highly esoteric yogic exercizes but also a special transmission of spiritual power from an enlightened guru. For this reason the guru occupies in the Vajrayāna an even more exalted position than in the other *yānas*, being regarded as the Buddha Himself in human guise. Various forms of Vajrayāna can be distinguished. These are not doctrinal schools but lines of spiritual transmission which, so far as the human plane is concerned, originated with one or another of the Eighty-four Siddhas, prominent among whom were Padmasambhava or Padmakara and Sarahapada.

IX. The Spiritual Life

While the experience of Enlightenment is instantaneous, the approach to it is always gradual. In Buddhism, therefore, the spiritual life consists essentially in the following of a path, the

---

[1] E. Conze, *A Short History of Buddhism* (Chetana, Bombay, 1960), p. x.

successive steps and stages of which have been carefully mapped out by tradition in accordance with the spiritual experience of the Buddha and His disciples, both immediate and remote. As temperaments and methods of practise differ, this path can be formulated in various ways and the number and order of its constituent factors determined and described from various points of view. Thus it comes about that we have not only the Āryan Eightfold Path and the Path of the Ten Perfections and Ten Stages—two of the best-known formulations—but also the Path as consisting of seven stages of purification, thirteen "abodes" (*vihāra*), fifty-two *yānas*, and so on, the list being practically interminable. What we may call the architectonic of the Path, however, does not vary, just as the different types of bridges, built in accordance with the same principles of mechanics and for the same purpose, reveal the same basic structure. This architectonic is most clearly exhibited in the formula of the Three Trainings (*triśikṣā*), namely Morality (*śīla*), Meditation (*samādhi*) and Wisdom (*prajñā*), which according to one tradition was the recurrent theme of the discourses delivered by the Buddha during His last tour, and concerning which He is represented as declaring, "Great becomes the fruit, great the advantage of samādhi, when it is set round with śīla. Great becomes the fruit, great the advantage of prajñā when it is set round with samādhi."[1]

In its primary sense *śīla* means "behaviour" and in its derived sense "good behaviour." All behaviour, good or bad, is the expression of a mental attitude. Despite the formidable lists of precepts with which, in practise, Buddhist ethics has tended to become identified, *śīla* is in the last analysis defined in purely psychological terms as those actions which are associated with karmically wholesome mental states and dissociated from those which are karmically unwholesome. What constitutes a wholesome mental state differs from one *yāna* to another; or rather, there is a difference of emphasis. For the Hīnayāna, good actions are those connected with the wholesome mental roots of non-greed (*alobha*), non-hate (*adveṣa*) and non-delusion (*amoha*)—for the Mahāyāna and Vajrayāna, those inspired by love (*maitrī*) and compassion (*karuṇā*) for sentient beings. Bodily and verbal ac-

[1] *Dīgha-Nikāya* ii. 81 *et seq.*

tions being the extensions of mental states, these states can be induced by the performance of the actions, whether good or bad, self-regarding or altruistic, which are their natural expression. In this fact lies the importance of *śīla* as a preparation for *samādhi*.

Samādhi or Meditation (the translation is approximate only) comprizes the exercizes by means of which the practitioner attains mental concentration and the superconscious states, as well as these states themselves. It is the heart and centre of the Buddhist spiritual life. In the words of a modern authority, its significance is that "It uses concentrated force to investigate Buddhist philosophic truth and transform it from being abstract perception into a concrete inner realization whereby liberation from sorrows and false views, embodiment of Nirvana, and the functions of salvation are all attained."[1] Broadly speaking, in the Hīnayāna the term *samādhi* generally refers to the practise of the meditation exercizes, and in the Mahāyāna to the spiritual states attained by such practise. Thirty-eight or forty meditation exercizes are enumerated, but in fact there are more. Among the most popular are the contemplation of the ten stages of decomposition of a corpse, by means of which craving (*lobha*) is destroyed, the cultivation of loving-kindness (*maitrī*) towards all sentient beings, which destroys hate (*dveṣa*), and mindfulness of the bodily movements and the process of respiration, which leads to the destruction of delusion (*moha*). The Mahāyāna makes use of the same exercizes but combines them with the practise of Śūnyatā. In the Vajrayāna, Meditation includes the repetition of the mantras of the Buddhas and Bodhisattvas and the visualization of Their forms which, after being conjured forth from the voidness, worshipped, and meditated upon, are resolved back into it again. There are also various exercizes which, by manipulating the gross energies of the physical body, aim at activating their subtle and transcendental counterparts. Whatever the type of exercize may be, the aim of it is to attain a state of purity and translucency of mind wherein the Truth can be as it were reflected.

In general *prajñā* or Wisdom is threefold, as based upon

[1] C.M. Chen, *Buddhist Meditation, Systematic and Practical.* Kalimpong, 1967.

learning (literally "hearing"), upon independent thought and reflection, and upon meditation (*bhāvanā*, that which is (mentally) developed, or "made to become"). Here the third kind or Wisdom proper is to be understood. This may be described as a direct, non-conceptual apprehension of transcendental Reality. For the Hīnayāna such apprehension arises when things and persons are viewed exclusively in terms of the *dharmas*, or ultimate elements of existence; for the Mahāyāna, when the *dharmas* themselves are seen as Śūnyatā. In either case, the result is a permanent disruption of the web of illusion resulting in one instance in the attainment of Arahantship and in the other of Supreme Buddhahood. What, for want of a better word, we are compelled to term Buddhist philosophy is, in fact, essentially the conceptual formulation of the non-conceptual content of Wisdom or Enlightenment. Correctly understood, the Sarvāstivāda, the Sautrāntika, the Yogācāra or Vijñānavāda and the Mādhyamika are not rival systems of thought, one of which must be true and the rest false, but expressions on the intellectual plane of successively more advanced degrees of spiritual insight. The technique is for a philosophy pertaining to a more advanced degree of insight to utilize the formulations of a less advanced degree in order to undermine its basic assumptions, thus impelling the practitioner to move from a more to a less limited experience of Reality.

X. Nirvana

Although the state of perfection attained by following the Path is said to be ineffable, it is referred to in the Scriptures by a bewilderingly rich variety of names. The best known of these in the West is Nirvana, from the root *vā*, meaning to blow, and the prefix *nir*, out or off. Its Pali equivalent Nibbāṇa is made up of the negative particle *ni* and *vana* meaning selfish desire or craving. Hence the traditional explanations of Nirvana as the "blowing out" of the fires of greed, hatred and delusion and as the state wherein the thirst for sensuous experience, for continued existence, and even for non-existence is altogether absent. Notwithstanding these etymologies, however, the goal of Buddhism is far from being a purely negative state, a metaphysical and psychological zero wherein individuality disappears, as some of the older orientalists maintained that the Buddhists believed. What does not in reality exist cannot be said to cease to exist: all that is extinguished is the false assumption of an individual being distinct from and independent of the psycho-physical processes of which it is composed. Positive descriptions of Nirvana are in fact of no less frequent occurrence in the Scriptures than negative ones, though in both cases it must be borne in mind that these are not so much definitions in the logical sense as conceptual-cum-verbal signposts pointing in the direction of a realization which leaves them far behind. No necessary connection exists between the word "orange" and the fruit of that name; but one who has been told that it is a golden nearly globose fruit belonging to the genus *Citrus* may be able, with the help of this description, to identify it and experience its unique and indefinable flavour for himself. Psychologically, Nirvana is a state of absolute illumination, supreme bliss, infinite love and compassion, unshakeable serenity, and unrestricted spiritual freedom. Ontologically, it is for the Hīnayāna the eternal, unchanging, extra-mental spiritual entity wholly unconnected with the cosmic process, and for the Mahāyāna the Absolute Reality transcending all oppositions including that between itself and the Saṁsāra. As the supreme object of the spiritual consciousness, or Dharmakāya, it is the embodiment of Great Wisdom and Great Compassion and embraces all possible virtues and perfections. It is the Infinite Light (Amitābha) which shines not without sentient beings but within and the Boundless Life (Amitāyus) which has nothing to do with personal immortality.

XI. Art

Consideration has been given to the general nature of the relation between Buddhism and Art in the author's essay "Buddhism and Art." Here it need only be observed that, great as the æsthetic value of Buddhist art may be, it is a functional and religious art deeply rooted in conceptions belonging to the transcendental order and designed as a means not so much of æsthetic enjoyment as of spiritual realization. Thus the *vihāra*, *saṅghārāma* and *lena* are places for living the communal religious life, the Buddha or Bodhisattva image an object of worship, whether private or public, the sculptured gateway and the frescoed wall a series of lessons in the previous lives of the Śākyamuni, the *stūpa* simultaneously a reliquary, a focus of popular devotion and a synthesis of cosmic symbology, and the illuminations of manuscripts a guide to the visualization of divine forms in the realms of meditative consciousness. Buddhist art, in other words, is primarily Buddhist and only secondarily art. Failure to take this fact fully into account is bound to result in a serious collapse of understanding. This is particularly so, perhaps, in the case of the art of Tibet, which according to Chögyam Trungpa is "entirely based on the spirituality of Buddhism."[1]

XII. Social and Political Ideals

As a teaching aiming at the experience of Enlightenment, Buddhism has no direct concern with the collective life of man on the social and political level. It does not tell its followers how many wives they may have or what forms of government they should support. At the same time, as the existence of the Monastic Order indicates, external conditions are by no means irrelevant to the development of the wholesome mental attitudes on which the experience of Enlightenment depends. A minimum of social and political teachings are, therefore, scattered here and there throughout the Tipiṭaka. That notwithstanding the example of Asoka they were never taken up and systematically developed in India is perhaps due to the predominantly philosophical and other-worldly tendency of the Indian Buddhist mind. Matters of everyday social ethics apart, the social teachings of Buddhism concentrate upon two vitally important issues: caste and means of livelihood. The Buddha rejected the system of hereditary caste. A man's position in society, he maintained, is determined not by birth (*jāti*) but by worth, by conduct (*caraṇa*) and character (*caritra*) rather than by descent. Brahminical pretensions to hereditary holiness were therefore dismissed with ridicule, and membership of the Buddhist community, whether as monks or lay devotees, thrown open to all who took refuge in

---

[1] *Visual Dharma: The Buddhist Art of Tibet.* Shambhala, Berkeley and London, 1975.

The Three Jewels and were prepared to observe the *śīla* appropriate to their vocation. Means of livelihood (*ājīva*) are of two kinds, right (*samyak*) and wrong (*mithya*). The Buddha refused to concede that a man's life could be compartmentalized, with his professional conduct governed by one set of standards and his private life by another, or that the former constituted a neutral field to which ethical considerations need not apply. He went so far, indeed, as to prohibit essentially unethical occupations, such as those of the butcher, the dealer in poisons, and the weapon-maker, and to make Right Means of Livelihood (*samyak-ājīva*) the fifth member of the Aryan Eightfold Path.

In the sphere of politics Buddhism holds that the government should promote the welfare of the people (not excluding animals) by all possible means. Religion is to be made the basis of national life. In particular, morality is to be encouraged and the Sangha supported. This simple but sublime ideal finds picturesque embodiment in the figure of the Cakravarti-rāja or Dharmarāja (the latter representing, perhaps, the most distinctively Buddhist phase of the conception) as described, for example, in the *Mahāsudassana Suttanta.*[1] Historically speaking, it receives splendid exemplification in the person of Asoka, who in his Thirteenth Rock Edict renounces war and proclaims the ideal of *dharma-vijaya* or victory through righteousness, as well as being cultivated with varying degrees of success by later rulers, both Indian and non-Indian, who strove to emulate the most illustrious of the Mauryas.

Yet despite the greatness of his achievement it is doubtful if even Asoka—not to mention Kaniṣka, Duṭugämuṇu, Srongtsan Gampo, and Shōtoku Taishi—fully realized the potentialities of the Buddha's Teaching as a catalyst of social as well as individual transformation. Those potentialities could be realized, perhaps, only at the present time, when we confront the same problems as Asoka did but on an infinitely vaster scale—when the choice is not between war and peace in a particular part of a particular country but between the destruction and the continued existence of humanity itself. It is therefore not surprizing that, although the Buddha's Teaching long ago disappeared from India (to be revived there in our own lifetimes), and although in

[1] *Dīgha-Nikāya,* Sutta 17.

the rest of Asia institutional Buddhism has been seriously weakened—in large areas virtually wiped out—by more militant creeds, the importance of Buddhism as a spiritual teaching should be more widely recognized than ever at the present time, particularly in the West. Indeed, Buddhism is increasingly seen as holding the key not only to the spiritual development of the individual but to the creation, in the world, of that Sangha or Spiritual Community the presence of which is alone able to counteract the forces of destruction. In these circumstances it is natural that we should look in the direction of the East and make a "Survey of Buddhism."

CHAPTER ONE

THE BUDDHA AND BUDDHISM

I. The Approach to Buddhism

THE importance of Right Motive, of a correct attitude of mind, is emphasized more strongly in Buddhism than in any other form of traditional teaching. Bodily and vocal actions are regarded not as so many detachable appendages of personality, but as a true expression of our subjective selves, as the externalization of our innermost thoughts and desires, and they are judged and evaluated accordingly. It would be strange if the very study of Buddhism—the taking, that is to say, of the Dharma itself as subject of investigation—should be exempted from the application of this principle. There are wrong as well as right motives, bad as well as good mental attitudes, with which the study of the Teaching may be taken up; and the importance of Right Motive and correct mental attitude is stressed here as elsewhere, not out of any abstract notion of respect due to the Dharma, but simply and solely because it is quite impossible to understand the Dharma truly without them.

At the risk of appearing dogmatic (not that dogmatism, in the sense of an intellectually precise formulation of spiritual certainties, is necessarily a bad thing) we have to insist that inasmuch as the Dharma is the means of emancipation, the Raft that ferries us across the waters of birth-and-death to the Farther Shore of Nirvana, the state of Matchless Security, the only possible Right Motive with which the study of Buddhism can be undertaken is the hope that through such study Enlightenment may ultimately be attained. "Just as the great ocean, O Monks, has one taste, the taste of salt," declared the Buddha, "even so, O Monks, this Doctrine and Discipline have one taste, the taste of Emancipation."[1]

To ignore or to lose sight of this explicit and quite unambiguous statement of the sole function which the Dharma is meant to

---

[1] *Vinaya*, II. 239.

perform, and either consciously or unconsciously to regard it as possessing any other significance or value whatsoever, is a wrong mental attitude that can result in nothing but the gravest misunderstanding.

Does this mean that the scientific study of Buddhism, to which several generations of illustrious scholars have devoted their lives, is a mistake, a procedure which should now be as much as possible discouraged, and finally abandoned altogether? Is the orthodox study of the Dharma as the means of emancipation so intolerant of humanistic rivalry that, like the Turkish monarch of eighteenth–century belief, it can bear "no brother near the throne" of its supremacy? Our meaning need not be construed so drastically. We do not wish that the scientific study of Buddhism should be abolished, but that it should be relegated to its proper place in the hierarchy of disciplines, where it may continue to perform its useful but distinctly subordinate function. Like many other things it is wrong not in itself, but only when it is put in the wrong place. Lucifer, to borrow an illustration from the Hebrew tradition, was an angel of light so long as he remained content with his own place in the celestial hierarchy; he became the Prince of Darkness only when he sought to usurp a position higher than the one which had been allotted him. In order that all possibility of misunderstanding may be precluded, it is not only necessary to insist that the scientific study of Buddhism be relegated to its proper place in the scale of values, but at the same time to indicate the nature and scope of such a study and to define clearly its lateral limitations.

Before this can be done it will be necessary for us to remind ourselves of the nature of the scientific method generally. It is intellectual. It believes, or at least its procedure is based on the conscious or unconscious assumption, that the unaided intellect is capable of penetrating to the truth about the subject of its researches. The scientific study of Buddhism will, therefore, be *a priori* limited to those aspects of the Dharma which are susceptible of an intellectual understanding, while the Dharma as a whole, being concerned exclusively with the Path of Emancipation, and more particularly with those actualities which, we are expressly told, exist "beyond the reach of reasoning" (*atakkavacaro*), will transcend the sphere of its investigations. What remains as a legitimate subject of scientific enquiry, after the spiritual essence, the transcendental core, of Buddhism has been excluded from its purview, are the various spatial and temporal forms which even a purely transcendental Teaching is compelled to assume in order to accommodate itself to the capacities of human beings.

Spiritual teaching is often imparted through the medium of language, and the nature of the language used, its origin and development, its grammatical structure, literary forms and influence upon other languages are legitimate subjects of scientific research. Science may even be permitted to arrive at conclusions about them, provided that such conclusions are strictly philological and make no attempt to trespass on spiritual preserves. Similarly, the traditional Buddhist fine and applied arts and other æsthetic expressions of the Dharma, Buddhist archæology and epigraphy, together with the history of Buddhism on its institutional side (in its essence, being a space-and-time-transcending spiritual experience, Buddhism has no history) may be regarded as subjects which it is within the competence of the scientific method to examine. Indeed, such scientific studies may be, when they do not seek to extend their "vast prerogative" if not "so far as Jove" then at least certainly beyond the proper sphere of its authority, not only useful but almost necessary even from the strictly Buddhist point of view. Unless we happen to be Bodhisattvas, in which case we should be able to see the Buddha in His Sambhogakaya and hear Him preaching to the assembly of Bodhisattvas in one of the celestial realms, we are dependent for our knowledge of the Dharma upon an acquaintance with the various spatio-temporal forms in which it has found embodiment. It is for this reason that Buddhists down the ages have had of necessity to concern themselves with subjects which, having become detached from the main body of Western traditional knowledge to which they originally belonged, are now regarded as independent "sciences." Many orthodox commentators are fond of indulging in a little amateur philology. The philology is often bad; but the lessons they draw from it are generally excellent. The ancient world, if the choice had been placed before it, would no doubt have preferred bad philology with good doctrine to bad doctrine (sometimes no doctrine at all) and good philology. The modern world plumps for good philology regardless of consequences. There is of course no reason why our sciences and our doctrine should not both be sound; but if one of the two must be sacrificed, then by all means let it be the less valuable.

We believe, however, that the scientific study of Buddhism within the limits necessarily imposed upon it by the nature of the scientific method itself need not be considered irreconcilable with the traditional approach to the Dharma. (We distinguish "Buddhism" from "the Dharma" and link it with "scientific study" because the term is itself a product of scientific modes of thought and has, if all its connotations are taken into account, no traditional equivalent, though "Dharma" is more often than not mistakenly regarded as such.) All that we insist is that the two methods can be used together only when the scientific study of Buddhism is recognized as possessing a merely subordinate and instrumental value and is not permitted to transgress its own clearly defined limits. The Teaching, it is true, exists in texts, and these texts are written in languages which may be learned with the help of dictionaries and grammars. But we refuse to admit that merely because he understands the language in which Buddhist texts are written, even though it be to the point of being able to "translate" them into a modern language, the mere scholar may for this reason alone be considered equal to the task of exploring the spiritual significance of those texts or of explaining it to others. Much less still can we agree that one who refuses to accept the existence of a transcendental Principle, whether in the Buddhistic sense or in some other way, can ever hope to understand a doctrine whose sole concern is with the realization of such a Principle. It may even be said that a student belonging to a non-Buddhist tradition which affirms the existence of a spiritual world beyond the physical senses and the mind, in however crude and exclusive a form the affirmation may be made, has sometimes a better chance of understanding the Dharma than a conscientiously impartial person who has no belief in the reality of such a world. Of course, should the tradition concerned formulate its affirmation in so chronically exclusive a manner that any genuine recognition of the spiritual value of an alternative formulation is rendered impossible from its point of view, then misrepresentations far more serious than those of our "impartial" materialist will inevitably arise.

During the last hundred years, which is the length of the

period for which the Bodhi-Dharma, transformed by modern science into "Buddhism," has been known to the Western world and its Westernized dependencies (both political and cultural) in the East, the Doctrine of the Enlightened One has had to suffer misrepresentation at the hands of friends and foes alike. *Avidyā* (ignorance), *moha* (delusion), or *mithyā-dṛṣṭi* (wrong understanding) is the intellectual counterpart of lust-and-hate (*lobha-dveśa*), and though ultimately the feeling of attraction is inseparable from that of repulsion, the immediate genesis of ignorance may be from either of them separately. There are those who dislike Buddhism for the right reason as well as those who like it for the wrong reason, and which form of misunderstanding is ultimately more fatal to the Dharma it would be difficult to say. One thing, however, is clear. With the marvellously increased dissemination of factual knowledge about Buddhism which has been witnessed in both East and West during the last few years, the malicious misrepresentations, the deliberate distortions, of Buddhist doctrine, which certain interested persons and parties strove so sedulously to circulate only a few years ago, are finding it more and more difficult to win credence. A great deal of the original hostility to Buddhism has gone underground and reveals itself not in open criticism of Buddhist doctrine so much as in underhand attempts to hinder the efforts made by Buddhist organizations to propagate the Dharma. In fact, so far as the West is concerned, open misrepresentation of the Dharma has almost disappeared from intellectually responsible quarters, and would appear to be largely confined to pulp magazines and Protestant Christian missionary literature.

Nowadays Buddhism has more often to pray for protection from its friends than from its enemies. The number of those who like Buddhism for the wrong reason, or who, more correctly, are attracted by what they wrongly imagine is Buddhism, is increasing, and by reason of their very sincerity they constitute a growing threat to the purity and integrity of the Doctrine which they profess to support. Such people will generally be found to have developed strong religious convictions prior to their study of Buddhism. These convictions they do not wish to have unsettled, and although genuinely attracted by certain aspects of the Dharma they do not hesitate to challenge, misinterpret or simply "explain away" whatever other aspects of the Teaching are in conflict with their preconceived ideas. One of the most original contributions of the Buddha to human knowledge is the discovery of the fact that theories are rooted in desires, and the very tenacity with which, in the face of the clearest textual evidence to the contrary, such students persist in clinging to their erroneous interpretations of the Dharma, is an unmistakable indication of the extent of their emotional commitment. Theories of a personal God and an immortal soul are so deeply rooted in the soil of the human heart that belief in them has often been regarded as synonymous with religion itself. Such belief is not synonymous with the Dharma. The Buddha in fact taught that belief in a personal God and an immortal soul were rationalizations of desires, of our craving for love and protection, our attachment to our own personalities and our thirst for life. Enlightenment can be attained by the renunciation not only of selfish desires but of the religious theories or "views" (*dṛṣṭi*) which are based on those desires. Belief in personal God and immortal soul are not helps but hindrances to one who would follow the Dharma, and the student who is strongly attached to such beliefs and who feels at the same time attracted by certain aspects of Buddhism, or who shrinks from the suggestion that so distinguished a tradition should deny his most cherished convictions, will be compelled by his emotional needs to blunder into misunderstandings and misinterpretations of the Dharma. "The Buddha *must* have believed in God," cry some such people, "He *could not* have denied the existence of the Atman," protest others; but unfortunately for them the Buddha did do both "shocking" things. The Wisdom of the Tathagata is not to be measured by the yardstick of human intelligence, nor limited by the cravings of the human heart.

The ideal student of Buddhism would be one who, whether scientifically trained or not, was prepared to admit the possibility of a spiritual experience which would transcend the physical senses and the rational mind, and who would be willing to give unprejudiced consideration to the Buddha's claim that He had achieved this experience Himself and that by following His Teaching others might achieve it for themselves too. Such a person would not commit the mistake of thinking that the intellect, though capable of performing useful preliminary work, was able to penetrate the inner meaning of Buddhism, or that Truth would reveal itself to any faculty save to intuition awakened by spiritual practice. He or she would be free from beliefs which, though they pass for religious doctrines in the world, are in fact born of fear, craving and other egocentric emotions. Resolved fearlessly to pursue, frankly to examine and faithfully to accept and follow, whatever the truth about Buddhism might turn out to be, such an ideal student could be said to be fairly well equipped for the study of Buddhism, and to approach the Dharma with at least an approximation to Right Motive in the specifically Buddhist sense.

We are not unaware that it will be objected, and objected with good reason, that very few students of Buddhism can be expected to meet the somewhat exacting demands that we have made of them; but we have enunciated the principle involved with the minimum of compromise, not because we expect that it will in all cases be lived up to, but in order to insist upon the limitations of the merely scientific approach to the study of transcendental doctrines, and to combat, if only to the extent of explicit contradiction, the modern tendency to believe that spiritual truths can be understood by those who have not been spiritually trained. All intending students of Buddhism would do well to remember, however, that the Heart of the Dharma, the spiritual essence which underlies and interpenetrates all doctrinal formulations, metaphysical disciplines and æsthetic expressions, will be revealed, not in proportion to the bulk of our scholastic equipment, but only to the extent to which we have cultivated Right Motive.

If we render Right Aspiration (also known as Right-Mindedness, etc.) back into the original Pali or Sanskrit term, and adopt the analysis given in the ancient texts, we shall see that *Sammā-sankappo* or *Samyak-saṁkalpa* is said to comprise the mental states of *alobha* (non-greed), *adosa* (non-hatred) and *ahiṁsa* (non-injury). From the modern point of view it might seem strange that a certain purity of mind should be helpful, even indispensable, to the proper understanding of traditional teachings. If so, it would indicate the greatness of the extent to which modern life and thought had lost their anchorage in Tradition. From the viewpoint of traditional spirituality, as it exists in varying degrees of purity in all the great religions of the world, the way in which a man lives is not unrelated to his capacity for the apprehension of Truth, and his ability to understand doctrines of a transcendental nature is thought in part to be determined not only by the integrity of his approach to these doctrines themselves but also by the integrity of his character in all the relations of life. Even a tradition so well barnacled with theistic accretions as Christianity has not forgotten that it is the "pure in heart" who shall "see God." Our study of the Dharma will be fruitful only if we ourselves have some hankering after the spiritual life.

II. The Study of the Dharma: Methods and Materials

Though it may be true that the most serious obstacles to the proper understanding of Buddhism are those which exist in the student's own mind, and though it may be a fact that psychological obstructions are generally much more difficult to remove than any merely physical barrier erected by circumstances or forces outside us, it would be a mistake to assume for this reason that obstacles external to the mind of the student do not exist, or that once he is furnished with the key of Right Motive no further difficulties will be encountered—that every door will yield at his approach, every lock fly open before him. With the key of Right Motive in his hand the student of Buddhism may indeed draw near the dragon-warded portals of the Palace of Wisdom with the confidence that he has only to "turn the key softly in the oilèd wards" for the adamantine doors to swing open at a touch. But what if he stands at the wrong door? What if he tries to insert the right key into the wrong lock?

The obstacles to which, with the help of a traditional similitude, we are now drawing the reader's attention, are not unrelated to the merely intellectual, scientific, or non-traditional approach to the study of Buddhism discussed in the foregoing pages. Scientifically trained scholars not only conduct researches into Buddhism but also publish the results of their labours in books and magazines. Under modern conditions, such publications are generally for a long time the sole sources of knowledge available to the student, who, with his unreflecting worship of scientific methods and academic qualifications, is in any case predisposed to accept them at their face value, and to regard them as authentic expositions of the Dharma. So long as the works in question recognize the limitations of the scientific method, and confine themselves to those aspects of Buddhism which are susceptible of a purely intellectual approach, the student suffers little positive harm. He is deprived, indeed, of a great positive good, that of an acquaintance with the Dharma as the source and means of spiritual life; but if he is himself spiritually perceptive he will sense it, like an invisible perfume in a musty chamber, underneath the layers of arid exposition and dusty comment; and in any case the possibility of such acquaintance at some time in the future is not precluded. Meanwhile, he may be obscurely aware that he is being offered, in gospel phrase, a stone instead of bread, and he may even join the poet in his lament

Oh what a dusty answer gets the soul
When hot for certainties in this our life!

Unfortunately, few of the numerous "scholarly" books on Buddhism are content to remain within the proper limits of scientific investigation. The majority of them appear to be quite unconscious that there are realms into which the intellect is powerless to penetrate, and rarely, if ever, do they refrain from dogmatizing in the most pontifical manner on the fundamental verities of Buddhism. Should the unwary student be so unfortunate as to encounter, at the outset of his career, works of this misleading kind, irreparable harm may be done; for he would have to be possessed of "roots of merit" of quite extraordinary strength to be able to surmount so huge an obstacle and arrive, eventually, at a true understanding of the Dharma.

We therefore emphasize how important it is for the student to avoid from the very beginning practically all books which are merely "about" Buddhism, and to place instead almost his whole reliance upon the actual Word of the Buddha and on the sayings and writings of His enlightened disciples through the ages. The temptation to derive knowledge and guidance from popular manuals, especially from those written by non-Buddhists, should be firmly resisted; for such productions are generally little more than compilations from a number of scientific works, usually old ones, and possess little originality apart from their own contribution of misunderstandings and mistakes. The ideal method of studying Buddhism would be to read in the original language a number of carefully selected texts belonging to the

Pali, Sanskrit, Chinese, Tibetan, Mongolian or Japanese canonical Buddhist literature. Should this for any reason be deemed impracticable (under modern conditions it will be so for all save the most diligent and earnest students) the next best method of learning the Dharma is by studying some of the numerous translations of such texts which now exist in many modern languages, both European and Asian. Preference should be given, in those cases where the purely scientific qualifications of the translators are more or less equal, to versions of Buddhist texts which have been made, if not by professed Buddhists, then at least by persons sympathetic towards Buddhism. Indeed, it may even at times be found that translations which are, from the literary point of view, uncouth and clumsy in the extreme, but which have been made by persons possessed of genuine insight into the Dharma, are capable of opening the inner eye of the student in a way which the most exact and polished translation made by the mere scholar is powerless to effect. Wong Mow Lam's English version of *The Sutra Spoken by the Sixth Patriarch (Wei Lang) on the High Seat of the Gem of Law* (Shanghai) is an excellent example of this type of translation. Despite bad grammar, faulty syntax and wrong use of words (to say nothing of printer's errors, coarse paper and unattractive binding of the original edition) there shines through its pages a light which is not of this world, so that it enjoys among many English students of Buddhism—some of whom owe to it their first glimpse of Enlightenment—an esteem which is hardly equalled by that of the most scholarly translations from the Buddha-Word itself. It should not be thought, though, that by reading a Buddhist text in translation the student is excused from all knowledge whatsoever of the language in which it was originally composed. There are key-words in the Indo-Aryan language or languages in which the Buddha preached that cannot be satisfactorily rendered by a single equivalent in any modern tongue not in the line of direct descent from the languages of ancient India. The meaning of these key-words, such as *Nirvāṇa, saṁsāra, citta, dharma, prajñā, mokṣa* and many more must the student learn, not by consulting dictionaries merely, but by carefully noting the various contexts in which they occur, and by systematically meditating upon the actualities of which they are symbols. Inasmuch as even the richest languages of modern Europe are woefully deficient not only in such "religious" or "philosophical" terms, but even in a term to describe such terms (for strictly speaking they pertain neither to religion nor philosophy as understood in the West, but to something including and transcending both, which can be described only as "Dharma"), the most painstaking translation of a Pali or Sanskrit text into French or German or any other modern European language is by the very act of translation distorted to a degree of which the student is generally quite unaware. The greater the number of "key-words" translated, and the more "understandable" the translation appears at the beginning to the student, the greater the degree of distortion is likely to be. Such a danger is to be guarded against by leaving all key-words untranslated (a number of approximate equivalents may be given within brackets the first time each such word occurs), by which means the student will gradually learn to accustom himself to their use and in time will grow familiar with their significance. Should it be objected that such a method of study will impose great difficulties on the student, we shall reply that it is better to arrive with difficulty at a true understanding of the Dharma than to arrive with ease at an understanding that is wrong and false.

Smooth the descent, and easy is the way;
But to return, and gain the cheerful skies,
Therein the toil and mighty labour lies.

Renderings of Buddhist texts which fail to leave untranslated the Indo-Aryan key-words, and books on Buddhism which, instead of employing such terms, not only make use of Western religious and philosophical expressions—many of which have acquired a Christian connotation quite foreign to the spirit of Buddhism—but also attempt to reduce the Dharma to some modern 'ism or 'ology, should be either scrupulously avoided or employed with the utmost circumspection. Where it is difficult or impossible for the student to read either original text or reliable translation of a portion of the Buddhist Canon he should as far as possible confine himself to books by professed Buddhists, preferably by members of the Sangha. This we say not out of sectarian prejudice, nor from any desire to aggrandize a particular body of men, but simply and solely for the reasons to which we have already sought to give clear expression, namely, that inasmuch as the Dharma is a way of life aiming at

Enlightenment it can be best understood and expounded by those who in both theory and practice accept and follow it as such. Members of the Sangha, the Holy Order of the monastic disciples of the Lord Buddha, for this reason have ever been revered in the Buddhist lands of Asia as the custodians of the Dharma, and regarded as being, by reason of their special vocation, more qualified to teach it than other people. In some such countries a Buddhist layman will, even now, speak in public on the Doctrine only with the utmost diffidence, and never without first making it clear that whatever he says is subject to correction by the Sangha.

Though the student may grasp the necessity of Right Motive in the study of Buddhism, and also understand the importance of having right material for study, there remain some minor occasions of misunderstanding against which also he must be on his guard. We have said that the best way of studying the Dharma is to rely first on the Buddha-Word in the original language, secondly upon translations which are from the traditional point of view reliable, and thirdly on books about Buddhism which have been written by men possessing the traditional qualifications for teaching the Dharma. Here, "best way" includes not only the material but the method of study, and between the ancient and traditional and the modern and non-traditional methods of studying a scriptural text there exists, though the fact is often lost sight of, a very great deal of difference. In ancient India to learn a text did not mean to read it by oneself. It meant to learn, recite, study and meditate upon it at the feet of one's teacher. In fact, learning and hearing were represented by the same word, and a learned man was not one who had read many books but one who had "heard" much. This idiom did not arise solely from the lack of writing materials but, in the case of spiritual lore at least, out of the very nature of the spiritual experience itself and of the inexorable laws governing the transmission from one human being to another of knowledge pertaining to the means whereby Truth may be realized. In all traditional civilizations the relation between Master and disciple was one of the basic facts of life, and to be without a teacher was synonymous with being without education or culture of any kind. Though much that does not directly pertain to the Path of Liberation may now be learned by the private perusal of printed literature, the traditional practice of studying scriptural texts with a teacher who has more than a theoretical knowledge of them is still the best method of penetrating into the essence of the Dharma. Under the conditions which generally obtain in modern society it will but rarely be possible for the student to live either in his master's house, as was the Brahminical practice, or in a monastery dedicated to the use of the Sangha, as was and to a great extent still is the custom in many Buddhist countries. In those places, however, where the traditional Buddhist way of life has not yet capitulated to the forces of materialism and secularism it will still be possible for him to go and sit for regular instruction at the feet of a qualified teacher, be it Ceylon *bhikkhu* or Tibetan *gelong*, and in this way to learn the correct interpretation of the text selected for study. Students of Buddhism who have the misfortune to live in places where the light of the Dharma does not yet shine in its full glory should at least take full advantage of the temporary presence of those members of the Sangha who follow the Buddha's exhortation to go forth and preach "out of compassion for the world, for the welfare and happiness of gods and men" (*Vinaya, Mahavagga*). However short the duration of the visiting *bhikkhu's* stay may be, it should be utilized to the full for clearing up doubts, resolving difficulties, and in short for gaining a clearer comprehension of the Dharma. Earnest students of Buddhism living in a non-Buddhist environment should meet for discussion, as well as for group study and meditation, as often and as regularly as possible. As soon as their resources permit, they should make arrangements for periodical visits by a qualified member of the Sangha. Eventually, as their numbers grow, they will feel the need of having in their midst a permanently resident monk to provide them with continuous spiritual guidance. Without a personal teacher the study of the Dharma is beset with many difficulties; but in the absence of a guru progress in the higher spiritual life is rendered almost impossible. As Sarahapada sings in the *Dohākosha* or Treasury of Songs:—

It is This that's read and This that's meditated;
It's This that's discussed in treatises and old legends.
There is no school of thought which does not have This
as its aim,
But one sees it only at the feet of one's master.

Students who have no means of direct contact with a teacher, and who are therefore obliged to study alone, should not, however, despair of making good progress. Taking the Dharma itself as their guide, they should diligently apply themselves to the accumulation of a stock of merit (*punya-sambhāra*) with the firm conviction that, as an ancient adage says, "When the disciple is ready the Master will be there."

The student who is possessed of Right Motive and who is acquainted with the right materials and knows the right method for the study of the Dharma, needs to be warned against one more misconception. This, like the misconception just now discussed, pertains not to motive or material but to method, and though seemingly the most innocuous is in reality (at least in its ultimate foundations and eventual consequences) the most dangerous of all, being in fact one of the symptoms of a disease which today afflicts, in one form or another, practically the whole of Occidental humanity, as well as a growing section of the peoples of the Orient, namely, the progressive dissociation of more and more activities of life from the unifying and integrating dominance of Tradition. In a traditional civilization every branch of knowledge, and every kind of activity, is integrated with conceptions of a metaphysical order. Every aspect of life, even the lowest and most mundane, is given a transcendental orientation which enables it to function, in a general way, as a support, if not for the actual living of the spiritual life, then at least for a more or less constant awareness of the existence of spiritual values. In such a civilization, religion (to use the narrow modern term) is not something from which a man can escape, even if he wants to; for it encounters him at every step, with the familiar objects of home and the accustomed routine of daily life. Nurtured in such an environment, in which the whole of existence appears to be a great Smaragdine Tablet, constantly reminding us that "the things below are copies" and that the originals are above, sensitive hearts and minds become more subtle and sensitive still. To them "rocks, and stones, and trees," and other natural objects, are not simply lumps of matter of various shapes and sizes, but "huge cloudy symbols of a high romance" traced, not by the "magic hand of chance," but by the irresistible finger of omnipresent spiritual law. Nature is not dead, but alive with many voices, and to an eye accustomed to see and to hear things that point beyond themselves even

An old pine-tree is preaching wisdom,
And a wild bird crying out truth.

Through the non-traditional civilization of the modern West, however, the sledge-hammer blows of science have driven a wedge that threatens to split asunder the whole fabric. "Religious" and "secular," "sacred" and "profane" interests and activities are sharply distinguished and ruthlessly divided the one from the other. The sphere of "religion" has progressively shrunk, so that it now has little or no connection with, or influence over, the vast majority of the activities in which men at present engage. It may no longer be compared with the ocean-bed which supports (*Dharma* is derived from a root meaning "to support") the mighty mass of waters rolling above, but to a small volcanic island reeling and shuddering beneath the relentless impact of the hostile element by which it is surrounded and well-nigh overwhelmed. For the modern man there is in the common things of life no hint of aught beyond; for him there falls, like moonlight upon shifting leaves, no steady radiance of the Eternal upon the flickerings of his days. He is the true descendant of Peter Bell, in whom Wordsworth, writing when the smoke of the Industrial Revolution had already begun to darken the skies of England, described a type of humanity now fast becoming universal:—

A primrose by the river's brim
A yellow primrose was to him
And it was nothing more.

Religion, banished from the affairs of men, sits dark and solitary in the temple. Life goes on, or seems to go on, as before; but that which was "the life of life" is no longer there, and it is problematical how long the ghastly simulacrum will be able to continue its antics.

Such a displacement of civilization from its age-old foundations in spiritual values, and the consequent opening of a breach between the "religious" and "secular" aspects of life, will inevitably find a counterpart not only in the student's life but in his approach to the study of Buddhism. Brought up in a non-traditional environment, wherein few objects and activities have any significance beyond themselves, he will be naturally prone to think that the study of Buddhism is one activity among many, to be pursued without the necessity of considering either what influence it may have on other activities or what effect they may have upon it. In a traditional society such negligence would not have very serious consequences; for, as already stated, in such a society everything receives, ultimately, a transcendental orientation, and few activities other than those which violate the moral law could be positively deleterious in their effect upon the study of Buddhism. The "spiritual" life and "religious" studies point in the same direction as the "worldly" life and its duties; but one points directly, the other indirectly. In a non-traditional society, however, there is a constant tug-of-war between those departments of life which have been dissociated from their transcendental principles, on the one hand, and the isolated remnants of tradition on the other. Even the sincerest student cannot entirely withdraw himself from activities which, being no longer traditional, are in principle, or rather because of their very lack of principle, at variance with the proper method of studying the Dharma. His life, lacking a common guiding principle for all its activities, will be to some extent disintegrated. He will be like a man who, clinging desperately to a rock in midstream, feels against his body the mighty rush of waters which seeks to tear him from his refuge and whirl him to destruction. In order to integrate his life and strengthen his hold upon the unshakeable rock of the Dharma, the student will have to withdraw himself from as many profane activities as possible, and to reinforce the traditional supports not only of his own life but, as far as he can, of society as well. He should take part, and encourage others to take part, in traditional observances of all kinds; taking care, first, to understand the meaning and value of each observance. Worship of the image of the Lord Buddha with the traditional offerings of flowers, lights and incense; paying homage to spiritual teachers, to sacred objects and buildings, and to elders and members of the Holy Order, in the manner traditionally prescribed; the wearing of the traditional costume (in societies that still have one); participating in celebrations such as those held in honour of the Lord Buddha's Enlightenment—in these and many other similar ways can the student, by multiplying opportunities for contact with Tradition and consequent recollection of the Dharma, effect at least a partial integration not only of his own life but also, albeit to a lesser extent, of the lives of his associates. On the other hand, abstention from participation in untraditional activities of all kinds, particularly from forms of entertainment which are calculated to excite the senses and stimulate the lower mind, is no less essential to the successful study of the Dharma than are the more positive methods already described. Should the student think that if he devotes an hour a day or two or three hours a week to the study of the Dharma it will be sufficient, and that when not so engaged he will be free to spend his time in competitive games, or with a trashy novel, or under the hypnotic influence of the latest popular film, he would be making a very great mistake. It is no accident of language that the words "whole" and "holy" are etymologically connected, or that one of the definitions of "holy" should be "spiritually whole." The quest for holiness, which the study of the Dharma subserves, is a quest for spiritual wholeness, for complete integration of the "personality" not with any subjective principle merely, but with Reality. The more faithfully the study of Buddhism is pursued, the more difficult will it be to allow even activities of minor importance to remain outside the circle of its influence. Only from the intellectual or dogmatic scientific point of view is it possible to regard Buddhism as being merely one among hundreds of other possible subjects for scholarly research and doctoral dissertation. To one who studies it with some attempt at approximation to the fully traditional method we have endeavoured to describe, it can appear as nothing less than what it actually is, the dominating and controlling influence of the whole of life.

III. History *versus* Tradition

(i) The Universal Context of Buddhism

That no phenomenon arises without cause, and that things exist not in isolation but connected with every other thing in the universe, so that each influences and acts upon all and all influence and act upon each, is, as we shall see later, the cardinal principle of Buddhism. As a historical phenomenon, as an event occurring at a certain point in space and time, the origin of Buddhism itself, especially the career of the Founder (or Re-

Discoverer, as He would be more properly termed), is an exemplification of the law of the mutual dependence and interconnection of all things. Though in essence infinite and eternal, transcendent over the categories of space and time, the Dharma on its phenomenal side, as it was made known to gods and men, must be viewed not in isolation but against a definite background of historical events and geographical conditions. Our picture of the Dharma must not be a sharp silhouette, which reveals nothing of the object save its outline from merely one point of view, but a work of art that ranges up and down the whole gamut of colours (colour is a sensation produced by the *impact* of light from the object upon the retina—another example of interconnection) and that shows us the object in all its relations, with the present impinging on it from every side, with the past stretching out far behind it, and with the future at its feet. Buddhism must be viewed in context and in perspective.

So much will no doubt be conceded as axiomatic, for probably no one would seriously argue that Buddhism ought to be considered in entire isolation from other events. But when we come to inquire into the extent and range of that context and that perspective important differences of outlook, as between scientific history on the one hand and "unscientific" tradition on the other, will at once be disclosed. History plots the rise of civilization and culture, of which Buddhism is considered to form a part, from century to century: whatever happened more than ten thousand years ago is handed over to the sister sciences of astronomy and geology as their concern. Anthropology declares that though there are innumerable forms of life inferior to man, there is none superior; he is "the roof and crown of things": the "supernatural" beings which play such an important part in religion, mythology, folklore and other forms of tradition the world over are dismissed as products of primitive "superstition" which simply do not exist. Buddhist tradition, on the other hand, as embodied in the texts which preserve for us the Word of the Master, maintains that not merely sentient, but also intelligent, forms of life have existed in this universe and this world, and in the countless universes and worlds which preceded them, not for a few score millennia but for vast periods of time which are to be measured only by means of units comprising hundreds of millions of years. It moreover asserts that, although man is the highest of beings in the sense that the Nectar of Immortality can, with certain rare exceptions, fill only the vessel of a human body, there nevertheless exist higher and happier worlds than his which are inhabited by beings endowed with immeasurably greater longevity, beauty, happiness and power than he is. ("Rebirth" into these worlds is the result of meritorious actions performed on earth: when the result of such actions is exhausted rebirth in a human body again takes place; but these are points of doctrine with which we are not now concerned.) Moreover, besides the states of painful existence "below" that of the human race (rebirth into which inevitably follows the performance of demeritorious deeds) there are countless planes of existence, each inhabited by its own creatures, as it were intersecting the plane inhabited by man. For Buddhism, as for the classical and Christian traditions of the West (where the Church has preserved this fragment of traditional lore in a rather distorted form),

Millions of spiritual creatures walk the earth

and Buddhist canonical texts in Pali, Sanskrit, Tibetan and Chinese, as well as later Buddhist literature in a score of other languages, record numerous encounters between human and non-human beings. The world of man is in fact axial to all other planes of existence, from the "highest" abode of bliss to the "lowest" realm of suffering. This is due not merely to its intermediate position, or because the higher Transcendental Paths are attainable only on earth, but because in this world alone a Supreme Buddha can arise; and the Diamond Throne (*vajrāsana*) on which He sits for the re-discovery of the long-lost and long-forgotten way to Nirvana is regarded as the spiritual centre of the universe: it was the first spot to solidify when the earth arose out of the fire-mist at the beginning of the æon, and at the end of the æon it will be the last to pass away. The Buddha's attainment of Enlightenment has significance not for this world only but for the whole cosmos. He is *Satthādevamanussā,* the Teacher of gods no less than of men. The oldest written records of His life and teachings are replete with accounts of the numerous visits He paid to the worlds of the gods, and of the visits they paid Him when He was dwelling in the Jeta Grove at Savatthi, in the Bamboo Grove at Rajagaha, and at numerous other places. The *Maṅgala Sūtta,* said to be one of the most popular discourses in the Pali Canon, was addressed to a deva; and according to the Theravada tradition the *mātikas* or outlines of the *Abhidhamma Piṭaka* were first expounded by the Lord in the *Tāvatiṁsa*-devaloka, to the being who in her previous birth had been Maya Devi, the Bodhisattva's mother. Moreover, when, a few months after His Enlightenment, the Buddha sent forth His first sixty Arahant disciples to preach the Dharma which was "lovely in its origin, lovely in its progress and lovely in its consummation," they were bidden to preach to gods as well as to men. At every step of His career the Buddha was watched over and waited upon by millions of beings invisible to mortal eye: the intervention of Brahmā Sahampati immediately after the Enlightenment is well known. At every discourse He delivered the celestial audience was invariably far greater than the terrestrial one; those possessed of the Divine Eye (*divya-cakṣu*) could see, ranged and ranked about the Master in ever wider and higher circles that stretched from earth to the uttermost heaven, innumerable great and radiant beings that, as the glance swept upward, merged into one indistinguishable blaze of glory.

How poor and narrow in comparison with this magnificent panorama, this revelation of the cosmic significance of the Buddha and His Dharma, is the hasty snapshot that confronts us when we open the album of scientific history! The gods have vanished, and even the men have shrunk in stature. Instead of the Buddha, the Enlightened One, we find a person, no doubt amiable and agreeable enough, who believed that he had gained enlightenment. In place of the practice of meditation and the attainment of supernormal states of consciousness, we find hallucinations induced by means of autohypnosis. Psychic powers and supernatural beings are roundly dismissed as impossibilities, and all references to them—and they occur on almost every page of the scriptures—are accounted for either as products of self-deception or as later interpolations. This method of dealing with traditional records is termed scientific, and is said to be distinguished by objectivity, impartiality and complete freedom from presuppositions of any kind. The truth of the matter is, however, that prejudice and prepossession reign in all minds which have not been purified by means of spiritual practice, and even "scholars" in Buddhism are no exception to this rule. They bring with them to the study of the Dharma a host of preconceptions. Most of them are convinced in advance that Nirvana is merely a psychological, not to say psychopathic, state; some of them equate it with the unconscious of modern psychology, for, they argue, since there is in Nirvana no consciousness of self, and since consciousness is always *self*-consciousness, Nirvana must be a state of unconsciousness. Few of them (we are not speaking of professed followers of the Dharma) seem ever to have paused to consider whether syllogistic reasoning is an adequate instrument for the exploration and elucidation of a teaching which claims to go beyond logic. Historical and anthropological conceptions acquired in the course of a general education are moreover responsible, as we have already noticed, for many misrepresentations. One would not feel so strongly about the matter if scholars in Buddhism said plainly that the Buddhist texts refer to, and Buddhists have always believed in, the existence of supernormal attainments and supernatural beings, but that they themselves were unable to accept such a belief. But instead of adopting this straightforward course, which would have the merit of at least not attempting to conceal the gulf between traditional beliefs and the modern scientific outlook, some scholars reason that since devas, for example, do not exist, and since the early Buddhists *could not* have believed in them, all references to them in the texts *must have been* interpolated at a later date and should therefore be expunged. The scientific method thus becomes a veritable Bed of Procrustes in which Buddhism, the unfortunate victim, is either crushed or stretched, but in any case severely mutilated, in accordance with the whim of the investigator. And it is such people whom we are asked to regard as "authorities" on Buddhism, and to whom the Buddhists are expected to be grateful for what they have done for their religion! The reader will probably no longer feel astonished that we have advised the student of Buddhism to avoid, as far as possible, books written by such people and to stick, instead, to traditional expositions of the Dharma.

The omission, by many translators, of the conclusion of the *Dhammacakkappavattana Sūtta,* the First Discourse delivered by the Lord after His Enlightenment, is an instance, only one among many, of the cavalier treatment of Buddhist records to which we refer. Some scholars omit the last four or five paragraphs of this Discourse without comment; one, at least, frankly declares that since they are "mythological" they must be accretions to the original text, and therefore drops them without further ceremony. But is such a procedure justifiable? Has the conclusion of the Discourse, though strikingly different from the rest of the text, no significance and no value at all that it should be thus rudely dismissed? We shall try to answer this question first by recalling the significance of the Discourse itself and then by quoting the conclusion in full.

As the first public utterance of the Buddha's career, the Discourse on the Foundation of the Kingdom of Righteousness or, more literally, the Setting in Motion of the Wheel of Dharma, occupies a unique position among the discourses of the Pali Canon. So much at least will be conceded even by those who regard the Buddha merely as a kind of Indian Socrates Who is historically important by reason of the extent of His influence over the life and thought of Asia. The compilers of the Pali Canon have not failed to recognize, in their own way, the uniqueness of this Sutta; for the title it bears refers neither to the persons to whom it was addressed nor to the subject with which it deals, but to its significance as the first proclamation of the liberating Truth discovered by the Buddha during His meditation beneath the Bodhi-tree. The extent of this significance will of course vary in accordance with the intrinsic value attributed to the Dharma, as well as with the relative breadth or narrowness of vision with which the context of Buddhism is envisaged. To the scientist, its significance is purely historical and human; but to the Buddhist, with his conviction that in His First Discourse the Buddha made again available, not merely to men but to gods, the highest Truth, it possesses in addition a significance which is transcendental and universal. After exhorting the five monks to avoid the extremes of self-indulgence and self-torture and to follow instead the Middle way (*majjhimā paṭipadā*), or Noble Eightfold Path (*ariyo aṭṭhaṅgiko maggo*), the Buddha proclaimed the Four Noble Truths (*catāri ariya saccāni*) of Suffering (*dukkha*), the Arising of Suffering (*dukkha-samudaya*), the Cessation of Suffering (*dukkha-nirodha*) and the Path leading to the Cessation of Suffering (*dukkha-nirodha-gāminī paṭipadā*), declaring that so long as His knowledge and insight into these Four Noble Truths under their three aspects (*tiparivaṭṭaṁ*) and twelve modes (*dvādasākāra*), and in their essential nature, were not perfectly purified, so long He did not profess among the Devas, Māras and Brahmas, among the hosts of recluses and brahmins, including gods and men, that He had attained the Incomparable Supreme Enlightenment. Now, however, having thoroughly purified both knowledge and insight, He does make such a profession. He knows that His liberation of mind (*cetovimutti*) is unshakeable, that it is His last birth, and that there will in future be no rebirth (*punabbhava,* "again-becoming") for Him. The five monks were delighted with the Lord's utterance. In the venerable Koṇḍañña arose the pure and immaculate Eye of Truth (*dhamma-cakkhu*) that whatever is liable to origination is also liable to cessation. Here, according to those who believe that whatever smacks of "mythology" is necessarily a later addition, the Discourse in its original form ends. The text of the Sutta as handed down by the Theravada concludes, however, with the following paragraphs:—

Thus when the Wheel of the Doctrine was set turning by the Lord, the earth-dwelling gods raised a shout: "This supreme Wheel of the Doctrine has been set going by the Lord at Banares at Isipatana in the Deer Park, a Wheel which has not been set going by any ascetic, brahmin, god, Māra, Brahmā, or by anyone in the world." The gods of the heaven of the four Great Kings hearing the shout of the earth-dwelling gods raised a shout. . . . The gods of the heaven of the Thirty-three hearing the shout of the gods of the four Great Kings . . . the Yāma gods . . . the Tusita gods . . . Nimmānarati gods . . . the Paranimmitavasavattin gods . . . the gods of the Brahma-world raised a shout: "This supreme Wheel of the Doctrine has been set going by the Lord at Banares at Isipatana in the Deer Park, a Wheel which has not been set going by any ascetic, brahmin, god, Māra, Brahmā, or by anyone in the world."

Thus at that very time, at that moment, at that second, a shout went up as far as the Brahma-world, and this ten-thousandfold world system shook, shuddered and trembled, and a boundless great light appeared in the world surpassing the divine majesty of the gods.

The Sutta returns to earth with the words:

So the Lord uttered this fervent utterance: "Verily Koṇḍañña has attained the knowledge; verily Koṇḍañña has attained the knowledge." Thus Aññāta-Koṇḍañña became the name of the elder Koṇḍañña, "Koṇḍañña who has attained the knowledge."[1]

Important as the doctrinal matter contained in the body of the

---

[1] *Saṁyutta-Nikāya,* V. 420.

Discourse undoubtedly is, the conclusion is in its own way hardly less deserving of attention. The account of how the news of the Buddha's setting again in motion the Wheel of the Dharma was echoed from heaven to heaven clearly indicates that the event was of significance not only to the five monks who were the immediate recipients of the Teaching, or even to humanity at large, but to the whole inhabited universe. Whether they are understood literally or symbolically, the threefold shaking of the ten-thousandfold world system, and the appearance of the boundless great light, enable us to realize that the delivering of the First Discourse was, like the Birth, Enlightenment and Passing Away of the Lord Buddha, an event not of merely human and historical, but of cosmic, importance. Thus the conclusion of the Sutta, far from being an unnecessary addition by mythologizing aftermen, much less still a mere literary flourish, is a revelation of the true context of Buddhism, and, as such, indispensable to the proper understanding of the significance of the Dharma itself. To delete it, or minimize its importance, or even to attempt to understand the meaning of the Sutta without reference to it, will be to commit, even though unintentionally, one of those Procrustean distortions and mutilations of Buddhism to which we have already adverted.

IV. History *versus* Tradition
(ii) The Cosmological Perspective

No less serious than the failure to envisage the Dharma in its true context is the refusal to view it in correct perspective. Perhaps the second mistake is even more serious than the first; for though the Dharma may be understood and practised, to some extent, even out of context, inability to see it in perspective will, by obscuring the real nature of the Buddha's attainment, not only undermine our faith by depriving its object of almost all definite content, but also shake to its foundations our confidence in the Dharma as the means to Enlightenment. Buddhist "faith" or *saddhā* (Skt. *śraddhā*) is quite a different thing from the first of the Christian theological virtues. Far from being a substitute for knowledge, it is in fact based on it. As knowledge becomes clearer, faith grows firmer. Faith in the Buddha, therefore, presupposes knowledge of His special qualities, attributes and functions. So long as we do not possess a clear and correct understanding of these we shall have faith, not in the Buddha, but in something else to which the appellation "the Buddha" has been attached. Though we may know thoroughly, and even intensely admire, the life and teachings of the Buddha from the human and historical point of view, unless we view them and their promulgator in the traditional perspective we may have faith in Gautama the Rationalist, or in Gautama the Reformer, and so on, but faith in Gautama *the Buddha* we shall not have, though it is faith in this sense alone that conduces to Enlightenment. To envisage the Buddha and His Dharma in correct perspective is, therefore, no less necessary than viewing them in their proper context.

At a time when the rest of the world, including even Greece and China, Egypt and Babylonia, were calculating the dimensions and duration of the physical universe in terms of hundreds of thousands of miles and years, the Indian mind, long accustomed to revelling in the concept of infinity, had, by the bold use of imagination, by the exercise of supernormal faculties, and by the conservation of fragments of incredibly ancient traditionary lore, attained to a vivid apprehension of the vastness and incommensurability of the sphere of mundane existence in time as well as in space. This apprehension, purified and perfected by the supernormal vision of the Buddha and His Arahant disciples, is clearly reflected in Buddhist literature, especially in texts belonging to the Mahāyāna (which strongly emphasized the universal background and cosmic significance of the Dharma), though it is certainly not absent from Theravada works. To pass from the narrowly geocentric conceptions of Semitic "religious" literature, especially the Bible, to the far horizons and limitless vistas opened up in the Buddhist scriptures, is like stepping out from a windowless cabin into the open air and gazing up into the midnight sky

Thick inlaid with patines of bright gold.

The cosmic perspectives which provide the background of the Dharma in general, and particularly of the Buddha's career as a Bodhisattva, are in fact, in broad outline at least, strikingly similar to those disclosed by modern astronomy. We are far from desiring, however, to convert this circumstance into an argument for the truth of Buddhism, which, being concerned primarily with the transcendental verities (*lokuttara-dhammā*) is not demonstrable by such means. We mention the resemblance only as an *upāya,* as an accommodation to the mentality of the reader, who, provided he does not look for similarities in matters of detail or credit the ancient Buddhists with scientific leanings, will be enabled better to understand the nature of the conceptions involved by the citation of a parallel in modern knowledge with which he is familiar. With this proviso it may be said that for Buddhism, as for modern science, the material universe consists of an infinity of world-systems (*cakkavālas*) scattered through boundless space and coming into existence and passing away through beginningless and endless time. According to the Buddha the beginning of the Samsara (i.e., the whole of phenomenal existence, of which the universe known to science is but the lowest of thirty-one planes) is incalculable; it has no perceptible beginning; in His own words:

> *A world-without-end (*ana-matta 'gga*—"incalculable is the beginning"), is this round of birth and death. No beginning can be seen of those beings hindered by ignorance, bound by craving, running through the round of birth and death.*

To measure the course of events, including the evolution and involution of worlds, taking place in the Samsara, units of unthinkable magnitude are required. The text from which we have just quoted, after attempting to indicate the immensity of the number of rebirths through which the disciples of the Buddha, like other human beings, had passed, by declaring the amount of mother's milk drunk, and the tears shed, during all these previous existences, to be greater than the waters of the four mighty oceans, proceeds to relate how a certain *bhikkhu* once asked how long the *Kappa* (Skt. *Kalpa*) or ordinary unit of measurement for vast periods of time really was. The Lord replied:—

> *"Long indeed is the æon, brother: it is not easy to reckon it in this way: 'So many years, so many centuries, so many millennia, so many hundred thousand years.' "*
>
> *"But can an illustration be given, Lord?"*
>
> *"It can, brother," replied the Exalted One. "Just as if, brother, there were a mighty mountain crag, four leagues in length, breadth and height, without a crack or cranny, not hollowed out, one solid mass of rock, and a man should come at the end of every century, and with cloth of Benares should once on each occasion stroke that rock: sooner, brother, would that mighty mountain crag be worn away by this method, sooner be used up, than the æon.*
>
> *"Thus long, brother, is the æon: of æons thus long many an æon has passed*

away, many a hundred æons, many a thousand æons, many a hundred thousand æons." (Saṁyutta-Nikāya, *it. 178 ff.) (Woodward's translation)*[1]

This authoritative text makes it clear that the length of a kalpa is to be grasped, if it may be grasped at all, not by any process of mathematical computation, but by a flight of the spiritual imagination. Poetry may succeed where logic fails. The word here translated as 'æon' has also been rendered, by other translators, as "world-period," and this alternative rendition of the term gives us a further clue to its meaning in the original language. A kalpa is the period of time required—not, indeed, for the world, but—for a whole world-system to evolve from, and to involve back into, what Buddhist texts call the Brahma-world, the highest and subtlest plane (in fact three planes) of phenomenal existence. Each kalpa is subdivided into four periods: æon of involution (*saṁvaṭṭa-kappa*); continuance of involution (*saṁvaṭṭa-tthāyī*); æon of evolution (*vivaṭṭa-kappa*); and continuance of evolution (*vivaṭṭa-ṭṭhāyī*). The length even of these subdivisions of the kalpa, says the Buddha, is not to be reckoned in terms of hundreds, or of thousands, or even in hundreds of thousands, of years.[2]

Though we have used "evolution" and "involution" as equivalents of *saṁvaṭṭa* and *vivaṭṭa,* it should not be supposed that these modern scientific terms correspond at all closely to their ancient Aryan originals. Unlike science, Buddhist cosmology posits a subjective spiritual world or plane (the *Brahma-loka*; not to be confused with the transcendental non-dual state of Nirvana) in addition to the objective world or plane of "matter," and it therefore maintains that the line of biological development from amœba to man is not single but double, being the joint product of a process of spiritual degeneration or involution, on the one hand, and of material progress or evolution, on the other.

The first of the four *asaṁkheyya-kappas*, the "aeon of involution," is the vast period of time during which the previous *cakkavāla* or world-system is completely destroyed, or resolved into its constituent elements. The majority of the "beings" inhabiting its various planes are at this time reborn into the

---

[1] *Some Sayings of the Buddha* (Oxford University Press, 1951, pp. 184-85).
[2] *Aṅguttara-Nikāya,* IV. 156.

Brahma-world, which alone does not undergo the process of dissolution. What happens to the beings who are not so reborn the Pali texts, at least, do not reveal; but we may assume that they pass to other world-systems and are reborn there in accordance with their deeds. During the second *asaṁkheyya-kappa*, the period of "continuance of involution," we therefore find on the one hand the residual energy of matter, representing the limit of objectivity, and on the other hand the Brahma-world and its inhabitants, representing the extreme of subjectivity, both existing in complete isolation at opposite poles of phenomenal existence. The process of interaction does not begin until long after the commencement of the third *asaṁkheyya-kappa*, the "æon of evolution," when the world-system re-evolves from the residual energy of matter and the majority of the beings inhabiting the World of the Radiant Brahmas are reborn on earth, where for an immense period of time they follow the same mode of life as they did before in heaven, being mind-made, self-luminous, and nourished by rapture. The earth is described as being at this time dark and covered with water, which, as a contemporary Buddhist writer has pointed out, is an exact description of the early phase of the earth before the rays of the sun had dissipated the steam filling its atmosphere. The radiant beings from the Brahma-world were then sexually undifferentiated. As ages pass, however, the earth begins to appear (in the expressive metaphor of the *Aggañña Sūtta* of the *Dīgha-Nikāya*, our chief source of information in Pali on the subject of cosmogenesis) "as scum forms on the surface of boiled milky rice that is cooling," and on this scum they began to nourish themselves. Finding the sensation of taste pleasant, they became filled with craving. Being filled with craving for the scum, and depending more and more upon it for nutriment, their formerly light and ethereal bodies became gross and solid, and in course of time differences in their shape and beauty became manifest. Meanwhile the earth became still more separated from the waters, the mist cleared away from its face, and the sun and the moon were seen shining down upon it. As the process of "evolution" continued, first lichenous or fungoid growths, then creeping plants, and finally cereals, appeared on the earth, and as the formerly bright and radiant beings learned to feed on each of them in succession they became more and more gross and solid, more and more conscious of differences, until at last they became differentiated not only into various species but into sexes. The Fall of Man was now well-nigh complete. For in the train of bi-sexuality came lusts and passions, hatred and enmities, sexual morality, the institutions of family and property, law and crime, and finally government and social distinctions, and, in fact, that same world of the last few hundred thousand years which appears in the foreshortened annals of anthropology and the blood-smeared pages of history. The fourth and last *asaṁkheyya-kappa*, the period of "continuance of evolution," somewhere on the fringes of which we are now living, is the time for which the world-system holds itself at the stage of evolution attained in the previous period until the commencement of a new *mahākalpa*, when the process of evolution and involution already described takes place once again.

It should now be obvious why we have asserted that the line of biological development is not single but double. Every step in the evolutionary process results from a coalescence between an upward movement of material progress and a downward movement of psychic or spiritual degeneration. Man is not only risen ape but fallen angel, and the history of the human race may be summarized as a spiritual involution within a biological evolution. (Such, indeed, on an infinitely larger scale, is the history of the world-system of which the puny planet inhabited by man is an infinitesimally tiny part.) The fact that modern science devotes its whole attention to his material ancestry, ignoring the joint existence of a line of existence which is spiritual, is yet another instance of its inability to perceive those limitless vistas revealed by the Buddhist scriptures of which we have just attempted an indication.

The Samsara, the totality of phenomenal existence, may be imagined as a boundless ocean of waters. Incessantly rising and falling upon its surface are an infinite number of waves. Each wave represents a *cakkavāla* or system of ten thousand worlds. The rising of the wave corresponds to the period of evolution; its falling, to the period of involution. Just as all the infinitely numerous waves of the ocean do not rise and fall simultaneously, but at different times, even so some world-systems will be re-emerging from their respective chaoses while others are sinking back again into them. Shelley makes use of the same kind of image, though on a reduced scale ("worlds" instead of world-systems) in the famous lines:—

Worlds on worlds are rolling ever
From creation to decay,
Like the bubbles on a river,
Sparkling, bursting, borne away.

When it is remembered that a kalpa is the period of time which elapses between the complete destruction and the complete renovation of one world-system, and that the world-systems are being destroyed and renovated as incessantly as waves rise and fall on the surface of the ocean, even an unimaginative person will be impressed by the boldness with which the Buddha and His disciples formulated their cosmological conceptions.

Ability to deal with infinitudes did not, however, lead to the neglect of what were, comparatively speaking, matters of detail. Having divided the kalpa into four *asaṁkheyya-kappas,* the Pali texts proceed to still further refinements of classification. Each *asaṁkheyya-kappa* is subdivided into twenty *antara-kappas,* which is the period that elapses while the age of man increases from ten years to $10{,}000{,}000^{20}$ (1 followed by 140 ciphers), and then decreases to ten again, and each *antara-kappa* is subdivided into eight *yugas* or ages. But with these details we are not now concerned. The sole reason for which we have sketched in the cosmological background of Buddhism, and attempted to elucidate the conception of kalpas, is that without a preliminary grasp of these matters the true nature and function of a Buddha cannot be understood.

V. The Lineage of the Enlightened One

The use of the indefinite article before the appellation "Buddha" indicates the important fact that there is not one Buddha but many. Although in ordinary parlance, and for all practical purposes, "the Buddha" means Gautama the Buddha, in Whose era and under Whose dispensation we are now living, this is only a usage analogous to that whereby, when speaking of "the King" or "the Queen," we refer to the reigning monarch of England without our words being understood as a denial of the existence of previous wearers of St. Edward's crown. And just as even the most junior English schoolboy knows, when the monarch's birthday is being celebrated, that he or she is only the latest of a long line of kings and queens of England, just so—if so Homeric an extension of our simile be permissible—even the least instructed Buddhist knows that Gautama the Buddha, though historically a unique being, cosmologically speaking is but the latest scion of the Dynasty of the Buddhas, the most recent representative of a longer and more illustrious line than any earthly king can claim to be descended from. This fact, whereof Mahayana Buddhists received constant iconographical reminders, is witnessed to by Theravadins in their daily worship of the Triple Gem (*Tiratana-vandanā*), wherein they offer their homage to the Buddhas of the past, the present and the future. Indeed, in many Buddhist lands the images of Dīpankara, Gautama and Maitreya, representing the Buddhas of the three times, form a popular triad that symbolizes concretely, in terms which all can understand, the truth that the attainment of Enlightenment is a constantly recurring event in the universe, and the advent, after the elapsing of vast periods of time, of an enlightened human being, an integral part of the structure and workings of phenomenal existence.

Despite the assurance of many Mahayana texts that the Buddhas are in number "incalculable as the sands of the Ganges," the number of world-systems is so immense, and the duration of even a single kalpa so unthinkably long, that the appearance of a Buddha, a Tathagata, is, from the merely human point of view, an extremely rare event. So rare, indeed, that not every kalpa is so fortunate as to give birth to a Buddha: such unfortunate æons are known as *suñña-kappas* or "empty æons." Those kalpas which are blessed by the advent of a Buddha are termed *asuñña-kappas* or *Buddha-kappas*. There are five kinds of *Buddha-kappa*: *Sāra-kappa*, in which one Buddha appears; *Maṇḍa-kappa*, in which two appear; *Vara-kappa*, in which appear three; *Sāramaṇḍa-kappa*, which is sanctified by the advent of four; and *Bhaddha-kappa* or *Mahābhaddha-kappa* (Skt. *Mahābhadra-kalpa*) which is an æon blessed by the appearance of no less than five Buddhas, and which is therefore most fittingly termed a "Greatly Auspicious Æon." The Pali texts, with their usual temperance and reticence, confine their attention to our own world-system, and reveal, besides the names of Gautama and Maitreya, the "present" and the next of the "future" Buddhas respectively, the names of only twenty-seven "previous"

Buddhas. Mahayana texts, being much more communicative, give in addition the names of a very large number of past, present and future Tathagatas belonging to other world-systems. Into these further details we need not now enter: their existence is acknowledged as an additional evidence of the grandeur of the Buddhist cosmological perspective. References to the seven Buddhas from Vipassī to Gotama (Skt. Gautama) are of frequent occurrence in what scholars consider to be the earlier Pali scriptures. The names of the twenty-one Buddhas from Tanhaṁkara to Tissa, the immediate predecessor of Vipassī, are found in what are generally considered to be later works. These twenty-nine Buddhas are in Theravadin tradition distributed over a truly immense number of kalpas. To begin with, the interval of time which elapses between one Buddha-kalpa and the next varies from one *Mahā-kappa* to an *asaṁkheyya* of *Mahā-kappas*. The first four of the twenty-seven "previous" Buddhas belonged to a *Sāramaṇḍa-kappa* the date of which was four *asaṁkheyyas* of *Mahā-kappas* plus one hundred thousand *Mahā-kappas* ago. It was at this unthinkably remote period, during the lifetime of Dīpankara, the fourth of this group, that the being subsequently honoured as Gautama Buddha, but who was in that birth known as the ascetic Sumedha, resolved upon the attainment of Enlightenment. For the prodigious period of one *asaṁkheyya* of *Mahā-kappas* after Dīpankara no Buddha arose to lighten the darkness of the world-system. But at last the Sun of Truth once more dawned on a cosmos awakening from the spiritual slumber of ages: nine *Buddha-kappas* then elapsed, containing between them the eighteen Buddhas from Koṇḍañña to Vipassī; but we are told nothing about the number of Buddhas belonging to each kalpa, or the number of *suñña-kappas* from one *Buddha-kappa* to the next. Coming to what, from the traditional Buddhist viewpoint, may be thought of as "our own times," twenty-nine *suñña-kappas* elapsed between the last *Buddha-kappa*, which was a *Maṇḍa-kappa* of two Buddhas, Sikkhi and Vesabhu, and the *Buddha-kappa* in which we are now living, which happens to be a *Mahābhaddha-kappa*, or Greatly Auspicious Æon of five Buddhas, Kakkusandha, Konagamana, Kassapa, Gotama, our "own" Buddha, and Metteya (Skt. Maitreya), the Buddha yet to be.

The contrast between the historical view of the Buddha as

merely the son of Suddhodana, the descendant of a line of kings and warriors, and the traditional recognition of the cosmic significance of His life and mission, is nowhere more sharply delineated than in the famous scene, recounted in the Pali scriptures, which brings face to face for the first time in seven years the earthly father, with his limited knowledge and narrow loyalties, and the enlightened Son. The story is essentially dramatic, for it involves a clash of values of two very different orders, and in *The Light of Asia* Sir Edwin Arnold, with his usual competence, has not failed to exploit the dramatic possibilities of the situation. Seeing the Buddha begging in the streets of Kapilavastu, Suddhodhana bursts into sorrowful and scornful reproach:—

> *"Thou should'st have come apparelled in thy rank,*
> *With shining spears, and tramp of horse and foot.*
> *Lo! all my soldiers camped upon the road,*
> *And all my city waited at the gates;*
> *Where hast thou sojourned through these evil years*
> *Whilst thy crowned father mourned? and she, too, there*
> *Lived as the widows use, foregoing joys;*
> *Never once hearing sound of song or string,*
> *Nor wearing once the festal robe, till now*
> *When in her cloth of gold she welcomes home*
> *A beggar-spouse in yellow remnants clad.*
> *Son! why is this?"*
> *"My Father!" came reply,*
> *"It is the custom of my race."*
> *"Thy race,"*
> *Answered the King, "counteth a hundred thrones*
> *From Mahā Sammāt, but no deed like this."*
> *"Not a mortal line," the Master said,*
> *"I spake, but of descent invisible,*
> *The Buddhas who have been and who shall be,*
> *Of these am I, and what they did I do. . . ."*[1]

With these emphatic words, which reproduce the spirit of the original text with a force and a felicity which more than compensate for their lack of verbal equivalence, does the Buddha, in the very first year of His Enlightenment, unmistakably place Himself against the vast cosmological background, and in the universal perspective, the main outlines of which we have already attempted to sketch in. Whether we accept, or do not

---

[1] *The Light of Asia,* Book VII.

accept, the descriptions and classifications of kalpas, and the numbers and names of Buddhas, as found in the Buddhist Scriptures, none can refuse to be impressed by the grandeur of the whole conception, or fail to recognize its essential truth. Be the traditional Buddhist cosmology a sober statement of scientifically verifiable fact, or a delirious flight of poetic imagination, it reflects on its own level a law whose operation is as the heartbeat of Buddhism, the law that when the conditions for the production of a phenomenon—from the falling of a leaf to the birth of a Buddha—are present, the effect will inevitably follow. The ultimate significance of the traditional Buddhist cosmological teachings, and the way in which they light up the serene and majestic figure of the Master, has to our knowledge been nowhere better explained than by Lama Anagarika Govinda in the course of an article on "The Buddha as the Ideal of the Perfect Man and the Embodiment of the Dharma" which appeared in the Vaisakha Number of the *Maha Bodhi Journal* for the year 2498 (May-June, 1954). He writes:—

The so-called historical facts of the Buddha's life, however, were regarded as of so little importance that, up to the present day, it is impossible to ascertain the exact year of the Buddha's birth. Even the century in which he lived is a matter of controversy between the various Buddhist Schools. They do not even agree with regard to the name of Siddhartha's wife, or whether Rahula was born before or after the Bodhisattva left his home.

In what they all agree, however, is that the Buddha proclaimed the same eternal Dharma, preached by his spiritual predecessors in this world-cycle (kalpa) as well as æons ago, and that this doctrine will be preached again by the future and last of the five Buddhas of this kalpa, namely Maitreya, whose advent is announced by Buddha Sakyamuni's prophetic utterance in Dīgha-Nikāya, *XXVI. In a similar way he frequently speaks about the Buddhas of the past and compares their lives and actions to his own; in fact, it is only in this connection that we learn about the main events of his own life. The names of the Buddhas of this and previous æons are known to all Buddhist traditions.*

In other words, more is known and said about the Buddha's spiritual lineage than about his descent, though the fact that he came from a royal (or at least noble) family should have made it easy to record the lineage and the historical background of his forefathers. This shows clearly that his spiritual lineage, which might rightly be called his universal background, was regarded as being far more important than the historical and material one.

This universal background reveals one of the most profound ideas of Buddhism, which raises its teachings above the narrow concepts of dogmatic sectarianism, namely, the inescapable conclusion that the quality of enlightenment is inherent in the universe, or more correctly, latent in every form of consciousness, and therefore must come to maturity, according to universal law, whenever the conditions are favourable. That this law does not work with the mechanical regularity of clockwork, proves it to be a living force and explains why every kalpa does not produce the same number of Buddhas. According to the Theravadins, there may even be kalpas without Buddhas.

Thus the human life of a Buddha must be seen in an entirely different perspective: it becomes a mere fraction of a far bigger and more important development, in which the human element is essentially the vehicle for the rediscovery of the universal (and in this sense "transcendental") character of mind or consciousness, which according to the Prajñāpāramitā-Sūtra *is "inconceivable" in its true nature.*

This "rediscovery of the universal" is not the achievement of a day, nor yet of a single lifetime. The goal is indeed "attained" at a particular instant of time, and the anniversary of that instant is rightfully observed as the most important date in our calendar; but the attainment itself depends upon the exertions not of one life only, but of many lives. As the avalanche that suddenly descends upon the sleeping hamlet has been slowly gathering weight from the continuous falling of innumerable tiny flakes of snow, so the attainment of Enlightenment, by which desire, anger and ignorance are swept away, is the cumulative effect of the efforts and aspirations of countless lives dedicated to the attainment of the one supreme objective: Enlightenment for the sake of all sentient beings. Just as the career of a Bodhisattva is unthinkable apart from the conception of Buddhahood as the goal before it, so the attainment of a Buddha is inconceivable without the ideal of the Bodhisattva's career behind it. Though Buddhahood is logically "prior" to Bodhisattvaship, in experience the former is necessarily preceded by the latter, which is in fact related to it as cause to effect. We have, therefore, to see the latest of the Enlightened Ones not only as "the successor of the Buddhas of old" but as the inheritor of the results of actions performed during an incalculably long series of lives. Metaphors derived from kingship are inappropriate here. The double line of descent may be illustrated instead by a republican similitude. A president of the United States, for instance, may be considered both as the successor of previous presidents and as the descendant of his own ancestors, and he may have his biography written as a private person or as a public figure. Eventually, of course, the two lines of descent converge. In the case of a Buddha they coalesce: His Buddhahood is the ultimate significance of His Bodhisattvaship. The human and historical biography of

Gautama the Buddha is the story of the mystic marriage of the human and the divine, the individual and the universal, the terrestrial and the cosmic, the immanent urge and the transcendental ideal. Stretching back behind Him into the infinite past are the lives of His sublime predecessors, the Buddhas, and His own previous births as a Bodhisattva, and, as Lama Anagarika Govinda has pointed out, more is known about His spiritual lineage than of His human descent. Though the Pali canon contains interesting fragments describing various episodes of His last life on earth, it contains no connected biography of the Master in the modern sense. It does, however, contain the *Buddhavaṁsa*, in which are set forth the lives of the previous Buddhas, His spiritual ancestors, and it does contain the *Jātaka* book, which recounts the story of no less than five hundred and fifty of His own previous lives as a Bodhisattva, during all of which he practised the Ten Perfections (*daśa-pāramitā*). Moreover, scattered here and there in the Pali Canon are references to His own past lives not found in the *Jātaka* book. For instance, speaking of the profit of good works the Buddha says:—

> *"I myself, brethren, can bear witness to having reaped for many a long day the profit of good works—a thing desired, beloved, dear and delightful. For seven years, I practised kindly thought, and (as a result) I came not back into this world for seven æons of the unrolling and rolling up of the world (*Saṁvaṭṭa-vivaṭṭa*, "involution and evolution"). When the æon had unrolled, brethren, I became one of the Splendid Devas. When the æon had rolled up, brethren, I was born in the Highest Abode (*Brahmā-vimāna*). There was I a Brahmā, a great Brahmā conquering, and unconquered, the all-seeing Controller.*
>
> *"Thirty and six times, brethren, was I Sakka, Lord of the Devas. Countless hundreds of times was I a rajah, a world-ruler, a righteous monarch, victorious over the four quarters, ruling a realm that enjoyed the blessing of the security: possessed of the seven gems was I: (such a ruler was I)—not to speak of (mere) provincial rule."*
>
> (Itivuttaka, *22. Woodward's translation*)[1]

VI. Gautama the Buddha: His Greatness and Role

When boundless space and infinite time have been revealed as the background and setting of the great drama of Enlightenment, we can realize for ourselves how ridiculous are all attempts to dwarf and dwindle the majestic figure of the Bud-

---

[1] *Some Sayings of the Buddha*, p. 172.

dha, before the calm determination of Whose gaze have passed the pageants of a million births, into a mere *jīvanmukta* or liberated being. That which would be the greatest praise of any other creature is the least of the achievements of the Buddha. The Buddhas are born not for Themselves alone, but for the sake of all sentient beings, out of compassion for the world, for the welfare, profit and happiness of gods and men. They are World Teachers, and Their Teaching, though ever the same, has to be discovered afresh by each of Them before it can again be made known to the world. Truth, though not in essence at least in its manifestations, is like all other things subject to vicissitudes of fortune. As time progresses and as human beings become more and more degenerate, little by little the Dharma disappears from the hearts and minds of men, and in the end ceases to exist even as a memory of the righteousness of former ages. The disappearance of the Dharma means that Nirvana is rendered impossible of access; emancipation from the round of births becomes a dream; for the Dharma, as we were studious to insist at the very outset, is in essence the means to Emancipation, which is the one flavour (*ekarasa*) of the whole Teaching. No event occurs, no phenomenon arises, except in dependence on causes. The Dharma is the complex of causes and conditions indispensable for the attainment of Enlightenment.

It cannot be argued that, inasmuch as there are other ways to Enlightenment than that taught by the Buddha, the disappearance of His Teaching from the earth is not equivalent to a temporary obscuration of the Path to Peace. For the Dharma is not a way among ways, but The Way. This fact we assert not out of sectarian bigotry, or dogmatic prejudice in favour of the Teaching which claims our own allegiance, but because the Dharma states with a precision and clarity which, in Christian lands, are considered the prerogatives of science rather than of religion, those universal laws in accordance with which the attainment of Enlightenment by a human being takes place, and, therefore, the conditions upon which it depends and the means by which it must be achieved. It is thus not just one more path to Nirvana, but the underlying principle, the *rationale*, of all paths. The disappearance of the Dharma means essentially the disappearance of the principial knowledge of the means to Enlightenment and not merely of any particular application of that means. Outside the Dharma it is impossible to go, for it presents in their most universal, and hence in their most individual aspect, those Teachings which in other religions are more often found in fragmentary and distorted forms.

By the disappearance of the Dharma, then, we mean not merely the passing away of this or that religion, but the total eclipse of that knowledge of the means to Emancipation which constitutes, at least ideally, the essence of all traditions and all religious teachings. The period of darkness which then ensues, during which the Path to Nirvana is completely forgotten, may last, as we have already seen, for hundreds of millions of years. The importance of the advent of a Buddha, by Whom the way to Emancipation is rediscovered, retrodden and reproclaimed, may therefore be readily grasped. His greatness consists, not in the fact that He attained Nirvana, but that, after the lapse of untold millennia, He rendered the attainment of Nirvana once more practicable, not for Himself alone, but for countless millions of human beings. Wherever man seeks to extend the domain of knowledge, to widen the field of human achievement, or to fling farther into the territories of the impossible the frontiers and banners of possibility, it is upon the sturdy shoulders and stubborn head of the pioneer that inevitably the heaviest weight and fiercest shock of battle fall. To the height whereon he has planted the flag of victory, perhaps at the cost of his life, ten thousand may thereafter ascend with ease. In the lonely footsteps of the few a multitude may follow. What the genius of one man alone could discover—maybe a Plato brooding upon the Theory of Universals, or a Newton

Voyaging through strange seas of thought alone

in quest of the Theory of Gravitation—may be understood, once it has been discovered, by all who are possessed of sufficient concentration of mind to follow the steps of a demonstration. It is not when we merely do a thing, but when we do it *for the first time*, that the most formidable obstacles are encountered. We therefore honour the Master not only as an Arahant, or one by Whom Nirvana has been attained, but as a Buddha, as one Who, having qualified Himself for the superhumanly difficult task by practising the Ten Perfections for an incalculable number of lives, without a teacher and without a guide breaks through the obstacles which block the road to Nirvana and throws it open once more to the traffic of humanity.

This view of the true significance of the Buddha's life, and the real value of His work for humanity, is corroborated by a number of Pali scriptural texts. We leave aside for the moment Sanskrit sources, as these are generally considered to contain, at least in their present literary forms, later versions of material originally common to all Buddhist schools. In the *Saṁyutta-Nikāya* we are told that the Buddha once asked the brethren what the distinction, the specific feature, the difference was between the Tathagata Who, being Arahant, was a Fully Enlightened One, and the brother who was freed by insight. Replying that for them things were rooted in the Exalted One, and that they had Him for their guide and resort, they requested Him to reveal to them the meaning of His utterance. Having exhorted them to close application of mind the Lord proceeded:—

"The Tathagata, brethren, who, being Arahant, is Fully Enlightened, He it is who doth cause a way to arise which had not arisen before: who doth bring about a way not brought about before: who doth proclaim a way not proclaimed before: who is the knower of a way, who understandeth a way, who is skilled in a way. And now brethren, His disciples are wayfarers who follow after Him. That, brethren, is the distinction, the specific feature which distinguishes the Tathagata who, being Arahant, is Fully Enlightened, from the brother who is freed by insight."

(Saṁyutta-Nikāya, *III. 66. Woodward's translation)*[1]

Even more emphatic, and more impressive, than this, is the Buddha's declaration, in a later section of the same *Nikāya*:—

"So long, brethren, as moon and sun have not arisen in the world, just so long is there no shining forth of great light, no shining forth of great radiance. But gross darkness, the darkness of bewilderment, prevails. Neither night nor day is distinguishable, not the month nor the half-month nor the seasons of the year are to be discerned.

"But, brethren, when moon and sun arise in the world, then is the shining forth of great light, of great radiance, and gross darkness, the darkness of bewilderment, is no more. Then are distinguished the night and the day, then are discerned the month and the half-month and the seasons of the year.

"Just so, brethren, so long as a Tathagata arises not, an Arahant, a Buddha Supreme, there is no shining forth of great light, of great radiance, but gross darkness, the darkness of bewilderment, prevails, and there is no proclaiming, no teaching, no showing forth, no setting up, no opening up, no analysis, no making plain of the Four Ariyan Truths.

---

[1] *Ibid.*, pp. 289-90.

"But, brethren, so soon as a Tathagata arises all these things take place, and then there is a proclaiming, a teaching, a showing forth, a setting up, an opening up, an analysis, a making plain of the Four Ariyan Truths."
(Saṁyutta-Nikāya, *V. 442. Woodward's translation)*[1]

Again in the same *Nikāya*, the Buddha, after describing His Enlightenment in terms of a penetration into the origin and cessation of suffering through a progressive understanding of the third to twelfth *nidānas* of the *paṭicca-samuppāda* or conditioned co-production—in consequence of which there arose in Him a vision into things not before called to mind, as well as knowledge, insight, wisdom and light—illustrates His discovery by the following parable:—

"Just as if, brethren, a man travelling in a forest, along a mountain height, should come upon an ancient road, an ancient track, traversed by men of former days, and should proceed along it: and as he went should come upon an old-time city, a royal city of olden days, dwelt in by men of bygone ages, laid out with parks and groves and water tanks, and stoutly walled about—a delightful spot.

"Then suppose, brethren, that this man should tell of his find to the king or royal minister, thus: 'Pardon me, sire, but I would have you know that while travelling in a forest, along a mountain height, I came upon an ancient road. . . . (as above) *. . . a delightful spot. Sire, restore that city.'*

"Then suppose, brethren, that king or royal minister were to restore that city, so that thereafter it became prosperous, fortunate and populous, crowded with inhabitants, and were to reach growth and increase.

"Even so, brethren, have I seen an ancient Path, an ancient track traversed by the perfectly Enlightened Ones of former times. And what is that Path? It is this Ariyan Eight-fold Path."

(Saṁyutta-Nikāya, *II. 104. Woodward's translation)*[2]

The difference between a Buddha and an Arahant was not only clearly stated by the Master, but recognized and deeply felt by His disciples. Even when they had themselves attained to that freed state of consciousness which was the goal of the Teaching, they seem to have continued to feel that in some indefinable manner His realization immeasurably transcended their own. Hence the expressions of reverence, devotion and love for the personality of the Buddha which burst from the lips of Theras and Theris after the dawning of their own heart's emancipation. Hence the pæan which drew down upon the devoted head of Sāriputra—who in the fervour of his faith had declared that

[1] *Ibid.*, p. 32.
[2] *Ibid.*, p. 36.

there never had been nor ever again would be anyone like the Buddha—the smiling rebuke of his Master. Hence that feeling of wondering regard, not without a touch of awe, which years of the closest daily companionship were unable to dispel. A Napoleon may not be a hero to his valet; but a Buddha remains a Buddha even to His personal attendant. Shortly after the Lord's Parinirvana, a brahmin named Gopaka Moggallana asked the elder Ananda whether there was a single monk entirely and completely endowed with all the qualities of the Buddha. Ananda replied without hesitation in a manner which suggests that thirty years of intimacy had not dimmed the original brightness of his conviction that between the Master and even His enlightened disciples there lay an impassable gulf of difference.

"There is no single monk, brahmin, who is entirely and completely endowed with all those qualities with which the Lord, the Arahant, the all-enlightened, was endowed. For the Lord was the producer of the unproduced Way, the originator of the unoriginated Way, the preacher of the unpreached Way, the knower, cognizer, perceiver of the Way. But now the disciples abide following the Way, being endowed with it afterwards."

(Gopaka-moggallāna-Sūtta, Majjhima-Nikāya, *III. 7)*

From these quotations, and from the outline of Buddhist cosmology given in Sections IV and V, it will be evident that several things can be affirmed of the Teaching with sufficient certainty to warrant their being made the basis of further conclusions about the nature of Buddhism generally. To begin with, the immeasurably superior status of the Buddha in relation to all other beings, not excepting Arahants, is categorically asserted. The essence of the distinction between Him and His enlightened disciples is said to consist in the priority of His attainment, in the fact that the Way to Nirvana was first discovered and opened up by Him: others merely follow in His footsteps. Within the context of scientifically verifiable "history" the Buddha and His Dharma are unique. But the historical context is itself contained within a context which, as we have seen, coincides with the whole cosmos, with the immeasurable extent and duration of the entire world-system. Consequently the Buddha's discovery of the Way to Nirvana is held to be a re-discovery, and His proclamation of the Dharma a re-proclamation. Within this infinitely enlarged context His attainment, far from being a unique occurrence, is the latest confirmation of a law which acts wherever and whenever conditions permit, and His Teaching, far from being absolutely original, is new only in the sense that it is never out-of-date.

The Dharma taught by the Buddha is termed *sanātana*, eternal, and *akālika*, timeless, not because it has little to recommend it except its age, but because it is the formulation in this Buddha-period of principles which are true at all times and in all places. It is not merely "handed down" from one Buddha to another, like a family heirloom: all discover it afresh for Themselves. The unity of Their Teaching is due not so much to the faithfulness with which They have preserved a common tradition as to the definiteness with which They have imposed upon it the stamp of a common experience. They have not merely transmitted the imprint, but found and used the die. That a teaching has come down from remote antiquity is not necessarily an argument in its favour; for error is coeval with truth, and Wrong Views are twin-born with Right Views. The Dharma is said to be *sanātana* not so much because it is eternal, though that is the literal meaning of the word, as because it is of universal applicability. This universality is the hallmark of the Teaching. External forms may change, and one formulation of Buddhism succeed another; but these are only adaptations to the various cultural and social expressions of a common human need. Beneath all such changes the Dharma remains unchanged, not as a fossil but as an inexhaustible fountain of spiritual life; for it is based not upon the accidents but upon the essentials of existence, upon truth which has outlived the dissolution of millions of world-systems, being in its widest sense identical with that very Law which renders the origin and dissolution of world-systems possible.

VII. Historical Uniqueness of the Dharma

Just as it is impossible to regard the Buddha as a mere liberated being, even so it is impossible to regard His Dharma as the development of any previous teaching. This is an obvious corollary from the fact that the Master is not merely Arahant but Buddha, the re-discoverer of the Path to Nirvana. He could hardly have called Himself the discoverer of what was known already, and since the Dharma is above all else the Means to Enlightenment it follows that the finding of the Path is equivalent to the penetration of the Dharma. The historical uniqueness of the Buddha and the originality of His Teaching are inseparable. Once we admit the first, the second will inevitably follow. The mere scholar cannot believe that the Dharma was rediscovered by the Buddha, because he does not accept the "legendary" or "mythical" (words for him synonymous with imaginary) Buddhist accounts of its existence in previous world periods. Hence his "scientific" concern to trace the process of its development from historically earlier teachings, and his pathetic eagerness to explain how the transcendental swan of the Dharma, its unequalled insight into the fundamental nature of existence, could ever have come to be hatched from the mundane duck's egg of what were, though sincere and genuine searchings after truth, in comparison with the Buddha's Teaching but partial glimpses rather than the full and perfect vision.

For the Buddhist, however, the conclusion is inescapable. Taking refuge as he does not in Gautama the Rationalist, or Gautama the Reformer, or even in Gautama the Arahant, but in Gautama *the Buddha*, the re-discoverer of the Path to Nirvana, he is bound to regard the Dharma as a historically unique phenomenon, affiliated not to any contemporary teaching by which the Buddha might have been influenced, but only to the eternal Dharma preached by His predecessors, the previous Buddhas. *Pacceka-* (Skt. *Pratyeka-*) Buddhas or Privately Enlightened Ones did indeed live before the Buddha, perhaps even within historical times, but by very definition they are incapable of preaching to others the truth which they have discovered, and hence of founding any tradition from which a Samyak Sambuddha, or Fully Enlightened One, such as the Sakyamuni was, might subsequently borrow.

The relation between Buddhism, on the one hand, and the various philosophical speculations and religious practices flourishing in North-Eastern India in the sixth century B.C.E., on the other, may be compared to that existing between a seed and the soil of the pot in which it is planted. The seed is not *produced* by the soil, but it could not germinate, or put forth roots and shoots, or go through all the remaining stages of a plant's unfoldment, unless the soil was there to supply it with nutriment.

Buddhism, in the sense of the Way to Nirvana, was not a product of its environment, nor the development of any other Indian teaching; but the high standard of intellectual inquiry and ethical endeavour prevailing at the time was undoubtedly, if not the principal cause, at least one of the prime conditions, of the re-emergence of the light of the Dharma from the darkness of oblivion. Hundreds of years of religious and philosophical development had left on the intellectual soil of India a rich and fertile deposit of ideas and ideals which was the best possible matrix into which the seed of the Dharma could fall. Greece, China, Egypt and Babylonia, for all their loftiness of thought, had not attained to the same quality of vision as the forest- and mountain-dwelling sages of Jambudvīpa. In the north-eastern corner of India alone could be found materials which might contribute to the growth and development of the germ of Enlightenment which had been borne, like a winged seed from distant fields, from worlds in space and time infinitely remote from ours.

These materials were of two kinds: those which contributed to the Buddha's attainment of Enlightenment, and those which, after His Enlightenment, He incorporated into the fully articulated body of His Teaching. Though historically distinct, the two are in principle not logically distinguishable; for the Master found certain contemporary teachings helpful before He sat down on the Vajrāsana as a Bodhisattva for the same reason that He found them acceptable after He had arisen from it a Buddha: they were conducive to the attainment of Nirvana. As we shall see in detail later on, the Dharma, as the means to Enlightenment, is divided into successive stages, and though it remained for the Buddha to re-discover the Way to the Transcendental, many were the doctrines and methods current in His time which led to the farthest reaches and uttermost verge of the mundane. At present, however, we are concerned not so much with the Buddhist evaluation of the specific teachings of this or that school of thought—consideration of which would carry us far beyond our scope—as with the nature of the general principle in accordance with which some doctrines and methods were recognized by the Buddha as belonging to True Dharma while others were condemned and rejected.

The principle which the Buddha employed before Enlightenment was purely empirical: it was the method of trial and error. Finding that a life of ease, comfort, luxury and pleasure led only to a feeling of disgust and that, far from being able to give any lasting peace and happiness, it was merely "a path for the dust of passion," He followed the time-honoured Indian practice, cut off His hair and beard, put on the yellow robes and went forth from a house to the houseless life. During the six years which elapsed between His great Renunciation and His Enlightenment He resorted to many different methods of attainment of the Deathless State of Nirvana, all of which failed, and made a number of mistakes. Self-torture availed Him no more than self-indulgence had, and both, therefore, were afterwards condemned, in the opening words of the First Discourse at Sarnath, as extremes which should not be followed by one who had gone forth as a wanderer. The teachings of Ālāra Kālāma and Uddaka Rāmaputta, under whom the Bodhisattva learned the techniques of Indian Yoga, proved inadequate rather than wrong: they led not to Nirvana, which was His goal, but merely to exalted yet still mundane states of consciousness for which no terms exist in any non-Indian system of psychology. After His Enlightenment the Exalted One remembered His old teachers, and thought that they would be the worthiest recipients of the Truth He had discovered; but, perceiving that they were dead, He went in search of the five disciples who had left Him when He had abandoned as useless the life of self-torture, intending to impart it to them instead. The deep-rooted Indian conviction that purification from desires was essential to the perception of Truth (which came to Siddhartha, according to one tradition, as an actual sight of the composed and peaceful appearance of a wandering ascetic), and the methods traditionally prescribed for concentrating the mind, probably helped the Buddha along for a few steps in His career; but hardly more than this could He learn from His contemporaries. In the end they deserted Him; He was left alone; and it was out of that loneliness and solitude, of heart and mind no less than of body, that there came His great discovery, or re-discovery, of the Way from the mundane to the supramundane, the Way to Nirvana, the state of completely free and radiant Mind, which for countless generations had remained unknown to the sons of men, and which is the pith and kernel of the Doctrine of All the Buddhas.

The method adopted by the Tathagata after His Enlightenment was in a sense no less empirical than that employed before; but it was empirical with a difference. Though continuing to depend upon experience, it was the experience not of a Bodhisattva but of a Buddha, not of one who was still seeking but of one who had found the Truth; and hence it was not a method of trial and error, involving both loss of time and waste of energy, but an immediate spiritual perception on the basis of which the Buddha could affirm with certainty that *these* doctrines and methods were conducive to Enlightenment, while *those* were the reverse. Among the Ten Powers and Four Confidences of a Tathagata, as enumerated in the *Mahāsīhanāda Sūtta* of the *Majjhima-Nikāya*, are the power of knowing rightly whither all paths of conduct lead, the power of rightly knowing the purity or impurity and growth of the trances, releases, concentrations and attainments, and the confidence that the rebuke, "Though you claim that you have stated those things that are hindrances (to the religious life), they are not really hindrances," will not be rightly uttered against Him. For His own disciples, who believed the Buddha to be omniscient regarding the Means to Enlightenment, such an affirmation would suffice: they would be prepared to reject this method and accept that on His authority alone. But for the sake of those who had not yet taken the refuge in Him the Buddha was compelled to make explicit the general principle in accordance with which He, as King of the Dharma, adjudicated between the conflicting claims of the various rival sectarian teachings of that time. Hence to the Kālāmas of Kesaputta, who had been bewildered by the disputes of recluses and brahmins, He said:—

> *"Now Kālāmas, do not ye go by hearsay, nor by what is handed down by others, nor by what people say, nor by what is stated on the authority of your traditional teachings. Do not go by reasoning, nor by inferring, nor by argument as to method, nor from reflection on and approval of an opinion, nor out of respect, thinking a recluse must be deferred to. But, Kālāmas, when you know, of yourselves: 'These teachings are not good; they are blameworthy; they are contemned by the wise: these teachings, when followed out and put in practice, conduce to loss and suffering'—then reject them."*
>
> (Aṅguttara-Nikāya, *I. 188. Woodward's translation)*[1]

[1] *Ibid.*, p. 283.

The real import of this oft-quoted but much misunderstood passage should be carefully noted. It was not intended as a vindication of "free thought"; neither does it give a *carte blanche* to rationalistic scepticism. Rationalism is in fact explicitly rejected. The Kālāmas were no more disposed to question the possibility of a transcendental attainment than the Buddha Himself was; but they were confused by the impossibility of reconciling the claims made on behalf of one method of reaching the goal with the claims made on behalf of other methods. All the rival teachers could not be speaking the truth. If one was right, the others must be wrong. The Buddha's reply is not an invitation to question the existence of a transcendental state, nor an encouragement to doubt whether the realization of such a state is within the reach of human effort. It simply affirms that we are to decide between the rival claims of religious teachings, firstly on the basis of their results as revealed in our own experience and secondly (a statement which is almost always ignored) in accordance with the testimony of the Wise. Who the Wise are, and how we may recognize them, is told elsewhere. One of their characteristics is that, unlike the recluses and brahmins who had disturbed the minds of the Kālāmas, they do not indulge in acrimonious disputes.

The Buddha's reply to Mahā-Pajāpati, the Gotamid, who had asked Him to show her a teaching, hearing which from the lips of the Exalted One she might dwell "alone, solitary, zealous, ardent and resolved," formulates in much more positive terms, and in a more definitely Buddhist context, the general principle which was the burden of His discourse to the Kālāmas.

"Of whatsoever teachings, Gotamid, thou canst assure thyself thus: 'These doctrines conduce to passions, not to dispassion; to bondage, not to detachment; to increase of (worldly) gains, not to decrease of them; to covetousness, not to frugality: to discontent, and not content; to company, not solitude; to sluggishness, not energy; to delight in evil, not delight in good': of such teachings thou mayest with certainty affirm, Gotamid, 'This is not the Norm. This is not the Discipline. This is not the Master's Message.'

"But of whatsoever teachings thou canst assure thyself (that they are the opposite of these things that I have told you),—of such teachings thou mayest with certainty affirm: 'This is the Norm. This is the Discipline. This is the Master's Message.' "

(Vinaya, *II. 10. Woodward's translation)*[1]

[1] *Ibid.*, pp. 278-79.

These well-known passages from the Pali Canon make perfectly clear the nature of the principle by which the Buddha's attitude towards contemporary teachings was governed. He was prepared neither to accept nor to reject them absolutely. With complete intellectual detachment and freedom from preconception, He surveyed them all from the standpoint of Enlightenment—just as one who has ascended a mountain height can look back and see clearly that, of the numerous paths winding up from the valley below, some come to an end at the edge of a precipice or a foaming torrent, while others lead safely to the summit—and followed the Middle Path of accepting as part of His own Teaching whatever was conducive to the attainment of the beyondless heights of Liberation, and rejecting as false and wrong whatever hindered, or retarded, or even merely did not help, in the process of spiritual ascent.

Thanks to the unexampled intellectual fertility of the Indian mind in that age, and to the unrestrained exuberance of its religious imagination, which ran riot through a thousand brillantly coloured forms and fancies, as well as to the fanatical enthusiasm with which a thousand zealots experimented with the most fantastic methods of salvation, there was no lack of material for the Buddha to work upon. What He Himself described as the "jungle of views," which flourished so richly and so rankly in those days, seems to have produced the sublime and the ridiculous, the more than divine and the hardly less than bestial, in the way of religious ideals, with the same perfect indifference with which the great subtropical forests of the Himalayan region produce at the same time the marvellous blossoms of the rare and lovely orchid, and the monstrous growth of the common poisonous *dātura*. This luxuriant crop of ideas the Buddha had partly to uproot, partly to prune, and partly to train to grow in the right direction. One has only to read the *Brahmajāla Sūtta*, the opening discourse of the *Dīgha-Nikāya* (collection of "long discourses") with which the *Sūtta Piṭaka*, the first of the three great divisions of the Pali canonical scriptures, begins—where no less than sixty-two contemporary "false views" are classified—to realize the immensity of the work of religio-philosophical criticism accomplished by the All-knowing One. It may, in fact, be said, that it was He Who laid down the main lines for the development of Indian spirituality, not only in its Buddhist but in its non-Buddhist forms, for thousands of years to come.

Though the Buddha rejected in the most categorical manner a great many of the beliefs and practices current in His time, references to which will be found scattered all over the pages of the scriptures, it should not be concluded that His attitude towards contemporary trends of thought was entirely negative, much less still unsympathetic or hostile—words which have no meaning in relation to a Fully Enlightened and Wholly Compassionate One. He was as ready to accept as to reject; in fact, more ready. For He knew that a positive method of teaching was more appealing, more likely to find entrance into the hearts and minds of His auditors, than a purely negative and destructive one, however correct and logical the latter might be. Consequently we find the Buddha constantly putting—if we may be permitted a metaphor which He probably would not have used, even if He had known it—the new wine of His Teaching into old bottles. He does not condemn the practice of ceremonial ablution, for instance, so much as insist that real purification comes by bathing, not in the Ganges as people thought, but in the cleansing waters of the Dharma. He does not ask the brahmin to give up tending the Sacred Fire, with which so many ancient traditions and so much religious emotion were bound up, but to remember that the true fire burns within, and that it feeds not on any material object but solely on the fuel of meditation. These examples of the Buddha's capacity to utilize Indian traditional practices for the purposes of His own Teaching could be paralleled by a hundred others from the same canonical sources. Though self-torture had been definitely rejected as a means to Enlightenment, He permitted thirteen ascetic practices, called *dhutangas*, out of hundreds of similar ones, to the members of His Order, not because He considered them necessary, but because there was a popular demand for them and because they were in any case not positively harmful.

This spirit of adaptation and assimilation was one of the causes which enabled Buddhism to spread so rapidly and easily, and with the minimum of opposition, among races and peoples whose traditions and cultural background were in many ways quite different from those of India. The Dharma, while remaining in essence changeless, was capable of assuming a thousand forms, because, as we have already seen, it is in principle simply the Means to Enlightenment. With this criterion constantly in view, Buddhism, both in India and abroad, was able not only firmly to reject beliefs, customs and observances which hindered the living of the holy life, but also freely to accept those by which it was helped, regardless of their origin. The illustration by means of which we sought to elucidate the relation of Buddhism to contemporary teachings may here be of further service to us. In the soil of the pot, there are found not only particles of earth which contain various nutritious elements, but also potsherds and fragments of stone containing none. Among the doctrines current in North-Eastern India during the life of the Buddha, there were some which could provide materials for the growth and development of the seed of the Dharma, and others which could not provide such materials. The former were of course utilized, and not so much incorporated into the Buddha's Teaching as recognized as being in truth already a part of it. The latter were simply picked out and thrown away.

What we need most of all to remember is the fact that whatever the part played by the contents of the pot may be, the seed out of which grew up the mighty spreading Banyan tree of the Dharma came not from inside but from outside it. Only if we grasp this idea will it be possible for us to comprehend the traditional conception of the Buddha and His Teaching.

VIII. Ineffable Nirvana

Having dealt with the cosmic setting and significance—the external relations, as it were—of the Buddha's achievement, it becomes necessary to direct attention to what may be called its internal dimensions. What is the nature of Nirvana? Granting that the Buddha did attain such a state (an admission which does not necessarily depend upon an acceptance of the traditional views regarding the place of His attainment in history), this is the question with which we are now confronted. At this point occurs the transition from mundane context to transcendental text. We have begun to hear, as though from a great distance, the muffled heartbeat of Buddhism.

At the outset of our enquiry we are confronted by what at first sight appears an insurmountable obstacle. In common with other teachings of the kind loosely described as "mystical," Buddhism solemnly affirms that the Ultimate Experience is beyond the reach of speech, and that words are powerless to describe it. In fact it cannot even be thought about; for the entire cessation of all thought-constructions, including even the distinction—so fundamental to existence in the phenomenal world—between "self" and "not-self," is the principal condition of its attainment. The ineffability, not only of Truth (a word sufficiently colourless for our present purpose), but also of the Tathagata, the One by Whom Truth has been attained, is a topic upon which Buddhist literature of all schools tends to expatiate at a length which might seem to the uninitiated not altogether appropriate. Says an early Buddhist text:—

Since a Tathāgata, even when actually present, is incomprehensible, it is inept to say of him—of the Uttermost Person, the Supernal Person, the Attainer of the Supernal—that after dying the Tathāgata is, or is not, or both is and is not, or neither is nor is not.

(Saṁyutta-Nikāya, *III. 118. Horner's translation)*[1]

The condition of an Enlightened One after the death of the physical body seems to have been a question about which the Buddha's contemporaries were deeply concerned. The Buddha, however, declared it to be one of the "undetermined questions" (*avyākṛtavastūni*), that is to say, a question which could not be answered by means of any form of logical predication. The condition of the Tathagata after death is incomprehensible because even during life His nature cannot be fathomed by the intellect. He is not to be measured, any more than the waters of the mighty ocean are, or the infinite expanses of the sky. The Master's reply to Upasiva, who had asked whether one who had attained the goal was non-existent or whether he enjoyed a perpetuity of bliss, makes it quite clear that this incomprehensibility, far from being peculiar to a Buddha, in the full traditional sense of that term, is a characteristic shared by all who have realized the Truth. It also states the reason why nothing can be affirmed or denied of an Enlightened One:—

---

[1] *Buddhist Texts Through the Ages,* p. 106.

There is no measuring of man,
Won to the goal, whereby they'ld say
His measure's so: that's not for him;
When all conditions are removed,
All ways of telling are removed.
(Sūtta-Nipāta, *1076. E.M. Hare's translation)*[1]

"Words cannot describe the unconditioned," as the translator tersely paraphrases the last two lines of the stanza.

The Sanskrit texts of the Mahayana schools, which are on the whole of much later date than the Pali scriptures from which we have quoted, continue to affirm the same truth. That Nirvana is inexpressible (*niṣprapañca*) is the first of the eight points of agreement between the various conceptions of this most exalted state which are, according to Dr. Nalinaksha Dutt, to be found in Hinayanic and Mahayanic works.[2] During the centuries which elapsed between the compilation of the Pali Canon and the composition of the Sanskrit sutras which embody the fully developed Mahayana doctrine, a shift of emphasis had, however, taken place. It was not the inexpressibility of Nirvana, or even of the Enlightened Man, that was now so much affirmed, as the indefinability of the real nature of things, which was declared to be uniformly identical with voidness (*śūnyatā*), and the "elusiveness," as Conze aptly terms it, of Perfect Wisdom (*prajñāpāramitā*), the "faculty" or "organ" for the apprehension of that real nature. The development was natural, even inevitable. By rendering fully explicit all the implications of the early Buddhist conception of Reality, the Mahayanists made possible the extension of the principle of indefinability from the transcendental sphere to the mundane sphere, which had, in fact, already been declared identical with, or at least "not different" from, each other. What formerly had been applicable to a strictly limited number of cases was now expanded into a universal law. Inexpressibility was no longer a special characteristic of Nirvana. All *dharmas* (things or phenomena in general) were unthinkable and indefinable in their essential nature, and therefore Nirvana, as well as the Buddhas and Bodhisattvas, and whatever else might be named,

---

[1] *Woven Cadences* (Oxford University Press, 1947), p. 155.

[2] *Aspects of Mahayana Buddhism in its Relation to Hinayana* (Luzac, 1930), p. 198.

being *dharmas* were unthinkable and indefinable too. One of the oldest and most authoritative of the numerous texts dealing with Perfect Wisdom contains the following dialogue between the Buddha and His disciple Subhuti:—

Subhuti: 'It is wonderful to see the extent to which the Tathāgata has demonstrated the true nature of all these dharmas, and yet one cannot properly talk about the true nature of all these dharmas (in the sense of predicating distinctive attributes to separate real entities). As I understand the meaning of the Tathāgata's teaching, even all dharmas cannot be talked about in any proper sense?'

The Lord: So it is, for one cannot properly express the emptiness of all dharmas in words.

(Ashṭasahāsrikā, *XVIII. 348. Conze's translation)*[1]

The elusiveness of Perfect Wisdom is hymned by Rāhulabhadra, a writer of the third century, in the following verses:—

Saviours of the world, from pity,
So that men might understand,
Speak of Thee, observing custom,
Yet of Thee they do not speak.

Who is able here to praise Thee,
Lacking signs and featureless?
Thou the range of speech transcending,
Not supported anywhere.

(Prajñāpāramitāstotra, *vv. 18, 19. Conze's translation)*[2]

Perhaps more prosaic, but even more impressive philosophically, is a further dialogue between the Buddha and Subhuti which occurs in the great scripture from which we have already quoted. Almost liturgical in their solemnity are the profound questions put by the disciple and the Master's even profounder replies. Deep seems to be answering deep from abysses of realization unfathomable by thought:—

Subhuti: 'Deep is the essential nature of the dharmas.'
The Lord: 'Because it is isolated.'
Subhuti: 'Deep is the essential nature of perfect wisdom.'
The Lord: 'Because its essential nature is pure and isolated.'
Subhuti: 'Isolated in its essential nature is the perfection of wisdom. I pay homage to the perfection of wisdom.'
The Lord: 'Also all dharmas are isolated in their essential nature. And the isolatedness of the essential nature of all dharmas is identical with the perfection of wisdom. For the Tathāgata has fully known all dharmas as not made.'

---

[1] *Buddhist Texts,* p. 179.
[2] *Ibid.,* p. 149.

Subhuti: 'Therefore all dharmas have the character of not having been fully known by the Tathāgata?'

The Lord: 'It is just through their essential nature that those dharmas are not a something. Their nature is non-nature, and their no-nature is their nature. Because all dharmas have one mark only, i.e., *no mark. It is for this reason that all dharmas have the character of not having been fully known by the Tathāgata. For there are not two natures of dharma, but just one single one is the nature of all dharmas. And the nature of all dharmas is no-nature, and their non-nature is their nature. It is thus that all points of attachment are abandoned.'*

Subhuti: 'Deep, O Lord, is the perfection of wisdom!'

The Lord: 'Through a depth like that of space.'

Subhuti: 'Hard to understand, O Lord, is the perfection of wisdom!'

The Lord: 'Because nothing is fully known by the enlightened.'

Subhuti: 'Unthinkable, O Lord, is the perfection of wisdom!'

The Lord: 'Because the perfection of wisdom is not something that thought ought to know, or that thought has access to.'

(Ashṭāsahāsrikā, *VIII. 192. Conze's translation)*[1]

This deeply esoteric teaching has found popular expression in a saying, widely current among Mahayana Buddhists in China and Japan, that from the day of His Enlightenment to the day of His Final Passing Away, the Buddha has not uttered even a single word.

Since nothing could be predicated absolutely of Nirvana, as all Buddhist schools agreed, or of the essential nature of *dharmas*, as was concluded by the texts dealing with Perfect Wisdom, it was naturally felt that what in Western lands was known at the *via negativa*, the way of negation, was the best means of indicating the goal of the "religious" life. Nirvana was sought to be described, not in terms of what it was, but in terms of what it was not. Positive concepts are of course derived from our experience of the phenomenal world. The premise that nothing positive could really be predicated of Nirvana was followed logically, or at least psychologically, by the conclusion that it was a state of "existence," or a range of "experience," austerely aloof from the polluting touch of the mundane. This exclusively transcendental (*lokuttara*) conception of Nirvana led, in certain early Buddhist schools, to a one-sided emphasis on the merely negative aspects of the religious life, and to an exaggerated and harmful "otherworldliness." To this subject we shall return in our next

---

[1] *Selected Sayings from the Perfection of Wisdom* (The Buddhist Society, London. 1955), p. 51.

chapter, when dealing with some of the important factors in the rise of the Mahayana.

The Buddha Himself and His immediate disciples appear, at least in the Pali Scriptures, to have been more concerned with the delineation of the Path than with descriptions of the Goal; though it is untrue to say, as people sometimes do, that when questioned about the nature of Nirvana the Buddha invariably remained silent. The texts dealing with this subject may not seem very numerous when compared with those treating of other topics, but they are much more plentiful than is generally supposed, and certainly sufficient to give us a tolerably adequate account of what the limitations of language compel us to refer to as the Buddha's "conception" of Nirvana. In a well-known and oft-quoted text the Blessed One declares:—

"There is, monks, the stage where there is neither earth nor water nor fire nor wind nor the stage of the infinity of space nor the stage of the infinity of consciousness nor the stage of neither consciousness nor non-consciousness; neither this world nor the other world nor sun and moon. There, monks, I say there is neither coming nor going nor staying nor passing away nor arising. Without support or going on or basis is it. This indeed is the end of pain.

"There is, monks, an unborn, an unbecome, an unmade, an uncompounded; if, monks, there were not here this unborn, unbecome, unmade, uncompounded, there would not here be an escape from the born, the become, the made, the compounded. But because there is an unborn, an unbecome, an unmade, an uncompounded, therefore, there is an escape from the born, the become, the made, the compounded."

(Udāna, *VIII. 1 and 3. Thomas's translation)*[1]

Even in the absence of other texts the second part of this quotation is sufficient evidence for the fact that though Nirvana is a conceptually negative state, in the sense that no attribute can be predicated of it, nevertheless inasmuch as it constitutes the very basis of the possibility of emancipation from phenomenal existence it may be described as spiritually positive, in the sense of being the definite goal of the religious life. In a dialogue occurring in the *Saṁyutta-Nikāya*, however, Sāriputra, who is traditionally regarded as having developed the more analytical aspects of the Buddha's Teaching, in the absence of any explicit statement to the contrary might appear to come dangerously

[1] *Early Buddhist Scriptures* (Kegan Paul, 1935), pp. 110-111.

near to suggesting that negations completely exhaust the content of Nirvana.

A wanderer who ate rose-apples spoke thus to the venerable Sāriputra: "Reverend Sāriputra, it is said: 'Nirvana, Nirvana.' Now, what your reverence, is Nirvana?"

"Whatever, you reverence, is the extinction of passion, of aversion, of confusion, this is called Nirvana."

(Saṁyutta Nikāya, *IV. 251. Horner's translation.)*[1]

Before proceeding to Mahayana texts on the subject we shall collate from a late Pali scholastic work a few of the more negative and transcendental synonyms for Nirvana. The Summum Bonum of Buddhism is spoken of as the Uninterrupted (*accanta*), the Uncreate (*akata*), the Infinite (*ananta*), the Inextinguishable (*apalokita*), the Cessation of Suffering (*dukkha-kkhaya*), the Freedom from Longing (*anāsa*), the Uncompounded (*asankhata*), the Farther Shore (*para*), the Beyond (*pāra*), the Deliverance (*mokkha*), the Extinction (*nirodha*), the Indiscernible (*anidassana*), the Unoppressed (*aryāpajja*), the Absolute (*kevala*), the Unendangered (*anītika*), the Unattached (*anālaya*), the Deathless (*accutta*), the Release (*vimutta*), the Liberation (*vimutti*), the Final Deliverance (*apavagga*), the Dispassionate (*virāga*), the Stillness (*santi*), the Purity (*visuddhi*), and the Allayment (*nibbuta*).

The negations of the Mahayana scriptures, which in most cases had behind them several centuries of Buddhist tradition, are naturally much more systematic, elaborate and prolix than those of the earlier Pali works. As with the question of the indefinability of Nirvana, however, a shifting of interest had taken place, and it was now not Nirvana, but *dharmas* in general, and Perfect Wisdom in particular, that became the object of their negations. Besides containing the very oldest distinctively Mahayana scriptures, the *Prajñāpāramitā* corpus of Sanskrit texts has many claims to be considered the heart of Mahayana Buddhism. The heart of the *Prajñāpāramitā* literature is the *Hṛdaya Sūtra*, a summary dating from the fourth century of the common era, which Conze describes as "one of the finest and most profound spiritual documents of mankind."[2] Though covering only two pages, it is too long to be given in full, and we

---

[1] *Buddhist Texts,* p. 94.
[2] *Ibid.,* p. 74.

shall therefore quote only the negations with which we are now concerned. Addressing Śāriputra (a detail not without significance) the holy Lord and Bodhisattva Avalokita says:—

"Here, O Sariputra, all dharmas are marked with emptiness, they are neither produced nor stopped, neither defiled nor immaculate, neither deficient nor complete. Therefore, O Sariputra, where there is emptiness there is neither form, nor feeling, nor perception, nor impulse, nor consciousness; no eye, or ear, or nose, or tongue, or body, or mind; no form, nor sound, nor smell, nor taste, nor touchable, nor object of mind; no sight-organ element, and so forth, until we come to: no mind-consciousness element; there is no ignorance, nor extinction of ignorance, and so forth, until we come to, there is no decay and death; there is no suffering, nor origination, nor stopping, nor path; there is no cognition, no attainment and no non-attainment."

(Prajñāpāramitāhṛdaya, *Conze's translation*)[1]

From the *Saptaśatikā* comes the following series of negations regarding Perfect Wisdom. The Bodhisattva Mañjuśrī, who is specially associated with the *Prajñāpāramitā*, and who is iconographically represented as bearing in his left hand a lotus flower whereon rests a copy of this Sutra, demands of the Buddha:—

"How can one speak of the qualities or advantages of a perfect wisdom which is incapable of doing anything, neither raises up nor destroys anything, neither accepts or rejects any dharma, is powerless to act and not at all busy, if its own-being cannot be cognized, if its own-being cannot be seen, if it does not bestow any dharma, and does not obstruct any dharma, if it brings about the non-separateness of all dharmas, does not exalt the single oneness of all dharmas, does not effect the separateness of all dharmas, if it is not made, not something to be done, not passed, if it does not destroy anything, if it is not a donor of the dharmas of the common people, of the dharmas of the Arhats, of the dharmas of the Pratyekabuddhas, of the dharmas of the Bodhisattvas, and not even of the dharmas of a Buddha, and does not take them away, if it does not toil in birth-and-death, nor cease toiling in Nirvana, neither bestows nor destroys the dharmas of a Buddha, if it is unthinkable and inconceivable, not something to be done, not something to be undone, if it neither produces nor stops any dharmas, neither annihilates them nor makes them eternal, if it neither causes to come nor to go, brings about neither detachment nor non-detachment, neither duality nor non-duality, and if, finally, it is non-existent?"

(Saptaśatikā, *326.* et seq. *Conze's translation*)[2]

The Buddha replies that Mañjuśrī has well described the qualities of perfect wisdom, and declares that he should train in it in the manner of no-training. No less radical than these are the

---

[1] *Ibid.*, p. 152.
[2] *Selected Sayings*, pp. 77-78.

negations of a work belonging to the same corpus. The Blessed One says:—

> *"The perfection of wisdom should not be viewed from duality nor from non-duality; not from a sign nor from the signless; not through bestowal nor through withdrawal; not through subtracting something nor through adding something; not from defilement nor from non-defilement; not from purification, nor from non-purification; not through abandoning nor through non-abandoning; not from taking one's stand nor from not taking one's stand; not through junction nor through no-junction; not through a connection nor through a non-connection; not through a condition nor through a non-condition; not from dharma nor from no-dharma; not from Suchness nor from no-Suchness; not from the reality-limit nor from the no-reality-limit."*
>
> (Kauśika, *I. Conze's translation)*[1]

Much terser, but no less emphatic, than the passages we have quoted, is a text from the *Sūrangamā Sūtra*. As in the earlier Buddhist scriptures, Nirvana is once more the object of conceptual negations:—

> *The comprehension which takes place as a result of perception does not imply an understanding of the reality (of the thing perceived). What you perceive without perceiving—that is Nirvana, also known as deliverance.*[2]

Here negation passes into paradox, which, as we shall see in Chapter II, was a method of approach to Reality systematically cultivated by some Mahayana schools. For the present we are concerned with certain consequences of the method of unqualified negation.

IX. The Charge of Nihilism

It must be admitted that those consequences were not always satisfactory. However natural the *via negativa* may have seemed to the Buddhists themselves, and of howsoever great practical spiritual help they may have found it, to their opponents, and even to the weaker among their own brethren, it was everlastingly a stumbling block and a rock of offence. Effectively to distinguish between thoughts and things, between the concepts which merely indicate realities and those realities themselves, is an art belonging to a highly advanced stage of philosophical discipline and spiritual culture. Such a stage had not been attained by all the Buddha's contemporaries, and after His death it seems to

---

[1] *Ibid.*, pp. 78-79.

[2] BLOFELD, *The Path to Sudden Attainment* (Buddhist Society, London. 1948), p. 13.

have become increasingly difficult of access not only to the followers of non-Buddhist schools of thought but also to certain sections of His own disciples. That Nirvana, or an Enlightened One, or the essential nature of all dharmas, was beyond the reach of all possible predications, that it was not any object denoted by any word in any language, appeared to some uncomprehending critics equivalent to a declaration of nihilism. Overlooking the fact that not only positive but also negative terms had been rejected as inadequate, such persons maintained that Nirvana was a state of absolute annihilation, and that a man who had attained Nirvana was no longer in any sense of the word existent. The unqualified language of Śāriputra, who, as we saw in the preceding section, gives in the passage quoted no hint of a *spiritually* as distinct from a conceptually positive state behind his triple negation, and of Manjusri, by whom Perfect Wisdom is explicitly said to be "non-existent," are examples of the kind of texts which could easily be misconstrued by those who were neither intellectually acute nor spiritually very developed. But neither the Pali nor the Sanskrit text has, in fact, failed to indicate that after all negations (including the negation of negation itself) there remains a spiritually positive residue. The "wanderer who ate rose-apples," having received an apparently quite negative reply to his question about the nature of Nirvana, asks Śāriputra whether there is "a course for the realization of this Nirvana." Śāriputra replies that there is, and that it is the Aryan Eightfold Path, the stages of which he proceeds to enumerate.[1] Nirvana, then, was evidently for Śāriputra the goal of the religious life, and therefore hardly a state of complete non-existence, spiritual as well as conceptual. Similarly the Buddha, after listening to Manjusri's astounding series of negations, simply accepts his description of the qualities of Perfect Wisdom with the comment:—

"But nevertheless a Bodhisattva should train in just this perfection of wisdom, in the manner of no-training, if he wants to train in, and to accomplish, that concentration of a Bodhisattva which allows him to see all the Buddhas, the Lords, if he wants to see their Buddha-fields, and to know their names, and if he wants to perfect the supreme worship of those Buddhas and Lords, and firmly to believe in and to fathom their demonstration of dharma."[2]

---

[1] *Buddhist Texts,* p. 94.
[2] *Selected Sayings,* p. 78.

Here the goal of the Bodhisattva's career is very far from being a state of non-existence. But despite the concreteness of the Buddha's description it would be a mistake to assume that it was therefore a positive state in the conceptual sense of the term. Manjusri has already shown that Perfect Wisdom is free from all determinations, both positive and negative, and the Buddha's reply is not simply a reversion to that same conceptual use of terms which had just been so categorically repudiated. As so often happens in the Mahayana Sutras, we find ourselves in this passage in a purely spiritual world which transcends thought and speech. Words are used not conceptually but symbolically, and their truth is not the scientific truth of the intellect but the poetic truth of the imagination. We are in the realm of the spiritually positive, a world glowing with colour and flashing with light.

These purely symbolical, as distinct from merely logical, affirmations, were, however, a feature of the literary products of a much more developed form of Buddhism than that which we find in the comparatively early texts of the Pali Canon. Not that clearly symbolical positive descriptions of Nirvana and the state of the Enlightened Man are entirely absent from the Pali Scriptures. As we shall shortly see, such is far from being the case. Descriptions of this kind occur quite frequently; but they do not occur, as they do in the Mahayana Sutras, expanded into an elaborate mythology and adorned with every rhetorical artifice: they are almost always found condensed into a metaphor or a single epithet. Moreover, in the doctrinal discussions out of which the charge of nihilism seems originally to have arisen, the Buddha appears definitely to have preferred the negative method of determination—if that can properly be called negative which negates even negation. The charge of nihilism could therefore be levelled against Him with a semblance of justice and, although most strenuously repudiated, it crops up again and again through the centuries. Indeed, in India the misunderstanding (artificially aggravated, no doubt, by brahminical hostility) persists, and the belief that Buddhism teaches nihilism is still very widely current among the Indian public. Examples of the misunderstanding may be found, to mention only two sources, not only in the commentaries of Śaṅkara but in the more recent writings of Sri Aurobindo, both of whom were highly intelligent men and should have known better. Error is tenacious of existence. Nor is the misunderstanding confined to India. It flourishes in Europe too, though perhaps with less vigour than in its native clime. However, since of late its progress has been considerably checked, and since the most illustrious of those who fostered its growth are long since dead, we shall for the present confine our attention to the way in which it first struck root in the soil of India.

The Pali word for nihilism is *ucchedadiṭṭhi*, the belief or "view" that after death the soul or life-principle is annihilated. At the time of the Buddha this belief existed in two forms, one of which was the doctrine taught by Pakudha, Ajita Kesa-Kambalin and other teachers, the other a doctrine attributed to the Buddha Himself by His enemies and, on one occasion at least, by the more obtuse among His own disciples. According to Ajita, the vital principle (*jīva*) was identical with the physical body (*sarīra*), at the death of which both the foolish and the wise were "cut off" (the literal meaning of the verbal root whence *ucchedadiṭṭhi* derives) and destroyed. This wrong belief the Buddha rejected in terms of the strongest condemnation, teaching instead the doctrine of the Middle Way which avoids the two extremes of nihilism (*ucchedadiṭṭhi*) and eternalism (*sassatadiṭṭhi*) and setting forth His own peculiar and distinctive discovery of the conditioned co-production (*paṭicca-samuppāda*) of all phenomena. This discovery, as we shall see later, was of the very essence of His Enlightenment.

The second kind of *ucchedaditṭṭhi,* which was the annihilation doctrine wrongfully attributed to the Buddha, maintains that after death a Tathagata, or released person, no longer exists. As we saw in the last section, the condition of an Enlightened One was declared to be unthinkable even during His lifetime, and whether after the dissolution of His physical body either, or both, or neither of the terms existent and non-existent could be applied to Him was stated to be one of the four undetermined questions (*avyākṛtavastūni*) to which no answer ought to be made. Though the view that after death the Tathagata no longer exists is thus unequivocally rejected, both disciples and non-disciples sometimes insisted in deducing from the Buddha's position a completely nihilistic conclusion. We are told that the monk Yamaka, for example, had formed such an evil view as this, that he understood the doctrine as taught by the Lord to be "that a monk in whom the *āsavas* are destroyed at the dissolution of the body is cut off and destroyed and does not exist after death." Śāriputra, who had taken him to task for his misconception of the Buddha's teaching, counters his argument by forcing him to admit that a Tathagata, or released person, being neither identical with nor different from, the aggregates of body, feeling, perception, karma-formations and consciousness either individually or collectively, is even in this very life "not to be apprehended in truth and reality."[1] Having granted that the condition of the Tathagata is unthinkable during life, Yamaka has no alternative but to admit that it is equally unthinkable after death, and that negative predications are as much out of the question as positive ones.

A similar case is that of the wanderer Vacchagotta. Approaching the Buddha, he enquires whether or not He is of the view that the universe is eternal, that the universe is finite, that the vital principle is identical with the body, and that the Tathagata exists after death. Nor are the two remaining forms of predication recognized by Indian logic, namely, the both affirmative and negative and the neither affirmative nor negative, forgotten by the industrious inquirer, who seems to have been anxious to get to the bottom of the matter and have it settled one way or another once and for all. But the Buddha refuses to accept any of them, and Vacchagotta therefore asks what danger He sees in such views that He thus entirely avoids them. The reply he gets is in principle pragmatic. The Buddha refers to each doctrine in turn, and after describing it as "a view, a thicket of views, a wilderness, jungle, tangle, fetter of views, full of pain, vexation, trouble and distress," declares that it "does not tend to aversion, absence of passion, cessation, tranquillity, higher knowledge, enlightenment, Nirvana." Having exhausted all possible views on the four problems which he had raised, Vacchagotta is left no alternative but to ask the Buddha whether He even has any view. He is answered by an emphatic negative and a succinct summary of the Doctrine: the Tathagata has seen the body, sensation, perception, the karma-formations and consciousness, and He has seen their origin and disappearance; a released person is

---

[1] *Saṁyutta-Nikāya,* III. 110.

released upon the complete abandonment of "all imaginary and confused leanings to conceit in a self or in anything belonging to a self." Vacchagotta is quick to put another question: Where is the monk who is thus released reborn? But the Buddha retorts that to say that he is reborn does not fit the case. Neither does it fit the case to say that he is not reborn, or that he both is and is not reborn, or that he neither is nor is not reborn. At this point Vacchagotta breaks down and admits that his mind has become completely confused, and that the measure of faith which he had in the Buddha as a result of their former conversation has now completely disappeared. The Buddha then solemnly utters a warning which may seem stern, even harsh, to those who imagine that the Dharma can be understood without difficulty even by those who have not taken effective refuge in the Buddha, the Dharma, and the Sangha, and who neither believe in nor attempt to practise the Teaching. It is a warning they would do well to remember:—

> *"Profound is this doctrine, Vaccha, hard to see, hard to comprehend, good, excellent, beyond the sphere of reasoning, subtle, to be understood only by the wise.* For you it is hard to understand, who hold other views, other inclinations, other likings, another training, and another master."

Eventually, after being interrogated by the Buddha, who makes His position clear by means of a stock comparison, that of the fire which, upon the exhaustion of its fuel, cannot be said to "go" anywhere, Vacchagotta understands the truth of the matter. At last he realizes that, in the words of the Buddha,

> *"A released person, . . . released from what is called body, . . . is profound, immeasurable, hard to fathom, and like the great ocean. To say he is reborn does not fit the case; to say that he is not reborn, that he is reborn and not reborn, that he is neither reborn nor not reborn does not fit the case."* [1]

Once again all possible forms of affirmative and negative predication are decisively rejected. This time, however, Vacchagotta, having shed his false views, instead of being confused feels like a great *sāl* tree from which branches and leaves, bark and shoots and decayed wood, have fallen away, and which "stands established pure in its strength."

Since the position that upon his release from the body the released person is not reborn is one of the wrong views rejected

---

[1] *Early Buddhist Scriptures*, p. 196.

by the Buddha, it is a matter for regret that modern expositions of Theravada Buddhism, which claims to be based on the very Pali texts from which we have quoted, and which moreover professes absolute and exclusive purity of doctrine, should frequently be found deviating from the Middle Way and inclining towards the nihilistic position that, upon the dissolution of the physical body, one who has attained Nirvana is not reborn again. Even so scrupulous and conscientious a scholar as Nyanatiloka Maha Thera seems inadvertently to have fallen into this wrong view. In a recent publication he speaks of Nirvana as "the ultimate and absolute deliverance from all future rebirth."[1] Instances of this slight but nevertheless quite definite tendency towards a nihilistic interpretation of Nirvana could easily be multiplied from popular manuals, pamphlets and magazine articles by Theravadin writers. Such eroneous expositions of the Dharma are certainly to be numbered among the causes by which the misconception that Buddhism is nihilism is still kept alive. When such a tendency is active in Hinayana circles even today, it is not difficult for us to reconstruct the circumstances leading to the rise of Mahayana Buddhism, which was from one point of view a protest against the increasingly negative attitude of the Hinayanists and an attempt to recapture the spirit of the Original Teaching.

That this Teaching, being difficult to grasp, was open to misunderstanding, was realized by the Buddha as early as the seventh week after His Enlightenment, when He was undecided whether or not to reveal the Truth He had mastered to a deluded and infatuated generation. Long afterwards, in consequence of the heresy of Ariṭṭha, who had misinterpreted the Master's teaching about the dangers of craving and the reality of the "hindrances" as such, He declared that the Dharma was as difficult to grasp rightly, and as dangerous to grasp wrongly, as a poisonous water snake.[2] The misconceptions that flourished among His critics and opponents were certainly no less known to Him than those which were sometimes entertained even by His own disciples, and the accusation of nihilism was on more than one occasion declared by the Buddha to be absolutely without

[1] *Buddhist Dictionary* (Colombo, 1951), p. 93.
[2] *Majjhima-Nikāya,* I. 132.

foundation. He understood, though, how it had arisen, and in an important passage explicitly connects the charge of being a preacher of the doctrine of annihilation with His teaching about the nature of the released person.

"A monk whose mind is thus released cannot be followed and tracked out even by the gods including Indra, Brahma, and Prajapati, so that they could say, 'There rests the consciousness of a released person.' And why? Even in this actual life, monks, I say that a released person is not to be thoroughly known. Though I thus say and thus preach, some ascetics and brahmins accuse me wrongly, baselessly, falsely and groundlessly, saying that the ascetic Gotama is a nihilist, and preaches the annihilation, destruction and non-existence of an existent being. That is what I am not and do not affirm. Both previously and now I preach pain and the cessation of pain."

(Majjhima-Nikāya, *I. 135. Thomas's translation*)[1]

Though the Buddha insisted that undetermined questions should be allowed to remain undetermined, and though undetermined they remained wherever His disciples were true to the spirit of His Teaching, it would be a serious mistake to jump, as some have done, to the conclusion that His position was one of mere agnosticism, and that certain questions were left unanswered out of ignorance. Omniscience, in the sense of simultaneous awareness of all possible objects of knowledge, the Buddha never claimed to possess. In fact, He repudiated the ascription of all-knowledge as a slander. What He did claim to possess was the Threefold Knowledge, (*i*) that He remembered numberless past existences, as far back as He wished, (*ii*) that with His divine eye He could see beings passing away and being reborn according to their karma, and (*iii*) that with the destruction of the *āsavas* of craving for sensuous pleasure, craving for existence, and ignorance, He had of Himself attained and realized release of mind and knowledge in this life and abode therein.[2] According to the Pali texts the Buddha refused to answer the undetermined questions for two reasons. One was that the holy life was not dependent upon the truth or falsity of any of the four propositions; the other, that the questions dealt with matters which were not susceptible of logical treatment. Believing that these two reasons are contradictory, certain writers have sought to make a distinction between the position that the undetermined

[1] *Early Buddhist Scriptures*, p. 107.
[2] *Majjhima-Nikāya*, I. 482.

questions *ought not* to be answered and the position that they *cannot* be answered. They believe that in the second position the other, earlier doctrine has hardened into dogma. But in fact the distinction is only apparent and cannot in any real sense be maintained. The holy life does not depend upon the establishment of any of the sixteen modes of the four undetermined questions for practically the same reason that those questions themselves cannot be answered: one aims at, while the other attempts to deal with, realities which are beyond the scope of reasoning. The second method of approach is theoretical and negative, and insists upon the limitations of logic; the first is practical and positive, discouraging the disciple from attempting to solve by means of logic problems which are logically insoluble and reminding him that only at the supra-logical goal of the holy life will the "answer" be found. Though fully realizing the limitations of logic, neither the Buddha nor His disciples were so ignorant of the elementary principles of reasoning as to think that the undetermined questions could not be answered because they ought not to be answered. Their true position was that they ought not to be answered because they could not be answered, which, whatever modern critics may think, is a rather different thing.

The texts do not anywhere suggest that the Buddha did not know the answers to the undetermined questions. This does not imply that the correct answer was to be found among the four possible modes of stating each question, for the Buddha had unambiguously rejected each and every one of them as out of the question. Rather does it draw attention to the fact that His knowledge was of an altogether transcendental kind, and that the questions concerned, being by their very nature not susceptible to logical treatment, could be "answered" only by ascending to a supra-logical spiritual "plane" where they simply did not arise. As far as the fourth undetermined question, at least, was concerned, this plane was identical with the object with which the question itself dealt. The question concerning the nature of the Tathagata, and His condition after death, was to be answered by becoming a Tathagata oneself. That the Buddha, far from being an agnostic, was possessed of full spiritual knowledge and transcendental wisdom, is indicated, not only by the title by which He is most often referred to, but also, as we shall hereafter see, by the whole trend of His Teaching, which throughout insists that Enlightenment is the true goal of human life. From the next section onwards we shall be dealing with the doctrines arising out of the Buddha's Enlightenment, as well as the methods He prescribed as necessary for the attainment of Enlightenment by His disciples. The whole of the remainder of this book is therefore in a sense a vindication of the Buddha's absolute Wisdom and a refutation of the charge of agnosticism.

X. The Positive Aspect of Nirvana

Though the Buddha and His immediate disciples defined Nirvana only negatively, thus exposing themselves to the charge of nihilism, it would be wrong to assume that in the Pali texts no positive symbolical indications of the goal of the Aryan Eightfold Path are given. Rhys Davids collates from his wide and detailed knowledge of the *Tipiṭaka* a number of epithets for the state attained by the released person. Nirvana is described as

the harbour of refuge. the cool cave, the island amidst the floods, the place of bliss, emancipation, liberation, safety, the supreme, the transcendental, the uncreated, the tranquil, the home of ease, the calm, the end of suffering, the medicine for all evil, the unshaken, the ambrosia, the immaterial, the imperishable, the abiding, the further shore, the unending, the bliss of effort, the supreme joy, the ineffable, the detachment, the holy city.[1]

Some of these epithets are clearly akin to the negative determinations of Nirvana with which we have already dealt. Others are obviously positive. A small number of epithets belonging to the second class, such as those which celebrate Nirvana as the cool cave, the farther shore, and the holy city, must be regarded as poetical descriptions rather than logical definitions. Their function is to awaken the dormant spiritual energies of the disciple not by addressing his intellect but by making an appeal to his imagination. Such poetical epithets the Buddha sometimes expanded into similes of more than Homeric amplitude, and into parables which flash among the unattractive repetitions of the Pali "Scriptures" (originally not written texts but memorized sayings) like multi-faceted jewels. We have quoted in an earlier section the Parable of the City and the Ancient Road, wherein the Truth rediscovered by the Buddha is likened to one of those

---

[1] *Early Buddhism,* p. 172.

"lost cities" which even in modern times are sometimes found lying silent, deserted and overgrown with vegetation in the midst of dense jungle. From the wealth of parables and similes by means of which the Master has given positive indication of the nature of Nirvana, two jewels may be selected at random. The first, a fully developed parable, compares Nirvana to "a delightful stretch of level ground." In the second, which is an unexpanded simile, Nirvana is described as the incomparable isle of refuge.

What has been called the Parable of the Two Paths comes as the climax of the Buddha's exhortation to His cousin Tissa, who, as the introduction to this discourse informs us, had reached a crisis in his spiritual life.

"Suppose now, Tissa, there be two men, one unskilled and the other skilled in wayfaring. And the one who is unskilled asks the way of the other who is skilled in that way. And that other replies: 'Yes. This is the way, good man. Go on for a while and you will see the road divide into two. Leave the path to the left and take the right-hand path. Go on for a little and you will see a thick forest. Go on for a little and you will see a great marshy swamp. Go on for a little and you will see a steep precipice. Go on for a little and you will see a delightful stretch of level ground.'

"Such is my parable, Tissa, to show my meaning and this is the meaning thereof. By 'the man who is unskilled in the way' is meant the manyfolk. By 'the man who is skilled in the way' is meant a Tathāgata, an Arahant, a Fully Enlightened One. By 'the divided way,' Tissa, is meant 'the state of wavering.' The 'left-hand path' is a name for this false eightfold path, to wit: the path of wrong views, wrong intention, and so forth. The 'right-hand path,' Tissa, is a name for this Ariyan Eightfold Path, to wit: Right Views, and so forth. The 'thick forest,' Tissa, is a name for ignorance. The 'great marshy swamp,' Tissa, is a name for the feeling-desires. The 'steep precipice,' Tissa, is a name for vexation and despair. 'The delighful stretch of level ground,' Tissa, is a name for Nibbana."

(Saṁyutta-Nikāya, *III. 106*)[1]

Chapter V of the *Sutta-Nipāta,* a collection of discourses in prose and verse embodying what are believed to be some of the earliest versions of the Teaching, is entitled "The Way to the Beyond." Therein the sixteen brahmin pupils of Bāvarin are sent by their master to interrogate the Buddha. Each in turn puts a question. The tenth disciple, Kappa, asks the Enlightened One to tell him of an isle of refuge from the flood of decay and death. The Lord replies:—

[1] *Some Sayings of the Buddha,* pp. 325-326.

"In midstream standing, in the fearsome flood,
For those o'erwhelmed by decay and death,
I'll tell thee of an island, Kappa (said
The Exalted One)—I'll tell thee of an isle,
Where all these things shall be no more.

"Possessing naught, and cleaving unto naught—
This is the isle, th' incomparable isle.
That is the ending of decay and death.
Nibbana do I call it, Kappa (said
The Exalted One)—that is the isle."

(Sutta-Nipāta, *V. 1092-93*)[1]

Symbolical indications such as these were undoubtedly called for by the exigencies of the spiritual-pedagogic situation. Nirvana was in the highest sense devoid of all qualities, both positive and negative. Nothing could be predicated of it. Even silence, literally interpreted, might be misunderstood. Yet on the phenomenal plane, amidst the objects of the external world, including our own bodies—all seemingly so solid and so real—the holy life had, conventionally speaking, to be lived, and Nirvana, though in the absolute sense not definable even as the goal had, in a relative sense, to be attained. Paradoxes of this kind were transformed by some of the later Mahayana spiritual masters into extremely fruitful subjects for meditation. The Buddha, like the more dialectically inclined among His followers, seems to have in practice observed a sharp distinction between the absolute truth of the total negation of all qualifications, negative ones included, and the relative truth of the symbolical indications, both positive and negative. This distinction between *paramattha-sacca* (Skt. *paramārtha-satya*) and *sammuti-sacca* (Skt. *saṁvṛti satya*) or absolute truth and relative truth, despite important differences of interpretation, has remained throughout the long "history" of Buddhism fundamental to all schools of Buddhist thought. As we have seen, in discussions of the nature of Nirvana and the condition of the Released Person, the Buddha tolerated no predicate of any kind; but when rousing the dormant spiritual energies of His disciples He depicts Nirvana in the concretest forms and in the strongest and most brilliant colours. After the Parinirvana of the Master the "contradiction"

[1] *Ibid.*, p. 331.

between the two kinds of truth, which had hitherto created in the spiritual life of the disciple only a certain needful tension, led to a rupture between two rival groups in the Sangha. One group, while agreeing that the conventional expressions of ordinary speech, including epithets and metaphors and other poetical figures, were not literally and absolutely true, nevertheless contended that doctrines such as the Four Aryan Truths possessed not merely relative but absolute validity. A "man" was unreal, but the five aggregates of which he was composed did really exist. Nirvana was of course not literally a cave or an island or a delightful stretch of level ground, but it was in truth and fact the entire cessation of becoming. To the other group, spiritually subtler and intellectually more acute than their opponents, Nirvana itself, also called by them the Voidness, was the sole Absolute Truth, and even the most abstract intellectual indications of the goal were as much a matter of relative truth as the concretest imaginative ones. From one point of view the history of Buddhist thought, and of the various schools which contributed to its development, is the history of the setting up for practical purposes of one indication of Reality after another, each to be ruthlessly discarded the minute it came to be regarded as true in the absolute sense. As Buddhism, in its highest sense of the realization of the Truth, rolled victorious through the centuries, it left behind it a long trail of deposed "definitions." This inherent antagonism between the literal and figurative interpretations of doctrinal terms was, as we shall see more narrowly later on, one of the main factors leading to the emergence of the Great Vehicle.

Though the Buddha's own symbolical indications of Nirvana were generally of a sensuous and poetic nature, others of a more abstract and conceptual character are by no means entirely absent from the Pali Scriptures. One of the most interesting and, bearing in mind later historical developments, doctrinally most important of these, is a short but tremendously significant text in which the mind or consciousness is declared by the Buddha to be radiant or luminous (*pabhassara*) in its essential nature.

*"This consciousness (*citta*) is luminous, but it is defiled by adventitious defilements. The uninstructed average person does not understand this as it really is. Therefore I say that for him there is no mental development.*

"This consciousness is luminous, and it is freed from adventitious defilements.

The instructed Ariyan disciple understands this as it really is. Therefore I say that for him there is mental development."

(Aṅguttara-Nikāya, *I. 10 Horner's translation)*[1]

This same intrinsically pure and radiant consciousness was at a later stage in the development of Buddhist thought not only explicitly identified with Nirvana but regarded as of all designations of Reality the most significant and appropriate. To the Vijñāna-vādins, as we shall see in Chapter III, absolutely undifferentiated consciousness, free from the distinction of subject and object, alone was real. Nothing existed save Thought (*cittamātra*). The hint given in the Pali Scriptures was expanded into an elaborate metaphysics and epistemology. Similarly, the text's assertion that "mental development," as the translator has it, is possible only for one who understands consciousness to be in its intrinsic nature undefiled, was on the practical side developed into an elaborate system of spiritual training, culminating in the intensive practice of certain forms of meditation.

Historically important as this early conception of an intrinsically pure and radiant consciousness undoubtedly is, it occupies a comparatively insignificant place in the Pali Canon. Modern students have sometimes even wondered whether these teachings are the *ipsissima verba* of the Buddha, or whether they represent interpretations current among His immediate disciples. We have cited them as evidence of the fact that positive symbolical indications of Nirvana are not absent from texts traditionally regarded by the Theravada as being the very Word of the Buddha, and which even modern scientists, with all their scepticism, agree to contain some of the earliest records of the Master's Teaching. Incomparably more important, however, and of incontestably greater antiquity and authority—belonging as it does to the earliest strata of Buddhist tradition, where it is found occurring innumerable times—is the description of the goal of the holy life as Bodhi, enlightenment, supreme knowledge, wisdom, or spiritual illumination. The importance of this description, the positive complement of Śāriputra's negative indication of Nirvana from a psychological point of view, is attested by a number of circumstances, among them the facts that from this term are derived both the appellation by which

---

[1] *Buddhist Texts,* p. 33.

the Buddha Himself is most widely known and most often referred to, and the most popular designation for His Dharma. According to the Pali texts Bodhi or Enlightenment is of three kinds: the enlightenment of a disciple; private or merely personal enlightenment, and Supreme Perfect Enlightenment (*sāvaka-bodhi, pacceka-bodhi,* and *sammā-sambodhi*). The first is knowledge and illumination obtained by following the teaching of a Perfect Buddha (*sammā-sambuddha*); the second is knowledge and illumination which, after being obtained without a teacher, is not imparted to any disciple; the third and last is the supreme knowledge and illumination of a Perfect Buddha, Who, after winning Enlightenment without the aid of a teacher, out of compassion shows to others the way to that same transcendental experience. In the Pali Canon and its commentaries the difference between these three kinds of Bodhi is said to be merely extrinsic and adventitious. As a purely spiritual state Bodhi is not three but one; it becomes differentiated into three kinds only in accordance with the manner of its acquirement, as in the case of all three kinds, and with the special powers, attributes and cosmic functions which may be associated with it, as in the case of the Supreme Perfect Enlightenment of a Buddha. The later Sanskrit texts of the various Mahayana schools, however, make for methodological reasons a real distinction between the enlightenment of disciples and *pratyeka* Buddhas, on the one hand, and the enlightenment aimed at by Bodhisattvas, and attained by Buddhas, on the other. By the time these texts were composed the "disciple" and the *pratyeka* Buddha had come to be regarded as representing a type of spiritual attitude which, the Mahayanists thought, needed to be sharply distinguished from that of the genuine Buddhist. The kind of Bodhi associated with their names was therefore considered an inferior ideal. As we shall see in the next chapter, this apparently radical re-evaluation of the first two kinds of Bodhi, far from being an arbitrary manifestation of sectarian prejudice, was in fact a protest against the increasingly narrow interpretations given by some Hinayanists of the true goal of the Buddhist life. For the present, however, we shall take Bodhi in its original sense of the full spiritual illumination attained by Master and disciple alike. Texts which appear to be among the earliest parts of the Pali Canon do not, in fact, always distinguish clearly between the three kinds of

Enlightenment, and the Arahant is not infrequently spoken of as attaining Sambodhi, which the Hinayanists were later on to consider exclusively the prerogative of Perfect Buddhas. In both Pali and Sanskrit texts the seven groups of practices which, shortly before His Parinirvana, the Buddha exhorted His disciples to grasp, follow, practise and cultivate,[1] are termed collectively the *bodhipakkhika-dhammā,* teachings conducive to, or qualities comprising, Enlightenment. The fact that these thirty-seven items were as practices recommended to the śrāvakas, while as qualities they were regarded as constituents of the Enlightenment of the Buddha Himself, strongly suggests that at the time they received their collective designation (originally applied to one only of the seven groups) no essential difference between the three kinds of Bodhi had been recognized by any of the Buddhist schools.

Their aim being not theoretical but practical, not definition but description of the Goal, a certain imprecision in the use of terms—perhaps deliberate—in fact on the whole pervades the earlier, non-scholastic, portions of the Pali Canon and distinguishes them from the evidently later commentarial accretions. Though definite shades of meaning are sometimes quite clearly discernible, a number of important terms appears to be treated as more or less interchangeable. In His First Discourse the Buddha, speaking of His realization of the Four Aryan Truths, says: "O Bhikkhus, concerning things unheard before, there arose in me vision, knowledge, understanding; there arose in me wisdom; there arose in me light."[2] In the original text the words are *cakkuṁ* (literally, "the eye"), *ñānaṁ, paññā, vijjā* and *āloka,* all of which appear to be synonyms for Bodhi. As we have seen, our inquiry into the nature of Nirvana is for practical purposes identical with that into the nature of Enlightenment. Similarly, our investigation into the nature of Bodhi is by no means unrelated to the meaning of the various terms which are used interchangeably with it.

"Wisdom (Pali paññā, *Skt.* prajñā*)," according to the useful scholastic definition of Ācārya Buddhaghosa, the greatest commentator on the Theravada* Tipiṭaka, *"has the characteristic of penetrating into dharmas as they are*

---

[1] *Mahāparinibbāṇa Sutta, Dīgha-Nikāya,* II. 119.
[2] *Saṁyutta-Nikāya.* V. 420.

themselves. It has the function of destroying the darkness of delusion which covers the own-being of dharmas. It has the manifestation of not being deluded. Because of the statement: 'He who is concentrated knows, sees what really is,' concentration is its proximate cause."[1]

Bearing in mind the fact that the term Bodhi appears to indicate the predominantly static, wisdom the predominantly kinetic aspect of the spiritually positive content of Nirvana, this definition of Prajna may be applied, *mutatis mutandis*, to Bodhi as well. *Bodhi is insight into the true nature of phenomena* (*dharmā*). Figuratively speaking it is, as the Buddha in His First Discourse did not fail to indicate, the Supreme Light, subsequently symbolized as Buddha Amitābha. From this point of view the words "Enlightenment" and "Illumination" may be regarded as quite adequate renderings of the term Bodhi. More abstractly, Bodhi is the state of Supreme Knowledge, imperturbable and absolute, which arises in the concentrated mind, that is to say, in consequence of the attainment of a state of profound meditation or *samādhi*.

Before proceeding further, we have to be on our guard against a possible serious misunderstanding. Bodhi, it must be emphasized, does not consist in the knowledge of, or union with, an Absolute, but in an understanding of, and a penetration into, the real nature of phenomena. As we have so often had occasion to remind ourselves, Nirvana, being a state transcendent over all conceptual determinations, can be realized only by means of the complete cessation of all thought-constructions, both positive and negative, from the comparatively concrete to the most refined and abstract. The Absolute conceived by philosophers and metaphysicians belonging to the various schools of idealistic monism, Eastern as well as Western, are to the Eye of Enlightenment not realities, but mere "views," forms of that same "eternalism" (*sassatavāda*) which, with the doctrine of annihilation (*ucchedavāda*), is one of the two extreme views to be avoided by the disciple. Living as he already does in the midst of phenomena which are ultimately wrong mental constructions, the true disciple does not set up fresh barriers by seeking to elicit from them by means of a process of progressive abstraction a concept which, merely because it possesses the highest possible degree of

[1] Quoted by Conze, *Buddhism: Its Essence and Development*, p. 105.

generality, he regards as being ultimately real, nor does he tighten his bonds by endeavouring to "realize" or to attain union with that concept. This would be to build within the prison of the senses a second and stronger prison of the mind. Instead, the disciple, holding himself aloof from all conceptional constructions, follows the shortest possible path and attains Nirvana *through insight into the real nature of phenomena*. Though indispensable to a proper understanding of Buddhist "philosophy" (that is to say, of its systematic conceptual indications of Reality), so different is this teaching from all other metaphysical doctrines, so directly contrary, so opposed to, the natural tendency and workings of the unenlightened human mind, that it is not to be grasped even partially without strenuous study and prolonged and intense contemplation. The reader would at this stage do well to recall and ruminate the observations on Right Motive which we made in the first section of this Chapter.

XI. The Essence of Enlightenment

If Bodhi is insight into the true nature of phenomena, what is the nature of that insight? Before attempting to answer this question, around which revolves all that is most vital in Buddhism, we must clearly understand that this insight is a purely spiritual attainment, and that it has nothing to do with any kind of conceptual construction. Though described by the Buddha in terms comprehensible to the intellect, it would be a mistake of the most disastrous kind to imagine that it was even remotely akin to the intellectual understanding of phenomena possessed, for example, by students of physical science. Such descriptions are symbolical merely, reflecting, as though through darkness well-nigh impenetrable, only a faint glimmer of the infinite light of His realization. Having given this preliminary warning, we may state that the knowledge and insight attained by the Buddha beneath the Bodhi Tree at Gayā consisted in what, by way of an accommodation to the "normal" conceptual mode of human thought, He described as the truth that all phenomena arise in dependence on conditions. In the original Pali, all *dhammā* are *paṭicca-samuppanna*. This is the great Buddhist doctrine of *paṭicca-samuppāda*, a term variously rendered by scholars. Conze translates it as conditioned co-production, an equivalent more accurate and euphonious than many others. As the primary formulation of the Buddha's Enlightenment on the intellectual plane, it is the historical and logical basis of all later developments in Buddhist philosophy. In a text which we shall quote later on it has been equated with the Dharma itself.

The general formula of the doctrine occurs a number of times in the Pali Canon, where it is repeated in a set form of words that appears to have been recognized from the earliest times as a standard expression of the Buddha's insight. We quote this formula in Pali not only because of its intrinsic sacredness, but also in order that the reader may be afforded an opportunity of acquiring merit by reading and reciting it in the original language:—

"Imaṣmiṁ sati, idaṁ hoti, imass' uppādā, idaṁ uppajjati; imasmiṁ asati, idaṁ na hoti; imassa nirodhā, idaṁ nirujjhati."

(This being, that becomes, from the arising of this, that arises; this not becoming, that does not become; from the ceasing of this, that ceases.)[1]

No less famous is the great verse in which the Arahant Assaji, one of the Buddha's first five disciples, summarized for the benefit of Śāriputra, then a wandering ascetic, the Message of his incomparable Master. The popularity of this verse, upon hearing which Śāriputra immediately attained to the First Stage of Sanctification (*sotāpatti-magga*), is evinced not only by its frequent occurrence in Pali and Sanskrit Buddhist books, but also by the fact that chiselled in rock, inscribed on plates of copper or silver or gold, and stamped deep into tablets and seals of baked clay, it is found thousands of times in places all over the Buddhist world, from the crumbling grottoes of Afghanistan to the temples of Japan, from the *gompas* of Tibet to the ruins of Nalanda. The verse in Sanskrit runs:—

Ye dharmā hetuprabhavā hetuṁ teṣāṁ tathāgataḥ hyavadat,
Teṣāṁ ca yo nirodha evaṁ vādī mahāśramaṇaḥ.

(The Tathagata has explained the origin of those things which proceed from a cause. Their cessation too He has explained. This is the doctrine of the great Śramaṇa.)

That these great Mantras do indeed formulate the essence of the Master's realization, and that the Enlightenment which He

---

[1] *Majjhima-Nikāya,* II. 32; *Saṁyutta-Nikāya,* II. 28, etc.

attained beneath the Bodhi Tree did in truth consist in knowledge and insight into the conditioned co-production of all phenomena, is demonstrated by a tradition handed down by all schools of Buddhism.

As is well known, after His Enlightenment the Buddha hesitated to preach the Dharma to mankind, thinking that it was too profound and subtle for worldly beings to understand. Only at the entreaty of Brahma Sahampatti, Lord of a Thousand Worlds, who pleaded that there were beings of little impurity perishing through not hearing the Doctrine, did the Lord, after surveying the world with His Buddha-vision, out of compassion consent to make known the Truth which He had discovered and open wide the doors of the Immortal (*amata*) to devas and mankind. What exactly was the Dharma which He hesitated to preach? Towards the end of an extremely important autobiographical discourse preserved in the Theravada *Tipiṭaka* the Buddha, after describing His quest for, and attainment of, Supreme Enlightenment, proceeds to deal with this crucial episode in His career, when for a few moments the spiritual destinies of the worlds hung trembling in the balance. It is an awe-inspiring glimpse into the mind of a liberated and enlightened being that in this passage we are privileged to take, and one which will benefit us in accordance with the purity of our approach.

*"Then, monks, I thought, 'Now I have gained the Doctrine (Dharma, Reality), profound, hard to perceive, hard to know, tranquil, transcendent, beyond the sphere of reasoning, subtle, to be known only by the wise. Mankind is intent on its attachments, and takes delight and pleasure in them. For mankind intent on its attachments it is hard to see this principle, namely conditionedness, origination by way of cause (*paṭicca-samuppāda*). This principle, too, is hard to see, namely the cessation of all compound things, the renunciation of all clinging to rebirth, the extinction of craving, absence of passion, cessation, Nirvana.' "*

(Ariyapariyesana Sūtta, Majjhima-Nikāya, *I. 167*)[1]

The same reflection having spontaneously presented itself in verse, the Buddha's mind, so the text proceeds to relate, turned to non-action, not to preaching the Dharma. It may be observed that the concluding sentence of the passage quoted, being an unambiguous statement of the chain of reaction set up when the law of the conditioned co-production of all phenomena is

[1] *Early Buddhist Scriptures,* p. 23.

penetrated, is at the same time a clear indication of the practical purpose for which it was eventually preached.

In order that the disciple might have a clearer comprehension of the principle of conditionedness, the general abstract formula of the Pratitya Samutpada was frequently applied to different concrete groups of phenomena, the origination of which in dependence on causes was thus made more clearly manifest. The Buddha's Enlightenment itself is occasionally described not as the comprehension of the general formula of Conditioned Co-production but in terms of an understanding of one or other of its several special applications. Thus in another autobiographical discourse the Lord says:—

"Before my enlightenment, monks, when I was unenlightened and still a Bodhisattva, I thought: 'Into wretchedness, alas, has this world fallen, it is born, grows old, dies, passes away, and is reborn. But from this pain it knows no escape, from old age and death. When indeed from this pain shall an escape be known, from old age and death?'

"Then, monks, I thought, 'Now when what exists do old age and death exist, and what is the cause of old age and death?' And as I duly reflected, there came the comprehension of full knowledge: it is when there is rebirth that there is old age and death. Old age and death have rebirth as cause.

"Then, monks, I thought, 'Now when what exists does rebirth exist, and what is the cause of rebirth?' And as I duly reflected there came the comprehension of full knowledge: it is when there is becoming (or desire to be) that there is rebirth, rebirth has desire to be as cause.

"In the same way desire is said to be caused by grasping, grasping by craving, craving by feeling, feeling by contact or stimulation of any of the senses, contact by the six sense-organs, the six sense-organs by mind-and-body (nāma-rūpa)*, mind-and-body by consciousness, consciousness by the aggregates, and the aggregates by ignorance.*

"Thus with ignorance as cause there are the aggregates, with the aggregates as cause there is consciousness [etc., down to], with rebirth as cause there is old age and death. Even so is the origin of this whole mass of pain.

"The origin, the origin: thus as I duly reflected on these things unheard before, vision arose, knowledge arose, full knowledge arose, understanding arose, light arose.

"Then, monks, I thought: 'Now when what does not exist do old age and death not exist, and with the cessation of what do old age and death cease?' Then as I duly reflected there came the comprehension of full knowledge: when there is no rebirth there is no old age and death, and with the cessation of rebirth there is the cessation of old age and death.

"Then, monks, I thought: 'Now when what does not exist does rebirth not exist, and with the cessation of what does rebirth cease?' Then as I duly reflected there came the comprehension of full knowledge: when there is no desire to be there is no rebirth, and with the cessation of the desire to be there is cessation of rebirth.

(Then with the cessation of grasping follows the cessation of the desire to be, with the cessation of craving the cessation of grasping, with the cessation of feeling the cessation of craving, with the cessation of contact the cessation of feeling, with the cessation of the six sense-organs the cessation of contact, with the cessation of mind-and-body the cessation of the six sense-organs, with the cessation of consciousness the cessation of mind-and-body, with the cessation of the aggregates the cessation of consciousness, and with the cessation of ignorance the cessation of the aggregates.)

"Thus with the cessation of ignorance there is the cessation of the aggregates, with the cessation of the aggregates the cessation of consciousness, with the cessation of consciousness the cessation of mind-and-body, with the cessation of mind-and-body the cessation of the six sense-organs, with the cessation of the six sense-organs the cessation of contact, with cessation of contact the cessation of feeling, with the cessation of feeling the cessation of craving, with the cessation of craving the cessation of grasping, with the cessation of grasping the cessation of desire to be, with the cessation of the desire to be the cessation of rebirth, with the cessation of rebirth the cessation of old age and death. Even so is the cessation of this whole mass of pain.

"Cessation, cessation: thus as I duly reflected on these things unheard before, vision arose, knowledge arose, full knowledge arose, understanding arose, light arose."

(Saṁyutta-Nikāya, *II. 10)*[1]

In yet another autobiographical discourse the Buddha's attainment of Enlightenment is described as taking place in consequence of His understanding of the conditioned co-production not of twelve causal stages, as in the passage just quoted, but of ten only, the first two, ignorance and the karma-formations, not being mentioned at all. "Discrepancies" such as this seem to have perplexed more than one non-Buddhist translator of the ancient texts, some of whom, unwilling to confess that a doctrine so profound that the Buddha Himself hesitated to preach it should be beyond the reach of *their* understanding, take refuge in the suggestion that the simpler applications of the general formula must be the Buddha's own, and the more elaborate ones the work of His disciples. Others go so far as to maintain that the various expositions of the principle of Pratitya Samutpada found in Buddhist literature are "contradictory." Any absurdity rather than admit their own incomprehension! Such people genuinely think it more likely that the Buddha did not understand His own Doctrine than that they should have failed to understand it. Profane impertinence could hardly go farther than this. As

---

[1] *Early Buddhist Scriptures,* pp. 119-121.

we have already emphasized, the Sambodhi attained by the Buddha consisted of a purely transcendental, non-conceptual insight, and the general formula of the doctrine of Conditioned Co-production was an attempt to formulate that insight in intellectual terms. Phenomena being innumerable, the applications of that formula, which as a universal law was equally true of all conditioned things, were in theory innumerable too. In practice, however, the Buddha applied it only to the most salient and striking experiences of human life, for He knew that only by bringing His Doctrine home to men's business and bosoms in this way could He make it comprehensible to them. A perfect sphere at rest on an absolutely level surface can be rolled with equal ease in any direction. Similarly, the Buddha's realization of the Truth symbolized on the intellectual plane by the doctrine of Conditioned Co-production could be with equal facility applied to explain and make clear the contingent nature of any particular phenomenon. Transcendental Wisdom must be distinguished from its conceptual symbols, and the general formula of the Pratitya Samutpada from the different particular applications made necessary by the circumstances of human life and the different temperaments of disciples. If we learn to pass from a knowledge of the conditioned nature of particular groups of phenomena to an understanding of conditionedness as a universal law, and from an understanding of this law to a realization of the supra-logical Truth which it represents, then we shall see the texts dealing with the doctrine of Conditioned Co-production not as a tangle of "contradictions" but as the complementary aspects of a wonderfully consistent and profound teaching.

Once we have grasped this principle we shall no longer be astonished to find the Buddha's Enlightenment at times described, not in terms of the general formula of Conditioned Co-production, or its application to the twelve or ten causal stages in the evolution of the so-called individual being, but in terms of an awakening to the Four Aryan Truths of Suffering (*dukkha*), the Origin of Suffering (*dukkha-samudaya*), the Cessation of Suffering (*dukkha nirodha*) and the Way to the Cessation of Suffering (*dukkha-nirodha-gāminī-paṭipadā-magga*). The Buddha's First Discourse at Sarnath, to which reference has already been made, is of all the texts belonging to this class one of the most important.

Another autobiographical discourse in which the Buddha describes His attainment of Sambodhi in terms of a perception of the Four Aryan Truths is the *Mahāsaccaka Sutta* of the *Majjhima-Nikāya*. After relating to a Jain ascetic the terrible austerities He had undergone, far outdoing others in austerities, He tells of the saner way by which He eventually realized the Truth, concluding:—

"Then with thought steadied, perfectly purified, and made perfectly translucent, free from blemish, purged of taint, made supple and pliable, fit for wielding, established and immovable, I bent down my mind to the recalling of my former existence. I recalled divers births . . . evolutions and involutions of æons . . . conditions of births . . . and experiences in such . . . the rise and fall of beings and their characteristics in the different worlds with the eye divine.

"Then I perceived the Four Aryan Truths . . . the destruction of the asavas . . . *and I knew this: 'Destroyed is rebirth for me. Lived is the holy life. Done is my task. For life in these conditions there is no hereafter.'* "[1]

Quotations need not be multiplied. The doctrine of the Four Aryan Truths is obviously an extension of the principle of universal conditionedness to the problem of suffering, and therefore no less valid as a formulation of the Buddha's insight into the essential nature of phenomena than any other. The detailed working out of the correlations between the general formula of Conditioned Co-production and its application to particular groups of phenomena in the doctrines of the Twelve Causal Nexuses (*nidāna*) in the individual life-continuum and the Four Aryan Truths will engage our attention in a later section. Suffice it here to affirm the absolute unity on the transcendental plane of all such conceptual formulations of the Buddha's Supreme Enlightenment.

That this Enlightenment was a knowledge and an insight into the essentially contingent and conditioned nature of all dharmas is further demonstrated by the fact that in innumerable discourses the Buddha has indicated comprehension of the Pratitya Samutpada in one form or another and perception of the Four Aryan Truths as the Goal of the disciple's career. Rebuking Ananda for having said that the doctrine of Conditioned Co-production, though in appearance and in reality profound, was nevertheless quite easy to understand, out of the depth of His own realization the Lord declares:—

---

[1] *Some Sayings of the Buddha,* pp. 25-26.

"Say not so, Ananda! Say not so! Deep indeed is this Causal Law, and deep it appears to be. It is by not knowing, by not understanding, by not penetrating this doctrine, that this world of men has become entangled like a ball of twine, become covered with mildew, become like munja grass and rushes and unable to pass beyond the doom of the Waste, the Way of Woe, the Fall, and the Ceaseless Round (of rebirth)."[1]

Similar is His declaration regarding the Four Noble Truths:—

"Through not understanding, through not penetrating the Four Aryan Truths, brethren, we have run on and wandered round this long, long journey (of rebirth), both you and I."[2]

The combination of these two formulations in the following passage, which describes the Aryan Disciple's knowledge of the Pratitya Samutpada in terms of the Four Truths is, as a further vindication of the essential unity of all such formulations, of special interest and significance:—

"*. . . . Now, brethren, inasmuch as the Aryan Disciple knows the Law of Causation thus, knows the arising of causal relation thus, knows the ceasing of causal relation thus, knows the Way leading to the ceasing of causal relation thus, this one is called, brethren, the Aryan Disciple who has attained Vision, who has attained Insight, who has reached the Good Norm (*saddhamma, *the Truly Real), who sees this good Norm (True Reality), who has become possessed of the Knowledge of the Trained Disciple (*sekho*), who has attained the Norm-Stream (current of Reality), who is an Aryan fastidious in his wisdom, who stands having reached the Threshold of the Deathless (*amata-nibbāṇa*).*"

(Saṁyutta-Nikāya, *II. 41. Woodward's translation, revised)*[3]

Pali canonical texts describing stage by stage the career of the disciple, from his renunciation of the household life, through his progressive training in bodily restraint, mindfulness and concentration, to the moment of his supreme victory over the world, when, growing ever faster and more frequent, the flashes of insight at last expand into the limitless light of Sambodhi, and he comprehends the essential nature of all dharmas in terms of the twelvefold, tenfold, or fivefold Pratitya Samutpada, or in terms of the Four Aryan Truths, are far too numerous and far too lengthy to be quoted here. Reference need only be made to the *Sāmaññaphala Sūtta* (*Dīgha-Nikāya,* I. 47) and the *Satipaṭṭhāna Sūtta* (*Majjhima-Nikāya,* I. 55) in order to show that among these

[1] *Ibid.*, p. 213.
[2] *Ibid.*, p. 13.
[3] *Ibid.*, p. 50.

texts are some of the most important discourses in the whole *Tipiṭaka*.

In view of the arguments brought forward, and texts quoted, in support of the answer we have sought to give to our original question concerning the nature of Nirvana, Bodhi or Prajna, we need not be astonished to find Dr. Nalinaksha Dutt clinching his arguments concerning the agreement between Mahayanists and Hinayanists regarding the Four Truths and what he terms the Causal Law with a quotation which will fittingly close our own discussion of the subject. Dr. Dutt summarizes his findings as follows:—

The Hinayanists and the Mahayanists differ as regards the Truth but they agree that the Truth, as conceived by them, is attainable through the comprehension of the causal law, and so the Buddhist texts, whether Hinayanic or Mahayanic, are unanimous in holding—

Yaḥ pratītyasamutpādaṁ paśyati sa dharmaṁ paśyati, yo dharmaṁ paśyati, so Buddhaṁ paśyati.

He who realizes the causal origination of things sees the Truth; one who sees the Truth sees the Buddha.[1]

XII. The True Nature of All Dharmas

As we hope has been made quite clear, Supreme Wisdom does not consist in the knowledge of an Absolute but in the understanding of the true nature of dharmas. But what are dharmas? To this question a brief reply at least must be essayed before we pass on to a more detailed enquiry into the application of the principle of Conditioned Co-production to the causal stages in the life of an individual being.

Dharma (Pali *dhamma*) is the key-word of Buddhism. So great if the frequency with which it appears in the texts, and so numerous the vitally important ideas connoted by its various shades of meaning, that it would scarcely be an exaggeration to claim that an understanding of this protean word is synonymous with an understanding of Buddhism. For all its laconic diction and telegraphic abbreviations, The Pali Text Society's *Pali-English Dictionary* has found it impossible to dispose of all the meanings, applications and combinations of this term in an article of less

[1] *Aspects*, p. 51. The extent of the author's Pali and Sanskrit references for this quotation should be carefully noted.

than 6,000 words. An attempt to discuss even superficially all the connotations of dharma is out of the question here. Though such a discussion would be quite useful, inasmuch as the various applications of the word are interconnected and an understanding of one of them is helpful to the understanding of all and *vice versa*, we shall have to limit ourselves to that application with which we are immediately concerned. Buddhaghosa (a much more reliable guide through the labyrinth of the *Tipiṭaka* than many a modern commentator) groups the various meanings of the term under four main heads: (1) *pariyatti*, or doctrine as formulated; (2) *hetu*, or condition, causal antecedent; (3) *guṇa*, or moral quality or action; and (4) *nissatta-nijīvatā*, or "the phenomenal" as opposed to "the noumenal," "animistic entity." Following the compilers of the *Dictionary*, who observe that "(2) and (3) really constitute but one main implication considered under the two aspects of Doctrine as taught and Doctrine as formulated," we may interpret dharma as being in the first place the Doctrine or Teaching of the Buddha (in essence identical with that of all previous Buddhas); in the second, as right, or righteousness, in the double sense of individual behaviour and cosmic law; thirdly, as condition (already discussed as the Pratitya Samutpada); and fourthly, as phenomenon. Our concern is with the fourth of these divisions.

Turning from Buddhaghosa to Webster, we find that, being the neuter present participle of *phanesthai* ("to appear"), passive of *phainein* ("to show"), the word *phainomenon* or phenomenon in the broadest sense denotes any observable fact or event whatever. In the original Greek usage, however, it connoted a fact or an event in the changing and perceptible forms, as distinguished from the permanent essences of things. Webster explains:—

There was a double but related antithesis in the ancient conception, phenomena being the mutable, caused or developing aspects of things as opposed to their fixed and substantial natures, and also their perceptible aspects or appearances as opposed to their true or ideal being. The phenomenal world was thus distinguished both from the ontal world of permanent being and the ideal world of permanent truth.

Against this sort of antithesis, which vitiates practically the whole of Western philosophy, ancient, and modern, from before the time of Plato to after that of Hegel, at whose hands it received supreme apotheosis, is Buddhaghosa's double negative definition of dharma-as-phenomenon directed. Whatever his failings as a philologist might have been, the great Theravadin commentator had an eye for essentials, and in this terse definition he has not failed to counter what to the Eye of Enlightenment is the greatest delusion that the aspirant can entertain, the most dangerous obstacle on the path of discipleship: the belief that terms such as *attā* (self), *satta* (being), *jīva* (anima), *purisa* (man) and so on refer not to groups of conditioned and conditioning phenomena merely, but to independent and unchanging realities existing "within" or "beyond" or "above" such groups of phenomena. By dharma-as-phenomenon Buddhaghosa means dharmas which neither support (dharma is derived from *dhṛ*, "to hold" or "to support") as noumena other phenomena nor are themselves supported by noumena. Noumena do not exist. Only dharmas exist and support dharmas. Here, as in many other places, Buddhaghosa speaks not for one school of Buddhism but for the whole Buddhist tradition, thus amply vindicating his right to be called Buddha Ghosa, the "Voice of the Buddha."

The delusion of the noumenal "fixed and substantial natures" of things being as it were double-faced, the Buddhist offensive against the spiritual foe proceeds simultaneously from two directions. Every "thing" can be viewed under two aspects, each of which is in turn twofold. First it can be regarded as it were spatially and in relation to itself; secondly, dynamically and in relation to other "things." The wrong belief which Buddhism, singling out its most prominent and important form as representatitive, terms *attavāda* or "noumenalism," therefore comprises both a belief in the indivisible and irreducible "atomic" essences of things and a conviction that the life, energy or motivating power of an object comes not from outside it but from within. The first prong of the Buddhist attack is directed against the first of these wrong ideas, and hence Buddhaghosa defines dharmas as *nissatta*, without permanent essence; the second prong of the attack is intended to destroy the other wrong idea, and hence the Acarya in addition defines dharmas as *nijīvatā*, not themselves the source of their own life-energy. We therefore find in Buddhism, corresponding to this double-facedness of error, a twofold method for destroying delusion and seeing things as in reality they are. One method may be termed spatio-analytical, the other dynamic-synthetical.

The first of these consists in the progressive analysis of the phenomenon-as-fact into ever smaller constituent parts. As he perseveres in this exercise, which, inasmuch as all objects are infinitely divisible, may be continued indefinitely, the disciple slowly awakens to the important truth that phenomena are not simple but composite, and that however far he proceeds with his analysis, on whatever level of existence, he will nowhere encounter any object, or any part of an object, so minute that it cannot be subjected to the process as easily as a lump of dried clay is crumbled between the fingers into millions of fragments. Buddhist literature is replete with examples of the application of this analytical procedure to phenomena. The Simile of the Chariot, now rather hackneyed after centuries of repetition and elaboration, may be cited in its earliest and simplest form as the classic illustration of the analytical procedure. Sharply rebuking one who had asked about "this being," questioning who had wrought it, where its maker was, and where its origin and its cessation, the Buddha replies:—

"Why do you harp on being?
It is a false view for you,
A mere heap of samkharas, this—
Here no 'being' is got at.

"For as when the parts are rightly set
We utter the word 'chariot,'
So when there are the khandhas—,
By convention, 'there is a being' we say."
(Saṁyutta-Nikāya, *I. 135. I.B. Horner's translation)*[1]

Later versions of the simile enumerate the component parts of the chariot, with a particularity which might seem excessive, did we not remember the function of the figure to be not rhetorical but religious, that it was not a literary ornament but a spiritual device. Whether simplified or elaborated, the main purpose of the exercise is clear. We are attached, not to the components of a thing, but to the whole we imagine to exist apart from those

[1] *Buddhist Texts,* p. 80.

components and which we wrongly conceive of as constituting both their true nature and their relatively unchanging essence. By enabling us to see that terms such as "man," "woman," "child," "house," "soul" and so on denote not things-in-themselves but only a transitory assemblage of evanescent parts, the method of analysis causes our attachments as it were to disintegrate by revealing the unreality, in fact the non-existence save as mere names, of their assumed objects. Analysis of phenomena is to be continued without intermission until the last trace of attachment to "objects" is destroyed. The five *khandhas* mentioned in the second of the verses quoted represent the basic Buddhist formula of the process as applied to the so-called individual. They are *rūpa* (body, form, corporeality or materiality in general), *vedanā* (feeling or sensation), *saññā* (perception), *sankhārā* (complexes, impulses, karma-formations or volitions) and *viññāṇa* (consciousness). What the meaning of these divisions is we shall see in Section XVIII of this Chapter. None is of course ultimate. They belong to the first stage of the analytic process, when the "being" is broken down into its physical and psychical components and the latter group resolved into four components of its own. Each of the five is susceptible of further division *ad infinitum*. The subdivision of *rūpa*, in the sense of the physical body, being a comparatively simple affair, we shall give two more examples, with illustrations, of the analytic method of attacking the delusion of selfhood. Both are from the *Satipaṭṭhāna Sūtta* of the *Majjhima-Nikāya*:—

"And further, monks, a monk reflects on just this body enveloped by the skin and full of manifold impurity, from the soles up, and from the top of the hair down, thinking thus: 'There are in this body hair of the head, hair of the body, nails, teeth, skin, flesh, sinews, bones, marrow, kidneys, heart, liver, pleura, spleen, lungs, bowels, intestines, mesentery, fæces, bile, phlegm, pus, blood, sweat, solid fat, liquid fat, saliva, mucus, synovial fluid, urine.'

"Just as if, monks, there were a basket with two openings, full of various kinds of grain, namely, hill-paddy, paddy, green-gram, cowpea, sesamum, rice; and a man with sound eyes, having opened it, should reflect thus: 'This is hill-paddy; this is paddy; this is green-gram; this is cowpea; this is sesamum; this is rice.' In the same way, monks, a monk reflects. . . .

"And further, monks, a monk reflects on just this body according as it is placed or disposed, by way of the material elements: 'There are, in this body, the element of earth, the element of water, the element of fire, the element of wind.'

"Just as if, monks, a clever cow-butcher or a cow-butcher's apprentice, having

slaughtered a cow and divided it into portions, should be sitting at the junction of four highroads, in the same way a monk reflects. . . ."

(Soma Thera's translation.)[1]

The second method may be termed dynamic-synthetical because it emphasizes, on the one hand that nothing lives or moves by its own power, and on the other that phenomena arise in dependence not upon a single cause but upon a multiplicity of conditions. Just as the first method at each stage analyses the phenomenon-as-fact into the sum of its internal parts, so the second resolves the phenomenon-as-event into the sum of its external relations. The two methods are interconnected. Between the parts into which a given object may be analysed a number of relations exist; similarly, the relations between objects may be analysed into various kinds. Ultimately, the two methods are one, and in the higher stages of insight "fact" is as indistinguishable from "event" as in advanced physics "particle" is indistinguishable from "wave." The function of both pairs of words is merely instrumental; both point beyond themselves to a certain kind of insight into the nature of things, but whereas one is transcendental the other is mundane.

Since the brief exposition of the twelve links of the Pratitya Samutpada which will be given in the following section may be regarded as a unilateral illustration of the multilateral relations of phenomena, we shall cite here no example of the dynamic-synthetical method, and for further information on the subject refer the reader to Dr. Conze's perspicuous article on "Conditions and the Unconditioned."[2] Before attempting an answer to the question proposed at the beginning of this section it remains for us only to observe that the double method of analysis and synthesis is in Buddhism applied not only to the external phenomena of nature but to the internal phenomena of mind, and that a thought no less than a thing, an idea equally with an empire, is resolved into a complex of infinitely extensive relations between infinitesimally small parts. Both the infinite and the infinitesimal are, however, only theoretically accessible. In practice analysis has to stop at components not really

[1] NYANAPONIKA THERA, *The Heart of Buddhist Meditation* (Colombo, 1953), pp. 131-32.

[2] *The Maha Bodhi,* Vol. 62, p. 159 (May-June, 1954).

ultimate, which have then to be synthesized into relations which are actually not exhaustive. The various Buddhist schools have for practical purposes drawn up definite lists of "parts" and "relations." Theravada scholasticism, for instance, enumerates twenty-four kinds of relation (*paccaya*), the *Abhidharma* works of the Sarvastivadins four, the *Laṅkāvatāra Sūtra* six, and so on. Similarly, the *Abhidhammattha Sangaha,* a mediæval compendium of the Theravadins, declares the whole phenomenal world can be analysed into 169 component parts, reckoning 89 types of consciousness (*citta*), 52 psychic factors (*cetasika*), and 28 material qualities (*rūpa*). These, together with the two kinds of Nirvana (*Nibbāṇa*), make up the 171 "realities" of this school. Sarvastivadin works such as the *Abhidharmakośa* and the *Mahāvibhaṣa-śāstra* enumerate only 75 such realities. Despite divergencies in matters of classification between the various schools, they were unanimous in holding that Wisdom was to be cultivated by learning first how to analyse phenomena into the "realities" of which they were composed and then how to relate these realities to each other in various ways. The nature of dharmas should now be obvious. They are theoretically the infinitesimally small "facts" or infinitely evanescent "events" which are all that phenomena really are. Practically they are the definite numbers of "realities" into which the various Buddhist schools analysed the world and all that in it is for the purpose of providing a definite basis for the demolition of the wrong belief in an *atta* or noumenon through the systematic development of analytical insight. As we shall see later, there gradually grew up among the Hinayanists generally an increasingly strong tendency to stress the spatio-analytical method at the expense of the dynamic-synthetical. Against this onesidedness the Mahayanists protested with such vigour that in the end some of them were carried to the opposite extreme. The best Buddhist tradition has always sought to preserve a balance between the two methods. It may be said, however, that *on the whole* the Hinayana is predominantly analytical, while the Mahayana is *on the whole* more synthetic. Of the Hinayana schools, the Sarvastivada, which developed a system of pluralistic realism, was much more explicitly and dogmatically analytical than the Theravadins, though much of the scholastic literature of the latter is infected by the same tendency. Among the Mahayana schools, the Mādhyamikavāda, which was preoccupied with the conditionality of dharmas, resorted chiefly to the synthetic method, and the Vijñānavāda, one of whose problems was the explanation of the origin of apparently objective phenomena from pure undifferentiated consciousness, by the method of analysis. The refrain of the following two inspired stanzas by Buddhaghosa may be cited as a succinct example of that double insight into the empty and the conditioned nature of dharmas which the Buddhist tradition as a whole aims at developing:—

No doer of the deeds is found;
No one who ever reaps their fruits:
Just bare phenomena roll on—
This view alone is right and true.
No god, no Brahma, can be found,
No maker of this wheel of life:
Just bare phenomena roll on,
Dependent on conditions all.[1]

This conception of, or rather insight into, the nature of phenomenal existence, is not readily comprehensible to the mundane intelligence. In fact, save through meditation it is hardly to be understood at all. An illustration from the art of painting may be found helpful. The Impressionists made great use of a method of painting called divisionism. Colours were separated into their component hues, and these, in pure colour, laid side by side on the canvas. One form of this method was pointillism, in which the colours were laid on in dots. Viewed from a distance of a few yards, a picture painted by this method would appear to depict natural objects in the usual manner. As the spectator drew nearer, however, trees, houses and human figures would gradually dissolve into an apparently meaningless chaos of colour-dots. These dots are the dharmas. To the worldling, who sees as it were from a distance, the phenomenal world seems to be composed of a number of real "things." The

---

[1] *Visuddhi Magga,* XIX. Since one of the meanings of dharma is "mental object," "representation" or "idea of sense," it will be at once apparent that Buddhaghosa's conception of *suddhadhammā* is in this sense identical with Vasubandhu's conception of *vijñaptimātra,* the "mere idea." The great Theravadin commentator seems to have come very much under the influence of the Yogācāra, the school to which Vasubandhu belonged.

noble disciple, however, who takes a closer and more penetrating view, seeing things not as they seem but as they are, knows that "things" are unreal and that only dharmas exist. The illustration is far from perfect. The colour-dots of an Impressionist picture are relatively static things. In order to make our illustration complete we shall have to set it in motion. This we can do by superimposing upon it the Bergsonian image of the cinematograph. Instead of a picture imagine a technicolour cartoon film produced by the pointillist method. Those sitting at the back of the theatre will see a moving image of the external world, with men and women eating, drinking, laughing, crying, making love and undergoing the pangs of separation and death. It will seem vivid and real, and they will follow with intense interest the unfolding of the drama. The spectator seated down at the front will see only a succession of reds and blues and yellows flickering and flashing across the screen with inconceivable rapidity. He will watch the scene with perfect indifference until it is time to leave the theatre.

XIII. Conditioned Co-production: The Twelve Links

In common with other Indian traditions, Buddhism teaches what is popularly known as rebirth. Buddhist texts, however, make use of the rather more precise term of *punabbhava* (again-becoming), and their description of the rebirth-process is far more detailed and elaborate, and their discussion of the metaphysical issues involved much more thoroughgoing, than what is found in the writings of other schools. The twelvefold Pratitya Samutpada is, as we have already seen, an application of the principle of conditionality to the lives of the so-called individual as in accordance with the results of his karma he passes from birth to birth. The purpose of the application is twofold. Firstly, by pointing to a definite series of concrete instances it enables the disciple to develop a clearer insight into the universal law of the impermanent and conditioned nature of all phenomena. Secondly, by showing how birth, old age, disease and death, and the rest of the woes inherent in phenomenal existence, arise in dependence upon conditions, and how in the absence of those conditions they cease, it offers an intelligible explanation of human suffering, and points out a way of escape from the mundane to the transcendental, from the bondage of Samsara into the state of perfect Freedom which is Nirvana.

But why are twelve *nidānas* enumerated? Could the number possibly be either augmented or reduced, or must there always be exactly twelve? As we tried to make clear in Section XI, when we referred to alternative fivefold and tenfold formulations, Pratitya Samutpada is essentially the general principle of conditionedness rather than any specific sequence of conditions within this or that phenomenon. The factors conditioning the life of the individual at any given moment are innumerable. The twelve *nidānas* recognized by all Buddhist schools, whether of the great or lesser vehicle, as the standard application of the law of Conditioned Co-production to the birth-and-death process of the individual, are no more than a selection, from the factors operative at certain stages of his development, of those which are of crucial importance in determining the next stage. If the principle governing the selection be not immediately apparent, and if our very superficial survey gives the reader the impression that they were more or less arbitrarily chosen, let him remember that the selection was made by the superhuman intelligence of the Buddha, and that, far from being of merely theoretical interest and value, the twelvefold Pratitya Samutpada has for five and twenty centuries provided millions of human beings with a philosophy of life and served as the methodological basis of Buddhist realization.

As an illustration of the popularity and importance of this formulation reference may be made to its iconographical representation in Tibetan Buddhism. Painted on the wall of the vestibule of every Tibetan monastery is a picture of the so-called Wheel of Life, more properly Wheel of Becoming (*bhavacakra*). Held fast in the clutches of the demon Impermanence, whose fanged jaws project over the top, while his reptilian tail is visible below, the Wheel is divided by five or six spokes into an equal number of sections. In the topmost section are depicted the heavenly mansions of the gods; in the second, the realm of the *āsuras* (titans); in the third, the animal kingdom; in the fourth and bottommost section the hot and the cold hells; in the fifth the abode of the *pretas*, beings with pot bellies and needle-eye mouths; and in the sixth and last section the world of men. At the hub of the Wheel, biting each other's tails are a cock, a snake and a pig, representing greed (*lobha*), anger (*dveṣa*) and ignorance (*moha*). Round the rim, which is divided into a dozen sections, runs a series of pictures, each of which stands for one of the twelve links of Conditioned Co-production. Reckoning clockwise, these are ignorance (*avidyā*), a blind man with a stick; the karma-formations (*saṁskārāḥ*), a potter with a wheel and pots; consciousness (*vijñāna*), a monkey climbing a flowering tree; "name-and-form," mind and body (*nāma-rūpa*), a ship (body) with four passengers (the four mental aggregates) one of whom (consciousness) is steering; the six sense-organs (*ṣaḍāyatanāni*), an empty house; contact (*sparśa*), a man and woman embracing; feeling or sensation (*vedanā*), a man with an arrow in his eye; thirst or craving (*tṛṣṇā*), a woman offering a drink to a seated man; grasping (*upādāna*), a man gathering fruit from a tree; coming-to-be (*bhava*), a pregnant woman; birth (*jāti*), a woman in childbirth; finally old age and death (*jarā-maraṇa*), represented by a man carrying a corpse to the burning ground. Impelled by greed, anger and ignorance, worldly beings "transmigrate" through the six spheres of phenomenal existence in accordance with the law of Conditioned Co-production.

Another indication that the twelve links or causal stages are by no means intended to be exhaustive, is furnished by the fact that, according to the oldest traditional explanation—common to all schools—they are distributed over not one life but three lives. The first and second belong to the last birth, the eleventh and twelfth to the next birth, and the remainder to the present life. Each existence, therefore, may be regarded as possessing two or eight or a second pair of two causal stages, as it is viewed as past, present or future. Thus if the three divisions are combined each life can be regarded as possessing twelve links or causal stages, and three lives as possessing thirty-six, each link occurring thrice.

Though ignorance is enumerated first, it is not therefore to be interpreted as the ultimate origin, the absolute first beginning, of the individual. Neither does it have a cosmological significance. The rim of a wheel cannot be said to begin at a particular point: it is continuous. So with the twelve links of the "chain" of Conditioned Co-production. The enumeration of the whole series may begin at any one of them.

Regardless of which link is counted first, the series can be reckoned in four ways: in direct order (*anuloma*), when we pass from cause to effect; in reverse order (*pratiloma*), from effect to cause; positively, when the existence of the cause determines the existence of the effect, or when the existence of the effect is seen to depend upon the existence of the cause; and negatively, when owing to the nonexistence of the cause the effect is not produced, or when the non-production of the effect is seen to be due to the non-existence of the cause. (There being no single English word for the "thing conditioned," we have used the correlatives cause and effect. But by "cause" is to be understood causal ground or condition, rather than cause in the strict, Western philosophical sense.[1])

1. *Āvidyā* (Pali *avijjā*), the "first" of the twelve *nidānas*, is ignorance in the sense of spiritual unawareness. Though the Transcendental, being beyond all determinations, can have no opposite, from the mundane point of view ignorance may be regarded as the antithesis of Bodhi. Hence Enlightenment or Supreme Wisdom being the goal of the disciple's career, the state of ignorance, of total deprivation of Bodhi, is methodologically the starting-point of the entire Teaching. *Āvidyā* is positive as well as negative. The worldly person is not only unenlightened; he entertains wrong views about the nature of phenomenal existence which are contrary to the right views held by Aryans. He views the conditioned as unconditioned; imagines noumena where there are only phenomena; sees the impermanent as permanent, the painful as pleasant, and the impure as pure. He is either an eternalist (*sassatavādin*) or an annihilationist (*ucchedavādin*). He may believe in the existence of God and the soul; have faith in the efficacy of prayer and self-mortification, and hold fast to the wrong opinion that certain external acts, such as bathing in "sacred" rivers, and certain ethical observances, such as the giving of alms, are in themselves of spiritual value. We have seen that the conceptual content of Bodhi may be formulated intellectually in various ways. Similarly *āvidyā* is not only the stage of general deprivation of Wisdom; it is specifically ignorance of the doctrine of Conditioned Co-

---

[1] Theravadin works state by way of which of the twenty-four conditions (*paccaya*) each of the twelve links is related to the one succeeding.

production, of the Four Aryan Truths, and other cardinal tenets of Buddhism, and scholastically is always so defined.

2. The relation between *āvidyā* and *saṁskārāḥ* (Pali *sankhāra*), the second of the *nidānas* belonging to the "previous" birth, may be compared to that which exists between the state of drunkenness that makes a man forget himself and the irrational actions he performs while in such a condition. Meaning literally "preparation, get-up," *saṁkhārāḥ* has been rendered in modern languages by a great variety of "equivalents," none of them very satisfactory. In its applied sense of "aggregate" it means the conditions necessary to bring about a certain result, in this case the aggregate of mental conditions which, under the law of karma, are responsible for the production of the first moment of consciousness in a "new" life. Essentially it stands for the acts of will associated with a particular state of mind or consciousness, and for this reason has been defined by the commentators as *karma-cetanā*, "volitional action." This volitional action may be bodily, vocal or merely mental. It can be either meritorious, in the sense of arising in association with "wholesome" mental states and making for a "good" rebirth, or demeritorious, arising in association with "unwholesome" states of consciousness and making for a "bad" rebirth. The volitional actions associated with the ethically neutral mental states of the Arahant are not conditions making for rebirth in any sphere of phenomenal existence.

3. Dependent upon the karma-formations of the "previous" birth arises the third causal state, *vijñāna* (Pali *viññāṇa*) or consciousness, the first of the causal stages belonging to the "present" existence. Unlike the modern science of Biology, Buddhism teaches in addition to physical heredity a heredity which is purely psychical. Conception takes place only upon the conjunction of the three necessary factors: when father and mother copulate; when it is the mother's season; and when there is a "being" to be reborn. By "being" is meant here the last moment of consciousness belonging to the "previous" birth. Conception does not take place, despite the presence of the other factors, when there are no "aggregates" which have been "prepared" or "got up" for the physical heredity, parentage, environment, etc., pertaining to birth of such and such parents. Between the cessation of the last moment of consciousness

belonging to the last birth, and the arising of the first moment of consciousness of the present birth there is, according to the modern Theravada, no interval.

What is reborn? To say that the "being" reborn is identical with the being lately dead would be the extreme of eternalism. To say that he was not identical would be nihilism. Avoiding these two extremes, the Buddha teaches the Middle Way, namely, just this doctrine of Conditioned Co-production, "This being, that becomes; from the arising of this, that arises, etc." Rebirth takes place, but in reality no "being" is reborn. Going as it does so much against the grain of our deep-rooted attachment to the delusion of permanent individuality, this application of the Pratitya Samutpada to the rebirth-process is one of the hardest ideas to grasp in the whole range of Buddhist teaching. It is not to be understood even intellectually without careful and *impartial* study and a certain amount of meditation.

The karmically neutral resultant (*vipāka*) consciousness which begins functioning at the very instant of conception comprises eye-, ear-, nose-, tongue- and body-consciousness, together with certain associated mental phenomena.

4. Dependent upon this consciousness (*vijñāna*) arises *nāma-rūpa* (equal in Pali and Skt.), by which is meant the (at first embryonic) physical body (*rūpa*) and the remaining three mental (*nāma*) "heaps" or *skandhas* (Pali *khandhas*): feeling or sensation (*vedanā*); perception or *samjñā* (Pali *saññā*); and volitional activities (*saṁskārāḥ*). The *skandha* of consciousness (*vijñāna*) being reckoned as the "cause" cannot be enumerated in the "effect." This division into five heaps, one material and four mental, is the primary Buddhist analysis of the human so-called personality, the first step in its analytical onslaught against "noumena." What arises in dependence upon consciousness at the fourth causal stage is, therefore, the whole psycho-physical organism. A slightly more detailed account of the five *skandhas* will be given in Section XVIII.

5. Dependent upon *nāma-rūpa* arise the *śaḍāyatana* (Pali *saḷāyatana*), the six "bases," that is to say, the five physical sense organs and the mind (*vijñāna*) considered as the organ for the perception of mental objects. It should be noted that here "mind-base" stands for the different types of consciousness represented by the *vijñāna-skandha* which, having not been enu-

merated at the last causal stage, reappear in this one. The apparently simple formula for the fifth *nidāna* conceals an extremely complicated network of conditions. *Nāma* and the mind-base, *nāma* and the five physical sense-organ bases, *rūpa* and the mind-base, and *rūpa* and the five physical sense-organ bases, are all interrelated in very many different ways. Objection may be made that consciousness (*vijñāna*) has been in existence ever since the third causal stage, and that it cannot without contradiction be said to arise at the fifth stage. The objection would hold good only if we were here concerned not with conditionality but with causality. According to the Theravada tradition, conditions are of twenty-four kinds. The kinds of conditions upon which *vijñāna,* as mind-base, has arisen at the fifth causal stage are different from those upon which it now arises at the third. Hence instead of a contradiction we find, on closer examination, only further evidence of the depth and complexity of this doctrine.[1]

6. Dependent upon the *ṣaḍāyatana* arises *sparśa* (Pali *phassa*), contact or impression, the sixth *nidāna,* which is of six kinds (eye-contact, ear-contact and so on), each kind consisting of a combination of the organ, the object and the impression. This is elementary psychology such as even worldlings can understand. Only one point needs comment. Buddhist psychology treats consciousness (*vijñāna*), as being from one point of view an organ or sense (*manāyatana*), with its own mental objects or dharmas (another application of this multi-significant term). Hence it speaks also of the mental contact or impression produced by their mutual impingement.

7. Dependent upon *sparśa* arises *vedanā* (equal in Pali and Skt.), feeling or sensation. Like the last *nidāna, vedanā* is with regard to its place of origin sixfold: born of eye-contact, born of ear-contact, and so on. Each of these six kinds can be pleasant, or painful. Having, like the six "bases" and contact, already arisen simultaneously with consciousness, with which it is inseparably connected, feeling in the seventh *nidāna* is conditioned not by way of simultaneity but as karma-result.

---

[1] NYANATILOKA'S *Guide Through the Abhidhamma-Pitaka* (Colombo 1938), pp. 150-151, contains fuller information on this point.

8. Dependent upon karma-resultant *sparśa* arises *tṛṣṇā* (Pali *taṇhā*), hunger and thirst, or craving for excitement; the fever of unsatisfied longing. It is the flame of desire that burns unsatisfied from birth to birth until once and for all extinguished in the cool waters of Nirvana. In an interesting comment on this word, The Pali Text Society's *Pali-English Dictionary* says:—

The figure (of "thirst") is a strong one, and the word Taṇhā is found mainly in poetry, or in prose passages charged with religious emotion. It is rarely used in the philosophy or the psychology.

The Buddha's use of a poetic rather than a scientific expression for the eighth *nidāna* is not without significance. *Tṛṣṇā* being unwholesome affectivity in its most vehement and violent form, a metaphor gives a richer and more suggestive indication of its nature than a definition. The six objects of craving are the five physical sense-objects and ideas, the object of the mind-organ. Its three modes are *kāma-tṛṣṇā,* when craving for a particular form, sound, etc., arises together with desire for sensuous pleasure (*kāma*); *bhava-tṛṣṇā,* when it arises in association with the wrong belief in eternal personal existence (*bhava*), or theological dogmas such as that of the "immortality of the soul"; and *vibhava-tṛṣṇā,* when it is connected with the false view that personality is annihilated at death. As we shall see later, the *nidānas* are of two kinds: belonging to the karma-process (*karma-bhava*); and belonging to the rebirth-process (*utpati-bhava*). The five *nidānas* from consciousness to feeling represent the rebirth process of the present life; being the resultants of the karma-process set up in the previous existence they are ethically neutral. With *tṛṣṇā,* however, begins the karma-process of the present life, upon the setting up of which depends the rebirth-process of the future existence. For this reason the eighth *nidāna* appears also as the Second Aryan Truth, the Truth of the Origin of Suffering.

"What, O Monks, is the origin of suffering? It is that craving which gives rise to ever fresh rebirth and bound up with pleasure and lust, now here, now there, finds ever fresh delight." (Dīgha-Nikāya *XXII*)

The transition from sensation to craving, from passive feeling to active desire, is the psychological fact standing behind all myths of the Fall of Man from paradise to earth, from a blissful to a miserable state and sphere of existence. The interval between these two *nidānas* is the battlefield of the spiritual life and to experience feelings yet check desires is that victory over oneself which the Buddha declared to be greater than the conquest of a thousand men a thousand times. According to another well-known image, craving is the poisoned arrow embedded in the flesh of the disciple's heart which must be pulled out before he can be restored to the state of perfect spiritual health or holiness which is Nirvana.

9. Should that arrow remain stuck fast, then the next causal stage inevitably follows: Dependent upon *tṛṣṇā* arises *upādāna,* grasping, clinging or attachment. Of this there are four kinds: attachment to sensuous pleasure (*kāma*); to *dṛṣṭi* (Pali *diṭṭhi*) or "views": mere "metaphysical" speculation, groundless belief, unfounded opinion, dogma; to ethics (*śīla*) and external observances (*vrata*), merely for their own sakes; and to the wrong belief in the existence of noumenal residues in phenomena (*atmavāda*), especially in the form of a soul, self or ego separate from the phenomena of "personality." The greater importance assigned at this causal stage to the various types of "intellectual" attachment—all differentiations of that "original" basic ignorance which underlies the whole Samsaric process—serves to underline the very great importance of Right Veiws, True Doctrine or, in a word, of a correct theoretical and intellectual grasp of the Dharma. Mere "goodness" does not avail to deliver from the round of birth and death.

10. Dependent upon *upādāna* arises *bhāva* (Pali *bhava*), "becoming," in the sense of life in, or rebirth into, any "sphere" or "plane" of phenomenal existence. According to the division adopted in this *nidāna,* these planes are three in number: that of desire (*kāma*), comprising existence as titans, animals, human beings, beings in hell, hungry ghosts and gods of the lower heavenly realms; that of form (*rūpa*) comprising life in the intermediate heavens; and formless existence (*arūpabhava*), comprising rebirth at the apex of the pyramid of phenomenal existence in the highest celestial abodes. Inasmuch as within each individual life, regardless of plane, there is a double process of rebirth-producing volition (*cetana*) and karma-resultant (*vipāka*) mental and physical phenomena, *bhava* is also said to be twofold, consisting of the karma-process (*karma-bhāva*) and the rebirth process (*utpati-bhāva*). The term is also taken to mean conception, for at the tenth causal stage begins the "future" life.

11. Dependent upon *bhāva* (in the sense of *Kamma-bhava*:

being a resultant, the rebirth-process is causally inefficacious) arises *jāti,* or birth, here understood not in the sense of actual parturition but as—in the case of beings of the human species, and most other mammals—the simultaneous appearance of the five *skandhas,* body, sensation, perception, constructive volition and consciousness, in the mother's womb.

12. Dependent upon *jāti* arises *jarā-maraṇa,* or decay-and-death, with sorrow, lamentation, pain, grief and despair in its train. The connection here is obvious. "Thus"—that is to say, by way of these twelve causal stages—"arises this whole mass of suffering", as the conclusion of the canonical formula for the whole series has it.

The Wheel of Becoming has now made one complete revolution; the *nidānas* from ignorance to decay-and-death have been enumerated positively in direct or progressive order; the great fact that, far from being due to fate or chance or the fiat of the creator-god, human bondage to phenomenal existence is the product of human volitional action, has now been made plain.

The secret of bondage is also the secret of liberation. By exerting a force stronger than that of hate, stronger than desire, stronger even than ignorance, the Wheel of Becoming can be made to revolve in the opposite direction; the *nidānas* can be enumerated negatively in reverse order: from the cessation of birth comes the cessation of decay-and-death; from the cessation of becoming, the cessation of birth; from the cessation of attachment, the cessation of becoming; from the cessation of craving, the cessation of attachment; from the cessation of feeling, the cessation of craving; from the cessation of contact, the cessation of feeling; from the cessation of the six bases, the cessation of contact; from the cessation of name-and-form, the cessation of the six bases; from the cessation of consciousness, the cessation of name-and-form; through the cessation of the constructive volitions, the cessation of consciousness and through the cessation of ignorance, the cessation of the constructive volitions. "Thus," in the triumphant words of the old text, "is the cessation of this whole mass of suffering."

"Many a House of life
Hath held me—seeking ever him who wrought
These prisons of the senses, sorrow-fraught;
Sore was my ceaseless strife:

"But now,
Thou Builder of this Tabernacle—Thou!
I know Thee: Never shalt Thou build again
These walls of pain,
Nor raise the roof-tree of deceits, nor lay
Fresh rafters on the clay;
Broken Thy house is, and the ridge-pole split:
Delusion fashioned it:
Safe pass I thence—deliverance to obtain."[1]

XIV. Samsara and Nirvana

Cessation is, however, far from being the last word of Buddhism. Though indicated mainly by negative expressions, Nirvana, the goal of the disciple's career, is not in itself a state of mere non-existence. Similarly, the process of cessation one by one of the twelve causal stages, though described exclusively in terms of extinction, is certainly not to be understood as a gradual approximation to a state of absolute annihilation. What the disciple achieves with the breaking of the last link of the chain binding him to phenomenal existence can be described not only as the cessation of ignorance, but also, more positively, as the attainment of Supreme Enlightenment—Sambodhi; or Wisdom—Prajna. A positive formulation of the Pratitya Samutpada in reverse order, when the Wheel of Becoming rolls away from Samsara to Nirvana, should therefore be possible; at each causal stage it should be possible to speak, not only of a cessation of this or that condition making for rebirth, and hence for suffering, but also of the production of positive factors which progressively augment one another until with the realization of Sambodhi the whole process reaches its climax.

Such a formulation has indeed been recorded in the Pali Scriptures; but as far as we know only once. Being without parallel in the *Tipiṭaka,* and moreover completely out of line with the one-sided negativism which came increasingly to dominate the Hinayana schools, including the Theravada, this doctrinally very important text was for centuries neglected and ignored. Attention was first drawn to it in modern times by Caroline Rhys Davids, who in the Preface to the second volume of her translation of the

---

[1] The Buddha's "Song of Victory": *Dhammapada,* verses 153-54; *The Light of Asia,* Bk. VI.

Saṁyutta-Nikāya, in which division of the Scriptures the passage may be located, recognizes its importance and who, not without a slight intemperance of expression, refers to it as an "oasis" of affirmation in the midst of an arid desert of negation.

According to the *Nidāna-Vagga* of the above mentioned Nikaya, the process of Conditioned Co-production consists of a series of twenty-four causal stages. One slight difference in terminology apart, the first half of the series is identical with the more common series of twelve links enumerated and described in the last section. The twelfth of the longer series of twenty-four causal stages is not, as might have been expected, *jarā-maraṇa,* "decay-and-death," but simply *duḥkha,* suffering. The change is slight but significant: *duḥkha* is the first of the Four Aryan Truths. If one out of the two most important formulas for the principle of universal conditionality can be interpreted positively, why not the other also? Why should there not be a positive as well as a negative application of the formula of the Four Truths? We must be careful however, not to hang too long a chain of deductions from the difference, which is after all only a difference of terms. By the figure of speech known as synecdoche "decay-and-death" stands for all those unpleasant and painful experiences of life which are collectively called *duḥkha* or suffering. Dependent upon *duḥkha* arises *śraddhā* (Pali *saddhā*) or faith, the first of the second series of twelve causal stages or associations. Then dependent upon faith arises joy (*pamojjā*); dependent upon joy arises rapture (*pīti*); dependent upon rapture arises serenity; dependent upon serenity arises happiness; dependent upon happiness arises concentration; dependent upon concentration arise knowledge and vision into things as they really are; dependent upon knowledge and vision into things as they really are arises repulsion; dependent upon repulsion arises passionlessness (*virāga*); dependent upon passionlessness arises liberation; dependent upon liberation arises knowledge of the destruction of the *āsravas* (Pali *āsavas*): the intoxicants of sensuous craving, thirst for existence, and ignorance.[1] Sambodhi has been attained; but this time the succession of causal stages has been described not negatively but in purely positive terms. The difference between the positive and the

[1] C. A. F. Rhys Davids, *Book of the Kindred Sayings.* Vol. II, pp. 25-6.

negative formulation of the Pratitya Samutpada in reverse order is, however, much more than a difference of terminology, and the importance of the text in question, as an evidence that the later more richly affirmative Mahayana descriptions of the Path are anticipated in the oldest records of the Teaching, is therefore enormous.

The Buddha illustrates the whole process of Conditioned Co-production, or, as Mrs. Rhys Davids translates the term, causal association, in its extended twenty-fourfold formulation, with one of those graphic similes which are among the chief beauties of Pali literature.

"Just as when, brethren, on some hilltop when rain is falling in thick drops, that water, coursing according to slope, fills the hillside clefts and chasms and gullies, these being filled up fill the tarns, these being filled up fill the lakes, these being filled up fill the little rivers, these being filled up fill the great rivers, and the great rivers being filled up fill the sea, the ocean—even so, brethren, there is causal association of activities with ignorance, of consciousness with activities, of name-and-shape with consciousness, of the sixfold sense-sphere with name-and-shape, of contact with the sixfold sense-sphere, of feeling with contact, of craving with feeling, of grasping with craving, of (renewed) becoming with grasping, of birth with (renewed) becoming, of sorrow with birth, of faith with sorrow, of joy with faith, of rapture with joy, of serenity with rapture, of happiness with serenity, of concentration with happiness, of the knowledge and vision of things as they really are with concentration, of repulsion with the knowledge and vision of things as they really are, of passionlessness with repulsion, of liberation with passionlessness, of knowledge about extinction (of intoxicants) with liberation."[1]

That there exists within the Pratitya Samutpada this second positive, progressive, "spiritual" and, as it were, spiral series of causal stages, and that it, and not the mere process of cessation, is the true counterpart of the cycle of births and deaths which make up the first series, has been demonstrated by one of the greatest Buddhist scholars and thinkers of modern times, Dr. Beni Madhab Barua. In his Dona Alphina Ratnayake Lecture on "Buddhism as Personal Religion" Dr. Barua has sought to define the logical relation between the Pratitya Samutpada and Nirvana which, as he observes, are the two central points in the Buddha's personal religion. Is the abiding order of cosmic life expressed by the Buddha's doctrine of Conditioned Co-production (rendered by him as "causal genesis") an all-inclusive reality? "If so," he

---

[1] *Ibid.*, Vol. II, p. 27.

asks, "does it or does it not include *Nirvāṇa* in it? If it precludes *Nirvāṇa* or any other experience, material, mental, moral or spiritual, it cannot be an all-inclusive reality. Further if it is not all-inclusive, it does not deserve the name of reality at all. To be a reality it must be not only a fact but the whole of the fact, known or knowable, actual or potential."[1] The only *caveat* we would wish to add here is that the the question at issue is not so much whether the Pratitya Samutpada is an all-inclusive reality as whether it is an all-inclusive formulation of reality, a distinction which, in the light of our previous remarks on the need for distinguishing between thoughts and things, will be seen to be not without importance. Dr. Barua observes that the problem of the relation between the Buddha's two principal doctrines created a puzzle and a difficulty in His personal religion, and that it divided the Buddhist teachers into two sharply antagonistic schools of thought. One of these maintained that Nirvana, representing the counter-process of cessation, was logically excluded from the Buddha's doctrine of Pratitya Samutpada, which was concerned solely with the phenomenal. Even Buddhaghosa did not grasp the logical and metaphysical difficulty of the matter. The direction from which Dr. Barua has approached what he terms the Buddha's personal religion is different from our own; but at this point the two lines converge, and his own solution of the problem which baffled even the intelligence of Buddhaghosa so closely corroborates our own previous findings, and is moreover of such intrinsic interest, that we reproduce it as fully as space permits. After informing us that light on the problem comes from the intellectually gifted early Buddhist sister Dhammadinnā, whose views were fully endorsed by the Buddha with the remark that He had nothing further to add to them, Dr. Barua embarks upon the following brilliant exposition:—

*As interpreted by her, Buddha's Causal Genesis admits of two different trends of things in the whole of reality. In one of them, the reaction (*paṭibhāga*) takes place in a cyclical order between two opposites (*paccanīkas*), such as pleasure and pain (*sukha-dukkha*), virtue and vice (*puñña-pāpa*), good and evil (*kusala-akusala*). This is aptly termed by Buddhaghosa as* visabhāga-paṭibhāga. *In the other, the reaction takes place in a progressive order between two*

[1] *The Maha Bodhi,* Vol. 52, p. 62 (March-April, 1944).

counterparts or complements or between two things of the same genus, the succeeding factor augmenting the effect of the preceding one. This is what Buddhaghosa terms paṭibhāga. *By the term "world," as distinguished from* Nirvāṇa, *we are to understand the first trend in the causal genesis where we revolve within the cycle of reaction between the opposites.* Nirvāṇa *represents the other trend in the causal genesis in which the course of reaction lies from strength to strength, good to further good, from that to still greater good, from pleasure to joy, from joy to gladness, from gladness to happiness, from happiness to bliss, from bliss to beatitude, from intuitive knowledge (*vijjā*) to the feeling of emancipation (*vimutti*), from that to self-mastery (*vasībhāva*) or self-consciousness as to the acquisition of the free state, and from that to the fullest enjoyment of the bliss of* Nirvāṇa. *In reply to the question as to what follows by way of the reaction from* Nirvāṇa *Dhammadinnā wisely said that* Nirvāṇa *was generally regarded as the final step in the process in order to avoid an infinite regress—for the sake of* pariyanta-gahaṇam *in her own language. But she has not failed to indicate that even if there be any further reaction, that also takes place in the line and whatever follows therefore will also appertain in* Nirvāṇa *and, therefore, will partake of its nature. . . .*

If such be the correct interpretation of the philosophical position of Buddha's causal genesis both Samsāra *and* Nirvāṇa *may be consistently shown to be included in it, both as possibilities in one and the same reality. That this was the exact position may be realized from the fact that the entire mode or method of religious training which was the outcome of Buddha's personal religion was based upon the second trend, the second line of reaction implying the procession from good to greater good, from the wholesome to the more wholesome. The rotatory play or strife between the opposites is restricted to the* kāma *or non-jhānic non-reflective spheres of consciousness.* Akusala, *the immoral or unwholesome reaction of mind, is given no place in the jhānic or reflective spheres of consciousness and religious experience admitting of infinite gradations, though for convenience sake or scientific purpose these are reduced to sixteen or seventeen successive stages of progress in the life of an aspirant.*

Given these two trends within the order of becoming, as discovered by Buddha, and clearly held before us as such, it is up to us all to decide for ourselves which of them to seek and which not. And here lies the scope of the freedom of the Will. Had Buddha's been simply the Heraclitean view of change, compelling us to rotate off and on with the cycle of the opposites, the grand conception of the progressive path of life as outlined by the Aṣṭamārga, *better the* Daśamārga, *which emanated out of* Buddha-jñāna, *would have been logically impossible.*[1]

It should now be possible for us to synthesize our own and Dr. Barua's findings into a fairly complete account of the conceptual content of the Buddha's realization according to the oldest records available. Reality being ineffable, positive and negative definitions are equally out of place. By following a Middle Path between affirmation and negation the Buddha's insight may,

[1] *Ibid.*, pp. 63-4. See also *Ceylon Lectures* (Calcutta 1945), pp. 155-162.

however, be formulated as the principle of universal conditionality, Pratitya Samutpada, or Conditioned Co-production. This doctrine is an all-inclusive Reality, or formulation of Reality, within which are included two trends or orders of things, one cyclic between opposites, the other progressive between factors which mutually complement and augment each other. The second trend is not merely the negative counterpart of the first, but possesses a positive character of its own. Upon this second trend the spiritual life is based. In relation to the first trend Nirvana may be described only negatively, in terms of cessation; from the viewpoint of the world it will inevitably appear as a purely transcendental and, as it were, "static" state. In relation to the second trend Nirvana may be described as the farthest discernible point of the increasingly positive and progressive series of reactions away from the Samsara; here it appears as "dynamic" rather than static, the archetype of time rather than of space. The advantages of this binocular view of Reality are enormous. Instead of being a mere defecation of things evil the spiritual life becomes an enriching assimilation of ever greater and greater goods. The *Via Affirmativa* is no less valid an approach to the goal than the *Via Negativa*.

Unfortunately, this perfect equilibrium of opposite but complementary spiritual forces and methods could not long be sustained, and in view of certain shiftings back and forth of emphasis which later on took place in the Buddhist schools, Dr. Barua's central thesis, that in the Buddha's personal religion Samsara and Nirvana were both possibilities in one and the same reality, and that this reality was the Pratitya Samutpada, is not only very important practically but also of great theoretical interest. As we have already had occasion to point out, the Pali texts of the Theravada *Tipiṭaka* which establish as the counterpart of the process of rebirth not merely a process of cessation but something positive and progressive are exceedingly rare. Much more numerous are texts describing the Path and the Goal exclusively in terms of extinction. The unmistakable preference shown by the Hinayana schools for the negative side of the Buddha's teaching is both the cause and the effect of this very great difference between the number of "negative" and the number of "positive" texts which have been transmitted by their traditions. The Mahayana schools have on the whole been more faithful to the spirit of the Original Teaching. In a paper on *"Philosophy and Religion in Original and Developed Buddhism"*[1] we have tried to show that what Buddhaghosa calls *visabhāga-paṭibhāgas,* reaction in a cyclic order between opposites, corresponds to what Nāgārjuna and his disciples term *saṁskṛta-śūnyatā,* or the emptiness of the composite, and the former's *sadisa-paṭibhāga,* or reaction in a progressive order between two counterparts of complements, to the *asaṁskṛta-śūnyatā,* or emptiness of the incomposite, of the latter sage. We have also pointed out that just as in the Buddha's personal religion Samsara and Nirvana were both possibilities in one and the same reality, so in the Vijñāṇavāda philosophy the seeds of defilement (*sāsrava-bīja*) and the seeds of purity (*anāsrava-bīja*) are both contained in the *Ālaya-Vijñāna* or Storehouse Consciousness. Those who are interested in the matter are referred to this study for fuller information. We must now turn from the Pratitya Samutpada to the second most important formulation of the principle of universal conditionality.

XV. The Four Aryan Truths

It will be remembered that the Buddha's insight into the true nature of phenomena found its most highly generalized expression in a fourfold formula. (1) A certain thing exists, or event occurs; (2) the existence of that thing, or the occurrence of that event, depends on the existence or occurrence of a particular cause or condition; (3) in the absence of this cause or condition it ceases to exist or to occur; (4) the phenomenon in question does not exist or is not produced. This formula, expanded into the twelve *nidānas* of the Pratitya Samutpadá, was applied to explain the bondage and liberation of the so-called individual. The first proposition has its counterpart in those *nidānas* which make up the karma-process; the second in those comprising the rebirth-process. The third and fourth propositions have their respective counterparts in the cessation of these two processes. Though the Path to Liberation had been explained by the Buddha not only in terms of the second half of the general formula but also in terms of the first half, that is to say, as positive growth, as well as

[1] *The Buddhist,* Colombo, 1950.

negative cessation, the Hinayana schools relegated the positive applications exclusively to the "world" and the negative ones exclusively to "Nirvana," thus seriously upsetting the equilibrium of the Teaching with regard to both Doctrine and Method. As we shall now see, the same fate befell what is, apart from the twelvefold Pratitya Samutpada, historically the most important application of the general principle of conditionality: the doctrine of the Four Aryan Truths, which in the words of Nyanatiloka Thera is considered by many Buddhists, both Theravadins and Mahayanists, as "the briefest synthesis of the entire doctrines of Buddhism."[1]

The Four Aryan Truths, as generally stated, are *duḥkha* (Pali *ḍukkha*), pain or suffering; *samudaya* (equal in Pali and Skt.), the origin of pain or suffering; *nirodha,* its cessation; and *marga* (Pali *magga*), the means, literally path or way, to its cessation. It will be observed at once that only the First Truth has a definite content; the rest are all formulæ. The content of the First Truth can, however, be varied. In a text of the *Majjhima-Nikāya,* Sariputra, while giving an exposition of Right View (*sammādiṭṭhi*), takes up, for example, *āhāra* (food), *dukkha* (pain or suffering), *jarā-maraṇa* (decay-and-death), *taṇhā* (thirst or craving), *nāma-rūpa* (name and form) and *avijjā* (ignorance), applying to each in turn the fourfold formula of existence, origin, cessation and means to cessation. From this it should be immediately apparent that the Aryan Truths are not a doctrine but formulæ for application to everything perceived, a fact which according to Dr. Nalinaksha Dutt "has been brought out very clearly in many Buddhist texts."[2] Since Sariputra finds it possible to define Right View not only in terms of pain or suffering, but also, for example, as understanding of food, how food originates, how it ceases, and what the means to its cessation are, Right View clearly consists not in the comprehension of this or that particular application, but in insight into the spirit of the general formula of conditionality. As in the case of the Pratitya Samutpada, however, the distinction between general formula and specific application was rarely borne in mind, and for Buddhists both ancient and modern the Four Aryan Truths are simply the Truth of Pain, the Truth of

[1] *Buddhist Dictionary,* p. 132.
[2] *Aspects,* p. 206.

the Origin of Pain, the Truth of the Cessation of Pain, and the Truth of the Way leading to the Cessation of Pain. We are obliged to follow a tradition of such venerable antiquity, even though it represents a deviation from the Buddha's Teaching taken as a whole, and to discuss the Four Truths solely in terms of suffering; even errors must be respected when they are more than two thousand years old. But first we shall endeavour to guard against the misconceptions which such a procedure might otherwise entail by showing as clearly as possible how the selection of pain or suffering as the standard or normal subject for the application of the Four Truths was dictated by considerations of a predominantly methodological nature. By opening our eyes to the limitations on the metaphysical side of the most widely current form of the "doctrine" of the Four Aryan Truths, such a precaution will enable us not only to avoid the one-sidedness of the Hinayana schools, but also to accord other aspects of the Dharma more adequate recognition than generally they receive.

Throughout the entire Buddhist Tradition there runs a clear distinction between what pertains to Doctrine, theory, or rational understanding, on the one hand, and what pertains to Method, practice or spiritual realization on the other. The Pali texts of the Theravada *Tipiṭaka* abound in references to the "Doctrine and Discipline" (*dhamma-vinaya*). Similarly, the Mahayana Sanskrit texts speak repeatedly of Wisdom (*prajñā*) and Skilful Means (*upāya*) as the twin aspects of the Buddha's Teaching. It should be noted that we speak of a distinction, not of a difference; for here we are concerned not with a division between different things of the same order, or even between different parts of the same thing, but simply with a certain doubleness of aspect under which the Dharma, while remaining in itself unaffected, necessarily presents itself to human understanding. Corresponding to these two aspects of the intrinsically impartite Dharma there are two procedures, methods of approach, or points of departure, the "view" of the Dharma obtained from one differing from that obtained from the other in much the same way as the countryside as seen from the top of a high mountain differs from the countryside as seen from the mountain's foot. Or each view is "reversed" in relation to the other, like the image of a thing reflected in a mirror: that part of the object which is nearest to the spectator, supposing the object to be between him and the mirror, appears as farthest from him in the reflection. If the Dharma is viewed under the aspect of Wisdom, then Nirvana is "near" and Samsara "far"; if under the aspect of Method, then Samsara is "near" and Nirvana "far." The distinction with which we are here concerned is obviously of the same order as the distinction between logical priority and priority in experience, between the *a priori* and the *a posteriori* kinds of reasoning, and between the deductive and inductive methods of arriving at truth. Since on the plane of His compassionate action the Buddha was concerned with the "realities" of the immediate human situation, not with things as they might or ought to be but as they actually are, He was obliged to present the Dharma more often under the aspect of Method than under that of Doctrine. Worldlings could be shown the mountain peak only as it appeared from the valley in which they dwelt. Nirvana must be presented as "far" and Samsara as "near." The "world" being a positive datum of experience, and mankind having on the whole no knowledge of anything beyond the world, Nirvana had necessarily to be descirbed to them in terms of the cessation of the world, hence in a predominantly negative manner. Thus for purely practical reasons the Dharma confronts humanity under the aspect of Method, while the Sāsana or Dispensation which is the current manifestation of the Dharma under the modes of space and time appears as possessing a predominantly empirical, inductive and *a posteriori* character.

But why *duḥkha*? Even granting that for pedagogic reasons the Buddha was obliged to place Samsara rather than Nirvana in the forefront of His Teaching, and to speak of the former in positive and of the latter in predominantly negative terms, why should He and His followers have selected, out of all the multifarious experiences of life, suffering as the content of the First Aryan Truth? We have already tried to find an answer to this question in a paper on *"Where Buddhism Begins—And Why It Begins There."*[1] Two main arguments are adduced therein. Firstly, by beginning with a feeling rather than an idea Buddhism avoids needless controversy. It may be doubted whether we really exist

[1] *The Aryan Path,* Vol. XXIII, pp. 55-61 (February, 1952). See also *The Path of the Inner Life* (FWBO Publications, London, 1975), pp. 48-49.

because we think; but none can deny that he experiences pain. Moreover, both philosophical enquiry and religious aspiration arise out of pain or suffering, out of a feeling of profound dissatisfaction with the present state of knowledge or mode of being. "Buddhism solves the problem of where philosophical exposition is to begin by identifying the psychological starting-point of philosophical activity itself with the logical starting-point of philosophical exposition."[1] Secondly, man being a desiderative rather than a rational animal,

> *. . . it is his emotions, his desires, his experience of pleasure and pain which ultimately determine his behaviour, (and) it is only by somehow appealing to and utilizing them that human behaviour can be influenced and changed. Most of all must religion, which seeks to work in human nature the most radical of all possible changes, be able not only to scratch the rational surface but also penetrate the desiderative depths of the psyche.*
>
> *By beginning with the fact of pain Buddhism involves the whole nature of man from the very outset. Recognition of the First Noble Truth comes not as a pleasant intellectual diversion but as a terrible emotional shock. The scriptures say that one feels then like a man who suddenly realizes that his turban is in flames. Only a shock of this kind is strong enough to galvanize the whole being into action. The most astonishing intellectual discovery is no more than an agreeable titillation in the region of the cerebral hemisphere. Only when a man feels strongly will he act effectively. It is for this reason above all others that Buddhism starts not with a concept but with a feeling, not with intellectual postulation but with emotional experience.*[2]

It might be objected that our arguments have succeeded in showing why Buddhism begins with emotional experience, but not why it begins with *painful* emotional experience. We meet the objection by recalling that we are at present in the realm of Method. From the "metaphysical" point of view Buddhism does not deny that pleasant emotional experiences do occur; it even admits that for persons of a certain temperament such experiences may predominate over the painful ones. But since under its aspect of Method the Dharma is concerned to inculcate aversion to, and consequent renunciation of, the Samsara, under this aspect it directs attention to the painful rather than to the pleasant experiences of life.

It cannot be too strongly emphasized that while the general formula of conditionality which constitutes the framework of

---

[1] *Ibid.*, p. 58.
[2] *Ibid.*, p. 61.

the commonly accepted version of the Four Aryan Truths pertains to Doctrine, their specific content pertains only to Method. Unless this distinction is made and continually borne in mind serious misrepresentation and distortion of the Dharma will inevitably ensue. The charge of pessimism so often brought against Buddhism is a case in point. Now pessimism is a philosophical doctrine which holds that reality is not good but evil, and that the painful experiences of life overbalance the pleasant ones; it is obviously akin not to Method but to Doctrine. Buddhism maintains neither that reality is evil nor that life is on the whole unpleasant, and to accuse it of pessimism simply because of its purely methodological preoccupation with suffering is absurd. Nor is the accusation rightly disproved by arguing that though the First Aryan Truth recognizes the experience of *duḥkha,* the Fourth Truth points out the way to its cessation. Such a rejoinder, though mitigating to some extent the severity of the charge, fails to recognize the true nature of the misunderstanding from which it proceeds. Being ignorant of the distinction between the Dharma as Doctrine and the Dharma as Method, the defence, like the attack, takes up its stand on the methodological plane and is, *ipso facto,* superficial. A man whose mother is dead need not reply, when accused of beating her, that he does not possess a stick.

Another instance of this type of confusion between metaphysics and methodology which, though not directly connected with the Four Truths, is serious enough to merit at least a passing reference, relates not to pain and pleasure but to ugliness and beauty. There are in Buddhism numerous meditational exercises in which the disciple directs his attention away from the attractive towards the repulsive aspects and functions of the human body. Here we are concerned, obviously, not with any doctrine but simply with a perfectly valid method of diminishing, and eventually destroying, sensual desire. Yet some Hinayanists, including many modern Theravadins, unable to distinguish between what pertains to methodology and what to metaphysics, persist in drawing from this exercise the fantastic conclusion that ugliness is real and beauty unreal. Even apart from the fact that the Pali scriptures contain a number of texts which clearly show the Buddha's own appreciation of the charms of nature or the beauties of art,[1] the distinction which we have shown to exist between what pertains to Doctrine and what to Method should be sufficient to expose the fallaciousness of such a view.

Having now indicated the strictly methodological function of the content of the Four Aryan Truths, thereby defining the limitations of that content on the metaphysical side (the doctrinal framework alone being unlimited), and being now in no danger of misinterpreting them, we must next give some explanation of each of the Four Truths in turn. The explanations will be very brief. For one reason, the doctrinal framework of the Truths is simply the general formula of conditionality already described in Sections XII-XIV. For another, their specific content, pertaining, as we have just seen, strictly to Method, requires very little comment. Finally, hardly a book on Buddhism has been written which does not contain an account, varying in length from a few lines to a whole chapter, of this teaching. To these works the reader may be referred with the caution that since, as far as we know, none of them draws clearly the distinction between Doctrine and Method, all tend to present, whether explicitly or by implication, the Four Truths not as a methodological but as a metaphysical world-view, and that if serious misunderstanding is to be avoided all are therefore to be read with full mindfulness of their limitations.

The *locus classicus* for the teaching known as the Four Aryan Truths is the *Dhammacakkappavattana Sutta,* the Buddha's First Discourse at Sarnath, wherein the general principle of conditionality constituting the conceptual expression of His Enlightenment received for the first time methodological application to a specific content in accordance with the temperament of disciples. We quote only the first part of the discourse.

Thus have I heard: at one time the Lord dwelt at Benares at Isipatana in the Deer Park. There the Lord addressed the five monks:—

"These two extremes, monks, are not to be practised by one who has gone forth from the world. What are the two? That conjoined with the passions and luxury, low, vulgar, common, ignoble, and useless, and that conjoined with self-torture, painful, ignoble, and useless. Avoiding these two extremes the Tathagata has

---

[1] See our booklet *The Meaning of Buddhism and the Value of Art.* Maha Bodhi Society of India, Kalimpong Branch, 1956.

gained the enlightenment of the Middle Path, which produces insight and knowledge and tends to calm, to higher knowledge, enlightenment, Nirvāṇa.

"And what, monks, is the Middle Path, of which the Tathāgata has gained enlightenment, which produces insight and knowledge, and tends to calm, to higher knowledge, enlightenment, Nirvāṇa? This is the noble Eightfold Way, namely, right view, right intention, right speech, right action, right livelihood, right effort, right mindfulness, right concentration. This, monks, is the Middle Path, of which the Tathāgata has gained enlightenment, which produces insight and knowledge, and tends to calm, to higher knowledge, enlightenment, Nirvāṇa.

*(1) "Now this, monks, is the noble truth of pain: birth is painful, old age is painful, sickness is painful, death is painful, sorrow, lamentation, dejection, and despair are painful. In short the five groups of grasping (*khandhas*) are painful.*

(2) "Now this, monks, is the noble truth of the cause of pain: the craving, which tends to rebirth, combined with pleasure and lust, finding pleasure here and there, namely, the craving for passion, the craving for existence, the craving for non-existence.

(3) "Now this, monks, is the noble truth of the cessation of pain, the cessation without a remainder of craving, the abandonment, forsaking, release, non-attachment.

(4) "Now this, monks, is the noble truth of the way that leads to the cessation of pain: this is the Noble Eightfold Way, namely, right views, right intention, right speech, right action, right livelihood, right effort, right mindfulness, right concentration."

*(*Saṁyutta-Nikāya, *V. 420)*[1]

(1) Pain being a sensation, and hence indefinable, it will be observed that the text of the First Truth is not so much a definition as simply an enumeration of some of the most prominent occasions, forms and expressions of suffering. Little explanation is therefore required. Being now in the realm of Method we are concerned not with the elucidation and theoretical understanding of concepts but with the concentration of the mind upon certain select aspects of experience. Refinements in theoretical analysis may sometimes become a means not of understanding facts but of escaping from them, especially when they happen to be unpleasant. The Buddha in His wisdom therefore "explained" the First Aryan Truth by simply elaborating its description of the different types and phases of suffering.

*"What, now, is Birth? The birth of beings belonging to this or that order of beings, their being born, their conception and springing into existence, the manifestation of the Groups of Existence (*khandhas*), the arising of sense activity:—this is called birth.*

"And what is Decay? The decay of beings belonging to this or that order of

[1] *Early Buddhist Scriptures,* pp. 29-31.

beings, their getting aged, frail, grey and wrinkled; the failing of their vitalforce, the wearing out of the senses:—this is called decay.

"And what is Death? The departing and vanishing of beings out of this or that order of beings, their destruction, disappearance, death, the completion of their life-period, the dissolution of the Groups of Existence, the discarding of the body:—this is called death.

"And what is Sorrow? The sorrow arising through this or that loss or misfortune which one encounters, the worrying oneself, the state of being alarmed, inward sorrow, inward woe:—this is called sorrow.

"And what is Lamentation? Whatsoever, through this or that loss or misfortune which befalls one, is wail and lament, wailing and lamenting, the state of woe and lamentation:—this is called lamentation.

"And what is Pain? The bodily pain and unpleasantness, the painful and unpleasant feeling produced by bodily impression:—this is called pain.

"And what is Grief? The mental pain and unpleasantness, the painful and unpleasant feeling produced by mental impression:—this is called grief.

"And what is Despair? Distress and despair arising through this or that loss or misfortune which one encounters, distressfulness and desperation:—this is called despair.

"And what is the 'Suffering of not getting what one desires'? To beings subject to birth there comes the desire: 'Oh that we were not subject to birth! Oh that no new birth was before us!' Subject to decay, disease, death, sorrow, lamentation, pain, grief and despair, the desire comes to them: 'Oh that we were not subject to these things! Oh that these things are not before us!' But this cannot be got by mere desiring; and not getting what one desires, is suffering.

"And what, in brief, are the Five Groups of Existence? They are corporeality, feeling, perception, (mental) formations and consciousness."

(Dīgha-Nikāya, *XXII. Nyanatiloka's translation.)*[1]

It is as though the Buddha wanted us to form a mental image or picture, or better, series of pictures, of the ills that flesh is heir to, rather than merely indulge in abstract speculations about them. At other times He speaks of the pain of being separated from what is dear, pleasant, beloved and sweet, and of being conjoined with what is disagreeable, unpleasant, hateful and repulsive. The list of sufferings might be extended indefinitely, for even the pleasant things of life, being ephemeral, are potentially sources of pain.

When you are joyous, look deep into your heart and you shall find it is only that which has given you sorrow that is giving you joy.

When you are sorrowful, look again in your heart, and you shall see that in truth you are weeping for that which has been your delight.[2]

---

[1] *The Word of the Buddha* (11th ed. Colombo, 1952), pp. 3-4.

[2] KAHLIL GIBRAN, *The Prophet,* p. 26.

Speaking "metaphysically," pleasure and pain are inseparable. As the same poet says, "When one sits alone with you at your board, remember that the other is asleep upon your bed."[1] On the plane of Method, however, we have to bear in mind the second of the aphorisms quoted, rather than the first, and learn to concentrate and meditate on the fact that the pangs of bereavement will be commensurate with the delight of possession. Only one exceptionally deep in love with life will find that it is the sweeter for its transitoriness, and that death gives a keener edge to joy; only such a one will be able to sing, with Tagore:—

We hasten to gather our flowers lest they are plundered by the passing winds.
It quickens our blood and brightens our eyes to snatch kisses that would vanish if we delayed.
Our life is eager, our desires are keen, for time tolls the bell of parting.
Brother, keep that in mind and rejoice.[2]

The refined hedonism of these lines is far removed from the sane and vigorous ascesis of Buddhism, which instead of making the transitoriness of pleasure an incentive to still more headlong enjoyment, transforms it into a means of deflecting the energies of the disciple away from the ignoble pursuit of ephemeral pleasures towards the noble quest (*ariyapariyesana*) of that ineffable and time-transcending bliss of Nirvana, which, compared with all lesser satisfactions, is as the sun to shadows. For this strictly methodological reason does the Buddha, without denying that mundane pleasures are delectable of their kind, urge upon the disciple the necessity for regarding the whole of phenomenal existence, from its highest to its lowest plane, as being either actually or potentially painful. Most statements of the First Truth therefore conclude with the succinct statement, "In short, the five *khandhas* are painful."

The disciple is exhorted to increase his awareness of the painfulness of existence by forming a mental picture not of the sufferings of a single human life, but of the whole Samsaric process. As Nyanatiloka Thera says:—

Saṁsāra is the unbroken sequence of the fivefold Khanda-combinations, which, constantly changing from moment to moment, follow continually one upon the other through inconceivable periods of time. Of this Saṁsāra a single

[1] *Ibid.*, p. 27.

[2] *The Gardener*, p. 68, Verse 3.

lifetime constitutes only a tiny fraction. Hence to be able to comprehend the first Noble Truth, one must let one's gaze rest upon the Saṁsāra, upon this frightful sequence of rebirths, and not merely upon one single lifetime which, of course, may be sometimes not very painful.[1]

The following example of this type of reflection, or mental picture-making, indicates clearly enough the nature and purpose of the practice:—

"Which do you think is more: the flood of tears which, weeping and wailing, you have shed upon this long way—hurrying and hastening through the round of rebirths, united with the undesired, separated from the desired—this, or the waters of the four oceans?

"Long time have you suffered the death of father and mother, of sons, daughters, brothers and sisters. And whilst you were thus suffering you have, indeed, shed more tears upon this long way than there is water in the four oceans.[2]

"Which do you think is more: the streams of blood that, through your being beheaded, have flowed upon this long way, these, or the waters of the four oceans?

"Long time have you been caught as robbers, or highwaymen, or adulterers; and, through your being beheaded, verily, more blood has flowed upon this long way than there is water in the four oceans.

"But how is this possible?

"Inconceivable is the beginning of this Saṁsāra, not to be discovered is any first beginning of beings who, obstructed by ignorance and ensnared by craving, are hurrying and hastening through this round of rebirths."[3]

"And thus have you long time undergone suffering, undergone torment, undergone misfortune and filled the graveyards full; truly, long enough to be dissatisfied with all the forms of existence, long enough to turn away and free yourselves from them all."[4]

(2) The Second Aryan Truth, the Truth of the Origin of Suffering, which is *tṛṣṇā* or craving, having already been discussed as the eighth *nidāna* of the twelvefold Pratitya Samutpada, need not be discussed again here. The stereotyped descriptive formulæ are the same in both contexts.

(3) We therefore pass on to the Third Aryan Truth, the Truth of the Cessation of Suffering, which is deduced from the First Truth by a process known to Western logicians as immediate inference. Where there is no craving there is no suffering either. The cessation of desire is the cessation of pain. Indeed for one who has conquered desire there is not only

---

1 *The Word of the Buddha*, p. 14.

2 *Saṁyutta-Nikāya*, XV. 3.

3 *Ibid.*, XV. 13.

4 *Ibid.*, XV. 1.

cessation of pain but cessation of phenomenal existence. The Third Truth therefore corresponds to the purely negative and transcendental aspect of Nirvana. As we saw in Section IX, Nirvana is not a state of absolute annihilation. Both the positive and the negative synonyms for the Goal are not definitions but descriptions, symbolical indications of That which is ineffable, and neither are to be understood literally. For certain practical, spiritual purposes, Nirvana may be described as the cessation of greed, anger and ignorance, but description should not be confused with definition, and though the cessation of all such unwholesome states of mind is the condition precedent for the attainment of Nirvana, it would be a mistake to think of Nirvana as being in itself merely the cessation of the phenomenal. For this reason we were in that section careful to insist upon the spiritually, as distinct from the conceptually, positive character of the Goal, and to point out that important positive indications, such as the term Sambodhi, though naturally rarer than negative ones, were by no means entirely absent from the earliest written records of the Teaching. Just as the First Truth relates to one aspect only of phenomenal existence so the Third Truth is concerned with one side only of the spiritual life. Once again methodological limitations must be borne in mind if doctrinal misunderstandings are to be avoided. Craving having been posited as the cause of suffering, the nature of the general formula constituting the doctrinal framework of the Four Truths requires that the cessation of suffering should depend upon the cessation of desire. The positive side of the spiritual life has not been mentioned. Unless the distinction between what pertains to Method and what to Doctrine has been clearly drawn the Third Aryan Truth may be the subject of no less serious misunderstanding than the First. As we have written in the paper already quoted:—

It is easy . . . to make the mistake that Buddhism is concerned only with the removal of suffering, and it is a mistake which certain Buddhists frequently make. Just as the particular kind of pain incidental to bodily existence is a symptom of physical ill health, so is the wider and more inclusive pain of existence itself a sign that there is something radically wrong with life as a whole. In both cases we are confronted not simply with the straightforward task of relieving pain, but also with the infinitely more difficult and complex one of readjusting the unbalanced somatic and psychological condition which is its cause, thus rendering the patient spiritually healthy, hale or whole.

Suffering is important not for its own sake, but only because it is a sign that we are not living as we ought to live. Buddhism does not encourage morbid obsession with suffering as though it were the be-all and end-all of existence. What we really have to get rid of is not suffering but the imperfection which suffering warns us is there, and in the course of getting rid of imperfection and attaining perfection we may have to accept, paradoxically enough, the experience of suffering as indispensable to the achievement of final success. True it is that by the experience of pain we are compelled to enter upon the Path, and true it is that when we arrive at the goal there will be no more pain; but if we think that following the Path means nothing more than the studious avoidance of painful experiences we are making a mistake of astronomical dimensions, and plunging headlong down the path of a spiritual selfishness so utterly diabolical that it is frightful to contemplate even the idea of it.

The essence of Buddhism consists not in the removal of suffering, which is only negative and incidental, but in the attainment of perfection, which is positive and fundamental. The Bodhisattva is not afraid of suffering. He accepts it joyfully if he thinks that it will assist him in the attainment of his great goal of "Enlightenment for the sake of all sentient beings." The Christian mystic would continue to love God even though cast down into Hell, for he loves God for His own sake, not for the sake of any reward, not even happiness (though he is not unhappy, for love is happiness). It is only the spiritual individualist, the typical Hinayanist of Buddhist tradition, who "loves" God for the sake of escaping the pains of Hell. Not for our own sake, not even for the sake of "others," should we seek to attain the Divine, but simply and solely for its own irresistible sake.[1]

Having shown in the last section that the Pratitya Samutpada is an all-inclusive reality within which even Nirvana has a place, it may appear a work of supererogation for us to point out here, in connection with the Third Aryan Truth of the Cessation of Suffering, that the realization of Nirvana, like the other phenomena of the spiritual life, depends not upon chance or fate, much less still upon divine grace in the sense of the arbitrary favour of an anthropomorphic deity, but upon conditions which have been ascertained by the Divine Eye of the Buddha with the same type of precision that the material conditions necessary to bring about a release of atomic energy, for example, are calculated by the atomic scientist. The analogy should not, however, be pressed too far; the spiritual life is not a mechanical process, and spiritual attainments do not pour forth merely upon the pressing of some yogic button. Only at the preliminary ethico-meditative stages of the Path is it helpful to speak of spiritual attainments as depending on definite conditions, and to stress

---

[1] *The Aryan Path,* Vol. XXIII, pp. 59-60 (February, 1952).

the fact that these conditions depend on the will of the disciple. Should this mechanistic and individualistic manner of speaking be too literally understood self-reliance will harden into self-sufficiency and at his entrance upon the supreme gnostic stage of his career the disciple will be threatened by difficulties and dangers largely of his own creation. In the sublimer realms of spiritual experience the ego-sense becomes attenuated to such a fineness, transparency and luminosity, that the terms "self" and "non-self" lose their ordinary meanings, and it becomes no less difficult to speak of the spiritual life in terms of self-effort than to speak of it in terms of reliance upon divine grace, sometimes more difficult, in fact. For this reason the Shin Sect of Japan does not hesitate to drop entirely the language of self-reliance and to speak instead solely in terms of dependence on the Original Vow of Amitabha, the Buddha of Infinite Light. Even such a formulation, however, can be included within the framework of the general principle of conditionality, and is therefore to that extent fully in accordance with tradition. The Third Truth declares, broadly speaking, that the spiritual life, like every other phenomenon, is dependent on conditions. More specifically, it points to the cessation of suffering as being dependent upon the cessation of desire. As we have tried to make clear in this section, negative formulations of the Four Truths do not preclude positive ones. There is no *a priori* reason why the factor termed the Original Vow, or Grace, of Amitabha, should not be as much a condition for the cessation of suffering as the extinction of desire.

(4) The Fourth Aryan Truth is the Truth of the Way leading to the Cessation of Suffering. From the remarks already made, as well as from the general character of the eight stages into which the Way is divided, it should be obvious that in the Fourth Truth we are concerned with much more than the cessation of suffering. Fundamentally our concern is not with any merely negative process but with the positive attainment of Sambodhi.

The eight stages of the Way are *samyakdṛṣṭi* (Pali *sammā-diṭṭhi*), right view in the sense of correct understanding of doctrine, regarded as of the very first importance; *samyak-saṁkalpa* (Pali *sammā-sankappa*), right aspiration or resolve; *samyak-vācā* (Pali *sammā-vācā*), right speech; *samyak-karmanta* (Pali *sammā-kammanta*), right action; *samyak-ājīva* (Pali *sammā-ājīva*), right means of livelihood; *samyak-vyāyāma* (Pali *sammā-vāyāma*), right exertion or effort; *samyak smṛti* (Pali *sammā-sati*), right mindfulness; *samyak-samādhi* (Pali *sammā-samādhi*), right concentration of mind. For the Hinayana these eight stages comprise the entire Buddhist scheme of spiritual training. The Mahayana, however, while not neglecting the Way as eightfold, on the whole prefers to speak of it in terms of the six or ten *pāramitās*. As we shall see in Chapter IV, both formulations are elaborations of the basic triad of *śīla, samādhi* and *prajñā* which in the earliest records of the Teaching occupies a position of very great importance. After concluding this section with a brief description of the eightfold Way we shall therefore attempt, in the section that follows, a more systematic discussion of the Fourth Aryan Truth in terms of Morality, Meditation and Wisdom.

(a) Right Understanding (having given the original Pali and Sanskrit terms we shall now make use of their already quite familiar English equivalents), the first stage of the eightfold Way, is most often defined as penetration of the Four Aryan Truths. In other words, the very first step on the Path consists in acquiring a clear understanding of the various doctrines which express, in one way or another, the central Buddhist principle of universal conditionality. This understanding, at first merely rational, is gradually transformed under the pressure of spiritual practice into insight, and at the eighth stage, the stage of deep meditation, the disciple realizes in his own spiritual experience the truth which in the first stage he had comprehended intellectually through its doctrinal symbols.

(b) Right Aspiration may be described with accuracy sufficient for our present purpose as the volitional counterpart of Right Understanding. The stereotype Pali formula defines it as thoughts that are free from desire, free from ill will, and free from cruelty.

(c) There are four principal kinds of Right Speech, a fact that draws attention to the number of evils for which that small and seemingly insignificant member, the tongue, is responsible. The disciple should abstain from false and lying speech; he should not commit perjury. What he has heard in one place he does not repeat in another so as to cause dissension; he is neither a bearer of tales nor a backbiter. Instead, he delights in spreading concord and amity by his words. Avoiding harsh language, he speaks only such words as are gentle, soothing to the ear, loving, going to the heart, courteous, friendly and agreeable to many. He abstains from the different kinds of idle talk (the list of which is naturally quite a long one), speaking instead at the right time, speaking what is in accordance with facts, useful, about the Doctrine and Discipline. His speech is like a treasure, uttered at the psychological moment, accompanied by arguments, moderate and full of sense.

(d) Right Action is defined in this context as abstention from killing, stealing and unlawful sexual intercourse. In connection with the first of these three items the more positive virtues of conscientiousness, sympathy and anxiety for the welfare of all living beings, are also mentioned.

(e) Right Livelihood means gaining one's living by fair methods. Deceit, treachery, soothsaying, trickery and usury should not be resorted to. Five trades have been specifically prohibited to all Buddhists: trading in arms, in living beings, in flesh, in intoxicating drinks and in poison. Military service, and the work of hunter, fisherman, etc.; are understood as also included in this list.

(f) Right Effort is fourfold: the effort to prevent the arising of unarisen evil thoughts; to suppress arisen evil thoughts; to develop unarisen good thoughts; and to maintain arisen good thoughts.

The seventh and eighth stages of the Way will be discussed in detail in the next section. They are:

(g) Right Mindfulness and

(h) Right Concentration.

Each of the above eight stages is again twofold, in accordance with the two different types of persons by whom it may be practised. When practised by the holy ones, technically called Aryans, of whom there are four kinds, it is known as the transmundane (*lokuttara*) or transcendental eightfold Way; when practised by non-Aryans, that is to say by *pṛthagjana* (Pali *puthujjanas*) or worldlings, it is known as the mundane (*laukika*) eightfold Way. The point of this distinction is the difference between a virtue consciously and deliberately practised, with more or less success, as a discipline, and a virtue that is the natural expression, the spontaneous overflow, of an inner realization. The worldling treads the Path, and without doubt reaps the fruit of his treading; but the Aryan, following the advice of *The Voice of the Silence,* has "become that Path itself."

XVI. The Threefold Way—The Middle Path—Morality

The Buddha's First Discourse at Sarnath, which we quoted in the last section as the *locus classicus* for the formula for the Four Aryan Truths, speaks of the two extremes to be avoided by one who has gone forth as a wanderer, and announces His discovery of a Middle Path which produces insight and knowledge, and tends to calm, to higher knowledge, to enlightenment and Nirvana. This Middle Path is then explained as the Aryan Eightfold Way. Before dealing with the Fourth Truth, the Truth of the Way, in terms of the triad Morality, Meditation and Wisdom, it will be necessary for us first to examine it as the Middle Path.

We have already been at some pains to make clear the difference between transcendental truths and their mundane indications or symbols, both abstract and concrete. Going a step farther than we went before, each truth may be said to possess, in accordance with the plane of existence from which it is apprehended, the aspect or angle from which it is viewed, and the level of experience on which it is applied, not one but many symbols. The Middle Path is a truth of this kind; consequently, its definition is a matter of exceptional difficulty. In the space at our disposal we can give no more than a hint of the general principle involved and the nature of some of its most important applications.

The Middle Path is in its highest sense a synonym for the Goal of the disciple's career. Transcending as it does both affirmative and negative predications, Nirvana may be thought of as occupying a middle position "between," or better still "above" the two extreme conceptions of existence and non-existence. Metaphysically this amounts to a repudiation of eternalism and nihilism and their respective progenies of wrong views. Doctrines and methods which adopt an intermediate position between conflicting extremes are the manifestations, within their own more or less limited fields, and at their own higher or lower levels of application, of the Middle Path in its highest, transcendental aspect. All extreme or one-sided views and practices are manifestations of either eternalism or nihilism, the two basic errors. Within every sphere of thought and field of action we are confronted by one mode or another of the same triadic principle; at every stage of the spiritual life we are faced by the necessity of making a choice between either of two opposites, on the one hand, and the mean which reconciles the opposition by transcending it, on the other. The following of the Middle Path, in the sense of the term which coincides with the import of the Fourth Aryan Truth, the Truth of the Way, in essence consists in making this crucially important decision at ever higher levels of existence; at each level the opposites become more seductive, more "spiritual," and the mean more elusive, more difficult to perceive; at last only one choice remains to be made: on the right, eternalism in its subtlest and most principial forms: the Absolute, pure Being, Godhead, Divine Ground; on the left, the archetypes of nihilism: annihilation of the soul in God, the dissolution of the lower self in the Higher Self, the merging of the drop into the Ocean; above and between them both, like the full moon between the piercing brightness of the eastern and the western stars, the principial Middle Path in all its purity, untarnished by even the shadow of a positive or negative concept.

Descending stage by stage from the higher to the lower levels of application, we find that from the spiritual point of view the most important manifestations of the triadic principle are three in number: there is a modality of the Middle Path in metaphysics, in psychology, and in ethics. At each level there is a correspondence, in the strict Hermetical sense of the term, not only between the higher and lower manifestations of the Middle Path itself, but also between the higher and lower modalities of both extremes. There is as it were a vertical alignment of hedonism with lack of belief in a soul apart from the body, and of this belief with the wrong view that Nirvana is a state of absolute annihilation, on the one hand; on the other, of asceticism with belief in an immortal soul separate from the body, and of this with the wrong belief that Nirvana is a state of absolute existence. The lower, that is to say, the relatively more concrete and more highly differentiated manifestation of a principle, cannot be understood more than superficially in the absence of an understanding of the manifestation of the next in order above it; whereas the knowledge of the higher contains principially the knowledge of the lower, and the realization of the highest comprehension of all. Few modern exponents of the Dharma, particularly those who take their stand on the Theravadin texts alone, fail to commit the mistake of commenting upon this aspect of the Fourth Truth from an exclusively ethical point of view. And the result? One of the profoundest teachings of Buddhism is degraded to the practice of an undistinguished mediocrity.

The doctrine of the Middle Way is in fact co-extensive with the Dharma, so that to penetrate one is simultaneously to penetrate the other. Phenomena arise in dependence on conditions. This thesis, as we now hardly need insist, is the essence of the Teaching, realization of which constitutes Enlightenment. Inasmuch as they arise in dependence on conditions phenomena can be described neither as existent nor as non-existent: they are *śūnya,* empty of self-nature. This *śūnyatā* or emptiness of phenomena coincides with the reality indicated by the term Nirvana; for the attainment of Nirvana depends upon the realization of the conditionality of all phenomena.

Since the true nature (which in terms of existence and non-existence is non-nature) of phenomena is indefinable, transcending the extremes of being and non-being, it may be spoken of as the *madhyama mārga.* Following the Middle Path in metaphysics consists in understanding that reality is not to be expressed in terms of existence and non-existence and in recognizing that the positive and negative indications of Nirvana, whether concrete or abstract, sensuous or conceptual, possess not absolute but only relative validity.

As with phenomena in general, so with the phenomena, both physical and mental, of the so-called personality. Even consciousness, as the enumeration of *viññāṇa* as the third *nidāna* makes perfectly clear, far from being an unchanging entity arises, like any other phenomenon, in dependence upon conditions. It is not the principle of personal identity but simply the uninterrupted procession of a certain kind of mental states, all of infinitesimally short duration. These caused and conditioned "flashes" of consciousness, together with other no less evanescent mental states and functions, constitute "personality" on the psychic side. Since the fivefold phenomena of personality (*rūpa, vedanā, saṁjñā, sankhāra,* and *vijñāna:* the *pañca-skandhā*) one and all arise in dependence on causes and conditions, and since what we term personality, individual being or selfhood is only the sum total of these caused and conditioned psycho-physical phenomena, the five *skandhas* are not nucleated by a permanent, unchanging soul, self or ego-entity. The *anātmavāda,* the categorical denial that any of the phenomena of personality are exempt from the operation of the law of conditionality, is the psychological counterpart of the great metaphysical conception of *śūnyatā,* and constitutes the Middle Path in the sphere of mental science. It avoids both the wrong extreme of identifying personality with the body, which would amount to materialism—hence to a form of nihilism—whether of the mechanistic or the dialectical variety, and the no less grievous error of postulating behind the flux of psychophysical phenomena an immortal soul, or changeless self, or any other kind of static "spiritual" entity—which would be tantamount to the extreme of eternalism.

How absolute is the dependence of the Middle Path in ethics upon the Middle Path in metaphysics and in psychology, and how indispensable comprehension of the latter to understanding of the former, should now be apparent. The belief that behind the bitter-sweet of human life yawn only the all-devouring jaws of a gigantic Nothingness will inevitably reduce man to his body and his body to its sensations; pleasure will be set up as the sole object of human endeavour, self-indulgence lauded to the skies, abstinence contemned, and the voluptuary honoured as the best and wisest of mankind. Similarly, the contrary belief that the macrocosm is grounded upon absolute Being, whether personal or impersonal, is automatically adumbrated in the sphere of psychology as the belief that above or behind the microcosm, the little world of human personality, there exists a soul or self which is on the one hand related to absolute Being, whether by way of ultimate identity, as in the non-dualist Vedanta, or as its part or product, as held by other schools, and which is on the other hand quite different from, and independent of, the physical body. In this case matter will be considered illusory or evil or both, and the body regarded as the principal cause of man's non-realization of his identity with or dependence on the Divine. The object of the spiritual life will be held to consist in effecting a complete disassociation between spirit and matter, the real and the unreal, God and the world, the temporal and the eternal;

whence follows self-mortification in its extremest and most repulsive forms. In the East, particularly in India, various exaggerated forms of asceticism have long enjoyed great popular esteem. Even Buddhism, despite the general sanity and moderation of its methods, was not able entirely to escape their influence. For the West, however, self-mortification as a religious discipline lost all significance centuries ago, and at present only a mild historical interest attaches to it. Modern churchmen read of hair shirts and "disciplines" with a smile. Certain Roman Catholic religious orders apart, both in precept and in practice Christianity on the whole falls far short of the healthy asceticism which the Greeks in their best days recognized as indispensable to the ethical life. The only lasting concord which Christendom seems to have been able to bring about is the peace between God and Mammon.

With this rudimentary account of the Middle Path by way of introduction we may now proceed to a somewhat more ample treatment of the Fourth Truth, the Truth of the Way, in terms of its fundamental threefold division into the successive stages of *śīla, samādhi* and *prajñā.*

Śīla in its primary sense denotes "nature, character, habit, behaviour" in general, as when a person of stingy or illiberal character is spoken of as *adānaśīla.* Its secondary meaning, doctrinally the more important one, is "moral practice, good character, Buddhist ethics, code of morality." Provided that Christian, especially Protestant, connotations are not superimposed upon the English word, the Pali term may be rendered as Morality, with an initial capital letter to indicate its importance. (Morality is the Latin *moralis,* from *mos, moris,* meaning "manner, custom, habit, way of life, conduct," and is thus in its original classical sense almost identical with the primary denotation of *śīla.*) Like other traditions, Buddhism has for reasons of practical convenience reduced the ethical part of its teaching to various sets of rules or precepts, most of them negative or prohibitory in character. These ethical formulæ are common to all branches of Buddhism, and whether it be in Tibet or Ceylon, Burma or Japan, when Morality is spoken of it is generally these specific ethical requirements which are meant. The *dasa-śīla* or ten items of good character (*not* "commandments," as The Pali Text Society's *Pali-English Dictionary* so rightly insists), and the *pañca-śīla*, or five items of good behavior or training, are the best-known codes or formulæ of this type. In the first are included (we give the traditional interpretations) abstinence from taking life (*pāṇâtipātā veramaṇī*); from taking what is not given (*adi-'nnādānā*); from misconduct—or, in the case of monks and nuns and for lay devotees on holy days, from any kind of indulgence—in sexual desires (*kāmesu micchācārā*); from telling lies (*musāvādā*); from slander (*pisuna-vācāya*); from frivolous and senseless talk (*samphappalāpā vācāya*); from covetousness (*abhijjhāya*); from malevolence (*byāpādā*); and from wrong or false views (*micchā-diṭṭhiyā*). The second comprises the first four items of the *dasa-śīla* together with the precept of "abstaining from any state of indolence arising from (the use of) intoxicants" (*surā-meraya-majja-pamādaṭṭhānā veramaṇī*). This fivefold formula embodies the minimal ethical requirements of Buddhism, which all practising Buddhists (a nominal follower of the Dharma is really no follower at all) are expected to make strenuous efforts to fulfil.

A Buddhist is technically one who takes the Three Refuges, in the Buddha, the Dharma and the Sangha, and observes, or tries to observe, the Five Precepts. Our roots of goodness planted in past lives being weak, and our bad desires strong, it is not astonishing that we are frequently unable strictly to observe even these simple rules. In many Buddhist lands the practice of "taking" the Refuges and Precepts from a member of the Sangha on solemn occasions such as the first and fifteenth days of the lunar month therefore prevails. Though in such countries the practice is followed by the whole Buddhist community, including those whose precepts are intact, it may be regarded as a more or less formal and explicit recognition of the fact that failure to observe the precepts amounts to ceasing, for the period of such non-observance, to be a Buddhist, and that a fresh acceptance and renewed observance of these rules is required to effect a restoration to our original, genuinely Buddhist status.

Mention should also be made of the Eight Precepts observed by lay devotees on full- and new-moon days, as well as on other auspicious occasions, and of the Ten Precepts of the novice. The former comprises the Five Precepts together with the three additional rules of abstaining from (1) untimely food, from (2) dancing, singing, instrumental music, shows, garlands, scents, cosmetics and various kinds of personal adornment, and from (3) large and lofty beds. These Eight Precepts, together with the rule of abstaining from handling gold and silver, make up the Tenfold Training of the novice, the seventh precept having for the purposes of this formula been divided into two separate rules. Consideration of the 227 monastic rules observed by members of the Theravada branch of the Sangha, and the 250 which are binding upon those belonging to the Mahayana branch, must be postponed till we have guarded ourselves against two misunderstandings which might arise in the course of our consideration of this aspect of the first of the three stages of the Way.

The fact that sets of numbered rules occupy so important a place in Buddhist religious life and literature should not cause us to interpret *śīla* or Morality as mere ethical formalism. Neither should we think that the exclusively negative character of these rules means that Buddhist morality consists merely in abstention from evil, without the necessity of doing good. Superficial appearances to the contrary notwithstanding, Buddhist ethics is essentially an ethics of intention, and taken as a whole its requirements comprise both positive and negative elements. Actions themselves are neither good nor bad: for the Buddhist even more than for Shakespeare, "thinking makes them so." *Kauśalya* (Pali *kusala*) and *akauśalya,* literally skill and unskill, the more precise Buddhistic expressions for what is morally good and morally bad, are terms applicable only to karma-producing volitions and their associated mental phenomena. By the figure of speech according to which qualities belonging to the cause are attributed to the effect, an action is termed immoral when it springs from a mental state (really a congeries of states) dominated by the three unskilful or "unwholesome" roots of greed (*lobha*), hatred (*dveṣa*) and delusion (*moha*), and moral when it proceeds from mental states characterized by the opposites of these, that is to say, from non-greed, non-hatred and non-delusion. The Buddhist position in ethics is not, however, one of antinomianism. It does not maintain that one may commit what are conventionally regarded as sins provided that he does so with the best of intentions. Had this been its position Buddhism would have confined itself to questions of psychology and left the uninteresting task of drawing up lists of ethical rules and framing codes of conduct to less emancipated teachings. The connection between thoughts and deeds, between mental and material action, is not fortuitous. One is in fact a prolongation of the other. It is not possible to commit murder with a good heart because the deliberate taking of life is simply the outward expression of a state of mind dominated by hate. Deeds are condensations of thought just as water is a condensation of air. They are thoughts made manifest, and proclaim from the housetops of action only what has already been committed in the silent and secret chambers of the heart. One who commits an act of immorality thereby declares that he is not free from unwholesome states of mind; conversely, a being of purified and radiant consciousness, in whom all unskilful thoughts and feelings are extinct, is incapable of committing any such act. The Buddha tells a monk quite categorically:

"Thus, Cunda, should you reply, concerning the Arahant, to those of other views:

'Friend, a brother who is Arahant, one in whom the āsavas *are destroyed, who has lived the life, who has done his task, who has laid down the burden, who has reached his own welfare, who has utterly destroyed the bond that binds to becoming, who is released by the knowledge,—such an one is incapable of behaving in nine ways, to wit:*

'Intentionally taking the life of a creature;
Of taking by way of theft what is not given;
Of practising the sexual act;
Of telling a deliberate lie;
Of indulging in intoxicants;
Of storing up (food) for the indulgence of appetite, as he did before when he was a householder;
Of going on the wrong path through hatred;
Of going on the wrong path through delusion;
Of going on the wrong path through fear.' "

(Dīgha-Nikāya, *III. 133. Woodward's translation)*[1]

Though the Arahant is "beyond good and evil" only in the sense of transcending the wholesome volitions which result in "good" rebirth no less than the unwholesome ones which result in rebirths that are "bad" and not in the sense of being capable of both virtuous and sinful acts, there is still a vast difference between the *śīla* of an Arahant and the *śīla* of an ordinary person. It is not merely a difference of degree, that one is

---

[1] *Some Sayings of the Buddha,* p. 269.

perfect and the other imperfect. The *śīla* of the Arahant or of any other Aryan disciple, is the spontaneous outward expression of an emancipated mind; that of the worldling a disciplinary observance. A poem, or any other work of art, is the embodiment of a certain mood, which by reading the poem we capture for ourselves. The poet passes from intensely felt emotion to its embodiment in imagery, rhythm and words as a poem; his reader passes in reverse order from the words of the poem to the sentiment by which it was inspired. Morality is, as it were, the words of that most perfect of all poems, the holy life, the language which makes intelligible the secrets of spirituality. Meditation and Wisdom, the two remaining stages of the Way, are its rhythm and its imagery. The Arahant passes poet-wise from "inspiration" to "expression"; the worldling readerlike from "expression" to "inspiration," from *śīla, samādhi* and *prajñā* to Enlightenment, just as a person who is himself incapable of generating poetic emotion may induce it by reciting the words of a great poem. Action being the extension of thought, thought is the intension of action. Conduct influences states of mind just as states of mind determine behaviour. An angry person will instinctively grasp a stick; and one who handles a stick will naturally feel like striking something. When the mind is deep in meditation the trunk automatically becomes rigid, the lids closed, the gaze fixed, the respiration light, and the hands folded loosely in the lap; contrariwise, the adoption of these postures has even without any further exercise a tendency to pacify the mind. *Śīla* is prescribed for the worldling not as an end in itself but as the means of weakening the unwholesome states of mind from which wrong speech and wrong bodily action proceed; Morality is the indispensable stepping-stone to Meditation. Our minds being usually in a thoroughly unwholesome state, burning with the threefold fire of greed, hatred and delusion, inevitably the actions which we commit are nearly always unskilful. Abstention from evil is therefore the first stage of spiritual progress, and it is for this reason above all others that the elementary ethical requirements of Buddhism, as expressed in the formulæ just now discussed, have been cast in a predominantly negative form. In the words of a celebrated stanza of the *Dhammapada,* we must "cease to do evil" before we "learn to do good."[1] The literal meaning of the second half-line, in the original Pali *kusalassa upasampadā,* is "the acquiring of good," which refers to the development of wholesome states of mind through the practice of Meditation, the second stage of the Way. For Buddhism the significance of Morality resides principally in the fact that without the good life for basis the state of superconsciousness or *samādhi,* which in its turn is the foundation of Wisdom, is impossible of attainment. Attempting the practice of Meditation without first having purified one's Morality is like seizing the oars of a boat and trying to row before one has unhooked the hawser. This principle, which we may term the principle of ethical instrumentality, is recognized by all schools of Buddhism. Texts which appear to countenance even the slightest infringement of the moral law should be interpreted symbolically, as in the case of Padmasambhava's Biography, or understood either as being a purely hyperbolical glorification of Compassion, as when it is said that the Bodhisattva (from whom is required the strict practice of Morality as the second of the Six Perfections!) in his eagerness for the salvation of all beings is ready even to commit a sin, or as being a reaction against the setting up of ethical codes as ends in themselves and a reassertion of the principle of instrumentality, an attitude that was occasionally found necessary by some of the followers of certain Tantric schools. The Teaching as a whole distinguishes quite clearly between what the Theravada tradition terms *paṇṇatti-śīla* and *pakati-śīla,* conventional morality and natural morality, and though the former is declared to be karmically neutral, the latter, which comprises all the most important precepts, including the Five Precepts, with the above-mentioned exceptions is universally regarded as an integral part of that eternal and immutable order of the universe, simultaneously physical and mental, natural and supernatural, which is one aspect of the connotation of the all-comprehensive reality termed Dharma in accordance with which a man must live to attain the Highest.

That the observance of Morality is a preparation for the practice of Meditation can be inferred from what are known as "the four kinds of Morality consisting in Purity" (*parisuddhi-śīla*):

---

[1] *Dhammapada,* v. 183.

(a) Restraint with regard to the (monastic) Obligations (*pāṭimokkha saṁvara-śīla*); (b) Restraint of the senses (*indriya-saṁvara-śīla*); (c) Purity in one's means of livelihood (*ājīva-parisuddhi-śīla*); and (d) Morality in respect of the four (monastic) requisites (*paccaya-sannissita-śīla*). With these four kinds of morality, which should be practised, at least in principle, by all who are sincerely desirous of progressing on the Path and which all monks are expected faithfully to observe, we come as far as ethics can take us, and approach the frontiers of the second stage, the stage of Meditation, in which the mind, purified by disciplinary ethical observance from the most unwholesome kind of mental states, is gradually established in states of superconsciousness. The following brief account of the four kinds of Morality consisting in Purity may be viewed as propædeutic to the survey of Meditation which will be given immediately afterwards.

(a) The "Obligations" is the name given to a collection of rules found in the *Vinaya Piṭaka,* or Book of the Discipline, which were recited by the monks on Uposatha (new-moon and full-moon) days for the purpose of confessing any infringement. Many of them were no doubt instituted by the Buddha Himself. Others must have been added later. As preserved in the *Suttavibhanga* of the Theravadins this collection consists of 220 precepts divided into eight sections according to the penalty incurred through failure to observe them. The first and most important group are four rules the breaking of which involves permanent expulsion from the Sangha. These are the rules forbidding sexual intercourse, taking what has not been given, intentionally depriving a human being of life or inciting to suicide, and boasting of possessing supernormal powers. The breaking of the remaining seven groups of rules involves such punishments as calling an assembly of the Sangha (for this purpose all the monks residing within a certain prescribed area), forfeiture, expiation (the largest group), and confession. In addition to the 220 rules to be observed by the monk in his individual capacity there are seven more that are binding upon the Sangha collectively.

Other Hinayana schools, such as the Mahāsaṁghikas and the Sarvastivadins, were in possession of similar codes of discipline. As observed by the Chinese pilgrim I-tsing, the Mahayanists, who had no separate Vinaya of their own, followed the Vinaya of the Hinayanists.[1] This is a state of affairs which continues to prevail in Mahayana countries. In Tibet, for instance, the Gelugpa branch of the Order follows a Vinaya originally belonging to a sub-school of the Sarvastivada. These ecclesiastical minutiæ—doubtless but little relished by most readers—need to be borne in mind if we are to understand the vitally important fact that there is in Buddhism really only one Sangha. A Mahayana bhikshu is not one who belongs to a Mahayana Order in the sense of a separate religious corporation, but simply one who, observing in fundamentals the same monastic discipline as his Hinayana brother, devotes himself to the study and practice of the Mahayana Sutras. Similarly a Hinayana monk is simply one who follows the Hinayana Sutras. No Buddhist country, regardless of the school to which it belongs, has a monopoly of the Vinaya. But it must be admitted that between the Mahayana schools on the one hand, and certain modern representatives of the Theravada, the only surviving Hinayana school, on the other, there does exist a considerable difference of attitude towards the observance of the monastic code. The Mahayanists, their spiritual life dominated by the absolute altruism of the Bodhisattva Ideal, are on the whole much more deeply aware of the instrumental character of ethics, and when circumstances demand it do not hesitate to augment, modify and even to abrogate the minor rules, particularly if the promotion of the spiritual welfare of beings seems to require it. Quite contrary to this is the attitude of most Theravadins. Fully convinced that every one of their 220 rules was promulgated by the Buddha Himself, they profess to insist upon rigid observance of the whole code. In practice this generally means that observance of the letter of the Vinaya is regarded as an end in itself. Exaggerated importance is attached to the observance of quite minor rules, while offences against the major precepts, provided they are committed quietly, pass unnoticed. More than once has the writer been told by monks from Ceylon that in that home of pristine Buddhism eating after midday is regarded as a more serious offence than indulging in sexual intercourse with a woman. We must admit with regret that in the Theravada

[1] *Aspects*, p. 290.

Buddhist countries the first kind of Morality consisting in Purity has degenerated, a few noble exceptions apart, into the systematic practice of hypocrisy as one of the Buddhist Fine Arts, into an ostentatious parade of empty and meaningless ecclesiastical formalism of the most frivolous kind. Only if there is a radical change of attitude towards the Vinaya, and recognition of the need for a drastic revision of some of the minor precepts—in short, only if there is a return to a more truly traditional understanding of ethics—can we hope that Restraint with regard to the Obligations will again function as a help, rather than as a hindrance, to the spiritual life of the Theravada Sangha.

(b) The second kind of Morality consisting in Purity carries a stage farther the practice of restraint begun in the first. Having learned to abstain from all unskilful deeds, the monk must now trace the evil back even closer to its source and check it at an even earlier stage of its development. The senses must be prevented not only from seizing hold of their objects but even from turning towards them. The attention must be diverted from its natural outward-going tendency and turned within. Only when there is no longer any response to external stimuli, whether physical or mental, the mind being as it were at rest within itself, can there take place that expansion, elevation and intensification of consciousness beyond the limits of the personal wherein consists the essence of Meditation. The Pali Scriptures contain the following account of how restraint of the senses should be exercised:—

Now, in perceiving a form with the eye—a sound with the ear—an odour with the nose—a taste with the tongue—an impression with the body—an object with the mind, he cleaves neither to the whole, nor to its details. And he tries to ward off that which, by being unguarded in his senses, might give rise to evil and unwholesome states, to greed and sorrow; he watches over his senses, keeps his senses under restraint. By practising this noble Restraint of the Senses he feels in his heart an unblemished happiness.

(Majjhima-Nikāya,*XXXVIII. Nyanatiloka's translation (revised)*[1])

As the text indicates, before the senses can be restrained their movements must be watched. This practice of watching the senses is a preliminary exercise in mindfulness. Changing by

[1] *The Word of the Buddha,* p. 85.

imperceptible degrees, Morality has now almost completely merged itself in Meditation. The two remaining kinds of Morality consisting of Purity, which are of comparatively minor importance, will therefore not detain us long.

(c) Purity with regard to one's livelihood is generally held to mean that the monk should not support himself in a manner incompatible with his vocation. More liberally interpreted, it means that Right Livelihood—which, as we saw in Section XV, is the fifth stage of the Aryan Eightfold Path—is an essential part of ethics, and Purification of one's means of Livelihood is therefore indispensable to the successful practice of Meditation.

(d) Morality in respect of the four (monastic) requisites, which according to the austerest form of the Teaching are the only indispensable material accessories of the holy life, is described thus in the texts:

> *Wisely reflecting he makes use of his robes . . . merely to protect himself against cold and heat, etc. Wisely reflecting he makes use of his alms-food . . . merely as a prop and support to his body. . . . Wisely reflecting he makes us of his dwelling . . . merely to keep off the dangers of weather and to enjoy solitude. . . . Wisely reflecting he makes use of the necessary drugs and medicines, merely to suppress feelings of sickness that arise, and to reach perfect freedom from suffering.*
>
> (Majjjima-Nikāya, *II (condensed). Nyanatiloka's translation)*[1]

Upon this kind of Morality consisting in Purity, also, a more liberal construction may be put: we can interpret it in terms of a wise and thoughtful use of all material possessions. Nevertheless for the householder, cumbered as he is with all manner of worldly goods and gear, the principle will be much more difficult of application than for the homeless and well-nigh possessionless wanderer, especially as the former often happens to have so many things for which the only use is an unwise one. How much more difficult for him therefore the practice of Meditation!

XVII. Meditation

Like many other Pali and Sanskrit Buddhist terms the word *samādhi,* by which is indicated the second stage of the Way, possesses both a narrow and precise denotation and a wide and diffuse connotation. Literally it means "firm fixation," in the

---

[1] *Buddhist Dictionary,* p. 148.

sense of the firm fixation of the mind on a single object. Hence the traditional definition of *samādhi* as *cittass' ekaggatā,* one-pointedness of mind or, more simply, as "concentration." This concentration is of two kinds, according to whether it is associated with a karmically wholesome or with a karmically unwholesome state of consciousness. The first kind is known as *samyak samādhi,* or Right Concentration—the last stage of the Eightfold Way—and it is with this that we propose to deal in the present section. Unless an explicit statement to the contrary has been made, by the term concentration without any qualification, the student of Buddhist texts is invariably to understand Right Concentration. *Samādhi* we may therefore define as being in its narrowest and most exclusive sense essentially the wholesome concentration of the mind on a single object. To disentangle its connotations is less easy. Variations in the meaning of the term as it appears now in this, now in that "universe of discourse" are considerable. Reckoned as the eighth step of the Aryan Eightfold Way, *samādhi* does not include *smṛti* or mindfulness, which is reckoned separately as the seventh step. When the eight steps are distributed between the three stages, however, the seventh and eighth steps are both included in the third stage, that is to say, in the stage of *samādhi.* Obviously the meaning of the term is much narrower in the first usage than in the second. *Samādhi* in its widest sense traditionally comprises: mindfulness and self-possession; contentment; emancipation from the hindrances; preliminary exercises for the development of one-pointedness of mind; the degrees and kinds of concentration; the various ascending states of superconsciousness to which concentration is capable of leading; and the different supernormal powers for the development of which these states are the basis. With each of these we shall therefore deal in turn. When *samādhi* in the narrower sense is in question we shall speak of it as concentration; otherwise we shall employ the more nebulous term "Meditation."

Mindfulness and self-possession, with the practice of which the second stage of the Way not only begins but must begin—a fact the unwisely enthusiastic novice in meditation is often inclined to overlook—is thus described by the Buddha in an important discourse on the disciple's career addressed to Ajātasattu, Ruler of Magadha:—

"And how, O king, is a monk endowed with mindfulness and self-possession? In this case a monk is self-possessed in advancing or withdrawing, in looking forward or looking round, in bending, or stretching his limbs, in wearing his inner and outer robes and bowl, in eating, drinking, masticating, and tasting, in answering the calls of nature, in walking, standing, sitting, sleeping, waking, speaking and keeping silence. Thus, O King, is a monk endowed with mindfulness and self-possession."

(Dīgha-Nikāya, *I. 47. Thomas's translation*)[1]

Our actions are generally impulsive. Desires are immediately translated into deeds, without a thought being given to the question of whether they are fit for the change or not. When we act with mindfulness, however, analysing motives before allowing them to influence conduct, there accrues not only the negative gain of abstention from unskilful courses of action but positively the acquisition of an undisturbed and tranquil state of mind. By carrying on even the commonplace activities of life in a clearly conscious manner we introduce as it were an interval of inactivity between thought and deed, intention and execution. In the gulf of this interval, if a mixture of temporal and spatial metaphors be deemed permissible for the elucidation of one of the technicalities of concentration, our unwholesome impulses expend their force. The tempo of existence slackens. Behaviour becomes smoother, slower and more deliberate. Life proceeds at a pace like that of a mild and majestic elephant. As J. Evola finely says of the practice:—

It can easily be seen that by following such a path a man transforms himself into a kind of living statue made up of awareness, into a figure pervaded by composedness, decorum and dignity, a figure which inevitably calls to mind not only the whole style of the ancient Aryan aristocracy but also that made famous by the ancient Roman tradition in the original type of the senator, *the* paterfamilias *and the* maiores nostri.[2]

Bodily composure, though itself the product of a certain mental attitude, turns round as it were and, reacting on the mind, produces an even deeper quietude of spirit than before. It should moreover be noted that through the practice of mindfulness and self-possession the most trivial occasions of life are invested with a halo of sanctity. Eating, drinking and dressing, the processes of excretion and urination even, are transformed

[1] *Early Buddhist Scriptures,* p. 62.
[2] *The Doctrine of Awakening,* p. 171.

from hindrances into helps to concentration; from interruptions of the spiritual life they become its continuation under another form. Obliterated is the distinction between things sacred and things profane. When Morality is pure, and clear consciousness in all activities firmly established, from morning to night not a minute is wasted; uninterrupted from dawn till dusk flows the current of spiritual life, the stream of constant striving after holiness; and even in sleep, if the practice be intense enough, that clear consciousness is still shining, even as shines the moon amidst the darkness of night.

In the wake of mindfulness and self-possession comes contentment (*santuṭṭhi*). The monk is described as being content with the robe that protects his body and the bowl in which he collects food. "Wherever he goes," says the beautiful simile of the Pali texts, "he is provided with these two things; just as a winged bird in flying carries his wings along with him."[1] At least in principle, contentment is a virtue that can be practised regardless of the number of one's possessions, by a householder no less than by a monk, by a prince as easily as by a pauper. But in practice philosopher kings and householder bodhisattvas are remarkably rare. Generally speaking, the greater a man's possessions, the less likely he is to be contented with them; not because riches and contentment are necessarily incompatible; but because the accumulation of wealth is possible only to one who is discontented with poverty. Despite the contrary professions of philanthropic millionaires, a man who makes money disinterestedly is harder to discover than the phœnix sitting on its Arabian tree. Harder still to find is one to whom the making of money has, in itself, brought contentment. Just as a fire fed with dry sticks is not extinguished, but burns even more brightly, so the acquisition of wealth, instead of bringing contentment, increases discontent a thousandfold. The *Dhammapada* compresses a great deal of wisdom into three Pali words when it asserts that contentment is itself the greatest wealth—*santuṭṭhi paramaṁ dhanaṁ.*[2]

Concentration may now be developed; the disciple takes his seat for the practice of the particular exercise for inducing one-pointedness of mind prescribed for him by his teacher. First

[1] *The Word of the Buddha,* p. 85.

[2] *Dhammapada,* v. 204.

the five (mental) hindrances or obstacles (*nīvaraṇa*) have to be at least temporarily inhibited. These are lust (*kāmacchanda*), ill-will (*vyāpāda*), sloth and torpor (*thīna-middha*), restlessness and anxiety (*uddhacca-kukkucca*), and doubt (*vicikicchā*). In the expressive simile of the Pali texts, trying to meditate while the mind is disturbed by the hindrances is like expecting to see the reflection of one's face in water wherein various colours have been mixed, or in boiling water, or in water covered by aquatic plants, or in water whipped up into waves by the wind, or in water that is turbid and muddy. Therefore, say the Scriptures,

He casts away lust; he dwells with a heart free from lust; from lust he cleanses his heart.

He casts away ill-will; cherishing love and compassion towards all living beings, he cleanses his heart from ill-will.

He casts away sloth and torpor; loving the light, with watchful mind, with clear comprehension, he cleanses his mind from sloth and torpor.

He casts away restlessness and anxiety; dwelling with mind undisturbed, with heart full of peace, he cleanses his mind from restlessness and anxiety.

He casts away doubt; dwelling free from doubt, full of confidence in the good, he cleanses his heart from doubt.

(Majjhima-Nikāya, *XXXVIII. Nyanatiloka's translation (revised).)*[1]

Though merely one of the stages preparatory to the actual development of concentration—admittedly the last of them—the suppression of the five mental hindrances is not such a simple matter as it might appear to be. The various habits, practices and reflections strengthening or weakening each of these five obstacles to concentration have received in the Pali Canon careful and detailed, in its commentaries quite elaborate, treatment, so that the literature on the subject is by no means small. A number of important passages, canonical and extra-canonical, have been collated and systematically arranged by the Venerable Nyanaponika. To his useful booklet, *The Five Mental Hindrances and Their Conquest by Buddhist Spiritual Training*,[2] those interested in the actual practice of meditation are referred for guidance.

In principle, any material or mental object, from a matchbox to the loftiest philosophical conceptions, may serve as the external basis for the development of one-pointedness of mind. The

---

1 *The Word of the Buddha*, p. 86.

2 Buddhist Literature Society, Colombo, 1947.

possible supports for concentration are infinite. An awe-inspiring stretch of mountain scenery, with snow peaks dazzlingly upthrust into the sunshine, a swiftly flowing stream

That to the sleeping woods all night
Singeth a quiet tune,

or the faint glimmerings of light upon a pool at eventide, are all means of inducing at least partially that undistracted attention to one object in which the essence of concentration consists. Buddhist hagiography abounds in anecdotes of disciples who attained insight on the basis of concentration developed in this natural, and at times quite spontaneous, manner. There is nothing so homely that it cannot function, if rightly used, as one of the instruments of liberation. Cooking pots and grindstones, the dripping of water through an unthatched roof and the sudden extinction of a lamp, have all at one time or another played their part in the spiritual life of the Holy Ones. Buddhist tradition, however, universally recognizes certain "classical" and archetypal objects as being of very special efficacy as supports for the development of concentration. The Theravada commentator Buddhaghosa, the second part of whose great original work the *Visuddhi Magga*, or "Path of Purity," is particularly rich in information relating to the practice of meditation, collates from the Pali texts forty such supports, all recommended by the Buddha Himself, and applies to them the term *kammaṭṭhāna,* literally "place of work," in this case the work of concentration. These forty simple supports, the bare branches of the tree of Buddhist meditation, enable us to see the structure, to grasp the underlying principle, of the whole system of practice, all the more clearly for their being naked of that luxuriant crop of special methods and elaborate techniques which later on sprang up, like an exuberant growth of leaves, on the basis of the broad principles indicated by the prescriptions of the original teaching.

The forty *kammaṭṭhānas* comprise the Ten Devices (*kasina*), the Ten Impurities (*asubha*), the Ten Recollections (*anussati*), the Four Sublime Abodes (*brahma-vihāra*), the Four Formless Spheres (*arūpâyatana*), together with Perception of the Loathsomeness of Food (*āhāre patikkūla-saññā*) and Analysis of the Four Elements (*catudhātuvavatthāna*), each of which is reckoned as one support.

The ten "devices" for concentrating the mind and for attaining, ultimately, the four superconscious states, are the elements earth, water, fire and air; the colours blue, yellow, red and white; space and consciousness. It will easily be seen that the brilliantly coloured representations of various divine beings which play such an important part in Tantric meditation are not, as is so often ignorantly supposed, concessions to popular polytheism, but more richly diversified and elaborate forms of colour-devices, possessing, as the earlier and more abstract forms do not, the additional advantage of deep philosophical significance and profound emotional appeal. The mandalas or "magic circles"—as uncomprehending observers call them—of Mahayana Buddhism, and of the Theravada too, in the days when it practised meditation more extensively than now, are also devices of this kind.

According to Buddhaghosa, the Ten Impurities are the various disgusting aspects of bodily existence. In the Pali canonical texts, however, mention is made of the different stages in the decomposition of a corpse, from the day it is seen lying on the charnel ground "swollen, blue, and festering," as the *Satipaṭṭhāna Sutta* says, to that on which it is finally reduced to a handful of fine dust. Whether the impurities of the living or of the dead body are taken as one's "support," the object of the practice remains the same. Not only is the mind concentrated but, going a little beyond the second stage of the Way, it is gradually compelled to give up its inordinate attachment to the body by realizing its essentially compound and transitory nature. There is nothing morbid in the practice, as some of those hostile to Buddhism, with their suppressed fear of death, and their horrified recoil from anything that might even remotely remind them of the grisly fact that they must one day die, seem to think and to want others to think. For chronic diseases drastic remedies are required. The malady of attachment to this bag of impurities, as Buddhist texts call the body, being as it were endemic in the whole human race, the powerful prophylactics originally prescribed by the Great Physician occupy a prominent place in the pharmacopœia of every form of Buddhism. In Tibet, where fear is not allowed to veil the process of dissolution in the name of decency, the charnel ground is still the resort of those bent on subjugating all attachment to the flesh. "Verily, this body of mine, too, is of the same nature, it will become like that and will not escape it"—thus, with corpses in various stages of decomposition scattered around him, the yogin reflects. Strange as the fact may seem to those unfamiliar with this practice, it has a tonic effect on the system bracing and invigorating the mind of the practitioner, immensely enhancing his spiritual vitality, and leaving him as it were inflated with the exhilaration born of self-conquest as a balloon with air. According to tradition, by taking the Ten Impurities as supports for concentration one can attain the first stage of superconsciousness, but not any of the remaining stages.

The Ten Recollections are on the whole much less fearsome. They are the Buddha, the Doctrine, the Order, Morality, liberality, the goods, death, the body, respiration, and the peace of Nirvana. Of these the ninth recollection, mindfulness, or watchfulness (as the term is variously rendered) of the process of respiration (*ānāpāna-sati*), is undoubtedly the most important. It occurs as the chief external support of concentration in the famous system known as the four Foundations of Mindfulness, concerning which the Buddha said:—

> *"This is the only way, monks, for the purification of beings, for the overcoming of sorrow and lamentation, for the destruction of suffering and grief, for reaching the right path, for the attainment of Nibbana, namely the four Foundations of Mindfulness."*
>
> (Satipaṭṭhāna Sutta, *Soma Thera's translation)*[1]

During the last fifty years the practice of Respiration-Mindfulness has undergone a remarkable revival in Burma, and appears to be slowly spreading among small but influential groups of earnest monks in other Theravada lands. Several centres wherein is given practical instruction in this method of developing concentration have been established by the Union Government of Burma; many private institutions also exist. One of the most promising features of the revival, from the purely spiritual point of view, is the fact that the meditation-masters of modern Burma have not hesitated to introduce variations of the practice of which no mention is made in the Pali canonical and commentarial literature. So much so, that the method of inducing

---

[1] NYANAPONIKA THERA. *The Heart of Buddhist Meditation* (Colombo, 1954), p. 125.

concentration through mindfulness of the process of in- and out-breathing now most widely in use is termed by Nyanaponika Thera the New Burman Satipatthana Method. The reason for this development is not far to seek. Instead of relying exclusively on books, a habit which for centuries has been the bane of the Hinayana form of Buddhism, the contemporary heirs of the Arahants of old are supplementing scriptural knowledge by personal experimentation and experience. If the movement gathers strength and is allowed to exert its influence beyond the sphere of technical concentration-exercises the dry and dusty pitchers of modern Theravada may well present once again to the parched lips of humanity a brim overflowing with the waters of spiritual life. Though the practice of Respiration-Mindfulness is capable of inducing all four stages of superconsciousness, the New Burman Method, it is said, proceeds directly from concentration to the development of insight into Reality. The rest of the Ten Recollections lead only to what is technically known as neighbourhood-concentration (*upacāra-samādhi*), a stage intermediate between a distracted and an undistracted state of mind of which an explanation will shortly be given.

Love (*mettā*), Compassion (*karuṇā*), Sympathetic Joy (*muditā*) and Equanimity (*upekkhā*) towards all beings are the four Sublime Abodes wherein the monk is admonished constantly to dwell. The fanning of the cold embers and grey ashes of the heart until, by degrees, the coals of affection smouldering beneath are blown first into a fiery blaze, then into a white-hot incandescence of love that radiates far and wide a beneficent spiritual heat, is not only enumerated but also to be practised first. Without Love, Compassion will turn to contempt, Sympathetic Joy to vicarious satisfaction, and Equanimity to heartless indifference. The texts therefore invariably describe first the cultivation of Love, after which they repeat the same formula, with the variation of one term only, for the other three abodes.

Having his mind accompanied by love he abides pervading one quarter, likewise the second, the third, the fourth, above, below, around, everywhere, entirely he abides pervading the entire world with his mind accompanied by love, with abundant, great, immeasurable freedom from hatred and malice. Having his mind accompanied by compassion he abides . . . accompanied by sympathetic joy . . . by equanimity, with abundant great immeasurable freedom from hatred and malice.

Just as if there were a lotus pool of clear, sweet, cool water, limpid, with good steps down to it, of charming aspect; if a man were to come from the east, overcome and suffering from the heat, exhausted, parched and thirsty, on coming to the pool he would quench his thirst and relieve his exhaustion from the heat. If he came from the west . . . the north . . . the south . . . from wherever he came he would quench his thirst and relieve his exhaustion from the heat. Even so, if one of a family of the warrior caste (etc.) has gone forth from a house to a houseless life, and having come to the Doctrine and Discipline taught by the Tathāgata has thus practised love, compassion, sympathetic joy, and equanimity, he acquires inward peace, and with inward peace he has followed the proper path of an ascetic.

(Majjhima-Nikāya, *I. 281. Thomas's translation*)[1]

As pointed out by Dr. Conze in the first of his three essays on Love and Compassion in Buddhism,[2] the exceedingly ambiguous English word love is an extremely unsatisfactory equivalent for the much more precise Indo-Aryan word *mettā* or *maitri,* which is not so much ordinary human affection, even in sublimated form, as a detached and impersonal benevolence raised to the highest possible pitch of intensity. Literally, *mettā* means "friendliness"—"Friend" being *mitta* or *mitra*—and the Buddhist texts carefully distinguish the emotion indicated by this term from *pema* (Skt. *prema*), by which is meant a feeling of sexual or quasi-sexual affection. "From affection (*pema*)," declares the Lord in the *Dhammapada,* "is born grief; from affection fear is begotten."[3] *Mettā,* however, leads to the state of union with Brahma. It is interesting to note, in this connection, that the Buddha, far from denying the existence of the theistic god, points out to the disciple the path by which he may become united with him. The Pali texts nevertheless firmly put Brahma in his proper place; he is neither omniscient nor omnipotent, and his present position, like that of other beings, is the result of karma. He inhabits a lofty, but still mundane, plane of being—the objective correlative of what subjectively speaking is a superconscious state of mind—beyond which is the immeasurably higher—really a different "dimension" altogether—state or sphere designated Nirvana. The actual practice of *mettā-bhāvanā* has two aspects, one being the intensification internally, the other the external radiation, of Love. The feeling that was

---

[1] *Early Buddhist Scriptures,* pp. 80-81.
[2] *The Middle Way* (February, 1954), p. 134.
[3] *Dhammapada,* v. 213.

directed, at the commencement of the exercise, towards one person, is not divided but rather multiplied, by being radiated towards all. As Shelley so emphatically says:—

True love in this differs from gold and clay,
That to divide is not to take away.
Love is like understanding, that grows bright,
Gazing on many truths; 'tis like thy light,
Imagination! which from earth and sky,
And from the depth of human phantasy,
As from a thousand prisms and mirrors, fills
The universe with glorious beams, and kills
Error, the worm, with many a sun-like arrow
Of its reverberated lightning. Narrow
The heart that loves, the brain that contemplates,
The life that wears, the spirit that creates,
One object, and one form, and builds thereby
A sepulchre for its eternity.[1]

The chief difference between *pema* and *mettā* is that while one is exclusive, at best an *égoisme à deux,* the other is inclusive. Love, in the Buddhist sense of the term, is love only when it is felt impartially for all living beings. From this exalted and wholly spiritualized emotion it is obviously only a step to Equanimity, the fourth of the Sublime Abodes. Compassion and Sympathetic Joy are closer still at hand, for the first of these is only Love's response to the sufferings of others, the second its reaction to their joys. Each of the four "infinitudes" or *appamaññā,* as the four *brahma-vihāras* are also called, has a "near-enemy" and a "far-enemy." The "far-enemy" of Love is, of course, hate; its "near-enemy"—by reason of its proximity still more insidious—is "affection." Every precaution should therefore be taken to prevent the development of Love from degenerating into mere intensification of carnal attachment. For this reason the practitioner is cautioned that the first person, after his own self, towards whom Love is developed, should be a living friend *of the same sex.* According to commentarial traditions, the cultivation of *mettā, karuṇā* and *muditā,* either jointly or individually, leads as far as the third stage of superconsciousness; the practice of *upekkhā* alone leads to the fourth stage.

Buddhism divides the Samsara, or totality of phenomenal existence, on the objective side, "vertically" into three principal

---

[1] *Epipsychidion,* lines 160-173.

planes, each having numerous subdivisions: *kāma-loka,* or "world of desire"; *rūpa-loka,* or "world of form"; and *arūpa-loka* or "formless world." Each of these planes of existence has as its subjective counterpart a state of consciousness. Attainment of a more exalted state of mind, and entrance into a loftier realm of being, are at bottom synonymous expressions. "Rebirth" or "again-becoming" at a certain level of phenomenal existence is simply the inevitable "result" of our being, at the moment immediately succeeding that of death, in a particular mode of consciousness. If one side of a coin faces the table, the other necessarily looks at the ceiling. The four stages of superconsciousness, to which we have more than once referred, correspond to the four main divisions of the "world of form." In the same way, corresponding to the four main divisions of the "formless world" there are four additional stages of superconsciousness. Each of these four stages is developed by taking the one immediately preceding as "support" and by eliminating certain of its features. For this reason the four Formless Spheres or formless states are reckoned as the fourth group of classical "supports" of concentration, though with them we have of course gone far beyond concentration in the restricted technical sense of the term.

Just as sexual desire can be checked by concentrating one's mind on the repulsive, rather than on the attractive, aspects of bodily existence, so can the no less intense craving for food (closely connected, according to Indian yogic tradition, with sexual appetite) be brought under control by focusing attention on the disgusting instead of the enjoyable concomitants of the process of eating. Perception of the Loathsomeness of Food, is, therefore, also reckoned as one of the objects by means of which fixation of consciousness, in this case to the point of "neighbourhood-concentration," may be attained.

The last of the forty *kammaṭṭhānas* is analysis of the Four Elements, or the mental separation, with regard to the body, of the parts pertaining respectively to the four great elements, earth, water, fire and air. In the simile of the *Satipaṭṭhāna Sutta,*

> *Just as, O monks, a skilled butcher, or butcher's apprentice, having slaughtered a cow and divided it into separate portions, sits down at the junction of four highroads (to sell the flesh), so does the disciple contemplate this body with regard to the elements.*

On this passage, which, incidentally, shows clearly enough that the eating of beef was a common practice in Ancient India, Buddhaghosa comments in the following characteristically sardonic manner:—

To the butcher, who rears the cow, brings it to the slaughter-house, ties it up, puts it there, slaughters it, or looks at the dead and slaughtered cow, the idea "cow" does not disappear so long as he has not ripped open and dismembered the body. As soon, however, as he has sat down, ripped open, and dismembered it, the idea "cow" disappears for him, and the idea "meat" arises in its place, and he does not think, "a cow do I sell," or "a cow do they buy." Even so, when the monk was still living an ignorant worldling, whether layman or homeless one, the ideas "living being," "man" and "individual" do not disappear so long as he has not taken this body—whatever position or direction it might have had—to pieces and analyzed it part by part. As soon, however, as he has analyzed this body into its elements, the idea of "living being" disappears for him, and his mind becomes established in contemplation of the elements.[1]

Analysis of the Four Elements, also, leads to the attainment of neighbourhood-concentration only.

From the forty classical supports of concentration we now turn to a brief consideration of the degrees and kinds of concentration to which they can give rise. Before so doing, however, we hasten to assure those for whom this section may possess more than a theoretical interest, that in order to develop concentration it is no more necessary for *one* person to have resort to *all* the *kammaṭṭhānas* than for a sick person to swallow all the medicines in the pharmacopœia. Theravada commentarial tradition enumerates six different *caritas* (Skt. *caritras*)—literally "characters"—or psychological types to which human beings belong. Each of the forty supports is particularly suited to persons of a particular character-type; a few are adapted to the needs of all. When a disciple came to Him for instruction in meditation, it was the Buddha's practice first to observe his temperament, then to prescribe for him a particular support for the development of concentration, and finally, to question him from time to time about his progress in the practice, giving further instruction and exhortation whenever necessary. The same procedure is followed, even today, by meditation-masters in all parts of the Buddhist world.

Supposing the red colour device, for example, to have been

[1] *Visuddhi Magga,* XI.

given the novice yogin as his "place of work," the method of developing concentration is as follows. The practitioner first sets up, at a certain distance from the meditation-seat, and at eye level, a red disc of prescribed size. On this disc, technically known as the *parikamma-nimitta,* or preparatory image, he focuses his attention, endeavouring to shut out, not only from his field of vision, but also from his very thoughts, everything except that dancing disc of colour. Gradually, as his concentration becomes more and more firmly fixed, the preparatory image becomes steady and his attention unwavering. He has attained *parikamma-samādhi,* or preparatory concentration, the first of the three stages in the development of mental one-pointedness. Then, closing his eyes, he will gradually be able to perceive a mental counterpart of the original, material image having the same size, colour and shape as the first. This mental image, known as the *uggaha-nimitta,* or acquired image, now becomes the support of concentration. The second stage of concentration, technically known as "access" or "neighbourhood-concentration" (*upacāra-samādhi*) arises when, after the yogin has remained for some time absorbed in the preceding stage, there emerges from the mental image—as the moon freed from clouds, or a sword flashing from its sheath, according to the traditional similes—that luminous disc termed the *paṭibhāga-nimitta* or reflex image. Upon the cessation of the reflex image, and suspension of the five-sense consciousness, there now arise, with *appanā samādhi* or full concentration as their nucleus, those progressively "higher" states to which, with deliberate imprecision, we have hitherto referred as stages of superconsciousness.

The original Pali word for these exalted and supernormal—but, as we must repeatedly insist, still entirely natural and mundane—modes of being, is *jhāna,* perhaps better known under its Sanskrit form *dhyāna;* and the reason for which we have so far refused to commit ourselves to any of the numerous English equivalents put forward by scholars is that they are all entirely unsatisfactory, if not downright misleading. "Trance," "rapture," the impossibly feeble "musing," to say nothing of *versenkungen,* with its suggestion of sinking into unconscious depths, even in combination are powerless to reproduce the meaning of *jhāna.* In fact, the Pali term itself, which means to think over, or to brood upon, something, will mean little, if anything at all, to those who have not themselves practised meditation and attained some degree of concentration, however well versed they may be in the Pali language and its literature. Imaginative description sometimes succeeds, however, where logical definition fails. After giving the stereotype formula of the four *jhānas,* which is of frequent occurrence in the *Suttas,* we shall quote four similes, of astonishing power, beauty and spiritual suggestiveness, by means of which the Buddha sought to indicate the individual quality, the unique flavour, of each of these states:—

"Free from sensual desires, free from evil thoughts, he attains and abides in the first jhāna *of joy and pleasure, which is accompanied with reasoning (*vitakka*) and investigation (*vicāra*) and arises from seclusion [here identical with* samādhi*]. He suffuses, pervades, fills, and permeates his body with the pleasure (*sukha*) and joy (*pīti*) arising from seclusion, and there is nothing in all his body untouched by the pleasure and joy arising from seclusion.*

"Again the monk with the ceasing of reasoning and investigation, in a state of internal serenity, with his mind fixed on one point, attains and abides in the second jhāna *of joy and pleasure arising from concentration, and free from reasoning and investigation. He suffuses, pervades, fills, and permeates his body with the pleasure and joy arising from concentration, and there is nothing in all his body untouched by the pleasure and joy arising from concentration.*

"Again the monk with indifference towards joy, abides with equanimity, mindful and self-possessed, and with his body experiences the pleasure that the noble ones call, 'dwelling with equanimity, mindful, and happy,' and attains and abides in the third jhāna. *He suffuses, pervades, fills, and permeates his body with pleasure without joy, and there is nothing at all in his body untouched by his pleasure without joy.*

"Again the monk, with the dispelling of pleasure and pain, and even before the disappearance of elation and depression attains and abides in the fourth jhāna *which is without pain and pleasure and with the purity of equanimity and mindfulness. He sits permeating his body with mind purified and cleansed, and there is nothing at all in his body untouched by his mind purified and cleansed."*[1]

Thus in the first *jhāna* there are present reasoning, investigation, joy, pleasure and concentration; in the second, joy, pleasure and concentration; in the third, joy and concentration; in the fourth, equanimity and concentration. We should beware, however, of too literal an interpretation of this analysis. As The Pali Text Society's *Pali-English Dictionary,* speaking of the *jhānas,* warns us, "The whole really forms one series of mental states, and the stages might have been fixed at other points in the series." Other

---

[1] *Early Buddhist Scriptures,* pp. 63-64.

texts, in fact, by reckoning the cessation of reason and the cessation of investigation as separate stages, arrive at a scheme of five *jhānas* instead of four.

The above formula speaks of each of the four *jhānas* as suffusing, pervading, filling and permeating the monk's body, a fact that should be noted: as even the allopathic branch of medical science now admits, health of body and "health" of mind are interrelated, so that we need not be astonished to find the attainment of superconscious states having a tonic effect not only upon the mental but also upon the physical constitution of the practitioner. The function of the four similes that follow is to indicate, in the case of each *jhāna,* the mode of permeation taking place. Far from being arbitrarily chosen, the distinctive features of each comparison correspond in a very definite and detailed manner to the unique qualities of each state of *jhāna*-experience, and should therefore be minutely observed.

As an expert bath attendant, or bath attendant's apprentice, puts soap powder into a dish, soaks it with water, mixes and dissolves it in such a manner that its foam is completely permeated, saturated within and without with moisture, leaving none over, even so the monk suffuses, pervades, fills and permeates his body with the pleasure and joy arising from seclusion, and there is nothing in all his body untouched by the pleasure and joy arising from seclusion. . . .

As a lake with a subterranean spring, into which there flows no rivulet from East or from West, from North or from South, nor do the clouds pour their rain into it, but only the fresh spring at the bottom wells up and completely suffuses, pervades, fills and permeates it, so that not the smallest part of the lake is left unsaturated with fresh water, even so the monk . . . permeates his body with the pleasure and joy arising from concentration. . . .

As in a lake with lotus plants some lotus flowers are born in the water, develop in the water, remain below the surface of the water, and draw their nourishment from the depths of the water, and their blooms and roots are suffused, pervaded, filled and permeated with fresh water, so that not the smallest part of any lotus flower is left unpermeated with fresh water, even so the monk . . . permeates his body with pleasure without joy. . . .

As a man might cloak himself from head to foot in a white mantle, so that not the smallest part of his body was left uncovered by the white mantle, even so the monk sits having covered his body with a state of extreme equanimity and concentration. . . .[1]

With the attainment of the fourth *jhāna,* in which, as J. Evola finely says,[2] the body is not only pervaded but also covered by the new force, as if it was not the body that contained the force

---

[1] *Dīgha-Nikāya,* II. 82.

[2] *The Doctrine of Awakening,* p. 196.

but the force that contained the body, the path divides and the disciple is confronted by the necessity of making a choice. On one side is the path leading to the four *arūpa* or formless *jhānas,* on the other, the road leading to the development of various supernormal powers. Should he be bent solely on attainment of the transcendental stage of Nirvana, however, he will turn his back on these lofty, but still mundane, possibilities, and retrace his steps as far as the stage of neighbourhood-concentration. For it is at this stage, according to the Teaching of the Buddha, that the development of liberating insight, or Wisdom, begins, and the transcendental path (*lokuttara-magga*) of the Noble Ones, the Way to Enlightenment, opens out. In accordance with whether insight is developed by contemplating the painful (*dukkha*) transitory (*anicca*) or egoless (*anattā*) nature of phenomena three kinds of concentration can now be distinguished, *appaṇihita-samādhi, animitta-samādhi,* and *suññatā-samādhi.* By means of these three kinds of concentration, Nirvana may be realized, according to Theravada teaching, under its three aspects, either as aimlessness, or as signlessness, or as emptiness. Just as the stage of Morality overlapped the stage of Meditation, the stage of Meditation has now overlapped the third and last stage, that of Wisdom. But before in imagination accompanying the disciple upon that steep and hazardous ascent to the summit of Being—and beyond—we shall go back to the fourth *jhāna* and survey the landscapes that would have disclosed themselves to him had he chosen to proceed along either of these two forks in the road.

As we have already seen, each stage of superconsciousness is the subjective counterpart of an objective higher "world." By developing repugnance for the four lower stages, as well as their corresponding "realms," and by means of the idea "infinite is space," the yogin attains the sphere of Infinite Space (*ākāsânañcâ-yatana*), the first if the four "formless" *jhānas.* By realizing that his consciousness, inasmuch as it has for object the infinity of space, is also infinite, he attains the sphere of Infinite Consciousness (*viññāṇañcâyatana*). After that there rises for him, at the idea "Nothing is there," the sphere of Nothingness (*ākiñcaññâyatana*), and then, last of all, the sphere of Neither-perception-nor-non-perception (*saññā-n'asaññâyatana*), with which he reaches the limit of mundane existence. Not only the four lower, but also the four higher *jhānas* were well known in India long before the advent of the Buddha, and actual attainment of these exalted states was at that time, as even now to a lesser extent is the case, by no means a rarity among Indian yogis. From His first teacher, Alara Kalama, the Lion of the Sakyas learned the technique for the attainment of the Sphere of Nothingness, and from His second teacher, Uddaka Ramaputta, the method of reaching the Sphere of Neither-perception-nor-non-perception. But finding that neither of them conduced to aversion, absence of passion, cessation, tranquillity, higher knowledge, Nirvana, He abandoned in disgust the doctrines of these two teachers and, plunging into the jungle, entered upon that long course of terrible austerities that led Him, eventually, to the foot of the Bodhi Tree. There, without a teacher and without a guide, relying solely upon His own heroic fortitude and strength of mind, He discovered the Path of Insight, the Path trodden by His predecessors the Buddhas of old, and with the complete extinction of the *āsavas* attained supreme Enlightenment. Thereafter He proclaimed Wisdom, in the sense of insight into the true nature of phenomena, as the sole means to Emancipation, declaring that outside this Path there could be no deliverance for any being. However, the doctrines of Alara Kalama and Uddaka Ramaputta still live on in India. The four lower *jhānas* are now collectively known as *savikalpa-samādhi,* their objective counterpart being the *saguṇa-brahman,* or theistic god, while the higher *jhānas* are termed *nirvikalpa-samādhi,* the corresponding "world" or plane of existence being the *nirguṇa-brahman,* or godhead. The dualist teachings of Rāmānuja, Madhva, Niṁbārka, Vallabha and Chaitanya all regard, in one way or another, the *saguṇa-brahman* as the ultimate object of the religious consciousness and *savikalpa-samādhi* as the highest state attainable by man; Śaṅkara, going a step farther, proposes instead realization of the *nirguṇa-brahman* by means of *nirvikalpa-samādhi* as the supreme goal of human existence. Strictly speaking, inasmuch as concentration and equanimity, the constituents of the fourth *rūpa-jhāna,* are both present in the "formless" states of superconsciousness, the four higher *jhānas* are regarded as belonging to the last of the four lower *jhānas.* For this reason many Buddhist texts refer not to eight but to four states of superconsciousness.

The various supernormal powers known as the six *abhiññā*

(Skt. *abhijña*), literally "higher knowledges," are frequently described and alluded to in Pali and Sanskrit texts. Since it is not these powers themselves, but the correct evaluation of them, which is the more important, we shall content ourselves with the minimum of description. With the exception of the last, the six supernormal powers are all mundane; their development is a consequence not of transcendental insight but of attainment of the fourth *jhāna.* The stereotype text for the Siddhis, or psychic powers, the first of the "higher knowledges," describes the monk as multiplying his body, passing unobstructed through walls and mountains as though through air, walking on water as on earth and diving into earth as though into water; as floating cross-legged through the air like a bird, and touching with his hand the sun and the moon. Even up to the world of Brahma, declares the text, does such a monk have mastery over his body. This body is not, of course, the material body, but a mind-made or mind-formed (*manomaya*) body which is produced from the physical body, according to the traditional similes, like a sword from the sheath, pith from a reed, or a snake from its basket. The production of such a body, elsewhere described as radiant or luminous, is referred to in unmistakable terms by several Pali texts of the Theravada Canon. For the Mahayana schools this highly esoteric practice, described in detail in the *Guhyasamāja Tantra* and other Tantras of the *Anuttara* class, possesses tremendous doctrinal significance, for it is by means of his glorified "mental" body that the Bodhisattva, after reaching a certain stage of his career, carries on his work for the emancipation of all sentient beings. The second *abhiññā,* known as the "divine ear" (*dibba-sota*), corresponds to what we should nowadays term clairaudience. The third is knowledge of the minds of other beings (*parassa cetopariya-ñāṇa*), or telepathy; the fourth, remembrance of former births or, more literally, "abodes" (*pubbe-nivās ânu-sati*). The fifth and last in the list of mundane supernormal powers is the "divine eye" (*dibba-cakkhu*), possessed of which the monk beholds beings vanishing from one sphere of existence and reappearing in another in accordance with the results of their bodily, verbal and mental actions. This is a more highly developed and comprehensive form of clairvoyance. The development of the sixth *abhiññā,* destruction of the *āsavas,* has for basis not attainment of the fourth *jhāna* but insight into the true nature of phenomena. It is therefore not mundane but transcendental. Once again we have passed from the stage of Meditation to the stage of Wisdom.

The supernormal powers (except the last) being for Buddhism not an irruption from the transcendental but a prolongation and extension of the mundane, it follows that their acquisition is devoid of spiritual significance. Though they are within the disciple's reach, he should not commit the mistake of regarding them as desirable; if they happen to arise spontaneously, he should look on them with indifference, even with disgust. Certainly he should never exhibit them for the sake of impressing people; not even for the sake of "converting" them, such conduct being regarded as in the highest degree reprehensible. Orthodox Christians believe that because Jesus of Nazareth worked miracles he was the Son of God. To the Buddhist, if this fact has any value at all, it is not as a proof of the alleged divinity of the Founder of Christianity but as an evidence of the spiritual immaturity of his followers. Far from teaching that the acquisition of mundane psychic powers was a matter for self-congratulation, the Buddha declared that He regarded them with contempt and loathing. The only true miracle, the only one that really counts, is when a man turns from an ignoble to a noble way of life.

XVIII. Wisdom and the Arahant Ideal

"He who is concentrated sees things as they really are."[1] With these words does the All-knowing One indicate not only the essence of Meditation and the essence of Wisdom, but also the nature of the relation between them. Just as only a well-tempered, finely ground and carefully sharpened blade of best-quality steel is capable of cutting smoothly and easily through some solid object, so is it only the concentrated mind that penetrates reality. Concentration, not excluding that of the *jhānas,* is not an end in itself but a means to an end. That end is Wisdom, the seeing of things as in truth and reality they are. In fact, with the sole exception of neighbourhood-concentration, though the various stages of *samādhi* are a means to the devel-

[1] *Saṁyutta-Nikāya,* XXII. 5.

opment of liberating insight, in the sense of occupying an intermediate position between Morality, the first stage of the Way, and Wisdom, the third, they are even as a means not indispensable. Hence two kinds of disciples are distinguished. There are those who attain the transcendental paths (*ariya-magga*) with "tranquillity" as their vehicle (*samatha-yānika*) and those who, on the other hand, attain them by means of bare insight alone (*suddha-vipassanā-yānika*), without having passed through any of the *jhānas.* To get "stuck in" a superconscious state—the fate that befalls so many mystics—without understanding the necessity of developing insight, is for Buddhism not a blessing but an unmitigated disaster.

The nature of the insight developed by the disciple in the course of the third and last stage of the Way forms the subject-matter of Sections X-XV, wherein Bodhi, or Enlightenment, was explained as understanding of the conditionality of all dharmas, and wherein the various conceptual formulations of this principle, the intellectual symbol of the Buddha's realization, were dealt with more or less comprehensively. What was said then need not be repeated now. *Dīgha-Nikāya,* XXXIII, distinguishes three kinds of knowledge or wisdom (Pali *Paññā,* Skt. *Prajñā*): based on thinking (*cintā-mayā*), on learning (*suta-mayā*), and on "mental development" (*bhāvanā-mayā*), here equivalent to Meditation. They are thus explained by Buddhaghosa:—

> *"Based on thinking" is that knowledge (or wisdom) which one has acquired by one's own cogitation, without having learned it from others. "Based on learning" (literally "hearing") is that knowledge which one has learned ("heard") from others. "Based on Meditation" is that knowledge which one has acquired through "mental development" in this or that way, and which has reached the stage of attainment-concentration (*appanā-samādhi*)*[1].

When, with his concentrated mind, the disciple penetrates the true nature of dharmas, his erstwhile distracted and merely "intellectual" understanding of the Teaching becomes transformed into Transcendental Wisdom. In those texts wherein the steps of the Eightfold Path are distributed into three stages the order of stages is not, as one might expect, Morality, Meditation, Wisdom, but Wisdom, Morality, Meditation. Here by wisdom is meant "learning"; for intellectual comprehension of the Doctrine,

---

[1] *Visuddhi Magga,* XIV.

though in itself powerless to effect Liberation, must precede any attempt to put into actual practice even its most elementary tenets. In this particular permutation of steps and stages Meditation is therefore understood to include not only concentration but also the insight based on concentration. The importance of acquiring by means of a rigorous course of scriptural study, preferably at the feet of a teacher, thorough intellectual comprehension of the Doctrine, has during the long history of Buddhism rarely been underestimated. Only if one has taken refuge in an enlightened Master, capable of providing at each stage of the disciple's career the appropriate instruction, are there adequate grounds for dispensing with these preliminaries. Otherwise even though the disciple succeeds in developing concentration it will be of no more use to him than a sharpened pencil to a man who can neither read nor write. Wisdom, the ultimate stage of the threefold Way, does not consist in the comprehension of truths superior to those which form the subject-matter of Sections X-XV but in making those truths themselves the object, not of a distracted mind, as was hitherto the case, but of a mind concentrated by the practice of Meditation. Knowledge stops short at conceptual symbols; Wisdom passes beyond them to apprehension of the realities indicated by the symbols. But if the nature of that realization is to be communicated, recourse to those same symbols must again be had. Hence all that we can offer as a description of the third stage of the Way is a recapitulation of the summary of Buddhist doctrine already given. But if the reader will be so kind as to reread the Sections referred to, and to transpose them from the intellectual to the intuitive mode, we shall be delivered from the necessity of repeating ourselves. In this case we shall be required only to round off our survey of the three stages of the Way with a reference to some of the stereotyped formulæ with which the Pali texts bring to a conclusion the disciple's career, after which we shall deal with a few matters of more general import.

The *Samaññaphala Sutta* and other texts which describe the stages succeeding attainment of the *jhānas* in terms of the six *abhiññā,* or supernormal powers, naturally speak of Wisdom as culminating in knowledge of the destruction of the three *āsavas* of sensual desire, desire for existence, and ignorance. In a sense, however, the sixth *abhiññā* is the effect of Wisdom, its reaction upon the character of the disciple in the form of a complete and permanent extinction of all unwholesome states of mind, rather than Wisdom itself. In some texts, therefore, destruction of the *āsavas* is prefaced by understanding of the four Aryan Truths. This important formulation of the central Buddhist principle of universal conditionality has already been discussed in Section XV. Here we shall speak of *vipassanā,* which may perhaps be regarded as the more active and causally efficacious aspect of Wisdom, as insight into the three characteristics (*ti-lakkhaṇa*) of all phenomena, a formula recognized by the vast majority of Buddhists as the keystone of the whole arch of Buddhist doctrine. In words which ring triumphantly down the ages the Lord declares in the *Dhammapada*:—

> " *'Impermanent are all component things.' He who perceives this with insight becomes thereby immediately unmoved by suffering. This is the Path of Purity.*
>
> " *'Involved in suffering are all component things.' He who perceives this with insight becomes thereby immediately unmoved by suffering. This is the Path of Purity.*
>
> " *'Unsubstantial (*anattā*) are all dharmas.' He who perceives this with insight becomes thereby immediately unmoved by suffering. This is the Path of Purity.*"[1]

The first of these theses being logically prior to the others we shall have to devote to it a little more space than need be given to them. The words of the Pali original are "*Sabbe sankhārā aniccā.*" By *sankhārā* is meant, in this context, not the "setting up," by means of volition, of conditions leading to rebirth, as is the case when the term occurs as the second "link" in the chain of the twelvefold conditioned co-production, but rather whatever has been "set up," put together, formed or compounded, by such an aggregation of causal factors. Like the English word "formation," by which the Pali term is sometimes translated, *sankhārā* connotes both the act of forming and the passive state of having been formed. It is with the second of these meanings that we are now concerned. "Compounds" or "formations" are impermanent because whatever has been put together must one day be taken apart; the principle of creation is identical with the principle of destruction; we die the moment that we are born. That alone is eternal which is uncompounded; only the unborn can never die. Nirvana is Deathless (Pali *amata,* Skt. *amṛta*)

---

[1] *Dhammapada,* verses 277-279.

because it is the Unconstituted (Pali *asankhata,* Skt. *asaṁskṛta*). Every state and form of phenomenal existence, from the shortest-lived of the ephemerids to the longest-lived of the gods—whose lifetimes are reckoned not by thousands but by millions of years, and who behold unmoved the wreck of universes and the crash of worlds—is perishable, and must one day end. Nirvana alone endures. As he penetrates, by means of his concentrated mind, into this liberating truth of the transitoriness of all phenomena, the disciple becomes free from desire for, free from attachment to, any created thing. Turning his back upon the world, he enters the stream that leads to Nirvana—"where the Silence lives."

If it were in fact possible to remould this sorry scheme of things "nearer to the heart's desire," and if the impermanent could by some magic of transmutation be made permanent, then there might not be any harm in our enjoying this or that object of the senses. But things being constituted as they are, the objects of enjoyment disintegrate in our very grasp, as ice melts when clasped in a warm hand, and the result is suffering. Happiness can be attained either when existence accords with our desires, or when our desires are in harmony with existence. True, the second alternative is difficult; but the first is impossible. If we cannot gain happiness by refashioning the world we shall have to find it by reforming ourselves. Compound things are indeed painful because they are impermanent; but that impermanency is not so much the cause as the occasion of our suffering. The root cause is desire. Happiness comes only when we desire and are attached to—nothing. And that happiness is eternal.

Dharmas are *anattā* for two reasons, one of which represents the static, the other the dynamic, aspect of the doctrine of unsubstantiality. Things have no "own-being," no permanent identity or unchanging selfhood, firstly because each one of them is merely the sum of its components, apart from which it is merely a name, and secondly because it is not self-originated (a contradictory conception) but produced by a momentary collocation of exterior causal factors. When the doctrine of *anattā* is considered under its first aspect, compounds are impermanent because they are unsubstantial; under its second, unsubstantial because they are impermanent. We shall deal with these two aspects in reverse order. Risking a generalization, it may be said that in Indian thought the idea of selfhood is closely connected with the idea of mastery or ownership. That over which we cannot exercise complete control does not pertain to our self. The body, obviously, as all the non-materialist schools admit, is not the self, because, among other reasons, it is not fully subject to the will. Whether we like it or not, eventually it falls sick, grows old, and dies. Buddhism, pursuing this line of reasoning to its logical conclusion, asserts that not only the material processes of the body, but also the mental processes which make up the so-called "mind" do not belong to us, are not our own, because they arise in dependence on conditions over which we have, with few exceptions, no control whatever. None of the phenomena of personality can be regarded as the self because none of them "belongs" to us, and apart from these phenomena personality does not exist. This truth is to be realized only by insight into the unsubstantiality of things. None but the fool, the man devoid even of an intellectual understanding of the doctrine of *anattā,* will think that anything belongs to him. As the *Dhammapada* says, "Even his self is not his own. How then a son? How wealth?"[1] Because, in the last resort, we have no possessions, in the ultimate analysis we have no self either. The monk's renunciation of all worldly goods is the living symbol of this truth. He is called *akiñcana,* "man-of-naught," not merely because he is civilly a pauper, but because in the far deeper, psychological and metaphysical sense of the term, he does not regard any phenomenon, however exalted, as his own, but abides free from grasping, and therefore aloof from pain. Hence the great exhortation

"Form is not yours, O Monks. Give it up! Sensation, perception, the formations and consciousness are not yours. Give them up!"

Because things are impermanent they can be taken away from us; what can be taken away from us is not our own; and what is not our own cannot be regarded as our self. Thus is the unsubstantiality of phenomena deduced from their impermanence.

Mention of the five *skandhas* brings us to the static and analytical aspect of the doctrine of *anattā* in which it is not the conclu-

---

[1] *Dhammapada,* verse 62.

sion but the major premise of the doctrine of *anicca.* Things are transitory because they are compounded. But how are they compounded? What, for instance, are the elements of personality? To the second of these questions, from the spiritual point of view decidedly the more important, the Buddha's classification of the psycho-physical phenomena of so-called individual sentient existence into five "heaps" supplies the answer. We render *skandhas* (Pali *khandhas*) by its most literal English equivalent for a definite reason. *Rūpa,* or form, for example, is not a phenomenon but a "heap" of phenomena; not "matter" but simply a congeries of events of the "material" order. Similarly, the word *vijñāna* (Pali *viññāṇa*) or consciousness, does not represent a permanent unchanging element or ultimate principle of consciousness, but is simply the collective term for all our evanescent mental states. The different heaps of grain in a chandler's shop are ticketed "rice," "maize," "millet," and so on. These labels do not stand for so many entities of the cereal order but simply for the various heaps, each one of which is composed of millions of tiny grains. With this illustration in mind should the following brief description of the five *skandhas* be understood.

Rūpa, form or corporeality, comprises not only the four primary material phenomena, that is to say, the forces of cohesion, undulation, radiation and vibration, but also four-and-twenty secondary material phenomena. Apart from the five physical sense-organs and sense-objects the latter comprises, according to Theravada tradition, masculinity and femininity; the physical base of mind; bodily and verbal expression; physical vitality; (limited) space; physical buoyancy, plasticity, adaptability, integration and continuity; decay; impermanence; and physical nutriment. By *vedanā,* the second "heap," is meant simply bodily and mentally pleasant, painful and neutral feeling. The third "heap" consists of the six different kinds of *saṁjñā* (Pali *saññā*) or perception, that is to say, the perception by their respective sense-organs of form, sound, odour, taste, bodily impression and mental impression ("ideas" being regarded, it will be remembered, as objects of a special mind-organ). The *saṁskāras,* or formations (in the active, not the passive, sense of the term), comprise—again according to the Theravada (other schools differing a little in detail but with exception of the Vatsiputriyas and Sarvastivadins, not at all in principle)

—50 mental phenomena of which 11 are general psychological elements (5 of them being present in all stages of consciousness), 25 lofty moral qualities, and 14 qualities that are karmically unwholesome. In the Pali Suttas six classes of consciousness are distinguished, each representing the series of infinitesimally brief "flashes" of consciousness that arises in dependence on the conjunction of a sense-organ with its particular sense-object. The Theravadin Abhidhamma, however, bent on exorcising even the faintest ghost of an ego-entity by means of still more dreadful analytical incantations, distinguishes within the "heap of consciousness" no less than 89 different types of "grain," each consisting of an infinite number of infinitesimally minute "particles." Of these, 21 are karmically wholesome, 12 unwholesome, and 55 neutral. It should be added that some of these 89 items, since they are capable of entering into more than one of the three principal kinds of combination just now mentioned, are enumerated more than once. This may be taken as another opportunity of reminding ourselves that we are here concerned not with specified numbers of combinations between solid and discrete things, but with an uninterrupted succession of permutations of an only more or less stable number of *processes*. Personality being neither simple, nor composed of elements that are simple, it follows that personality is a complex and compound thing; being compound it is transitory; because it is transitory it is a source of suffering. Thus from the static aspect of the characteristic of unsubstantiality are deduced the two remaining characteristics of all phenomena.

References to the five "heaps" of psychic and somatic "events" occur again and again in all branches of Buddhist literature, and the importance of a right understanding of the truth symbolized by this ubiquitous formula cannot be overestimated. If the twelvefold Conditioned Co-production be regarded as the rim of the great Wheel of the Dharma set rolling by the Buddha in the Deer Park at Isipatana, five-and-twenty centuries ago—that Wheel which, once set revolving, neither gods nor men can stay—and if the eight steps of the Way be taken as its spokes, then the doctrine of the five "heaps" will be the hub of the Wheel, and the doctrine of unsubstantiality the empty space in the centre of the Wheel, without which it would be not a wheel but only a useless disk.

Insight consists in seeing, wherever one looks, whether within or without, not a "self," "soul," "ego," or "living being," but simply five "heaps" of psycho-physical phenomena. Like Avalokita in the *Prajñāpāramitāhṛdaya Sūtra,* the disciple, coursing in the Wisdom that has gone beyond, looks down "from on high" and sees merely five heaps, all of which he recognizes as being in their own-being empty. Astonishing to the common run of idealist and materialist alike though the fact may seem, in the Buddha's estimation, to regard the "form-heap" as one's self was less inexcusable than to identify it with any of the immaterial "heaps." The body, after all, does possess a certain relative stability; but the mind does not persist in the same state for even two consecutive seconds. The more obviously evanescent a thing is, the less difficult should be recognition of its unsubstantiality. As an illustration of the way in which the disciple contemplates the three characteristics of all phenomena another graphic simile may be quoted from the Pali texts.

Suppose a man not blind were to observe the multitudinous bubbles being borne rapidly along on the surface the river Ganges, and should watch and carefully examine them. After he has carefully examined them they will appear to him empty, unreal and unsubstantial. In exactly the same way does the monk behold all corporeal phenomena . . . all feelings . . . all perceptions . . . all mental formations . . . and all states of consciousness, whether they be of the past, the present, or the future . . . far or near. He watches and carefully examines them, and after he has carefully examined them, they appear to him empty, unreal, and unsubstantial.[1]

Vivider still is the simile which compares *vipassanā* to the lightning that, on a dark night, lights up for an instant with dazzling brilliance the whole surrounding countryside. Insight comes, not all at once, but in a series of "instantaneous," that is to say, time-transcending "flashes" that are as it were not continuous with, but utterly discrete from, the phenomenal order. These flashes, coming with ever-increasing frequency, gradually merge first into a series of more and more sustained emissions of radiance, and then into the unbroken and wholly transcendental illumination of Perfect Wisdom. Progress on the Path is not sudden, but gradual. Says the Buddha:—

"Just as, brethren, the mighty ocean deepens and slopes gradually down, hollow after hollow, not plunging by a sudden precipice—even so, brethren, in this

[1] *Saṁyutta-Nikāya,* XXII. 95.

Norm-Discipline the training is gradual, progress is gradual, it goes step by step, here is no sudden penetration to insight."

(Udāna, *V.5, and* Vinaya, *II.9. Woodward's translation*[1])

The Zen Buddhist doctrine of Sudden Enlightenment does not mean that the Goal of the holy life can be attained quickly and easily. It merely insists that inasmuch as the mundane and transcendental "planes" are discontinuous there can be from the mundane side no question of a greater or less degree of approximation to insight, whether in the form of a "flash" or as a "stream" of illumination. Either it is there or it is not there. No intermediate positions are possible.

Development of insight being a gradual process, the stage of Wisdom is divided, as were the stages of Morality and Meditation, into a number of sub-stages. By referring to these divisions of the Transcendental Path the precise extent of the disciple's progress in Wisdom can be ascertained. Four in number, they are named after the appellations received by the disciple as he enters upon each of them in turn. Thus there are the Path and Fruit of Entrance upon the Stream (leading to Nirvana) or *sotāpatti-magga* and *-phala*; the Path and Fruit of One Return (*sakadāgami-magga* and *-phala*); the Path and Fruit of Non-Return (*anāgami-magga* and *-phala*) and the Path and Fruit of Holiness (*arahatta-magga* and *-phala*). The difference between the two subdivisions has been explained with his usual authority and lucidity by Nyanatiloka.

*According to the Abhidhamma, "supermundane path," or simply "Path" (*magga*), is a designation of the moment of entering into one of the four stages of holiness—Nirvana being the object—produced by intuitional Insight (*vipassana*) into the impermanency, misery and impersonality of existence, flashing forth and for ever transforming one's life and nature. By "Fruition" (*phala*) are meant those moments of consciousness, which follow immediately thereafter as the result of the path, and which under circumstances may repeat for innumerable times during lifetime.*[2]

The particular sub-stage of Wisdom at which the disciple stands depends upon the pitch of intensity, the degree of strength, to which insight has been developed. That strength is measured against the standard of the Ten Fetters (*dasa-saṁ-*

---

[1] *Some Sayings of the Buddha,* p. 249.

[2] *Buddhist Dictionary,* p. 17.

yojana), a certain number of which are to be burst asunder at each sub-stage. The Stream-Entrant, or Sotāpanna, has developed insight sufficiently powerful to break, completely and finally, the three fetters of wrong belief concerning the nature of individuality (*sakkāyadiṭṭhi*), "sceptical doubt" (*vicikicchā*) in the sense of wilfully incomplete, or hesitant, acceptance of the Doctrine, and dependence upon mere morality and external ascetic observances (*sīlabbata-parāmāsa*) as though they were by themselves a sufficient means to Enlightenment. Such a disciple is exempt from rebirth in any of the lower worlds, and has not more than seven lives to pass through, all on the human and divine planes, before attaining the total emancipation of mind which is Nirvana. His characteristics are unshakable faith in the Buddha, the Dharma and the Sangha, and absolutely unblemished Morality. The Sakadāgāmi, or Once-Returner, succeeds in weakening, though not in actually breaking, the fourth and fifth fetters of sexual desire (*kāma-rāga*) and ill-will (*vyāpāda*). One more rebirth as a human being awaits him: in his next life he will attain Full Enlightenment. The Anāgāmi, or Non-Returner, having burst all five lower fetters, is reborn in one of the Pure Abodes, five heavens at the summit of the "world of form," and there attains Nirvana without the necessity of incurring another human birth. The Arahant, or Holy One, shattering by means of his fully developed and irresistible insight the five remaining "higher" fetters—desire for existence in the world of form (*rūpa-rāga*), desire for existence in the formless world (*arūpa-rāga*), conceit (*māna*) or the idea of himself as superior, inferior or equal to others, restlessness (*uddhacca*), and ignorance (*avijjā*)—in this very life wins emancipation from the bondage of phenomenal existence and straightway plunges into the Deathless State, Nirvana. These four kinds of persons (or eight, if we take into account the division of each sub-stage according to *magga* and *phala*), technically known as the Ariya-Puggalā or Noble Ones, comprise the Ariya-Sangha or Noble Order which is, as every Buddhist knows, the third of the Three Gems to which go for refuge both monk and lay disciples of the Enlightened One. They alone are "saints" in the only sense in which this term, soaked as it is in Christian and nebulously mystical connotations, can be used by the writer on Buddhism. Hence on His very deathbed the Buddha addressed to His last convert this emphatic declaration, the meaning of which cannot possibly be in doubt:—

*"In whatsoever norm-discipline, Subaddha, the Ariyan Eightfold Path is not found, therein also no recluse is found, either of the first, the second, the third, or the fourth degree [*i.e., *the Sotāpanna, etc.] and in whatsoever norm-discipline, Subaddha, the Ariyan Eightfold Path is found, herein also is found a recluse of the first, second, third and fourth degrees. Now in this Norm-Discipline (of mine), Subaddha, the Ariyan Eightfold Path is found. Herein also is found a recluse of these four degrees. Void of recluses are the other sects of disputants. But if, Subaddha, in this one brethren were to live the perfect life, the world would not be void of Arahants."*

(Dīgha-Nikayā, *II. 148. Woodward's translation)*[1]

With the attainment of Arahantship the disciple reaches the climax of his career. Conquering himself—a conquest more glorious, according to the *Dhammapada,* than conquering in battle a thousand men a thousand times—he has conquered the universe, and becomes worthy of the homage, worthy of the adoration, of gods and men, a field of merit unsurpassed for the world. There is nothing above him, nothing beyond him, now; bearing witness to his attainment, he declares, "Destroyed is rebirth, lived is the holy life, done is what I had to do, there is no more existence for me in conditions such as these." The Buddha Himself is superior to the Arahant, not in transcendental attainment but only in respect of cosmic function. *Namo Tassa, Bhagavato, Arahato, Sammāsambuddhassa*—Homage to Him, the Exalted, the Holy, the Fully Enlightened One—runs the formula of adoration in use all over the Buddhist world: the Buddha Himself is Arahant. The sole difference between Him and His enlightened disciples consists in the priority of His attainment, and in the fact that they attained Nirvana with, He without, the aid of a Teacher.

There are no valid reasons for regarding the attainment of Buddahood and the attainment of Arahantship as two different, even contradictory, spiritual ideals—much less still for regarding the latter as a synonym for spiritual selfishness. To the Aryan Disciple Nirvana is not an object that can be grasped; neither does he think that it can be made his individual possession. Only from the standpoint of relative truth is it possible to speak of this or that person as attaining Enlightenment: such expressions are

---

[1] *Some Sayings of the Buddha,* p. 353.

not to be understood literally. In reality, the gaining of Enlightenment consists, not in the addition of a certain transcendental attainment to an actually existing individual self, but rather merely in the cessation of the delusion that any kind of self exists at all. A striking passage from the Pali Canon makes it clear that, for the Arahant disciples of the Buddha, at the level of the first *jhāna,* even, the idea of individual attainment had vanished.

"Serene, pure, radiant is your person, Sariputta; where have you been today?" asks one Chief Disciple of the other.

"I have been alone, in first jhāna *brother, and to me never came the thought:* I *am attaining it;* I *have emerged from it. And thus individualizing and egoistical tendencies have been well ejected for a long while from Sariputta."*[1]

Even more emphatic is the following excerpt, in which two disciples bear witness to their attainment of Nirvana.

"Lord, he who is Arahant, who has destroyed the āsavas, *who has lived the life, who has done that which was to be done, has laid aside the burden, has won his own salvation, has utterly destroyed the fetters of becoming, is by perfect knowledge emancipated, to him it does not occur: 'There is, who is better than* I, *equal to* me, *inferior to* me.*' " So saying, they made obeisance and went out.*

*And the Master said, "Even do so men of true breed declare the gnosis they have won; they tell of their gain (*attha*), but they do not bring in the ego (*attā*)."*

There being in the realization of Nirvana no question at all of an "I," it follows that to represent the ideal of Arahantship taught in the oldest portions of the Pali Canon, in all probability the closest approximation we have to the form in which the Buddha's Message was originally cast—as being a "self-regarding" ideal, and as inculcating a cold and uncompassionate attitude towards human suffering, is an inexcusable misinterpretation of the Teaching. At the hands of certain Hinayana schools, the Arahant ideal did, indeed, receive an individualistic twist that provoked, and still provokes, justifiable protests from the Mahayanists. But in the Pali Canon, as the Theravadins themselves have preserved it, there is no trace (if we except obviously apocryphal accretions) of that extreme spiritual individualism with which the Arahant ideal later on became identified. Though the language of the Pali Scriptures is much less exuberant, emotional and highly coloured than that of the later Sanskrit texts, there can be no doubt, even on the evidence of these more restrained and "classical" records, that after their

[1] *Saṁyutta-Nikāya,* III. 235.

Enlightenment, compassion was the motive power behind the lives and activities of the Buddha and His disciples. Out of compassion for those who were but a little immersed in the mire of worldliness did the Lord agree, at Brahma Sahampatti's request, to open wide the Door of the Immortal to mankind; out of compassion did He do, for His disciples, "all that a teacher could do," and addressing His first sixty Arahant disciples, did He not exhort them to go forth on their journey, not coldly and indifferently, but "for the profit of the many, for the happiness of the many, *out of compassion for the world,* for the welfare, the profit, the happiness, of gods and men"? Indeed, there is an unmistakable thrill of urgency in His voice as He concludes His charge with the words, "There are beings with but little dust of passion on their eyes. They are perishing through not hearing the Norm. There will be some who will understand. I myself, brethren, will go to Uruvela, to the suburb of the Captain of the Host, to proclaim the Norm." Surely it is a spirit very different from individualism, on however exalted a level, that breathes in the words of this almost passionately compassionate exhortation.

In the *Sutta-Nipāta,* unquestionably one of the oldest and most authentic recensions of the Teaching, occurs a description of the Arahant which, breathing poetry into the prosaic catalogue of stages and sub-stages, still has the power of awakening into vivid life the highest ideal of Early Buddhism. Replying to a question concerning the vision and virtue of the Man of Calm—here equivalent to the Arahant—the Buddha says:—

Who conquers craving ere he crumble up,
Who trusts not first things nor the last, nor counts
The middle things: he hath no preference.

Gone wrath, gone fear, gone boasting, gone remorse,
Sooth-speaking, mild: that sage doth curb his talk.

Hoping for naught to come, he mourns no past;
Seer of th' aloof 'mid touch, views lead him not.

Guileless, apart, not found nor envious,
Nor loth nor forward, not to slander giv'n;

Not fain for pleasures nor to pride inclined,
Gentle yet quick, no dupe, dispassionate;

He traineth not in hope of gain, nor moved
Is he at getting none; no craving stirs
His placidness; he hankers not for tastes.

Poised, e'er alert, he deems not in the world
Things "equal," "notable" nor "lacking worth,"
For him there are no thoughts of "prominence."

Who trusteth not, knows not a thing on trust,
Thirsts not about becoming a decay,

I call him man-of-calm; not heeding lusts,
Without a knot, he hath the foul mire crossed.

No sons, kine, fields, nor property are his;
Naught to assume or to reject he finds.

Between folk's words, or brahman or recluse,
No choice hath he, hence talk doth move him not.

Gone envy, greed, the sage speaks not of "high,"
"Low," "equal," seeking not time's web, weaves none.

Who here hath naught, nor grieves o'er loss, nor goes
To views, he truly man-of-calm is called.
(Sutta-Nipāta, *849-61. Hare's translation)*[1]

Though compassion is not explicitly mentioned selflessness undoubtedly is; and that the realization, through Wisdom, of the selflessness of all phenomena, including these of one's own personality, brings about a spontaneous release of compassion, no school of Buddhism has yet denied.

XIX. The Foundations of Buddhism: Early Schools

The teachings outlined in this Chapter are Basic Buddhism; for upon them rest, as on an unshakable foundation, the loftiest superstructures and dizziest pinnacles of later Buddhist Doctrine and Method. The fruit, says Hegel, does not deny the flower, and the "developed" and "expanded" form of Buddhism known as the Mahayana, or Great Way, does not destroy but brings to fulfilment the Original Teaching.[2] Just as a flower, though its birth means destruction for the seed from which it sprang, nevertheless bears within its heart a seed of the same species, so the Mahayana, which is born of the true seed of the Original Teaching, casts away the withered husk of Hinayana dogmatism only to enshrine within its heart the living vital germ of the

---

[1] *Woven Cadences,* pp. 126-27.

[2] This Original Teaching, or Original Doctrine, corresponds to what Conze terms "archaic Buddhism." See *Buddhist Thought in India,* p. 31 *et seq.*

Dharma. Even of schools most extremely divergent from, and most deeply involved in contradictions seemingly irreconcilable with what some are pleased to call "pure" Buddhism, does this assertion hold good. The Pali Scriptures do not, it is true, contain any mention of Sukhāvatī, the Happy Land of Amitābha, and we shall in vain search their pages for any trace of trees made of gold, silver and all manner of precious stones, or for lotus flowers ten miles in circumference, or rivers fifty miles wide and twelve miles deep whose perfumed and music-producing waters, in which are bunches of flowers adorned with jewels, flow calmly between banks planted with yet more jewel-trees.[1] But that is not the point. The real point of the description is that the silver bells hung on the jewel-trees, and millions of golden-bodied Buddhas seated at the end of each of the millions of light-rays proceeding from every lotus, and the sound made by the waves of the rivers, all proclaim, as though with one voice, the same truths that were taught in the Bamboo Grove at Rajagriha and in Jeta's Park at Sravasti—the eternal and immutable truths of the painful, impermanent and unsubstantial nature of all phenomena. The Mahayana emancipates Buddhism from its comparatively drab terrestrial and historical context and transfers it to a celestial context of dazzling beauty and irresistible emotional appeal; it mounts the priceless jewel of the Dharma in a ring of gold. Like the princess in the fairy tale, who was brought up by a swineherd as his own daughter, Buddhism, though the offspring of the Eternal Truth and Law, had for some time to wear the coarse habiliments of its apparent place of origin; it was the Mahayana who wove for it the sumptuous robes befitting its true birth.

From the fact illustrated by these metaphors (which summarize more succinctly than any prose the position more amply set forth in Chapter II) it follows that without a previous knowledge of the earlier formulations of the Buddha's Teaching as preserved in either the Hinayana or the Mahayana collections of canonical literature, understanding of the later and often more elaborate formulations is impossible. For most English-knowing students of Buddhism this in effect means that study of the Theravada Pali Canon, at least in translation, must precede the study,

[1] See, however, "Mahāsudassana Suttanta," *Dīgha-Nikāya* XVII.

whether in the original or in modern-language versions, of the surviving Mahayana Sanskrit texts and the Mahayana Canons in Chinese, Japanese, Tibetan and Mongolian. To attempt to understand the special teachings by which Zen, or Shin, or some other school of comparatively recent origin, has become differentiated, with regard either to Doctrine or Method, from the main body of Mahayana Teaching, without first having covered thoroughly the common ground which it shares with other schools, both earlier and later, is a course even more likely to end in disaster than the one just described. Yet this, too, is a mistake often committed. Buddhism is nowadays by no means wanting in students, especially Western students, who, not content with the spacious staircases that lead from the lower to the higher storeys of the Palace of the Dharma, hastily scramble up the tree of their own intellect and try to leap therefrom headlong through the window of one of the topmost towers. They cut themselves on the broken glass or crash ignominiously to the ground. Needless to say, these observations apply chiefly to the independent student; of the accepted disciple of a living Master (not an imaginary one, or one who speaks from "the other side") of whatever school, they may of course not always be true.

According to the Pali Scriptures, the term by which the Buddha most often referred to His Teaching was Dhamma-Vinaya, now almost uniformly rendered by English translators either as "Norm-Discipline" or by the more sonorous Miltonic "Doctrine and Discipline." When, in the centuries immediately following the Maha Parinirvana of the Blessed One, the various schools of reciters began to bring the floating mass of oral traditions into a number of more or less fixed and systematic arrangements, teachings pertaining to Dhamma were included in what became known as the *Sutta-Piṭaka* or Collection of Discourses, while those treating of, or having some bearing on, matters of Vinaya, were included in the *Vinaya-Piṭaka*, or Collection of Disciplinary Precepts. These two collections, or the sources upon which they drew for their material, did not belong to any one school, but were the common property of all schools. The disputes which rent the Sangha from the beginning of the second century after the Great Decease owed their origin not to multiplicity of traditions but to differences of opinion regarding the correct interpretation of, and the proper attitude to be adopted towards, the identical body of doctrinal and disciplinary Teaching which all members of the Sangha regarded as authentic, and to which every party appealed in support of its views. Even after their emergence as separate branches, all the various schools continued to preserve, not merely their own distinctive teachings, but also their own versions of the common stock of primitive traditions; each, while putting forth its own leaves and flowers, continued to clasp firmly the parent trunk. The close similarity, amounting at times almost to identity, between the *Sutta-* and *Vinaya-Piṭakas* of the Theravadins and Sarvastivadins, in contrast to the wide divergences of arrangement and material found in their respective *Abhidhamma-Piṭakas,* or Collections of Higher Doctrine, may be cited as an example of this characteristically Buddhist process of development by accretion: obviously, each of the two schools had made a third collection after they had branched off from one another, and in it each had included not only its own systematization and interpretation of the Doctrine but also its refutations of views of other schools. The Mahayanists acted in accordance with the same principle. They took over from the older schools the whole common stock of primitive tradition, much exegetical apparatus, a large number of new technical terms, and all the earlier doctrinal developments which were not at variance with their own views. To this already imposing accumulation of material they added refutations of the misinterpretations which had brought about their own emergence as an independent movement, together with their unsurpassed original contributions to the profounder understanding and more ample practice of the Teaching.

The origins of the early Buddhist schools are with few exceptions involved in baffling obscurity, while the nature of the views they held, and the relative order of their appearance, more often than not afford material for speculation rather than ground for certainty. Eighteen or twenty are generally enumerated, but the lists rarely coincide, and in all there must have been almost double that number. Three schools, however, are of outstanding importance: the Theravadins (Skt. Sthaviravadins), the Sarvastivadins, and the Mahasanghikas. They represent the principal trends of thought in Early Buddhism, to one or another of which all the remaining schools owed their origin. Before concluding this chapter with a brief characterization of each of these three main currents of monastic thought, we must emphasize the fact that we speak of "schools" and not of "sects" because we are here concerned, not with a number of independent religious corporations, mutually exclusive in respect of teaching and membership, so much as with different lines of pupillary succession, each with its own increasingly distinctive emphasis on this or that aspect of the Teaching, all existing side by side within the one—as yet—undivided Sangha.

For more than a century after the Maha Parinirvana of the Blessed One perfect unanimity seems to have prevailed among His followers. The first great division was that between the Theravadins and the Mahasanghikas, which took place in connection with the Second Council, the Council of Vaisali. Whether the Mahasanghikas seceded from the Theravadins, or the Theravadins from the Mahasanghikas, is a matter of opinion to be settled, for most of us, in favour of whichever party we think was in the right. The immediate occasion of the split was the famous Ten (or Five) points put forward on behalf of the Vaiśālī party by the monk Mahādeva, whom the Theravadins accuse of parricide, incest and schism, and whom a modern Mahayana scholar eulogizes as "one of the most remarkable thinkers India has produced."[1] According to the Theravadin chronicles, there were ten points at issue, all relating to quite minor disciplinary precepts; Mahayana records, however, state that between the two parties there were five points of difference, all doctrinal, and all reflecting the dissatisfaction of the Vaiśālī monks with the current interpretation of the Arahant ideal. Bearing in mind the developments subsequently taking place in these schools, it is by no means impossible that the Sangha was agitated by controversies both doctrinal and disciplinary at about the time, perhaps during the actual proceedings, of the Second Council. The Theravadin party, which was the smaller of the two, rejecting the Ten (or Five) Points of Mahādeva and his associates, insisted—according to their own account—on an unmodified observance of the disciplinary precepts, or—according to the Mahayana version of the episode—on the Arahant's freedom from the imperfections attributed to him by the

[1] YAMAKAMI SOGEN, *Systems of Buddhistic Thought* (Calcutta, 1912), p. 5.

majority party. Whether this tradition is true or that, or whether both are true or both untrue, the attitude adopted by the Theravadins, not only at that time but ever afterwards, was indisputably one of unintelligent conservatism. As we have been at pains to insist, the Mahayanists by no means rejected the earlier traditions, and in this sense were themselves conservatives. Theravada conservatism was of a different type. It believed that the spirit of the Teaching would be best preserved by the preservation of its letter, that the permanence of the Doctrine was inseparably connected with the immutability of its outward forms. Hence it was in principle opposed to fresh interpretations and new developments of any kind. Owing to its inability to adapt itself to changing conditions the Theravada disappeared from India earlier than most other schools; but it was successful in establishing itself in Ceylon, Burma and Siam, as well as in a few smaller states, in all of which countries the general level of intelligence and standard of spiritual culture were considerably lower than those of India. Having changed, about five hundred years after the Maha Parinirvana of the Blessed One, from an oral to a written tradition, it became the means of preserving until modern times a larger and more complete collection of primitive formulations of the Teaching than any other school. Even unintelligent conservatism is not without its compensations! In this case, however, the compensations were of the historical rather than of the spiritual order. Theravada Buddhism on the whole resembles the tombs of the Egyptian kings; faithfully embalming against decay the outward forms of spiritual life, it has not succeeded in preserving that life itself; its boasted immutability is the settled and frozen immutability of death. The Mahayana schools, on the other hand, may be compared to the contemporary descendants of the ancient Egyptians; their features do not always resemble those gilded masks that stare up at us from the stone sarcophagi, but they have at least the merit of being alive. As for modern Theravadins, their attitude is even more unintelligently conservative than was that of their forebears. Not only do they believe, in the face of even canonical evidence to the contrary, that every word of the Pali *Tipiṭaka* was uttered just as it stands today, by the Enlightened One Himself, but they vehemently insist that their form of Buddhism alone is orthodox, and that all other schools—which nowadays they never study—are corruptions and degenerations of the original Teaching. Just as the development of the flower cannot be understood without reference to the seed, so the significance of the seed cannot be understood apart from the flower. Only an influx of Mahayana Buddhsm as a living spiritual force will save the Theravada countries from the stereotyped scholasticism that now passes for Doctrine and the rigid formalism that has taken the place of Method, and enable them fully to appreciate the real significance and true value even of their own tradition.

The Sarvastivada was geographically the most widespread and historically the most important among the early schools. Emerging as a distinct movement soon after the Council of Vaisali, it continued to flourish in India long after the disappearance of the Theravada. The Council convened by Kanishka in the sixth century of the Buddhist Era was a Sarvastivadin assembly; for centuries the school had powerful establishments not only in Central but in many parts of South-East Asia. Differing from the parent body, so we are told, in respect of only three doctrines, one alone of which concerned the Way, the Sarvastivadins may be regarded not as an independent school but rather as the more liberal and progressive wing of the Theravada. The analytical and expository material contained in their Abhidharma literature, which was much more systematic and philosophical than its Theravada counterpart, was the weightiest contribution made by the Hinayanists to the development of Buddhist thought. Taken over and incorporated into their own doctrines by the Mahayana schools, who of course regarded it as pertaining not to absolute but to relative truth, it has remained a permanent element in any curriculum of philosophical studies. Unlike the Theravadins, who upheld the Arahant ideal alone, the Sarvastivadins thought it possible for the disciple to aspire not only to Arahantship but also to Pratyeka and Samyak Sambuddhahood. They therefore regarded the scriptural account of the Bodhisattva's career as being not merely a description of the previous lives of the Buddha, as the Theravadins taught, but as also depicting a universally valid spiritual ideal. This doctrine, too, was incorporated by the Mahayanists, who after revealing its full significance placed it in the very forefront of their teaching.

Over one point, however, the Mahayanists and Sarvastivadins were in irreconcilable opposition. This was the famous doctrine of *sarvam asti,* or "everything exists," after which the great Hinayana school received its distinctive appellation. By this enigmatic proposition, which seemingly resulted from an attempt to give adequate philosophical consideration to the problem of time, the Sarvastivadins meant (though different sub-schools had their own interpretations) that the substance of the seventy-five *dharmas* recognized as ultimate by their school had a permanent existence throughout the three periods of time. Against this movement in the direction of psycho-physical atomism, which, as its opponents were quick to perceive, was in effect a repudiation of the fundamental Buddhist doctrine of universal unsubstantiality, a group within the Mahasanghika school entered an emphatic protest. Hence in the words of Dr. Nalinaksha Dutt,

> *We may say that the Mahayana is a continuation of the Buddhological speculations of the Mahāsāṅghikas and their offshoots, and a revolt against the Astitvavāda of the Sarvāstivādins—a dogma which appeared to the Mahayanists as an utter distortion of (the) Buddha's teachings.*[1]

The main stream of Buddhist tradition flows from the Sarvastivadins through the Mahasanghikas to the Mahayana schools. The Theravada may be regarded as a quiet but stagnant backwater.

The Mahasanghikas, as we saw, were the majority party at the time of the Council of Vaisali. Their outlook, scholars tell us, was more "liberal" and "progressive" than that of the Theravadins, though we may be sure that it was neither liberal nor progressive in the current sense of these terms. Like all other schools, both early and late, it was concerned to keep open the Way to Enlightenment; it differed from the Theravadins only in believing that the spirit of the Dharma could be best preserved by a readiness to modify, adapt, and supplement its external forms in accordance with changing social conditions and psychological needs. To accuse the Mahasanghikas of wanting to alter the Teaching is more than a dangerous over-simplification of an obscure sequence of historical events: it involves serious misunderstanding of the Doctrine. The Dharma is a Raft; the perpetuation of the Dharma means the perpetuation not of obsolete

---

[1] *Aspects,* p. 27.

secondary forms but of the principal Means to Enlightenment. Because they realized this the Mahasanghikas, and the Mahayanists after them, were in reality more faithful to the Buddha's Teaching, and therefore more truly traditional and conservative, than the Theravadins, for all their vaunted obsession with the letter of the Doctrine, ever succeeded in being. The Mahasanghikas disappeared from India only with the disappearance of Buddhism. Despite their "liberal" attitude, they were responsible for fewer doctrinal developments than might have been expected. The Lokottaravadins, their most important branch, taught what Western scholars in Buddhism generally regarded as a docetic theory of the Buddha's mundane personality, though the implied comparison with early Christian speculation cannot be sustained in detail. According to this school, the nature of the Buddhas is wholly transcendental; phenomena defile them not; they are capable of multiplying their bodies an infinite number of times, and their power and longevity are without limit; neither sleeping nor dreaming, they remain ever absorbed in *samādhi;* they comprehend all dharmas in a single moment of thought, and are continuously engaged in preaching the Doctrine. The Bodhisattva, which for the Lokottaravadins, no less than for the Theravadins, is simply the Buddha's designation during the time immediately preceding His Enlightenment, descends from the Tusita Heaven by an act of deliberate choice; with full consciousness he enters the womb, remains there for the period of gestation, and is born. We should not think that merely because the Buddhology of the Mahasanghikas is more aloof from current scientific and humanistic modes of thought than are the much more naturalistic Theravadin views on the same subject, that the former is thereby proved either less true or less likely to be the genuine teaching of the Buddha. There is no evidence that the traditions preserved by the Mahasanghikas were later or less reliable than those of the Theravadins. Apart from their general attitude towards the Dharma, their dissatisfaction with the Theravadin interpretation of Arahantship, and their contributions to Buddhology (which were afterwards incorporated by the Mahayana), there was little to distinguish the Mahasanghikas from their opponents of Theravada schools. The Mahasanghikas are, in fact, so important and significant chiefly because their school was the matrix of that profounder and more universal, and at the same time more deeply authentic and spiritually efficacious interpretation of Buddhism which called itself the Great Way, *Mahāyāna.* How and why the Mahayana arose, and what its teachings were, we shall see in Chapter II.

CHAPTER TWO

HINAYANA AND MAHAYANA

I. Is Buddhism One or Many?

THE distinction between individual and social is one which applies not only to man but to all human activities, including religion, each of which has, like man himself, a twofold aspect. Poetry, for instance, is simultaneously "expression" and "communication." Politics speaks of both rights and duties. Ethics is concerned not only with the significance of our actions for ourselves, but also with the way in which they affect the lives of other sentient beings. The first person clearly and adequately to distinguish between the two "faces" of religion was William James, to whom we owe the (from the viewpoint of Method very useful) distinction between what he terms "Personal Religion" and "Institutional Religion." So far as Buddhism is concerned, however, the distinction was already implicit in the twin terms *Dhamma-Vinaya,* or Doctrine and Discipline, comprehending the two main aspects of Early Buddhism. James's terms, being the products of generalizations about the nature of Christianity, a very different kind of tradition, do not, it is true, coincide very exactly with the Pali expressions. Neither are they so precise. But their very imprecision perhaps renders them all the more useful when attempting to characterize the various seemingly divergent movements and tendencies which, spanning five-and-twenty centuries, make up Buddhism in the widest and truest sense of the term.

Institutional religion is the form which a traditional teaching assumes in order to be able to act from the objective material order of things subjectively upon the hearts and minds of men. All the outward, organizational and social supports of the Doctrine, such as temples, monastic orders, vestments, canonical languages, sacred art and music, together with traditional customs and observances of every kind, are to be included under this aspect. So far as Buddhism is concerned, personal religion covers the study, understanding and practice of the teachings pertaining to Morality, Meditation and Wisdom.

As even the most superficially interested visitor cannot fail to observe, the Dharma assumed in every land in which it took root a distinct, unique and unmistakable national form and local coloration. The history of the stupa, as it evolves from its spheroid Indian original into the bell-shaped beauty of its Sinhalese type, the waisted *chortens* of Tibet, the almost Gothic perpendicularity of the graceful gilded Siamese *chedis,* the streamer-swathed *chaityas* of Nepal, each of their four sides alive with a pair of hypnotically staring eyes, the city-like formations of Java and Cambodia, and the many-storied pagodas of China and Japan, may be taken as an architectural illustration of the richness and diversity of the Dharma on the institutional side. Of India one does not speak: though later systems incorporated a number of its teachings, here Buddhism as an institutional religion no longer exists. Let us go southward to Ceylon, for centuries the stronghold of Theravada, and where even now are to be found the most intelligent and cultured exponents of this ancient school. The sky is an abyss of cloudless blue, and our eyes are almost blinded by the sunlight reflected from the dazzling white walls of squat, bungalow-like *vihāras,* each with red-tiled roofs and deep verandahs, and of the larger and grander temple buildings nearby: the *dagobas* are so white that they seem flat rather than round, shapes cut out of enormous sheets of white paper and pinned on to the landscape. Coconut palms are everywhere—in groves, in clumps and clusters, and singly. Their trunks are bent at angles of various degrees of acuteness towards the earth, and when silhouetted against the sky seem to be interlaced; their plumes sweep the ground; the green nuts are high up, hanging in clusters, and seem quite small until we see a tiny turbaned figure scramble up and start hurling them to the ground. It is still early morning. Slowly and quietly there comes along the road—so slowly and so quietly that at first there seems to be only a patch of colour in almost imperceptible motion—a figure draped in brilliant yellow with bowed and shaven head. He clasps in his two hands a large black bowl. His countenance is impassive. His eyes seem to be shut, for they are fixed upon the ground in front of him. With dignity and deliberation he moves from door to door, and is received with respectful salutations. Halting for a moment, he lifts the lid of the bowl to receive the alms of the faithful, who, from their reverential demeanour, evidently feel that they are indebted to him rather than he to them. More and more yellow figures as it were materialize on the scene, appearing in the alternate bars of brilliant sunshine and purple shadow lying along the dusty road like the silent unfolding of yellow flowers. They are not seen for long, though, and as the sun mounts and the shadows shorten no human figures are visible save a few Tamilian coolies whose blue-black bodies, glistening with sweat, stagger along under enormous loads. The rickshaw puller sleeps between the shafts of his vehicle in a scrap of shade. Earth and sky begin to vibrate with heat. Presently a haze flickers in front of the eyes, blurring the landscape, which now jumps and dances as though seen through a tongue of flame. . . . Perspiration . . . exhaustion . . . prostration . . . The click of the fan above the bed . . . then unconsciousness.

When we awake the land is steeped in deep, cool shadows. A light breeze brings unimaginable refreshment. The palm trees rustle above our heads, and looking up through the fronds we see that the unclouded sky is ablaze with stars. The tom-toms begin to throb from the temple nearby; the clarinets wail; the air, that had vibrated all day with the intensity of heat, now vibrates with the fury of sound. Already white figures are flitting through the shadows of the trees. Each one bears a tray on which is a heap of five-petalled temple flowers—ah! the incredible sweetness of their fragrance as it floats through the dusk—a few sticks of incense and a tiny lamp. Let us follow them to the temple. We shall bow down together at the feet of the Exalted One. Squeezing in, we find that the shrine is densely packed with white-clad worshippers, and the air oppressive with the fumes of thousands of brightly burning lamps of coconut oil. Progress is slow; the men and women are either silent or muttering prayers; there is no impatience, no pushing. Inch by inch, we move forward with the crowd; at last the pressure relaxes; we find ourselves standing with waist pressed against the edge of the great altar. Flowers are everywhere; the smell of the incense is overpoweringly sweet; thousands of candles splutter and burn. Lifting our eyes we see behind the altar, clad in robes of the same brilliant yellow, a dozen or so serene figures who smile benignly at the worshippers. Above and beyond them towers the brightly painted image of the Buddha, upon its face the smile of eternal peace. But our contemplation cannot last long. A gentle pressure from behind reminds us that it is time to give place to others, and before many minutes have passed we find ourselves outside in the cold night air. We stand beneath the palm trees watching the streams of worshippers passing through the temple gates. A line of elephants, gorgeously caparisoned and surrounded by troops of excitedly shouting boys, comes swaying through the darkness, their triumphal progress illuminated by flaring torches. Parties of strongly built male dancers, with black oil-bright bodies that reflect the ruddy glare of the torches and fantastic headdresses, pirouette on either side, their bare feet stamping upon the hard ground in time with the rhythm of the tom-toms. The tumult is deafening. But only for a few moments. As swiftly as it had come the procession disappears from sight. In an hour's time the last worshippers have left the temple and gone home. Silence reigns. But hour after hour, and even long after we have gone to bed, we can still hear the faint insistent beat of the tom-tom . . . *tom-tom . . . tom-tom. . . .*

Geographically speaking, the distance between Ceylon, the Theravada stronghold, and Tibet, the inmost citadel of Mahayana tradition, is only two thousand miles. But on the spiritual plane, at least so far as the institutional aspect of religion is concerned, the gulf dividing them is seemingly immeasurable. Crossing the snow-clad peaks of the Himalayas, the largest and the loftiest mountain barrier in existence, we find ourselves on the Roof of the World. An icy wind blows furiously, cutting through quilted garments and furs; lightly but steadily comes the snow, driven almost horizontally by the wind. Soon our eyes are sore with looking at the blinding whiteness of the earth and the pitilessly brilliant blueness of the sky. Every now and then the tempest shrieks suddenly past, giving mighty buffets as though it were a legion of devils seeking to send us rolling from our horses down the five-thousand-foot precipice yawning beneath our feet. We cling on tightly, gripping the horse's mane with numbed fists. At last we feel the animal between our knees slithering down the stony slopes of the mountain-side . . . our three-weeks-long journey to the Land of Religion is nearing its end. Painfully we open our gummed lids with the help of our fingers. Around us the unbroken circle of the horizon makes a sharp edge against the sky. We realize that we had never known before the meaning of space. Here and there are patches of light green colour; but no trees, hardly a shrub. Only a vast expanse of waving grass as smooth and flat as a billiard table, with what look like specks of stone but are really Tibetan homesteads, and the black dots of grazing yaks and nomad tents scattered over it at enormous intervals: they are so small that at first sight the landscape seems deserted.

As we ride forward, and as the days pass, what at first had seemed a slight corrugation of the horizon becomes a long low range of mountains blue-black in the far distance. Gradually, as we approach, they thrust themselves higher and higher into the sky, and eventually the central peak towers above our heads seemingly halfway up to heaven. Saddle-sore, we dismount at the foot of a flight of stairs hewn as though for the feet of a giant out of the rock. Slowly we ascend. Each turn of the path reveals a fresh flight and each flight contains thousands of steps. We dare not look down. At last, on the next ridge, only a few hundred feet above our heads, we see red and white striped walls and gilded roofs. Where the mountain ends and the monastery begins is difficult to say, though, for they are built of the same material and on the same colossal scale. The black mouth of an enormous door yawns before us. Stalwart figures are mounting guard on either side, their bulk prodigiously increased by swathings of maroon-coloured woollen cloth, their already exceptional stature heightened by yellow headgear shaped like the helmet of Achilles, and yet more terrible; in their hands are enormous staves studded with brass. As we approach their eyes narrow suspiciously in their grimy faces; but they say nothing, and we are allowed to pass. The iron door slams shut behind us; there is a rattling of chains. After a full half-minute has passed the sound is echoed as though from the very heart of the earth. Slowly we grope our way forward through the pitch darkness, tripping and stumbling over the uneven ground. We are aware of flittings to and fro on either side of us; suddenly a hand seizes hold of our arm, and we are pulled roughly along. A misty light shines forth; a door has opened. With the sudden lifting of a curtain the mist becomes a blaze and a deep roaring and groaning noise of trumpets, inexpressibly moving, that had been hitherto muffled by the thickness of the stone walls, blares mournfully in our ears.

We find ourselves in an enormous chamber. On the floor sit rows and rows of maroon-coloured figures: there must be thousands of them. From the ceiling hang huge cylinder-shaped Banners of Victory, every flounce of a different colour. Before each monk is a bowl of steaming tea; some are sipping, some adding their voices to the deep-throated rumbling chorus that the assembly sends rolling wave-like from one end of the long chamber to the other. Armed with a whip, a figure resembling those we saw at the main entrance strides up and down the central aisle. A few vertical shafts of misty sunshine, penetrating from some aperture above, illumine the faces of the celebrants, some of whom are obviously very old, others astonishingly youthful; but all, despite bent backs and rounded shoulders, are sturdily built and all are shaven-headed. In the far distance, ranked on a long narrow table running almost the entire width of the room, hundreds of golden butter-lamps are steadily burning. Behind them is the altar, whereon have been arranged various artistically moulded offerings. To the left, high above the heads of the worshippers, is a magnificently carved, painted and gilded throne. In front of this, a white silken scarf in our hands, we now find ourselves. Cross-legged upon its brocade cushions sits an old man, magnificently clad in garments of dark red silk. The smile with which he looks down at us as we make our obeisance is not of this earth; it is the smile of Enlightenment. Far more brightly than any ray of earthly sunshine it penetrates our heart. Within his small, twinkling eyes all knowledge seems to dwell, and we are aware that not even our most secret thoughts are hidden from him; yet we do not feel afraid.

When, a few minutes later, we stand in front of the main altar, it is the same smile which, as though from the moon itself, calmly and tenderly shines from the central face of the eleven-headed white image behind the glass doors of the tabernacle. A thousand arms, each ending in a hand which either bears an emblem or makes with tapering fingers a graceful symbolical gesture, radiate from its shoulders like spokes from the hub of a wheel. We are face to face with Universal Compassion.

Five minutes later we are face to face with Death. After being hurried through dimly lit corridors, the noise behind us receding farther and farther into the distance, we are ushered into a small black hole. A single lamp is burning. Fearfully, as though in unwilling obedience to a command, a monk lifts the heavy curtain of iron rings that hangs before the inmost shrine. Involuntarily we recoil from the sight. The figure that stares down upon us with bulging eyeballs is full of menace. His huge, powerful body, deep blue in colour, is festooned with garlands of skulls. His four arms are raised threateningly, and his hands grasp various weapons. One brawny knee is uplifted as he tramples upon the enemies of the Dharma. His face is that of a horned beast, and his red tongue lolls out from between his rows of gleaming fangs as though thirsty for blood. Round his waist is a tiger-skin. Clinging to his bosom, her slender arms clasped tightly round his bull-neck, her legs wrapped round his thighs, and her mouth strained passionately to his, is the small white figure of his consort. They are locked in sexual embrace. Round them roars a halo of flames. Terrible but strangely fascinating, vibrant with power incalculable, are the Father and the Mother, the transcendental Pair whose union symbolizes the inseparability of Wisdom and Compassion, of Doctrine and Method—or, returning to the much more limited point of view wherefrom we started—the metaphysical unity of the institutional and personal aspects of religion—as they tower in all their preternatural vigour before us until, with a ringing clash, the curtain falls, and we are left with the smoky lamp throwing against the ceiling the fantastic shadows of the huge stuffed animal carcases suspended there.

Two strikingly dissimilar pictures indeed! Could a greater contrast be imagined, the reader may wonder, than that between the Buddhism of Ceylon and the Buddhism of Tibet? For, though we may freely own up to a deliberate heightening of colour, a calculated distribution of lights and shades, the diptych we have painted is nevertheless a faithful illustration of the differences prevailing at the institutional level between the various distinct and mutually independent branches of Buddhist tradition. No wonder, then, that those who have been born or brought up within an environment dominated, from the religious point of view, by any one form of institutional Buddhism, to the exclusion of the rest, should find it difficult to avoid falling into the pitfall of thinking that the form with which they have been familiar since childhood is the one true form, while less familiar forms are false. Most superficial observers, in fact, tumble headlong in, roundly declaring (rather like the Master of Balliol College in the limerick) that what they do not know about Buddhism is simply not Buddhism at all, or, as in their saner moments they sometimes admit, is merely a corrupt, degenerate and perverted form of Buddhism. Like the objects of Bacon's reprehension, whose—according to him—superficial understanding of the laws of nature inclined them to atheism, even serious students who succeed in penetrating a little deeper, though still not deep enough, through the institutional supports and symbols of the Dharma to the intellectual formulations whence they derive their significance and their utility, find not a resolution but an intensification of the discords that seem to dominate Buddhism at the institutional level. A little learning is not merely dangerous; it is even more dangerous than complete ignorance. The common man, aware of external differences only, may indulge the charitable hope that the Colonels' ladies and the Judy O'Gradys of religion are all sisters under their institutional skins. Such charitableness seldom troubles the more scholarly student. With an extensive, though not profound, understanding of the tenets of his own school and an inadequate and frequently erroneous knowledge of the tenets of other schools for his premises, he does not find much difficulty in arriving triumphantly at the conclusion that as regards both Doctrine and Method the teaching of the school he honours with his allegiance is alone the genuine article and that the teachings of other schools are the shoddy and worthless imitations with which impostors have flooded the credulous markets of less favoured parts of the nominally Buddhist world.

Yet the poor well-frog, imprisoned within his own school, is not altogether to be blamed for his inability to realize that the mighty ocean of the Dharma cannot be measured by the yardstick of his little well. We can even excuse him for losing his temper and kicking out that well-meaning intruder the ocean-frog, who comes with tall stories about a body of water many times bigger than any that he, the well-frog, had ever seen! For although, as we insisted in the concluding section of Chapter I, there does exist a Basic Buddhism which is the common foundation of all schools, the doctrines by which one line of tradition is distinguished from another are almost always placed, by those belonging to that line, at the very centre of their picture of Buddhism, and receive the high light, while the remainder, their shapes hardly discernible in the gloom, are distributed towards the circumference, some in fact being cut in half owing to the necessity of having a frame. It is hardly astonishing, therefore, that even a conscientiously impartial student of the Buddhist schools should discover, more often than not, mutual opposition and contradiction rather than agreement and harmony. Differences regarding doctrine, no less than a variety of institutions, do exist: the fact cannot be ignored; and of those who become aware of them without having transcended the intellectual standpoint what can we expect but a violent reaction towards an even more bigoted belief in the exclusive truth and authenticity of the traditions of their own school?

Modern Theravadins, insisting that progress upon the path depends solely upon one's own efforts, wax eloquent over the fact that every man is his own saviour, that we ourselves are the architects of our fortunes, the captains of our souls and the masters of our fates, and that heavens and hells are the creations of our own good and evil deeds. The Buddha is simply a guide pointing out to us the path, which, whether we like it or not, we must perforce tread with our own two feet. He is like a schoolmaster (a comparison for which several exponents of this school exhibit a special fondness) who can explain to us a difficult algebraical problem on the blackboard but who cannot, unfortunately, give us the intelligence with which to do our own sums. One of their favourite texts is *Dhammapada* Verse 165, which says:—

> *Evil is done by self alone, by self alone is one stained; by self alone is evil left undone, by self alone is one purified. Purity and impurity depend on one's own self. No man can purify another.*

This individualistic doctrine the Jodo Shin school repudiates as dire heresy. Emancipation, it believes, depends not on our own efforts but entirely upon the grace of Amitabha Buddha; attempting to save ourselves is as ridiculous as trying to hoist ourselves up into the air by tugging at our own bootlaces. Good deeds, far from being of any help, only intensify the feeling of individual selfhood, thus obstructing the operation of the saving grace or "other power" of Amitabha. Hence the paradoxical saying, no less popular with Jodo Shin followers than the *Dhammapada* verse is with Theravadins, "Even the good man will be saved. How much more so the evil man!" Instead of striving to win Enlightenment in this world and in this life by means of our own unaided efforts, we should, with a heart full of love and faith, simply invoke the name of Amitabha and pray to be reborn in Sukhāvatī, the Land of Bliss He has established in the West.

No less extreme is the difference which exists between certain Tantric schools, on the one hand, and the non-Tantric schools on the other, regarding the importance of Morality. Though both parties agree in recognizing the instrumental function and relative value of ethical observances, the recognition is accorded from positions so wide apart as in effect to amount to a radical divergence of views. To the non-Tantric schools, the fact that Morality is a means to Enlightenment adds to, rather than detracts from, its importance; for in the absence of the proper means, the desired goal becomes impossible of attainment. Morality is not only the means, but the indispensable means to Enlightenment; hence it is an absolute value. Some of these schools therefore strive for a rigid observance not only of the major precepts of morality but even of the minor monastic obligations which, though many of them are in reality without ethical significance, are all comprehended in the traditional Buddhist conception of Morality. Against this view, which can so easily harden into a petrified ethical formalism, the followers of various Tantric schools contend that the fact of Morality being only a means to an end instead of proving its absoluteness demonstrates its relativity. The sole absolute value is Compassion; even Wisdom is only a means for the realization of that supreme end. However indispensable at the time of sickness, medicines may be emptied down the drain when we are restored to health; the Perfected Ones, having by means of ethical observances attained full Enlightenment, thereafter have personally no further use for them, and henceforth may act according to circumstances either in an "ethical" or in an "unethical" manner. Their sole concern is with the welfare of all sentient beings, for the sake of which they are prepared to sacrifice every other consideration. If by their merely apparent violation of the ethical precepts they can assist in his progress along the path a single pilgrim soul they do not shrink from committing what, in the case of an unenlightened person, would be a deadly sin, even though they thereby forfeit their own reputation for sanctity (one of the subtlest fetters, this) and incur the disapprobation of society. The biography of more than one Tantric teacher is replete with episodes in which he deprives animals and even human beings of life, appropriates to his own use the property of others, freely indulges in sexual intercourse, tells lies, and partakes of strong drink to the point of inebriation. We appear far indeed from the sobriety and restraint, the almost pathetic eagerness to "keep up appearances" in the eyes of the world, even though not always in the mirror of one's own conscience, which characterizes the followers of other schools! Where even the major ethical precepts are treated with so little ceremony, the minor monastic obligations, indeed the very idea not only of monasticism but of any formally religious life at all, can expect nothing but a rude dismissal. All pretences to respectability are abandoned; dignity, decorum and even ordinary decency, are flung to the winds. In place of the noble bearing and refined manners of the true monk we see the reckless demeanour and hirsute behaviour of the outcastes of society. Among non-Tantric schools, the appearance of saintliness is easily achieved even by those who are in reality farthest from saintliness; in some Tantric schools, however, the opposite is the case: the saintliest appear as the least saintly. It is not difficult to see that the doctrine of ethical relativism is fraught with grave dangers; the frailty of human nature is only too willing to believe that since the Perfected Ones may, upon occasion, act "unethically," one who acts unethically is a Perfected One, and that the easiest and the quickest way of gaining Enlightenment is by breaking, one after another, all the moral laws. In the Tantric schools, too, may be found those who follow the letter rather than the spirit of tradition. Whatever our own attitude towards ethical relativism may be, the fact is that in the extreme form which we have described it the doctrine is far from being upheld by all Tantric schools, the majority of which are as exacting in their ethical demands as any of the schools belonging to the non-Tantric group.

Differences of this kind are by no means rare in Buddhism;

the two somewhat extreme cases we have described, far from being exceptional, are only illustrative of a hundred divergencies of opinion on doctrinal issues—some of them of fundamental importance. Ere long the student of the Dharma discovers, rather to his amazement, that whereas the dharmas are for one school realities, for another they are merely words; on the one hand he is exhorted to work out his own salvation with diligence, on the other to dedicate his life to the emancipation of all sentient beings; for *this* school the Buddha is merely a man who attained Enlightenment, while for *that* He is the wholly transcendental and eternally enlightened Reality Itself in human form; one party tells us that Meditation and Wisdom are inseparable, and that with the attainment of the former the latter is attained automatically, but this view the opposite party denies, saying that Meditation is not necessarily associated with Wisdom; *here* we see vegetarianism upheld, *there* meat-eating permitted; one school defines Reality as absolute consciousness, another as complete emptiness; in some teachings Nirvana and Samsara are identical, in others an irreducible duality; on one side we see a celibate monastic order, on the other an association of married priests. And so on. The catalogue is without end.

Divergencies in both institutional religion and personal religion being so numerous, and in many cases so radical, are we justified in speaking of Buddhism at all? Or are we not rather concerned with a number of practically independent religious movements, all more or less nominally Buddhist? Is Buddhism one or many? Obviously, there is no external uniformity. There is not always even unity of Doctrine. What, then, constitutes the fundamental ground of unity in Buddhism?

II. The Transcendental Unity of Buddhism: The Dharma as Means

The unity of Buddhism consists in the fact that, through differences and divergencies of doctrine innumerable, all schools of Buddhism aim at Enlightenment, at reproducing the spiritual experience of the Buddha. The Dharma is therefore to be defined, not so much in terms of this or that particular teaching, but rather as the sum total of the means whereby that experience may be attained. Hence it can even be considered as being in principle and function, though not always in institutional form and specific intellectual content, as identical for all schools of Buddhism. The Pali Scriptures represent the Buddha as emphasizing the instrumental character and relative value of the Dharma by means of a striking parable.

"Using the figure of a raft, brethren, will I teach you the Dhamma, as something to leave behind, not to take with you. Do you listen to it. Apply your minds. I will speak."

"Even so, Lord," replied those brethren to the Exalted One.

The Exalted One said: "Just as a man, brethren, who has started on a long journey sees before him a great stretch of water, on this side full of doubts and fears, on the further side safe and free from fears: but there is no boat to cross in, no causeway for passing over from this side to the other side. Then he thinks thus: 'Here is a great stretch of water . . . but there is no boat. . . . How now if I were to gather together grass, sticks, branches, and leaves, bind them into a raft, and resting on that raft paddle with hands and feet and so come safe to the further shore?'

"Then, brethren, that man gathers together sticks . . . and comes to the further shore. When he has crossed over and come to the other side he thinks thus: 'This raft has been of great use to me. Resting on this raft and paddling with hands and feet I have come to the further shore. Suppose now I were to set this raft on my head or lift it on to my shoulders and go my way?'

"Now what think ye, brethren? Would that man in so doing have finished with that raft?"

"Surely not, Lord!"

"Doing what then, brethren, would that man have finished with that raft? Herein, brethren, that man who has crossed and gone to the further shore should think thus: 'This raft has been of great use to me. Resting on it I have crossed to the further shore. Suppose now I haul up this raft on the shore, or sink it in the water and go my way!' By so doing, brethren, that man would have finished with that raft.

"Even so, brethren, using the figure of a raft have I shown you the Dhamma, as something to leave behind, not to take with you. Thus, brethren, understanding the figure of the raft, ye must leave righteous ways behind, not to speak of unrighteous ways."

(Majjhima-Nikāya, *I. 134. Woodward's translation)*[1]

That the teaching of the Enlightened One, far from being an end in itself, is only a means to an end, could hardly have been made clearer than this. One therefore would not have expected to find, in certain Buddhist lands, quite so many people busily engaged in carrying hither and thither upon their heads on *this* shore the very Raft which, according to the Buddha, should be

---

[1] *Some Sayings of the Buddha,* pp. 316-17.

abandoned even after crossing over to the Other Shore.

From the fact that the Dharma is, as the Buddha explicitly declares in the above-quoted passage, essentially that which conduces to the attainment of Enlightenment, it necessarily follows that whatever conduces to the attainment of Enlightenment is the Dharma. Another Pali text cited in Chapter I may be repeated here as it in fact represents the Buddha as drawing this very conclusion. To Mahā-Pajāpati, the Gotamid, the Master says:—

> *"Of whatsoever teachings, Gotamid, thou canst assure thyself thus: 'These doctrines conduce to passions, not to dispassion; to bondage, not to detachment; to increase of (worldly) gains, not to decrease of them; to covetousness, not to frugality; to discontent, and not to content; to company, not to solitude; to sluggishness, not to energy; to delight in evil, not delight in good': of such teachings, Gotamid, thou mayest with certainty affirm 'This is not the Dhamma. This is not the Vinaya. This is not the Master's Message.'*
>
> *"But of whatsoever teachings thou canst assure thyself (that they are the opposite of these things that I have told you)—of such teachings thou mayest with certainty affirm: 'This is the Dhamma. This is the Vinaya. This is the Master's Message.' "*
>
> (Vinaya, *II. 10. Woodward's translation*)[1]

The criterion of what is or what is not Buddhism is ultimately pragmatic. The question with which we concluded the last section is to be settled, in the last resort, not by an appeal to logic but by an appeal to spiritual life.

This does not mean the setting up of mere subjective feeling as our criterion. All those who are enlightened think that they are enlightened—of course not in an egoistic sense; but not all those who think that they are enlightened are so in reality. Our spiritual experience must be in accordance with the spirit of the Scriptures, and, what is more necessary still, its authenticity must be attested by one whose own enlightenment has been the object of similar attestation. Ultimately, this chain of pupillary succession is stapled onto the rock of the Buddha's own Enlightenment, which is at once the support and the criterion of all succeeding attainments. Personal experience, or the realization of the individual Buddhist, will, if genuine, be in line with tradition, not, indeed, with—or not necessarily with—tradition in the merely bookish sense of the term, the authority of which the Buddha in fact repudiated, but rather with tradition in the sense

---

[1] *Ibid.*, pp. 278-79.

of that unbroken succession of enlightened beings upon whose existence the very life of the Dharma depends, and who, as torches that are lit from torches in a midnight marathon, alone illumine the darkness of the ages.

These doctrines and methods which do not have for their ultimate object Enlightenment in the specifically Buddhist sense of the term cannot be regarded as belonging to the Buddhist tradition. Conversely, those teachings are to be accepted as Buddhist which, regardless of whether they were originally given out by the Master Himself or by His enlightened disciples, both immediate and remote, are in practice found to be conducive to the realization of that very Sambodhi which He attained beneath the Bodhi Tree at Gayā. The sole test of the genuineness of any school of Buddhism is its capacity to produce enlightened beings. Whether we are making a study of the institutional and personal aspects of the Dharma as they are found in Ceylon or as they are found in Tibet, or whether we are attempting to arrive at a true evaluation of the Doctrines and Methods of the Tantric schools or of the Jodo Shin Shu, the orthodoxy and authenticity of this or that line of the Buddhist tradition is to be judged not in accordance with the alleged antiquity of its literature, nor by means of any other criterion of a merely external and historical nature, but solely in accordance with its present poverty or richness in respect of transcendental attainments. The Buddha-Dharma, far from being confined to any one body of sacred texts, however ancient, or limited to any one set of traditional observances, dating from however early a period, "in its full breadth, width, majesty and grandeur comprises," as Dr. Conze so well says, "all those teachings which are linked to the original teaching by historical continuity, and which work out methods leading to the extinction of individuality by eliminating the belief in it."[1] That schools which for one reason or other have lost faith in the possibility of attaining to realizations of the transcendental order should venture to impugn the orthodoxy of schools whose faith is still green is therefore one of the greatest paradoxes of the whole course of Buddhist history.

Such minor, and in any case comparatively modern, deviations

[1] *Buddhism: Its Essence and Development,* p. 28.

from genuine orthodoxy apart, however, Buddhists of all schools, taking to heart the Buddha's admonition, have applied their minds to the understanding and practice of the teaching contained in the Parable of the Raft. So much so, indeed, that still more beautiful variants for it have been produced, among them the well-known Japanese Buddhist simile of a finger that points out the moon. To look at the finger, representing the Dharma, instead of gazing at the moon, which stands for Enlightenment, is no less foolish than carrying the raft about on one's own shoulders, and for no other reason. The doctrine which both parable and simile are designed to illustrate is, in fact, vitally important in Buddhism, being one of the factors responsible not only for the rich efflorescence of schools and teachings which marked all spiritually active periods but also for the extraordinary mutual tolerance by which their relations with one another were distinguished. Unlike the followers of certain non-Buddhist religious traditions, the spiritual heirs of the Enlightened One have as a whole clearly understood that not only the various observances comprising Morality, not only the different practices which constitute Meditation, but even the whole of those doctrinal formulations which are—not indeed Wisdom itself but—the conceptual indications of Wisdom, possess not an absolute but only a relative and instrumental value. This understanding is a direct consequence of the realization that, as we saw in Chapter I, Section VIII, Nirvana is ineffable, being equally beyond the reach of positive and negative predications, or even of no predication at all. Far from detracting from the value of right doctrine, or abrogating the need for it, much less still blurring in any way the distinction which at the intellectual level undoubtedly does exist between right doctrine and wrong, the way in which what may be termed the instrumental attitude insists upon the remoteness of the Goal only serves to emphasize the necessity of having a Raft and of its being constructed of the right materials. True doctrine is only relatively true, and false doctrine only relatively false, but the former must be upheld against the latter because, as Nāgārjuna says, the relative truth is the means to the realization of the Absolute Truth. Right doctrine indicates Reality though it is powerless to describe it, but wrong doctrine can neither indicate it nor describe it.

All Buddhist schools, whether of the Mahayana or of the Hinayana, were concerned not with the theoretical determination of truth as an end in itself, but with its practical realization in life. What divided them, therefore, was not differences of opinion over what was true and what untrue in the scientific, descriptive sense of that term—for all agreed that truth being indescribable was a matter for personal experience—but differences regarding which doctrines, as well as which ethical observances and which meditational techniques, could in practice function as the means for the attainment of Enlightenment. Whether they were aware of what was happening or not, it was due to the conjunction of their understanding of the relativity of the Dharma with a compassionate desire to share the experience of Enlightenment with as many sentient beings as possible, that led to the springing up within the rapidly widening field of Buddhism of those rich crops of "methods leading to the extinction of individuality by eliminating the belief in it" in which every school, but especially the schools of the Mahayana, were so astonishingly fertile. As might have been anticipated by anyone familiar with the forty classical supports of concentration enumerated, and to some extent described, in Section XVII of the preceding Chapter, it was within the sphere of Meditation that such productivity was most marked. As we then observed, the supports of concentration are potentially infinite; consequently, as the teachers of meditation were not slow in realizing, the possibilities of adding to the number of traditionally sanctioned aids to mental one-pointedness are without limit. The *sādhana* class of literature is an example. A *sādhana* is a text describing the shape, colour, insignia, attributes, etc., of a Buddha, a Bodhisattva, a Guardian Deity, or of a member of one of the various other classes of divine beings, for the purpose of visualizing them in meditation. Directions of a general nature, as well as doctrinal teachings, are often given. In Tibetan alone, both inside and outside the three hundred and odd volumes of the Sacred Canon, there must be several thousand of these texts, some indigenous; probably even the most learned *geshe* could not say exactly how many there are. All are applications, in accordance with the diverse needs of devotees of many different temperaments and character-types, of one unchanging central principle: the principle that concentration, without which Wisdom cannot be attained, consists in the undistracted wholesome fixation of the mind on a single object. Developments within the sphere of Morality were much less spectacular. Again as might have been anticipated, they pertained more to details of casuistry than to ethical principles. The Theravadins, for instance, discovered that it would be wrong for a monk to pull his mother out of a pit by the hand, should she be so unfortunate as to fall into one, as that would be a violation of the monastic obligation to refrain from physical contact with women. Certain Mahayanists, on the other hand, started teaching that monks might possess wealth and property, even gold, silver and silken clothes, as such possessions would allow them to be more useful to others and to help them.[1] Generally speaking, the Hinayanists were interested more in the personal, the Mahayanists more in the social, side of ethics. The contrast is, however, far from being absolute, for the Mahayana conception of Morality was on the whole remarkably balanced and harmonious, being based on a well-nigh perfect correspondence between the self-regarding and other-regarding aspects of the moral life. Doctrinal developments—developments within the sphere of Wisdom—while naturally much less numerous than those in Meditation, were considerably in excess of what took place within the domain of Morality. Statistics are, however, not the best instrument for gauging the influence or plumbing the depth and significance of teachings pertaining to the transcendental order. The quite extensive doctrinal developments which occurred not only in India but also in Japan, and to some extent in China too, took place partly by way of an attempt to push to their ultimate logical conclusion the teachings attributed to the Buddha, many of which were suggestive rather than exhaustive in nature, partly because of the need for building up for the Doctrine a systematic rational basis from which the tenets of Buddhism could be defended and the theories of non-Buddhist schools attacked. The fact that the two forks of a road have branched off at the same spot does not prevent them, after they have proceeded almost parallel with each other for a mile or two, from ultimately diverging in opposite directions. Similarly, given the same doctrine, it is possible for different persons to arrive, in the end, at conclusions which to the intellect appear

[1] *Ibid.*, p. 57.

contradictory. Shin and Zen, the two principal schools of present-day Japanese Buddhism, have with the same Indo-Chinese Mahayana tradition as their foundation succeeded in erecting thereon doctrinal superstructures between which there is no more resemblance than between a classical frieze and a baroque altar. The former, as we have already noted, believes that emancipation consists in a wholehearted surrender to the "other power," in an unconditional faith in and dependence on the saving grace of Amitabha, while the latter maintains that it can be won only by means of a complete reliance on "self-power," on the unaided and unsupported efforts of the individual devotee.

Contradictions of this kind should not dismay us. Realities of the transcendental order are no more susceptible of fully adequate intellectual formulation as doctrine than a three-dimensional body can, without distortion, be represented on a two-dimensional surface. Do not Australia and South America look, in Mercator's projection of the globe, as though they were situated at opposite ends of the earth? A flat-lander, ignorant of the existence of a third dimension, would probably conclude that the nearer one went to the Antarctic, the further he would be going from South America. In one sense, indeed, his conclusion would be true, though it would not be the whole truth; for the addition of a third dimension does not contradict the other two so much as deepen their significance. It is quite possible that doctrines which, like the "other-power" teaching of Shin and the "self-power" teaching of Zen, on the intellectual plane are in complete mutual opposition, should both be the means of attaining to that supra-rational, purely transcendental "experience" known as Enlightenment. Like all other Buddhist traditions, both schools do in fact propose Enlightenment, in the sense of Supreme Buddahood, as the final goal of the religious life, a circumstance which should be in itself sufficiently arresting to make us pause and reflect before jumping from premises merely intellectual to sweeping conclusions on the subject of which schools are to be regarded as genuinely Buddhist and which are not. The Dharma is essentially the means to Enlightenment and, intellectual difficulties notwithstanding, schools which have transmitted the experience of Enlightenment must be assumed to have transmitted the Dharma too. We should have the courage not of our intellectual convictions but of our transcendental realizations. The doctrinal differences existing between the various schools of Buddhism ought to delight rather than dismay us, for we are thereby stung into keener awareness of the limitations of the intellect, startled into livelier recognition of the purely instrumental nature of the Dharma, and at last awakened into a clearer comprehension of the great truth that, as Buddha Himself said repeatedly, Nirvana is *attakkavācara,* beyond the reach of reasoning.

Accordingly, we find the *Prajñāpāramitā* literature rejecting Formal Logic and revelling in a mystifying and bewildering "logic of contradictions" which, to a mind suckled at the breast of Dame Syllogism, and nicely brought up on Barbara, Celarent and Darii, will seem like the nightmare ravings of a lunatic logician. The Law of Identity states that A is A; the Law of Contradiction, that A cannot be both B and not-B; and the Law of Excluded Middle, that a thing must be either B or not-B; but the *Prajñāpāramitā,* the texts relating to Perfect Wisdom, declare: "Beings, beings, O Subhuti, as no-beings have they been taught by the Tathāgata. Therefore they are called 'beings.' "[1] Symbolically, A is B because it is not B. In the dimension of Emptiness, wherein the Bodhisattva courses with a coursing that is a non-coursing, and wherein he cognizes that Truth by means of a cognition that is a non-cognition, contradictory terms are identical. So long as the mind oscillates between contradictory statements, trying to determine which of them is true and which false, the aspirant remains immured within the mundane; but no sooner does he embark upon a bold identification of opposites than, by-passing the intellect, he disappears from the phenomenal plane and reappears in the Transcendental, in the domain and dimension of Emptiness.

On the same principle on which it is possible for both the Shin and Zen teachings to be genuine Buddhism, it should be possible for an individual Buddhist to be simultaneously a follower of both schools, to rely on the "other power" at the very moment that he relies on the "self-power"—not, indeed, by way of some painfully laborious process of intellectual syncretism, but by means of an experience transcending the plane of dualistic thought-construction. Out of its profound realization of this

[1] *Selected Sayings from the Perfection of Wisdom,* pp. 101-2.

truth Zen Buddhism teaches that one should rise above the limitations of the intellect by means of a deliberate cultivation of "contradictory" attitudes. The unremitting struggle to resolve at the intellectual level a contradiction which at that level cannot possibly be resolved, produces a certain psychological tension which, being stepped up by degrees, finally results in a shattering explosion: we find that the walls are all down, and we have only to step over the debris in order to be able to move about freely in the realm of the Transcendental. One of the Zen sub-schools goes so far as to regard meditation on problems or situations embodying an insoluble contradiction as the main spiritual exercise. Of these problems, technically known as *koan,* there are said to be several thousands—further evidence of the astonishing richness of Buddhism in the field of Meditation. Dr. Suzuki's writings have been the means of familiarizing English-knowing students not only with this type of support for the development of insight, but also with many other Zen practices, all of which have, as the reader now need hardly be reminded, the attainment of Enlightenment as their ultimate objective. The *koan* of the goose in the bottle is a well-known example. A goose, confined in a bottle when it was quite young, has grown so big that it is now quite impossible for it to squeeze through the neck. How is it to be set at liberty without breaking the glass? The symbolical nature of the *koan* will be apparent even to the rational mind, though we should be going far astray indeed if we thought that the ultimate meaning of the symbolism was therefore within the reach of reason. Other examples are still more elusive. What is the sound made by the clapping of one hand? Such are the seemingly nonsensical problems upon which the Zen disciple meditates. Readers in search of fuller information on the subject are referred to the works of Dr. Suzuki, who writes with equal charm and brilliance—and at equal length—on the ineffability of Zen and on the complete uselessness of attempting either to speak or to write about that ineffability. Once again it is a case of a finger pointing to the moon.

Unless he has succeeded in grasping the principle which we have endeavoured to set forth in the present section, the principle of the transcendental unity of all schools of Buddhism, the reader will feel only bewilderment when, in Section III, he is at last confronted by that greatest of all *koans,* the difference, amounting at times to unmitigated contradiction, between the Hinayana and the Mahayana.

III. Hinayana and Mahayana: The Three Vehicles

By the Hinayana is meant that form of Buddhism which prevails in Ceylon, Burma, Siam, Cambodia and Laos, the literary basis of which is the texts of the Pali Canon. Its popularization in the West through the writings of several generations of Orientalists notwithstanding, the term Hinayana remains in general unacceptable to the followers of this school, many of whom nowadays prefer to describe themselves as belonging to the Theravada, or School of Elders. As we saw at the conclusion of Chapter I, the more conservative wing of the Sangha divided, in the course of the century following the decisive break which took place at, or in connection with, the Second Council, the Council of Vaisali, into a number of schools, one of which was the Theravada. Whether the form of Buddhism now prevailing in Ceylon, Burma and the rest of the so-called Theravadin domains is in fact the descendant of this ancient school is far from being as self-evident as the people of these countries believe. From the tenor of its teaching, however, we may at least infer with certainty that it is descended from one of the Hinayana schools, as the sole survivor of which there is some justification for our continuing the usage of applying to it the designation originally covering the whole group. By the Mahayana is meant the form of Buddhism flourishing in Nepal, Tibet, Mongolia, China, Japan, Korea and parts of Central Asia, its literary basis being the voluminous texts of the Chinese and Tibetan Sacred Canons, the bulk of which are translations from Sanskrit originals in nine cases out of ten no longer extant. The complete Mongolian version of the Tibetan Canon and the Japanese version of the Chinese Canon, in all of which additional strata of indigenous material have been deposited, are of secondary importance. Historically, the schools and sub-schools of the Mahayana, numbering in all probability nearly a hundred distinct branches of the parent trunk, are the spiritual descendants of the Mahasanghikas or Great Assemblists, representing the more progressive wing of the Sangha at the time of the Council of Vaisali. Despite the fact that certain scholars, misled by a merely intellectual criterion, have on the grounds that there is little distinctively Mahayana in their doctrines insisted on classifying the Mahasanghikas and their offshoots as Hinayanists, we prefer to follow the Mahayana tradition which, applying the criterion not of doctrinal identity but of continuity of spiritual life, has ever regarded them as Mahayanists. Which procedure is more in accordance with the principle laid down in the last section, and hence more genuinely Buddhist, the reader may decide for himself. At any rate, none can gainsay the fact that the Mahasanghikas and their immediate offshoots no longer exist as an independent body because that small residue of distinctive doctrine which, surviving the most vigorous shakings of the scientific sieve, still remains to their credit, was taken up and developed not by any of the admittedly Hinayana schools but exclusively by schools belonging to the Mahayana. What these schools were, and what they taught—and still teach, for unlike the Hinayana schools they have not yet fallen into the sere and yellow leaf—we shall see in Chapter III. In the present chapter our concern is, firstly, with the general nature of the Hinayana-Mahayana conflict—for on the intellectual level a conflict undoubtedly it was and still is—disregarding whatever complications might have been introduced by the peculiarities of this or that individual school, whether Hinayanist or Mahayanist; secondly, with what we may call Basic Mahayana, or the tenets which are common to all Mahayana schools in the same way that the doctrines and methods described in Chapter I, comprising what we there termed Basic Buddhism, are common to all Buddhist schools without exception.

While the term Mahayana means, literally, the Great Way, or Superior Vehicle, the literal meaning of Hinayana is the Small Way, or Inferior Vehicle. From the nature of the distinction involved in this nomenclature, a number of less invidious alternatives to which occur in the Sanskrit texts, one easily infers not only that it originated with the Mahayanists but that it was intended to characterize a difference felt to be acute. The word *yāna,* though in all probability never used in its later, technical sense by the Buddha Himself, was familiar to all schools of Early Buddhism, all of which recognized the existence of three *yānas*: *Śrāvakayāna, Pratyekabuddhayāna* and *Bodhisattvayāna,* meaning the Path, Vehicle or Career—this last perhaps being the most satisfactory English equivalent—of the Disciple, of the "Private" Buddha, and of the Bodhisattva. References to these three classes of aspirants, and to their respective "vehicles" (as, in anticipation of an important parable, we shall generally render the term) occur very frequently in almost all Mahayana scriptures, commentaries and expository works. By the Sravaka (Pali *Sāvaka*, "Hearer") or Disciple is signified one who attains any of the four stages of Holiness, up to and including Arahantship, only after having "heard," that is to say learned, about the Transcendental Path from a Buddha or from a Buddha's disciple. The Pratyekabuddha (Pali *Paccekabuddha*) on the contrary attains Arahantship in complete independence of all external supports; living not only without a teacher but without a pupil, he makes no attempt to share with others his self-acquired knowledge of the Path to Nirvana. He is therefore fittingly termed an "Individual," "Private," "Solitary" or "Silent" Buddha. A Bodhisattva (Pali *Bodhisatta*) is one bent on attaining Supreme Enlightenment (the literal meaning of the term) not merely for his own sake but for the sake of all sentient beings. His career lasts for hundreds of thousands of births, in every one of which he prepares himself for his great achievement by the practice of the Six Perfections on a heroic scale. In his last human birth he attains Enlightenment in the same way as the Pratyekabuddha, without the guidance of a teacher, but instead of enjoying "the sweet but selfish rest of quiet wilds" He rises from His seat at the foot of the Bodhi Tree and goes forth as the Teacher of Gods and Men. Since the *Bodhisattvayāna* has for its goal the attainment of Supreme Buddahood it is also known as the *Buddhayāna* or *Tathāgatayāna*. According to the Pali Scriptures the Buddha recognized no essential difference between His own Insight and that of His disciples; the only difference was the accidental one of relative priority and posteriority of attainment; references to Paccekabuddhahood are rare. In the eyes of the early Buddhist schools, however, the difference loomed much larger, and Arahantship, Pratyekabuddhahood, and (Supreme) Buddhahood gradually assumed the character of three distinct and mutually independent spiritual ideals. Once they had been thus discriminated, a corresponding difference of opinion as to which of the three should be followed at once arose. The Theravadins, on the grounds that the *Bodhisattvayāna* was not a universally valid ideal but only a description of the Path followed by Tathāgatas, whose appearance in the universe was a miraculously rare event, maintained that the Buddha had taught only the Path to Arahantship and that with the exception of the infinitesimal minority bound for Supreme Enlightenment all Buddhists should tread this Path and this Path alone. To the Sarvastivadins, however, all three ideals are equally valid; some Buddhists follow one, some another, and the difference of paths is due to a difference of temperaments. In their efforts to explain the nature of this difference of temperaments and why it should exist, the Sarvastivadins became entangled in a number of doctrinal difficulties which, together with other problems of a similar kind, were inherited by the Mahayanists, who ultimately solved them by the simple expedient of adopting a point of view from which they no longer had any meaning. Incidentally it is curious to find at least one prominent modern exponent of the Theravada form of Buddhism, not unnaturally impressed by the subliminity of the Bodhisattva ideal, preaching in the name of pure Buddhism the distinctively Sarvastivadin doctrine of the equal validity of all three ideals. The fact is significant, for it suggests that the usual Theravadin doctrine does not command the full support even of its own scriptures in Pali. Against both Theravadins and Sarvastivadins the Mahayanists strenuously upheld the universal validity of the *Bodhisattvayāna*, maintaining that every Buddhist ought to aspire to Supreme Buddhahood. The Path of the Disciple and of the "Private" Buddha, they contended, led to the liberation of one person only, to mere individual enlightenment, in their eyes a narrow, not to say selfish, ideal. The Path of the Bodhisattva, on the contrary, though incomparably more arduous, led in the end to the emancipation of an infinite number of living beings, to universal enlightenment; it represented an ideal of unbounded altruism, obviously the highest and noblest ideal of all. To the *yānas* of the Disciple and the "Private" Buddha, since they were restricted in scope, was applied the epithet *hīna,* meaning low, small or inferior; to that of the Bodhisattva, in scope unlimited, the epithet *mahā,* sublime, great or superior. Thus the terms Hinayana and Mahayana give expression to the fundamental antagonism which exists between the spiritual ideals of the two great branches of Buddhism, between the ideals, that is to say, of individual enlightenment on the one hand and universal enlightenment on the other.

What was said in the last section concerning the possibility of contradictory doctrines leading to the same transcendental realization should, however, be neither lost sight of nor forgotten. Though their opponents were invariably blind to this higher third dimension of the problem, the Mahayanists on the whole kept it clearly and conspicuously in view, declaring in the emphatic words of the *Saddharma Puṇḍarīka Sūtra,* one of the most impressive and important of all Mahayana Scriptures—"In the whole universe there are not even two vehicles, how much less a third."[1] This momentous doctrine of the identity, on the transcendental plane, of the three *yānas,* the *Saddharma Puṇḍarīka Sūtra* makes clear by means of a magnificent parable well known throughout the Far East. The Blessed One, seated on the Vulture Peak in the midst of an "ocean-wide" assembly of Bodhisattvas, gods, serpent kings, demon kings and their followers (the "arahants" having walked out in disgust!), is represented as addressing the Elder Sariputra.

"Śāriputra! Suppose, in a (certain) kingdom, city, or town, there is a great elder, old and worn, of boundless wealth, and possessing many fields, houses, slaves and servants. His house is spacious and large, but it has only one door, and many people dwell in it, one hundred, two hundred, or even five hundred in number. Its halls and chambers are decayed and old, its walls crumbling down, the bases of its pillars rotten, the beams and rooftrees toppling and dangerous. On every side, at the same moment, fire suddenly starts and the house is in conflagration. The boys of the elder, say, ten, twenty, or even thirty, are in the dwelling. The elder, on seeing this conflagration spring up on every side, is greatly startled and reflects thus: 'Though I am able to get safely out of this gate of this burning house, yet my boys in the burning house are pleasurably absorbed in amusements without apprehension, knowledge, surprise, or fear. Though the fire is pressing upon them and pain and suffering are instant, they do not mind or fear and have no impulse to escape.'

"Śāriputra! This elder ponders thus: 'I am strong in my body and arms. Shall I get them out of the house by means of a flower vessel, or a bench, or a table?' Again he ponders: 'This house has only one gate, which is moreover narrow and small. My children are young. Knowing nothing as yet and attached to their place of play, perchance they will fall into the fire and be burnt. I must speak to them on this dreadful matter (warning them) that the house is burning, and that they must come out instantly, lest they be burnt and injured by the fire.' Having reflected thus, according to his thoughts, he calls to his children: 'Come out quickly, all of you!'

---

[1] W.E. Soothill, *The Lotus of the Wonderful Law* (Oxford, 1930), p. 69.

"Though their father, in his pity, lures and admonishes with kind words, yet the children, joyfully absorbed in their play, are unwilling to believe him and have neither surprise nor fear, nor any mind to escape; moreover, they do not know what is the fire (he means), or what the house, and what he means by being lost, but only run hither and thither in play, no more than glancing at their father. Then the elder reflects thus: 'This house is burning in a great conflagration, if I and my children do not get out at once, we shall certainly be burnt up by it. Let me now, by some expedient, cause my children to escape this disaster.' Knowing that to which each of his children is predisposed, and all the various attractive playthings and curiosities to which their nature will joyfully respond, the father tells them saying: '(Here are) rare and precious things for your amusement—if you do not (come) and get them, you will be sorry for it afterwards. So many goat-carts, deer-carts, and bullock-carts are now outside the gate to play with! All of you come quickly out of this burning house and I will give you whatever you want.' Thereupon the children, hearing of the attractive playthings mentioned by their father, and because they suit their wishes, every one eagerly, each pushing the other, and racing one against another, comes rushing out of the burning house.

"Then the elder, seeing his children have safely escaped and are all in the square, sits down in the open, no longer embarrassed, but with a mind at ease and ecstatic with joy. Then each of the children says to the father: 'Father! please now give us those playthings you promised us, goat-carts, deer-carts, and bullock-carts.' Śāriputra! Then the elder gives to the children equally each a great cart, lofty and spacious, adorned with all the precious things, surrounded with railed seats, hung with bells on its four sides, and covered with curtains, splendidly decorated also with various rare and precious things, draped with strings of precious stones, hung with garlands of flowers, thickly spread with beautiful mats, and supplied with rosy pillows. It is yoked with white bullocks of pure (white) skin, of handsome appearance and of great muscular power, which walk with even steps, and with the speed of the wind, and also has many servants and followers to guard them. Wherefore? Because this great elder is of boundless wealth and all his various storehouses are full to overflowing. So he reflects thus: 'My possessions being boundless, I must not give my children inferior small carts. All these children are my sons, whom I love without partiality. Having such great carts made of the seven precious things, infinite in number, I should with equal mind bestow them on each one without discrimination. Wherefore? Because, were I to give them to the whole nation, these things of mine would not run short—how much less so to my children!' Meanwhile each of the children rides on his great cart, having received that which he had never before had and never expected to have."[1]

Every detail of this great parable, retold in the *gāthā* or verse portion of the text in an even more highly embellished style, is fraught with meaning, to be teased out only by patient and thoughtful study. The rich elder, as the Sutra itself explains at length is, of course, the Buddha; the burning house, with its decayed old halls

[1] *Ibid.*, pp. 86-89. See also *The Threefold Lotus Sutra* (New York/Tokyo, 1975), pp. 85-87.

and chambers, the various realms of phenomenal existence, all transitory and on fire with greed, hatred and delusion; the thoughtless boys, joyfully absorbed in play, are sentient beings; the promised goat-carts and deer-carts are the vehicle of the Disciples and the vehicle of the Pratyekabuddhas, while the magnificently adorned bullock-carts, in which all the children eventually ride, are the Great Vehicle, the Vehicle of the Bodhisattva. Though from the point of view of Method the Sutra admits the existence of three Vehicles, so far as Doctrine is concerned it recognizes one only. The difference of *yānas* is a device made necessary by the fact that, from the standpoint of relative truth, beings are of different dispositions; at the level of absolute truth, however, where there obtains not even a real difference of beings, there can be no question of distinction of temperaments and vehicles. Like the *Satipaṭṭhāna Sutta* of the Pali Canon, the *Saddharma Puṇḍarīka Sūtra* teaches that, in the words of the former, there is "only one way . . . for the purification of beings, for the overcoming of sorrow and lamentation, for the destruction of suffering and grief, for reaching the right path, for the attainment of Nibbana." This "one way" (*ekayāna*) consists, according to the Pali text, in the cultivation of mindfulness of the body, especially of the process of respiration; of feelings, whether pleasant, painful or neutral; of thoughts, whether defiled or undefiled by greed, hatred and delusion; and of *dhammas,* in the sense of the whole body of conceptual formulations of the Teaching, such as the doctrines of the five "heaps," the seven constituents of Enlightenment, and the four Aryan Truths. The first three bases for the development of mindfulness coincide, not only in principle but often in detail also, with Meditation, the second stage of the Way; the fourth basis is plainly identical with Wisdom, which is the third stage. Morality, the first of the three stages, though not explicitly mentioned in this fourfold scheme of spiritual training, obviously has been tacitly assumed as the indispensable prerequisite of all the practices mentioned. As we shall see in Chapter IV, the six perfections practised by the Bodhisattva are an amplified version of the three stages of the Way traversed by the Arahant—not the spiritual individualist of Hinayana tradition but the true Arahant, peer of the Buddha Himself in transcendental realization, as depicted in the Master's own Teaching as handed down even in the much-edited texts of the Theravada Canon in Pali. The Mahayana schools taught, just as the Buddha did, that in the ultimate sense there was only one Way, or one Vehicle, to Enlightenment; that all the minor paths rendered necessary by idiosyncrasies of individual temperament eventually converged into a single unique path running without deviation broad and straight until it reached the City of Nirvana. Not only the Parable of the Three Vehicles but the whole teaching of the *Saddharma Puṇḍarīka Sūtra,* in its extant literary recension one of the oldest documents of the Mahayana movement, must in fact be regarded as the outward and visible sign of an inward and a spiritual return to, or rather (for the Mahayanists at least, had never lost it) a reaffirmation of, the transcendental quintessence of the Dharma as taught by the Buddha, and as embodying a powerful protest against the failure of the Hinayanists to rise above the contradictions inherent in a merely intellectual approach. Without going back on the principles adumbrated in the last section, thereby in effect repudiating the whole transcendental content of the Dharma, there is no escape from the conclusion that the Mahayana, and not the Hinayana, is the main channel for the transmission of those mighty waters of which it was said that even as the waters of the ocean have only one taste, the taste of salt, so do they have only one taste, the taste of emancipation—the life-giving waters of the Truth taught by the Buddha.

IV. Factors in the Emergence of the Mahayana

The Parable of the Three Vehicles, like all non-conceptual modes of doctrinal instruction, is richly suggestive, so that lessons not at all apparent to the casual reader may sometimes be drawn from it by the careful student. In his eagerness to save his children from the fire, the rich elder promises them goat-carts, deer-carts and bullock-carts; but after they have come safely out of the burning house he presents all of them with bullock-carts, of course much larger and more beautifully decked than they could possibly have imagined. Why did the Sutra, written as it is in such an exuberant and highly coloured style, deliberately refuse to embrace the opportunity of heightening the effect of the passage, and thus of bringing its meaning still more prominently into view, by representing the boys as eventually riding not in bullock-carts but in horse-carts, or upon the backs of elephants, or in some conveyance even more imposing? The fact that at the time when the rich elder and his children are confined within the burning house, typifying phenomenal existence, the bullock-carts are referred to as only one out of three possible modes of transportaion, whereas when they are outside the burning house, on the transcendental plane, the same bullock-carts are spoken of as being the one and only mode, suggests that the Mahayana itself has a dual aspect, or a double significance. At the intellectual level on which are formulated these sometimes contradictory conceptual indications of transcendental realities familiar to us as the doctrines of Buddhism, the Vehicle of the Bodhisattvas is distinct from the Vehicle of the Disciples and of the Pratyekabuddhas—Mahayana is opposed to Hinayana; but at the transcendental level, where all intellect-born contradictions are finally resolved into a state of unimpeded mutual solution, the Mahayana transcends even its own opposition to other schools, thus revealing its essentially non-conceptual character. It is in the fact that, while making use of conceptual formulations of the Doctrine, it is not limited by them, that the superiority of the Mahayana consists. There are thus in a sense two Mahayanas, one not limited to any form of Buddhism but coextensive with the whole Tradition, not inimical to any school but accepting all, embracing all and ultimately transcending all; the other, the Mahayana which, in Doctrine and Method, in Canon and geographical distribution, often differs from the Hinayana. The transcendental Mahayana, being in essence identical with the Eternal Dharma, has neither beginning nor end, existing in timeless perfection without history and without vicissitude; its manifestation in time and space possesses, just like the manifestation of the Dharma, as a distinct historical movement not only a more or less definite point of origin, in this case the Vaisali split, but also a specific conformation that has been determined by the nature of the historical circumstances due to which it arose. Without some understanding not so much of specific doctrinal deviations from the Teaching of the Buddha, but rather of the spirit behind these deviations, and of the far deeper problem of the whole Hinayana attitude towards the Dharma at the time of the rise of the Mahayana, it is impossible to understand why the Mahayana arose or what, historically speaking, it stands for.

The most serious charges against the Hinayana may be formulated as follows:—

At the time of the rise of the Mahayana it had become

(a) Conservative and literal-minded, adhering to the letter rather than to the spirit of the teaching, and on the whole averse to change;

(b) Scholastic, over-occupied with the analysis and classification of mental states;

(c) One-sidedly negative in its conception of Nirvana and the Way;

(d) Over-attached to the merely formal aspects of monasticism; and—probably the gravest charge of all—

(e) Spiritually individualistic.

We shall deal with each of these charges in turn, for inasmuch as they may be laid to the account not only of the extinct Hinayana schools against which the original Mahayana protest was made, but also to the account of a great deal of current Theravadin exposition of the Dharma, there attaches to them not only a dead historical interest but also an interest which is contemporary and living. Modern Theravada, by reason of the fidelity with which it continues to represent the original Hinayana attitude, may in fact be regarded as constituting a kind of living evidence of the necessity of the Mahayana movement. The most convincing of all arguments in favour of the Mahayana is in fact—the Hinayana.

(a) By characterizing the Inferior Vehicle as conservative and literal-minded we should not be understood as objecting to it on the score of failure to conform to modern notions of Progress; for Progress being an un-Buddhistic, not to say anti-Buddhistic, conception, the following of such a procedure would require nothing less than a complete abandonment of the strictly traditional view-point so far adopted in this work. The issues here involved are more far-reaching than any that the blinkered vision of Technology, for whom progress means the constantly accelerated multiplication of gadgets, can possibly envisage. We have already seen that the Dharma, with its threefold division into Morality, Meditation and Wisdom, was taught by the Buddha—using the figure of a raft—as something to be left behind, not as something to be taken with one; as being essentially the Means to Enlightenment, but not the Goal itself, and as therefore possessing not an absolute but only a relative and instrumental value. The literal-mindedness of the Hinayana consists of its habit of regarding intellectual formulations of the Doctrine as valid in the ultimate sense, as being not merely the conceptual symbols of Reality, and thus the theoretical supports for its practical realization, but as constituting a fully adequate description of Reality. In other words, its conception of Truth was in effect merely rational. The Buddha had, for instance, demonstrated the essential unreality of the so-called individual being by analysing it into its most prominent constitutent phenomena, His purpose of course being the purely pragmatic one of eradicating craving and attachment. The Hinayanists, however, especially the Sarvastivadins—though the trait is by no means absent from the Theravadins—started treating these psycho-physical phenomena, technically known as *dharmas,* as being themselves ultimately real, thus developing a pluralistic metaphysical outlook far remote from the Buddha's own uncompromising abjuration of all "views." In order to rectify this deviation from the purport of the Original Doctrine the Mahayanists taught, as we shall see more fully hereafter, insubstantiality (*śūnyatā*) not only of the personality (*pudgala*) but also of its constituent physical and mental states or *dharmas.* A number of Mahayana teachings are to be understood not as developments taking place *in vacuo* but as protests against the taking of historically earlier doctrines in so literal a sense as to preclude the possibility of their functioning as the means to Enlightenment. Having identified Truth with its conceptual formulations, it was not long before the Hinayanists took the next step of equating the conceptual formulations of Truth with their verbal expressions and, after the oral tradition had been committed to writing—an unmistakable sign of spiritual deterioration—with the very letters of the written text. Failing to realize that, in the words of Hui Neng, "The profundity of the teachings of the various Buddhas has nothing to do with the written language,"[1] they shut their Buddhism up between the gorgeously lacquered covers of a book, where it has remained ever since. The rabidly aggressive conservatism—the very antithesis of the genuinely traditional outlook—which distinguishes certain Theravada groups even today is the direct consequence of the general failure of the Hinayana schools to understand that, as the Buddha says in their own scriptures, the Dharma is simply a Raft. Had the Buddhists of Burma, for instance, been able to grasp this vitally important teaching, they would never have spent ten million rupees on the so-called Sixth Buddhist Council in order to determine whether a certain letter of the texts was a '*t*' or a '*d*.' No wonder Christmas Humphreys wrote, after attempting in vain to persuade them to accept his Twelve Principles of Buddhism, that he had not thought that in the Buddhist world there were people so wedded to the letter of tradition.[2] To the extent that the conceptual formulations and verbal expressions of the Teaching are treated as though they possessed not relative but absolute validity, and are regarded as being not symbolical indications but scientific descriptions of Reality, the way to the actual realization of their transcendental import is cut off. The claims of those who, though they treat the Dharma not as a Raft but as a permanent fixture of the hither shore, nevertheless profess to have reached the Other Shore, cannot be taken at all seriously. Identifying as they do Truth with its conceptual formulations, it is hardly surprising that they mistake rational comprehension of the Doctrine for its actual realization.

(b) Thus we come to the second charge against the Hinayana, the charge of scholasticism, signifying in this context over-occupation with the theoretical analysis and classification of physical and mental states, particularly of the latter. Since they treated them as realities the Hinayanists naturally thought that by making an exhaustive enumeration of the *dharmas* and by cataloguing each and every one of their numerous permutations, it would be possible to arrive at a complete picture of Reality. Acting on this assumption both Theravadins and

---

[1] *The Sutra of Wei Lang* (Luzac and Company, Ltd., London. 1947), p.64.
[2] *Via Tokyo,* pp. 147-9.

Sarvastivadins embarked upon the compilations of voluminous works belonging to their respective *Abhidharma Piṭakas* or Collections of Higher Doctrine, as well as upon the composition of exegetical manuals innumerable, a process that was continued, in the case of the Theravada, down to the present day. The view that the whole *Abhidharma Piṭaka,* whether that of the Sarvastivadins or that of the Theravadins—for the two canons are by no means identical—embodies the direct utterance of the Buddha Himself is, however, even on the internal evidence of these *Piṭakas* themselves, in the historical sense in which the claim is made, quite untenable. Several of the early Hinayana schools, especially the Sautrāntikas, in fact refused to accept the Abhidharma as the authentic Word of the Buddha, declaring that only the Vinaya and the Sutta could be so regarded. We need not adopt such an extreme position. As the Venerable Nyanatiloka maintains: "... In spite of this fact [of its later origin] it [*i.e.,* the *Abhidhamma Piṭaka*] is nevertheless in no way to be considered as a corruption or distortion of the Buddha's doctrine, but rather an attempt to systematize all the doctrines laid down in the Sutta, and to elucidate them from the philosophical or, more correctly psychological and physiological standpoint."[1] Though a development of the Buddha's Teaching, the Abhidharma may be regarded as a quite legitimate, indeed necessary and helpful, development, so long as it does not start treating methodological categories as metaphysical realities, thus reducing the Scriptures to a gigantic card-index system, and substituting for penetrating Insight a retentive memory. That this still happens, and that the Mahayana criticism is therefore still entirely justified, is revealed by the Venerable Nyanatiloka's attempt to explain the difference between the Sutta and the Abhidhamma.

> *The subject in both is practically the same. Its main difference in treatment, briefly stated, may be said to consist in the fact that in the Sutta the doctrines are more or less explained in the words of the philosophically incorrect "conventional" everyday language* (vohāra vacana) *understood by anyone, whilst the Abhidhamma, on the other hand, makes use of purely philosophical terms true in the absolute sense* (paramattha vacana). *Thus, in the Sutta it is often spoken of "individuals," "persons," of "I," "you," "self," even the rebirth of "self," etc., as if such so called individualities really existed. The Abhidhamma, however, treats of realities* (paramattha dhamma), i.e., *of psychical and physical phenomena, which alone*

[1] *Guide Through the Abhidamma Piṭaka* (Colombo, 1938), p. 1.

may be rightly called realities, though only of momentary duration, arising and passing away every moment.[1]

This is pluralistic realism with a vengeance! The Venerable Nyanaponika Thera, a disciple of the Venerable Nyanatiloka Maha Thera, upholds the contrary view: only in Buddhism do intellectual differences fail to disrupt the teacher-pupil relation—a tacit admission, this, of the relativity of all conceptual formulations of the Doctrine. Referring to "the danger inherent in a purely analytical method" he writes:—

> *This danger consists in erroneously taking the "parts," resulting from analysis, for genuine separate entities, instead of restricting their use to methodical and practical purposes: to the purpose of classification* (i.e., *orientation*) *and of dissolving the component units, wrongly conceived as ultimate unities. . . . To this danger already early Buddhist schools have submitted,* e.g., *the Vaibhasikas, better known as Sarvastivadins, which belong to the so-called Hinayana. . . . The teachings of these schools have been probably the reason why Hinayana in general has been denoted as a "pluralistic" doctrine, by Mahayanistic thinkers as well as by some modern writers. But this statement is certainly not justified with regard to the Theravada School and still less with regard to the Pali Canon itself. . . . We wish to emphasize once more that the genuine tradition of Theravada is, in our opinion, not affected by that criticism provided that its standpoint is formulated with due caution,* i.e., *by using both the analytical and synthetical method, as done by the Buddha in Sutta as well as in Abhidhamma. By following, in this respect too, the Master's great example, the danger of converting, or perverting, concepts of relative validity into entities of ultimate reality will be avoided.*[2]

This is, of course, precisely the position of the Mahayana, which, far from rejecting the Abhidharma, has incorporated it, in its more highly developed Sarvastivadin form, into its own tradition. Here as elsewhere, what divides the Hinayana and the Mahayana is not so much a difference of doctrine as the evaluation of doctrine. Both Hinayanists and Mahayanists accept the Abhidharma classification of *dharmas;* but whereas to the former they are realities, to the latter they are not.

We may not be drawing too far-fetched a conclusion if we see in the exaggerated scholasticism of the Hinayana one of the main factors contributing to the almost total neglect of the practice of Meditation which is so striking a feature of modern Theravada Buddhism. Once we have started regarding as a true picture of Reality a list, or even a chart, of *dharmas,* fully com-

---

[1] *Ibid.,* p. 3.

[2] *Abhidhamma Studies* (Colombo, 1949), pp. 18-19.

prehensible to the rational mind, the need for the development of Wisdom, and therewith for the practice of Meditation, tends to become obscured. Not without significance is the fact that, according to the Venerable Nyanaponika Thera, the New Burman Satipatthana Method "does not aim at attaining the highly focused concentration of the meditative absorptions (*jhāna*), but leads directly to liberating Insight (*Vipassanā*)."[1] Insight may indeed be developed without the *jhānas* having been attained *in this life;* but the fact that Abhidharma "studies" of a certain kind are widely popular in Burma naturally strengthens the suspicion that theoretical knowledge, in the debased modern usage of both terms, has been in some instances mistaken for Wisdom.

(c) Its one-sidedly negative conception of Nirvana and the Way, which is the third ground of complaint against the Hinayana, is closely connected with its scholasticism. According to the Abhidharma there are two primary classes of *dharmas, saṁskṛta* or compounded and *asaṁskṛta* or uncompounded. In the latter class only two *dharmas* are included, one of these being the transcendental element of Nirvana. All the remaining *dharmas,* seventy-three in number according to the Sarvastivada, are compounded, for which reason they are not transcendental but mundane. In the classification of these mundane *dharmas* lies the real concern of the Abhidharma; of Nirvana, once it has been duly enumerated, hardly any further mention is made, and it is allowed to recede into the background of the picture. Such being the case, it is in effect the mundane or conditioned *dharmas* which are treated by the Hinayanists as ultimate realities, and it is the rational understanding of these "realities," in their various permutations, which they mistake for Wisdom. When conditioned *dharmas* are defined as actually existent entities there is no alternative save to describe the transcendental element of Nirvana in terms of non-existence and non-entity. This conclusion was of course not explicitly drawn by the Hinayanists, who continued to assert, with Nāgasena, "Nirvana is"; but the influence of what was in effect a complete acceptance and systematic application of this point of view in the end outweighed that of a merely formal disclaimer.

[1] *The Heart of Buddhist Meditation,* p. 87.

Samsara being regarded as existent, and Nirvana as therefore relatively non-existent, the attainment of Nirvana inevitably came to be interpreted exclusively in terms of the cessation of the Samsaric process, as the extinction of the phenomenal. Owing to their habit of emphasizing the negative aspect of the Buddha's Teaching at the expense of the positive, grave distortions of the Doctrine eventually gained currency in Hinayana circles. As we saw in Chapter I, the Buddha attained Enlightenment as a result of His insight into the principle of universal conditionality, the conceptual expression of which is the fundamental Buddhist doctrine of Conditioned Co-production, variously formulated as a "chain" consisting, according to the context, of five, eight, ten, twelve, or twenty-four "links." The last of these formulations, which is the most comprehensive, consists of two series of twelve causally associated stages, the first explaining the origin and cessation of the round of phenomenal existence, from ignorance to suffering, the second describing the successive arising of psychic factors, such as faith and joy, which progressively augment each other until they culminate in the attainment of Nirvana. Because of their marked preference for the negative side of the Teaching the Hinayanists, ignoring the second series of twelve links, which depicts the Way to Nirvana positively, in terms of growth and development, fastened their attention exclusively upon the first series, which represents it as being nothing but a process of extinction. For the same reason the Four Aryan Truths, which were only a formulation and application of the principle of universal conditionality from a specific methodological standpoint, came to occupy a place at the very forefront of Hinayana doctrine, whereas, as we have reasons for believing, they held no such position in the Buddha's own Teaching. Though they explained the Fourth Truth, the Truth of the Way to the Cessation of Suffering, in terms of the Eightfold Path, which comprises both positive and negative practices, the fact that all these were held to contribute to the realization of a state which, according to this formulation, was the merely negative one of the total extinction of the suffering inherent in phenomenal existence, inevitably decreased the weight which might otherwise have attached to their admission of at least some positive factors into the spiritual life. Even the Eightfold Path, as depicted in the Pali texts, is on the whole rather a negative affair. Right Understanding is explained as understanding of the Four Truths; Right Aspiration as abstention from greed, anger and cruelty; Right Speech as abstention from lying, talebearing, harsh language and idle talk; Right Action as abstention from taking life, from taking what does not belong to one, and from unlawful indulgence in sexual intercourse; and so on. The impression created by such a representation of the Way is that the Buddhist life is one of unmitigated negation—hardly an inspiring prospect. Such an impression is not, however, produced by a reading of the complete Pali Canon, which, even after having passed through the hands of generations of Hinayana *rédacteurs,* is still far from deficient in teachings of a more positive character. The fact that, largely owing to the labours of the Pali Text Society, practically the whole *Tipiṭaka* is available in competent editions and English translations, may well make possible in future a more balanced presentation of the Dharma from these sources than is now given by the majority of Theravadins.

(d) Over-attachment to the merely formal aspects of monasticism, the fourth charge against the Hinayana, follows inevitably in the footsteps of the charges already preferred. Adherence to the letter rather than to the spirit of the Teaching leads, sooner or later, to the undue predominance of the institutional aspect of religion over the personal. Scholasticism, by exalting rational understanding above realization, inhibits both the practice of Meditation and the attainment of Wisdom, thereby not only depriving Morality of its transcendental sanction but dispensing with the need for any ethical training other than a merely external conformity with the disciplinary precepts. Exclusively negative conceptions of Nirvana and the Way lead to a misinterpretation of the ideal of renunciation, "giving up the world" being regarded as synonymous with a life of idleness and inactivity. These factors, in combination with others less important, are responsible for that identification of the religious life exclusively with the formal aspects of monasticism which is so prominent a feature of the Hinayana. Rigid observance of the strict letter of the Vinaya, at least while under public surveillance, is all that is expected of the monk in most parts of the so-called Theravada world today. In most cases the monk accepts the rôle allotted him by society, and plays it extremely well, with the result that the Theravada Sangha has become a veritable hothouse for hypocrisy in all its most orchidaceous varieties. Exquisite and extraordinary blossoms of monastic formalism which, parasitic upon the mighty trunk of the Dharma, suck from it all vitality and strength, can be gathered by the basketful by any observant pilgrim to the home, or rather homes, of "pure Buddhism." He will be informed, with an air of infinite satisfaction and superiority, that Theravada monks eat only once a day and do not handle money. Admiration quickly changes to astonishment, when it transpires that the said monks consume three heavy meals a day, all reckoned together as technically only one meal inasmuch as they are all eaten before noon. With the same rigidity they accept gifts of cash in such a manner that their fingers are not brought into direct contact with the contaminating lucre, a piece of cloth sufficing to protect the purity of their observance; the richer and more scrupulous brethren conduct all their fiscal business through banks. Robes are no longer made from rags; pieces of fine linen, or costly silk, are cut into rectangles and then *stitched together again;* sometimes complicated seams are made on the sewing machine without the material having been divided at all. Made in this way, a monk's outfit, technically the badge of poverty, can be four or five times as costly as that of a middle-class layman. Similarly, the *vihāra,* originally a leaf-thatched hut on the fringes of the primeval forest, has become a commodious and well-furnished bungalow wherein the monk is supplied with every comfort and convenience free of charge. At the time of the Buddha, and in all likelihood for several centuries afterwards, there was an element of risk and uncertainty in adopting the monastic life; the Master Himself, so we are told, occasionally returned from His begging round with an empty bowl—a circumstance attributed by the commentators to the personal intervention of Māra—and the experience of the Master must have been with even greater frequency the experience of His disciples too. An empty begging bowl is unheard of in Theravadin countries today. From the day of his ordination to the day of his death the monk is maintained certainly in comfort, perhaps even in luxury, without the necessity of his having so much as to lift a finger for the good of the community which supports him. In such countries the monastic life, from being a spiritual adventure, has degenerated into a safe investment. Strange as the fact may seem, the monastic life, in the way in which the Buddha, according to the Pali Scriptures themselves, intended it to be lived, can be more faithfully pursued in a country such as India, where Buddhism in the institutional sense no longer exists, than in Ceylon or Burma or Siam. Paradoxically, the spiritual standard of the Sangha may be higher when it is dependent for its subsistence upon a population which, though sympathetic towards Buddhism, is technically either not Buddhist at all or not exclusively Buddhist. Once Buddhism is set up as the State religion of any country, which in effect means that the economic security of the Sangha is ensured, the monastic life automatically ceases, in the vast majority of cases, to have any spiritual significance, becoming little more than a convenient means of livelihood for idle people. While this is, at least to some extent, the tragedy of the Sangha in all parts of the Buddhist world, the Mahayana branches of the Order have generally made some efforts to adapt themselves to changed conditions, so that even in the face of the fact of Buddhism being the established religion and the Sangha an endowed body the economic insecurity and thereby the spiritual freedom of the individual monk might be to some extent safeguarded. The Theravada branches of the Sangha, being in principle opposed to adaptation of any kind, on the contrary have kept up on a basis of complete economic security the formal aspects of a way of life based on absolute economic insecurity. Small wonder, then, that Hinayana monastic life should today be vitiated from top to bottom by the most consummate hypocrisy, or that the Vinaya should have been reduced, for all practical purposes, to a single obligation: the obligation of not being found out.

(e) Literal-minded adherence to the letter rather than to the spirit of the Teaching; scholasticism, in the sense of over-occupation with a merely rational analysis and classification of mental states; one-sided negativism in respect of Nirvana and the Way; inordinate attachment to the merely formal aspects of monasticism—these are charges in all conscience grave enough; but graver still is the fifth and last charge brought by the Mahayana against the Hinayana: the charge of spiritual individualism. If, as we have seen, there exists a kind of peripheral interconnection between the various Hinayana attitudes against which the first four charges are directed, one giving rise to and producing another, the attitude of spiritual individualism which provokes the fifth charge may be said to be connected with each one of them directly as its ultimate root, source and centre. For this reason do the Mahayana *Prajñāpāramitā* texts, perhaps the earliest literary evidence of reaction away from the narrowness of the Hinayana back to the breadth and amplitude of the original Teaching, not only enlarge upon the "selfishness" of the Disciples and Pratyekabuddhas as the first and the most fundamental of their numerous shortcomings, but moreover contrast it with the unbounded altruism of the Bodhisattva, thus in effect representing the spiritual individualism of the Hinayana as the basic cause of conflict between the two schools. Says the Lord in the *Ashṭāsāhasrikā*:—

A Bodhisattva should not train in the same way in which persons belonging to the vehicle of the Disciples and Pratyekabuddhas are trained. How then are the Disciples and Pratyekabuddhas trained? They make up their minds that "one single self we shall tame, one single self we shall pacify, one single self we shall lead to Nirvana." Thus they undertake exercises which are intended to bring about wholesome roots for the sake of training themselves, pacifying themselves, leading themselves to Nirvana. A Bodhisattva should certainly not in such a way train himself. On the contrary, he should train himself thus: "My own self I will place into Suchness, and, so that all the world might be helped, I will also place all beings into Suchness, and I will lead to Nirvana the whole immeasurable world of beings." With that intention should a Bodhisattva undertake all the exercises which further the spiritual progress of the world.[1]

The *Pañcaviṁśatisāhasrikā* illustrates the difference between the two ideals by means of a striking simile:—

A glowworm, or other luminous creature, does not think that its light would illuminate the continent of Jambudvipa, or radiate over it. Just so the Disciples and Pratyekabuddhas do not think that they should, after winning full enlightenment, lead all beings to Nirvana. But the sun, when it has risen, radiates its light over the whole of Jambudvipa. Just so a Bodhisattva, after he has accomplished the practices which lead to the full enlightenment of Buddhahood, leads countless beings to Nirvana.[2]

The real point at issue between the Hinayana and the Mahayana could hardly have been stated more explicitly or with greater force than in these words. But the statement of a fact is one thing and its explanation quite another. We are told that the

[1] *Selected Sayings*, pp. 32-33.
[2] *Ibid.*, p. 33.

Hinayana was spiritually individualistic; but how and why it became so, or more correctly, why there developed within Buddhism that trend of spiritual individualism known as Hinayana—that we are never told. The sole concern of the Mahayana texts being with eternal verities they are apt to discard as irrelevant all considerations of a merely psychological or historical nature. Nevertheless, in the eyes of the present generation, burdened as they are with more knowledge and less wisdom than their forefathers, and in whom intellectual curiosity is so much more awake than transcendental insight, the question assumes not only a historical interest but even a definite spiritual significance. An understanding of the origins of spiritual individualism may help us in our own progress along the Path. Some answer, however provisional, to the question already propounded, or some explanation, however inadequate, of the phenomenon therein involved, must therefore be attempted. Why, then, did one line of Buddhist tradition develop into a spiritual individualism—or, more accurately, into a pseudo-spiritual individualism—of the Hinayana type? How did there ever come to be heard, amidst the jubilant chorus of Buddhist altruism, the shrill, despairing cry "One single self we shall tame, one single self we shall pacify, one single self we shall lead to Nirvana"?

More than one answer could of course be given; for this phenomenon, like all other phenomena in the universe, from ideas to empires, is dependent for its origin not upon one isolated and indisputable cause but upon causal factors and conditions innumerable, every one of which contributes jointly to the production of the total effect. Four such factors by reason of their special importance may be selected for particular mention.

(i) As we saw in Chapter I, the periodical disappearance of the Dharma from the earth calls for the periodical appearance of a Buddha in order that the Dharma may be rediscovered and reproclaimed. Truth, no doubt, is eternal; but of the mundane vehicles and manifestations of Truth it must be admitted that "sad mortality o'ersways their power." However high the point attained by a projectile fired from the earth may be, sooner or later the forces of gravitation assert themselves and, describing a magnificent parabola, it falls to the ground. There is a sort of gravitational pull, as it were, not indeed upon the lofty transcendental "states" which it is the object of the Buddhist life to attain, but certainly upon those conceptual and verbal indications of those states which constitute the mode in which the Dharma exists at the phenomenal level, and which, after all, derive their existence not from the heavens but from the earth.

The basis of phenomenal existence is the wrong assumption of a separate, eternal, individual self or ego; the basis of Nirvana, the highest transcendental "state," is complete freedom from any such assumption. (The Mahayana would, of course, warn us that such a basis is in reality a no-basis.) Between the phenomenal and the transcendental, *laukika* and *lokottara,* there exists, from the methodological standpoint at present adopted—though not in reality—an irreducible dualism. Every mundane thought, word and deed is individualistic, has for its origin and end attachment to the delusion of an *ātman.* Every transcendental, or transcendentally inspired, thought, word and deed, is on the contrary non-individualistic, having for its basis a realization of the fundamental egolessness and "emptiness" of all existence. Along with the delusion of "I" arises that of "mine": ignorance is twinborn with desire. Hence we find that greed (together with anger, or desire frustrated) is the most typical mental attitude of worldly beings, even as grasping is their most characteristic activity. Though the Dharma was preached by the Lord Buddha as the Means to Enlightenment, that is to say, as the means for the realization of a state wherein not even the faintest shadow of the ego-concept would obtain, it was not long before the Dharma itself, coming under the influence of the gravitational pull to which we have already alluded, began to be treated as something that could be grasped. The transcendental realities which it was the business of the Dharma to indicate, having become identified with their conceptual formulations by reason of a subtle change of attitude that came over a certain section of the Sangha, began to be thought of as objects which could in reality be brought within the possession of the individual. Nirvana came to be regarded as a state that could in reality, and not merely in a manner of speaking, be possessed by the person attaining it. "I" and "mine" being inseparable, the reality of possession implies the reality of the possessor. If "my" realization is real then "I" must be a reality. In this way the attainment of Nirvana, and in fact the whole spiritual life, came to be looked upon as an individual affair, and the possibility of one's attainment being divorced from the rest of humanity, not only admitted but positively asserted. Though the Mahayanists, like the Hinayanists, spoke—as indeed the very structure of the language forced them to speak—of Enlightenment as though it could be an individual attainment, not only were they careful to balance the statement that the Bodhisattva should think "My own self I will place into Suchness" by the counter-statement, "I will also place all beings into Suchness," but they clearly taught the essential voidness of both self and others, the inexpressibility of Truth, and the relativity of all concepts and verbal expressions.

This is not to suggest that spiritual individualism of the Hinayana type is to be found either in what appear to be the oldest portions of the Pali Canon, or that the best Theravadin commentarial and exegetical literature, such as the writings of Buddhaghosa, does not in its own way guard against the dangers of individualism with hardly less care than do the Mahayana scriptures. Nevertheless, it must be admitted, with regret, that much current Theravadin exposition of the Dharma is markedly individualistic in tone, and that in certain quarters attacks on the Bodhisattva ideal are by no means unheard-of. No more effective retort can be made to those who, in the name of a pseudo-Arahant ideal, venture to impugn the orthodoxy and historicity of the doctrine of unbounded altruism, than that of Lama Anagarika Govinda. Referring to the Pali *Jātakas,* the five hundred and fifty tales illustrating the Buddha's practice of the Bodhisattva career in His previous births—tales accepted by all Theravadins as part of the genuine Buddha-Word—the great artist-scholar remarks, not without a touch of asperity, "It is hardly possible to think that the Buddha told these stories merely for the sake of entertainment."[1] The question of the alleged individualism of the Early Buddhist ideal of spiritual life will, however, be discussed in greater detail in Chapter IV, wherein we hope to demonstrate the basic unity, so far as their ultimate transcendental objective is concerned, of the Arahant

[1] "Origins of the Bodhisattva Ideal." (*Stepping-Stones,* Vol. II, p. 244). Strictly speaking, only the verses of the Pali Jātaka Book are regarded as canonical.

ideal as preached in numerous texts of the Theravada Pali Canon and the Bodhisattva ideal as proclaimed by all branches of Mahayana tradition.

ii) As the first of the five charges against them has already informed us, the followers of the Hinayana formed the habit of understanding the Buddha's words in an exclusively literal manner, with the consequence that, in the end, they started treating intellectual formulations of the Doctrine as possessing ultimate validity. This literal-mindedness was undoubtedly a factor in the development of that attitude of spiritual individualism with which we are at present concerned. Language is the child not of transcendental knowledge but of mundane necessities. Words and concepts, as we have insisted more than once in the course of this study, far from being able to describe realities, can at best only indicate them, and hence must be understood not literally but symbolically. Once we start taking at their face value the frail words of human speech by means of which the Buddha, or any other enlightened teacher, endeavours to make clear to unenlightened beings the nature of Reality, we are compelled to fall from the transcendental import of those words back to their original mundane significance. Passages innumerable of the Pali scriptures inform us that such and such a person attained Nirvana, gained Arahantship, won release, *et cetera:* names and other personal details are given. So far as grammer is concerned, there is no difference between entering Nirvana and entering a house: the sentences "He attained Enlightenment" and "He went home" employ the same parts of speech in exactly the same syntactical order. But metaphysically there is a whole world of difference. One sentence describes an activity accompanied, so far as worldly beings are concerned, by the delusion of individual existence, the other indicates the final extinction of that delusion. If we take literally the words of the first sentence, "He attained Enlightenment," we shall be forced to concede the separate real existence firstly of the person attaining, secondly of the object attained, and thirdly of the act of attainment, a position in diametrical opposition to the orthodox teaching. And this is in effect exactly what the Hinayanists did. Understanding literally the Buddha's use of proper names, or of the personal pronoun, with reference to transcendental attainments, they not only began to look upon such attainments as being the property of a real individual being, but also to regard the spiritual life as consisting exclusively in the accumulation of such pieces of property. Spiritual individualism consequently became rampant in Hinayana circles.

(iii) Emotional, no less than intellectual factors, must, however, be taken into consideration. Whether operating on the material, or on the intellectual, or on the spiritual plane, one endeavours to help those in trouble because one to some extent participates in their sorrows and sufferings and feels them as his own. The word sympathy, by which we denote our emotional response to the woes of others, means literally "suffering with." Now whereas in modern Theravada teaching—not in the Pali Canon, which contains strong indications of a more altruistic attitude—sympathy, pity, or—to pronounce at once the most beautiful of all words of human speech—compassion (*karuṇā*), is regarded as being merely one wholesome mundane state of mind among a number of other such states, in all branches of Mahayana tradition it is on the contrary regarded as coordinate with Wisdom itself, and hence as being by nature purely transcendental. For the Mahayanist, Wisdom and Compassion, as the static and kinetic modes of one Reality, are inseparable. Consequently, the Bodhisattva, in aiming at the attainment of Wisdom aims also at the development of Compassion, or, what is in effect the same thing, in aiming at his own emancipation by means of the one he aims simultaneously at the emancipation of all sentient beings through the other. The literal-mindedness and scholasticism of the Hinayana, having led to a rationalistic identification of the conceptual formulations of Reality with Reality itself, so that Wisdom became confused with knowledge, realizations of the transcendental order were rendered, in the circles where this confusion prevailed, impossible of attainment. Without Wisdom there could be no Compassion, without Compassion no concern either for the material or for the spiritual welfare of others. This total deprivation of Compassion, in the transcendental sense of the term, which was itself the product of the spiritual individualism of the Hinayana, having become complete, powerfully reinforced that individualism and, like a rotten fruit that, falling from the bough, nourishes with its decay the tree that bore it, contributed to the further development of that one-sided conception of the Arahant in which the spiritual ideals of this school—such as they were—eventually came to be embodied.

(iv) In close parallelism to the above considerations is the last of the four most important factors responsible for the Hinayana defection from the altruistic attitude which was so prominent a feature of early Buddhism. We say "attitude" and not "teaching" advisedly; for in the Pali texts, as now extant, Compassion is revealed in the lives rather than recommended in the lectures of the Buddha and His disciples. The term generally used for Compassion is not *karuṇā,* however, but *anukampā,* a word derived from a verb meaning literally to shake with, or to tremble with, an idiom which presents an obvious analogy with the English "sympathy." As I. B. Horner, in a characteristically pithy article on "Compassion," points out:—

> *The Buddha urged his first five followers—all of them arahats—to go forth and teach out of* anukampā *for the world (*Vinaya, Mahavagga, *I. ii, 1). He is further recorded to have said: "Anyone speaking truly of me would say, 'A being not liable to intellectual confusion has arisen in the world . . . out of* anukampā *for the world' " (*Majjhima, Sutta *4). He also, out of* anukampā *for his disciples, put before them the aim of becoming heirs of Dhamma in him, not heirs of the material things of the world (*Majjhima, Sutta *3). And again in pointing out to them empty places in which to meditate, he said on a number of recorded occasions: "All that teachers can do out of* anukampā *for their disciples, that I have done for you; meditate, monks." And so on.*[1]

These citations from the Scriptures, though by no means exhaustive, may be held sufficient to our present purpose. Compassion was not only the guiding spirit, the motivating force, behind the Buddha's own activities, but was moreover to be the dominating power in the lives of His disciples. The Hinayanists, however, being interested in the precepts rather than in the practice of the Master, were more intent on understanding the Buddha-Word than in following the Buddha-Way. Instead of seeking inspiration from the Buddha's own example they sought to tread the Way to Nirvana exclusively by means of information derived from the oral traditions and, at a later date, from the written records of His supposed utterances. Hinayana interpretation of the texts being, as we have already noticed, literal and narrow enough, it is not astonishing that sooner or later a sharp divergence should occur between the

[1] *Stepping-Stones,* Vol. II, p. 16.

Path of unbounded altruism followed, as all schools admitted, by the Buddha Himself, and the Path of spiritual individualism which, according to the Hinayanists, He prescribed for the inferior capacities of His disciples. Ordinary mortals, they contended, should aim not at Buddhahood but at Arahantship (now regarded as a distinct ideal) and hence should concern themselves not with the liberation of others, responsibility for which rested with the Buddhas, but exclusively with their own salvation.

Though, in the passage above quoted, I. B. Horner cites texts pertaining to the manifestation of Compassion in life rather than to the determination of its essential nature by thought, it need not for this reason be concluded that the Pali Canon contains no theoretical discussion of the place and importance of Compassion in the disciple's career. Miss Horner refers to the *Mahāgovinda Suttanta* of the *Dīgha-Nikāya,* wherein the monk Mahāgovinda, having spent the four months of the rainy season practising the meditation of Compassion, was suddenly visited by Brahmā Sanankumāra, the Eternal Youth Recovering from terror, he asked the Brahmā a question, the gist of which was: "Is a mortal able (to reach) the undying Brahma-world?" (*pappoti macco amatam Brahma-lokam.*) The Brahmā replies: "Having put away egotism (*mamattā*), having become concentrated (in meditation), being intent upon compassion . . . training himself thus, the mortal is able (to reach) the undying Brahma-world." As Miss Horner so pertinently comments, "Here the individual cannot gain his desired end unless he is aware, among other things, of the needs of others and the wish to console and protect them in the distress and anxiety to which all mortality is subject."[1] This is, of course, the whole sum and substance of the Mahayana attitude. That such a passage should occur in the Pali Canon is a challenge to the orthodoxy of the Hinayana ideal of spiritual individualism which its modern Theravadin proponents cannot afford to ignore.

V. What is Mahayana Buddhism?

To the question which stands as the heading of this section answer may be returned in a twofold manner. Firstly, by way of

[1] *Ibid.*, p. 19.

an enumeration of the general characteristics developed by the Mahayana in reaction against those Hinayana deviations from the spirit of the Original Teaching which were summarized in the five charges preferred in the last section. Secondly, by way of an account of the teachings which, in addition to the basic Buddhist doctrines and methods described in Chapter I, were held in common by all schools and offshoots of the Mahayana. In this section the subject will be dealt with in the first manner; the remaining sections of this chapter will be devoted to a discussion of it in the second manner.

The Hinayana being conservative and literal-minded, scholastic, one-sidedly negative in its conception of Nirvana and the Way, over-attached to the formal aspects of monasticism, and spiritually individualistic, the Mahayana, as a movement of reaction against the Hinayana, was naturally compelled to emphasize the importance of whatever qualities and characteristics were the exact opposite of these. It was therefore:

(a) Progressive and liberal-minded, caring more for the spirit than for the letter of the Scriptures, willing to write fresh ones whenever the need of recasting the outward form of the Teaching arose;

(b) More highly emotional and devotional in attitude, with a deeper understanding of the value of ritual acts; and

(c) More positive in its conception of Nirvana and the Way;

(d) While continuing to cherish the monastic ideal it gave increased importance to a dedicated household life; and

(e) It developed the altruistic aspect of Buddhism and preached the Bodhisattva Ideal.

Inasmuch as the account given in the preceding section of the general characteristics of the Hinayana constitutes, at the same time, a negative description of the characteristics of the Mahayana, knowledge of the former automatically throwing a partial illumination upon the latter, an examination of the above five distinguishing features of the Great Vehicle as detailed as that which was accorded the five principal charges against the Little Vehicle would be superfluous. Besides, the remaining sections of this work, since they treat exclusively of the Mahayana, are in a sense all illustrative of the facts which it is now the business of this section to establish.

(a) Once again the possibility of serious misunderstanding must be guarded against, and just as in the corresponding paragraph of the last section we had to point out that the Hinayana was not accused of being unprogressive in the modern sense, so must we now insist that although characterizing the Mahayana as progressive and liberal-minded we do so only after injecting these terms with a distinctly Buddhist connotation. By the progressivism and liberalism of the Great Vehicle, no more—and no less—is meant than its constant awareness, its vivid realization and effective recognition, of the fact that the Transcendental is ineffable and that all possible conceptual formulations and verbal expressions possess in relation to it a merely symbolical significance.

Says the Lord in the *Laṅkāvatāra Sūtra*:—

"Mahāmati, words are not the highest reality, nor is what is expressed in words the highest reality. Why? Because the highest reality is an exalted state of bliss, and as it cannot be entered into by mere statements regarding it, words are not the highest reality. Mahāmati, the highest reality is to be attained by the inner realization of noble wisdom; it is not a state of word-discrimination; therefore discrimination does not express the highest reality."[1]

But though the indescribability of the "state" or "reality" designated by such words as Nirvana, Tathatā, Śūnyatā, Dharmakāya and Chitta, and the elusiveness of Perfect Wisdom, is one of the favourite topics of Sanskrit Buddhist literature, especially of the *Prajñāpāramitā* group of texts, the anti-literalism of the Mahayana consists as much in the vigorousness and systematicality of its application of this truth as in the prolixness of its appreciation. Almost every important Mahayana sutra, while conscious of its own indispensability, is also instinct with a sense of its own inadequacy; every doctrine is as it were window-like, transparent, inviting the eye to look not at it but through it and beyond it into that heaven of Pure Consciousness where the Sun of Truth, transcending the clouds of discrimination, shines with undimmed glory. Compassion springs up in the Void as a lotus in the water, and all Mahayana expedients for the attainment of the Supreme

---

[1] *The Lankavatara Sutra*, translated by DAISETZ TEITARO SUZUKI (London, 1932), p. 77. For an unambiguous statement of the Mahayana attitude towards even their own scriptures see p. 167, where the Buddha declares: "The Bodhisattva-Mahasattva is not to become attached to the words of the canonical texts."

Buddhahood— every one of which is wrought and devised by compassion—are saturated with the consciousness of their own relativity. The more emphatically a text enjoins upon us a certain practice, the more vigorously does it exhort us constantly to remember that, from the transcendental view-point, the practice is quite meaningless. Indeed, we are sometimes even told that the success of the practice depends upon our realization of the impossibility of success in the ultimate sense. While one text, with typical exuberance of expression, declares that (relatively speaking) in Buddha-lands numberless as the sands of the Ganges countless Buddhas deliver for incalculable æons discourses innumerable, another, with no less typical austerity, assures us that (in the absolute sense) from the night of His Supreme Enlightenment to the night of His Final Passing Away, the Tathagata has not uttered even a single word. How different is such an attitude from that of the Hinayana! On the one hand we find unbounded confidence in the spirit of the Teaching leading to a marvellous flexibility of the letter, to an opening up in all directions of ever wider and wider approaches and avenues to the Truth; on the other, a slavish dependence on the letter of the Teaching resulting in an almost total evacuation of the spirit, in a gradual narrowing—culminating at last in a complete blockage—even of the Path recognized as taught by the Buddha and professedly followed. Should there be for a Buddhist no choice save between sacrificing the spirit to the letter of the Teaching, on this side, or the letter to the spirit, on that, we hope that we should have the strength to reject the former alternative in order to embrace the latter. Happily, though, modern scientific research, by enabling us to study side by side the Hinayana and the Mahayana, has spared us the pain of making so invidious a choice. The spirit of Buddhism, as transmitted by the Mahayana, can now be studied in the light of its letter as preserved by the Theravada,[1] and *vice versa.* An intelligent and informed Buddhist, though he may follow in practice, as indeed follow he must, the doctrines and methods of the particular line of Buddhist tradition best adapted to his

[1] But it should not be forgotten that very early material exists, in translation, in the Chinese Canon, and also preserved in the original Sanskrit in the sometimes fragmentary literary remains of non-Theravadin Hinayana schools.

individual requirements, can no longer regard as valid the claim of any school to the exclusive possession of the whole truth about Buddhism.

(b) In the eyes of those to whom reason and emotion are, if not contradictories at least inimical to each other, it is one of the paradoxes of the Mahayana that, while giving a much greater scope to the free play of emotion than the Hinayana, it is at the same time much more rigorously intellectual. This phenomenon may to some extent be accounted for by remembering that the Mahayana was, as we shall see more fully later on, not merely a sporadic movement of reaction against the Hinayana but also a more or less systematic development of the whole body of Early Buddhist teaching. Contrary to the received opinion, certain pages of the Pali Canon thrill with a quiet enthusiasm, or glow with a serene happiness, or flash out in dazzling ecstasy, while striking expressions of faith in, and devotion to, the person of the Buddha are by no means wanting. Like a vibration of a pitch too high to be perceived as sound by human ears, the very delicacy and refinement of the emotional element in the Pali Scriptures, wholly free as it is from the turbidity and violence of ordinary human passion, has perhaps caused it to escape attention. At any rate, according to both Pali and Sanskrit Buddhist Scriptures, reason and emotion, Wisdom and Faith, must be developed, not one-sidedly but in perfect equilibrium. A completely harmonious development of the cognitive, conative and affective aspects of personality is in fact necessary at each and every stage of the life spiritual. As a perusal of the *Bodhicaryāvatāra* of Shantideva will suffice to indicate, the fervent emotionalism of the Mahayana never went to the extreme of anti-intellectualism. Even the Jodo Shin Shu, which professes to teach salvation by simple faith, does so against the background of a profound and subtle metaphysic. Though the emotionalism of the Mahayana stands in contrast to the one-sided scholasticism and rationalism of the Hinayana, it should never be forgotten that the Mahayana not only incorporated into its own teaching the bulk of Hinayana scholasticism but also developed schools of philosophy which, for sharpness of dialectic, boldness of speculation and sustained awareness of that which transcends philosophy, have rarely, if ever, been equalled in the world.

Every emotion being of a triune nature, inasmuch as it may be directed towards an object inferior, equal or superior to the subject, we find taking place in Mahayana Buddhism a threefold development of emotion as Compassion (*karuṇā*), Love (*maitri*) and Devotion (*bhakti*). Owing to the very nature of Buddhist thought, however, Devotion and Compassion, which are in a sense complementary, sprang up much more luxuriantly than Love. The novice Bodhisattva, for whose edification most of the Mahayana Scriptures were intended, found himself occupying as it were an intermediate position. Below him, swept struggling along by the torrent of Samsara, were untold millions of miserable worldly beings; while, above, smiling and resplendent upon their lotus-thrones, Buddhas and Bodhisattvas innumerable rose tier upon tier to the zenith. Adoration for the latter, Compassion for the former, were his dominating sentiments, the height and depth of his spiritual life. Love was a sentiment to be felt either between worldly beings (though their very worldliness would generally make them incapable of love) or between the enlightened members of the transcendental hierarchy.

Since emotion, as we know it, can be felt not for things but only for persons, the development of devotion naturally led to a multiplication of the objects of devotion, namely, of Buddhas and Bodhisattvas, so that we find in the Mahayana transcendental beings innumerable who are quite unknown to the Teaching in its earlier form. Again, emotion naturally tending to seek an outlet in action, the sentiment of adoration, as its intensity increased, inevitably found expression in a variety of outward forms of worship. These forms, being inoculated with metaphysics, became possessed of a deep symbolical significance, and the ritualistic aspect of the Mahayana developed in dependence upon devotion as one of its conditions. The value of ritual acts in helping to induce certain correspondent states of consciousness was fully appreciated by the Mahayana, in consequence of which they made extensive use of supports of this kind. The Hinayanists, not feeling so strongly the devotional impulse, stopped short at ceremony, and failed to make any contribution to the ritualistic aspect of Buddhism. In the Theravada as it exists today, however, especially in Ceylon, Siam and Cambodia, the effect produced on the mind by the dignified and decorous proceedings of the Sangha is sometimes in nature strangely similar to, though feebler in intensity than, that of Mahayana ritual. But it should not be forgotten that whereas the more diffuse benefits of Theravada ceremonies are largely confined to members of the Sangha, Mahayana rituals are vehicles of a concentrated transcendental power available to all who are qualified by initiation for its reception.

(c) Coming now to the third general characteristic of the Mahayana, its more positive conception of Nirvana and the Way, we must again beware of identifying the teaching of the Great Vehicle with any one-sided or extreme position merely because its emergence on the phenomenal plane was bound up with a movement of opposition to certain aspects of Hinayana doctrine and discipline. That Nirvana was ineffable was axiomatic for all schools. Consequently all recognized, at least in theory, the impossibility of regarding positive statements about its essential nature as being more valid than negative ones, or *vice versa.* This is the position of both the Pali and Sanskrit Scriptures, and if certain of the latter appear to be one-sidedly negative in their mode of expression, the appearance is superficial, being in reality due to their confirmed habit of negating even negation.

Mahayana positivism is of two kinds: doctrinal and methodological. As we saw in Chapter I, the Hinayana gradually became prey to the habit of regarding the negative characterizations of Nirvana as being not descriptions but definitions, and as therefore possessing not a relative but an absolute validity. Against this dangerous tendency the Mahayana entered a vigorous protest, maintaining that, from the standpoint of Doctrine, all conceptual formulations of Reality, whether positive or negative, were equally invalid. At the same time it maintained that from the standpoint of Method, positive formulations, being more easily understood and more attractive than negative ones, were generally of greater practical help to the average Buddhist. This dual standpoint was adopted by the followers of the Great Vehicle because on the one hand they wanted to safeguard the profundity of the Doctrine and on the other to guarantee the amplitude of the Method. Wisdom demanded that the positive should be defended against the encroachments of the negative indications of Nirvana; Compassion, going a step farther, pleaded that the positive indications, though admittedly no more valid in the ultimate sense than their negative counterparts, were much more efficacious as supports of the spiritual life. Consequently we have as the metaphysical background of Mahayana Buddhism the all-dominating conception of *Śūnyatā*, or Voidness, the state wherefrom all conceptions, including that of Voidness itself, have been prescinded. Against this background of absolute (not relative) negation stands out that rich efflorescence of positive conceptions which constitutes the methodological foreground of the Mahayana. First, we see abstract conceptions such as *Citta* as Absolute Consciousness and *Mahāsukha* or Supreme Bliss; next quasi-religious conceptions such as the *Dharmakāya*, the Absolute Person wherein Wisdom and Compassion are united not mathematically but spiritually;[1] after that, an innumerable host of Buddhas, Bodhisattvas and other divinities, all personifications of various stages of the Path; and finally, legions of gods, demi-gods, guardian spirits, and so on, each of which embodies, at however low a level of phenomenal existence, some aspect of the Teaching. These positive conceptions stand out against the omnipresent background of Voidness not as actors against the drop curtain of a stage, but rather as panes of glass of gradually increasing degrees of opaqueness might stand out against the sunlit blue of the sky. The Light of the Void shines, in varying degrees of intensity, through them all; through the well-nigh perfect transparency of the most abstract positive conceptions with hardly any diminution of its brilliance; through the more concrete conceptions with more; but through all to some extent, so that all, to the measure of their capacity, may serve as indications for practical spiritual purposes of That which none of them is able to express.

Just as, in the case of the Hinayana, the conception of Nirvana as nothing but the complete cessation of phenomenal existence led to a one-sidedly negative presentation of the Way, so in the case of the Mahayana a more positive conception of Reality, even though that conception was admitted to possess only a relative validity, led to the formulation of an ideal of spiritual life much more positive, and hence infinitely more inspiring, than any preached by the Hinayana. This was the famous Bodhisattva ideal, the ideal of absolute altruism on the highest

---

[1] D. T. SUZUKI. *The Essence of Buddhism* (London, 1946), p. 19.

transcendental plane, constituting the practical side of the teaching of all schools of Mahayana Buddhism. Owing to the unique importance of the Bodhisattva Ideal, which has been truly described as the very heart of the Mahayana, we shall devote to it the whole of Chapter IV. To this chapter the reader is therefore referred for further information.

(d) Modern Theravadins often commit the mistake of thinking that the Mahayanists gave increased importance to a dedicated household life at the expense of the integrity of the monastic ideal and the purity of the monastic observance. One at times hears the absurd charge that Mahayanist monks have "no Morality" (in the technical Buddhist sense) and that "they do not observe the Vinaya." Though there are sections of the Mahayana Sangha against whom such charges might with justice be brought, they are no more true of Mahayana monks as a body than of their Theravadin counterparts. What is quite true, however, is that Mahayana Bhikshus (we exclude the Jodo Shin Shu clergy, who are not members of the Sangha) do not attach so much importance as the Hinayanists to what we have called the formal aspects of monasticism. Morality is not for them merely a matter of keeping up appearances in the eyes of the lay public, as it so often is in Theravadin lands. This healthier, and of course much more truly orthodox attitude, the Mahayana owes largely to the influence of the Bodhisattva Ideal. Once it has been admitted that a Bodhisattva may be either a monk or a layman it becomes impossible to identify the spiritual life exclusively with a life of monasticism. The Buddha Himself certainly did not do so, a fact which the following verse from the Pali *Dhammapada* should be sufficient to establish:—

"Even though a man be richly attired, if he develops tranquillity, is quite, subdued and restrained, leading a holy life and abstaining from injury to all living beings—he is a Brahman, he is an ascetic, he is a Bhikkhu."[1]

At the same time, the Mahayana refusal to regard the spiritual and the monastic life as necessarily synonymous, being the result of an emphasis on the essence rather than the accidents of the disciple's career, in practice brought about not a weakening but a strengthening of the integrity of the monastic ideal in the Mahayana and helped to safeguard the purity of the monastic

[1] *Dhammapada,* verse 142.

observance. Though according to some authorities the Bodhisattva may commit for the good of others actions generally regarded as sinful, statements of this type must be regarded as upholding the supremacy of Compassion rather than as being subversive of the moral order. Such Mahayana texts as deal with the subject on the whole demand of the Bodhisattva who is also a member of the Sangha as high a degree of asceticism as the Theravada Scriptures demand of the Bhikkhu who aims at Arahantship, the only difference being that for the novice Bodhisattva, unlike the would-be Arahant, the possibility of taking refuge in monastic formalism is by the very nature of the Mahayana precluded. Degeneration there may sometimes be in the Mahayana no less than in the Theravada branch of the Sangha; but hypocrisy as one of the fine arts is unheard-of there.

(e) Just as spiritual individualism is the gravest charge that can be brought against the Hinayana, so does the unbounded altruism of the Mahayana bespeak its greatest praise. In place of the ideal of the pseudo-Arahant, concerned primarily, if not exclusively, with his own emancipation from suffering, the Great Vehicle preaches the incomparable ideal of the profoundly wise and infinitely compassionate Bodhisattva, the great being who, in his eagerness to show to others the Way to Nirvana, is willing to sacrifice his own prospects of salvation. Yet it should not be supposed that because they took up a position diametrically opposite to that of the Hinayanists the Mahayanists therefore fell into the trap of committing the diametrically opposite error. Speaking conventionally, individual beings do exist, and to talk of gaining Enlightenment for oneself or of helping others to gain it are therefore on the level of conventional truth both quite valid modes of expression. Harm is done only when we begin thinking that such statements are true absolutely. Spriritual individualism of the Hinayana type developed partly because certain groups of early Buddhists insisted upon interpreting the Buddha's exhortations to self-effort and personal experience of the Truth in a grossly literal manner. But the Mahayanists, adhering firmly to both Doctrine and Method, taught that although from the standpoint of Compassion the Bodhisattva should resolve to emancipate all beings, from the standpoint of Wisdom he should at the same time reflect that in the absolute sense no beings exist. By means of a fearless acceptance of contradictory propositions of this kind did the Mahayana safeguard itself against misunderstandings such as those to which the more literal-minded and rationalistic Hinayana so easily fell prey.

Should we wish to parallel the four chief factors responsible for the rise of Hinayana individualism with four factors which, though neither historical sequence nor logical connection can be claimed for them, undoubtedly played an important part in the emergence of Mahayana altruism, it may be said, in brief, that the Great Vehicle

(i) Was better able to resist the "gravitational pull" already mentioned. This was no doubt because it

(ii) Was much more keenly aware of the purely relative value and symbolical significance of words and concepts in relation to the Absolute. That, moreover,

(iii) It gave a much more prominent place in the spiritual life to emotion, thus rendering possible the maximum development of Compassion, and

(iv) Attached at least as much importance to the personal example of the Buddha as to His precepts.

Having summarized the main points of divergence between the Hinayana and the Mahayana it must now be our endeavour to achieve a wider and more synthetic view of the relations between the two schools. One point has already emerged with sufficient distinctness. The Teachings of the Great and Little Vehicles are not mutually exclusive as regards either Doctrine or Method, and there is sufficient evidence to show that in Ancient and Mediæval India followers of various branches of both schools were sometimes found dwelling together as members of a single confraternity. Though the Hinayana repudiated as heretical the distinctively Mahayana teachings, as does the Theravada to this day, a number of them were too useful to be ignored and were in the end tacitly absorbed by the more conservative school. The Mahayana, on the other hand, had recourse to the much bolder expedient of incorporating the Hinayana wholesale into its own teachings. Tibetan Buddhists even today speak of their faith as the Triyana Tibetan Buddhism, the three *yānas* being in this case not those described in Section III, but the Hinayana, the Mahayana and the Tantrayana envisaged as the successively higher stages of a single path. Yet it would be a mistake to think that what we have termed the distinctively Mahayana teachings were altogether different from, or discontinuous with, the teachings incorporated from Hinayana sources. Sarvastivadin and Vijnanavadin scholasticism constitutes one continuous line of development, and however unorthodox certain Mahayana doctrines may appear in the eyes of modern Theravadins all of them can be discovered in germinal form in the pages of the Theravada Scriptures. Even the five general characteristics by means of which we have distinguished the Mahayana from the Hinayana could be illustrated with instances derived from the oldest strata of the Pali Canon. The Mahayana is a movement not of innovation but of development and unfoldment. Hardly astonishing, therefore, is the fact that more than one historian of Buddhism has found the similitude of a plant or a tree particularly appropriate. The Mahayana is related to the Original Teaching as a flower to its parent germ. And as the flower produces fresh seed so does the Mahayana contain within itself the possibility of perpetually renascent spiritual life. The Hinayana literalism against which the Mahayanists inveighed may be compared to the husk which, while it protects the seed in the early stages of its growth must be burst asunder and cast aside if the germinating life within is to find room for development. Whatever the verdict of historians may be, in the spiritual sense the Mahayana is not a departure from but rather a return to the Teaching of the Buddha.

The Mahayanists themselves have, in fact, always believed that the distinctive tenets of their school, far from being developments of or additions to the original Buddha-Word were actually taught by the Lord's own golden mouth. This point of view may be expressed in two different ways. According to the first, which is the account traditionally accepted by Mahayanists, the Sanskrit Sutras as we have them today are nothing less than the direct utterance of the Sakyamuni Himself: some might have been delivered earlier in His career, others later; but all are to be fitted in with the recorded events of His earthly existence and all to find a place in the catalogue of historical discourses. The second way of understanding the Mahayana point of view has been hit upon by certain modern Japanese Buddhist scholars, and is much more sophisticated. According to this interpretation, though the Buddha cannot be regarded as the author of the Sanskrit Sutras, the distinctively Mahayana doctrines embodied in these works were first taught by Him to the more advanced among His disciples, who then transmitted them esoterically from generation to generation until the time was ripe for making them public. By the publication of these hitherto carefully guarded traditions is of course meant the composition of the Sanskrit Sutras which, though they may not reproduce with stenographic fidelity the *ipsissima verba* of the Buddha, at least preserve the substance of authentic teachings. As expressed in the traditional way, the Mahayana point of view is quite unacceptable: the Sanskrit Sutras are unmistakably the work of a period much later than that of the Buddha. But as interpreted by the Japanese scholars it contains an important element of truth, and in this form, though difficult to prove, has at least the advantage of being impossible to disprove. The least that can be said for the Mahayanists is that they are undoubtedly right in claiming to be in the direct line of spiritual descent from the Buddha, though they must be understood as having transmitted, not this or that doctrine, in the sense of a more or less elaborate conceptual formulation of transcendental verities, but rather that to which all such formulations pertain and point, namely, the Buddha's own experience of Enlightenment. With the preservation of this experience the Mahayanists were from the very beginning of their career as an independent school chiefly concerned, the principal reason for their dissent from Hinayana literalism being their conviction that it rendered Enlightenment impossible of attainment.

This dissent naturally sought to justify itself in criticism. But the main object of Mahayana criticism was not the doctrines and methods of the Hinayana tradition but rather the attitude which the Hinayanists took up towards them and the manner in which they interpreted them. In fact, as we have already seen, instead of rejecting the Hinayana teachings the Mahayanists incorporated them into their own tradition, where they may still be found. Such criticisms of the Hinayana as occur in the Mahayana Sutras are therefore to be understood as directed not against the actual teachings of the Buddha as preserved, for instance, in the *Suttas* of the Theravada Pali Canon, so much as against the one-sided interpretations which had arisen in certain ancient schools, especially among the Sarvastivadins. Indeed, though the substance of the Mahayana criticism still holds good of certain vociferous and violent groups claiming to represent the modern Theravada, the only surviving Hinayana school, it is not at all applicable to what appear to be the oldest strata of the *Vinaya Piṭaka* and *Sutta Piṭaka* of the Theravada *Tipiṭaka*. Mahayana and Theravada, when correctly interpreted, are much closer to each other than is generally imagined, a truth to which some at least among the followers of both schools now seem to be awakening, especially in Japan and Ceylon, to both of which countries must be ascribed the merit of endeavouring to achieve a more synoptic view of Buddhism.

Disastrous as Hinayana literalism undoubtedly is, it should not be thought that liberalism is without its dangers. Eventually, after having flourished in the land of its birth for more than fifteen hundred years, the Mahayana carried liberalism to extremes and exalted the spirit above the letter of the teaching to such an extent that the latter was almost lost sight of and the Dharma deprived, at least on the mundane plane, of its distinctive individuality. This was one of the factors responsible for the decline of Buddhism in India and its ultimate disappearance from its native soil.

Hinayana and Mahayana may be regarded as representing two tendencies, one centripetal and the other centrifugal, in the teaching of the Buddha. While the first prevents disintegration, the second preserves from petrification. In the history of Buddhism we see the constant interplay of these two tendencies or forces, each of which exists in a subordinate manner within the sphere of influence of the other. As the existence of the solar system depends upon the maintenance of a perfect balance between the centripetal and centrifugal forces impelling the heavenly bodies of which it is composed, so the very existence of Buddhism depends upon the maintenance of an absolute equilibrium between the literalizing and the liberalizing influences which the Hinayana and the Mahayana respectively exert over the doctrines and methods constituting the Dharma. This fact the Mahayana realizes with much greater vividness than the Hinayana, so that, although historically speaking the Mahayana is opposed to the Hinayana, doctrinally it includes it. The Hinayana, which in the modern context means the Theravada, on the contrary generally regards the Mahayana as a degeneration of the Original Teaching, of which it claims to be the sole custodian, and the distinctively Mahayana doctrines and methods are repudiated as corruptions of "the Pure Dhamma." But as Dr. Conze says, "To regard all later Buddhist history as a record of the "degeneration" of an "original" gospel is like regarding an oak tree as a degeneration of an acorn."[1] The most reasonable course seems to take the Mahayana's own view of its relation to the Enlightenment of the Buddha on the one hand, and to the Hinayana on the other, and to regard its distinctive teachings as legitimate, helpful and indeed necessary developments. What exactly these developments were it will now be our business to enquire.

VI. The Trikaya Doctrine

Seemingly inexhaustible though the topics relating to Buddhism undoubtedly are, they may all be distributed under three heads: the Buddha, the Dharma and the Sangha. The *Triratna,* or Three Jewels, in fact constitute Buddhism. To accept Buddhism means, in traditional terminology, to go for refuge to the Enlightened One, to go for refuge to His Teaching, and to go for refuge to His Order. The developments which took place in the Mahayana may therefore also be classified under these headings. We shall accordingly discuss, in very general terms, firstly the distinctively Mahayana doctrines concerning the Buddha, secondly those pertaining to the Dharma, and thirdly those relating to the Sangha.

In the Hinayana the Buddha was generally regarded as a human being who, after passing through the normal experiences of life, had by means of His own exertions attained Enlightenment. The Mahayanists, however, as they penetrated deeper into the transcendental Reality behind the mundane appearance, gradually evolved the doctrine of the *Trikāya,* the three bodies or personalities of the Buddha: *Nirmāṇakāya, Sambhogakāya* and *Dharmakāya.* According to this doctrine the Buddha is not merely a human being but Reality Itself. This Reality, being not only Wisdom but Compassion, for the purpose of preaching the Dharma to all beings assumes innumerable forms. These forms, of which

[1] *Buddhism, Its Essence and Development,* p. 26.

Gautama Buddha is the one best known to us, are all identical with Reality and hence themselves wholly transcendental. Human birth and death are nothing but appearances. In reality the Buddha is never born and never dies. He never attains Enlightenment; for He is eternally enlightened, and in any case, according to the profoundest Mahayana teaching, Enlightenment is in the ultimate sense unattainable. His "attainment" under the Bodhi Tree at Gayā was, like all the other events of His earthly career, simply a skilful device (*upāya kauśalya*) for the encouragement of the ignorant. The historical personality of the Buddha is the particular mode in which unenlightened gods and men perceive the transcendental compassionate activity of the Absolute.

Presented in this bald fashion the Mahayana conception of the Buddha-nature seems at first sight to be more of the nature of a revolution than an evolution, more a radical departure than a natural development; but a number of intermediate stages do connect the Hinayana with the Mahayana conception, and perhaps the best method of comprehending the *Trikāya* doctrine in its fully developed form would be to trace these earlier stages of its evolution. For the sake of convenient exposition they may be regarded as four in number. We may describe them as the Early and Late Hinayana, and Early and Late Mahayana stages, respectively. The first stage is represented by the Theravada, the second by the Sarvastivada, the third by the Madhyamika and Mahasangha jointly, and the fourth by the Yogacara. Each of these schools, while taking its stand upon the teaching of its predecessors, added its own contribution to the development of the doctrine.

(a) A great deal of discussion revolved around the question of the exact meaning of the terms *Rūpakāya* and *Dharmakāya*. Though from the very beginning it was agreed that the Buddha possessed these two bodies, there was no unanimity of opinion regarding their nature and function. The Early Hinayanists, for instance, "conceived Buddha's *Rūpakāya* as that of a human being, and his *dharmakāya* as the collection of his dhammas, *i.e.*, doctrines and disciplinary rules collectively."[1] This is, generally speaking, the conception most often encountered in the *Nikāyas* of the Theravada Pali Canon; but, as the authority just cited

[1] DUTT, *Aspects*, p. 102.

points out, even in these works passages do occur which admit of a different interpretation.[1] To the monk Vakkali, who on his deathbed had ardently desired to see the Buddha in person, the Blessed One said, "He who sees the Dhamma sees Me. He who sees Me sees the Dhamma." Whether we interpret these words realistically or metaphysically will depend upon the nature of the general attitude we adopt towards Buddhism. If our attitude is literal, in the sense already defined, the word Dharma, which is the key word of the whole passage, will be interpreted literally: the Dharma will be identified with its conceptional and verbal formulations, and the Buddha's admonition to Vakkali will mean no more than that inasmuch as He is, metaphorically speaking, the embodiment of His various doctrines and disciplinary precepts, one who walks in accordance with them may be said to "see" Him. If on the other hand our attitude is liberal, and if for us the Dharma means not so much the words and concepts which indicate Reality but Reality Itself, then we shall see in the utterance of the Buddha a declaration of His essential identity with the Absolute, so that to "realize" the Dharma and to "see" the Buddha are not metaphorically but in actual fact the same thing, being simply alternative ways of expressing the ultimate transcendental experience.

(b) The Later Hinayana conception of the Buddha-nature, while continuing to adhere to the realistic interpretation of the *Rūpakāya* started interpreting the *Dharmakāya* metaphysically. In the *Abhidharmakośa* of Vasubandhu, the great Sarvastivadin doctor, two explanations of the *Dharmakāya* are given. According to the first one, the *Dharmakāya* is the sum total of the qualities (*dharmas*) constituting a Buddha or, what comes to the same thing, the aggregate of those qualities the acquisition of which is synonymous with the attainment of Full Enlightenment. Taking the first of the three refuges means taking refuge not in the Buddha, in the sense of a transient human personality, but in Buddhahood. Vasubandhu has in fact demonstrated that the very act of taking refuge in the Buddha implies a non-realistic interpretation of the *Dharmakāya*. Gautama Buddha is dead and gone. In what, then, shall we take refuge if not in the indestructible essence of Buddhahood? This means a metaphysical interpretation

[1] *Ibid.*, p. 98.

of the Buddha-nature. According to Vasubandhu's second explanation, which goes a step farther than his first, the *Dharmakāya* consists of

*a series of pure dharmas, or rather a renewal of the psycho-physical organism of the substratum (*anāsravadharmasaṁtāna, āśrayaparāvṛitti*). The Dharmakāya then signifies a new purified personality or substratum (*āśraya*) but it is pointed out that such a Dharmakāya is possessed also by an arhat.*[1]

The reader probably finds these technicalities rather obscure. What Vasubandhu means can perhaps be reduced to simpler, if less precise, language. The so-called individual is nothing but a succession or stream of material and mental events or *dharmas*. In the case of a worldly being, contaminated as he is by greed, hatred and delusion, these dharmas are said to be impure. In the case of a Buddha or an Arahant these impure *dharmas* have all been purified by Wisdom. The personality of an enlightened being is a succession or stream of pure *dharmas*. These pure *dharmas* are collectively termed the *Dharmakāya*. The *Dharmakāya* is the same for all Buddhas. Harivarman, the founder of the Satyasiddhi school, going a little farther than Vasubandhu, differentiates the *Dharmakāya* of a Buddha from that of an Arahant by making it consist not only in the qualities constituting Enlightenment but also in the qualities and endowments associated with the specific cosmic functions of a Buddha as rediscoverer and re-proclaimer of the Way.

(c) The Early Mahayana stage was mainly one of synthesis. The *Prajñāpāramitā* literature had already familiarized the Mahayana schools with a purely metaphysical interpretation of Nirvana, the goal of the Buddhist life, as the state or principle of *Śūnyatā* or Voidness. *Prajñā* or Wisdom was not simply an intuitive understanding of the true nature of phenomena but a transcendental faculty for the apprehension of that Reality—*Śūnyatā*—which all phenomena are in essence. The Madhyamikas revised the *Dharmakāya* doctrine in the light of these conceptions. According to them, the *Dharmakāya* of the Buddha consists chiefly of *Prajñā*. In other words, His personality is ultimately identical with the Cognition of Reality, or, since on the transcendental plane no distinction can be made between the subject and the object of knowledge, identical with Reality Itself. The

[1] *Ibid.*, p. 106.

metaphysical implications of the Buddha's declaration "He who sees Me sees the Dharma" have now been rendered fully explicit. No further development could therefore take place in this direction, so in the Early Mahayana stage we find the centre of interest shifts from the *Dharmakāya* of the Buddha to His *Rūpakāya*.

Discussions concerning the nature of the *Rūpakāya* were already rife in Hinayana circles. The Theravadins and Sarvastivadins had argued that the material body of the Tathāgata was really material, and not a transcendental entity as the Mahasanghikas in general, and their branch the Lokottaravadins in particular, believed. According to the more realistic view, which was the view of the Madhyamikas also, the Buddha's physical body was the product of His karmas in previous existences and before its birth, which took place in the natural manner, had gone through all the normal stages of intra-uterine development. These views scandalized the Mahasanghikas, who maintained the contradictory thesis that the Sakyamuni's body was an apparitional body which, after residing in the womb for a time one month in excess of the normal period of gestation, spontaneously made its appearance at the moment of parturition. "They conceived Buddha," says Dr. N. Dutt, summarizing the views of the Mahasanghikas and their followers:

> *as* lokottara *(transcendental), and Sakyamuni as only a phantom (Nirmāṇakāya). The transcendental Buddha has a rūpakāya which is limitless, everlasting, free from all sāśrava [impure] dharmas. He is always in samādhi, never sleeps or dreams, and can know everything in an instant of thought. He knows neither fatigue nor rest, and is ever busy in enlightening sentient beings. His power and his life are limitless. For the benefit of sentient beings, He appears at will in any one of the six gatis [realms]. Whatever he utters relates to the truth, though people may understand him differently. In short, the Mahasanghikas conceived Buddha as a totally supermundane being with illimitable powers and knowledge, who never desired to attain Nirvana.*[1]

Though this uncompromisingly transcendental conception of the Buddha-nature was incorporated into the *Trikāya* doctrine only during the third, or what we have termed the Early Mahayana stage, of its development, it dates from a much earlier period of Buddhist history. As we saw at the conclusion of Chapter I, the schism between the Theravadins and the Maha-

[1] *Ibid.*, p. 111.

sanghikas occurred about a century after the Buddha's Parinirvana, and there is sufficient literary evidence to show that by the time of Ashoka the Lokottaravadin conception of the Buddha-nature was fully developed. Indeed, it would seem that their transcendentalist doctrines were not altogether innovations upon the original Teaching but rather a systematic arrangement and an emphatic statement of traditions which had existed from the earliest times. Traces of these traditions are to be found even in the *Nikāyas* of the Theravada Pali Canon, and signs of a slight tendency towards a non-realistic conception of the *Rūpakāya* are by no means absent either from later Hinayana literature or from popular Hinayana belief even at the present day. According to the *Mahāparinibbāṇa Sutta* of the *Dīgha-Nikāya* the Buddha could, had He so wished, have remained in the world until the end of the kalpa or world-period.[1] His *Rūpakāya*, even if not everlasting as the Lokottaravadins claimed, must therefore have been of immense duration. Many of the numerous passages of the Pali Canon dealing with Meditation refer to the power—within the reach of all who succeed in attaining to the fourth *jhāna*—of producing a subtle body resembling the gross one in every particular except that whereas the former is made of matter the latter is made of mind (*manomaya*). The *Saṁyutta-Nikāya* records a dialogue on the subject between the Buddha and Ananda.

"Does the Exalted One fully know, Lord, how to reach the Brahma-world by magic power, by means of the mind-created body?"

"I do indeed know, Ānanda."

"Does the Exalted One fully know, Lord, how to reach the Brahma-world by means of this body which is compounded of the four great elements?"

"I do indeed know, Ānanda."

"A strange thing it is, Lord! A marvel it is, Lord, that the Exalted One has this knowledge!"

"Yes, Ānanda. Strange indeed are the Tathāgatas and endowed with strange powers. Marvellous indeed are the Tathāgatas and endowed with marvellous powers.

"Whenever, Ānanda, the Tathāgata concentrates body in mind and concentrates mind in body, and entering on awareness of ease and buoyancy abides therein, at such time, Ānanda, the body of the Tathāgata is more buoyant, softer, more pliable, and more radiant.

"Suppose Ānanda, a ball of iron is heated all day long. It becomes lighter,

---

[1] *Dīgha-Nikāya*, II 104-15.

softer, more pliable, and more radiant. Just so it is, Ānanda, with the body of the Tathāgata.

"Now, Ānanda, at the time when the Tathāgata so concentrates body in mind and concentrates mind in body, the Tathāgata's body with but little effort rises from the earth into the sky, and in divers ways enjoys magic power, to wit: being one he becomes many and so forth, and he has power over the body even up to the world of Brahma.

"Just as, Ānanda, a ball of cotton or thistledown, light and borne by the wind with but little effort rises from the ground into the sky . . . just so when the Tathāgata concentrates mind in body and body in mind . . . does he in divers ways enjoy magic power . . . even up to the world of Brahma."

Saṁyutta-Nikāya, *V. 283-4 (Woodward's translation)*[1]

According to Buddhaghosa, once, when the Buddha was engaged in preaching the Abhidhamma to His mother in the Tutsita heaven, He created a number of Nimmita Buddhas to take His place on earth.[2] All these mind-formed Buddhas were in speech, appearance and behaviour His exact replicas, even down to the rays of light issuing from their bodies and the difference between them and the Buddha's original body could be detected only by gods belonging to the higher ranks of the celestial hierarchy. With regard to the mode of the Sakyamuni's birth, the *Dīgha-Nikāya* says that an ordinary being enters the womb unconscious, so remains and so comes forth; the eighty great disciples enter the womb fully conscious, but remain in it and come forth from it unconscious of the past; the two chief disciples, in this case Sāriputta and Moggallāna, enter the womb fully conscious and so remain, but coming forth they lose recollection. A Buddha, however, in His last birth enters the womb, remains in it and comes forth from it with perfect recollection of His past career and fully conscious of His future greatness. Even according to Hinayana tradition, the Buddha's appearance in the world by no means took place in the normal manner. He issued from the right side of His mother, without pain, and with a great multitude of celestial beings in attendance. Says the poet Asvaghosha, whose great poem the *Buddha Carita* is from the doctrinal point of view probably a Sarvastivada work:

At the time the constellation Pushya was auspicious, and from the side of the queen, who was purified by her vow, her son was born for the welfare of the world, without pain and without illness.[3]

---

[1] *Some Sayings of the Buddha*, pp. 260-61.

[2] *The Expositor.*

[3] *Buddha Carita*, I. 25.

The words "purified by her vow" probably refer to the tradition, handed down by both Hinayana and Mahayana schools, that the conception of the Bodhisattva, the future Buddha, took place at a time when His mother, Maha-Maya, was observing the eight precepts. Since the third precept enjoins complete celibacy the Bodhisattva's conception obviously could not have taken place as the result of sexual intercourse. His body, therefore, not being the product of ovum and spermatozoon, could not have been material. It must have been non-material.

The non-realistic theses of the Lokottaravada were little more than a collation of common traditions of this kind. So far as we can judge from the existing literary remains, one such thesis alone seems not to have been directly implied by the Original Teaching. This was the Lokottaravadins' definite insistence that what appeared to be the physical body of the Buddha was in reality not mundane but transcendental. True, the Pali texts speak of a *manomayakāya* or mind-formed body, but the mind of an enlightened person, no less than His physical body, is mundane. A transcendental body can be the property only of one who has realized the Transcendental. Since according to the Hinayana teaching the Sakyamuni did not attain Enlightenment until He was thirty-five years of age He could not have attained a transcendental body until that time. Consequently, even though He might have been born with a mind-made body He could not have been born with one that was transcendental. The Lokottaravadins, however, maintained that the body of the Tathāgata was transcendental from the time of His apparent birth to the time of His apparent death. For was not the transcendental *Rūpakāya* possessed of endless life and infinite power? In order to safeguard the transcendental nature of the Buddha's *Rūpakāya* the Lokottaravadins were, logically speaking, compelled to regard the Buddha's Enlightenment as having taken place long before His present birth. We have no means of ascertaining whether such a conclusion was actually drawn at this stage, but during the Later Mahayana stage it was certainly drawn by the Yogacarins and constitutes one of the most important elements in the fully developed *Trikāya* doctrine. This process of antedating the Buddha's Enlightenment may have been facilitated by the development of the Bodhisattva doctrine, which, as a description of the career of Gautama the Buddha in His previous existences, was accepted even by the Theravada. *Dhyāna* or *Samādhi* is according to the Mahayanists, the fifth of the six or ten paramitas which the Bodhisattva must practise in order to prepare Himself for the attainment of Buddhahood. Though not enumerated in the corresponding Hinayana lists, its practice is implied by the inclusion of *mettā* and *upekkhā* both of which are forms of meditation, as well as by the inclusion of *Paññā* or Wisdom, for the attainment of which the practice of *Dhyāna* is indispensable. As we have already seen, the creation of a mind-formed body is within the reach of anyone attaining the fourth stage of superconsciousness. The Bodhisattva, having in the course of his previous existences perfected himself in Meditation, must be possessed of a mind-formed body by means of which it would be possible for him to appear first in the Tusita heaven and then on earth, wherein, as an actor on the stage, he would enact the drama of Birth, Enlightenment and Parinirvana. This mind-formed body could, however, he regarded as being of a transcendental nature, as the Lokottaravadins claimed, only if the Bodhisattva could be shown to have attained Nirvana, in the Hinayana sense of the term, at some time during the course of his previous career. This had to be demonstrated by the Yogacarins and others at the fourth and last stage in the development of *Trikāya* doctrine. Meanwhile, the achievement of the third stage may be held to consist in its synthesis of the Madhyamika conception of the *Dharmakāya* with the Lokottaravadin conception of the *Rūpakāya,* which, by a significant adjustment of terms, became known as the *Nirmāṇakāya* or Body of Transformation.

(d) If the Early Mahayana stage was chiefly one of synthesis, the Late Mahayana stage was mainly one of elaboration. Having clearly demonstrated the purely transcendental nature of the *Rūpakāya* or *Nirmāṇakāya,* the Mahayanists proceeded to distinguish the gross *Rūpakāya* from its subtle counterpart. This subtle *Rūpakāya* was then subjected to a further process of subdivision. These two developments, with which the *Trikāya* doctrine was brought to perfection, were both largely the achievement of the Yogacarins. We shall deal with each of them in turn.

As already indicated, without antedating the Buddha's attainment of Nirvana from His present life to one of His past lives it is impossible to establish the purely transcendental nature of

His *Rūpakāya*. That the Yogacarins were able to surmount this formidable obstacle was due to the developments which had taken place in Mahayana philosophy as a whole, particularly to the sharp distinction which came to be drawn between the Hinayana and Mahayana conceptions of Nirvana and to the more detailed and dogmatic treatment given to the various stages (*bhūmis*) of the Bodhisattva's career. Since the Mahayana ideal was not spiritual individualism but transcendental altruism, it naturally tended to relegate all merely individual gains to a comparatively inferior position in the hierarchy of spiritual attainments. Thus, though not denying the possibility of an individual Nirvana being gained by Sravakas and Pratyekabuddhas if they so wished, they refused either to consider such a state as identical with Reality or to regard its attainment as the ultimate objective of the Bodhisattva's career. This career consists of ten successive stages or *bhūmis*. According to the *Daśabhūmika Sūtra,* in which the fullest and most systematic treatment of the doctrine of *bhūmis* is found, it is at the eighth *bhūmi,* named *Acalā* or The Immovable, that the Bodhisattva definitely renounces the prospect of individual Nirvana, which is at this stage within his reach, and instead perseveres in his efforts to attain Full Enlightenment for the good of all sentient beings. We must beware, however, of understanding our conceptual formulations of these exalted experiences too literally. Though at the eighth stage of his career the Bodhisattva does not attain Nirvana in the sense in which it is attained by the Sravakas and Pratyekabuddhas, it must not be supposed therefore that he does not attain Nirvana in any sense. He attains whatever they attain, but with this difference, that whereas they, because they cherished an individualistic spiritual ideal, from the moment of their attaining Nirvana cease to exist so far as the phenomenal world is concerned, he, being supported by the sustaining power of the Buddhas and by his own age-old vow to lead all sentient beings to Enlightenment, simultaneously attains a transcendental body by means of which he continues to appear in the various realms of phenomenal existence. This doctrine is clearly enunciated in the *Laṅkāvatāra Sūtra,* wherein the Lord, discoursing to Mahamati on the ten stages of Bodhisattvahood says:—

"Further, Mahāmati, the Srāvakas and Pratyekabuddhas at the eighth stage of Bodhisattvahood are so intoxicated with the happiness that comes from the

attainment of perfect tranquillization, and, failing to understand fully that there is nothing in the world but what is seen of the Mind itself, they are thus unable to overcome the hindrances and habit-energy growing out of their notions of generality and individuality; and adhering to the egolessness of persons and things and cherishing views arising therefrom, they have the discriminating idea and knowledge of Nirvana, which is not that of the truth of absolute solitude. Mahāmati, when the Bodhisattvas face and perceive the happiness of the Samādhi of perfect tranquillization, they are moved with the feeling of love and sympathy owing to their original vows, and they become aware of the part they are to perform as regards the (ten) inexhaustible vows. Thus, they do not enter Nirvana. But the fact is that they are already in Nirvana because in them there is no rising of discrimination."[1]

The obtainment of the *Nirmāṇakāya* at this stage is clearly indicated by the text in the following verse:—

When those who are born of the Buddha see that the world is no more than Mind itself, they will obtain a body of transformation which has nothing to do with effect-producing works, but which is endowed with the powers, psychic faculties, and self-control.[2]

As Eliot, summarizing the *Trikāya* doctrine, tersely puts the matter,

According to the general opinion of the Mahayanists a Buddha attains to Nirvana by the very act of becoming a Buddha and is therefore beyond everything which we call existence. Yet the compassion which he feels for mankind and the good karma which he has accumulated cause a human image of him (Nirmāṇakāya) to appear among men for their instruction and a super-human image, perceptible yet not material, to appear in Paradise.[3]

Becoming a Buddha and obtaining Nirvana in the Hinayana sense however occurs, according to the Mahayanists, in the eighth stage of the Bodhisattva's career. Hence does Har Dayal, in his account of this stage as described in the *Daśabhūmika Sūtra,* declare, "This *bhūmi* is so important that it is called the Stage of Perfection, of Birth, of Finality."[4] Thereafter the Bodhisattva lives and works in a transcendental body, and it is apparently in such a body that, having obtained the *Dharmakāya* in the tenth stage of his career, he appears on earth as a Perfect Buddha. According to the *Daśabhūmika,* upon the attainment of the *Dharmakāya* the Bodhisattva attains a glorious body seated on a celestial

---

[1] SUZUKI, *The Lankavatara Sutra,* p. 184.
[2] *Ibid.,* p. 65.
[3] *Hinduism and Buddhism: An Historical Sketch* (London 1954), II. 35.
[4] *The Bodhisattva Doctrine in Buddhist Sanskrit Literature* (London, 1932), p. 290.

lotus adorned with jewels. The nature of the relation between this body and the body or bodies attained in the eighth stage does not seem to have been made the subject of investigation. Relating as it does to experiences beyond the power of heart to conceive or tongue to utter the matter is abstruse in the extreme. But it can at least be safely asserted that if the Nirvana attained in the eighth stage is transcendental the body then acquired must be transcendental too. At any rate, the Bodhisattva's career being thought of as infinitely long, and ages incalculable being considered to elapse from the attainment of one stage to the attainment of the next, there was a tendency on the part of the Mahayanists to think of the acquisition of the transcendental body as having taken place at an age infinitely remote from the present. Hence the great Bodhisattvas, such as Avalokitesvara and Manjusri, have no history. Practically speaking, they are purely transcendental personages—bright effluences of the "bright essence uncreate" of the Absolute—eternally existent outpourings of the Compassion which is Wisdom and the Wisdom which is Compassion—the everlasting saviours of mankind.

The doctrine of *bhūmis* having enabled the Mahayanists to antedate the Buddha's attainment of Nirvana, thus establishing the transcendental nature of His *Rūpakāya,* all that they had to do, in order to bring the *Trikāya* doctrine to perfection, was to subdivide the *Rūpakāya* into a gross and a subtle form. This development, the last of the long series, was again the work of the Yogacarins, who proceeded to distinguish between the personalities styled, when at a later period the terminology of the doctrine became more fixed, as *Sambhogakāya* and *Nirmāṇakāya.* The basis of this distinction is the idea that a Buddha or a Bodhisattva appears to different beings in different ways, according to their various tastes and temperaments and their various degrees of spiritual refinement. Indeed, it is not so much that Buddhas and Bodhisattvas assume different forms, as that the same transcendental compassionate activity of the Absolute is perceived in different ways by different minds, being thereby as it were broken up into a multitude of glorious figures in much the same way as a beam of light, on passing through a prism, is broken up into all the glowing iridescent hues of the rainbow. Carried to its logical conclusion, this would mean that there are as many Buddhas or Bodhisattvas as there are sentient creatures in the universe, each divine form being the mode under which the *Dharmakāya* exists for and through which it acts upon one particular person, or even one particular thing. From these premises the *Laṅkāvatāra* arrives at the conclusion that, just as the hand may be called *hasta* or *kara* or *pāṇi* and the body *tanu* or *deha* or *śarīra,* so may the Tathāgata "come within the range of hearing of ignorant people, in this world of patience, under many names, amounting to a hundred thousand times three asamkhyeyas," by which "they address Him not knowing that they are names of the Tathāgata."[1] Indeed, it roundly declares that even the names of various non-Buddhist deities, such as Brahma and Vishnu, as well as the numerous Buddhist and non-Buddhist designations of Reality, such as Nirvana, the Eternal, the Emptiness, the *Dharmadhātu,* the Formless, are all appellations of the Tathāgata.[2]

This dangerous doctrine, which ultimately helped to sap the foundations of Buddhism in India, did not all at once make its appearance. Since it was possible to divide sentient beings into two classes, the spiritually developed and the spiritually undeveloped, the primary division of the *Rūpakāya* was, as we have seen, into the *Sambhogakāya* or Body of Enjoyment, which is the *Dharmakāya* as perceived in the celestial realms by Bodhisattvas coursing in any one of the ten *bhūmis,* and the *Nirmāṇakāya,* which is the same reality as perceived on earth by Sravakas, Pratyekabuddhas, and ordinary folk, as well as by those Bodhisattvas who have not yet entered upon the first *bhūmi.* The *Sambhogakāya* again is twofold, consisting of the *Svasambhoga,* or form in which a Buddha is perceived by the Buddhas of other world-systems, and the *Parasambhoga,* or form perceived by Bodhisattvas. This refinement of analysis possesses, however, only a theoretical interest, and for all practical purposes the Buddha is regarded as possessing simply three bodies, the *Dharmakāya,* the *Sambhogakāya* and the *Nirmāṇakāya.* The nature of the first and the last of these having been explained when we dealt with the second and third stages in the development of the *Trikāya* doctrine the second one alone, that is to say, the *Sambhogakāya,* now claims our attention.

---

[1] *The Lankavatara Sutra,* p. 165.

[2] *Ibid.,* 166.

Just as the *Nirmāṇakāya* Buddha, in the sense of the human and historical Sakyamuni, is the central figure of the Hinayana, so is the *Sambhogakāya,* in one or another of its numerous resplendent manifestations, the dominating figure of the Mahayana. It is the *Sambhogakāya* which preaches the Mahayana Sutras, just as it is the *Nirmāṇakāya* which preaches those of the Hinayana. He is the supreme object of faith and devotion, the ultimate dazzling focus into which are concentrated, like innumerable converging beams of light, all those incipient strivings and yearnings of the heart, those half-blind impulses to perfection, those mighty soaring flights of love and adoration, which in less philosophical religions are directed towards more or less crude conceptions of the theistic order. His glorious body adorned with the thirty-two major and eighty minor marks of a Buddha, the illimitable radiance of which fills the entire cosmos, has ever been a favourite subject of Mahayana art, and the various transcendental forms in which it dawns sunlike above the horizon of the devotee's meditation have in the course of time been embodied in works of art which, apart from their value as supports of the spiritual life in general and the practice of meditation in particular, are acclaimed as being among the greatest artistic treasures of mankind.

So fervent was the devotion of the Mahayanists, so exuberantly creative their spiritual imagination, and so intensive their artistic activity, that the spacious Mahayana heavens speedily became populated with a glorious company of transcendental beings—Buddhas, Bodhisattvas and a host of lesser divinities—every one of whom possessed his or her distinctive attributes and individual personality. So numerous, indeed, did these *Sambhogakāya* forms eventually become that the Mahayanists began to feel the need for reducing them to some kind of order. Different systems of classification were accordingly adopted by different schools, the best known and most popular being a grouping into five "families" over each of which a particular Buddha presided. These five families were correlated with the five elements, the five *skandhas,* the five senses, and so on, as well as with various colours, letters of the alphabet, points of the compass, animals, etc. Vairocana, Amitābha, Ratnasambhava, Amoghasiddhi and Akshobhya are the five presiding Buddhas of this system, their families consisting of the great Bodhisattvas, each of whom is associated with this or that Buddha as his spiritual son, as well as of the female consorts which, at a later stage of development, each Buddha and Bodhisattva was considered to possess. Buddha Amitabha, for instance, presides over the Lotus Family; His colour is red, His direction the West, His paradise Sukhāvatī, the Land of Bliss. He is associated with the *saṁjña skandha,* or aggregate of perception. His consort is the goddess Pāṇḍarāvāsinī and the senior-most of His spiritual sons the Bodhisattva Avalokitesvara. The daughter of Avalokitesvara is the goddess Tārā. Moreover, since every *Nirmāṇakāya* was the reflection in the muddy waters of the world of one particular *Sambhogakāya,* who remains the while in moonlike splendour high in the heavens of the Transcendental, it was also possible to incorporate the various human if not always "historical" Buddhas into the scheme. For this reason the Śākyamuni is associated with Amitābha as that Buddha's most recent earthly manifestation, and since this is the latest manifestation of a *Sambhogakāya* to have taken place the present world-period is believed to be under the special protection of Amitābha and Avalokitesvara. In the system as a whole, however, Gautama the Buddha occupies a distinctly subordinate, indeed an almost insignificant position, and one is not unoften left with the impression that the Mahayana could now get on quite well without Him. As Conze says,

> *To the Christian and agnostic historian, only the human Buddha is real, and the spiritual and the magical Buddha are to him nothing but fictions. The perspective of the believer is quite different. The Buddha-nature and the Buddha's "glorious body" stand out most clearly, and the Buddha's human body and historical existence appear like a few rags thrown over this spiritual glory.*[1]

It is this spiritual glory and not the feeble glimmerings of historical evidence which, brought to a focus in the *Trikāya* doctrine, particularly in its conception of the *Sambhogakāya,* is the true light of the Mahayana. By its emphasis on the transcendental aspect of the Buddha-nature the Mahayana not only lifts Buddhism far above the plane of mere historicity, but also fully vindicates its eternal truth and universal significance.

---

[1] *Buddhism,* p. 38.

VII. The Two Truths: The Egolessness of All Dharmas

The Mahayana not only deepened the conception of the Buddha-nature but also developed doctrines which gave to the Dharma a profounder interpretation and a wider application than it had ever before received. On the theoretical side its insistence that just as the composite was empty of selfhood so were the components of the composite devoid of own-being made clear the Buddha's Cognition of Reality as expressed in His Teaching of universal conditionality, while on the practical side its emphasis on the universality of the Bodhisattva Ideal brought into bold relief the essential features of His conception of the spiritual life. Before embarking upon a brief exposition of these two outstanding doctrines, which are the most important of the distinctively Mahayana teachings concerning the second of the Three Jewels held in common by all schools of the Great Vehicle, it will be necessary to understand how the Mahayana could develop its own interpretation of the Dharma without altogether discarding that of the Hinayana. Hence brief reference must first be made to its distinction between relative and absolute truth.

This distinction had already been drawn by the Hinayana. According to the latter vehicle there are two kinds of truth or two modes of expression, one of which is true in the ultimate sense (*paramattha-sacca*) the other only in the conventional sense (*samutti-sacca*). To the Hinayanist, *dharmas* in the sense of the 165 (so the Theravada) or the 72 (thus the Sarvastivada) ultimate material and mental constituents of phenomena are realities, for which reason the only absolutely true description of a phenomenon is the one that tells us of which *dharmas* it is composed and in what way these are interrelated. Expressions such as "The monk goes for alms" or "He said he would do the work himself" are not true in the ultimate sense because the words "monk" and "self" do not refer to any correspondent realities. For the Hinayanist, the wheel, the axle, the linchpin, etc., are real, but the chariot is unreal. While descriptions of existence in terms of soul, self, ego, person, individual, etc., are valid only in the conventional sense, those which speak of it in terms of *skandhas, āyatanas,* and *dhātus,* or in terms of Conditioned Co-production or the Four Truths, are true in the ultimate sense. Hence according to the Hinayana by absolute truth (*paramattha-sacca*) nothing else is meant but these and the other important doctrines of Buddhism. According to the Mahayana, on the other hand, since the so-called ultimate *dharmas* of the Hinayana arise in dependence on causes and conditions they are not real but unreal by nature. This conditionality or unreality of all phenomena the Mahayanists indicate by the term *Śūnyatā* or Emptiness. Doctrines such as the Four Truths and the Conditioned Co-production since they refer to unrealities are themselves unreal in the ultimate sense, and whatever truth they possess is not absolute but only conventional. *Śūnyatā* or *Tathatā* is alone the Absolute Truth. For this reason the Mahayanists relegated the whole of the Doctrine to the domain of what the Madhyamikas called *saṁvṛti-satya,* conventional truth, or what the Yogacarins, again exhibiting their talent for elaboration, described as *parikalpita* and *paratantra,* illusory and contingent reality. Revolutionary though this development may seem, the Mahayana in fact does no more than give a metaphysical interpretation of the Buddha's Parable of the Raft: the Dharma is only a means. The answer to the question "What is the use of retaining doctrines such as the Conditioned Co-production and the Four Truths if they are only relatively true?" is therefore the same as the answer to "What is the use of a raft if we cannot take it with us after reaching the farther shore?" Far from repudiating the doctrines of Buddhism, the Mahayanists retained them because, according to them, only by means of the conventional truth could the Absolute Truth be realized; the one was the stepping-stone to the other. Moreover the Absolute Truth indicated by the words *Śūnyatā* and *Tathatā* being unique can be described only by means of an exhaustive series of negations. But in order to give a negative description there must be first of all something to negate. This "something" is the conventional truth. The doctrines of Buddhism are necessary, even though not absolutely true, because only by means of the negation of these doctrines can the only possible definition of Reality, namely a negative one, emerge. In this way the Mahayanists were able to develop their own distinctive doctrines without repudiating those of the Hinayana. Without comprehending the Mahayana version of the Two Truths full understanding of the relation between the two schools is impossible.

The first of the distinctively Mahayana doctrines held in common by all schools of the Great Vehicle, namely that of the egolessness and emptiness of all things (*sarvadharmanairātmya* and *sarvadharmaśūnyatā*), is closely connected with the doctrine of the Two Truths. We tried to show in Chapter I that the principle of universal conditionality, being the conceptual formulation of the Buddha's Enlightenment, was the central teaching of Buddhism, the chief plank of that Raft which is the Dharma, the one fundamental doctrine whence all other doctrines are derived and to which they may all be reduced. Even Nirvana, as the last of the series of causal stages wherein factors of the same kind progressively augment each other, falls within its scope. The Four Truths are the product of its application to the problem of suffering. And for what reason is the so-called person (*pudgala*) said to be devoid of selfhood (*anātman*)? Simply because in it there can be found no element, either material or mental, which does not arise in dependence on causes and conditions external to itself. Obviously the flesh is more than raiment and an understanding of the principle of universal conditionality of far greater moment to the spiritual life than an understanding of any of its specific applications, however important or interesting these might be, in the form of one or another of the doctrines of Buddhism. But this truth the Hinayanists speedily forgot. Neglecting the general principle, they directed their attention almost exclusively to that one among its numerous specific applications in which they were most deeply interested: the doctrine of the egolessness of the so-called individual (*pudgalanairātmya*). As a result of their marked preference for the psychological circumference rather than for the metaphysical centre of the Dharma they eventually promulgated two doctrines, both of which were in fact a denial of the spirit of the Original Teaching as well as fruitful sources of further misunderstanding and error. According to the first, the realization of *pudgalanairātmya* by means of a thorough-going analysis of the so-called self or *ātman* into its constituent *dharmas* is by itself sufficient to bring about the attainment of Nirvana. According to the second, the *dharmas* into which the self disintegrates when properly analysed constitute a definite limited number of ultimately real entities. These entities, technically known as *saṁskṛta-dharmas*, are recognizable by such signs (*nimitta*) as painfulness and impurity. Nirvana, the *asaṁskṛta-dharma,* is however devoid of such signs (*animitta*); it is a state of purity and bliss. One attains Enlightenment by gradually detaching the mind from the conditioned and directing it towards the Unconditioned. Thus the *dharmas* constituting personality being real the signs of such *dharmas* were real. Signs being real the absence of signs was also real. Both signs and absence of signs being real the difference between Nirvana and Samsara was a real difference, and hence abandonment of the one and attainment of the other was a real abandonment and real attainment.

Against these dualistic views, which obviously point in the direction of spiritual individualism and egoism, the Mahayanists entered an emphatic protest in the form of their doctrine of *sarvadharmaśūnyatā,* or the emptiness of all *dharmas* whatsoever, which was in effect a reassertion of the primacy of the principle of universal conditionality over its applications and a reminder of the relativity of all conceptual formulations. According to this doctrine the five *skandhas,* the twelve *āyatanas,* and the eighteen *dhātus,* together with their various subdivisions, into which the Hinayanists had so laboriously and elaborately analysed the so-called person, were not ultimate realities at all but only mental constructions. As was pointed out in the course of our discussion of the two kinds of truth, the *dharmas* constituting personality arise in dependence on causes and conditions. To be dependent means to be devoid of self-nature or own-being (*svabhāva*). What is devoid of self-nature is said to be empty (*śūnya*). Conditionality and emptiness are the same thing. A conditioned *dharma* is therefore an empty *dharma.* So much, indeed, even the Hinayanists admitted. But the Mahayanists, starting from the Hinayanic distinction between *saṁskṛta* and *asaṁskṛta dharmas,* the one possessing *nimittas,* the others devoid of them, went on to draw conclusions which horrified their opponents. They pointed out that negation was unthinkable without affirmation, and that the one was therefore dependent on the other. That which is devoid of signs is as it were bounded on one side by that which possesses signs. Nirvana therefore exists only in relation to the Samsara. Being relative it is dependent, since it is dependent it is conditioned, and because it is conditioned it must be regarded as empty. Having thus equated *dharmas* with

Emptiness on the one hand and Nirvana with Emptiness on the other the Mahayanists now took the even bolder step of equating Nirvana with the Samsara. If A and B both equal C then obviously A and B must themselves be equal. This daring identification of the world of phenomena with the Absolute is one of the most important and fruitful theses of the Mahayana. Besides contributing to the formation of still profounder philosophical conceptions, it is the foundation of the *Prajñāpāramitā* logic of contradictions, which asserts the identity of affirmation and negation, as well as the ultimate justification and explanation of a great deal of later Tantric theory and practice, particularly in the field of meditation and morals.

But perhaps the most striking consequence of the principle of universal emptiness was its application to the Mahayana conception of spiritual life, particularly as formulated in the Bodhisattva Ideal. All things, conditioned or unconditioned, being empty and therefore non-different from each other (*advāya*), the Mahayanists were able to assert not only the emptiness of all *dharmas* (*sarvadharmaśūnyatā*) but also, more positively, the sameness of all *dharmas* (*sarvadharmasamatā*). Since all things are in reality the same and since any discrimination between Nirvana and Samsara is, therefore, a delusion, it necessarily follows that in the ultimate sense there can be neither abandonment of the one nor attainment of the other. For this reason the Mahayana conception of Enlightenment differs radically from that of the Hinayana. Whereas the latter tends to think of it as involving a real transition (though not of a real person, as at least Buddhaghosa was acute enough to point out) from a real Samsara to a real Nirvana, for the former it consists in the absolute cessation of all such discriminations and the realization that undifferentiated and homogeneous Emptiness, Suchness, Sameness, or Consciousness, as it may be variously denominated, is the sole Reality. Even this realization is, of course, a non-realization, and only because it is a non-realization is it a realization. Similarly it would be a mistake to think of Emptiness as constituting the self-nature or own-being of *dharmas,* for there would then be no difference between the Buddhist doctrine of Emptiness on the one hand and conceptions such as the Nirguna Brahman of Sankara or the Substance of Spinoza on the other. All things are empty, therefore emptiness is itself empty and is not to be thought of as being in reality a sort of stuff or substance out of which *dharmas* have been manufactured and to which they can again be reduced, like pots to clay, much less still as a sort of substratum which somehow stands underneath things and holds them up. When the *Prajñāpāramitā* texts declare that the Bodhisattva takes Emptiness for the basis what they really mean is that he takes nothing whatever, conditioned or unconditioned, as his basis. Consequently there is in reality not only no attainment of Nirvana but even no aspiration towards that attainment. Realizing that all *dharmas* are eternally unproduced and that "all beings are from the very beginning the Buddha," the Bodhisattva remains in a state of profound quiescence, of absolute tranquillity and purity, undisturbed by dualistic concepts. But the Absolute Truth can be realized only by means of the truth conventional. At the same time, therefore, that he courses in the idea of non-attainment, or in Emptiness, the Bodhisattva makes strenuous efforts for the attainment of Enlightenment through the practice of the Ten Perfections and the fulfilment of the various other duties of a Bodhisattva. Indeed, if he is to avoid setting up a dualistic conception of non-attainment he must so practise. Non-attainment is not different from attainment. If it were, the doctrine of the absolute quiescence of all *dharmas* would lead, in practice, to some sort of quietism, which it has never done. On the contrary, it has ever inculcated an ideal of compassionate activity unparalleled in the history of religions. But the "basis" of this intensely active compassion, it should be remembered, is not any mundane and therefore at bottom egoistic "humanitarian" ideal, but the realization that all *dharmas,* including the so-called objects of compassion, are fundamentally empty and therefore unreal.

Such a conception of the spiritual life is poles apart from the starchy individualism of the Hinayana. Yet, great though the difference between spiritual egoism and transcendental altruism undoubtedly is, it is not so deep or so wide that it cannot be bridged over by the still greater latitude of Mahayana. The Path to Enlightenment, in the Mahayanic sense of the term, to be truly comprehensive must include all stages and degrees of the spiritual life, from the lowest to the highest. Even individualism must find a place. Consequently, just as on the theoretical side the Mahayanists had been able to include the Hinayana teachings in their own by means of the doctrine of the Two Truths, so on the practical side were they able to include the spiritual ideal of the Hinayana, as well as its insight and attainment, by the simple expedient of dividing the stages of the Bodhisattva's career into two series, a higher and a lower. This division is reflected in several schemes of spiritual practice. The meditation on Emptiness, for example, is divided into five stages. In the first the Bodhisattva realizes the emptiness of *dharmas,* in the second the emptiness of conditioned *dharmas,* and in the third the emptiness of those *dharmas* which are unconditioned. These stages belong to the Hinayana. In the fourth stage he realizes the absolute emptiness of all *dharmas* whatsoever. In the fifth even the conception of Emptiness is transcended, so that here nothing can be said. These two stages belong exclusively to the Mahayana. Again, the Ten Stages of the Bodhisattva's career are divided into two series, one consisting of stages 1-6, the other of stages 7-10. The first series corresponds to the first, second and third stages of the meditation on Emptiness, while the second series corresponds to the fourth and fifth stages. That is to say, one is Hinayanic and the other Mahayanic, although both belong to the Mahayana in the sense that the Bodhisattva is required to pass through both in the course of his career. According to the more developed and more truly orthodox teaching the face of Reality is doubly veiled. Behind the outer veil (*āvaraṇa*) of passions (*kleśa*) is the inner veil of ignorance, the veil obstructing true knowledge (*jñeya*). While admitting that the Hinayanists succeeded in removing the first veil by means of the realization of *pudgala-nairātmya,* or egolessness of the so-called person, the Mahayanists maintained that the second could be removed only by means of the realization of *sarvadharmanairātmya* or *sarvadharmaśūnyatā*—the egolessness and emptiness of all things whatsoever. In the sixth stage, the last of those constituting the lower series of stages in the Bodhisattva Path, the Arahant, having by the practice of the first three meditations on Emptiness destroyed his passions and realized the egolessness of personality, attains Nirvana in the Hinayanic sense. The Bodhisattva, however, rejecting individual emancipation, passes on to the higher series of stages, in the fourth and last of which, having by means of the last two meditations on Emptiness destroyed his ignorance and realized the truth of universal emptiness, he attains *Sambodhi* or Full

…ent, or in other words becomes a Perfect Buddha. … the Mahayanists able to accommodate Hinayana …sm as an intermediate stage of the Mahayanic Path of transcendental altruism. This in effect meant that the possibility of passing from the lower to the higher series was recognized, so that, according to some texts, the sixth stage could be transcended not only by one who had accepted the Bodhisattvic Ideal from the very beginning but also by a Sravaka who, after realizing Nirvana in the Hinayanic sense, discovered his mistake and saw that the attainment that he had hitherto believed to be ultimate was in fact not so. The *Saddharma Puṇḍarīka Sūtra* represents Sariputra, who in Mahayana texts often stands for the Hinayana point of view, as making this discovery. Having heard the Buddha tell the assembled Arahants, Bodhisattvas, gods and demi-gods,

> *Rejoice greatly in your hearts*
> *Knowing that you will become Buddhas*[1]

the great disciple reproaches himself for having been a follower of the Hinayana and for having imagined that he had attained Nirvana when real Nirvana was not that of the Arahants but that of the Buddhas. The Tathāgata then predicts that after infinite, boundless, inconceivable kalpas have passed away Sariputra will become a Buddha named Flower-light and that his Buddha-domain will be called Undefiled.[2] Since the Mahayanists held that both the Hinayana and the Mahayana Scriptures were preached by the Buddha the *Saddharma-Puṇḍarīka* has to give some explanation of the discrepancy between them, and that it proceeds to do by means of a variety of parables, one of which, the Parable of the Burning House, was quoted in Section III. But now that we no longer regard the Mahayana Sutras, in their present literary form, as the direct utterance of the Buddha, such explanations are no longer necessary. The Sariputra of the *Saddharma-Puṇḍarīka* is not a historical but a symbolical figure. He represents the literal, individualistic and negative interpretation of the Dharma popular in Hinayana circles at the time of the rise of the Mahayana. He does not represent the Original Teaching as preserved, at least

---

[1] *The Lotus of the Wonderful Law*, p. 80. See also *Scripture of the Lotus Bloom of the Fine Dharma*, p. 53.

[2] *Ibid.*, p. 55.

partially, in the Pali Canon of the Theravadins as it exists today. For there is no doubt that the historical Sariputra was, like the rest of his Arahant brethren, no less enlightened than Nagarjuna himself. Only later did the Arahant ideal harden into a doctrine of spiritual individualism. Just as the Mahayana criticism of the Hinayana applies not to the Original Teaching but to corruptions of the Original Teaching, so does its relegation of the Hinayanic Nirvana to the sixth stage of the Bodhisattva's career refer not to the Nirvana of the Buddha's own Arahant disciples but to the individualistic conceptions of later Hinayana scholasticism. Once again the Mahayana teachings are more concordant with those of the earliest portions of the Pali canon than is generally imagined.

The second of the distinctively Mahayana doctrines held in common by all schools of the Great Vehicle, namely, the Bodhisattva Ideal, is not only the result of a process of development and universalization similar to what happened in the case of the first, the doctrine of conditionality, but as it were its translation into terms of human life and spiritual action. However, since the Bodhisattva doctrine will be outlined in Chapter IV all that need be done now is to record the fact of its importance and pass on. One point only need be borne in mind. Whereas to the Hinayanists the term Bodhisattva means simply Gautama Buddha in the period prior to His Enlightenment, the Mahayanists apply it to any Buddhist devotee who accepts as his ultimate goal not individual emancipation but Full Enlightenment for the sake of all sentient beings. This distinction may in part explain what follows.

VIII. The Mahayana Sangha

Having deepened the conception of the Buddha-nature and given a more adequate and ample interpretation of the Dharma, it would be a matter for astonishment if the Mahayana had not simultaneously broadened the basis of the Sangha. In the Hinayana Sutras the Buddha is generally represented as expounding the doctrine to an assembly consisting chiefly of monks, and the residual impression left by such texts is that the Dharma is on the whole intended more for the members of the monastic order than for the laity. Mahayana Sutras, however, generally depict the Buddha in His *Sambhogakāya* preaching the Dharma to an "ocean-wide" assembly consisting, besides the Arahant bhikkhus, of innumerable Bodhisattvas, Guardian Kings, and gods and demi-gods of various orders. Sometimes the particular universe in which the assembly takes place finds difficulty in accommodating so great a multitude of beings, who arrive with their respective retinues from all directions of space. Consequently the visitors are sometimes obliged, like Milton's rebel angels, to reduce their dimensions before taking their seats. Celestial beings are of course among the auditors of many a Hinayana discourse. What differentiates the Mahayana from the Hinayana Sutras, so far as the composition of their respective audiences is concerned, is the fact that in the former the Bodhisattvas are more numerous and prominent than the Arahants and that they sometimes figure as their instructors. Moreover all these Bodhisattvas are represented iconographically as laymen, generally in the form of beautiful young princes, sixteen years of age, adorned with jewelled headdresses and strings of pearls. Difference of audience indicates a difference of attitude. As we have seen in Section IV, the fourth of the five charges brought by the Mahayana against the Hinayana was in respect of over-attachment to the merely formal aspects of monasticism. The Mahayana, on the other hand, as was explained in Section V, while continuing to cherish the monastic ideal gave increased importance to a dedicated household life.

This difference of attitude is reflected in their respective conceptions of the Arya Sangha, or Congregation of Saints, of which the third of the Three Refuges taken by all Buddhists essentially consists. According to the Hinayanists this spiritual aristocracy is made up exclusively of those who have entered upon the Four Transcendental Paths, that is to say Stream-Winners, Once-Returners, Non-Returners and Arahants, all of whom, with perhaps one or two exceptions in the lower grades, are members of the monastic order. Thus for the Hinayana the spiritual community is in effect a subdivision of the ecclesiastical corporation, so that both spiritually and socially monks occupy a more prominent position than laymen. In the Mahayana, however, the Arya Sangha consists exclusively of Bodhisattvas who have entered upon the second and higher series of the stages of the Path to Supreme Enlightenment. Some of these

Bodhisattvas may be living as monks, others as laymen. Thus for the Mahayana the spiritually advanced section of the ecclesiastical corporation is only a subdivision of the spiritual community, so that spiritually at least the position of the laity is no less prominent than that of the monks. Indeed, from the Mahayana point of view, though Arahants may be reckoned as Bodhisattvas of the sixth stage, laymen who have taken upon themselves the Four Great Vows of the Bodhisattva, even without having entered upon the first of the Ten Stages of the Path, are the spiritual superiors of monks who have made no such aspiration.

Apart from the fact that even according to the Hinayana Scriptures the Buddha Himself had emphasized that truth and righteousness were of far greater importance than the external habiliments of religion, two reasons may be assigned for this broadening of the basis of the Sangha by the Mahayana, with the consequent lessening of the essential difference, if not the external distinction, between monks and laymen. One is the Mahayana equation of Samsara and Nirvana, the other its doctrine that potentially all beings are Buddhas. Monastic life obviously involves the giving up of something. Thus it is based on a dualism, between God and the world, or spirit and matter, or, in the case of Hinayana Buddhism, between the transcendental order and the mundane. By asserting that Reality was the Non-Dual and that Nirvana and Samsara were not different from each other, thus relegating the whole Hinayana doctrine and discipline to the realm not of absolute but only of conventional truth, the Mahayana brought about as it were an easing of tension between the transcendental and the mundane, with a consequent weakening of the impulse for the attainment of one by the renunciation of the other. There does not seem to be much point in giving up the world when it is only God in disguise. If the Mahayana retained the monastic life it was for the same reason that it retained the Hinayana teaching, namely, that the relative truth is the indispensable stepping-stone to the Absolute Truth. In the spiritual life there are no short cuts. When, in the last stages of its career in India, certain pseudo-Tantric schools, forgetting this teaching, tried to make direct application of the doctrine of Non-Duality on the relative plane without first realizing its important, the result was speedy degeneration and collapse. The second reason for this lessening of the difference between monks and laymen, namely that all beings are potentially Buddhas, is the logical corollary of the Bodhisattva Ideal, as universalized by the Mahayana. All beings should traverse the Ten Stages of the Bodhisattva's career. All should aim at Supreme Buddahood for the sake of all sentient beings. All, in fact, *will* attain Supreme Buddhahood. However distant the day of Enlightenment may be, dawn it must for everyone, even if after the lapse of æons impossible to enumerate. Translated from the language of time into the language of eternity this means that speaking metaphysically, or from the standpoint of the highest truth, all beings are even now the Buddha, however unaware they may be of the fact. The only difference between the Buddha and an ordinary man is that the former knows that he is the Buddha whereas the latter does not. As the *Ratnagotra-vibhāga* says,

> *The element of Tathagatahood, as it is present in all, is immutable,*
> *and cannot be affected by either defilement or purification.*
> *Like the Buddha in a faded lotus flower, like honey covered by a*
> *swarm of bees,*
> *Like the kernel of a fruit in the husk, like gold within impurities,*
> *Like a treasure hidden in the soil, the fruit in a small seed,*
> *An image of the Jina in tattered garments,*
> *The universal monarch in the vile belly of a woman,*
> *And like a precious statue covered with dust,*
> *So is this element established in beings*
> *Who are covered with the stains of adventitious defilements.*
> (Ratnagotravibhāga, *I. 96-97. Conze's translation*)[1]

Both monks and laymen being equally the Buddha it is impossible to assert the superiority of one over the other, except in a purely social and conventional sense. Though even in the Mahayana, especially as it exists in Tibet, the spiritual community and the ecclesiastical corporation to some extent overlap, the general effect of the doctrines of Non-Duality and immanent Buddha-nature was to shift the centre of gravity in Buddhist society from the second to the first, with a consequent diminution of the importance of the monastic order and the monastic life.

Moreover, whereas in Hinayana lands the individual monk is submerged in the Sangha, which is treated as though it possessed a life and individuality independent of that of its members, in Mahayana lands it is certain leading members of the Sangha

[1] *Buddhist Texts,* p. 182.

who, in their individual capacities and by virtue of their transcendental attainments, occupy the foreground of the picture as religious teachers and spiritual guides. Such are Nāgārjuna, Aśvaghosa, Asaṇga, Vasubandhu, Hiuen Tsang, Atīśa, Milarepa, Kobo Daishi, Tsongkhapa and a host of others whose prestige and influence were in the eyes of the Mahayana public in no way contingent upon the fact that they had received monastic ordination. Again, whereas in the Hinayana schools all lineages, in the sense of the various lines of pupillary succession through which the Teaching has been handed down, are traced back to the Sakyamuni, that is to say to the Buddha's *Nirmāṇakāya,* in the Mahayana schools they are sometimes traced back to His *Sambhogakāya.* Thus Asaṅga, the co-founder with his brother Vasubandhu of the Yogacara, is traditionally supposed to have received the distinctive teachings of this school from the Bodhisattva Maitreya, while the "apostolical succession" of the Kagyu School of Tibetan Buddhism descends through Tilopa, its first human guru, directly from the Vajradhāra Buddha. The continued spiritual vitality of the Mahayana is largely due to the fact that again and again there welled up within it inspiration from these transcendental sources, which even today are by no means exhausted. Each and every founder of the numerous schools and sub-schools of the Mahayana was a channel for the transmission of the Wisdom and Compassion of the Buddha to mankind, and each, while taking up his stand upon these distinctive teachings of the Mahayana which were common to all its branches, at the same time developed his special doctrines and methods in accordance with the current requirements of sentient beings. What these special doctrines and methods were it will be out business to see in the next chapter.

CHAPTER THREE

THE MAHAYANA SCHOOLS

I. The Complexity of the Mahayana

SPEAKING of the reasons which had led him to abandon the study of Sanskrit in favour of Pali, the author of a well-known volume of selections from the *Tipiṭaka* has declared that whereas Pali literature is a cosmos Sanskrit literature is a chaos. As the reader no doubt recollects, the Canon of the only surviving Hinayana school, that of the Theravadins, has come down to us in Pali; the originals of the Mahayana Scriptures, on the other hand, are all in Sanskrit. This is perhaps more than just a coincidence. Hinayana Buddhism, with its closed Canon, its fixed conceptual formulations of the Doctrine, and its slavish adherence to the forms and precedents of past ages, is not only a cosmos but a cosmos frozen by the magic wand of scholasticism practically into immobility. Like the solar system, it consists of a limited number of parts arranged after a definite pattern, and is therefore easily described. But unlike the solar system it is standing still. Mahayana Buddhism, on the contrary, is not only, so far as appearances go, a chaos, but a chaos full of life and movement. Its elements are as numberless as the stars of the sky, and as impossible to enumerate. Like the stars they execute a dance the choreography of which is so intricate as to be mistaken for confusion. Not only the casual but even the close student of Buddhism is bewildered by the spectacle of hundreds of schools, possessing between them literally thousands of texts which in more than a score of languages recommend as essential to the emancipation of mankind doctrines and methods innumerable. Within the narrow compass of the few pages which make up the present chapter it will be impossible to give even the barest outline of all these. Condensation and summarization are therefore inevitable. Much must be omitted if much is not to be misunderstood.

But even a condensed and summarized account of the

Mahayana schools is not possible unless the term "Mahayana" is not just a convenient collective designation for a jumble of contradictory teachings having no clearly defined relations with one another and occupying no definite place in a single coherent scheme of doctrine and discipline. However accurate and entertaining a description of an ant, an eagle, an elephant and a human being might be, it would not be acceptable as a summary of biological science. For the various animal species are not merely a confused heap of living organisms but the mutually divergent manifestations of a single principle, of one supreme law, which despite or even because of their differences binds them together into unity. A summary of biology would necessarily consist of an explanation of this principle, which is of course the law of evolution, in the light of its most prominent exemplifications, and an understanding of these in the light of the principle. Without the law of evolution a summary of biology would not be possible, and we should be compelled to beat the track of an endless enumeration of animal species, though this would give us not understanding of life but only knowledge of its forms.

A similar situation confronts us in the present chapter. A condensed and summarized account of all branches of the Mahayana will be possible only if we can find a principle, analogous to the law of evolution, which will enable us first to schematize them in accordance with the main lines of their development and then to give brief descriptions of the most important schools. Even though we cannot enumerate all the stars in the Mahayana sky we should at least try to pick out for the guidance of travellers its most brilliant constellations. But does the kind of principle that we require exist? True, what we have termed the transcendental unity of Buddhism has already been established in the last chapter, and with it, we hope, the transcendental unity of all schools of the Mahayana. But this unity, alone and by itself, is not sufficient as a principle of schematization. To show that all schools lead, ultimately, to the same goal, to Enlightenment for the sake of all sentient beings, though a step in the right direction does not go nearly far enough. We must also explain why there should exist a specific number of paths, each converging upon the goal from a particular direction, and each with its still more numerous by-paths, and why each should follow the particular course it does in preference to all others. Though the principle of the transcendental unity of Buddhism makes it clear that despite contradictions at the intellectual level the Rinzai Zen Shu and the Jodo Shin Shu, for example, are equally means for the attainment of Enlightenment, it does not even attempt to explain why the differences between these two schools should have taken on the specific complexion and configuration that they did. At the conclusion of Section V of the preceding chapter we tried to support our assertion that Buddhism is a whole not merely by an appeal to its transcendental unity but by endeavouring to show that the Hinayana and the Mahayana represent the conservative and the progressive, the centripetal and the centrifugal tendencies or forces at work within the Dharma. By this means the differences between the two schools were not merely described but explained and justified. A similar principle is now needed to explain the development of the Mahayana schools.

II. The Five Spiritual Faculties

Such a principle exists, we believe, in the five spiritual faculties (*pañca-indriya*), mentioned not only by the Pali but also by the Sanskrit Buddhist texts. But before proceeding to explain how this group of faculties can be utilized as a principle for the schematization of the Mahayana schools the faculties themselves must be described. This procedure is called for not only because such a description will be of assistance in comprehending our subsequent schematization but also by reason of the intrinsic value of these five faculties as one of the earliest and most important classifications of the Buddha's teachings.

Just how important they are can be inferred from the fact that in the list known as the *bodhipakkhiya-dhammā*, or thirty-seven "principles conducive to Enlightenment," which purports to include all the doctrines of Original Buddhism, this group occurs twice over, once as the five faculties and once as the five powers (*balas*). Their importance moreover continues to be recognized today, for the band of distinguished scholars who edited *Buddhist Texts Through the Ages* thought them fundamental enough to constitute with the doctrines of Conditioned Co-production and Nirvana a summary of the entire Dharma from Theravada sources.

The word *indriya* occurs in the Vedas as an adjective meaning "belonging to Indra." Indra being considered the ruler of the gods, the word was able to acquire in Pali the specific sense "belonging to the ruler," that is to say, governing, ruling (as a noun), or ruling or controlling principle. According to *The Pali Text Society's Pali-English Dictionary* "Indriya is one of the most comprehensive and important categories of Buddhist psychological philosophy and ethics," meaning "controlling principle, directive force, *élan, dynamis,*" in the following applications: (a) with reference to sense perceptibility "faculty, function," often wrongly interpreted as "organ"; (b) with reference to objective aspects of form and matter "kind, characteristic, determinating principle, sign, mark" . . . ; (c) with reference to moods of sensation and (d) to moral powers or motives controlling action, "principle, controlling force"; (e) with reference to cognition and insight "category." The Pali texts contain a list of no less than twenty-two *indriyas* arranged in six independent groups. These are the six faculties of sense, a group consisting of femininity, masculinity and vitality, the five kinds of feeling, the five spiritual faculties, and the three supramundane faculties associated with various stages of the Transcendental Path. Thus *indriya* is a term of extremely wide connotation. The fifth group, consisting of the five spiritual faculties, coincides with application (d) of the *Pali-English Dictionary's* definition, given above, and it is with the *indriyas* in this sense, namely as "moral powers or motives controlling action" that we are now concerned. Both the contrast and the correspondence between the first and fifth groups of *indriyas* is well brought out by Dr. Conze, who says that, whereas before taking up the spiritual life a man is dominated by his five senses (or six, if we include mind), afterwards his conduct is increasingly guided by the five spiritual faculties.[1] When as a result of constant exercise these faculties have become so strong that they can no longer be crushed by the passions, they are termed *balas*, powers or forces.

The five spiritual faculties are faith (*saddhā*), vigour (*viriya*),

[1] *Selected Sayings,* p. 17.

mindfulness (*sati*), concentration (*samādhi*) and wisdom (*paññā*). A more or less stereotyped description of them in this order occurs in several parts of the Pali Canon. On one occasion the Buddha thus addresses His disciples:—

"There are five faculties, monks: what are the five? The faculty of faith, the faculty of energy, the faculty of mindfulness, the faculty of concentration, the faculty of full knowledge.

"And what, monks, is the faculty of faith? Herein, monks, the noble disciple is faithful. He has faith in the enlightenment of the Tathāgata, thus: the Lord, the arahat, the all-enlightened, endowed with knowledge and conduct, the Happy One, knower of the world, supreme charioteer of men to be tamed, teacher of gods and men, Buddha, the Lord. This, monks, is called the faculty of faith.

"And what, monks, is the faculty of energy? Herein, monks, a noble disciple dwells exercising energy. With the dispelling of bad thoughts and the gaining of good thoughts he is steadfast, advancing steadily, not throwing off the burden involved in good thoughts. This is called the faculty of energy.

"And what, monks, is the faculty of mindfulness? Herein, monks, a noble disciple is mindful, endowed with supreme skill in mindfulness, one who remembers and calls to mind both what has been done and what has been spoken long ago. This, monks, is called the faculty of mindfulness.

"And what, monks, is the faculty of concentration? Herein, monks, a noble disciple making relinquishment the object of his thought acquires concentration, acquires one-pointedness of mind. This, monks, is called concentration.

"And what, monks, is the faculty of full knowledge? Herein, monks, a noble disciple has acquired full knowledge. He is endowed with the higher knowledge of the rising and passing away of things, the noble higher knowledge which penetrates to the way leading to the complete destruction of pain. This, monks, is called the faculty of full knowledge. These, monks, are the five faculties."

(Saṁyutta-Nikāya, *V. 196. Thomas's translation*)[1]

Since faith, vigour, mindfulness, concentration and wisdom are not only faculties but categories for the classification of the most essential Buddhist doctrines and practices, some of them, as might have been expected, have turned up already in Chapter I, others the reader will meet again in Chapter IV. Just as the same mental factor (*cetasika*) enters into combination with a number of mental states (*citta*), so the same teaching can be included within the framework of a number of doctrinal schemes.

Nothing, however, has yet been said about the first of the spiritual faculties, faith, and this omission we shall have to make good before proceeding farther.

---

[1] *Early Buddhist Scriptures,* pp. 89-91.

Faith, as the foregoing quotation from the *Saṁyutta-Nikāya* should have made quite clear, is essentially faith in the Buddha. Faith in the Dharma and in the Sangha are secondary and derivative. But what is faith? To answer this question we shall first of all go back to the original Pali word.

Saddhā (Skt. *śraddhā*) is connected with a verb meaning "to place one's heart on." The connotation of the word is not cognitive but definitely emotional. Hence it is best rendered, not by "confidence," as some rationalizing interpreters of the Dharma would have us believe, but by the term that we have already employed, namely, faith. But this English word has a number of meanings and shades of meaning. Which of them, if any, coincides with the emotion to which Buddhists appropriate the term *saddhā*? According to *Webster's New International Dictionary* faith is primarily the "act or state of acknowledging unquestioningly the existence, power, etc., of a supreme being and the reality of a divine order." Buddhists, however, deny the existence of a supreme being. If faith is to be adopted as the equivalent of *saddhā* the dictionary definition must obviously be amended. For God we shall have to substitute the Buddha, not because of any similarity in their nature and functions, but because of the equipollency of their respective positions. Faith in the Buddhist sense then becomes the act (expressed by "taking refuge") or state (condition of being established in the refuge) of acknowledging unquestioningly that the man Gautama, or what appears as the man Gautama, is in possession of Full Enlightenment. Expressed in the traditional Buddhist terminology this is the great asseveration already quoted from the *Saṁyutta-Nikāya*, the asseveration which echoes from one end of the *Tipiṭaka* to the other, and which is today repeated by millions of Buddhists as part of their daily worship: *Iti 'pi so Bhagavā Arahaṁ Sammā-sambuddho Vijjā-caraṇa-sampanno Sugato Lokavidū Anuttaro Purisa-damma-sārathi Satthā-deva-manussānaṁ Buddho Bhagavā 'ti*—"He indeed is the Lord, the Arahat, the Fully and Perfectly Enlightened, the Endowed with Knowledge and Conduct, the Happy One, Knower of the World, Supreme Charioteer of Men to be Tamed, Teacher of Gods and Men, Buddha, the Lord."

This acknowledgment of the Buddha as enlightened is not, however, the result of an irrational impulse ungrounded in reason and experience. Faith in Him is not blind faith. It is not that "accepting . . . as real, true, or the like, that which is not supported by sensible evidence or rational proofs or which is indemonstrable" which is, according to the dictionary, one of the senses in which the word faith can be understood. Such faith may be necessary to accept the dogmas of Christianity, in which religion it indeed occupies a very prominent place; but there is no room for it in Buddhism. Buddhist faith, as we shall see later on, must be balanced by wisdom. Is there, then, any sensible evidence, are there any rational proofs, of the Buddha's Enlightenment, the existence of which might justify the claim that our acknowledgment of that Enlightenment is not a blind and ignorant but a clear-sighted and intelligent act? What, in other words, are the grounds of a Buddhist's faith in the Buddha?

They are firstly intuition, secondly reason, and thirdly experience. Since we are injecting into these words, all of which are very fluid in meaning, a specifically Buddhist content, a brief explanation seems called for. At the conclusion of Chapter II we saw that, according to the distinctively Mahayana teaching, all beings are in possession of the Element of Buddhahood. This Element is nothing but the reflection of the Absolute in the mirror of the so-called individual consciousness. Only because they are in possession of this reflected image do beings feel an affinity for Enlightenment. As the *Ratnagotravibhāga* says:—

> *If the Element of the Buddha did not exist (in everyone),*
> *There could be no disgust with suffering,*
> *Nor could there be a wish for Nirvāṇa*
> *Nor striving for it, nor a resolve to win it.*[1]

One of the strings of a musical instrument being struck, the corresponding string of the instrument beside it begins to vibrate. When the devotee hears the music of Enlightenment, when he stands in the very presence of the Buddha, his own Element of Buddhahood starts vibrating. Hence he knows that the great being before him is striking upon the strings of *His* own heart the mighty chord of Supreme Enlightenment. Even the mere utterance of the word "Buddha" was enough to call forth such a response from Anāthapiṇḍika:

" 'Householder, did you say *Buddha*?' " he asks in astonishment

---

[1] *Buddhist Texts,* p. 181.

of his brother-in-law, the banker of Rājagaha, when he first hears the marvellous word.

" '*Buddha* I did say, householder,' " replies his relation. Anāthapiṇḍika is so overwhelmed that he repeats the question thrice, and is answered thrice in the same manner. He then says:

> *"Even this sound,* Buddha, Buddha *is hard to come by in the world. Could I go and see this Lord, Arahant, perfect Buddha?"*
> *"Not now, but tomorrow early."*
>
> (Vinaya-Piṭaka, *II. 154. I. B. Horner's translation)*[1]

"So the householder Anāthapiṇḍika," relates the text, "lay down with mindfulness so much directed towards the Buddha that he got up three times during the night thinking it was daybreak."

It is this plangency of our own Element of Buddhahood when face to face with the Buddha which constitutes intuition in the present context, that is to say as the first of the grounds of our faith that the Buddha is in fact in possession of Supreme Enlightenment. Needless to say we stand face to face with the Buddha not only when we perceive his *Nirmāṇakāya,* or physical body, but also when, through the exercise of imagination or by the practice of meditation, we are able to behold, not with a fleshly but with a spiritual eye, His Body of Glory or *Sambhogakāya.* Seeing the Buddha as He really is, that is to say in His *Dharmakāya,* which takes place when we realize the import of the Teaching, belongs to a stage of spiritual life more advanced than that now under consideration.

However safe a guide mere intuition may be for the spiritually mature, in the case of the spiritually immature it is only too often a means of indulging mundane desires and justifying prejudices. Consequently faith in the Buddha is grounded not on intuition alone but also upon reason, which we here understand as including both sensible evidence and rational proofs. Now according to Buddhist logicians the basis of inference (*anumāna*) is the invariable concomitance (*vyāpti*) of the *probans (hetu)* and the *probandum (sādhya)* in the syllogism (*avayava*). Since there exists an invariable concomitance between Enlightenment, on the one hand, and various moral, intellectual and spiritual qualities on the other, we may infer, from our perception of these qualities

[1] *Ibid.,* pp. 17-18.

in a particular person, and our nonperception of their opposites, that he is enlightened. This principle is clearly enunciated in the Pali Canon. Addressing Cunda the Blessed One says:—

"Friend, a brother who is Arahant, one in whom the āsavas *are destroyed, who has lived the life, who has done his task, who has laid down the burden, who has reached his own welfare, who has utterly destroyed the bond that binds to becoming, who is released by the Knowledge—such an one is incapable of behaving in nine ways, to wit:*

Intentionally taking the life of a creature;
Of taking by way of theft what is not given;
Of practising the sexual act;
Of telling a deliberate lie;
Of indulging in intoxicants;
Of storing up (food) for the indulgence of appetite, as he did before when he was a householder;
Of going on the wrong path through hatred;
Of going on the wrong path through delusion;
Of going on the wrong path through fear."

(Dīgha-Nikāya, *III. 133. Woodward's translation)*[1]

That means that if a religious teacher in whose enlightenment we had conceived an intuitive faith were to commit any of the above actions we should have to conclude, however great his reputation and our own regret might be, that he was not enlightened, and that what we had thought was the vibration of our Element of Buddhahood was after all only a flutter of mundane emotion. Such a doctrine obviously precludes any form of antinomianism, for which reason teachers who claim that their lapses from morality are simply a means of testing the faith of their disciples should be treated as impostors. We acknowledge the Buddha to be enlightened, and we have faith in Him, not in spite of appearances but, partly at least, because of them. Being the premises from which we conclude that He was enlightened, our perception of the sensible evidences of His qualities and our knowledge that these qualities are invariably concomitant with Enlightenment constitute the rational proofs of the fact that He was enlightened and the ground of our rational faith in Him.

The concomitant qualities referred to are of two kinds, those pertaining chiefly to Compassion and those pertaining chiefly to

[1] *Some Sayings of the Buddha*, p. 269.

Wisdom. Among the first, which are to be seen manifested in His life, may be included kindliness, gentleness, serenity, dispassion, tact, urbanity, fearlessness and a host of similar qualities which, we should never forget, are not virtues in the merely ethical sense, but the expression on the mundane level of an insight purely metaphysical. The qualities pertaining to Wisdom, which are manifested in the Buddha's Teaching, are virtues in the intellectual sense. They too are the expressions of a realization pertaining to the transcendental order and as such have nothing to do with the mundane mental states and functions of the same name. Among them are complete freedom from prejudice, unfailing presence of mind, all-inclusive observation, infallible judgment, profound intellectuality, indefatigable power of analysis, perfect rationality and absolute freedom from misconception and error.

Just as faith grounded in intuition has to be tested by faith grounded in reason, so must faith grounded in reason be confirmed by faith grounded in experience. Out of a number of people passing us in the street we see one who, we feel certain, will be able to direct us to our destination. A brief conversation convinces us that he is well acquainted with the place we wish to reach, and we therefore follow his directions implicitly. On arriving at our destination we know that our confidence in him was justified, and that he really was acquainted with both the place and the route by which it might be reached. So with our faith in the Buddha. Only when, having practised His Teaching, we ourselves attain to a certain stage of the Path, do we know beyond all possibility of doubt that the Buddha had Himself attained it. Thus as we progress from stage to stage our faith becomes more and more firmly fixed until, with our own attainment of Enlightenment, it becomes unshakable. Of this faith which is rooted in experience does the Buddha speak after His conversation with the Brahmin Unnabha:—

"Brethren, just as in a peaked hut or a hall with a peaked gable, with a window facing east, when the sun comes up and its rays strike through the window, where do they alight?"

"On the western wall, Lord."

"Just so, brethren, is the faith of the brāhmin Unnabha in the Tathāgata settled, rooted, fixed, and strong, not to be pulled up by any one in the world, be he recluse or brāhmin, or deva or Māra or Brahmā.

"If at this time, brethren, the brāhmin Unnabha should come to die, there is no fetter, bound by which he would come back again to this world."

(Saṁyutta-Nikāya, *V. 219. Woodward's translation)*[1]

Unnabha being at least an *Anāgami* or Non-Returner, as the Buddha's concluding words imply, his faith was grounded not only in intuition and reason but also in experience.

Amplifying our former definition of *saddhā,* we may now say that it is an acknowledgment of the fact that Gautama is *the Buddha,* grounded, firstly on the intuitive response that arises out of the depths of our heart by reason of the affinity existing between His actual and our potential Buddhahood; secondly, on the sensible evidences and rational proofs of His Enlightenment afforded us by the records of His life and Teaching; and thirdly, on our own attainment of the successive stages of the Transcendental Path taught by Him as the Means to Enlightenment.

This acknowledgment of the Buddha's Enlightenment, though it includes cognitive elements, is primarily not an intellectual conviction but, as the etymology of the word *saddhā* itself implies, an emotional impulsion. This fact, so often overlooked by those who seek to equate Buddhism and Rationalism, is clearly evident from a number of *Tipiṭaka* passages. One will be sufficient for our purpose. At the end of the fifth and last book of the *Sutta-Nipāta,* one of the oldest portions of the Pali Canon, Bāvarin asks Pingiya, whom he had sent with fifteen other pupils to question the Buddha:—

How canst thou, Pingiya,
One moment stay from Him,
Sage of the quickening,
Seer of the quickening,
From Gautama, Who taught
Thee Dharma for both here
And now, and not anon,
For craving's end, for weal
Which nowhere hath a peer?

Pingiya replies that, in fact, he does not stay from the Buddha even one moment; for he sees Him in meditation:—

In mind I see Him as by eye,
In earnest, brahmin, day and night;

---

[1] *Ibid.,* pp. 204-5.

I brighten night in praising Him;
Hence not as absence deem I that.
With faith and joy and heart alert
Naught turneth me from His behest:
Unto what realm the quickening sage
Doth move, to that then I am drawn.
Since I am frail and worn with age
Thither my body goeth not,
But with strong purpose e'er I move
And so my heart is linked with Him.

While they talk the Buddha Himself appears to them and says:—

As Vakkalin, Ālavi-Gotama,
And eke Bhadrāvudha by faith did win
Release: so e'en by faith thou too shalt win
Release: and thou, O Pingiya, shalt go
To the beyond across the realm of death.

Pingiya replies with a pæan that may be ranked with the most precious gems of the world's devotional literature, and on this note of ecstatic devotion the *Sutta-Nipāta* fittingly ends:—

The sage's word I hear
And greater grows my faith!

With teeming, lucid thought
The All-awake rolled back
The veil; the deva-heights
He plumbed, and found and knew
The all of nigh and yon:

The quests of those who doubts
Confessed the teacher solved.
To that which naught can shake,
To that which naught can move,
Which nowhere hath a peer:
Lo! thither I shall go
And there my doubt shall end.
Think thus of me: a man
Intent on heart's release.

(Sutta-Nipāta, *1138-39, 1142-44, 1146-49. Hare's translation*)[1]

Here we are very definitely concerned, not with some lukewarm and feeble "confidence," but with an ardent and powerful emotion for which the best word at our disposal is faith.

Emotion means movement. As its etymology shows, it is an

[1] *Woven Cadences,* pp. 165-167.

outward-going motion, either of attraction towards a pleasant, or repulsion from a painful, object. Hence, according to Nāgasena, the distinguishing mark of faith is aspiration, which consists in a movement or, as he puts it, a "jump," from the mundane to the Transcendental.

*"As, sire [he is addressing King Milinda, the Menander of the Greeks], an earnest student of yoga (*Yogâvacara*), on seeing that the minds of others are freed, jumps (as it were) into the fruit of stream-winning or of once-returning or of non-returning or into arahatship and practises yoga for the attainment of the unattained, the mastery of the unmastered, the realization of the unrealized—even so, sire, is aspiration the distinguishing mark of faith."*

At the King's request Nāgasena gives one of those graphic illustrations which are the most charming features of the *Milindapañha:—*

"As, sire, when a great cloud pours down rain on a hill-slope, after the water, in flowing along according to the slope, had filled the clefts, fissures and gullies of the hill-slope, it would fill the river so that it would course along overflowing its banks; and then suppose that a great crowd of people were to come, but, knowing neither the width nor the depth of the river, were to stand afraid and hesitating on the bank. But then suppose a knowledgeable man were to come and who, on recognizing his own strength and power, should tie on his loincloth firmly and, jumping, should cross over. When the great crowd of people had seen him crossed over they too would cross over. This is the way, sire, that an earnest student of yoga, on seeing that the minds of others are freed, jumps (as it were) into the fruit of stream-winning and so on and practises yoga for the aims mentioned already. And this, sire, was said by the Lord in the Saṁyutta-Nikāya*:—*

By faith the flood is crossed,
By diligence the sea;
By vigour ill is passed;
By wisdom cleansed is he.

*(*Milindapañha*, 35-36. Horner's translation)*[1]

Thus faith in the Buddha is the motivating power of the disciple's life, the dominating and driving force which carries him through the successive stages of his career until finally, with the attainment of Supreme Enlightenment, he reaches his goal. Consequently, its importance is not to be underestimated. According to the *Sutta-Nipāta* "Faith is the wealth here best for man."[2] Har Dayal writes:—

The idea of bhakti *was not a borrowed feather, with which Buddhism adorned*

[1] *Buddhist Texts,* pp. 53-54.
[2] *Sutta-Nipāta,* p. 182.

itself. It was an integral part of the Buddhist ideal from the earliest times. In fact, the very word bhakti, *as a technical religious term, occurs for the first time in Indian literature in a Buddhist treatise and not in a Hindu scripture. The* Theragāthā *speaks of* bhatti: "so bhattimā nama ca hoti paṇḍito ñatvā ca dhammesu visesi assa" *(p. 41, lines 1-2). This anthology contains verses that go back to the earliest period of the history of Buddhism, and its final redaction took place in the middle of the third century* B.C. *But the idea of* bhakti *is found in the ancient Pāli* Nikāyas*: it was called* saddhā *in the fifth century* B.C. Saddhā *was a very important concept in early Buddhism. Faith in the Buddha is repeatedly declared to be essential for the spiritual development of the monks and the laymen. It can even lead to rebirth in a heaven. A novice must 'take refuge' first in the Buddha and then in the Doctrine and the Confraternity. It is a great mistake to underestimate the importance of* Saddhā *in early Buddhism, which has been wrongly represented as a dry 'rationalistic' system of precepts and theories. Even in the Pali Canon, the impression left on the reader's mind is that Gautama Buddha is the centre of the whole movement, and that the Doctrine derives its vitality and importance from his personality.*[1]

We have already seen that according to the *Saṁyutta-Nikāya* "By faith the flood is crossed." The *Majjhima-Nikāya,* comparing the Buddha to a good herdsman who sends his herd safely across a ford of the Ganges, bulls first, then sturdy kine and bullocks, then slim young calves, goes so far as to say:—

Just as the tender sucking calf, just born of its lowing dam, and carried along, crossed Ganga's stream . . . even so those brothers who follow the Norm and walk in faith, they too shall cross Mara's stream and come safe to the further shore.[2]

The terms *saddhānusārin* (walking according to faith) and *saddhā-vimutta* (emancipated through faith) are both found in the *Tipiṭaka.* According to the Hinayana scholasticism of a much later period, the first is a designation of those attaining the Path of the Stream-winner with a predominance of the faculty of faith, while the second is a designation of the same persons at certain higher stages of the Aryan Path. But the Buddhist doctrine of emancipation through faith is not in any sense the equivalent of the Protestant Christian dogma of justification by faith. For even in those who walk according to faith, or who are emancipated through faith, this faculty does not exclude but only slightly predominates over the faculty of wisdom. Conversely, those who are emancipated through wisdom (*paññā-vimutta*) are not totally lacking in faith: they are simply of a predominantly

[1] *The Bodhisattva Doctrine in Buddhist Sanskrit Literature,* p. 32.
[2] *Majjhima-Nikāya,* I. 34.

intellectual disposition. Faith, in fact, according to the Abhidhamma of the Theravadins, is the first of the twenty-five lofty qualities present in all wholesome states of consciousness. This alone should be sufficient to indicate its place in the spiritual life.

Having defined the nature and established the importance of faith we must now, eschewing the by-paths and retracing our steps back to the main track of our enquiry, attempt to understand the relation not only between faith and wisdom but also that between faith and the rest of the spiritual faculties. In an interesting text, quoted by Shantideva from the *Akṣayamati Sūtra*, we find all the five faculties treated as successive stages of the Path to Buddhahood. After defining faith as belief in karma and rebirth, in the mode of life of a Bodhisattva, and in the various formulations of the doctrine of universal conditionality, the text proceeds to say of one possessing such faith:—

> *He follows none of the false doctrines, and believes in all the qualities (dharmas) of a Buddha, his powers, grounds of self-confidence and all the rest; and when in his faith he has left behind all doubts, he brings about in himself those qualities of a Buddha. This is known as the virtue of faith. His* vigour *consists in his bringing about (in himself) the dharmas in which he has faith. His* mindfulness *consists in his preventing the qualities which he brings about by vigour from being destroyed by forgetfulness. His* concentration *consists in his fixing his one-pointed attention on these very same qualities. With the faculty of* wisdom *he contemplates those dharmas on which he has fixed his one-pointed attention, and penetrates to their reality. The cognition of those dharmas which arise in himself and which have no outside condition is called the virtue of wisdom. Thus these five virtues, together, are sufficient to bring forth all the qualities of a Buddha.*
>
> (Sikshāsamuccaya, *316. Conze's translation)*[1]

Besides bringing out the importance of faith, this passage clearly shows that in the five spiritual faculties are comprehended all the moral and spiritual conditions necessary to the attainment of Enlightenment and that in them a principle for the schematization of all the Mahayana schools may therefore be found.

Such a principle will emerge, however, when we remember that the five spiritual faculties can exist not only as the successive stages of a path, as explained by the *Akṣayamati Sūtra*, but also as psychic factors simultaneously present in the mind of the devotee. This co-existence of faith, vigour, mindfulness, concentration and wisdom is the key which, by opening the portals of

---

[1] *Buddhist Texts*, p. 186.

every Mahayana school, will reveal to us not only their essential unity but also the reason for their apparent divergence.

According to an early tradition the first, second, fourth and fifth *indriyas* can be arranged in two groups, one consisting of faith and wisdom, the other of vigour and concentration, with mindfulness as the supernumerary faculty. Between the members of each group there must be perfect harmony. A devotee in whom faith is strong but wisdom weak will speedily fall victim to blind credulity, dogmatism, bigotry and zeal for persecution. One in whom, on the contrary, wisdom is in full flower while faith is still in the bud will soon become a prey to no less blind rationalism, as well as to scepticism, cunning, chicanery and intellectual arrogance. Similarly, superabundance of vigour in combination with feebleness of concentration will lead to restlessness, instability and mere aimless activity, while the opposite condition, that of great power of concentration but little energy, is on the other hand apt to result in indolence and inertia. The devotee must, therefore, aim at what the Pali texts call *indriya-samatta,* or equalization of the faculties, so that faith and wisdom, vigour and concentration, may be held in a state of perfect equilibrium and balance. This equalization can be brought about only by means of mindfulness, the one faculty which does not go to extremes, of which there cannot be too much, and which therefore requires no counterbalancing faculty.

In various parts of the *Tipiṭaka* the Buddha is depicted as checking any tendency on the part of His disciples to develop one faculty at the expense of another. To Sona Kolivisa, who through excess of vigour in walking up and down had lacerated his feet, so that his ambulatory was dabbled with blood "like a butcher's shambles," the Master pointed out that the lute-strings are fit to play on only when they are neither over-taut nor over-slack, but evenly strung. Excess of vigour led to a self-exaltation, He said, while lack of zeal made one liable to sluggishness. Hence Sona should persist in evenness of zeal, should master his faculties, and make that his aim. In the same way Sariputra, who had declared it to be his faith that out of all the Buddhas of the past, the present and the future there was none to equal his own master, was brought back to a proper sense of proportion by being tartly questioned whether he had known all those Buddhas or whether he really knew even the Sakyamuni Himself! Incidents of this kind might be indefinitely multiplied not only from the Pali but also from the Sanskrit scriptures, as well as from later non-canonical sources.

Just as a gardener prunes a bush on the side on which it is of too exuberant a growth, so the Buddha and His enlightened disciples of all ages have sought to equalize faith and wisdom, vigour and concentration. This incidentally enables us to understand why different, even contradictory, instructions may be given to different pupils. One might be advised to devote more time to study, another to abandon it altogether. While one is admonished to bestir himself, another is advised to be less active. The nature of the advice given by the master depends upon the nature of the fault to be corrected in the pupil. Though the Doctrine is the same for all, the Method may be applied in a manner peculiar to each. For every kind of application, however, mindfulness is necessary. Whether the gardener eventually decides to trim on this side or on that the bush must first of all be carefully observed. Similarly, whichever pair of faculties the devotee has to equalize he must first of all be fully aware and completely mindful of the nature and extent of the disproportion between their members. In fact, mindfulness alone, if sufficiently prolonged and intense, is sufficient to equalize all the faculties. Of mindfulness itself there cannot be too much, for the idea that the four other faculties might become "too balanced" is obviously absurd. As soon as it exceeds the degree necessary for preserving an equilibrium between faith and wisdom, vigour and concentration, mindfulness, far from destroying the harmony it has helped to create, as it were overflows on a higher plane of consciousness and merges in meditation. Unless the faculties have first been equalized in this way entry upon the Path of Meditation is in fact impossible. In modern terminology, there can be no higher spiritual life for those who are not emotionally and intellectually balanced, or whose character is either one-sidedly introvert or one-sidedly extrovert.

III. The Schematization of the Schools

The nature, function and value of the five spiritual faculties having been made quite clear, and their internal relations indicated, we are now in a position to utilize them as a principle for the schematization of the Mahayana schools. It will have been noticed already that both individually and collectively these faculties possess a dual aspect, so that they may be simultaneously regarded from two points of view. In the first place they are those mental factors (*cetasika*) which even in their most rudimentary and undeveloped form must be held in equilibrium if further spiritual progress is to be made and which, when developed to their fullest possible extent, are equivalent to Enlightenment. In the second place they are the various methods by means of which these mental factors themselves are to be cultivated so that, as such, they constitute the whole body of the Buddha's teachings, which in fact consists solely of such methods. Being thus possessed of a subjective and psychological as well as of an objective and methodological aspect the five spiritual faculties are found not only in the individual devotee—indeed, in their most rudimentary state they are present in all human beings—but also in the Dharma as a whole. Buddhism contains within itself intellectual and emotional, passive and dynamic, elements, and like the individual it too sometimes experiences difficulty in rendering to each one its due while at the same time maintaining them all in a state of equilibrium. As far as the Original Teaching is concerned, the equilibrium between its various aspects and elements was necessarily absolute, for it was the product of an enlightened and hence perfectly balanced mind. Any appearance of disequilibrium would be due to the predominance of a certain type of defect in the minds of the disciples. If a teaching emphasizes, for example, the importance of vigour, we should not conclude that according to this teaching vigour is more important than concentration, but only that the person to whom it was originally addressed was particularly prone to the vice of indolence. Later on, however, as the implications now of this and now of that aspect of the Dharma were brought out and carried to their logical conclusion, the equilibrium of the Original Teaching was disturbed and the various schools of Buddhism, each of which eventually emphasized the importance and paid attention to the development of one spiritual faculty in particular, began to emerge. There being two pairs of faculties the equilibrium of which was liable to disturbance we find in the Mahayana four principal traditions, or four main schools nucleating clusters of sub-schools. The faculty of mindfulness, being incapable of going to extremes and therefore not requiring any counterbalancing faculty, could not lead to the formation of any school of its own. It is represented in the history of Buddhism by the various syncretist movements which from time to time endeavoured to bring the different schools into harmony.

Applying our principle of schematization in detail, we find that corresponding to the faculties of wisdom, faith, concentration and vigour there are in the Mahayana intellectual, devotional, meditative and activistic movements. These four movements eventually crystallized into the four main schools of Mahayana Buddhism, that is to say, into

(1) The New Wisdom School (*Mādhyamikavāda*),[1]
(2) The Buddhism of Faith and Devotion,
(3) Buddhist Idealism (*Yogācāra-Vijñānavāda*) and into
(4) The Tantra, or Magical Buddhism.

From the very outset of our attempt to describe these schools and their offshoots it must be emphasized that they are not sects such as are found existing in, for example, Christianity and Islam. A sect is an ecclesiastical corporation which enforces exclusiveness of membership, so that to belong to it automatically entails not belonging to any similar body, and which makes more or less comprehensive claim to possess the only true interpretation of scripture and a monopoly in the means of salvation. Except perhaps on one or two occasions in Japan, the Mahayana schools have never gone to such extremes. Though concentrating each one on the development of a particular spiritual faculty they did not lose touch with one another. In India the followers of different schools seem to have often lived, studied and taught side by side in the same monastery. Master and disciple did not always belong to a single school. Even today celebrated teachers like Nagarjuna and Asanga are included in the list of patriarchs not of one school only, but of many. All these facts indicate that the schools of the Mahayana are not mutually exclusive. They are complementary one to another. As faith needs to be

[1] The nomenclature follows that of Dr. Conze. A better adjective than "Magical" could perhaps have been devised for the Tantra.

counterbalanced by wisdom, and concentration by vigour, so Mādhyamika intellectuality without Jodo faith and devotion and Yogācāra mental quiescence without Tantric dynamism are alike one-sided and incomplete. Buddhism is a whole and must be followed as a whole. For the same reasons that he should simultaneously cultivate all the spiritual faculties, and not concern himself with the development of one only, the devotee is required to be a follower not of one school only but of all schools. Within the context of orthodox Christianity and Islam such a conception would seem utterly fantastic. One cannot possibly be at the same time a Roman Catholic and a Methodist. For Christianity is divided into mutually exclusive sects. Mahayana Buddhism, however, is distinguished into mutually complementary schools. The Mādhyamika, the Yogācāra, Devotional Buddhism and the Tantra, are the fully unfolded and perfectly developed forms of germinal elements contained in the Original Teaching. If the Mahayana is the fully open flower of Buddhism its four main schools represent the four petals of the flower and the faculty of mindfulness its calyx. Just as one who gazes at a single petal will never be able to appreciate the beauty of the rose, so he who studies the doctrines and follows the practices of one school only, ignoring the rest, will be unable to understand the Mahayana.

The petals of the rose (to pursue the comparison a stage further), though appearing to diverge from each other as they unfold, all open in accordance with the same law of growth. First they uncurl from the bud, then stretch, and finally expand. Similarly all four schools pass through three clearly marked stages of development. In the first stage there is a dogmatic[1] affirmation, from the standpoint of one particular spiritual faculty, of the Dharma or of some aspect of the Dharma. In the second we find an attempt at philosophical systematization. Lastly there is the stage of scholasticism. Each stage, while in one sense a development of the preceding stage, is in another sense a descent from it. While in the first stage the standpoint is intuitive and transcendental, in the second it is philosophic, and in the third merely rational and logical. Associated with each stage is a

[1] We are using the word in its non-derogatory sense of "not explicitly established by formal rational proofs."

particular type of literary composition: *sūtra, śāstra* and *ṭīkā* or *vyākhyā*. A *sūtra* is a discourse, usually of a very great length, purporting to have been delivered either by the Buddha Himself or by a great Bodhisattva speaking under His inspiration. The oldest of these *sūtras,* at least in their oldest portions, are roughly contemporaneous with the reduction of the Theravada Pali *Tipiṭaka* to writing (c. 80 B.C.), and therefore have an equal claim to represent the original gospel of Buddhism. Most Mahayana *sūtras* were delivered not by the *Nirmāṇakāya* but by the *Sambhogakāya* Buddha and the audience consisted not only of gods and men but also of innumerable Bodhisattvas with their retinues. The scene, when not laid on the Gṛdhrakūta or Vulture's Peak at Rajagriha, where many Hinayana discourses also were delivered, is some paradisaical-transcendental world beyond the confines of time and space. Here natural law is transcended, and the teaching is illustrated by marvels of profound symbolical significance. The mode of instruction in the *sūtras* is on the whole intuitive: the Buddha speaks directly out of the depth of His own innermost transcendental experience; sometimes he remains silent. There is very little attempt at argumentation; for the Buddha is endeavouring not to convince the minds of His auditors but to awaken their transcendental intuition. Recourse is often had to metaphor, simile and parable. Repetitions are very frequent, by which means the main points of the discourse are hammered ever deeper and deeper into the consciousness of the disciple. This fact to some extent accounts for their apparently inordinate length, and their carelessness of literary form. They have, however, a grandeur and a sublimity of their own. To read them, or to hear them read, is a unique and unforgettable experience. Each school derives its inspiration and support from one particular *sūtra* or group of *sūtras,* which is therefore the object of its special veneration. For example, the Mādhyamikas rely on the *Prajñāpāramitā* group of *sūtras,* the Yogācārins on the *Laṅkāvatāra* and the *Saṁdhinirmocana,* and the followers of the devotional schools on the Larger and Smaller *Sukhāvatīvyūha* and the *Amitāyurdhyāna.* At the same time each school accepts the scriptures of every other school as the genuine Word of the Buddha and venerates them accordingly.

While the editors or compilers of the *sūtras* in their present literary form are unknown the *śāstras* are the work of historical personalities. A *śāstra* is an attempt, often in the form of mnemonic verses, to summarize, elucidate and explain the teachings of a particular *sūtra* or group of *sūtras*. Though some *śāstras* are little more than lists of contents of the *sūtras,* others are cogent philosophical treatises. Their style is much more cryptic than that of the *sūtras,* and their appeal more to the understanding than to the intuition. Their authors, who are known as *ācāryas,* were not, however, philosophers in the modern Western academic sense of the term. They were sages who, through spiritual practice, had themselves actually realized the transcendental import of the *sūtras,* and who, for the benefit of an age more sophisticated than that to which the Buddha preached, gave to that import systematic philosophical expression. Great *ācāryas* such as Nagarjuna, Asanga, and Santideva are often referred to as Bodhisattvas, and the meagre records of their lives which have come down to us are quite sufficient, even apart from the testimony of their works, to convince us of their transcendental attainments. The *śāstra* literature, which is very voluminous, is not only expository but also polemical. Besides establishing the position of his own school,[1] each *ācārya* sought to demolish the positions of other schools, both Buddhist and non-Buddhist. This stimulated the growth of logic, which rapidly developed from a handful of rules of debate into a full-fledged science. The conflict among the schools was not personal but merely illustrative, so far as the schools of the Mahayana were concerned, of the inherently antinomical character of reason. Mahayana tradition as a whole venerates all the great *ācāryas* as equally enlightened. From what has been said about the relation between *sūtras* and *śāstras* it will be obvious that these great spiritual geniuses occupy in the history of Buddhism the position not of the founders of schools, much less still of sects, but of the givers of definitiveness and system to one particular line of Buddhist tradition. As such they rank second in importance to the Buddha Himself.

Of *ṭikās, vyākhyās* and similar types of literature not much need be said. They are commentaries on the *śāstras*, and though subordinate to them, are indispensable to a proper understanding of their meaning. Though commentators are not generally con-

[1] The Mādhyamikas are, strictly speaking, an exception. See *infra.*

sidered to be *ācāryas,* the authors of these works were often thinkers and writers of conspicuous ability. Between the authors of *śāstras* and commentaries no hard-and-fast line can, however, be drawn. Commentaries were written by authors of *śāstras,* and *śāstras* by writers of commentaries. Nagarjuna's is the most prominent instance of an *ācārya* commenting on his own works. *Ṭīkās, vyākhyās,* etc., are generally remarkable for uncompromising adherence to the tenets of their respective schools, rigorously intellectual approach, rigidly logical mode of treatment, and vigorous polemics. In the hands of the commentators the details of the position adopted by the schools were fully articulated and the whole system given its final shape.

IV. The Scriptures of Perfect Wisdom

The teachings of the Mādhyamika School being professedly a systematization of those set forth in the *Prajñāpāramitā Sūtras,* the Scriptures of Perfect Wisdom, a rudimentary knowledge of the extent, development and contents of these voluminous and uniquely important writings is obviously prerequisite to an understanding of the views—or rather of the entire repudiation of all views—of Nagarjuna and his followers.

According to Dr. Edward Conze, who has devoted the greater part of his life to studying, translating and interpreting this class of literature, the composition of the *Prajñāpāramitā* texts extended over about a thousand years, which period roughly speaking can be divided into three phases lasting two centuries each and one phase lasting five or six centuries. The first phase (c. 100 B.C. to A.D. 100) consists in the elaboration of the teaching in a basic text, the second (c. A.D. 100-300) in its expansion into three or four lengthy treatises, the third (c. A.D. 300-500) in its abridgement into a number of shorter treatises, and the fourth (A.D. 500-1200) in its condensation into Tantric *dhāraṇis* and *mantras.*

(1) Though many questions connected with the literary history of the *Prajñāpāramitā* corpus remain undetermined, it now seems fairly certain that the *Aṣṭasāhasrikā,* the Perfection of Wisdom "in 8,000 lines," is the oldest of the texts belonging to this class. Like other early Mahayana *sūtras* it grew by a process of accretion covering in this case perhaps two centuries. As might have been anticipated, it very likely had its origin among

the Mahāsanghikas, one of whose offshoots, the Prajñāptivādins, were from early times credited with the transmission of a teaching dealing with Wisdom. Geographically, the *Aṣṭasāhasrikā* probably came from a spot between the Godavari and the Kistna near Amaravati and Nagarjunakonda, in the Andhra country in South-Eastern India. As now extant, it consists of thirty-two prose chapters, the principal theme of which is, of course, the doctrine of emptiness. A verse summary of twenty-eight chapters, the *Ratnaguṇasaṁcayagāthā,* to which four chapters on the first five perfections were afterwards added, also existed originally. Only Haribhadra's eighth-century recension of this work has come down to us.

(2) The "Large *Prajñāpāramitā*" into which, about five centuries after the Buddha's Parinirvana, the *Aṣṭasāhasrikā* was expanded, is today represented by three different texts: the *Śatasāhasrikā,* the *Pañcavimśati,* and the *Aṣṭadaśa,* or Perfection of Wisdom "in 100,000 lines"—which even for a Mahayana *sūtra* is a prodigious length—"in 25,000 lines," and "in 18,000 lines," respectively. As Dr. Conze has pointed out, these three texts are really one and the same book, differing in the extent to which the "repetitions" have been copied out.[1] To this period also belongs the *Daśasāhasrikā,* or Perfection of Wisdom "in 10,000 lines," which incorporates material drawn from the Large *Prajñāpāramitā,* as well as several short independent treatises.

(3) During the third phase begins the process of contraction. By this time so formidable had the proportions of the Large *Prajñāpāramitā* become that they presented an obstacle even to scholars. Recourse was therefore had to two parallel methods of solving the problem, one by the compilation of short *sūtras,* the other by the composition of summaries of the expanded text. Undoubtedly the earliest and most celebrated of the abridged *sūtras* are the *Hṛdaya* or *Heart Sūtra,* in which is contained the concentrated essence of the Perfection of Wisdom teaching, and the *Vajrachhedikā* or *Diamond* (*-Cutter*) *Sūtra,* which "confines itself to a few central topics, and appeals directly to a spiritual intuition which had left the conventions of logic far behind."[2]

---

[1] *Selected Sayings,* p. 12.
[2] *Ibid.,* p. 14.

Scholars relegate both these documents to the fourth century A.D. Both are of the very highest spiritual value, and have for centuries wielded enormous influence throughout Central Asia and the Far East. To the Chinese translation of the *Diamond Sūtra* in fact belongs the distinction of being the oldest printed book known to us (May 11th, A.D. 868). Again both texts have won a perhaps premature popularity among some sections of Western Buddhists. Many other abridged *sūtras* have also come down to us. Among the summaries the most important is the *Abhisamayālaṁkāra,* a summary of the Perfection of Wisdom "in 25,000 lines" in the form of 273 memorial stanzas. Ascribed to Maitreyanātha, the teacher of Asanga, this brilliant piece of scholasticism—in the best sense of the term—is a noteworthy illustration of the close interconnections existing between the various schools. For whereas Maitreyanātha seems to have been the original inspirer of the whole *Yogācāra* movement the text which he subjected to systematic tabulation was one of those on which the Mādhyamikas based themselves. His disciple Asanga summarized the *Prajñāpāramitā* teaching in the form of a *śāstra* on the *Diamond Sūtra*. Other Yogācārins produced similar works.

(4) With the condensation of the *Prajñāpāramitā* into *dhāraṇis* and *mantras* the limit of contraction was reached. Though the *Heart Sūtra* concludes with a *mantra,* the famous "*gate gate pāragate pārasaṁgate bodhi svāhā,*" the *mantra par excellence* of the *Prajñāpāramitā,* most of these invocatory-meditative formulæ are found in the numerous short Tantric abridgements of the teaching which were produced during the final phase of the composition of the *Prajñāpāramitā* literature. One of these texts, the *Ekākśari,* goes so far as to assert that the Perfection of Wisdom is contained "in one letter," the letter "A." Eventually the *Prajñāpāramitā* was personified as a goddess, and her various iconographical representations were utilized as objects of worship and supports of different forms of concentration and meditation. With a group of texts, of the *sādhana* class, describing the attainment of the Perfection of Wisdom through these procedures, the production of this stupendous literature at last comes to an end.

Before venturing to give a brief exposition of the *Prajñāpāramitā* teaching we must clear up two points of comparatively minor importance connected with its literature. The first concerns

Nagarjuna's knowledge of the texts, the second their encrustation by successive layers of commentary and sub-commentary.

Nagarjuna, it is now generally agreed, "flourished" in the second century A.D.: the tradition which represents him as being alive some centuries later is due to a confusion with a Tantric adept of the same name. But the composition of the *Prajñāpāramitā* literature covers a period stretching from the 2nd century B.C. to the 12th century A.D. Obviously the Mādhyamika system could not have been based on the *Prajñāpāramitā* literature as a whole. The difficulty is more apparent than real. With the exception of some of the treatises of the fourth and last stage, in which the Perfection of Wisdom is viewed in the light of specifically Tantric modes of thought, the entire literature contains what is fundamentally the same teaching in various degrees of expansion and contraction. Nagarjuna's career falls within the second phase in the composition of the *Prajñāpāramitā*. He must therefore have been acquainted at least with the Perfection of Wisdom "in 8,000," "in 100,000," "in 25,000" and "in 18,000 lines." A commentary on the Large *Prajñāpāramitā* is in fact included among his works. Apart from texts of the *Prajñāpāramitā* class the only Mahayana *sūtras* with which Nagarjuna is definitely known to have been acquainted are the *Saddharma Puṇḍarīka,* from which he quotes, and the *Daśabhūmikā,* on which also he wrote a commentary. These works must have preceded and might have influenced him.

Bulky as the *Prajñāpāramitā sūtras* are, they are very far from exhausting the works belonging to this class of literature. As our reference to the writings of Nagarjuna suggests, almost every *sūtra* is plentifully supplied with commentaries and sub-commentaries. Now a commentary is at least twice as long as the original text; sometimes it is ten or twelve times as long. Sub-commentaries are, mercifully, in general much shorter. Adding *sūtras* to *śātras,* and *śāstras* to summaries, and all these to their respective commentaries and sub-commentaries, explanations and expositions, we find ourselves in the end confronted by a literature of truly staggering dimensions.

The principal teachings of the *Prajñāpāramitā* are, however, quite simple, though this is far from meaning that they can be understood by the average man, however high a degree of merely intellectual development he might have attained. They are in fact addressed to Bodhisattvas, or followers of the Mahayana, and it is expressly stated that they are not addressed to the Hinayanists, the followers of the lower ideals of an individual "Nirvana" and merely personal "enlightenment." This clear and emphatic delimitation of the kind of audience for which the *Prajñāpāramitā* teachings are intended reflects not only the historical circumstances of their origin but also what at every stage of progress is perhaps the central problem of the spiritual life, especially as it approaches the higher, purely transcendental realms of attainment. What is this problem? That the Means to Enlightenment, being regarded as an end in itself becomes an object of attachment, so that from a help it is transformed into a hindrance all the more dangerous for being in its subtler forms so very difficult to detect. As with his usual psychological perceptiveness Dr. Conze remarks,

> *The very means and objects of emancipation are apt to turn into new objects and channels of craving. Attainments may harden into personal possessions; spiritual victories and achievements may increase one's self-conceit; merit is hoarded as a treasure in heaven which no one can take away; enlightenment and the Absolute are misconstrued as things out there to be gained. In other words, the old vicious trends continue to operate in the new spiritual medium. The Prajñāpāramitā is designed as the antidote to the more subtle forms of self-seeking which replace the coarser forms after the spiritual life has grown to such maturity.*[1]

Inasmuch as the Means to Enlightenment is threefold, consisting of Ethics, Meditation and Wisdom, each of these individually can be regarded as an end in itself and become an object of attachment. While "the coarser forms of self-seeking" pertain to the first and second stages of the Path, the subtler forms pertain to the third, the stage of Wisdom. Now as it was our endeavour to demonstrate in Chapter I, the primary signification of Wisdom is insight into Reality, or, in terms more akin to those of the Original Teaching, into the true nature of phenomena. This insight, though strictly incommunicable, even as Reality is ineffable, finds expression in the various doctrines of Buddhism, which are not definitions of Reality but only symbols functioning as the intellectual supports for its realization. It is these conceptual symbols which, upon being regarded as faithful pictures of Reality, cause not Wisdom itself but the doctrines in which, for

[1] *Selected Sayings*, p. 18.

all practical purposes, it is embodied, to be transformed from the helps into the hindrances of the spiritual life.

For instance, the central doctrine of the Original Teaching was that of the conditionality of all phenomena. From the conditionality of phenomena followed their egolessness: that which was dependent on other things for its existence could have no absolute own-being. Since the human personality could be analysed into a number of material and mental elements, all of which originated in dependence on causes, it followed that it was devoid of independent selfhood; it was *ānattā* (Skt. *anātman*). So far so good. But in the centuries immediately following the Buddha's Parinirvana there developed within a section of the Sangha a tendency to regard Wisdom as consisting exclusively in the minute analysis of phenomena into their constituent material and mental elements, or *dharmāḥ*, as well as in the classification of the *dharmāḥ* themselves in accordance with various elaborate schemes. Even this development, which found expressions in the Abhidharma literature of the Theravadins and Sarvastivadins, was by no means entirely reprehensible: it carried to its logical conclusion what was definitely one aspect of the Original Teaching. Difficulties arose only when the followers of these schools, forgetting that the doctrines of Buddhism were symbols and supports, began to insist that the *dharmāḥ* were real entities and that the Abhidharma description of their various permutations could be accepted as a fully adequate account of Reality.

As was made sufficiently clear in Chapter II, this excessive literalism on the part of the most prominent Hinayana schools, by which they were eventually led into a form of pluralistic realism, was one of the main factors, if not the most important one, in the emergence of the Mahayana. For this reason the *Prajñāpāramitā* must be construed not only as a general warning against the inveterate human tendency of imposing upon Reality the categories of the understanding but also, more specifically, as an emphatic protest against the Abhidharma habit of treating the momentary discrete *dharmāḥ* not as concepts but as entities. The Hinayanists taught only the egolessness of the individual (*pudgala-nairātmya*). Having, in the interest of the doctrine of the conditionality and unsubstantiality of all phenomena, made an analysis of the so-called personality into its constituent material and mental elements, they paradoxically proceeded to forfeit the spiritual benefits of the analysis by asserting that though personality was unreal its constituent elements were real. The wrong conception of substantiality was simply transferred from the whole to its parts. Thus the Abhidharma eventually came to stand for the very substantialism which the Buddha had so categorically rejected. Wisdom, understood literally, became a hindrance to Wisdom. In order to counteract this misunderstanding the Mahayana taught not only the egolessness of the individual but also the unsubstantiality and emptiness of all phenomena (*sarvadharmaśūnyatā*). The locus of this teaching is, of course, the *Prajñāpāramitā sūtras,* which for this reason have as their principal theme the doctrine of *Śūnyatā.*

Though the Absolute being non-dual is not to be divided into species, twelve, sixteen, eighteen and even twenty modes of *Śūnyatā* are enumerated and described in the *Prajñāpāramitā* corpus. More convenient to our present purpose than this cumbrous classification, however, will be the three principal aspects of *Śūnyatā* as non-different from the universe of phenomena, as non-different from *Prajñā,* and as non-different from the *Tathāgata,* together with the five progressive stages of meditation on *Śūnyatā.* These two classifications will, between them, yield a more definite indication of the nature and purpose of the *Prajñāpāramitā* teaching.

(a) Phenomena are dependent for their existence upon causes and conditions. Being thus dependent they are devoid of independent selfhood. Consequently they are said to be *śūnya* or empty. Nirvana, being transcendent to all the categories of thought, is also *śūnya,* or rather it is *Śūnyatā* or emptiness itself. Both these propositions form an integral part of the Original Teaching. Partly in order to counteract the incipient dualism of the Hinayana schools, which regarded the distinction between the "compounded" and "uncompounded" *dharmāḥ* as possessing ultimate validity, and partly as a result of the inherent urge of the Dharma towards perfect unfoldment, the *Prajñāpāramitā* argued that if phenomena were *śūnya* and if Nirvana was *śūnya,* and if *śūnya* meant lack of individual selfhood, so that one could not say of a thing that it was really "this" or "that," then the emptiness of phenomena must coincide with the emptiness of Nirvana, so that in reality the universe was not different from the

Absolute. According to Dr. Conze "unconditioned identity of the conditioned and of the Unconditioned is the principal message of the *Prajñāpāramitā*."[1] Arguing from another point of view, it might be said that the conception of the Unconditioned having no meaning apart from that of the conditioned it was itself conditioned, hence dependent, and hence *śūnya*. The same conclusion is reached in either case: There is only one non-dual Reality, of which nothing can be predicated; Samsara and Nirvana, the relative and the Absolute, conditioned and Unconditioned *dharmāḥ*, are alike mere thought-constructions. These thought-constructions being ultimately empty are of course themselves non-different from Reality.

The most important practical corollary of this teaching is that if the Universe and the Absolute are in reality non-different, Enlightenment consists not in passing from one to the other, as though both were separate realities, but in the realization of their essential non-difference. Thus the spiritual life is in the highest sense an illusion. There is nothing to gain and nobody to gain it.

(b) The means by which, without there being any gainer, that which is not to be gained is gained by way of no-gaining, is designated *Prajñā*. Conventionally speaking, the object of *Prajñā* is *Śūnyatā*. But *Śūnyatā* being transcendent to all empirical determinations is not to be apprehended by means of any thought-construction, however subtle. Transcendental Wisdom consists in the complete cessation of all thought-constructions, the absolute abandonment not only of false but also of true doctrines; having crossed to the Other Shore, it follows the Buddha's advice and leaves behind it the Raft of the Dharma; it abandons even the idea of abandonment, for in reality there is nothing to be given up. From the absolute point of view *Prajñā* is not even that which apprehends *Śūnyatā*. In order to be an object of apprehension *Śūnyatā* would have to possess some kind of self-nature. But by definition it is the absence of self-nature. *Prajñā*, therefore, not being even that which apprehends *Śūnyatā*, cannot be said to have any being of its own. Having no own-being it is *śūnyā* or empty. *Prajñā* and *Śūnyatā* are non-different. In other words, *Śūnyatā* is to be realized by means of a

[1] *Ibid.*, p. 20.

faculty identical with itself. As Saraha more poetically expresses the matter,

> *Know your own Mind completely, O Yogin!*
> *Like water meeting with water.*[1]

Yet because in the absolute sense *Prajñā* is not something to be gained one should not relinquish one's efforts to gain it. For this would be to fall victim to those very dualistic modes of thought that *Prajñā* transcends. Formal Logic argues that if *Prajñā* cannot be gained no effort to gain it need be made. But the *Prajñāpāramitā* asserts that because it is unobtainable *therefore* we should strive to obtain it with all our powers. From the relative point of view, though Transcendental Wisdom ultimately goes beyond not only Ethics and Meditation but also Wisdom in the sense of an understanding of Reality in terms of the categories of the Abhidharma, it cannot arise except in dependence upon them. Only by means of the relative truth may the Absolute Truth be attained. Just as the *Prajñāpāramitā* literature is not to be fully understood except in the context of earlier tendencies towards literalism and scholasticism, so Transcendental Wisdom itself cannot be perfectly understood save as the culminating phase of a progressive series of preliminary spiritual endeavours.

(c) *Prajñā* being non-different from *Śūnyatā* the person who "attains" *Prajñā* is also in reality non-different from *Śūnyatā*. This aspect of the *Prajñāpāramitā* teaching, like the two aspects already considered, represents a return not only to the spirit but even to the letter of the Original Teaching. The Tathāgata is even during His lifetime incomprehensible. It cannot be said of Him that He exists after death, or that He does not exist after death, or both, or neither. In the terminology of the *Trikāya* doctrine, the Buddha is to be identified not with His *Rūpakāya* but with His *Dharmakāya*. As the Lord Himself is represented as saying in the *Vajrachhedikā Sūtra*,

> *"Those who by my form did see me,*
> *And those who followed me by my voice,*
> *Wrong the efforts they engaged in,*
> *Me those people will not see.*
> *From the Dharma should one see the Buddha,*

---

[1] *Dohokośa* 32. The Mind referred to is the Absolute Mind which is essentially non-different from *Śūnyatā*.

For the Dharma-bodies are the guides.
Yet Dharmahood is not something one should become aware of,
Nor can one be made aware of it."[1]

The last two lines are a warning against regarding Dharmahood as being in reality an object of apprehension, for this would be tantamount to attributing to it some kind of self-nature, in which case it would not be Reality. Being non-different from *Śūnyatā*, the Buddha can be "seen" only in the same way that *Śūnyatā* itself is to be "realized"—by the entire cessation of all thought-constructions, including that of "the Buddha." According to the *Prajñāpāramitā* teaching "*Śūnyatā*," "*Prajñā*" and "Buddha" are mere words. Only when, in the course of profound meditation, we entirely discard all such concepts, realizing that they represent no separate objectively existent things, but that like all other words they are only so many different designations of *Śūnyatā*, which is the Supreme Reality, may we be said to "realize" *Śūnyatā*, "attain" *Prajñā*, or "see" the Buddha.

This type of meditation, though the special province of Transcendental Wisdom, is, however, only the fourth of a progressive series of five meditations on *Śūnyatā*, all of which the *Prajñāpāramitā* literature recommends. The first, second and third correspond to the Hinayana conception of *Śūnyatā*, and their presence in the scheme is a reminder of the fact that the higher stages of insight and attainment must be securely based upon the lower. The fifth stage, as Dr. Conze remarks, is probably common to all schools of Buddhism.[2] A very short review of these five meditations will summarize the *Prajñāpāramitā sūtras* and conclude our sketch of the literature and its teaching.

(a) First, one meditates upon *Śūnyatā* as the absence of real selfhood and individuality. With the help of the categories of the Abhidharma the seemingly stable and homogeneous beings and objects of the phenomenal world are analysed until "men," "women," "houses," "trees" and other such common-sense notions disappear and a stream of momentary discrete mental and material events called *dharmāḥ* takes their place.

(b) Next, having distinguished between the conditioned and

---

[1] *Selected Sayings,* p. 111.

[2] "Meditation on Emptiness." *The Maha Bodhi,* Vol. 63, p. 201 (May, 1955).

unconditioned *dharmas,* one meditates upon *Śūnyatā* as the entire emptiness of the conditioned in respect of such attributes as permanence, happiness and purity, which are exclusively the property of the Unconditioned. Understanding the hollowness of every kind of mundane existence, one begins to feel the need for renunciation.

(c) In the third stage one meditates upon *Śūnyatā* as the emptiness of the Unconditioned in respect of the conditioned. Nirvana is regarded as absolutely other than and transcendent to the world. Having turned one's back upon all mundane things, one resorts to the practice of Morality, Meditation and Wisdom, and eventually progresses along the Transcendental Path as far as the attainment of Arahantship, or Nirvana in the Hinayanic sense.

(d) Passing from Wisdom to Transcendental Wisdom, one meditates upon *Śūnyatā* in the distinctively Mahayana sense of complete emptiness of all discriminations, particularly of the discrimination between the conditioned and the Unconditioned, which it is now realized are mere thought-constructions. Transcending logic, one reaches the realm of contradiction, wherein because there is nothing to be realized every effort to realize it must be made, and wherein for the very reason that no beings exist one must vow to lead them all to Supreme Enlightenment.

(3) Here nothing can be said, for meditating upon *Śūnyatā* as empty of *Śūnyatā* one transcends even Transcendental Wisdom. The Raft has now been completely abandoned.

V. The New Wisdom School

These profound teachings were given a more systematic and logical shape by one of the greatest spiritual geniuses and most brilliant thinkers the world has ever seen. Nagarjuna, the founding patriarch and well-nigh the perfecter of the Mādhyamika School, was born in a Brahmin family of Berar, Central India, probably about the middle of the second century A.D. Apparently he was active in both North and South, for tradition connects him not only with Nalanda, where he is believed to have propagated the *Prajñāpāramitā* teaching, but also with Amaravati, Dhanyakataka or Sriparvata, and Nagarjunakonda, in all of which places he may have lived. There seems no reason to doubt the story of his friendship with the Āndhra King Śātavāhana, to whom is addressed the *Suhṛllekha*, or Friendly Epistle, one of his minor works. His name, which is derived from *arjuna,* a kind of tree, and *nāga,* a serpent or "dragon" as the Chinese translations more expressively have it, refers to the "legend" (according to modern scholarship) that the sage was born beneath an Arjuna tree and that he visited the submarine kingdom of the Nāgas, where the Nāga kings transmitted to him the Large *Prajñāpāramitā Sūtra,* which had been entrusted to their care by the Lord Buddha. Indologists have been unduly perplexed by the symbolical elements in this story. As in almost all traditions, the Nāga or serpent stands for Wisdom. This the Buddha makes quite clear in a discourse belonging to the *Majjhima-Nikāya.* Explaining to Kumāra-Kassapa the meaning of a riddle which had been propounded to the monk by a certain deva, the Blessed One says, " 'The serpent,' brother, is a name for the brother who has destroyed the *āsavas.*"[1] By one who has destroyed the *āsavas* is of course meant an Arahant—not in the Hinayanic but in the Original Buddhist sense. The tradition that Nagarjuna had received the *Prajñāpāramitā* from the Nāgas therefore means that he had been the disciple of a community of Arahants who, owing to the dominant scholasticism of the period, were compelled to live not indeed at the bottom of the sea but in comparative seclusion. In another striking passage of the Pali Canon the *Dharma-Vinaya* is compared to the mighty ocean, and the Arahants and other classes of Aryan Disciples to mighty creatures such as the leviathan, the whale, and the great fish by which it is inhabited.[2] This could account for the association between the Arahants and the ocean. Or again, the ocean might be a symbol for the profundity of the Transcendental World, wherein in a quite literal sense the Enlightened Ones live and move and have their being. The tradition that the Nāgas had received the Larger *Prajñāpāramitā Sūtra* from the Buddha need not be understood too literally. What they received, and what they transmitted, was not so much a book as a teaching and a realization, though this again does not preclude the possibility of their having committed the teaching to writing and having

[1] *Majjhima-Nikāya,* I. 23.

[2] *Udāna,* V. 5 and *Vinaya,* II. 9.

transmitted it to Nagarjuna in both oral and written form. After studying this profound teaching and realizing its truth for himself, Nagarjuna decided that, in order to counteract the dogmatism of the Brahminical schools and the growing literalism and scholasticism of the Hinayana, the time had come for it to be made public. He therefore propagated the *Prajñāpāramitā Sūtra* and composed a number of original works on its teaching. For this service, by means of which the true interpretation of the Buddha's Teaching was preserved for humanity, Nagarjuna may well be regarded as the Second Founder of Buddhism.

The writings traditionally ascribed to Nagarjuna can, like the reputed works of most of the great *ācāryas,* be divided into three categories: authentic, doubtful and spurious. Without troubling ourselves about the third category, which contains a very large number of items, we shall first enumerate the works which by consensus of competent opinion are authentic and then mention one or two of the most important of those which are doubtful.

At the head of the authentic works of Nagarjuna stands the *Mūla-Mādhyamika Kārikās.* For intrinsic value and historical importance it is unsurpassed. Only the "Copernican revolution" brought about in Western philosophy by Kant's *Kritik der Reinen Vernunft,* the one work with which it can be to some extent compared, affords any parallel to its tremendous impact on all schools, both Brahminical and Buddhist, and its pivotal importance in the development of Indian thought. This great work, which unlike Kant's masterpiece is written in a supremely forceful and elegant style, consists of 448 verses distributed over twenty-seven chapters, each of which is devoted to the examination of a particular topic. Though the Brahminical schools are not spared, it is the categories of the Abhidharma which are the chief victims of Nagarjuna's powerful dialectic. Being the basic text of the Mādhyamika School, the *Kārikās* have naturally been the subject of extensive commentarial activity. Including the *Akutobhaya,* one of the doubtful works of Nagarjuna himself, there are eight commentaries by well known *ācāryas,* the best known and most authoritative being that of Candrakīrti, the *Prasannapadā* or "Clear-Worded," which alone survives in the Sanskrit original, the remainder being now available only in Tibetan translation. Probably next in importance to the *Kārikās* are the *Dvādaśa-Nikāya Śāstra* and the *Mahāprajñāpāramitā Śāstra,* both of which survive only in Chinese. The first is one of the *śāstras* accepted by the School of the Three *Śāstras* (Ch. San-Lun Tsung, Jap. San-Ron-Shu), the other two being the *Kārikās* themselves and the *Śata Śāstra* of Ārya Deva, and is therefore of great importance as having contributed to the expansion of the Mādhyamika teaching in China and Japan. The second is the commentary on the Large *Prajñāpāramitā* already mentioned. According to Dr. Conze, this gigantic work, which consists of a round hundred "volumes" in the Chinese version, "contains a staggering wealth of useful information."[1] Other authentic works of Nagarjuna are *Daśabhūmivibhāṣā Śāstra, Śūnyatā Saptati, Yukti Ṣaṣṭīka,* and *Vigraha Vyāvartanī.* The first deals with the ten stages of the Bodhisattva's career, the second with the doctrine of Emptiness. In the fourth, which is furnished with an auto-commentary, Nagarjuna replies to the various objections which might be raised against the purely negative method of establishing *Śūnyatā* employed in the *Kārikas.* Of more general interest are *Catuḥ Stava,* a kind of hymn in four parts, in which the great dialectician attains to unexpected heights of devotional expression, and the *Suhṛllekha,* or Friendly Epistle, a letter of moral and spiritual exhortation. Of the remaining authentic works of Nagarjuna only the *Vaidalya Sūtra and Prakaraṇa,* in which, we are informed, the author defends himself against the charge of perverting logic, and the *Ekaśloka Śāstra,* need be mentioned. Probably authentic are the *Ratnāvalī* and the *Bhavasaṁkrānti Sūtra Vṛtti.*

Since the teaching of Nagarjuna is in substance identical with that of the *Prajñāpāramitā sūtras,* we shall have to concern ourselves not so much with the general conclusions of the Mādhyamika School as with the particular method by which they arrived at them. Indeed, as we shall be able to appreciate more fully later on, the Mādhyamika is not so much a doctrine as a method. This method is generally described as dialectical. By comparing the Mādhyamika dialectic with the Socratic, a better known though less rigorous form of the same discipline, we shall be able to attain not only a clearer understanding of the fundamental principles of the dialectic of Nagarjuna and his followers but also a firmer grasp of its most important applications. Now Socrates, as

---

[1] *Selected Sayings,* p. 13.

is well known, by a series of apparently quite simple but in reality very adroit questions, was able to lead his interlocutors step by step away from their original propositions until, very much to their discomfiture, they found themselves maintaining in the end a thesis which was the exact contradictory of the one with which they had started. Here it is vitally important that we should understand that the Socratic method is not one of ingenious sophistry, as its victims sometimes felt: the two theses, though contradictory, are connected by a chain of reasoning in which the succeeding link depends quite logically upon the preceding one. Whether Socrates himself was fully aware of this may be disputed. At any rate, in the Dialogues of Plato he is represented as at one time leaving the threads of the discussion as it were hanging loosely in the air, at another as gathering them up into a knot of his own. Not so did Nagarjuna. The great Indian dialectician, having discovered that not merely some but all propositions passed, upon analysis, into their contradictories, had not only the boldness to declare that reason, being of an inherently self-contradictory nature, was incapable of arriving at the truth, but also the consistency to refrain from formulating any proposition of his own. Thus Nagarjuna's dialectic differs from that of Socrates not only in being more rigorous, systematic, and self-conscious, but also in being purely negative. Propositions are refuted not by other propositions but by themselves when carried to their logical conclusions. Reason does not succumb to external attack but is destroyed by its own internal conflicts. Not only is no proposition, whether affirmative or negative, true of Reality in the ultimate sense, but no combination of propositions, whether conjunctive or disjunctive, is applicable either.

The Buddha spoke of four possible modes of predication: A is B; A is not B; A both is and is not B; A neither is nor is not B. Applying this formula to the problem of the post-mortem condition of the Tathāgata, we get the well known declaration that it is inapt to say of such a being that He exists, or does not exist, or both exists and does not exist, or neither exists nor does not exist, after the dissolution of His physical body. His condition transcends thought. But whereas the Buddha, speaking from the standpoint of Transcendental Wisdom, confined Himself to stating that no proposition or combination of propositions was applicable to Reality—thus rejecting all possible philosophical "views" (*dṛṣṭi*)—Nagarjuna clearly demonstrated, for the first time in the history of Buddhist thought, just why they were inapplicable: they were inapplicable because they were self-contradictory. How could such conceptions as being and non-being, identity and difference, be considered valid in the absolute sense when, as soon as they were subjected to a thoroughgoing analysis, they were found to be riddled with contradictions and continually transforming themselves into their opposites? Like the Teaching of the Buddha, the dialectical method of Nagarjuna results in a thoroughgoing rejection of all views. The following of a Middle Path not only between but above the clash of all possible opposing doctrines is the most characteristic feature of the Mādhyamika School, from which, indeed, it derives its name. It would perhaps not be going too far to assert that Nagarjuna's dialectic, which exposes the antinomial structure of reason, being the logical equivalent of the Buddha's famous "silence" with regard to the four exhaustive modes of predication, the Mādhyamika School may be regarded as the transmitter of the correct interpretation of the Original Teaching.

That the Buddha's uncompromising abjuration of all views was transposed from the metaphysical to the logical mode was due partly to certain developments which, for two or three centuries before the advent of Nagarjuna, had been going on in the Buddhist schools, and partly to the Dharma's inherent need to attain full unfoldment and perfect expression within the sphere of every possible universe of discourse. Hinayana scholasticism, forgetting that Reality transcends thought and that the Dharma is only a Raft, had contracted the unfortunate habit of treating the doctrines and doctrinal categories of Buddhism as possessing absolute validity. In the Sarvastivada and Theravada Abhidharmas this habit had become positively vicious. Merely invoking the authority of the Buddha would have been useless; for His rejection of all views was found in the scriptures of the offending schools too, so that the very formulation of their realistic and pluralistic views by the Hinayana literalists showed that they had repudiated or at least ignored that authority. Nagarjuna therefore adopted the most effective method of dealing with the situation open to him. Without advancing any counter-proposition of his own, without even trying to turn the doctrines of one school against those of another (for the Hinayanists were far from agreeing among themselves), he simply showed the self-contradictory nature of every proposition that could be put forward. Though important categories of the non-Buddhist schools are subjected to the same ruthless analysis in the *Kārikās,* it is the traditional categories of Buddhism itself in general, and of the Abhidharma in particular, which are among the chief victims of his dialectic. For this reason, as well as because our primary concern is with the Buddhist schools, we propose to take as our examples of the application of the dialectical method Nagarjuna's examination of two of the most important categories of Buddhist thought: the Conditioned Co-production and Nirvana. It should not be forgotten, though, that this method is applicable to all propositions without exception. If it were not so, the dialectic of Nagarjuna would be able, like that of Socrates, to exhibit the invalidity of some propositions, but not to expose the absolute bankruptcy of reason itself.

The problem of causation occupies an extremely important place in Indian philosophy, and it is no doubt for this reason that the *Kārikās* open with a devastating attack on this category of the understanding. Only four views regarding the relation between cause and effect are possible: that cause and effect are identical; that they are different; that they are both identical and different; that they are neither identical nor different. The first view, technically known as *satkāryavāda,* was held at the time of Nagarjuna by the Sāṁkhya School; some centuries later Śaṅkara incorporated it into his non-dualist Vedanta: it may be regarded as the representative Brahminical view of causation. The second view, or *asatkāryavāda,* was upheld by the Sarvastivadins and Sautrāntikas, and is the representative Hinayana view. The third view, which attempts to synthesize the first and the second, is that of the Jainas, while the fourth, really a Humean repudiation of causation, may be ascribed to the Cārvākas. Of these the third, being beset by the difficulties attending both the first and the second views, does not call for separate examination, and the fourth, not being a genuinely philosophical position need not be subjected to serious criticism. We are left with *satkāryavāda* and *asatkāryavāda,* and it is against them that Nagarjuna launches his main polemic. He does not experience much difficulty in showing that the former, though purporting to be a theory of causation, is so badly riddled with contradictions that in the end it turns out to be a denial of causation. The latter theory fares no better. Since Nagarjuna's examination of the *asatkāryavāda* is not only a vigorous attack on Hinayana literalism, but also a denial of the ultimate validity of the central Buddhist doctrine of Conditioned Co-production, we shall have to devote a little more space to this phase in the application of the dialectic. Yet even so we shall be able to give hardly as much as a glimpse of the brilliance and dialectical acumen of the *ācāryas* of the Mādhyamika School.

Now the Sarvastivadins, having reduced the twenty-four *paccayā* or conditions of the Theravada to four only, had developed a theory of causation which, besides regarding cause and effect as different, also maintained that the effect could not be produced by a single entity. Nagarjuna exposes the absurdity of both these theses. If the cause is different from the effect no relation subsists between them, and anything can be produced from anything. A chip of gravel can sprout into a plant just as easily as a seed, for both the chip and the seed have the characteristic of being different from the plant. One of the corollaries of the first thesis is that with the production of the effect the cause ceases to exist. But causality is essentially a relation between two things, and unless those two things can exist not at different moments of time but together they cannot be related, in which case causality becomes unthinkable. Moreover, if an effect is produced by the co-operation of four factors, for the co-ordination of these factors a fifth factor would be necessary, and for the co-ordination of this with the first four yet another, and so on *ad infinitum*. By means of such arguments as these, all of which are worked out in great detail and with extraordinary subtlety, Nagarjuna and his followers succeeded in showing that the theory that cause and effect were different led to occasionalism, or a denial of causation. Thus the second of the four possible views concerning the nature of the relation between cause and effect is, like the first, vitiated by internal inconsistency. Having exposed the self-contradictions inherent in both *satkāryavāda* and *asatkāryavāda*, whether taken separately, conjunctively, or disjunctively, Nagarjuna concludes that causation is unreal, a mere thought-construction wrongly superimposed upon the objective order of existence. Phenomena in reality do not originate from themselves, or from others, or from both, or from neither. Origination being logically inconceivable causation is like a dream or an illusion.

Nagarjuna does not shrink from the conclusion that if causation is unreal the *Pratītya Samutpāda* is also unreal. In fact, he insists upon it, for according to him only by recognizing the merely relative validity of this teaching can its true import be preserved. The Hinayanists had interpreted the Buddha's Conditioned Co-production as the temporal sequence and spatial juxtaposition of ultimately real entities between which real causal relations obtained. Such an interpretation amounted to a repudiation of the fundamental Buddhist doctrine, of which, paradoxically, the *Pratītya Samutpāda* was intended to be an expanded statement—the doctrine of the essencelessness and unsubstantiality of all phenomena whatsoever. In the interests of the correct interpretation of the Dharma Nagarjuna showed that the *Pratītya Samutpāda* taught not a real causal relation between entities but their mutual dependence, hence their lack of independent selfhood, and that it therefore consisted of a sequence and juxtaposition not of realities, as the Hinayanists thought, but only of appearances. Consisting as it did entirely of appearances the *Pratītya Samutpāda* was itself merely an appearance; it was unreal; it could not be said to exist, or not to exist, or both or neither. Consequently it was to be equated with *Śūnyatā*. In this way did the dialectic of Nagarjuna, by exposing the contradictions inherent in the Buddhist doctrines themselves *when taken literally,* serve as a reminder of the supremely important fact that these doctrines, constituting the conceptual formulations of Wisdom, possessed not absolute but only relative validity, and were not ends in themselves but only means to an end. That end was of course Enlightenment. By shattering the hard shell of literalism in which Buddhism was then imprisoned Nagarjuna not only saved it from suffocation and probable death but also gave it room for future development. Recognition of the relativity of the means to a certain end leads, sooner or later, to the recognition of the possibility of there being a plurality of means. As far as the various methods conducive to Enlightenment are concerned, however, since they must pertain either to Morality, or to Meditation, or to Wisdom, all are included archetypally in the Means to Enlightenment proclaimed by the Buddha.

One of the principal charges brought by the Mahayanists against the Hinayanists was that the latter conceived Nirvana almost exclusively in terms of negation. They defined it either as the cessation of pain or of the five *skandhas* or of the *Pratītya Samutpāda* or some either supposedly positive entity or collection of entities: the Absolute was defined as privation of the contingent. Since the world, in the sense of the total aggregate of causally associated *dharmas,* was believed to be real, the cessation of the world was a real cessation and the definition of Nirvana in terms of such cessation therefore valid in the absolute sense. One of the results of Nagarjuna's dialectic was to render such a position quite untenable. *Pratītya Samutpāda* being ultimately unreal its cessation too was unreal; Nirvana could not, strictly speaking, be defined in terms of cessation. In fact it could not be defined at all. The twenty-fifth chapter of the *Kārikās,* which is devoted to an examination of the category of Nirvana, is a devastating attack on the concepts of being and non-being as applied, whether individually, conjunctively or disjunctively, to the ultimate goal of the higher Buddhist life. A few verses may be quoted from it in order to acquaint the reader, however imperfectly, with the qualities of Nagarjuna's style, which possesses both the scintillating brilliance and the incisiveness of a diamond. Owing to the terseness of the language, as well as the absence of exact English equivalents for the technical terms used, even in Sterbatsky's translation the verses necessarily remain more than a little obscure.

IV

Nirvana, first of all, is not a kind of Ens,
It would then have decay and death.
There altogether is no Ens
Which is not subject to decay and death.

V

If Nirvana is Ens,
It is produced by causes—
Nowhere and none the entity exists
Which would not be produced by causes.

VI

If Nirvana is Ens,
How can it lack substratum?
There whatsoever is no Ens
Without any substratum.

VII

If Nirvana is not an Ens
Will it then be a non-Ens?
Wherever there is found no Ens
There neither is a [corresponding] non-Ens.

VIII

Now, if Nirvana is a non-Ens,
How can it then be independent?
For sure, an independent non-Ens
Is nowhere to be found.

IX

Co-ordinated here or caused are [separate things]:
We call this world phenomenal;
But just the same is called Nirvana
When from causality abstracted.

X

The Buddha has declared
That Ens and non-Ens should be both rejected.
Neither as Ens nor as a non-Ens
Nirvana therefore is conceived.

XI

If Nirvana were both Ens and non-Ens
Final deliverance would be also both,
Reality and unreality together.
This never could be possible!

XII

If Nirvana were both Ens and non-Ens,
Nirvana could not be uncaused.
Indeed both Ens and non-Ens
Are dependent on causation.

XIII

How can Nirvana represent
An Ens and a non-Ens together?
Nirvana is indeed uncaused,
Both Ens and non-Ens are productions.

XIV

How can Nirvana represent
[The place] of Ens and of non-Ens together?
As light and darkness [in one spot]
They cannot simultaneously be present.

XV

If it were clear, indeed,
What an Ens means, and what a non-Ens,
We could then understand the doctrine
About Nirvana being neither Ens nor non-Ens.

XVI

If Nirvana is neither Ens nor non-Ens
No one can really understand
The doctrine which proclaims at once
Negation of them both together.[1]

According to the commentator Candrakīrti, the opening salvoes of this offensive are so far as the Buddhist schools are concerned directed against the Sarvastivadins who, though they regarded Nirvana as the cessation of all defiled (*āśrava*) *dharmas*, including even consciousness, did not regard it as the cessation of existence. As Nagarjuna points out in Verse V, however, the conception of Nirvana as some kind of positive entity conflicts with the Sarvastivadin assumption that it is unconditioned and unproduced (*asaṁskṛta, anutpādāna*).

A positive entity (*bhāva*) which is not dependent on conditions cannot be discovered. Even to speak of Nirvana as the cessation of the defilements is tantamount to admitting that it is conditioned; for such a cessation is an event occurring in time, which makes Nirvana not only conditioned but transitory. The *asaṁskṛta dharmas* are, however, by definition unconditioned and eternal. Consequently the Sarvastivadin conception of Nirvana as a positive unconditioned entity is self-contradictory. Moreover, Enlightenment according to the Sarvastivadins consists in a sort of switch over from a sequence of defiled and conditioned *dharmas* to a sequence of *dharmas* unconditioned and undefiled, the component *dharmas* of both sequences being regarded as

[1] *The Conception of Buddhist Nirvana.* For alternative translations, see Frederick J. Streng, *Emptiness—A Study in Religious Meaning* (New York, 1967) and Kenneth K. Inada, *Nāgārjuna: a Translation of his Mūlamadhyamakakārikā with an Introductory Essay* (Tokyo, 1970).

ultimate realities. Thus Enlightenment involves a change in the objective order. According to the Mādhyamikas the change is entirely subjective. What we have to change is not the world but ourselves. Enlightenment is obtained not only when, realizing that there is no difference between them, we cease to discriminate between Samsara and Nirvana, but also when, knowing that the Absolute is transcendent to thought, we abstain from thinking of it either in terms of existence or in terms of non-existence. By his brilliant exposure of the inconsistencies and self-contradictions inherent in both the Sarvastivadin and the Sautrāntika positions with regard to Nirvana Nagarjuna was able to bring Buddhism from the one-sided views of the Hinayana back on to the Middle Path of the Buddha which, henceforth, was to be identical with the Mahayana in general and the Mādhyamika school in particular.

Other important categories of the Abhidharma which Nagarjuna has subjected to dialectical treatment in the *Kārikās* are the six faculties of sense (*āyatanas*), the five aggregates (*skandhas*), and the six (not to be confused with the twelve) bases of existence (*dhātus*). All these categories are shown to be thoroughly inconsistent and self-contradictory; they are not realities, as the Hinayanists thought, but only appearances, and are therefore not absolutely but only relatively valid. He also applies the dialectical method to the various forms of substantialism upheld by the Brahminical schools, particularly to the conception of the *ātman* as the unchanging and identical substratum of experience. Having already given a few random examples of the way in which Nagarjuna reveals the total inadequacy of reason to formulate the real the details of these criticisms need not now detain us. The implication of them all is to establish *Śūnyatā* as the sole reality and phenomena as essentially non-different from *Śūnyatā*.

The *ācāryas* of the Mādhyamika School who succeeded Nagarjuna and who for more than a thousand years (if we include Tsongkhapa) illustrated the illustrious doctrine of the Middle Path were worthy disciples of their great master. Nagarjuna's immediate successor Ārya Deva, a Sinhalese by birth, was the author of the *Catuḥ Śataka*. In this celebrated work he has devoted even greater attention than Nagarjuna to the application of the dialectical method to the Sāṁkhya and

Vaiśeṣika systems of Brahminical philosophy, both of which at that time wielded great influence. According to tradition he was a formidable debater and many times vanquished his opponents in the public disputations which were so prominent a feature of the religious life of the times. For these and similar services he may be regarded as the co-founder with Nagarjuna of the Mādhyamika tradition.

With Buddhapālita and Bhāvaviveka, both of whom belonged to the fifth century A.D., occurs the first split in the school. According to the former the dialectical method was essentially negative; it consisted in showing the absurdity of the opponent's arguments on premises which he himself regarded as acceptable. *Śūnyatā* was not to be established as the sole ultimate reality on the strength of any logical, that is to say syllogistic, argument, but simply by exposing the essentially antinomial character of reason. Since Buddhapālita regarded *prasanga* or *reductio ad absurdum* alone as the genuine Mādhyamika method the school which he inaugurated is known as the Prāsangika. The latter *ācārya,* Bhāvaviveka, on the other hand, thought that *Śūnyatā* could be established by means of positive arguments. He also held what was for a Mādhyamika the heterodox view that realization of *Śūnyatā* was not indispensable for the attainment of Nirvana. His school is known as the Svātantrika.

If previous *ācāryas* had left any part of the Mādhyamika doctrine imperfect, incomplete or undeveloped their omissions were made finally good by Candrakīrti in the eighth and Śāntideva in the ninth centuries A.D. With these two *ācāryas,* both of whom were staunch upholders of the *prasaṅga* method, the Mādhyamika doctrine reaches the apogee of rigour and consistency. Candrakīrti's great commentary the *Prasannapadā* is accepted as the standard exposition of Nagarjuna's masterpiece, the *Mādhyamika Kārikās.* We should also mention his commentary on Ārya Deva's *Catuḥ Śataka* and his *Mādhyamikāvatāra,* an important independent composition, both of which works are now extant only in Tibetan translation. Besides criticizing Bhāvaviveka for his deviations from Mādhyamika orthodoxy, Candrakīrti turns his dialectic against the Vijñānavāda, then highly influential, going so far as to allege that its *vijñāna* was nothing but the *ātman* of the Brahminical schools in disguise. He also severely criticizes the Sautrāntikas. Largely owing to the genius of Candrakīrti the Prāsangika School became the norm of the Mādhyamika teaching not only in India, where it perished with the destruction of Nalanda in the twelfth century, but also in Tibet and Mongolia, where it still flourishes in the monastic universities. Śāntideva is, of course, well known as the author of the *Śikṣā-Samuccaya* and the *Bodhicaryāvatāra,*[1] two of the most popular works in the whole range of Mahayana literature. The first is an anthology of excerpts from important Mahayana *sūtras,* the complete Sanskrit originals of which are in most cases no longer available. A poem by Śāntideva prefaces the collection, each of its twenty-seven stanzas being subsequently utilized as the chapter heading of a particular group of excerpts. The *Bodhicaryāvatāra* is an original work. Though short, it is one of the brightest gems in the thickly studded tiara of Mahayana Buddhist literature. One of its most striking features is its unique combination of ecstatic devotion and penetrating philosophic insight. Śāntideva perhaps to an even greater extent than his master Nagarjuna, is both *Pater Ecstaticus* and *Pater Profundus.* He knows both the heights and the depths of spiritual experience. Chapter X of the *Bodhicaryāvatāra,* called *Prajñāpāramitā,* which contains a rigorous polemic against the Vijñānavāda, is a valuable source of information regarding Mādhyamika metaphysics.

With Śāntarakṣita, who belongs to the eighth century A.D., and his disciple Kamalaśīla, we pass from the stormy seas of controversy into the comparatively tranquil waters of philosophical syncretism. Candrakīrti had contended that the Sautrāntika and Vijñānavāda positions were not acceptable even as relative truth. The two latter-day *ācāryas,* with less rigour but perhaps greater subtlety, maintained that the Sautrāntika-Vijñānavāda views and the Mādhyamika repudiation of all views could both be accepted, the former as relative truth and the latter as Absolute Truth. Śāntarakṣita's *magnum opus* is the *Tattvasaṅgraha,* on which his disciple Kamalaśīla has written a *pañjikā* or commentary. Like the *Mādhyamika Kārikās* its principal concern is to expose the inconsistency of certain doctrines and doctrinal categories, both Brahminical and Buddhist. The number of schools having apparently increased considerably since the time of

[1] Recently translated into Sinhalese by Ven. Sasanasiri Maha Thera.

Nagarjuna, Śāntarakṣita's work is much more extensive in scope than that of his predecessor. In fact it is a kind of encyclopædia of refutations. That his school originated in an attempt to reconcile the two dominant Mahayana philosophies is indicated by its name, the Yogācāra-Mādhyamika-Svātantrika. Among its adherents were some illustrious men: Ārya and Bhadanta Vimuktasena, Haribhadra and Tsongkhapa. Syncretism is, however, generally an evidence of enervation and the precursor of decline. It is therefore not astonishing that with this school we reach the last phase in the long evolution of the Mādhyamika.

Though no new developments took place, the school of Nagarjuna did continue to exercise tremendous influence not only in Tibet and Mongolia, where it still supplies the philosophical basis of Mahayana Buddhism, but also in China, Japan and other Far Eastern countries. In India, practically all the Brahminical schools found it necessary to adapt the dialectic of Nagarjuna to their own needs. Gaudapāda and Śaṅkara, as is well known, borrowed much of their method and many of their conclusions from the Mādhyamikas. The Advaita system of Vedanta is in a sense a less rigorous and more compromising continuation of the Mādhyamika teaching.

VI. The Scriptures of Devotional Buddhism

Strange as the fact may seem to those who are incapable of understanding either the transcendental unity of Buddhism or the necessity of cultivating all five spiritual faculties simultaneously, the schools which upheld the supremacy of simple faith in and wholehearted devotion to the person of the Buddha were historically associated with the the Mādhyamikavāda, which insisted upon the primacy of Wisdom. So close, indeed, was the connection between them, and for so many centuries was the emotional overshadowed by the intellectual faculty, that in India the Buddhism of faith and devotion never evolved to the extent of being able to form an independent school. This development took place only much later, in China and Japan, where the average Buddhist monk and layman were on the whole much less susceptible to the charms of divine philosophy than their Indian brethren.

By nothing else, perhaps, is the tremendous depth of Nagarjuna's spiritual insight so much evinced as by his recognition that for those who seriously undertake to lead the Buddhist life two paths are open, the difficult path of self-reliance and the easy path of dependence on the compassion of the Buddhas. For this reason he is regarded as their first patriarch or founding father not only by the Mādhyamikas but also by the followers of the Jodo Shu and other predominantly or exclusively devotional schools of the Far East. The difficult and self-reliant path consists, according to Nagarjuna, in the practice of the Ten Perfections and the Four Abodes of Mindfulness, while the easy other-reliant path comprises simply the worship of the Buddhas Amitābha and Maitreya. Of these two great beings, the latter is spoken of as a Buddha only by anticipation; in fact he is not a Buddha but a Bodhisattva. He stands, however, on the threshold of Supreme Enlightenment, and according to both Hinayana and Mahayana traditions now resides in the Tuṣita Heaven, whence he will descend to earth towards the end of the present world-period for his final rebirth as a human being. After attaining Enlightenment beneath a tree which will thenceforth be associated with His name, He will be consecrated as their legitimate successor by all the Buddhas and from that time onwards until His Parinirvana preach the Dharma to gods and men. Maitreya enjoys the distinction of being the only Bodhisattva worshipped today in Theravada countries, for which reason it has been suggested that devotion to the ideal of Bodhisattvahood as exemplified in the career of Maitreya, the Loving One, the future Buddha, could be a unifying and harmonizing factor in modern Buddhism.

Amitābha, the Infinite Light, on the other hand attained Supreme Buddhahood an incalculable number of æons ago. Though the Larger *Sukhāvatī-vyūha Sūtra* tells us that He made His famous forty-nine vows under the Buddha Lokeśvararāja, who according to this text was the eighty-first in succession to Dīpankara, the name of Amitābha Himself is not included in any of the lists of *Nirmāṇakāya* or "earthly" Buddhas. He is a purely transcendental figure. Worshipped in India, Nepal, Tibet and Mongolia as one of the five principal *Sambhogakāyas* of the Buddha, He speedily came to be regarded in China and Japan as the supreme personification of the *Dharmakāya* Itself, eclipsing all rivals, and absorbing into Himself all the attributes of perfection. To His worshippers Amitabha is not one Buddha among many, not even *primus inter pares,* but Buddhahood Itself in the most beautiful and adorable form conceivable by the heart of man. He is Wisdom and Compassion not only in their fullness but in their overflowingness. He is the most highly transcendent and the most deeply immanent. In Him Absolute Reality manifests as the Supreme Beauty out of Infinite Love. Upon Him, therefore, gradually centred all those rays of devotion which had hitherto been dispersed over a multitude of Buddhas and Bodhisattvas until He had become the dazzling focus of the love and adoration of millions of Far Eastern Buddhist hearts.

According to Occidental scholarship, however, Amitabha is a myth, probably of Central Asian or Iranian origin. For what historical evidence is there that He ever existed? Such a view fails to take account of the distinction between the empirical truth of reason and the poetic truth of imagination. Whether Amitabha did ever live upon the earth as a human being is irrelevant. What is not only relevant but vitally important is the ideal which the myth, if it really is a myth, is intended to portray, the spiritual teaching which it imparts. We must not forget that Amitabha is the main object not of any system of philosophy but of the Buddhism of Faith and Devotion. What we are therefore concerned with here is an attempt not to convince the head but to move the heart. Since the heart is moved much more powerfully by a myth than by an argument the Buddhism of Faith and Devotion is necessarily in form mythical rather than historical, akin more to poetry than to logic. The substance of the myth, however, is nothing less than the Dharma itself in all its plenitude and in all its integrity. Just as the dialectic of Nagarjuna was a transposition from the dogmatic to the logical mode of the Buddha's teaching of the transcendence of the real to the rational, so devotional Buddhism in its last stages, especially in the teachings of Shinran Shonin, is a transposition of the whole Doctrine from the intellectual mode into the emotional. Speaking from another point of view it may be said that so vast, so comprehensive, was the Mahayana Buddhist ideal, so profound its philosophy, that no scientifically verifiable facts could provide them with an adequate concrete embodiment. A myth had therefore to be invented. Buddhism being the eternal and universal truth this myth was of cosmic dimensions. Not this world alone, but the whole universe was its background. Only infinite space and infinite time could provide a stage vast enough and a setting sufficiently magnificent for the presentation of the drama of universal emancipation. If we address the intellect the mere abstract notion of compassion will serve our purpose: "Be compassionate" is all that need be said; but if we speak to the heart, compassion must be shown revealing itself in a series of concrete acts. It is primarily to factors such as these that we must trace the origins of Devotional Buddhism, in which the Transcendental Truth shines no less brightly and certainly more beautifully through the medium of cosmic myth than it did through the conceptual formulations of the Doctrine.

The chief sources of the Amitabha myth, and hence the principal Scriptures of the Buddhism of Faith and Devotion, especially for its schools in China and Japan, are the Larger and the Smaller *Sukhāvatī-vyūha Sūtras,* or the "Array of the Happy Land," and the *Amitāyurdhyāna Sūtra,* or *Sūtra* of "Meditation on the Buddha of Infinite Life." A brief description of these fundamental texts, as well as a reference to a few devotional works of secondary importance, including those dedicated to other Buddhas and Bodhisattvas, must precede any attempt to elucidate the distinctive doctrines and methods of this school.

Though it is not possible to determine the date of the composition of the Larger *Sukhāvatī-vyūha Sūtra,* the later limit is definitely 186 A.D., in which year there died at Loyang the Yüeh-chih monk Lokaraksha, who was the first to translate the text into Chinese. As Lokaraksha's literary career spanned almost four decades, and as it would have taken at least a century for a *sūtra* to acquire sufficient prestige to be translated, we can safely assert that the original text could hardly have been composed later than the opening decade of the first century A.D. The Theravada Pali scriptures were first committed to writing in the year 80 B.C. Not more than a generation, perhaps much less, separates the *Tipiṭaka* and the *Sukhāvatī-vyūha* as literary compositions. Both are separated from the Parinirvana of the Master by more than four hundred years. Modern Theravadins maintain that during this period the traditions subsequently recorded in the *Tipiṭaka* were transmitted orally. Very likely they were. But what was there to prevent the teachings contained in the *Sukhāvatī-vyūha* from being transmitted orally too? Were retentive memories a monopoly of the Hinayana? The same line of argument which establishes the "authenticity" of the Pali *Tipiṭaka* can be utilized to establish the authenticity not only of the *Sukhāvatī-vyūha* but of any other Mahayana *sūtra* in Sanskrit. If a tradition can be transmitted orally for five hundred years it can be so transmitted for a thousand. The Scriptures of Buddhism stand or fall together. Any attempt to prove on textual grounds that one set of traditions is more authentic than another is likely to boomerang back upon the school by which it is made. Besides, the authenticity of a transcendental teaching is in the last resort to be determined by other than textual considerations.

Another indication of the comparatively early date of the text of the Larger *Sukhāvatī-vyūha Sūtra* is afforded by its prologue. Here the reader of Pali and Sanskrit scriptures finds himself on familiar ground. The Blessed One is dwelling in Rajagriha, on the sacred Vulture's Peak, and with him is a great company of 32,000 *bhikṣus,* all of whom except Ānanda are Arahants. Many noble-minded Bodhisattvas, led by Maitreya, are also present. The fact that thirty-one Arahant disciples are mentioned by name, whereas of the Bodhisattvas only their leader is so distinguished, is further evidence of the antiquity of this *sūtra.* Seeing that the face and body of the Tathāgata are bright and shining like the autumnal moon, or like a piece of gold fresh from the furnace, Ānanda asks Him whether He dwells in the transcendental state of a Buddha, and whether He contemplates the Tathāgatas of the past, future and present. After a short dialogue, in the course of which He stresses the rarity of a Buddha's appearance in the world, the Blessed One reveals to Ānanda, and to the whole assembly, the objective content of His contemplation. At this point the familiar ground melts beneath our feet. Rajagriha and the Vulture's Peak vanish, and we find ourselves in the midst of the unlimited vastness of the spiritual universe. We have passed out of time into eternity, from the mundane to the Transcendental, and from now onwards events are governed not by natural but by spiritual laws. History has been left far behind: the great Myth begins.

In the time of the Buddha Lokeśvararāja, the eighty-first in succession to Dīpankara, there lived a monk named Dharmākara.

One day this monk, after worshipping and praising the Buddha Lokeśvararāja, resolved in His presence to become a Buddha and requested Lokeśvararāja to describe to him the qualities of an ideal Buddha-country. Thereupon the Tathāgata Lokeśvararāja spent a full *koṭi* of years explaining to Dharmākara the excellencies and perfections of Buddha-countries belonging to 8,100,000 *niyutas* of *koṭis* of Buddhas. Having received the instruction for which he had asked, Dharmākara spent five kalpas mentally concentrating all the excellencies and perfections of all the Buddha-countries described by Lokeśvararāja into a Buddha-country eighty-one times more immeasurable, noble and excellent still. He then reappeared before his teacher, the measure of Whose life was full forty kalpas, and requested him to hear what his vows were, and what, after he had become a Buddha, his Buddha-country would be like. The forty-eight[1] vows which follow constitute the heart of the *Sukhāvatī-vyūha Sūtra* and the basis of the Pure Land teaching. Most important of them all is the eighteenth, which Genko, the teacher of Shinran, the founder of the Jodo Shin Shu, termed "The King of the Vows." The twentieth is of hardly less consequence. Nanjio renders them from Sanghavarman's Chinese translation as follows:—

18. "When I have obtained Buddahood, if those beings who are in the ten quarters should believe in me with serene thoughts, and should wish to be born in my country, and should have, say, ten times thought of me (or repeated my name),—if they should not be born there, may I not obtain the perfect knowledge;—barring only those beings who have committed the five deadly sins, and who have spoken evil of the good Law.

20. "When I have obtained Buddhahood, if those beings who are in the ten quarters, after they have heard my name, should direct their thoughts towards my country and should plant their roots of merit (or prepare their stock of merit), and should bring them to maturity with their serene thoughts, and wish to be born inmy country,—if they should not accomplish (their desire), may I not obtain the perfect knowledge."[2]

The conditional form in which not only these but the remainder of the forty-eight vows are cast is of the utmost significance. When, later on in the *Sūtra*, Ānanda questions the Buddha as to whether Dharmākara had by that time attained Supreme

[1] Thus the Chinese translations. They are forty-six according to the Sanskrit texts now extant.

[2] *The Sacred Books of the East*, Vol. XLIX, Pt. II, p. 73.

Enlightenment, and if so whether he had passed away or was still living, the Blessed One replies that Dharmākara had indeed attained the highest perfect knowledge, and that as the Tathāgata Amitabha He was then engaged in preaching the Dharma westwards in Sukhavati, the Buddha-country which He had established in accordance with His vows. Since Amitabha, as Dharmākara, had made His attainment of perfect knowledge conditional upon our being born in Sukhavati as soon as we repeat His name ten times, etc., and since according to the *Sūtra* He is already enlightened, it follows *sub specie temporis* that we have only to take His name in order to be reborn in the Happy Land, and *sub specie eternitatis* that we are already dwelling there. The reason why the spiritual life of the Shin Shu devotee centres round Amitabha's Vows is perhaps now more clearly apparent. We shall, however, defer further interpretation of this part of the myth till the next section, returning meanwhile to the story of the *Sūtra*. After he had made his forty-eight vows, and had received a miraculous assurance that he would become a Buddha, Dharmākara performed the duties of a Bodhisattva for a hundred thousand *niyutas* of *koṭis* of years. Here the compilers of the *Sūtra* insert a charming description of the Bodhisattva's career, the essence of which consists in following the Threefold Path of Morality, Meditation and Wisdom. That we are born rich or poor, beautiful or ugly, distinguished or undistinguished, as the result of actions performed in past lives is of course axiomatic for Buddhism. So well did Dharmākara fulfil the duties of a Bodhisattva, and so immense were the merits which he thereby accumulated, that wherever he happened to be reborn riches sprang to meet him out of the earth, while his mouth breathed forth a perfume excelling that of sandalwood and his head was redolent of the scent of lotus. Food and drink streamed from the palms of his hands. All this was only to prefigure the perfections of the Paradise which by virtue of his good deeds he would one day be able to create. Next comes the episode already referred to, in which the Buddha tells Ānanda that Dharmākara has attained Enlightenment as the Tathāgata Amitabha. Continuing, the Blessed One declares that the light and life of Amitabha are immeasurable, to which He adds the information that ten kalpas have elapsed since He arose and awoke to the highest perfect Knowledge. There now follows an account of Sukhavati, the Happy Land, which ranks with the most gorgeous examples of descriptive writing in the whole range of world literature. The Heavenly Jerusalem of the Book of Revelations is drab and insignificant in comparison. Sukhavati, which is inhabited exclusively by gods and men, is imagined as an immense plain, "level as the palm of one's hand," without mountains of any kind. Jewel-trees grow on all sides, and the whole Buddha-country is surrounded by golden nets and all round covered by lotus-flowers made of jewels. Some of the jewel lotuses are ten miles in circumference; from each one of them issue thirty-six thousand *koṭis* of rays, and in each ray sits a golden-coloured Buddha preaching the Dharma. The great rivers which flow through Sukhavati are up to fifty miles broad and twelve miles deep. On their perfumed waters float bunches of flowers to which jewels adhere. The music made by their waves puts one in mind of the deepest principles of the Dharma. All who have been born in Sukhavati are provided with subtle nutriment, perfumes, musical instruments, many-coloured garments, and magnificent palaces, as soon as they wish for them. Six times a day blow the winds, whereupon there rain down scented flowers by which the whole Buddha-country is covered seven fathoms deep. There is no fire, sun, moon, stars or darkness in Sukhavati; it is pervaded by an unimaginable radiance, which neither waxes nor wanes. Such, in brief, is the Happy Land—though no bald summary can hope to do justice to the glowing vividness of the description of its perfections given by the text. Those who are born there, the Buddha tells Ānanda, are irreversible from Enlightenment; their eventual attainment of Nirvana is assured.

After declaring that the praises of Sukhavati are inexhaustible, and that the name of Amitabha is glorified by the Buddhas of all the ten quarters, equal in number to the sands of the Ganges, the Blessed One announces that to those who had aspired to be reborn in His Happy Land, or who had meditated upon Him, Amitabha would appear surrounded by companies of *bhikṣus* at the time of their death. There follow a number of verses in praise of Amitabha and a further description of Sukhavati. In the course of this description occur the names of Avalokiteśvara and Mahāsthāmaprāpta, the two great Bodhisattvas specially associated with Amitabha. A marvellous phantasmagoria, of deep philosophical significance, such as the Mahayana *sūtras* excel in, is now revealed. Having on the Buddha's instructions worshipped in the direction of the West with a handful of flowers, Ānanda expresses a wish to see Amitabha, whereupon that Buddha sends forth from the palm of His hand a ray of light which illuminates not only His own but all other Buddha-countries of the universe. In this light not Ānanda alone but every living being can clearly see Amitabha and His retinue of Bodhisattvas in the Happy Land, while they in Sukhavati can clearly see the Buddha Sakyamuni and the whole Sahā-world. After asking the Bodhisattva Ajita (another name for Maitreya) if he sees the charming gardens, rivers and lotus-lakes of Sukhavati, and whether there is any difference between the gods called *Paranirmitavaśavartins,* and men in the world Sukhavati, the Blessed One explains that the beings who, being miraculously born in Sukhavati, appear seated cross-legged on open lotus-flowers, are the firm believers in Amitabha, while those who dwell shut up in the calyx of these flowers have entertained some doubt. Only after 500 years, when the lotus becomes full blown, will these latter be able to hear and see Amitabha. The Buddha in conclusion warns Ajita against harbouring doubts, tells him how many *koṭis* of Bodhisattvas will be reborn in Sukhavati from each Buddha-country, and, as is customary at the end of Mahayana *sūtras,* exhorts him to proclaim this treatise, the *Sukhāvatī-vyūha,* before the world together with the gods. Those who, having heard it with delight, read it, recite it, teach it to others, copy it and worship it, are assured of producing much good work. Finally, the Buddha utters some stanzas, and the compiler tells us that while this exposition of the Dharma was being delivered innumerable beings attained each of the stages of the Transcendental Path, the whole world-system shook, and various wonders took place. Gods and men applauded the speech of the Tathāgata.

The Smaller *Sukhāvatī-vyūha* is only one-eighth as long as the larger text, and probably belongs to approximately the same literary period. On this occasion the scene is laid at Śrāvastī, in the Jeta Grove, in Anāthapindika's Park, where the Blessed One was dwelling with a large company of *bhikṣus,* all Arahants, and many noble-minded Bodhisattvas. A great multitude of divine beings was also present. Addressing Śāriputra, His chief

Arahant disciple, the Bhagavat says that in the West there is a world called Sukhavati, the Buddha-country of the Tathāgata Amitāyus (the Infinite Life—a name of Amitabha). Apart from being much less elaborate, the description of the Happy Land which follows this declaration differs little from the one given in the Larger *Sukhāvatī-vyūha Sūtra*: instead of being level, it is adorned with terraces. Doctrinally, however, there is one very great and important difference between the two texts. The larger *sūtra* teaches that rebirth in the Happy Land is at least partially dependent upon the accumulation of a stock of merits. This its shorter counterpart explicitly denies. Says the Lord to Śāriputra:—

"Beings are not born in that Buddha-country of the Tathāgata Amitāyus as a reward and result of good works performed in this present life. No, whatever son or daughter of a family shall hear the name of the Blessed Amitāyus, the Tathāgata, and having heard it shall keep it in mind for one, two, three, four, five, six or seven nights, when that son or daughter of a family comes to die, then that Amitāyus, the Tathāgata, surrounded by an assembly of disciples and followed by a host of Bodhisattvas, will stand before them at their hour of death, and they will depart this life with tranquil minds. After their death they will be born in the world Sukhāvatī, in the Buddha-country of the same Amitāyus, the Tathāgata."

(The Smaller Sukhāvatī-vyūha Sūtra 10. *F. Max Müller's translation)*[1]

This teaching is not the antinomianism for which it might at first sight be mistaken. It is merely intended to assert the absolute discontinuity of the Transcendental and the mundane. The Real is not to be attained by means of a series of increments of the unreal. In the last resort emancipation depends upon the irruption into the universe of a factor that confronts our ego-consciousness as the Other Power. The significance of this profound teaching will be more fully dealt with later on.

The *Amitāyurdhyāna Sūtra,* the third of the three basic texts of Far Eastern Devotional Buddhism, occupies a doctrinal position intermediate between the respective positions of the Larger and the Smaller *Sukhāvatī-vyūha Sūtras.* It consists of the sixteen meditations which the Buddha taught to Vaidehi, the consort of King Bimbisāra of Magadha, as a means of visualizing the perfections of Sukhavati, wherein the miseries experienced by the Queen in the world were unknown. Those who wish to practise these meditations should firstly cultivate the threefold goodness

[1] *The Sacred Books of the East, Vol.* XLIX, Pt. II, p. 98-99.

of (1) supporting their parents, (2) serving and respecting teachers and elders, and (3) having a compassionate mind, abstaining from doing injury to living beings, and performing the ten wholesome actions; secondly, take refuge in the Buddha, the Dharma and the Sangha; and thirdly, give their whole mind to the attainment of Enlightenment, deeply believe in the law of cause and effect, and study and recite the Mahayana *sūtras*.

The First Meditation consists in concentrating one's mind upon the disk of the setting sun until it can be seen with equal distinctness whether the eyes are open or closed. This is obviously a form of *kasina* exercise such as was described in Chapter I, Section XVII. In the Second Meditation the *kasina* is first water and then ice. Having attained the reflex-image (*paṭibhāga-nimitta*) of ice one should imagine in it the colour of lapis lazuli. Every side of this ground of lapis lazuli, which extends to the eight points of the compass, consists of hundreds of jewels, every jewel has a thousand rays, and every ray 84,000 colours which, when reflected in the ground of lapis lazuli, look like a thousand million suns, so that it is difficult to see them separately. Across the surface of the ground of lapis lazuli are stretched golden cords crosswise, the squares thus made being subdivided by strings of jewels. The rays proceeding from these jewels form lofty towers, all adorned with flowering banners and musical instruments. When these instruments are played, they emit the sounds "suffering," "unreal," "impermanent," "non-self." In this way are the perfections of Sukhavati to be gradually visualized by the devotee. The Third to the Sixth Meditation consists in attaining a clear perception of the constituent parts of Sukhavati, such as its jewel-trees, jewel-lakes and jewel-lotuses, all of which one should be able to perceive vividly whether the eyes are open or closed. Whoever attains to these stages of meditation is assured of rebirth in the Happy Land regardless of the sins he might have committed. While the Buddha is speaking Amitāyus appears in the sky, with the Bodhisattvas Avalokiteśvara and Mahāsthāma attending on His right and left respectively. Their united radiance, a hundred thousand times brighter than gold, is of such dazzling intensity that the great beings can hardly be seen. Vaidehi then asks the Buddha how beings of the future should meditate so as to be able to see Amitāyus and His two attendant Bodhisattvas as clearly as she sees them now. The

Blessed One replies that those who wish to meditate on Buddha Amitāyus should first of all visualize a magnificent flowery throne. This constitutes the Seventh Meditation. A golden image of Amitāyus is then visualized sitting on the throne. Similar flowery thrones must be provided for Avalokiteśvara and Mahāsthāma, and their respective golden images visualized seated thereon to the right and to the left of their master. This is the Eighth Meditation. In the Ninth Meditation the devotee learns to perceive the bodily marks and the light of Buddha Amitāyus. The *Sūtra* says that those who have meditated on the Buddha's body will see also the Buddha's mind. In the Tenth Meditation he sees the bodily marks and the light of Avalokiteśvara and in the Eleventh Meditation those of Mahāsthāma. The constituent parts of all these visualizations are described with a wealth of florid detail. This is not mere "gushing eloquence" as F. Max Müller thought.[1] We should never forget that the dominant interest of these texts is not rhetorical but spiritual. The present text in particular is, as its very title indicates, a guide to meditation. The Happy Land is described with such vivid particularity simply in order to assist the process of visualization. Consequently it was very wrong of F. Max Müller to take the liberty of omitting from his translation several passages which seemed to him "unnecessary repetitions."[2] But in his time it was hardly possible for the real significance and function of the Mahayana *sūtras* to be understood. In the Twelfth Meditation the devotee should imagine that he has been reborn in Sukhavati, and that, after the lotus-flower upon which he is seated and which shuts him in has unfolded, he can see the Buddhas and Bodhisattvas that fill the sky, hear the sounds of waters and trees, the notes of birds, and the voices of many Buddhas preaching the excellent Dharma. Next, in the Thirteenth Meditation, he visualizes Amitāyus, Avalokiteśvara and Mahāsthāma together, in the same detailed manner that he had already imagined them in the Ninth, Tenth and Eleventh Meditations. In the last three meditations the devotee learns to perceive the three grades to Buddahood into which beings are reborn in Sukhavati. Each grade consists of three forms. Rebirth in the

---

[1] *Ibid.*, p. 175.
[2] *Idem.*

highest form of the highest grade is the result of observing the precepts, cultivating a right mental attitude, studying the Mahayana *sūtras,* practising different types of meditation, etc. One destined to such rebirth sees Amitabha and His attendant Bodhisattvas in all their glory at the time of death, is offered a diamond throne, and after dying is reborn seated on a diamond throne. Those who, being possessed of a smaller stock of merit, are destined to rebirth in the middle or lowest form of the highest grade, make their appearance in Sukhavati seated on thrones of purple and gold and of gold respectively. Thus as one's stock of merit decreases the panoply with which one is reborn into the Pure Land becomes less splendid. Even those who have no stock of merits at all, however, and who have committed the five deadly sins (unpardonable according to the Larger *Sukhāvatī-vyūha*), are destined to rebirth in the lowest form of the lowest grade to Buddhahood if only they repeat ten times before their death the mantra *Om Namo Amitābhāya Buddhāya,* "Adoration to Buddha Amitabha!" They will be reborn shut up within the calyxes of golden lotus-flowers. After ten great æons have passed these flowers will burst open, whereupon the Bodhisattvas Avalokiteśvara and Mahāsthāma, raising their voices in great compassion, will preach to them in detail the unsubstantiality of all phenomena and the law of the expiation of sins. Thus the *Amitāyurdhyāna Sūtra,* while apparently accepting the principle of karma, ingeniously modifies it to such an extent that its operation is practically suspended. Shinran carried the process to its logical conclusion by declaring that one was not reborn in the Pure Land even as the result of uttering the name of Amitabha. The compassion of Amitabha operated unconditionally.

Apart from the three *sūtras* just described, which together constitute the foundation of the Far Eastern Devotional schools, there are a number of other texts which are too popular and too influential to be omitted from even the sketchiest survey of the Scriptures of Devotional Buddhism. These may be divided into two classes, according to whether a Buddha or a Bodhisattva is the chief object of devotion. Owing to the deepened insight into the Buddha-nature which ultimately crystallized into the *Trikāya* doctrine it was, of course, impossible for Sakyamuni Buddha to be worshipped as the principal object of faith and devotion by any Mahayana school. In the *Sukhāvatī-vyūha* and *Amitāyurdhyāna sūtras* He figures simply as the revealer of Amitabha to the world. Nevertheless He is the recipient of some fine expressions of devotional fervour. Perhaps the most striking of these is the *Śatapañcāśatkastotra* of Mātṛceta, a work which vibrates throughout with the deepest organ-note of adoration.

Akṣobhya, "the Imperturbable," Whose Buddha-country Abhirati, the Land of Exceeding Great Delight, is situated in the East, seems to have been the central figure of a myth similar to that of Amitabha. According to Dr. Conze He is mentioned in quite a number of early Mahayana *sūtras*, from which we may infer that His worship must have been fairly widespread. Only fragments of His legend have, however, survived.[1] More fortunate was Bhaiṣajyaguru Vaidūryaprabha Tathāgata, the Lord of Healing, Who in the *sūtra* of that name is represented as making twelve great vows. His worship has enjoyed immense popularity in Mahayana countries down to the present day. Both Akṣobhya and Bhaiṣajyaguru may be regarded as only partially successful attempts to embody the conceptions which eventually found full and perfect expression in the myth of Amitabha. Maitreya occupies an intermediate position, being worshipped now as a Buddha, now as a Bodhisattva. In China, the chief centre of His worship, He is generally regarded as a Buddha and represented iconographically as a hilarious old man, of mountainous proportions, over whom a number of boys are clambering. This is Mi-lo Fu, otherwise known as the "Laughing Buddha."

Pre-eminent among Bodhisattvas stands Avalokiteśvara, the embodiment of Compassion, who has already made a brief appearance in the *Sukhāvatī-vyūha* and *Amitāyurdhyāna sūtras.* Throughout the Far East he ranks as an object of devotion second only to Amitabha. In Tibet he ranks second to none. The *Kāraṇḍavyūha Sūtra,* a summary of which is given in Chapter XV of Dr. E. J. Thomas's *History of Buddhist Thought,* is our primary source for His myth. An important secondary source is Chapter XXIV of the *Saddharma Puṇḍarīka Sūtra.* In this chapter, which really forms an independent work, Akṣayamati lauds Avalokiteśvara in a beautiful hymn. Far Eastern Devotional

---

[1] *Buddhism: Its Essence and Development,* p. 146.

Buddhism emphasized the maternal characteristics of Avalokiteśvara to such an extent that this definitely male Bodhisattva was eventually metamorphosed into a goddess known in China as Kwan Yin and in Japan as Kwannon—the "Regarder of the Cries of the World." Samantabhadra, another Bodhisattva, who figures prominently in the *Gaṇḍavyūha Sūtra,* where he makes a series of vows hardly less famous than those of Amitabha, in Japan was sometimes represented as a courtesan. In Tibet, Nepal and Mongolia, however, no such metamorphoses took place, probably because the presence of the Tārās, a group of twenty-one female emanations of Avalokiteśvara, rendered them superfluous. Of these goddesses the White Tārā and the Green Tārā are the most popular. The *Aryatārābhattarikānāmāshṭottaraśatakastotra,* in which Avalokita reveals to Vajrapāṇi the 108 names of the Green Tārā, is a hymn of uncommon pathos and beauty. Dr. Conze has included a very readable translation in his *Buddhist Texts Through the Ages.* Other Bodhisattvas who occupy a prominent place in Devotional Buddhism are Kṣitigarbha, Mahāsthāmaprāpta, Mañjuśrī and Vajrapāṇi, to each of whom pertains a legend and a literature.

VII. The Pure Land School

During the whole of its career in India Devotional Buddhism, including even the worship of Amitabha and Avalokiteśvara, existed not as an independent school but as an aspect of all schools. As we have already seen, the easy path of devotion to the Buddhas Amitabha and Maitreya was recommended by no less a personage than Nagarjuna. Tibet, Mongolia and Nepal still adhere to the Indian tradition. Only in China and Japan did Devotional Buddhism succeed in cutting the umbilical cord which united it to the parent body of the faith, though even in these lands it was only the movement of devotion to Amitabha which was thriving and vigorous enough to do so: the movements of devotion to Kshitigarbha, Samantabhadra, and other Bodhisattvas, though widespread and influential, were never able to raise themselves to the status of independent schools. Consequently when speaking of Devotional Buddhism as one of the four main schools of the Mahayana it is in effect to the worship of Amitabha that we refer. The historical fact that the worship of this Buddha was, while widely prevalent in India, there only an aspect of other schools, whereas in China and Japan it flourished independently, is reflected in the list of the Seven Fathers who, according to the Jodo Shin Shu, contributed most to the development of the Pure Land doctrine. The first two Fathers are none other than Nagarjuna, the founder of the Mādhyamika School, and Vasubandhu, the co-founder with Asanga of the Yogācāra movement. T'an Luan, Tao Ch'ao and Shan Tao, all of whom were natives of China, come third, fourth and fifth, while the seventh and eighth are Honen and his illustrious disciple Shinran, both of whom belonged to Japan. This list makes no mention of Hui Yüan, a Chinese monk who is generally credited with having raised the Pure Land movement to the status of an independent school. Probably the omission is due to the fact that Hui Yüan lived before Vasubandhu. According to Far Eastern Mahayana tradition the great Yogācāra doctor flourished in the latter half of the fifth century A.D., whereas Hui Yüan lived from 333 to 416. The Jodo Shin Shu list being chronological, thereby implying some sort of apostolical succession, though not in all cases a direct pupillary relation, between the relatively earlier and the relatively later Fathers, it would hardly have been possible to include Hui Yüan without excluding Vasubandhu, thus losing for the school the support of one of the most widely venerated names in Mahayana Buddhism. Alternatively, the omission might be due to the fact that though Hui Yüan was responsible for the school's independent existence as an organization his contribution to its doctrinal development was comparatively slight. From its association with Hui Yüan the school did, however, acquire the name by which it was for many centuries most widely known. In the grounds of the monastery in which he settled was a pond wherein white lotuses bloomed. Hence the brotherhood which he founded became known as the White Lotus School. The designation is perhaps not altogether fanciful. Lotus flowers are a prominent feature of life in the Happy Land, devotees of Amitabha being born from them according to the *Amitāyurdhyāna Sūtra,* and the white lotuses which bloomed in the quiet garden of Hui Yüan's retreat may have reminded him and his followers of the beauties of Sukhavati. At any rate, his famous hymn of praise to Amitabha, in which the wonders of the Happy Land are described in language no less glowing than that of the *Sukhāvatīvyūha Sūtra,* is popularly known as the White Lotus Ode, though the species of lotus referred to in the first verse, the *utpala,* is not white but blue. Other designations of the school are the Short Cut and the White Path. The second of these owes its origin to an allegory which Shan Tao (613-681 A.D.), the fifth of the Seven Fathers, has inserted into his commentary on the *Amitāyurdhyāna Sūtra.* In this allegory the repetition of the mantra *Namo Amitābhāya Buddhāya* is likened to a narrow white path, four or five inches wide, licked by a blazing stream of fire on one side and washed by a bottomless, turbulent stream of water on the other. Only by walking along this path can the traveller cross over from the hither to the farther shore. The name by which Hui Yüan's school is best known in modern times is the Pure Land School, and we have availed ourselves of this designation all the more readily because, owing to the fact that in India the movement of devotion to Amitabha never existed independently, no distinctive Sanskrit appellation for it is known. As the Pure Land School we shall therefore refer to it hereafter. A vast difference, however, separates the original Indo-Chinese form of the Pure Land doctrine from its Japanese offshoot. This later, profounder and more authentically Buddhist interpretation was largely the work of Shinran, the founder of the Jodo Shin Shu, or True Pure Land School, in which the movement of devotion to Amitabha after more than twelve centuries of development and preparation eventually reached its climax. Shinran's interpretation, being essentially a reading of the original Amitabha myth in the light of the loftiest transcendental conceptions, is not to be understood apart from the earlier traditions, out of which it sprang as naturally as a flower from the parent seed. Only after a brief outline of the Indo-Chinese form of the Pure Land doctrine has been given shall we be in a position to venture upon a somewhat fuller, though still inadequate, survey of the True Pure Land teaching.

The idea that the appearance of Buddhas was not limited to the present world-period, but that They had on the contrary already made Their appearance in previous world-periods was, as we saw in Chapter I, Section IV, according to the testimony of the Pali Canon an integral part of the Original Buddhist teaching. Developing this idea, both Mahasanghikas and Sautrāntikas asserted that if the advent of the Buddhas was regarded as unlimited by time it could also be regarded as unlimited in space: not only successive world-periods but also coexistent world-systems were presided over by different Buddhas. But though the world-systems which were subject to the influence and authority of one Buddha could coexist with those subject to the rule of another they could not, from the standpoint of relative truth at least, be regarded as coextensive with them. This problem the Mahayanists solved by explaining that though in His omniscience a Buddha comprehends the whole infinity of space, which is His field of knowledge, His spiritual authority is limited to a particular range of world-systems. This range of world-systems is known as His Buddha-field (*Buddha-kṣetra*) or Buddha-country. Although as may be inferred from the *Amitāyurdhyāna Sūtra,* a Buddha knows what is happening in other Buddha-countries, His responsibility for maturing and enlightening beings is confined to His own Buddha-country, which consists of not just a few hundred but of untold millions of world-systems. Now Buddha-fields are of two kinds, impure and pure. An impure Buddha-field is one inhabited by beings of all six realms of existence, that is to say, not only by gods and men, birth as either of which the average Buddhist layman ardently desires, but also by Titans, hungry ghosts, brutes and tormented beings, birth as any of which he fears and dreads as an unmitigated disaster. Impure Buddha-fields, such as that wherein we ourselves now live, are identical with one or another of the different ranges of world-systems belonging to the phenomenal universe. A pure Buddha-field, on the other hand, apart from its presiding Buddha and His glorious company of Bodhisattvas is inhabited exclusively by gods and men, all of whom come into being by apparitional birth and all of whom have male bodies. Sukhavati, the abode of Amitabha, is a Buddha-field of this kind, for which reason it is known as the Pure Land.

How a Pure Land—Sukhavati, though the most famous, is not the only one of its kind—comes to be established has already been described in the story of Dharmākara as revealed by the Sakyamuni, the presiding Buddha of our own impure Buddha-field—the *Sahāloka* or World of Tribulation—in the Larger *Sukhāvatī-vyūha Sūtra.* The reason for the establishment of a Pure Land is perhaps not quite so apparent. Yet it is in principle identical with the reason for which the Lord Buddha established that most familiar of all Buddhist institutions, the Sangha. Though instances of laymen attaining to advanced stages of the Transcendental Path are not entirely wanting in the Buddhist Scriptures, there was from the time of the Buddha Himself a widespread feeling in Buddhist circles that for one who had given "hostages to fortune" the undistracted pursuit of Wisdom was practically impossible. Domestic responsibilities, social obligations, above all the need for earning one's livelihood, were often incompatible with the perfect observance of the precepts of Morality, not to speak of the cultivation of purity and one-pointedness of mind by means of the regular and systematic practice of Meditation. The purpose for which the Sangha was founded was to create, for those who felt the pull of the Transcendental, a society within a society, almost a world within a world, which would provide them with an ideal environment for the living of the holy life. Membership in such a corporation makes the attainment of Enlightenment not more difficult but easier. A Pure Land is established on exactly the same principle. Seeing how hard it is for sentient beings, burdened as they are with the miseries of mundane existence, to find an opportunity even to hear the Dharma, much less to practise it, a certain Bodhisattva out of compassion makes a solemn vow that after he has attained Supreme Buddhahood he will establish a Buddha-field wherein conditions will be conducive in the highest possible degree to the winning of Enlightenment. Amitabha, as we know, went to the extent of making His attainment of Buddhahood contingent upon the establishment of a Buddha-field into which could be reborn, not merely the privileged few, but all sentient beings who (according to the Larger *Sukhāvatī-vyūha*) observed a few elementary ethical precepts, or who (according to the Smaller *Sukhāvatī-vyūha* and the *Amitāyurdhyāna*) simply invoked His name. Sukhavati may therefore be thought of as a kind of cosmic Sangha, unthinkably vaster and infinitely more perfect than the institution which is as it were its shadow here on earth. One who comes into being in this spiritual kingdom is free from the evil destinies; he has no more to fear rebirth as a Titan, as a hungry ghost, as an animal, or as a tormented being. Problems of food, clothing and means of livelihood perplex him not. His whole concern is with the attainment of Enlightenment, and of this—enjoying as he does the spiritual instructions of Amitabha and His Bodhisattvas—he is assured. From now onwards there can be no falling back. However many millions of years he may have to spend in the Pure Land he is destined to Supreme Buddhahood.

Such a conception of Sukhavati, as a plane of existence whence there can be no recession into inferior states of being, vividly recalls the Hinayana doctrine of the *Suddhāvāsa* or "Pure Abodes." It will be remembered that the *Anāgamī*, or "Non-Returner," is one who, having died with the five lower fetters broken, is reborn in the five highest heavens of the plane of form (*rūpa-loka*), whence he attains Nirvana without the necessity of undergoing another human birth. There is, however, some difference between this teaching and that of the Mahayana. Whereas the *Suddhāvāsa* are situated at the summit of the plane of form, Sukhavati belongs neither to the plane of desire, nor to the plane of form, nor yet to the formless plane; it is neither mundane nor transcendental. Again, the *Anāgāmi* has attained the third stage of the Transcendental Path, and because of this attainment is he born into the Pure Abodes; but beings are born in the Pure Land not by virtue of their own merits but by the power of Amitabha's compassion as expressed in His vows. Thus while Sukhavati is the penultimate goal of the easy path to Nirvana the *Suddhāvāsa* are the penultimate goal of the difficult path. The teaching of Shinran differs from both these conceptions in asserting that Sukhavati is itself the ultimate goal. Before attempting to elucidate this extraordinary thesis, which might at first sight appear to involve not only a denial of the transcendental content of Buddhism but also a painful relapse into the crudities of popular theism, we must round off our account of Indo-Chinese Devotional Buddhism with a few words on two points which, though to the mere scholar of academic interest only, are a matter of serious concern to the devotee. Firstly, granting for the sake of argument that the reason why a Bodhisattva establishes, or aspires to establish, a Pure Land, has been correctly explained above, is it really possible for him to create such a Buddha-field merely by wishing to do so? Can we believe that Sukhavati was *thought* into existence? Secondly, granting that such a place as Sukhavati exists, is it credible that beings can be reborn there simply by invoking the name of Amitabha as the

Smaller *Sukhāvatī-vyūha* and the *Amitāyurdhyāna* so confidently assert?

For one who recognizes the principle of karma, with its corollary that the sphere of one's rebirth is determined by one's deeds, the first question should present no difficulty. Dr. Conze answers it in such an admirably concise and convincing manner that we have no hesitation in preferring his words to our own:—

The creative power of ethically relevant actions is as axiomatic to the Buddhist, as it is strange to us. The environment in which beings have to live is to a great extent, especially in regard to its pleasantness or unpleasantness, determined by their deeds (karma). The various hells, for instance, are produced *by the deeds of the creatures who are reborn there. We have waterless deserts in our world because of our small merits. The world of things (*bhajana-loka*) is really nothing more than a kind of reflex of people's deeds. An environment can exist only as long as there are persons whose karma compels them to perceive it. In the same spirit one now claims that the merit of a Bodhisattva may be great enough to create a Pure Land not only for himself but also for others to whom he transfers it.*[1]

The existence of the so-called supernormal powers, described in Chapter I, Section XVII, can also be adduced in support of the Buddhist belief in the creative power of thought. One who has gained the fourth *dhyāna* is able not only to produce replicas of his physical body which are, to those less proficient in concentration, indistinguishable from the original, but also to "materialize" seemingly natural objects of every kind. Instances of such powers, far from being confined to the Scriptures, are known even today in all Buddhist lands where the practice of Meditation is still a living tradition. Perhaps the most remarkable exemplar of such powers in modern times was the late Tomo Geshe Rimpoche, a celebrated Tibetan yogin who died in the late 'thirties. Once, while travelling in Tibet with a large retinue, he caused to appear in the sky a wonderful phantasmagoria of the Buddha Maitreya and His attendant Bodhisattvas. This phenomenon, which was visible for miles around, lasted for several hours. Not only was the whole countryside bathed in celestial radiance, but flowers resembling lotuses came raining down onto the earth. These latter, though they could be picked up and handled, appeared to melt into the air after about half an hour. The whole incident, which was witnessed by hundreds

[1] *Buddhism: Its Essence and Development,* p. 156.

of people, has been depicted in the frescoes of the Dungkar Gompa, or "White Conch Shell Monastery," in the Chumbi Valley, Southern Tibet. In this monastery, which contains the embalmed and gilded body of the Rimpoche, His Holiness the Dalai Lama resided during the winter of 1950-51, while his government was negotiating with the Government of China. Many of those who were eye-witnesses to Tomo Geshe Rimpoche's extraordinary exploits are still alive, and the substance of their united testimony is not lightly to be rejected.[1]

The conclusion is obvious. If it is possible to produce a phantasmagoria which lasts a few hours and is seen by hundreds of people, it should be possible to produce one that will last for centuries and be seen by millions. If thought-power can create a flower it can, stepped up to the requisite degree of intensity, create a Buddha-field. The Smaller *Sukhāvatī-vyūha* is in fact explicit that the tribes of birds that sing in the groves of Sukhavati "have been made on purpose by the Tathāgata Amitāyus, and they utter the sound of the Law."[2]

The second question can, like the first, be partly answered by a reference to the law of karma or, more exactly, to the more general principle of causality, of which the law of karma is only a special case. Devotional Buddhism does not maintain that rebirth in the Pure Land takes place without a cause, but that the primary factor in its causation is the invocation of the name of Amitabha. Hence this school cannot be regarded as denying the general principle of causality. But is not the *Amitāyurdhyāna's* startling assertion that even one who has committed the ten evil deeds and the five deadly sins can, by taking the name of Amitabha, be reborn into the Pure Land, tantamount to a rejection of the law of karma as generally understood? If karma is interpreted in a strictly individualistic sense the objection is unanswerable. But such an interpretation would, by implying the ultimate reality of the individual, involve a repudiation of the very truth of which the principle of causality is the chief

[1] The Author has met and talked with several of them, with one exception all Tibetans. The exception is Lama Anagarika Govinda, a personal disciple of the Rimpoche who, it is to be hoped, will one day write the biography of his master.

[2] Smaller *Sukhāvatī-vyūha Sūtra,* 6.

conceptual formulation—the truth of *anātman* or *śūnyatā*. A nonindividualistic interpretation of the law of karma is provided by the doctrine of *pariṇāmanā* or "turning over" of merits. According to this doctrine the merits which one person has acquired by the performance of good actions can, if he so wishes, be transferred to another who is desirous of benefiting from them. Amitabha's stock of merits, accumulated during His career as a Bodhisattva, is so staggeringly immense that even after establishing the Happy Land an incalculably large surplus remains. By sincerely invoking His name, which is in reality identical with Amitabha Himself, we identify ourselves with Amitabha. As a result of this identification a portion of His merits is transferred to us. These merits, which are now ours, are sufficient not only to counterbalance the effects of our evil actions but also to ensure our rebirth in the Pure Land. The law of karma has not been suspended for our benefit. All that has happened is that a more powerful karma has cancelled out one that was weaker.

In the Indo-Chinese form of the Pure Land doctrine described above, Sukhavati, while standing as it were outside the three planes of existence into which the phenomenal universe is divided, nevertheless remains quite distinct from the transcendental state of Nirvana. Consequently it cannot be said to exist absolutely, but only in a relative sense, and this form of the Pure Land doctrine, being therefore concerned not with Reality but with what despite its beauty is only an appearance, must be regarded as an expression of the relative truth (*saṁvṛti*), not of the absolute truth (*paramārtha*). According to Shinran's interpretation, however, Sukhavati and Nirvana are identical—not because Nirvana is for him mundane, but because Sukhavati is simply a colourful symbol of the Transcendental. This later form of the Pure Land doctrine therefore expresses the absolute truth, and it is for this reason that Shinran designated his school the Jodo Shin Shu or *True* Pure Land School. Before reviewing the main features of the Pure Land myth in the light of Shinran's transcendentalism we must pause to acquaint ourselves with the leading events of his career, which in its early stages was closely bound up with that of Honen.

Shinran Shonin (Shinran the Saint), as he is known to his followers, was born in the year 1173, and died in 1262 at the age of ninety. Thus his life was practically conterminous with the richest and most creative period of Japanese Buddhism. While still quite young he adopted the monastic life, and devoted a number of years to mastering the *sūtras* and *śāstras* of the different Buddhist schools which had been introduced into Japan from the mainland. He also embarked upon the practice of a variety of spiritual disciplines. But neither by means of study nor by means of discipline, he found, was he able to win any nearer to Enlightenment. After spending several years in fruitless search for a teacher who could show him a way suited to his temperament, Shinran happened to meet Honen Shonin. Honen, then the greatest exponent and exemplar of the Pure Land doctrine in Japan, initiated him into the repetition of the mantra *Namo Amitābhāya Buddhāya,* and at last Shinran's troubled heart found peace. Renouncing the monastic vows, which he considered as pertaining to the path of self-reliance, Shinran spent the remaining sixty years of his long life travelling about the country preaching to the common people, many of whom became his friends and followers. In the year 1225 the Jodo Shin Shu was founded as an independent school. Today it is the largest of the Japanese branches of the Mahayana, possessing more temples and preachers, and claiming more adherents, than any other. So far as propagating the Dharma is concerned, Japanese Devotional Buddhism is on the whole more active than the three other most important schools of the Mahayana put together. In Western countries its efforts to enlarge the sphere of Buddhist influence are paralleled only by those of the modern Theravada.[1]

Sukhavati and Nirvana being according to Shinran synonymous expressions, the Jodo Shin Shu doctrine of rebirth in the Pure Land must not be construed as a re-emergence on some other plane of phenomenal existence, however exalted, as in the Indo-Chinese form of the teaching, but as identical with the attainment of Nirvana. "Rebirth . . ." (in the Pure Land), says Shinran, "is complete unsurpassed enlightenment."[2] Now all

[1] Both the Judo Shin Shu and the Theravada have now (1978) been overtaken by Tibetan Buddhism and Zen.

[2] *Shinshu Shogyo Zenshu,* Vol. II, p. 58. (Quoted by PHILIPP KARL EIDMANN. *The Simple Unimpeded Way,* p. 15. Issued Privately, 2497 Showa 281).

schools of Buddhism, regardless of the *yāna* to which they belong, unanimously hold that with the exception of *Anāgāmis* and beings reborn in Sukhavati enlightenment takes place during one's actual lifetime. Nirvana is attainable here and now. While in theory he did not deny this teaching, in practice Shinran minimized its importance by asserting that, humanity having seriously degenerated since the days of the Sakyamuni, such an attainment was now within hardly anybody's reach, certainly not the laity's. He therefore taught that we should seek to attain rebirth in Sukhavati, or enlightenment, not during our workaday lives, when there would be a multitude of distractions, but at the moment of death. All that we should seek to attain is an awakening of faith in Amitabha. By this awakening of faith will be produced an effect which, manifesting at the instant of death, will act as the condition for our immediate realization of Nirvana. In Shinran's usage not only rebirth and Nirvana, but death and Nirvana, are synonymous. Though the Pure Land School laid upon this teaching an unprecedented emphasis, the teaching itself is not original. Shinran in fact did not claim that it was original. Like all great Buddhist *ācāryas* he claimed only to interpret the words of the Scriptures. Evidence is not wanting, even in the Pali Canon, that the Buddha Himself had recognized the possibility of Nirvana being attained at the moment of death. Hence despite the striking, even startling, individuality of his teaching it would be unjust to accuse Shinran of being an innovator. He simply drew attention to a hitherto neglected aspect of the Buddha's Teaching.

Since the attainment of "rebirth" or Nirvana at the moment of death is dependent upon an effect produced by the awakening of faith during one's lifetime, it is evident that for the Shin devotee the awakening of faith is the axle upon which revolves the entire spiritual life. But this faith, the awakening of which can produce consequences of such magnitude, is not to be equated with mere belief, and it would be an egregious error if some slight coincidence in terminology should ever lead us to confuse the Shin doctrine of "salvation by faith" with the corresponding Protestant Christian dogma. To borrow the words of Philipp Karl Eidmann, "The awakening of faith in Shin Buddhism is an instant of pure egolessness."[1] This instant of

[1] *Ibid.*, p. 11.

pure egolessness occurs when, realizing that any attempt to gain Enlightenment by means of our "own" efforts will only strengthen our sense of separateness, we make an unconditional surrender to the Compassion of Amitabha, unreservedly relying upon it to carry us to Nirvana. By the word Amitabha Shinran does not denote any particular personality, not even a Buddha, but Buddhahood or Reality Itself. (It is significant that in Japan Amitabha and Amitāyus, the Infinite Light and the Infinite Life, have shed their suffixes and both become simply Amida, The Infinite.) Consequently the Compassion to which we surrender, and by which we are carried to Nirvana, is not the emotion of any individual, however exalted, but a cosmic principle. Absolute Reality, which as object of devotion is often called the *Dharmakāya,* is not only static but dynamic; it is both Wisdom and Compassion. Amida's Original Vow, which for the Indo-Chinese form of the teaching was a spatiotemporal phenomenon, according to Shinran's interpretation of the Amitabha myth is a symbol of the transcendental soterial activity of the Absolute. This activity is said to be eternal, not because it is prolonged for an undetermined period of time, but because it is not conditioned by time at all.

The Compassion of All the Buddhas, though transcending all the categories of thought, including those of subject and object, appears to our ego-distorted perception as a force which acts upon us externally—as the Other Power. This Shinran makes quite clear when he says "What is called external power is as much as to say there is no discrimination of this or that."[1] To surrender to the Other Power means to transcend the distinction between subject and object. As we identify ourselves with Amida, so Amida identifies Himself with us. What then takes place is not a transference of merits, in the sense of factors conducive to the attainment of phenomenal rebirth, but of the power of non-discrimination, or the Compassion of All the Buddhas. By this power are we eventually carried to Nirvana. Yet inasmuch as Compassion is coeternal with the Absolute its activity is not to be thought of as limited by time. In the symbols of the myth, Amida made His attainment of Supreme Buddhahood contingent upon beings obtaining rebirth in His Pure Land. Therefore since Amida is enlightened we also must be enlightened.

[1] *Ibid.,* p. 8.

Enlightenment being a transcendental state is to be thought of as being attained not in time but out of time. In reality we are eternally enlightened. Only through ignorance do we think of ourselves as unenlightened beings. When faith awakens, when we make the "crosswise leap" which lands us in the realm of the Transcendental without the need of intermediate steps (for the Absolute and the contingent are utterly discrete), we realize that, as the *Prajñāpāramitā* also teaches, Nirvana is not something that can be attained. Faith of this kind is not faith in the current sense of the term but the emotional counterpart of Wisdom. Though *Prajñā* is a word of predominantly intellectual connotation it would be committing a dangerous mistake to suppose that the transcendental faculty for which it stands is a species of intellection in the ordinary dualistic sense, or that it would not be possible to indicate that faculty by a word of predominantly emotional connotation instead.

As we have already observed, Devotional Buddhism in general, and the teachings of Shinran Shonin in particular, is a transposition of the whole Doctrine from the intellectual to the emotional mode. The transcendental realities indicated are the same, but in one case they are indicated by means of conceptual and in the other by means of imaginative symbols. Such a transposition is obviously attended by very great advantages. While a philosophy only titillates the rational surface of our being, poetry stirs it to its depths. Because they engage the darkest and most deeply submerged desires and urges of our personality the symbols of the Amitabha myth are collectively able to orient our whole being towards realization of the Transcendental.

At the same time the transposition has its disadvantages. From its doctrine of surrender to the Other Power of Amitabha the Jodo Shin Shu drew the logical, but completely false, conclusion that one should make no attempt to gain Enlightenment through one's own efforts. Under this misapprehension Shinran and his followers renounced the monastic ideal, including that indispensable prerequisite of any form of higher spiritual life, the observance of celibacy. Even the repetition of *Namo Amitābhāya Buddhāya* was regarded not as a spiritual exercise but as the spontaneous expression of the devotee's feeling of intense gratitude to Amida for having already accomplished our Enlightenment. The less logical but spiritually sounder and more orthodox view is embodied in the *Prajñāpāramitā's* classic assertion that while vowing to lead all sentient beings to Supreme Enlightenment one should reflect that in reality no sentient beings exist. Only by simultaneously adopting these two contradictory attitudes can we resolve, not logically but in our own spiritual life, the antinomies of the understanding and realize the Transcendental. Reliance upon the Other Power and upon one's own efforts, far from being incompatible, must go hand in hand. In the very act of vigorously practising the Threefold Path of Morality, Meditation and Wisdom, one must reflect that in reality one can do nothing and that the gaining of Enlightenment is dependent upon the Compassion of Amitabha. As we took special pains to point out in Section III of this Chapter, Buddhism is a whole and must be followed as a whole. Not only must Faith be balanced by Wisdom, and Concentration by Vigour, in the spiritual life of the individual Buddhist, but in the Dharma as a whole equilibrium must be maintained between the traditions corresponding to these four faculties. According to Nagarjuna the Absolute Truth is not to be realized except in dependence on the relative truth. Without accepting this point of view the Jodo Shin Shu can hardly avoid drawing the conclusion that Buddhism, whether regarded as a doctrine, a method, or an institution, is superfluous. If reliance on the Other Power in reality excludes reliance on our own efforts religion as a distinctive way of life, together with all distinctively religious acts, founders, and we are at once engulfed by the ocean of worldliness.

VIII. The Scriptures of Buddhist Idealism

While the Buddhism of Faith and Devotion grew up beneath the ægis of the Mādhyamika School, the Yogācāra or Vijñānavāda was in a sense a movement of reaction against it. The Way to Enlightenment is threefold, being divided into the successive stages of Morality, Meditation and Wisdom (*vide* Chapter I, Sections XVI to XVIII). Nagarjuna and his followers, while not wholly unmindful of the claims of Morality and Meditation, had shown a marked partiality for Wisdom, to the realization and elucidation of which they had indeed devoted the major part of their energies. In so doing they had remained true to the most strictly orthodox tradition, which ever since these teachings had issued from the Buddha's golden mouth had not only insisted that Wisdom alone was the immediate condition of Enlightenment, but had asserted also that in some cases Wisdom could be attained without prior practice of Meditation, at least in the present life. The Theravada Pali Canon speaks of two kinds of emancipation, known respectively as *ceto-vimutti* or emancipation of mind and *paññā-vimutti* or emancipation through Wisdom. By the second, termed in the commentaries *sukkha-* and *suddha-vipassanā,* or bare insight, is meant the emancipation which one attains without having passed through any of the four states of superconsciousness (*jhāna* or *dhyāna*). This type of emancipation is no doubt possible for persons possessing a certain kind of temperament. But the theoretical recognition of the possibility, by providing the merely intellectual with an apparently valid excuse for the neglect of Meditation, was potentially a source of danger. In the absence of any experience of the *jhānas* a merely rational understanding of the Dharma could easily be mistaken for insight. One might imagine that he was enlightened when he had only mastered the contents of a large number of books.

This was actually the case with some at least of the adherents of certain Hinayana schools, among whom there seem to have existed the spiritual ancestors of these militant modern Theravadins (fortunately a small, albeit sufficiently vociferous, minority), who on the strength of the fact that they can reel off list after list of the categories of the Abhidhamma expect us to believe that they have entered upon the Transcendental Path. It was because certain *ācāryas,* themselves closely connected with the Mādhyamika tradition, saw that though the teachings of Nagarjuna had not succumbed to this danger they were very much exposed to it, that the Yogācāra movement came into existence and gradually assumed the proportions of an independent school. The danger was in fact even greater for the Mādhyamikas than for the Hinayanists. For unless the *Prajñāpāramitā* teachings were envisaged in a lofty state of superconsciousness the dialectical method of Nagarjuna was liable to degenerate not only into scholasticism but even into scepticism. The Yogācārins therefore laid very great emphasis on the practice of Meditation, particularly as regards the attainment of states of superconsciousness, and it is to this emphasis that the school owes its name, meaning "The Practice of Yoga."[1]

Though the Yogācāra movement was in a sense a reaction against the Mādhyamikavāda, it was not a reaction against its general principles, most of which it found quite acceptable, but against its preoccupation with Wisdom at the expense of Meditation. Hence as far as the initial stages of the Yogācāra movement are concerned it would be a mistake to distinguish the two schools too sharply. G. Tucci, the great Italian scholar in Buddhism, is also of this opinion. He observes:—

It is generally said that Mahāyāna may be divided into two fundamental schools, viz., *Mādhyamika and Yogācāra. This statement must not be taken literally. First of all it is not exact to affirm that these two tendencies were always opposed to each other. Moreover . . . the antagonism between the Mādhyamika and the first expounders of the idealist school such as Maitreya, Asaṅga and even Vasubandhu is not so marked as it appears at first sight. . . . The fact is that both Nagarjuna as well as Maitreya, along with their immediate disciples, acknowledged the same fundamental tenets, and their work was determined by the same ideals, though holding quite different views in many a detail.*[2]

We shall be guilty of no serious error if, from the evidence already adduced in this Section, we conclude that the Yogācāra movement was originally a wing of the Mādhyamika which, while continuing to subscribe to its fundamental doctrines, emphasized the importance of Meditation. This emphasis upon Meditation, which in practice meant attainment of the *jhānas,* did however in the end influence the Yogācārins to such a degree as to modify their whole philosophy. As Conze remarks,

It was the function and purpose of the Yogacarins to give due emphasis to the outlook on the world revealed by withdrawal into trance.[3]

For this reason it is often asserted that there exists between the two schools not a difference of doctrine but of method. In the words of Dr. E. J. Thomas,

---

[1]Western readers are warned that this Yoga has nothing to do with the mysteries purveyed under the same name by non-Buddhist writers. In essentials it corresponds to Meditation as described in Chapter I, Section XVII.

[2] *On Some Aspects of the Doctrines of Maitreya [nātha] and Asaṅga* (University of Calcutta, 1930), pp. 2-4.

[3] *Buddhism,* p. 161.

While the school of Nāgārjuna started from the standpoint of logic, and showed the impossibility of making any statement free from contradictions, the Laṇkāvatāra *[according to the writer "the chief canonical text for the doctrine of subjective idealism"] started from a psychological standpoint, and found a positive basis in actual experience.*[1]

A difference of method may, however, if sufficiently insisted upon, in time develop into a difference of doctrine. As Tucci admits, the two schools held "quite different views on many a detail." These different views, though not fundamental, were sufficiently numerous and important to constitute the Yogācāra an independent school. Nevertheless it cannot be too positively affirmed that, to whatever extreme each might have developed its distinctive features, even at the period of their greatest divergence the Mādhyamika and the Yogācāra to a very considerable extent overlapped. Moreover, it should not be forgotten that the Yogācāra was not a simple logically coherent body of teaching. It was a movement which tended to think of the Transcendental in terms of Absolute Mind and which tried to explain why and how the seemingly objective universe came to evolve out of Absolute Mind. Within this movement there were several tendencies, some more, some less, sharply distinguished from and opposed to the Mādhyamika teaching. The term Vijñānavāda has been explained as denoting the school under its theoretical aspect, Yogācāra being understood to denote it under its practical aspect. The relation between the two terms is not quite so symmetrical. Probably Yogācāra is the older and less precise general designation for the whole movement, both in its earlier and in its later stages, whereas Vijñānavāda refers to the more specialized epistemic development of its teaching into the doctrine that the existence of phenomena is indistinguishable from our perception of them. This development, which recalls Berkeley's famous thesis *esse est percipi,* received its classic formulation at the hands of Vasubandhu, perhaps the greatest theoretician of the school, who asserted that the universe consists only of ideas (*vijñaptimātra*).

Partly because it started its career as the contemplative wing of the Mādhyamika School, partly because its original emphasis was upon individual experience rather than upon scriptural authority, the connection between the Yogācāra School and the

[1] *The History of Buddhist Thought,* p. 230.

sūtras which are said to form its canonical basis is not only looser, more nebulous and more difficult to grasp than that which exists between the Mādhyamika School and the *Prajñāpāramitā* texts, but perhaps less vitally important to determine. There is another reason for the comparatively loose connection between the Yogācāra and the *sūtras* of Buddhist Idealism. The intuitions in which these texts abound relate to a greater variety of topics than do those of the *Prajñāpāramitā sūtras.* In order to systematize them the Yogācārins had inevitably to make their own selection. Many teachings of importance were omitted. For this reason texts like the *Avataṁsaka* have sometimes been described as occupying an intermediate position between the Mādhyamikavāda and the Yogācāra. Other idealist scriptures have been dissociated from the school altogether. Our procedure will be less radical. We shall enumerate, and in part very briefly describe, the four or five *sūtras* recognized by tradition as forming the main canonical basis of the Yogācāra School.

With the exception of the *Saṁdhinirmocana,* the appearance of which was contemporaneous with that of the Large *Prajñāpāramitā,* the *sūtras* of Buddhist Idealism all belong to a period later than that of Nagarjuna. In the present state of our knowledge it would be unwise to attempt a strictly chronological survey of these texts, and we shall therefore describe them in the order best adapted to the purposes of exposition. Their compilation may, however, be safely regarded as having been distributed over the second, third and fourth centuries A.D.

While the *Saṁdhinirmocana Sūtra* has remained comparatively difficult of access, so that at present we can do no more than recognize its superior antiquity, the whole of the *Laṅkāvatāra,* as well as lengthy excerpts from the *Gaṇḍavyūha* and the *Surāṇgamā,* are well known even to Western Buddhists. The second of these texts, the *Gaṇḍavyūha,* is the last of a group of three *sūtras* known collectively as the *Avataṁsaka,* or "Ornament of Flowers." This magnificent work, the noble proportions of which are dwarfed only by those of the Large *Prajñāpāramitā,* is very highly esteemed by Far Eastern Buddhists, to many of whom it is the king of Mahayana *sūtras* and the summit of Buddhist thought. Though for the *Avataṁsaka,* as for the other *sūtras* of the Yogācāra School, Absolute Mind is the sole reality, its principal theme is the perfect mutual interpenetration of all phenomena. Since every object in the universe is devoid of self-nature, every object in the universe neither finds nor offers any impediment to penetrating or any impediment to being penetrated by every other object. Interpenetration, though involving loss of separateness, does not mean extinction of individuality. The idea is elucidated by means of a number of illustrations, one of the most famous of which is Indra's Net. Indra, the king of the gods, has a wonderful net made entirely of strings of jewels. Each jewel in the net both reflects and is reflected by all the other jewels. Thus all the jewels, though participating in one another's existence, mysteriously retain their own identity. Absolute Mind, while present in all phenomena, instead of obliterating them reveals their true significance. Though the doctrine of interpenetration was not taken up by the Yogācāra, so important a development could not be ignored indefinitely. We therefore find springing up in China at the beginning of the seventh century a school founded specially upon its teaching. This was the Hua Yen Tsung or *Avataṁsaka* School, the founder and first patriarch of which was Tu Fa Shun (557-640). Though on the wane by the tenth century, during the three centuries of its most creative period it produced some of the greatest thinkers in the history of Far Eastern Buddhism, among them being Chi-Yen (602-668), Fa Tsang (643-712), and Ten Kuang (738-839). In the year 735 the Hua Yen Tsung was introduced into Japan, where as the Kegon Shu—the Japanese form of its name—it still exists as a living though comparatively minor tradition. D. T. Suzuki, who regards the Kegon philosophy as the summit of Oriental thought, renders Fa Tsang's interpretation of the message of the *Avataṁsaka* as follows:—

There is one Mind which is ultimate reality, by nature pure, perfect, and bright. It functions in two ways. Sustained by it, the existence of a world of particulars is possible, and from it originates all activity, free and illuminating, making for the virtues of perfection (paramita). *In these two functions, which we may call existential and moral, three universal characters are distinguishable. Existentially viewed, every particular object, technically called "particle of dust"* (anuraja), *contains in it the whole Dharmadhatu. Secondly, from the creational point of view, each particle of dust generates all kinds of virtues; therefore, by means of one object the secrets of the whole universe are fathomed. Thirdly, in each particle of dust the reason of Sunyata is perceivable.*

Against this objective world so characterized the Bodhisattva practises four virtues: (1) the virtue of creative adjustment born of wisdom (prajna) *and love* (karuna), *(2) the virtue of morality by which the dignity of human life is preserved, (3) the virtue of tenderness towards others and of simple naturalness, and (4) the virtue of sacrifice or vicarious atonement. By the practice of these virtues the ignorant are saved from their delusions, passions are converted into rationality, defilements are thoroughly wiped off, and the mirror of Suchness is always kept bright and clean.*

The disciplining of oneself in these virtues is not enough to complete the life of devotion, for tranquillization (samatha) *is needed to keep one's mind in perfect harmony with the nature of Reality; not to be carried away into a world of multiplicities, but to hold one's light of the Unconscious*[1] *unspoiled and unobstructed. Tranquillization alone, however, may lead one to a state of self-complacency and destroy the source of sympathetic motivation. Hence the need of Vipasyana exercises.* Samatha *means "stopping" and* vipasyana *"seeing." The one complements the other. . . . To understand the* Avataṁsaka *these six contemplations are needed: (1) to look into the serenity of Mind to which all things return, (2) to look into the nature of the world of particulars which are because of Mind, (3) to observe that there is perfect mysterious interpenetration of all things, (4) to observe that there is nothing but Suchness where all the shadowy existences cast their reflections, (5) to observe that the mirror of identity holds in it images of all things each without obstructing others, and (6) to observe that the relation of master and attendants exists in a most exhaustive manner throughout the universe so that when any one particular object is picked up all the others are picked up with it.*[2]

The *Gaṇḍavyūha* or "Array of Flowers" is, as we have already seen, the last of the three *sūtras* collectively designated the *Avataṁsaka*. It is also the largest and probably the most important. In substance it is a description of the Bodhisattva ideal in the light of the doctrine of interpenetration, in form a narrative of the pilgrimage which on the advice of the Bodhisattva Mañjuśrī the youth Sudhana makes to various parts of India. The object of this pilgrimage is to achieve the highest knowledge of Enlightenment. One after another, Sudhana visits more than fifty teachers, male and female, human and non-human. All, however, possess only limited knowledge, and so, after instructing him to the best of their ability, all direct him to another teacher. In this way Sudhana finally meets the Bodhisattva Samantabhadra, who alone among them is in possession of the knowledge he

---

[1] This is Suzuki's rather misleading rendering of the *Wu-hsin*, literally "no mind," by which is meant a state of consciousness wherein the subject-object relation is transcended.

[2] *Essays in Zen Buddhism (Third Series)*. (Rider and Company, London. 1953), pp. 72-73.

seeks, and from him the young pilgrim eventually receives full instructions as regards his life of devotion, his knowledge, his vows, his supernormal powers, etc. No sooner has he realized the import of these profound teachings than Sudhana discovers that he is in a state of identity not only with the Bodhisattva Samantabhadra but with All the Buddhas. Like Theirs his body is of infinite extent, while his career as a Bodhisattva, his enlightenment, his bodies of transformation, his revolution of the Wheel of the Dharma, his eloquence, his voice, his faith, his abode, his love and compassion for sentient beings, and his emancipation and mastery over the world, are in no way different from Theirs. Despite the sublimity of this and many another teaching, the scene of the *Gaṇḍavyūha* is laid not on some remote plane of abstract thought, but in a concrete world of glowing particulars. Sudhana moves about in a world full of light and colour. For like the *Saddharma-Puṇḍarīka* and the Larger *Sukhāvatī-vyūha,* the "Array of Flowers" tries to indicate transcendental realities not by means of the conceptual symbols of thought but by means of the poetic symbols of the imagination. Important teachings are revealed through phantasmagoria of cosmic dimensions. Such a phantasmagoria is that which confronts Sudhana when, upon entering the Vairocana Tower of the Bodhisattva Maitreya, he finds that it has expanded to infinity, and that it contains, in a state of perfect mutual interpenetration, all the phenomena of the universe. This episode has been described in great detail by Suzuki, who in the work quoted above devotes three lengthy essays to the *Gaṇḍavyūha.* To these essays those who would like to know more about the contents of the *Gaṇḍavyūha* may be referred.

While the *Gaṇḍavyūha* establishes the reality of Absolute Mind by appealing to the imagination and the intuition, the method of the *Surāṇgamā* is predominantly psychological and discursive. In the former, we are rapt into a world of unthinkable dimensions, and the truth bursts upon us in a series of gorgeous apocalypses. In the latter, we find ourselves inside the hall of the Jetavana Monastery, looking out through the windows at the trees of Anathapindika's garden. It is a warm summer afternoon, and we listen quietly as the Buddha, step by step, leads Ānanda to the realization that in the ultimate sense only Absolute Mind exists. This dialogue, an English translation of which has been several times reprinted, occupies the first four chapters of the *sūtra,* which thereafter collapses into an amorphousness similar to that of the *Laṅkāvatāra.* The various arguments employed by the Buddha fall into three clearly marked divisions. First, He makes Ānanda admit that the mind cannot be regarded as being located inside the body, or outside it, or in between: it is not a spatially conditioned phenomenon. Next, He shows him the difference between the true mind and the false mind, the former being Absolute Mind itself, the latter the discriminative faculty. Finally, He declares that, like the hallucinations seen by a person with defective vision, the seemingly objective universe perceived by the discriminative faculty does not exist, and the sole reality is Absolute Mind. The effect which the Buddha's exposition produces is described by the compiler of the *Sūtra* in the following words:—

Ananda and all the great congregation . . . perceived that each one's mind was coextensive with the universe, seeing clearly the empty character of the universe as plainly as a leaf or trifling thing in the hand, and that all things in the universe are all alike merely the excellently bright and primeval mind of Bodhi, and that this mind is universally diffused, and comprehends all things within itself.

And still reflecting, they beheld their generated bodies, as so many grains of dust in the wide expanse of the universal void, now safe, now lost; or as a bubble of the sea, sprung from nothing and born to be destroyed. But their perfect and independent Mind [they beheld] as not to be destroyed, but remaining ever the same, identical with the ultimate reality of the Buddha.

With the *Saddharma-Laṅkāvatāra,* or "Entry of the True Doctrine into Laṅkā," the amorphousness which characterized the bulk of the *Surāṇgamā* becomes practically complete. The rare jewels of thought which it contains have not been mounted in the beaten gold of literary art to make for the glorious head of the Mahayana yet another glittering crown; they have been heaped pell-mell on the ground, and mixed with them are bits of glass and stone. Suzuki goes so far as to describe the *Laṅkāvatāra* as "a memorandum kept by a Mahayana master, in which he put down perhaps all the teachings of importance accepted by the Mahayana followers of his day."[1] The surmise may well be correct. Though the *sūtra* as now extant comprises nine chapters mainly in prose, together with a

---

[1] *The Laṅkāvatāra Sūtra: A Mahayana Text* (Routledge, London. 1932), p. xi.

verse supplement, most of the chapter headings (or colophons, for they come at the end), are related to the text in a rather indefinite manner. Apart from the Chapter on Meat-Eating and the Chapter on *Dhāraṇā,* both of which are later additions, the only chapter which possesses a definite literary form in the first, entitled both "The Invitation of Rāvaṇa" and "Rāvaṇa Asking for Instruction." This chapter in fact forms a complete piece of narrative by itself, having no doubt been incorporated into the *Laṅkāvatāra* at the time of the original compilation of the *sūtra.* Nevertheless between the first chapter and the remainder of the work exists a very close connection. Indeed the outward dissimilarity and the inner cohesion exhibited by these two divisions are interdependent. Whereas in "The Invitation of Rāvaṇa" the primary Yogācāra intuition, namely the sole reality of Absolute Mind, is presented as it were dramatically, so that we see before us the intuition itself, all that the succeeding chapters do is to talk "about it and about" from what is essentially the rational point of view. If we accept as correct Suzuki's vigorous contention that the *Laṅkāvatāra* was not written as a philosophical treatise to establish a definite system of thought, but to discourse on a certain kind of religious experience,[1] we may say that Chapter I contains the religious experience itself and Chapters II-VII do the discoursing. Chapter I is therefore obviously the most important part of the *Sūtra,* in the sense that it is the *fons et origo* of the ratiocinations of the work. It is in fact the *fons et origo* of the whole philosophy of the Yogācāra School, for this too is nothing but an attempt to discourse upon the same experience, the experience of the sole reality of Absolute Mind, which is represented by the *Sūtra* as befalling Rāvaṇa on the peak of Mount Malaya, but which according to the Yogācāra is the ultimate Buddhist attainment. Dr. E. J. Thomas's summary of "The Invitation of Rāvaṇa" will therefore provide us not only with a characterization of the chief subject-matter of the entire *Laṅkāvatāra* but also with an introduction to the more definitely philosophical teachings with which we shall be concerned in the next section.

When the sūtra opens Buddha was just coming out of the palace of the nāgas beneath the ocean, where he had been preaching for a week. He looked at

[1] *Studies in the Laṅkāvatāra Sūtra,* p. 72.

*Laṅkā and smiled, for he remembered that previous Buddhas had taught the doctrine there. Rāvaṇa, being inspired by the power of Buddha, invited him to come and teach the doctrine of inner perception and the real existence of mind (citta). Buddha then went to Laṅkā in Rāvaṇa's chariot, and he and his attendant Bodhisattvas were adorned by Yaksha girls and boys with necklaces of pearls and gems. He created other mountain peaks, on which he himself with Rāvaṇa was seen. Suddenly they all vanished, and Rāvaṇa found himself alone. He had a sudden revulsion of feeling (*Parāvṛitti*), and realized that what he perceived was only his own mind. Then through his former roots of goodness he was able to understand all treatises, and with his yoga power he could see things as they really are. He heard a voice from the sky saying, "it is to be known through the inner self," and Buddha explained to him that thus was the way of training. It is the way of the yogis, the sons of Buddha,* i.e., *the* Bodhisattvas, *who advance beyond the views and attainments of disciples, pratyekabuddhas, and heretics. This is the realization of the great yogis, who crush the doctrines of others, who destroy evil heresies, who are skilled in rejecting the heresy of a self and in producing a revulsion of mind by means of higher understanding.*

In this way Rāvaṇa was taught the two fundamental truths of this school, the truth that everything external is due to a wrong interpretation of inner experience, and the truth that the apprehension of reality is reached by a sudden revulsion in which the truth bursts upon the yogi (by which is meant the Bodhisattva) in his contemplation.

*The whole scene then reappeared to Rāvaṇa in all its glory, and Buddha laughed. The whole assembly laughed, but Buddha laughed loudest. The reason was, as Buddha explained, that Rāvaṇa wanted to ask a twofold question. He had already asked it of the Buddhas in the past, and he will ask it of the Buddhas to come. Rāvaṇa was then allowed to put his question on the duality of things. It is said that things and non-things are to be abandoned. How can they be abandoned if they do not exist? The answer is that duality is due only to the wrong imagination of the ignorant. Such people look upon the manifestations of mind as external things. They should be looked upon, like the horns of a hare, as belonging neither to reality nor non-reality, and in that consists their abandonment. He who thus sees, sees rightly. They who see otherwise move in false imagination, and grasp things as twofold, like a reflection of oneself in a mirror or in water, or one's shadow by the light of the moon or in a house, or like hearing an echo. Thus by grasping at their own false imagination they imagine things and non-things; they go on imagining, and never attain tranquillity. The word tranquillity means "having one point" (*ekāgra*). It is the entrance into the Tathāgatagarbha, the realm of the noble Knowledge of the inner self, whereby arises the highest concentration.*[1]

IX. The Yogacara School

Though Maitreya, the teacher of Asanga and the "founder" of the Yogācāra School, occupies according to Tucci a place in the

[1] *The History of Buddhist Thought*, pp. 231-32.

history of Indian philosophy not inferior to that of Nagarjuna,[1] we know less about him than about almost any other Mahayana *ācārya*. Only in the present century has the fact of his historical existence been clearly demonstrated. According to Chinese sources Asanga received the Yogācāra doctrines not from any human master but from the Bodhisattva Maitreya, whom he visited in the Tuṣita heaven. We now know that the circumstance that the historical Maitreya, who like Nagarjuna and other *ācāryas* was also styled Bodhisattva, bore exactly the same name and title as the future Buddha, had eventually led to the confusion of the two personalities. The *śāstras* which Asanga had quite correctly said were dictated to him by Maitreya the *ācārya* were attributed to Asanga himself, who was believed to have fathered them upon Maitreya the Bodhisattva either out of modesty or from a desire to enhance their prestige. But though Maitreyanatha (as, following Tucci, we shall now call him to avoid confusion) has been established as the name of an historical person that person remains little more than a name. Apart from the facts that he composed five *śāstras* and had one disciple, Asanga, all that we can with confidence assert of him is that he was born and that he died. Even the period at which he "flourished," generally said to be the beginning of the fourth century A.D., is not known with complete certainty. Any attempt to form an estimate of the man himself, his character and temperament, must therefore be based entirely upon the internal evidence of his works.

The evidence is in one respect unanimous. Says Tucci of Maitreyanatha:—

When we examine his works we cannot fail to notice a general and fundamental characteristic common to all. I mean the attempt for the conciliation of the various tendencies existent in Buddhism. . . . Between the monastic ideal represented by the arhatship and that of the bodhisattva there was a gulf. . . . Some texts tried to solve the apparent contradiction between Hīnayāna and Mahāyāna teaching by having recourse to the able theory of the double truth. . . . Later on a new doctrine was also elaborated according to which the different sutras were spoken by Buddha in three or even in five different times. . . . Such conciliatory steps were taken by the adherents of the Mahāyāna at a very early time, since the Ekayāna theory, as opposed to the Three-yānas theory, had already been enunciated in some of the oldest Mahāyāna sūtras such as the Saddharma-puṇḍarīka.

---

[1] *On Some Aspects of the Doctrines of Maitreya [nātha] and Asaṅga*, p.6.

*But, if it was relatively easy to assert this theory of the Ekayāna it was certainly difficult to combine in a logical way all practical, dogmatical, mystical and theological tenets representing the main characteristic of the two schools. This was attempted by Maitreya [nātha] in the Sūtrālaṅkāra and chiefly in the Abhisamayālaṅkāra, where the Hīnayāna as well as the Mahāyāna-*caryā *are combined in the* abhisamaya, *that is the mystical ascension towards the supreme realization.*[1]

Whereas Nagarjuna was by temperament decidedly analytical, Maitreyanatha was, it seems, more inclined to synthesis. The former dismissed all views as inadequate; the latter, while recognizing their inadequacy, thought that within a comprehensive scheme of spiritual progress a place could nevertheless be found for every one of them. Maitreyanatha's policy of conciliation and synthesis was, it seems, in principle ultimately triumphant, for as we saw in Section V even the Mādhyamika School eventually relaxed its rigorousness to the extent of admitting the relative validity of the Yogācāra teaching. In the same spirit did Atīṣa, as late as the first half of the twelfth century, declare that the Hinayana, the Mahayana and the Tantrayana were the successive stages of a single Path. As systematized by Tsongkhapa a century later, this view is still the official doctrine of the Gelugpa Order of Tibet.

Though Maitreyanatha is spoken of as the author of five *śāstras,* we need not regard his literary activity as necessarily limited to the composition of these works. According to Tibetan sources the five *śāstras* are the *Abhisamayālaṅkāra,* the *Mahāyānasūtrālaṅkāra,* the *Madhyāntavibhāga* (or *-vibhaṅga*), the *Dharmadharmatāvibhaṅga,* and the *Mahāyānāuttaratantra.* There are grounds for regarding the *kārikā* or verse portion of the *Yogācāryābhūmiśāstra,* a prodigious monument of scholasticism which treats of the Bodhisattva's career in seventeen successive stages, as being also a work of Maitreyanatha, but in the absence of conclusive evidence to this effect we shall confine ourselves to the first, second and third of the *śāstras* already enumerated—the fourth being inaccessible and the fifth according to Chinese authorities not the work of Maitreyanatha.

From both the literary and the doctrinal points of view the *Sūtrālaṅkāra* and the *Abhisamayālaṅkāra* have certain features in common. Both, as indicated by their titles, are *alaṅkā-*

[1] *Ibid.,* pp. 18-20.

ras, and both are attempts at synthesis. An authoritative definition of this type of *śāstra* has been given by Tucci:—

> *It is "an exegetical work which may be called a commentary, in so far as it explains either a particular book, as in the case of the Abhisamayālaṅkāra, or a class of books, as the Sūtrālaṅkāra but it is not a commentary in the usual sense of the word, because it does not explain any particular passage separately taken, but all the sūtra or the sūtras as a whole. Moreover the* alaṅkāras *are all in verses and they enumerate and classify the various topics contained in the sūtras. It is evident that the chief aim of the authors of these alaṅkāras was to bring some systematical arrangement in the clumsy and bulky Mahāyāna treatises and, while formulating a new system, to support their claim that the new ideas were all concealed in these venerable texts. . . . These alaṅkāras can rightly be considered as the link between the Mahāyāna-sūtras and the new philosophy of the Yogācāra."*[1]

As Tucci proceeds to point out, the *alaṅkāras,* being brief to the point of unintelligibility, required elucidation. To supply this want was the work of Asanga, who, on the basis of the oral explanations given him along with the *kārikās* themselves by his teacher, composed or compiled an elaborate commentary. In some cases, however, instead of writing the commentary himself he transmitted the explanation to his younger brother Vasubandhu, who afterwards committed it to writing. The possibility cannot be ruled out that explanations of other texts were transmitted in this way and at a much later date embodied in commentaries. From the fact that, in his commentary on the *Sūtrālaṅkāra,* Asanga cites not only the Mahayana *sūtras,* but also the *Āgamas,* which are the Sanskrit counterpart of the first four *Nikāyas* of the extant Theravada Pali Canon, we may infer that Maitreyanatha's verses are to some extent a synthesis of the Hinayana and Mahayana points of view. This is definitely the case with the *Abhisamayālaṅkāra,* or "Treatise on Re-union with the Absolute," in which the *Śrāvakayāna,* the *Pratyekabuddhayāna* and the *Bodhisattvayāna* are clearly recognized, not as alternative routes to the same goal, but as the successive grades of one all-inclusive Path. Additional evidence of the conciliating temper of Maitreyanatha's mind is the important fact that, though his teachings were the original impulse behind the whole Yogācāra movement, the *Abhisamayālaṅkāra* is a systematization, not of any idealist *sūtra,* but of the Perfection of Wisdom "in 25,000 Lines."

---

[1] *Ibid.,* pp. 10-11.

With Haribhadra's *Āloka,* which is at the same time a free commentary on the Perfection of Wisdom "in 8,000 Lines," the *Abhisamayālaṅkāra* "dominated the exegesis of the Large Prajñāpāramitā for centuries"[1] and is still one of the most important manuals studied in the monastic colleges of Tibet and Mongolia. It is, however, fundamentally a manual of yoga, and even if, as some have supposed, Maitreyanatha was no less representative of the Mādhyamika than of the Yogācāra, the fact remains that he graded the *Prajñāpāramitā* teachings in such a way as to emphasize Meditation, and that this emphasis was directly responsible for the marked difference of outlook which eventually distinguished the later from the earlier school.

This difference is clearly brought out by Maitreyanatha himself in the third of the three works we are now considering, the *Madhyāntavibhaṅga* (or *-vibhāga*), the title of which is plainly intended to provoke a comparison and a contrast with the *Mādhyamikākārikā* of Nagarjuna. According to Nagarjuna, following the Middle Path means refusing to think of Absolute Reality, *Śūnyatā,* either in terms of existence or in terms of non-existence. According to Maitreyanatha this is an extreme view, and as such to be rejected: Reality is both existent *and* non-existent. It is existent inasmuch as it constitutes the real being of phenomena, but non-existent inasmuch as in it the subject-object relation inherent in mundane experience does not obtain. His views are summarized in a verse of admirable conciseness which Tucci renders thus: "The unreal imagination is; duality does not exist in it, but voidness exists in it and it also (*viz.*, the unreal imagination) exists in this (*viz.*, the voidness)." Besides enunciating Maitreyanatha's own position the verse attacks rival positions and answers possible objections. The motive behind the affirmation with which it begins, that the unreal imagination exists (*Abhūtaparikalpo 'sti*) is practical rather than theoretical. Unless ignorance, in the sense of the wrong assumption of the independent existence of phenomena, is admitted somehow or other to exist, spiritual life, in the sense of the progressive elimination of ignorance and attainment of Enlightenment, becomes impossible. But although the unreal imagination, as a causally related succession of mental states, does exist, it exists devoid of the

---

[1] Conze, *Selected Sayings,* p. 14.

duality of subject and object (*dvayam tatra na vidyate*). In other words emptiness, which according to the commentators is here the negation of the subject-object relation, exists in the unreal imagination (*Śūnyatā vidyate tatra*), or, less cryptically, constitutes its real nature. Spiritual life is possible only because the unreal imagination exists; but it would be equally impossible if *only* the unreal imagination existed. For this reason Maitreyanatha posits *Śūnyatā* as existing in the unreal imagination, where it functions as the support of meditation and makes possible the attainment of Enlightenment. But if *Śūnyatā* is all the time present in the unreal imagination, why do we not all attain emancipation instantaneously without the troublesome necessity of ascending through the various stages of spiritual progress? Anticipating this objection, the great *ācārya*, having made liberation possible by asserting that *Śūnyatā* exists in the unreal imagination, concludes his verse by explaining that liberation takes place not all at once but progressively because the unreal imagination exists in *Śūnyatā* (*tasyām api sa vidyate*). This amounts to saying that the Absolute is obscured by ignorance, and that after the removal of the obscuration by means of spiritual practice It will again shine forth with undimmed glory. Whereas for Nagarjuna, Reality was neither positive nor negative, existent nor non-existent, for Maitreyanatha it was definitely positive. This positive Reality the Yogācārins, following the precedent already set by the idealist *sūtras,* identified with Absolute Mind. In so doing they were, like the compilers of the *sūtras,* attempting to take into consideration the fact that in the most exalted state of *samādhi,* whereas the distinction of subject and object vanishes, consciousness remains. Enlightenment does not consist in gaining any object, but simply in the realization, by means of methodical spiritual practice, of the essentially immaculate nature of our own Mind. That the Yogācāra is, like the Mādhyamikavāda, a development of one aspect of the Original Teaching, can be demonstrated even from the Pali Canon. In the *Aṅguttara-Nikāya* the Buddha says:—

"This consciousness (citta) is luminous, but it is defiled by adventitious defilements. The uninstructed average person does not understand this as it really is. Therefore I say that for him there is no mental development.

"This consciousness is luminous, and it is freed from adventitious defilements.

The instructed ariyan disciple understands this as it really is. Therefore I say that for him there is mental development."

(Aṅguttara-Nikāya, *I. 10. I. B. Horner's translation)*[1]

The word here translated as "mental development" is *bhāvanā*, which comprises both Meditation and Wisdom. Thus the Buddha makes it clear that spiritual life presupposes a recognition of the existence of what were afterwards termed Absolute Mind and the unreal imagination. Having affirmed this duality, the Yogācārins could hardly avoid giving some account of the relation between its members. This eventually beguiled them into attempting an explanation of the absolute first beginning of the universe, a purely theoretical question which the Buddha had dismissed with the remark that such a beginning was inconceivable. The final shape assumed by these speculations may, however, be more conveniently discussed in connection with the names of Asanga and Vasubandhu, to whose life and work we must now direct our attention.

These illustrious brethren, by whose names the fame of Maitreyanatha was for centuries eclipsed, were born towards the end of the fourth century A.D., in a Brahmin family of Peshawar, an important Buddhist centre since the days of Kanishka. Both began their religious career as Sarvastivadins. Asanga was the first whose views underwent a change, and he became, as we have seen, the disciple of Maitreyanatha. The philosophical development of Vasubandhu, though eventually leading to a form of idealism perhaps even more radical than that of Asanga, was much slower and more deliberate. During his Sarvastivadin phase he in fact composed an exposition of the Abhidharma which ranks as the fullest and most systematic the Buddhist world possesses. This was the celebrated *Abhidharmakośa*, based on the *Vibhāṣā* and *Mahāvibhāṣā* on the *Jñānaprasthāna-sūtra*. According to Paramārtha, the biographer of Vasubandhu, the 600 verses that comprise the nucleus of this great work were sent by the author to the monks of Kashmir. They approved of the composition but, finding the aphorisms too concise, asked for fuller explanations. Vasubandhu thereupon wrote a prose commentary; but since his views had in the meantime undergone

[1] *Buddhist Texts,* p. 33.

a change, he freely criticized any point in the Sarvastivada doctrine with which, at the time of writing, he no longer found himself in agreement. This unlooked-for way of acceding to their request not unnaturally gave offence to the monks of Kashmir, and Vasubandhu's new views were not allowed to pass unchallenged. The *Kośa,* however, stood firm as a rock in the midst of these commotions, and with Yaśomitra's *vyākhyā,* known as the *Sphuṭārtha,* ultimately became the foundation of an independent school known in China as the Kusha Shu. Only when well stricken in years, however, did the impetus of his own philosophical development and the earnest entreaties of his brother Asanga carry Vasubandhu from the Sarvastivada to the Yogācāra School. Though such an evolution (we refuse to call it a conversion) was by no means uncommon in that age, Vasubandhu is the only *ācārya* who enjoys equal prestige as an exponent of the two main branches of Buddhist tradition. With one foot planted firmly on the side of the Great, the other on the side of the Little Vehicle, he bestrides mediæval Indian Buddhism "like a Colossus."

Of the works composed by Asanga and Vasubandhu it is impossible, in the present state of our knowledge, to give a complete and accurate account. Apart from the initial difficulty that some are extant in Chinese and Tibetan translation only, while others have not survived in any form, we are confronted by the hard fact that only a small fraction of the works traditionally imputed to them can be regarded as being with complete certainty theirs. Probably we shall not be much mistaken, however, in accepting as the major opera of Asanga the commentarial portions at least of the *Yogācāryā-bhūmi,* the *Mahāyāna-sūtrālaṅkāra,* the *Dharmadharmatāvibhaṅga* and the *Mahāyānauttaratantra*[1]—the verse nuclei of all of which seem to have been the work of Maitreyanatha—and two independent treatises, the *Triśatikāyāḥ Prajñāpāramitāyāḥ Kārikā-saptati* and the *Mahāyāna-saṁparigraha.*

Coming to the works of Vasubandhu, we find among the drifting sands of uncertain ascription at least one spot of perfectly solid ground. This is the *Triṁśikā-vijñapti-kārikā,*

[1] This is not, as the title might suggest, a Tantric work, but an exposition of the Mādhyamika doctrine.

or "Thirty Stanzas on the Mere Idea," which fortunately is not only the most authentic but also by far the most important and influential of all the *śāstras* bearing the great *ācārya's* signature. Of the ten commentaries composed on this seminal work in India, only that of Sthiramati is extant in its entirety. All, however, were digested by the industrious Hiuen Tsiang, himself a staunch though not a rigorous advocate of the Yogācāra system, in a work known as the *Vijñaptimātratāsiddhi.* This compilation does not profess to strike a balance between the views of all ten commentators, but gives the greatest weight to those of Dharmapāla, abbot of Nalanda. As next in authenticity and influence we may no doubt reckon the commentary on Maitreyanatha's *Madhyāntavibhāga* which, as previously mentioned, Vasubandhu compiled from the oral explanations of his brother, and his commentary on Asanga's *Mahāyānasaṁparigraha.* There are also numerous minor works, out of which the *Trisvabhāvanirdeśa* may be selected as an authentic specimen.

Emphasis has already been laid on the fact that we are not to consider the Mahayana *ācāryas*—nor even the founders of schools—as original thinkers in the Western academic sense, but as systematizers of the traditional teachings embodied in the *sūtras.* Whatever originality they possessed found an outlet not in the excogitation of new doctrines but in the more perfect arrangement of the old. If the *sūtras* are mines of precious stones, the *śāstras* are single diamonds and rubies which by cutting and polishing have been made to scintillate. Moreover, just as a jeweller, though he does not *make* the stones, can select one of whichever variety he pleases, and give it whatever shape he thinks will most enhance its beauty, so the *ācāryas* were free to select, out of this *sūtra* or group of *sūtras* or that, whichever doctrines were to them most congenial, or of the greatest intrinsic value, or which they thought were being treated with misunderstanding or neglect. Such a state of affairs, though as contributing to the continuity of tradition it is to be praised rather than deplored, nevertheless tends to make the writing of an account such as we are trying to give in the present chapter very difficult. The line between the systematic and the unsystematic form of a teaching is not always easy to draw, nor is it possible to determine with exactness each *ācārya's* contribution to the work of systematization. A Mahayana school resembles a magnificent temple, different portions of which are known to have been built at different times by different people, though nobody can say with certainty that *these* pillars are the work of *this* architect and *those* domes of *that.* All that can be done in either case is to give a description of the structure concerned and an account of the men associated with its erection. This principle must be borne constantly in mind if we are not to commit the mistake of construing the development of the Mahayana schools in terms of a succession of purely individual speculative opinions such as on the whole constitutes the history of philosophy in Europe. The four doctrines of which a short introduction must now be given, though subjoined to an account of life and works of Asanga and Vasubandhu, must not for this reason be regarded as originating from them, though it was undoubtedly these two *ācāryas* who were responsible for their final systematization. Neither should it be supposed that either Asanga or Vasubandhu professed only the four doctrines mentioned. Like Maitreyanatha himself, though emphasizing a certain aspect of it, they accepted the whole Buddhist tradition. All four doctrines referred to are connected with the central thesis of the Yogācāra, namely that Absolute Mind is the sole reality. They are concerned with (*a*) the existence of mere ideas (*vijñāptimātratā*), of (*b*) the Store Consciousness (*ālayavijñāṇa*), (*c*) the three kinds of "own-being" (*svabhāva*), and (*d*) the triple body (*trikāya*) of the Enlightened One. The fourth doctrine, having been accepted by all schools of the Mahayana, was described in detail in Chapter II, Section VI, and need not be adumbrated here.

(*a*) One of the best ways of demonstrating the sole reality of Absolute Mind is by disproving the existence of matter. Though unacceptable to the Mādhyamikas, who believed that the antinomial character of reason precluded the establishment of positive truths by logical means, this line of argument appealed to the Yogācārins, particularly Vasubandhu, whose best known work, the *Triṁśikā-vijñāptimātratā,* is mainly an attempt to show that there is no such thing as a material substance, whether atomic or non-atomic, and that only ideas exist. Like the idealism of Berkeley, which in many respects closely resembles that of his great Indian precursor, the doctrine of *vijñāptimātratā* has been not only misunderstood but misrepresented. But Vasubandhu too is not refuted by striking one's foot against a stone, however forcibly. For what Vasubandhu, like Berkeley, denies, is not the existence of sensible qualities, of which solidity is one, but of the independent material substratum in which they are supposed to inhere. For both philosophers a flower, for example, is merely the sum total of certain visual, olfactory and tactile sensations; it is not a lump of matter which possesses these sensations as its attributes. Matter is an abstraction, a mere word. Strictly speaking, we should refer, not to having a perception *of a thing*, but only to having a perception. In Berkeley's language *esse est percipi* or *percipere* (to exist is to be perceived or to perceive); in Vasubandhu's *vijñāptimātra* (only ideas—that is to say perceptions—exist). Moreover, in endeavouring to establish the truth of their respective propositions, both the Irish bishop and the Indian *ācārya* were—as already hinted—influenced by practical and religious, rather than by theoretical and academic, considerations. Berkeley, to whom materialism was synonymous with atheism, atheism synonymous with irreligon, and all synonymous with vice, believed that by disproving the existence of matter he rendered materialism impossible, vindicated religion, and promoted the cause of virtue. According to Vasubandhu, when, like Rāvaṇa in the *Laṅkāvatāra,* we realize that the so-called objective universe exists nowhere save in our own mind, all attachment to it will be destroyed, and with the destruction of that attachment liberation will be attained. In the *ācārya's* own words, "Where there is nothing to grasp there is no more grasping."[1] Vasubandhu has, however, one very great advantage over Berkeley, for the Buddhist, unlike the Christian, idealist, can appeal for support in his conclusions not only to logic, not only to the analogy of dreams, but also to the testimony of the *yogin,* who in exalted states of *samādhi* perceives vivid sensuous impressions without there being any objective stimulus. Vasubandhu in fact suggests that only by personal experience of Meditation can one gain a living conviction of the truth of *vijñāptimātratā.* ". . . Before we have awakened from a dream," he says, "we cannot know that what is seen in the dream does not exist."[2]

(*b*) Granting that matter does not exist, and that except as the aggregate of our sensations the universe has no reality, why do

[1] *Triṁśikā,* p. 28.
[2] *Ibid.,* p. 16.

we *think* that matter exists? What is the *cause* of the illusion of objective existence? The doctrine of the *ālayavijñāna,* or Store Consciousness, is in one sense part of an attempt to answer this question in a systematic manner. Maitreyanatha, besides positing Absolute Mind as the sole reality, had also posited the existence of the *abhūtaparikalpa,* or unreal imagination, by which the radiance of Absolute Mind becomes obscured. These two principles, while in one sense identical, in another sense are different from each other. Regarding them as different, Absolute Mind is the static, and the unreal imagination the dynamic, or potentially dynamic, principle. Out of this dynamic principle, which comprises two aspects, eventually emerges the whole so-called objective universe, which is in reality nothing but a transformation of mind. The two aspects referred to are the *ālayavijñāna,* or Store Consciousness, and the *pravṛtti-vijñāna,* or evolving consciousness. Every willed action produces an effect, technically known as a *vāsanā.* These *vāsanās* are "stored" in the *ālayavijñāna* in the form of "seeds." As these seeds fructify and produce results, they develop touch, mental activity (*manaskāra*), feeling, perception, and will (*cetanā*)—corresponding to the five aggregates of the older tradition. This is the first transformation of consciousness. The second transformation takes place when *manas,* or ego-consciousness, evolves from the *ālayavijñāna,* and the third when, by means of the sixfold sense activity, perceptions of colour, sound, temperature, resistance, etc., arise and are wrongly interpreted as an objective and a subjective world, each independent of the other. Such is the genesis of the illusion of the reality of things and of the self. The *vijñānas* associated with the six faculties of sense together with the *mano-vijñāna,* or ego-consciousness, comprise the evolving consciousness (*pravṛtti-vijñāna*) already referred to, and these seven and the *ālayavijñāna* make up the eight consciousnesses of the Yogācāra School.

(*c*) While the doctrine of the *ālayavijñāna* is part of an attempt to explain the causal relation between Absolute Mind and its hypostases, the third of our three doctrines, that of the *svabhāvas,* differentiates their ontological status and determines the nature of their interrelations from the ontological point of view. The three *svabhāvas* are known as *parinispanna,* absolute reality, *paratantra* or relative reality, and *parikalpita,* imputed reality or mere illusion. The first corresponds to Absolute Mind, the second to the unreal imagination, and the third to the wrong notion of objective and subjective existence.[1] In this connection it should be noted that while for the Yogācārin the subject-object distinction is wholly unreal, the mind and the mental states on which it is superimposed are real in the relative sense. They are in fact identical with the *abhūtaparikalpa,* which is "unreal" only in comparison with the absolute reality of the One Mind. By admitting the relative reality of the mind and the mental states, the Yogācārins were able to incorporate, after suitable modifications, the Sarvastivadins' analysis and classification of *dharmas,* together with the bulk of their apparatus of scholasticism. Vasubandhu tries to explain the difference between the three *svabhāvas* by means of an illustration which, though of some interest, may not be found very illuminating. He says that by the power of a *mantra* a piece of wood may be made to appear in the form of an elephant. The non-existence of the elephant in the wood is the absolute reality, the form of the elephant the relative reality, and the elephant itself the imputed reality; the *mantra* corresponds to the *ālayavijñāna.*[2] Whatever the merits of this analogy, however, Vasubandhu makes it quite clear that the distinction between the three *svabhāvas* is pragmatic only; ultimately only the One Mind exists. Just as, when the illusory elephant and its form are no longer perceived, the piece of wood is seen, so when the imputed and the relative reality vanish the absolute reality is realized. The great *ācārya* describes the process of realization in the following beautiful verses, with which the *Trisvabhāvanirdeśa* fittingly concludes:—

*35. By restraining the opposite thought, seeing the vanity (of things) through the intellect, and by following the three kinds of knowledge (*i.e., *study, reflection and meditation), emancipation is attained without any effort.*

*36. Through the attainment of the state of Pure Consciousness, there is the non-perception of the perceivable; and through the non-perception of the perceivable (*i.e., *the object) there is the non-acquisition of the mind (*i.e., *the subject).*

*37. Through the non-perception of these two, there arises the realization of the Essence of Reality (*dharmadhātu*) and through the realization of the Essence of Reality, there occurs the acquisition of "the supernormal power of destroying ignorance and attaining prosperity (*vibhutta*)."*

[1] It is a great mistake to describe the Yogācāra as Subjective Idealism when it explicitly declares the subject to be an illusion.

[2] *Trisvabhāvanirdeśa,* p. 27, 28, 30.

*38. After having "the supernormal power of destroying ignorance and attaining prosperity," and having (thereby) attained a clear knowledge about oneself and others, the wise man realizes that Supreme Enlightenment (*bodhi*) which is embodied in three essential forms.*

The *ācāryas* who succeeded Asanga and Vasubandhu were no less illustrious, and no less numerous, than those who had continued the work of Nagarjuna and Ārya Deva. The names of Sthiramati, the commentator on Vasubandhu, and Dharmapāla, abbot of Nalanda, have already been mentioned. To them must now be added the names of Gunamati, another commentator, and Sāramati, author of the *Ratnagotravibhāga*. Śāntarakṣita and his disciple Kamalaśīla, though sometimes classified as Yogācārins, are perhaps correctly represented as synthesizing Mādhyamikas who accepted the Yogācāra doctrines as relative truth. The names of Paramārtha and Hiuen Tsiang are connected with the introduction of the Yogācāra School into China. Hiuen Tsiang, as we have already seen, besides translating Vasubandhu's *Triṁśikā* made a digest in Chinese of its ten Indian commentaries. This important work, known as the *Vijñāptimātratāsiddhi,* was the basic *śāstra* of a school known as the Fa Hsiang Tsung or Dharmalakshaṇa School, of which Hiuen Tsiang is regarded as the founder. His disciple Chi K'uei (632-685 A.D.), a brilliant thinker and prolific writer, was its chief exponent. During the middle of the seventh, and again at the beginning of the eighth century, the school was introduced into Japan, where it was known as the Hosso Shu. After flourishing for a while it gradually lost ground to more vigorous movements; today it survives as one of the numerically smallest branches of Japanese Buddhism.

Before bringing this section to a close notice must be taken of two movements of major historical importance, both of which may be classified, at least in their beginnings, as offshoots of the Yogācāra. They are the Indian movement which developed the Buddhist version of the science of Logic, and the Chinese movement which devoted itself to the practice of Meditation. Buddhist Logic began as a set of rules for public debate, proficiency in which was no less desirable in Mediæval India than in Ancient Greece, though in the former country its utility was not political but religious. By means of skilful argument unbelievers could be converted to the True Doctrine. The *Yogācāryā-*

bhūmi-śāstra, a comprehensive treatise on the Bodhisattva's career, therefore devotes one of its chapters to the eight kinds of rules to be observed by the Bodhisattva in the conduct of a debate. From these simple beginnings grew up the science of Buddhist Logic, which, due to the unprecedented dialectical competence of Vasubandhu's disciple Dignāga, and Dignāga's disciple Dharmakīrti—both of whom were Yogācārins with Sautrāntika leanings—administered to the non-Buddhist schools a shock even more violent than that which had been given them by Nagarjuna. It was not long, however, before logic and epistemology came to be studied, not as instruments of propaganda, but for their own sake, and it is for this reason that, despite the decisive part played by the Buddhist Logical School in the development of Indian philosophy during the mediæval period, we have here passed it over with no more than an honourable mention. Those who are interested in its doctrines will find a full account of them in Dr. Satkari Mookerjee's standard work *The Buddhist Philosophy of Universal Flux.*[1] The Meditation School, known in China as the Ch'an Tsung and in Japan as the Zen Shu, must unfortunately be dismissed with even less ceremony. Its connection with the Yogācāra is established by the fact that it began about 440 A.D. with a group of students of Gunabhadra's Chinese translation of the *Laṅkāvatāra Sūtra.* About three hundred years later it achieved the status of an independent school. For the last thousand years the Meditation School has exerted upon the course of Far Eastern religion and culture an influence equalled by no other branch of the Dharma. Thanks to the scholarly writings of Dr. D. T. Suzuki, Zen Buddhism, as it is now generally called, is widely known in the West. Unfortunately, however, by dissociating Zen from its traditional background certain Western Buddhists, with more enthusiasm than understanding, have created the erroneous impression that Meditation, or what they believe to be Meditation, can be practised as an independent discipline, without effective recourse either to Morality or to Wisdom.

Other fruits of the Yogācāra on Chinese soil include *The Awakening of Faith in the Mahayana,* a fifth-century systematization of the teachings of the *Laṅkāvatāra Sūtra.* This *śāstra* was

[1] *University of Calcutta,* 1935.

formerly believed to have been translated from a Sanskrit original by Asvaghosha; but recent investigations indicate that it is the work of a native Chinese author. Whatever its origin, it remains one of the best and most attractive expositions of Buddhist Idealism available.

X. Transition to the Tantra

In Section II we found that, excluding Mindfulness, the Five Spiritual Faculties made up two pairs, one consisting of Faith and Wisdom, the other of Concentration and Vigour. This coupling of faculties, far from being of merely psychological import, is exemplified by the historical connections between the corresponding schools of the Mahayana. Devotional Buddhism, as we saw in Section VI, was originally an aspect of the Mādhyamika School, which rightly upheld the supremacy of Wisdom. Similarly, Tantric or Magical Buddhism had, as we shall see in the course of this section, from the very beginning of its public career a particularly close connection with the Yogācāra. Owing to the accommodating spirit of the Mahayana, and the tendency of each school to "overlap" every other, this connection, however intimate, could not be exclusive. The Yogācāra itself, in fact, though concentrating upon the explication of its own idealist theses, had never dreamed of repudiating the absolutism of the Mādhyamikas, and the worship of Amitabha and Maitreya was no less warmly recommended by Vasubandhu than by Nagarjuna. Every school and sub-school of the Mahayana represented not a rejection of, but an accretion upon, the doctrines of earlier schools which, while in theory it accepted the whole previous tradition, in practice generally emphasized whatever aspect of tradition it thought most important. Direct connection with the Yogācāra implies indirect connection with both the Mādhyamika and the devotional schools. Conze therefore says, "The Tantra combines the devotional needs of the masses with the meditational practices of the Yogācāra school, and with the metaphysics of the Mādhyamikas."[1] Though this statement is quite true as far as it goes, it is far from being the whole truth, and it would indeed be a gross error to interpret

---

[1] *Buddhism,* p. 184.

Tantric Buddhism as a movement of popular syncretism. The Tantra represents, among the Mahayana schools, the Faculty of Vigour, traditionally defined as consisting in the maintenance and production of wholesome, and the elimination and obstruction of unwholesome, states of mind. By wholesome states of mind the *jhānas,* or *dhyānas,* in particular are meant. Consequently the dominating interest of the Tantra is not theoretical but practical. In default of the systematic practice of Meditation, the Mādhyamika doctrine, though indicating Absolute Truth, had sunk into scholasticism. The Yogācārin emphasis on Meditation, though originally a protest against this one-sidedness, ultimately met the same fate, being understood to mean not the actual attainment of *dhyāna* but a theoretical, not to say speculative, interpretation of existence in the light of this experience. The Tantra, though combining the distinctive doctrines of the earlier schools, differed radically from all of them in being concerned not with the further theoretical elaboration of these doctrines but with the application of the methods leading to the realization of the realities of which they were but the conceptual symbols. Thus the Tantra belongs not so much to the domain of Doctrine as to the domain of Method. Existing Buddhist traditions were accepted as providing not a starting-point for fresh speculative thought but a basis for action. More than any other school does the Tantra represent the practical side of Buddhism, and it is for this reason that, as Dr. Herbert V. Guenther insists, "It is in Tantrism that Buddhism finds its efflorescence and constant rejuvenation."[1] But though the Tantra stands for action, and hence for power in all its modes, it stands not for action in general, which would be better denominated mere activity, but in particular for ritual or sacramental action. In the light of this fundamental principle the *raison d'être* of more than one characteristically Tantric emphasis is clearly revealed. Action is of three kinds, physical, vocal and mental. Thought or mental action, of which concentrated thought is the most efficacious variety, determines speech and action; but at the same time speech and action influence thought. The sacramental action of the Tantra aims at bringing about a transformation of

---

[1] "The Origin and Spirit of Vajrayana," *Stepping-Stones,* Vol. II, p. 4 (May 1951).

consciousness by means of spiritually significant sounds and movements. By spiritually significant sounds we mean, of course, the various *dhāraṇis* or *mantras,* which, because of the tremendous effect their constant repetition has on the mind, occupy in Tantric Buddhism a position of extreme importance. Spiritually significant movements include those made by a part of the body, such as the *mudras* assumed by the hands, as well as those made by the whole body, such as the act of obeisance and dancing. Since ritual and sacramental actions can be performed only with the body, the Tantra far from depreciating the body hails it as the vessel of salvation and glorifies it to an extent unheard of in any other form of Buddhism. Moreover, not only is the body part of the material universe, but many material objects are employed for sacramental purposes; hence the Tantra regards the world too not as a hindrance but as a help to Enlightenment, eulogizing it as the theatre of salvation and the revelation of the Absolute. Instead of giving up the world one should live in it in such a way that the worldly life itself is transmuted into the life transcendental. Yet another fact which, in the eyes of the Tantra, invests the body with sacredness, is the possibility of our acting upon the mind not only by moving the limbs but by manipulating the breath and the seminal fluid, all of which are so intimately connected that by controlling any one of them the remaining two are automatically controlled. Again, being concerned less with broad philosophical generalizations than with the minutest details of spiritual practice, certain aspects of which were too complex, difficult and subtle to be committed to writing, the Tantras naturally insisted upon the necessity of receiving initiation and guidance from a qualified spiritual master. Some of these characteristically Tantric emphases will be examined more closely later on. Meanwhile we must endeavour to ascertain the particular aspect of earlier tradition which supplied the immediate theoretical basis of Tantric sacramentalism; for, as Conze pertinently observes, "If the Tantra expects salvation from sacred actions, it must have a conception of the Universe according to which such actions can be the lever of emancipation."[1]

We have already seen that the *Avataṁsaka Sūtra* has been spoken of as occupying an intermediate position between the

---

[1] *Buddhism,* p. 188.

Mādhyamika and Yogācāra schools. More properly might it be regarded as supplying the connecting link between the Yogācāra and the Tantra. The Mādhyamika had declared that all things were in reality *Śūnyatā.* The Yogācāra, after identifying *Śūnyatā* with Absolute Mind, had explained "the choir of heaven and furniture of the earth" as mere phenomena of consciousness. The *Avataṁsaka,* of which the *Gaṇḍavyūha* is a part, took up this idea of the essential non-duality of things and interpreted it, as we saw in our account of these *śūtras* in Section VIII, in terms of the unobstructed mutual interpenetration of all existing objects, both transcendental and mundane. Just as the jewels of Indra's Net reflect each other, so all things are reflected in Absolute Mind and Absolute Mind is reflected in all things. In the Far East this conception of mutual interpenetration fostered an attitude towards nature very similar to that expressed by Blake in his vision of "the world in a grain of sand" or by Tennyson when, contemplating the "flower in the crannied wall," he felt that if he could fully understand it he would know the true nature of God and man.

In India the same conception provided the doctrinal basis of an elaborate system of correspondences which acted as the fulcrum, as it were, of the Tantric lever of emancipation. Being concerned not with theory but with practice, the Tantra differed from the Chinese *Avataṁsaka* School in being quite indifferent to the metaphysical side of the doctrine of interpenetration. If transcendental realities were in truth reflected in the objects of the material world, the Tantra wanted to know exactly where to find them. It was not satisfied with vague general statements which, however adequate a basis they might provide for philosophical discussion, were quite useless as a guide to practice. If the transcendental reality designated Akṣobhya, for example, really existed, it should be possible to locate Him at a particular point in every form of phenomenal life and activity. The moon, though said to be reflected in a pool of water, was not reflected in the whole pool, but only in one particular part of it. To know that Akṣobhya was reflected in the phenomenal world was not enough. The world consisted of five *skandhas.* One of them must be the reflection Akṣobhya. Since the literal meaning of Aksobhya is "The Imperturbable," and since according to the Yogācārins consciousness in its fundamental nature is immutable, the Tantra identified Akṣobhya with the *vijñāna-skandha* or aggregate of consciousness. On these principles the Tantra built up an enormously complicated, but remarkably logical, system in which Buddhas, Bodhisattvas and innumerable Deities, all representing either different aspects of Reality or different stages of the Transcendental Path, were associated not only with an aggregate of Their own, but also with a particular *mantra, mudra,* element, direction, animal, colour, sense faculty, part of the body, etc. By repeating the *mantra* and assuming the *mudra* of any Buddha or Bodhisattva, as well as by the manipulation of the various phenomena in which He is reflected, one can not only place oneself in correspondence or alignment with the particular order of reality which He personifies but also be infused with its transcendental power. Tantric *pūjā,* or the ritual worship of a particular Transcendental Form or Group of Transcendental Forms, is not a mere outpouring of devotion, though devotion plays its part, but a systematic and, in its own way, scientific method of producing internal by means of external changes, or in other words of acting through the body upon the mind. After one's mind has been as it were "tuned in" by the performance of *pūjā* to a higher order of reality one can visualize in *dhyāna* the Transcendental Form Whose image or picture one has been worshipping. This Form is perceived even more vividly than the objects of the senses, and appears not less real than they are but more real. The purpose of the visualization is to teach the devotee, through his own personal experience, the fundamental tenet of the Yogācāra School that all the objects of perception, including his own body, are only transformations of consciousness. Like the visualized Transcendental Form, they are all the evolutes of his own Absolute Mind. He therefore meditates upon the voidness of the Transcendental Form, and then, having identified himself with the Form, upon the voidness of his own individuality too.[1] By this means he develops insight into what is not only the fundamental tenet of the Mādhyamika School, but also the ultimate basis of every form of Buddhism, namely, the unique principle of the egolessness and

---

[1] These sentences summarize a wide variety of lengthy and elaborate practices the essentials of which are fully dealt with in Tantric literature.

insubstantiality of all *dharmas*. Thus the Mādhyamika doctrine of *Śūnyatā*, the Yogācāra teaching of Absolute Mind, the *Avataṁsaka* conception of mutual interpenetration, the Tantric system of correspondences, and the Tantric practice of sacramental action, within which are included Yogācāra Meditation and Mādhyamika Wisdom, are links in the chain whereby Tantric Buddhism is indissolubly connected with the whole body of Mahayana teaching. This being so it is a serious blunder to represent, or rather misrepresent, the Tantra as a corruption or degeneration of Buddhism, or as being connected with it only by accident, or because of historical circumstances. As we have already insisted, the Tantra differs from earlier schools only in emphasizing the practical rather than the theoretical aspect of the Dharma, and it is this distinctive emphasis which is responsible for most of its characteristic features. Unless we can first recognize this fact all our efforts to understand the Tantra will be in vain.

XI. Tantric Texts, Teachers and Schools

As might have been anticipated even from the previous section, it is more difficult to give a general account of the Tantra than of any other school of Buddhism. The reasons for this are both intrinsic and extrinsic. To begin with, the Tantra, being concerned not with theoretical generalizations but with details of practice, was and to a great extent still is not an exoteric but an esoteric teaching, for centuries preserved exclusively by means of oral tradition and carefully shielded from profane curiosity. Materials for writing the history of an esoteric movement obviously will be very scanty, if not entirely non-existent. Even when literary records do start appearing they are not very helpful from the historical point of view. In addition to this, there is the fact that the Tantras and their supplementary texts, which for sheer quantity rival even the output of earlier schools, are largely unexplored in modern times, a few isolated fragments being all that is generally accessible. Yet since the language of the Tantras, even of their very titles, is often symbolical, not even the publication of the whole Tantric literature, so that whoever runs might read, could, in the absence of the oral tradition, avail to extricate us from our predicament. Moreover, as Lama Anagarika Govinda has so ably shown,[1] the biographies of Tantric teachers are replete with incidents which must be interpreted not literally but symbolically, so that without the necessary "key," which is generally to be found in certain highly esoteric forms of *yoga,* it is impossible to be sure with which order of reality one is dealing, the historical or the metaphysical. Again, since the Tantra is mainly concerned not with theory but with practice, the generalizations which in the case of other schools made it possible for us to dispose of ten centuries of philosophical development in as many pages cannot be resorted to. The more abstract a subject is, the more easily does it lend itself to condensation; as it becomes concrete, and deals with particulars, the difficulty of summarizing it undergoes a proportionate increase. In view of these circumstances, even so cursory an account as was given of the *sūtras, śāstras* and *ācāryas* of the foregoing schools will not be possible in the case of Tantric Buddhism. All that can be offered in this section is a reference to a few of the most salient and least disputed facts concerning its origin and development. In the next section it may be possible to recur to some of its special features.

We have been more than once reminded that the concern of the Tantra is principally with Method. No sooner do we attempt to probe the origins of Tantric Buddhism than this fact again emerges. Like almost all the Mahayana *sūtras,* the Tantras profess to be the Word of the Lord Buddha Himself. Before we dismiss the claim as preposterous, two facts must be taken into consideration. One has been adverted to already in connection with the question of the relative authenticity of the Hinayana and the Mahayana scriptures; the other is connected with the fact to which we have just alluded. In the first place, as we urged before, there can be no *a priori* objection to any Indian tradition, Buddhist or non-Buddhist, having been transmitted orally for five hundred or even for a thousand years. Indian memories were, and in traditional circles still are, extraordinarily retentive, and quite capable of preserving for a hundred generations teachings which among less gifted peoples would have been lost

[1] *Vide* his review of *The Tibetan Book of the Great Liberation,* with particular reference to the Biography of Padma Sambhava. *Maha Bodhi Journal,* Vol. 62, pp. 295-304 (August, 1954).

in ten. The circumstance that Tantric teachings were not committed to writing until a thousand years after the Parinirvana of the Blessed One therefore cannot be regarded as militating against their basic authenticity. In the second, those who have made the experiment know how difficult it is to practise successfully any form of Meditation, even the most elementary, simply by following the directions of a written text, however detailed these may at first sight appear to be. The temperaments and circumstances of the would-be practitioners of *yoga* are of so many kinds, and differ so widely, that even the most exhaustive treatise would be unable to make provision for all their special requirements. Instruction in Meditation was therefore given orally in all Buddhist schools—a tradition continued by the Mahayana down to the present day. Written instructions seem to have been intended not as a guide to novices but as an *aide-mémoire* to initiated pupils. Now the farther we go back in the history of Buddhist literature the scantier do these written or recorded instructions become, while on the contrary the nearer we draw to modern times the more numerous and copious do we find them. Despite their prolixity on all that pertains to Doctrine, both the Theravada Pali Canon and the classical Mahayana *sūtras* are strangely silent with regard to Method, particularly all that concerns the practice of Meditation. Yet we know that the Buddha Himself was in the habit of instructing His disciples in the use of a particular *kammaṭṭhāna* and of questioning them from time to time concerning their progress. Unless we are to suppose that all those instructions are lost, in which case it would be difficult to explain the astounding spiritual vitality of Buddhism, we can only assume that there existed side by side with the exoteric an esoteric tradition whose primary concern was with the correct transmission of the technique of various forms of Meditation. This tradition, though not incorporated into the canonical texts, gradually infiltrated into the commentarial and expository literature, both Pali and Sanskrit, and in the end became comparatively public in the Tantras.

Though *dhāraṇis* and *mantras* bulk large in the later chapters of many Mahayana *sūtras,* specifically Tantric works do not begin to make their appearance until about nine centuries after the Parinirvana of the Enlightened One, that is to say, until the beginning of the fifth century A.D. Their production continued with unabated vigour for upwards of 500 years, coming to an end only with the virtual disappearance of Buddhism from Indian soil. The earliest, and perhaps most authoritative of the Tantras is the *Tathāgataguhyaka,* or, as it is more generally styled, the *Guhyasamāja,* a work which in Nepal, Tibet and Mongolia is still regarded with the utmost veneration. The vast difference between the literal meaning and the symbolical interpretation of the mere title of this Tantra may be cited as an illustration of what has already been said about the difficulty, even the danger, of attempting a generalized account of Tantric literature without the support of the oral tradition. If we can trust the Sanskrit lexicons (and scholars generally trust them implicitly), *Guhyasamāja* may be rendered "Secret Assembly" or even "Secret Society," both of which "equivalents" are for prurient ears fraught with connotations of the most suspicious kind. According to the symbolical interpretation, the term *Guhyasamāja* signifies the esoteric (*guhya*) integration (*samāja*) of one's body, speech and mind with the body, speech and mind of the *Tathāgata,* that is to say, with His *Nirmāṇakāya, Saṁbhogakāya* and *Dharmakāya,* by means of certain extremely complicated yogic practices described in the Tantra. One of the most highly esoteric of these practices, or rather series of practices, consists in the creation of the transcendental body in which, after he has attained Supreme Buddahood, a Bodhisattva continues to exist for the sake of benefiting all sentient beings. Yet those are not wanting who, lacking the oral tradition, and misled by a grossly literal interpretation of the mere words of the Tantric texts, are loud in their condemnation of the "corruption" and "immorality" of the school of Buddhism by which they were produced! As might have been expected, the numerous Tantras which followed the *Guhyasamāja* were intended to cater to the diverse needs of a wide variety of aspirants. In accordance with the degree of realization which their practice confers,[1] they are distributed commonly into four main classes, or, more properly speaking, grades, respectively known as the Kriyā, Caryā, Yoga and Anuttara Tantra. The *Guhyasamāja* is a work of the fourth and highest class, the *Anuttara* or "Unsurpassed." In common with

[1] This is one explanation. There are others.

other schools, Tantric Buddhism suffered heavy literary losses at the time of the Muslim conquest of Northern India, and there is no doubt that many Tantras perished in the flames of Nalanda. Much, however, survived, and is still available either in Sanskrit or, as is more frequently the case, in Tibetan translation. Besides the Tantras themselves, there exist certain quasi-canonical texts, known as *Sādhanas,* which describe the correct procedure for worshipping a particular Transcendental Form. These texts are exceedingly numerous. Works of a more theoretical character, though not unknown, are comparatively rare: the Tantric *ācāryas* were not so much the authors of *śāstras* as adepts in a particular Tantra or group of Tantras.

Eighty-four *siddhācāryas*, or, more briefly, *siddhas* or Perfect Ones, as the Tantric adepts were called, are generally enumerated; but the number is not to be taken literally, eighty-four and its multiples by a hundred and a thousand being frequently mentioned in the Scriptures, especially in connection with groups of persons. As might have been expected, the *siddhas* all flourished during the same half-millennium that witnessed the production of the Tantras, that is to say, from the beginning of the sixth to the end of the eleventh century A.D. Unlike the *ācāryas* of the Mādhyamika and Yogācāra Schools, all of whom were monks, the Perfect Ones generally disregarded, not only the monastic obligations, but even the ordinary conventions of social life. Moreover, whereas Buddhist learning and spirituality had formerly been practically the monopoly of those who, like Nagarjuna, Ārya Deva, Vasubandhu and Asanga, had been born in Brahmin families, the *siddhas* frequently belonged to the most degraded and despised communities, and followed avocations which under Brahminism involved social ostracism. Some of the most famous of them, however, such as Indrabhūti, Padmasambhava, Naropāda, and Advayavajra, were for all their unconventionality extremely learned men, and composed various treatises analogous to the *śāstras* of other schools. But perhaps the most characteristic, certainly the most attractive, literary form employed by the *siddhācāryas* was the *dohā,* a rhymed vernacular couplet, meant to be sung rather than recited, in which the profoundest truths were expressed in concise and generally direct language for the benefit of the populace. These *dohās,* though often self-contained in meaning, could be strung together into a series not unlike the *rubāiyāt* of the Persian poets. The best-known collection is that of Sarahapāda, the earliest and perhaps most celebrated of the Perfect Ones, though many of his successors, such as Tillopāda, Śāntipāda, Kāṇhapāda, and Kukkurīpāda, also excelled in this species of composition. Owing to the overlapping of schools already referred to, we find in addition to the *siddhas* a group of *ācāryas* who, though nominally belonging to other schools, had not only mastered the Tantric teachings but expounded them in treatises. Thus Śāntarakṣita, the Mādhyamika-Yogācārin author of the encyclopædic *Tattvasaṅgraha,* wrote the *Tattvasiddhi,* a sort of philosophical defence of Tantric practices; while Ārya Deva, the disciple of Nagarjuna, was, according to a tradition not entirely undisputed, the author of the *Cittaviśuddhiprakaraṇa,* another standard work of the same type. Even *ācāryas* like Nagarjuna and Asanga, who are not credited with any works of a specifically Tantric character, are included in the Tantric succession on the grounds that they transmitted the teaching orally.

Apart from Sarahapāda, the most important *siddhācāryas* from the historical point of view are Padmasambhava, by whom the Tantra was introduced into Tibet, and Vajrabodhi and Amoghavajra, by whom it was first made known in China. About the first of these, who is respected throughout Tibet as Guru Rimpoche, or "The Precious Teacher," little can be said, for his "biography" appears to consist not of historical facts but of symbolical incidents. His name, which means "The Lotus Born," alludes to the tradition that he was not born of human parents but came into being by apparitional birth—one of the four kinds of birth recognized in Buddhism—from the calyx of a lotus on a lake in North-Western India. This lake is now popularly identified with that which gleams beside the Golden Temple at Amritsar, the holy city of the Sikh religion. Perhaps all that can be asserted of Padmasambhava with complete certainty is that he flourished in the eighth century, being the contemporary of Śāntarakṣita, and that his impact on the religious life of Tibet, where he spent in all only eighteen months, was so tremendous that he is honoured to this day as the "founder" of the Nyin-ma School in that country. He was able to exert so great an influence, not simply because of his learning and enlightenment, but because, as one of the greatest masters of *yoga* that India had ever known, he was in possession of extraordinary supernormal powers. Due to the impetus he gave it, the Nyin-ma, or "Old Style" School, so called for its adherence to the earlier, imperfect translations of the Tantras, is even today one of the major religious foundations of Tibet, where, though inferior in both numbers and prestige to the Gelugpa School, it still enjoys considerable influence. One of the main sources of its strength lies in the fact that it has successfully incorporated from the pre-Buddhist Bön cult a number of indigenous traditions.

A distinction is sometimes made between the Nyin-ma-pas and the Gelugpas on the ground that whereas the former are Tantrics the latter are not. This is a grave error. Tsongkhapa, the founder of the Gelugpa School, regarded the Tantra as the culminating phase of Buddhism, and as such his followers have regarded it ever since. Gelugpa ritual and meditation are almost wholly Tantric. The real point at issue between the two schools is one of interpretation. Certain Tantras recommend, so far as the word-meaning of the texts is concerned, sacramental indulgence in wine and sexual intercourse as highly conducive to the attainment of Enlightenment. According to the Nyin-ma-pas, such injunctions should be taken literally; but the Gelugpas maintain that they must be interpreted symbolically, and that they refer, not to bodily actions, but to *yogic* practices. Though much can be said on both sides of the question, which is a vitally important one, there is no doubt that the practical consequences of Nyin-ma literalism were frequently disastrous. Immorality was provided not only with an excuse but with a philosophy; the age-old tradition of sacerdotal celibacy was discontinued, the monk degenerated into a householder, and Buddhism in general and the performance of Tantric rites in particular, began to be utilized, not as a method of gaining Enlightenment, but as a means of supporting a family.

The other two *ācāryas,* Vajrabodhi and his disciple Amoghavajra, are almost as important for the history of Chinese as Padmasambhava is for the history of Tibetan Buddhism. Vajrabodhi was a South Indian Brahmin, while Amoghavajra is reported to have been a native of Ceylon. Together they arrived in China from the extreme south of India, perhaps from Malabar, in the year 719 A.D. Vajrabodhi died in 730, having translated several Tantras and *Dhāraṇis* into Chinese. His work was continued by Amoghavajra, who after his master's death spent several years in India and Ceylon collecting texts of the various Tantras, laden with which he eventually returned to China in 746. Until his death in 774 he was engaged in making translations, no less than 108 of which, mostly Tantric in character, have found a place in the Chinese *Tripiṭaka.* Amoghavajra's influence at Court was great, and it was he who, under Imperial patronage, was responsible for the introduction of the annual rites for the dead, which later became one of the most popular Chinese Buddhist festivals. The school which Vajrabodhi and Amoghavajra founded, and of which they are reckoned the first and second patriarchs, was known both as the Chên Yen Tsung, or "True Word" (*Mantra*) School, and as the Ni Chiao Tsung, or School of the Secret Teaching. The fourth patriarch, Hui Kuo, had for his disciple the brilliantly gifted Japanese monk Kobo Daishi, who in the year 806 introduced the school into Japan, where it became known as the Shingon Shu, the Japanese equivalent of Chên Yen Tsung. Next to Tibet and its cultural dependencies, Japan is today the most important centre of Tantric Buddhism, the Shingon Shu never having lost its position as one of the largest and most influential of the Japanese Buddhist schools. Owing to the inherent decorum of the Far Eastern followers of the school, the Tantra shed much of its sexual symbolism, with the result that in China and Japan its teachings were in this respect less exposed to misinterpretation than elsewhere.

Before bringing this section to a close mention should be made of the four main sub-schools into which, it is said, the original Indian Tantric tradition was divided. These are known respectively as the Mantrayāna, the Vajrayāna, the Kālacakrayāna, and the Sahajayāna. Perhaps it would be more accurate to describe these divisions not as sub-schools of the Tantra but as the successive phases of its development. The term Mantrayāna seems to have owed its origin to the necessity of distinguishing that branch of the Mahayana which advocated the repetition of the *mantras* as the principal means to Enlightenment from that which continued to emphasize the practice of the *pāramitās.* "This . . . Mantra-yāna school of Mahāyāna," says Shashi Bhusan

Dasgupta, "seems to be the introductory stage of Tantric Buddhism from which all the other offshoots of Vajra-yāna, Kālacakra-yāna, Sahaja-yāna, etc., arose in later times."[1] Nevertheless, as was the case with the Chinese and Japanese branches of the Tantra, the term Mantrayāna continued in use as a collective designation not only for the introductory but also for the later stages of the Tantric movement, and as such is sometimes employed today.

The Vajrayāna is the stage of full development, wherein what formerly were kindred tendencies converge into definite lines of thought and action, and wherein a multitude of seemingly discordant doctrines and methods are knit together in a complex but well ordered and coherent system: it is the norm of the Tantra. Vajra, literally the thunderbolt or diamond, is the most widely current Tantric synonym for *Śūnyatā.* Thus the term Vajrayāna connotes the vehicle, or *yāna,* by means of which one attains Enlightenment. This interpretation is confirmed by Indrabhūti, the royal *siddhācārya,* who says, "He who mounts the Vajrayāna will go to the other shore of the great ocean of this world of relativity, which is full of the currents of thought-constructions."[2] The theoretical basis of the Tantra is, however, as demonstrated in the foregoing section, a conception of existence according to which Reality is not only transcendent to phenomena but immanent in them. Absolute Mind, as by this time we need hardly insist, is reflected in all things, just as all things are reflected in Absolute Mind. To intensify their awareness of this truth the Vajrayānists prefixed the synonym *vajra* not only to their particular method of gaining Enlightenment but to every one of its accessories. Thus the spiritual teacher was the *vajrācārya,* the bell rung by the worshipper the *vajraghaṇṭā,* the meditation posture the *vajrāsana,* and so on. By employing the material and other accessories of the *sādhana* sacramentally, that is to say, with full consciousness of their transcendental significance as indicated by the *vajra* prefix, a *sādhaka* could, the Vajrayāna held, realize his own essentially transcendental nature, take possession of a transcendental body (*vajrakāya*), and be transformed into a transcendental being

---

[1] *An Introduction to Tantric Buddhism* (Calcutta, 1950), pp. 60-61.
[2] *Jñānasiddhi,* XI, 8.

(*Vajrasattva*). Among these accessories was included sexual intercourse with a virgin, technically known as the *vajrakanyā*. This important extension of Vajrayāna method, according to which awareness of the transcendental "correspondents" of the passions transformed them from hindrances into helps to the attainment of Vajrabodhi, will again engage our attention in the following section.

How the Kālacakrayāna ever came to be regarded as representing a distinct stage in the development of the Tantra, much less still a separate sub-school, in the present stage of our knowledge is far from clear. According to Shashi Bhusan Dasgupta, the only distinctive feature of the *Kālacakra Tantra*—the sole known representative of its class—is its emphasis on the control of the vital airs (*prāṇa* and *apāna*) and the results obtainable therefrom, and the texts he cites prove conclusively that the term *Kāla-cakra,* literally "Wheel of Time," is synonymous with *prajñā-upāya,* or that inseparable unity of Wisdom and Compassion which constitutes the essence of Enlightenment and at the realization of which the Vajrayāna aims.[1] Upon the Tantra, as upon every other school, there gradually came to be exerted that "gravitational pull" of literal-minded interpretation of which we have spoken before. Sacramentalism degenerated into ritualism in the derogatory sense of the term; the Tantric rites were performed mechanically, that is to say, without the performer being aware of their transcendental significance.

Against this degeneration the Sahajayāna seems to have been the protest. Sahaja means what is natural or innate, as opposed to what is artificial or acquired, and the Sahajayāna is so called, firstly because it seeks to realize the true innate nature of the self and things, and secondly because it believes that the best method of so doing consists not in obstructing but in following the ordinary course of human nature. Hence,

> *The exponents of the Sahajiyā school put the whole emphasis on their protest against the formalities of life and religion. Truth is something which can never be found through mere austere practices of discipline, neither can it be realized through much reading and philosophising, nor through fasting, bathing, constructing images and worshipping gods and goddesses and the innumerable other paraphernalia of rites and rituals prescribed in Vajra-yāna; it is to be intuited*

[1] *An Introduction to Tantric Buddhism,* pp. 72-77.

within in the most unconventional way through the initiation in the Tattva *and the practice of yoga. This makes the position of the Sahajiyas distinct from that of the Vajrayanists in general.*[1]

Though we have spoken of the Sahajayāna as the protest against a literal-minded interpretation of the Tantra, where and in what circumstances that protest was first made none can at present tell. Perhaps it would be more correct to regard it as conterminous with the whole Tantric tradition. The Sahajayāna represents not so much a stage in the development of the Tantra as its persistent awareness of the purely instrumental function and relative validity of its own specific methods. Owing largely to this awareness the efficacy of those methods has remained unimpaired down to the present day.

XII. Some Special Features of the Tantra

When we first attempted, in Chapter II, Section V, to find an answer to the question, "What is Mahayana Buddhism?" we discovered that, in contradistinction to the Hinayana, its conception of Nirvana and the Way included not only negative but also positive elements. From this more balanced tradition developed the distinctively Mahayana doctrine—common to all its schools—that Enlightenment consists not in Wisdom merely, but in the inseparability of *Prajñā* or Wisdom (*Śūnyatā*) and *Karuṇā* or Compassion. The conjunction of these two was termed *bodhicitta,* or Enlightenment-Mind, to the "arising" (*utpāda*) of which the Mahayanists attached, as we shall see in the next chapter, unprecedented importance, regarding it as the axis upon which revolved the whole Bodhisattva career. Compassion represents not only the positive but also the dynamic aspect of Enlightenment. By means of Wisdom, in the limited sense of insight into the unreality of the self, one could, the Mahayanists conceded, attain the peace of Nirvana.

But this one-sidedly transcendental state of personal emancipation from the round of birth and death was not, they maintained, the highest goal of Buddhism. The highest goal was Supreme Enlightenment for the sake of all sentient beings. This was attainable by Transcendental Wisdom, that is to say, by

[1] *Ibid.,* p. 77.

insight not only into the egolessness of the self but also into the unsubstantiality of all things (*dharmas*) and the consequent unreality of the distinction between Nirvana and Samsara. By his attainment of this non-discriminating Wisdom, the Bodhisattva, instead of remaining like the Hinayana "Arahant" immersed in the quiescent state of Nirvana, liberates a purely transcendental force, the dynamic aspect of Wisdom, by means of which he is able, even after attaining Supreme Enlightenment, to live and act in the universe for the benefit of all sentient beings. This transcendental force is Compassion.

In Tantric Buddhism the static and dynamic aspects of Enlightenment are generally referred to as *Prajñā* and *Upāya.* The term *upāya* means "device." By a variation of the figure of speech called metonymy, in which the instrument is substituted for the agent of an action, the "device" by means of which Compassion endeavours to lead beings unto the Path to Supreme Enlightenment has become the term for Compassion itself.

On the one hand accepting as it did the doctrine of interpenetration as the theoretical basis of its teaching, and on the other asserting that Reality was both static and dynamic, the Tantra inevitably regarded phenomena as reflecting not merely Absolute Mind but *Prajñā* and *Upāya* in indissoluble union. The four main reflections of this "duality," all of which play an important part in Tantric sacramentalism, may be termed respectively the cosmic, the Buddhological, the individual and the social. All are embodiments, on one level of existence or another, of the primordial two-in-one-ness of Wisdom and Compassion.

The cosmic reflection is the fact that the whole universe is divided into two complementary constituents, a passive and mental "womb-element" (*garbha-dhātu*) and an active and material "diamond-element" (*vajra-dhātu*). This conception of a cosmic reflection of Wisdom-Compassion is the principal teaching of the system of Amoghavajra, now represented by the Shingon Shu. According to this system it is the two "elements" which, in an infinity of combinations, constitute what it calls the cosmic body of Mahāvairocana, or the Great Sun Buddha, Who is the presiding Transcendental Form of this branch of the Tantra.

What we have termed the Buddhological reflection of Wisdom-Compassion consists in the fact that, both in the texts and iconographically, the Buddhas, Bodhisattvas and other Transcendental Forms—Who, as we saw, are personifications of the different aspects of Reality or the various stages of the Path—are represented as locked in sexual embrace with their female counterparts. Obviously, if one regards the glorified human body as the most fitting symbol of Enlightenment, and if one wishes at the same time to stress the inseparableness of *Prajñā* and *Upāya* under this image, not only the most natural but also the best and most effective way of so doing is to depict a male figure, representing *Upāya,* embracing and embraced by a female figure, representing *Prajñā.* Certain writers, incidentally, wrongly superimposing upon the Buddhist Tantra some of the conceptions of its Hindu analogue, have referred to the female counterparts of the Buddhas and Bodhisattvas as *Śaktis,* or as Female Energies, which they are not; for the Buddhist Tantra adheres to the psychologically sounder view that the active element is embodied in the male sex. By visualizing and meditating upon these sexually united Transcendental Forms the Tantric *sādhaka* realizes the truth that Wisdom and Compassion, as the static and dynamic, transcendent and immanent, aspects of Reality, are inseparable, and thereby attains Supreme Enlightenment.

Prajñā and *Upāya* are reflected in the individual, or rather in his physical body, as *lalanā* and *rasanā,* the nerves flowing from the left and the right side, respectively, of the nasal orifice. By means of a certain highly esoteric yogic technique the subtle energies of which these nerves are the conductors can be made to unite in the median nerve, known as *avadhūtī.* This unification of psychophysical energies sets up, in accordance with the general Tantric principle of acting from without within, a series of reactions first on the mental, then on the superconscious, and finally on the transcendental plane, as a result of which all the hitherto latent potentialities of the individuality are galvanized and integrated into a single unimpeded thrust of energy which pierces through layer after layer of darkness into the Infinite Light beyond. The method of gaining Enlightenment by manipulating the reflection of *Prajñopāya* in the individual is one of the most complex, difficult and dangerous in the whole range of Tantric yoga; he who practises it without the personal guidance of a competent teacher risks insanity just as certainly as he who touches a live wire without rubber gloves courts instant electrocution.

The fourth, and from the long and bitter controversies it has occasioned, most important, reflection of Wisdom and Compassion, is that which, perhaps rather misleadingly, we have termed the social. By this we mean the reflection of these twin aspects of Enlightenment in the field of human relations as the act of copulation. So bold an application of the doctrine of interpenetration and its corollary, the doctrine of correspondence, demands a treatment somewhat fuller than that accorded the three previous reflections.

Even the most hidebound critics of the Tantra may eventually be brought to admit, however grudgingly, that the sexual symbolism of what we have termed the Buddhological reflection of *Prajñopāya,* is a vivid and effective, even if (in their own cultural *milieu*) unconventional, means of depicting the inseparableness of Wisdom and Compassion. But how many of them can be persuaded even to consider the possibility of the "sacramental" performance of the sexual act being conducive to the attainment of Enlightenment? How many of them, even those who style themselves scientists, are prepared impartially and open-mindedly to investigate the nature of the general principle which the practice so hotly denounced involves? Some, indeed, go as far as to assert that this phase of Tantric method represents not the application of any principle, however remotely connected with the teachings of what they uphold as genuine Buddhism, but rather a total abandonment of all moral and spiritual principles.

Such merely emotional reactions, which sometimes reach the point of hysteria, are symptomatic of a deeply rooted complex of the very kind that the sexual sacramentalism of the Tantra is meant to cure. For this aspect of Tantric teaching, besides being based on a definite, experimentally verifiable principle, is designed as a means of solving an important problem of spiritual dynamics. This problem relates to the difficulty, with which every aspirant to Enlightenment is familiar, of fully and effectively mobilizing for spiritual purposes the emotional energies in general and the sexual energies in particular. Why is it that our theoretical understanding and practical realization of the Dharma are so rarely commensurate? Because realization requires energy, and by far the greater part of the total available energy of our personalities is as it were dammed up within mundane, especially sexual, channels, where it circulates without ever being able to contribute to the total momentum of the spiritual life. As we have pointed out elsewhere,

> *The central problem of the spiritual life is . . . not static but dynamic, not so much a matter of the intellectual understanding of this or that doctrine as of the concentration of the total psychic energy of the individual—now dissipated in so many directions—along the line of its eventual realization. Since this energy is nothing but the energy of desire in the widest possible sense of the term, and since emotion is only the "long-circuiting" of desire, it is with the concentration and sublimation of desire and the reorientation of emotion that the spiritual life is above all else concerned.*'[1]

This concentration and sublimation of desire the Tantra seeks to bring about by means of sexual sacramentalism. Because the act involved is a sexual act the dissipated psycho-physical energies are concentrated; because it is a sacramental act, an act possessed of the highest transcendental significance, they are not merely concentrated but sublimated as well. But can desire be sublimated, and our problem in spiritual dynamics thereby solved, in this way? The question can be answered in the affirmative only if the Tantra is in fact based, as claimed, on a definite, experimentally verifiable, principle. We believe that it is so based, and that the principle concerned is nothing but the dynamic counterpart of the doctrine of correspondence. Interpenetration is a transcendental reality. As such, it can be only imperfectly represented under the categories of human thought. Two of the most important of these categories are space and time. The doctrine of correspondence, according to which objects belonging to the transcendental are reflected in objects belonging to the mundane order and *vice versa,* is the spatial and static reading of interpenetration. It is only half the truth. What we may term the doctrine of transmutation, according to which a mundane energy may be actually changed into the transcendental energy with which it is in correspondence, is the other half. It is the temporal dynamic reading of interpenetration. All *dharmas* are *Śūnyatā*. But *Śūnyatā* is inseparable from *Karuṇā*. All *dharmas* are therefore *Karuṇā*. Since *Karuṇā* represents the dynamic aspect of Reality, it must be conceded that all *dharmas* are nondual not only in respect of essence but also in respect of energy. This means that one form of energy is convertible into

[1] "The Good Friend," *Stepping-Stones,* Vol. II, p. 125 (September 1951).

another; sexual desire can be transmuted into an aspiration for Enlightenment.

Does the sexual sacramentalism of the Tantra require the literal performance of the sexual act, or are its injunctions to be understood metaphorically? Contrary to the view generally accepted, not only by modern scholars but also by certain Tantric schools, a literal, that is to say physical, indulgence in sexual intercourse is not required. Our authority for this statement is, of course, the Tantras themselves. Says Shashi Bhusan Dasgupta:—

> *In the* Hevajra-tantra *it is clearly explained how to produce the gross Bodhicitta [*i.e., *the seminal fluid] through the physical process and how to turn it to the* Vivṛta *form through the yogic process. Pleasure may also be realized through the discharge of the Bodhicitta, but that has unreservedly been condemned by all the Buddhist Tantrikas and it has been said that instead of delivering a man it binds him to the realm of gross sense-pleasure. It is, therefore, that we find in all the texts repeated warnings not to discharge the Bodhicitta; if it be discharged, the* Mahāsukha *is never realised, the ultimate Sahaja-nature cannot be realised, a man is not liberated from the world of illusion.*[1]

The same author cites a verse quoted by the *Marma-kalikā Tantra,* as well as by the commentary on the *Dohākoṣa* of Kāṇha-pāda, where it is ascribed to the *Ādi-buddha Tantra,* according to which "There is no greater sin than discharge and no greater merit than bliss (arising from the motionless Bodhicitta)." No less emphatic is the *Kālacakra Tantra,* which definitely declares that salvation cannot be obtained through seminal discharge, for which reason the *yogins* should always shun worldly pleasure.[2] Yet despite the fact that, as implied by the unequivocal declaration of the Tantras, the literal performance of the sexual act is not requisite to the sublimation of desire, we should not therefore conclude that their injunctions concerning the practice of sexual sacramentalism have only a metaphorical significance. They are no more metaphors than are the energies which the practice is meant to sublimate. The act enjoined is a literal act, but it is to be carried out not physically but mentally, that is to say imaginatively. A physical performance of the sexual act, even with full awareness of its transcendental import (supposing awareness to be possible in such circumstances), would be of no

[1] *An Introduction to Tantric Buddhism,* p. 130 note.
[2] *Ibid.*

use, for in order to be sublimated the seminal fluid must be retained. The sexual sacramentalism of the Tantra therefore consists, correctly practised, in the concentration of the emotional, particularly sexual, energies, by means of an imaginative representation of the sexual act, and their sublimation by means of meditation on the transcendental significance of the act, that is to say, on the realities with which it is in correspondence—the inseparably united Wisdom and Compassion.

XIII. Integral Buddhism

We have now reached the end of our survey of the four main schools of Mahayana Buddhism. More than a thousand years of doctrinal and methodological development, to which contributed a succession of *ācāryas* of unrivalled brilliance, have been reviewed in a hundred pages. Yet despite our constant telescoping of important historical movements, and our wholly inadequate handling of philosophical themes, we hope the treatment accorded each school has at least been sufficiently ample to show that our use of the Five Spiritual Faculties as a principle for the schematization of the Mahayana schools was not an arbitrary procedure but grounded on the facts of history and the realities of spiritual life. Each school is the development of a particular spiritual faculty, and the Mādhyamika and the Buddhism of Faith and Devotion, the Yogācāra and the Tantra, are historically interdependent because the corresponding spiritual faculties are psychologically interdependent. The fact that, in our individual spiritual life, Faith must be equilibrated with Wisdom, and Meditation with Vigour, means, in the extended context of the Mahayana schools, that following one school does not prevent us from following another. The four principal schools of the Mahayana are not mutually exclusive; they are a whole and must be studied and followed as a whole. Strange as the fact may seem to those unacquainted with what we have termed the transcendental unity of Buddhism, this is the procedure generally followed in Mahayana lands, especially in Tibet and China. Just as the intra-uterine development of the individual recapitulates the development of the race, so before he can issue from the womb of ignorance, and be born into the World of Enlightenment, the student of the Dharma must recapitulate in his spiritual life the history of Buddhism. By virtue of the equilibrating faculty of Mindfulness there must be equal provision for the culture of Faith, Wisdom, Meditation and Vigour. Otherwise the spiritual life will be unbalanced. What that life is, according to the Mahayana, will be seen in the next chapter when we deal with the Bodhisattva Ideal.

CHAPTER FOUR

THE BODHISATTVA IDEAL

I. The Unifying Factor

IN Chapter I Buddhism was compared to a tree. Refining upon this similitude, it may be said that the Buddha's transcendental realization is the root, His Original Doctrine—the "Basic Buddhism" of Chapter II—the trunk, the distinctive Mahayana doctrines the branches, and the schools and sub-schools of the Mahayana the flowers. Now the function of flowers, however beautiful, is to produce fruit. Philosophy, to be more than mere barren speculation, must find its reason and its fulfilment in a way of life; thought should lead to action—Doctrine give birth to Method. The Bodhisattva Ideal is the perfectly ripened fruit of the whole vast tree of Buddhism. Just as the fruit encloses the seed, so within the Bodhisattva Ideal are recombined all the different and sometimes seemingly divergent elements of the Mahayana.

When discussing the origins of the Mahayana we saw that, in contradistinction to the Hinayana, it was progressive, devotional, positive, not exclusively monastic, and above all altruistic. The Bodhisattva Ideal fully exemplifies every one of these characteristics. "Progressive" means, in this context, realization of the relative validity of all conceptual formulations of Truth, the instrumental function of all spiritual practices, together with the consequent readiness to adopt fresh formulations and devise variants of the old practices whenever changed historical or psychological conditions call for a slightly different method of arriving at the same goal. *Upāya,* the seventh *pāramitā,* technically the device by means of which the Bodhisattva leads beings on the Path to Enlightenment, embodies this characteristic. As for the devotional content of the Bodhisattva Ideal, the Bodhisattva is not only himself the supreme exemplar of the devotional life; he is at the same time the highest object of devotion to the Mahayana devotee. Even as the New Moon, we are told, is worshipped in preference to the Full Moon, so are the Bodhisattvas worshipped more than the Buddhas. Again, the Bodhisattva Ideal is positive. Here "positive" means doing good rather than merely eschewing evil. Inasmuch as the Bodhisattva aims at attaining for all beings nothing less than the highest good, Enlightenment, his life is the most positive imaginable. Moreover the Bodhisattva Ideal is not exclusively monastic, for as we have already had occasion to point out, it can be followed not by the monk only but also by the layman. Finally, the Bodhisattva Ideal is altruistic. It is in fact altruism itself on the highest plane and the grandest scale. The Bodhisattva does much more than indulge in the pious hope that all beings may eventually be saved. He is prepared to sacrifice his life and limbs for others, to spend ages in torment if thereby he can help even a single creature to advance so much as one step along the path of Emancipation.

Besides exemplifying the general characteristics of the Mahayana, the Bodhisattva Ideal represents the perfect equilibrium of those four spiritual faculties which, inasmuch as it was their development which led to the formation of the Mahayana schools, as explained in Chapter III, also constitute the basis for the schematization of these schools. In the life of the Bodhisattva these four faculties are held in equilibrium because Faith and Wisdom, Meditation and Vigour, have all been developed to the fullest possible extent. As the *Prajñāpāramitā Sūtras*, the Scriptures of Perfect Wisdom, so often remind us, the transcendental archetypes of the intellectual and emotional elements of spiritual life—that is to say, Wisdom and Compassion—must be cultivated simultaneously. In one of the most famous of these texts the Buddha exhorts Subhuti:—

"One who has set out on the career of a Bodhisattva should reflect in such a wise: 'As many beings as there are in the universe of beings comprehended under the term "beings,"—egg-born, or born from a womb, or moisture-born, or miraculously born, with or without form, with perception, without perception, with neither perception nor non-perception,—as far as any conceivable universe of beings is conceived; all these I should lead to Nirvana, into the realm of Nirvana which leaves nothing behind.' But, although innumerable beings have thus been led to Nirvana, no being at all has been led to Nirvana. And why? If in a Bodhisattva the perception of a 'being' should take place he would not be called a 'Bodhi-being.' He is not to be called a 'Bodhi-being,' in whom the perception of a being should

take place or the perception of a living soul, or the perception of a person."
(Vajracchedikā, *VI. Conze's translation*)[1]

Out of Compassion the Bodhisattva aspires to emancipate all beings; by means of Wisdom he realizes that in truth no beings exist. Far from stultifying each other, these seemingly contradictory attitudes are interdependent, and must be cultivated simultaneously; for the Bodhisattva courses in a realm transcending logic. As with the emotional and intellectual, so with the static and dynamic, faculties. In the language of Jung's psychology, the Bodhisattva is both introvert and extrovert. He looks both within and without. External activities do not for him preclude internal calm and recollection, neither do his indefatigable exertions on behalf of all sentient beings prevent him from enjoying uninterruptedly perfect peace of mind. In the beautiful words of the *Ratnagotravibhāga*:—

Like a fire his mind constantly blazes up into works for others:
At the same time he always remains merged in the calm of the trances and formless attainments.
(Ratnagotravibhāga, *I. 73 Conze's translation*)[2]

Since we not only find that in the Bodhisattva all the general characteristics of the Mahayana are, as it were, in full bloom, but also that he holds in perfect equilibrium the four spiritual faculties in their highest possible state of development, it is but natural that the Bodhisattva Ideal should constitute, under one or another of its numerous guises, the practical or methodological aspect not merely of the Mahayana in general but individually of each and every one of the four main Mahayana schools, together with all their respective offshoots. Whether he studies the treatises of Nagarjuna or invokes the name of Amitabha Buddha, whether he sees with Rāvaṇa that the world is nothing but his own Mind or sings with Sarahapāda that Samsara and Nirvana are one, it is upon the glorious figure of the infinitely wise and boundlessly compassionate Bodhisattva that the eyes of the Mahayana devotee eventually come to rest. Just as the doctrine of universal conditionality, in one formulation or another, constitutes their theoretical aspect, so does the Bodhisattva Ideal

[1] *Buddhist Texts,* pp. 172-73.
[1] *Ibid.,* p. 130.

comprise the practical methodological aspect of all Mahayana schools. Doctrines and ideals can, of course, both function as unifying factors; but inasmuch as the heart of man is more profoundly moved and his conduct more powerfully influenced by the latter than by the former, it is the Bodhisattva Ideal which, for practical purposes at least, must be recognized as the unifying factor *par excellence.* Even the Hinayana schools, for all their individualism, could not altogether escape the influence of a way of life which, as their own scriptures affirm, the Lord Buddha had Himself followed in hundreds of births. The Sarvastivadins went so far as to maintain that, according to temperament, the devotee could either emulate the Master and pursue the Bodhisattva Path to Supreme Enlightenment, or imitate His disciples and attain the self-liberation of the Arahant—a point of view which modern Theravadins have shown an increasingly pronounced tendency to adopt. Thus the Bodhisattva Ideal is the principal unifying factor not only for the Mahayana schools but for the entire Buddhist tradition. As Lama Anagarika Govinda, after quoting the most common Pali formula of the Bodhisattva vow, very pertinently remarks:—

> *This ideal, which indeed deserves the name Mahāyāna, the great vehicle or the great, all-embracing way, is the living bridge between the Schools of "Northern" and "Southern" Buddhism. It is not at all the exclusive privilege of the so-called Northern Schools which, in spite of vast differences among themselves, have been classified under the general term "Mahayana," but it is something which each individual has to decide for himself.*
>
> *In other words: the Bodhisattva Ideal is not a dividing but a* uniting *factor in Buddhist life and thought. It has kept the widely divergent Schools of Northern Buddhism together, and it will remain the bond which will unite them with the traditions of the South.*[1]

If, therefore, we wish to transcend the intellectual barriers which seemingly separate school from school and *yāna* from *yāna* and know the heart, the essence of Buddhism as an integrated whole, we should contemplate their highest common factor, the Bodhisattva Ideal.

We should, however, take heed to contemplate it not in the abstract but in the concrete. The practice of *mettā-bhāvanā,* to cite an instructive parallel case of misunderstanding, consists not in

---

[1] "Origins of the Bodhisattva Ideal." *Stepping-Stones,* Vol. II, p. 245 (January 1952).

thinking of oneself as expanding the feeling of love until it becomes all-embracing but in expanding the actual feeling of love itself—a subtle but supremely important distinction. Similarly, the contemplation of the Bodhisattva Ideal, by definition the brightest facet of the Dharma under its aspect of Method, means the contemplation of the Bodhisattva's life, rather than the study of the doctrinal implications of his life. Flame is lit from flame, and ultimately life's inspiration springs not from theories about life but from life itself. The *Jātakas* and *Avadānas* are the basic scriptures of the Bodhisattva Ideal because instead of merely arousing our interest with a dissertation on the Bodhisattva doctrine they inspire us by showing, with shattering simplicity and truth, how the Bodhisattva actually lives, how not in one life only but through hundreds of lives he sweats and suffers for the ultimate good of all sentient beings. Small wonder, then, is it that, in the essay already quoted, Lama Anagarika Govinda should write,

> *The Jātakas are the divine song of the Bodhisattva ideal in a form which speaks directly to the human heart and which, therefore, is not only understandable to the wise but even to the simplest mind. Only the all-too-clever will smile at them indulgently. Up to the present day the Jātakas have not lost their human appeal and continue to exert a deep influence upon the religious life in all Buddhist countries. In Ceylon, Burma, Siam, and Cambodia crowds of people listen with rapt attention for hours when Bhikkhus during the full-moon nights recite the stories of the Buddha's former lives, and even in Tibet I have seen tears in the eyes of sturdy caravan men, when sitting around the camp-fire the Bodhisattva's suffering and sacrifices were retold. For these people the Jātakas are not literature or "folklore" but something that happens in their very presence and profoundly affects their own life. Something that moves them to the core of their being, because it is ever-present reality to them.*[1]

To be moved in this way one must read the *Jātakas* as one reads poetry, that is to say with a "willing suspension of disbelief" in whatever one on merely intellectual grounds is unable to accept. The beauty of Milton's Paradise moves us regardless of whether we accept or do not accept the Biblical account of creation. In the *Vessantara Jātaka,* one of the best known and most widely appreciated of all stories of the Buddha's previous births, Prince Vessantara, in fulfilment of his vow to give whatever he is asked to give, not only surrenders the palladium of his

[1] *Ibid.,* p. 244.

father's kingdom but even his own wife and children. Here the question of whether Vessantara had the right to dispose of his wife and children in this manner is irrelevant. The purpose of this *jātaka* is not to assert that a man's family is a species of movable property, to be given away or sold at will; its purpose is to show that absolute non-attachment to worldly things is an integral part of the Bodhisattva Ideal. In another *jātaka* the Bodhisattva sacrifices his body for the sake of a starving tigress who is unable to nourish her young. Human life is not less valuable than animal life. The *jātaka* inculcates absolute self-abnegation. Commenting on this episode, the deeply perceptive author of the essay already quoted says:—

> *To the modern man such a story may appear unreasonable and exaggerated . . . because he judges from a purely intellectual,* i.e., *external, point of view, according to which the sacrifice appears to be out of proportion to its cause. The preservation—or rather prolongation—of the life of some wild beasts does not seem to be worth the sacrifice of a human life.*
>
> *The Buddhist, however, sees this story in quite a different light. To him it is not the factual or objective reality that matters, but the motive, the power of compassion, which caused the Bodhisattva to act in this way, irrespective of external consequences. The spiritual and symbolical meaning of this deed goes far beyond the frame of its apparent cause.*
>
> *That the lives of the tigress and her cubs are saved, is not of such fundamental importance as that the Bodhisattva experiences within himself their suffering and despair in all its terrible reality, and that he proves by his deed that there is no more difference for him between his own suffering and the suffering of others.*
>
> *In his supreme sacrifice he overcomes the illusion of his own self, and thus he lays the foundation for his later Buddhahood.*[1]

If the modern man fails to be moved by the *jātakas* it is because he regards their picture of the Bodhisattva's life not as an ideal to be followed but as a doctrine with which one may agree or disagree on purely theoretical grounds. Seizing the letter, he misses the spirit of the Teaching. A Bodhisattva doctrine, in the sense of a conceptual formulation of the Bodhisattva's spiritual attitude, does indeed exist; but this doctrine, like all the doctrines of Buddhism, has a strictly pragmatic value: its function is to facilitate the realization of the Ideal. Though in the pages which follow, the expository nature of the present work will oblige us to discuss the Bodhisattva Ideal in terms of the Bodhisattva Doctrine, it should not for one moment be forgot-

[1] *Ibid.*, pp. 243-44.

ten that here our primary concern is not with the Doctrine but with the Ideal, and that even as the striking together of flint and steel has but one purpose, to produce a spark, so intellectual discussion has only one aim, the generation of the flame of transcendental life.

II. The Bodhisattva *versus* the Arahant

The essence of the Bodhisattva Ideal consists in the vow to attain Enlightenment not for oneself alone, but for the sake of liberating all sentient beings. As he contemplates this sublime Ideal, the heart of the devotee responds like a gong that has been struck. This response is of two kinds. The first, which may be termed the active or masculine response, consists in determining to become a Bodhisattva oneself and to take part in the great work of universal emancipation. The second, the passive or feminine response, consists in resolving to have complete faith in the power of the Bodhisattva's vow and to allow oneself to be saved by him. These two responses or reactions of the devotee when confronted by the Bodhisattva Ideal form the psychological basis of what Nagarjuna terms the "difficult path" and the "easy path." In the Hinayana, the distinction is between the Buddha, Who as emphasized in Chapter I is the Discoverer and Revealer of the Way, and His disciples, for whom "things are rooted in the Exalted One"—an oft-recurring phrase—and who, after "hearing" the Teaching from Him follow in His footsteps. In the Mahayana the distinction is between the Bodhisattva (or Bodhisattvas: the Ideal is singular only in the abstract) who out of compassion vows to establish a Pure Land and liberate all beings, and those who by virtue of their faith in him are reborn into that Pure Land. On the one hand we have the Teacher and the taught; on the other, the Saviour and the saved. But though this difference of function between the Buddha and the Bodhisattva gives rise to two different methods, one active, the other passive, the Goal of these methods is the same. The relation between The Enlightened and the unenlightened, since it involves transcendental realities, is ineffable. The "difference" between the two *yānas* really amounts to this: that whereas the Hinayana indicates the relation by means of concepts derived from the human and historical order, the Mahayana does so with the help of symbols belonging to the supra-historical realm of cosmic myth. Since in Chapter III, Section III, we have already dealt with the passive, devotional response to the Bodhisattva Ideal as represented by the second of the four great Mahayana schools, the School of Faith and Devotion, we intend for the rest of this chapter to continue the vigorous and self-reliant emphasis of the Original Teaching by confining ourselves to the active and gnostic modality of the Bodhisattva's career.

This career is described in a number of works, the earliest of which are the *Buddhavaṁsa* and the *Mahāvastu Avadāna.* The first of these texts belongs to the Theravadin *Sutta-Pitaka,* where it forms part of the *Khuddaka-Nikāya,* a collection of miscellaneous texts which includes the *Dhammapada* and the *Jātakas*; it describes the ten *pāramitās,* the eight qualities of a Buddha, and the Bodhisattva's decision to postpone his entry into Nirvana. The second text, which is much longer and more important, belongs to the Mahasanghikas; unlike the *Buddhavaṁsa* it describes the ten stages of the Bodhisattva's career.

Between these two texts and later Mahayana works such as the *Daśabhūmika Sūtra* and the *Bodhisattvabhūmi* (a portion of Maitreya's *Yogācārabhūmi Śāstra*) there is, so far as what may be called the general architectonic of the Bodhisattva's career is concerned, no essential difference. In both earlier and later works the Bodhisattva is represented as bent on the attainment not of individual but of universal Enlightenment, as practising certain perfections or *pāramitās* in an enormous number of successive births, and as passing through a series of stages (*bhūmi*) of spiritual progress. Differences regarding the number and order of the *bhūmis* apart, the later works are simply more detailed, systematic and comprehensive. The great dispute which for centuries raged between the Hinayana and the Mahayana was concerned not with the nature of the Bodhisattva Ideal, on which both parties were in basic agreement, but with the extent of its applicability. In the *Buddhavaṁsa* and the *Mahāvastu* the career set forth is merely that of Gautama Buddha in His previous births. Nowhere is it suggested that it constitutes an ideal to be followed by the ordinary Buddhist. Since there can be only one Supreme Buddha at a time there will be only one Bodhisattva. For the disciple is prescribed the Arahant Ideal. In the *Daśabhūmika* and the *Yogācārabhūmi,* as well as in all later Mahayana works, the Bodhisattva Ideal is on the contrary a universal ideal, to be followed according to their respective capacities by all Buddhists, whether monk or lay, male or female. Even those following the Arahant and Pratyekabuddha ideals will eventually find their paths broadening out into the One Supreme Way, the Way of the Bodhisattva. The inferior ideals are preached only as expedients.

As we saw in Chapter II, Section IV, the Mahayanists stressed the universality of the Bodhisattva Ideal in order to counteract the exaggerated and one-sided individualism of the Hinayana. Yet as demonstrated in Chapter I, Section XVIII, the Arahant Ideal preached by the Buddha Himself, though less explicitly endowed with the positive attributes of altruism than the Bodhisattva Ideal, was the antithesis of that spiritual selfishness with which it was later on to be confounded. The problem is at bottom one of language. According to the best traditions of all schools, the essence of the transcendental life consists not in making any addition to the self, even of attainments supposedly of the transcendental order, but simply in realizing that in the absolute sense the self is unreal: the true attainment is a no-attainment. At the same time, all schools were aware of the necessity for communication. But language, the usual medium of communication, is based upon the subject-predicate relation, and an "experience" which transcends the distinction between subject and object by realizing their unreality obviously cannot be expressed in terms of such a relation without undergoing serious distortions. The Original Teaching therefore asserts, on the one hand that the disciple should practise ethics, meditate, develop Wisdom, and attain Nirvana; on the other, that there is in reality no "I" to do any of those things. A merely theoretical knowledge of the unreality of the self, without practice of the Threefold Path, is of course useless. But practice of the Threefold Path without understanding that in reality no one practises or attains anything, is positively dangerous. For in the absence of such an understanding Morality, Meditation and (the conceptual formulations of) Wisdom instead of diminishing the sense of separate individuality will augment it, so that the Means to Enlightenment itself will be converted into an obstacle to the attainment of the Transcendental Path. One must therefore cultivate a double, indeed from the intellectual point of view a contradictory, attitude: "I will practise the Threefold Path to the fullest possible extent," yet "No 'I' exists." Such, so far as we can judge from later documentary evidence, seems to have been the Buddha's own position.

But in the centuries immediately succeeding the Parinirvana the doctrine that Nirvana was in reality not a personal gain was little by little forgotten, and in the hands of certain groups of monks the Arahant Ideal of the Original Teaching developed, or rather degenerated, into pseudo-spiritual Hinayana individualism. It was really against this misinterpretation of the Original Teaching, not against the Original Teaching itself, that the Mahayanists inveighed. Even the Hinayanists, however, despite the fact that they had reduced the goal of the spiritual life to mere individual enlightenment, either with or without the omniscience of a Buddha, had not been able to ignore the irreducible fact that the goal of the Buddha's own career had been Supreme Enlightenment for the sake of all sentient beings. In order to accommodate both ideals they had formulated the doctrine of the three *yānas,* according to which individual enlightenment, with or without omniscience (*i.e.,* the Pratyekabuddha and Arahant ideals), and universal enlightenment (*i.e.,* the Bodhisattva Ideal), were as goals of the spiritual life both valid—one for the vast majority, the other for the very, very few. The Mahayana protest, which so far as expression is concerned was in part conditioned by the nature of the historical context in which it was made, took the form of saying that, following the example of the Buddha Himself, every Buddhist should take the Bodhisattva vow of attaining Supreme Enlightenment for the sake of all sentient beings. But, as the *Vajracchedikā* for instance makes perfectly clear, at the same time as in the protest against Hinayana individualism they exhorted the disciple to deliver all sentient beings, the Mahayanists declared that in reality no sentient beings exist. Whereas the Original Teaching starts from the "self," the Mahayana starts from the "non-self." The Original Teaching, while exhorting the disciple to deliver himself, warns him that in reality there is no self to be delivered. In the same spirit does the Mahayana, though exhorting the novice Bodhisattva to save others, ask him to remember that there are no others to be saved. The purpose of both teachings is to make sure that the practice of the Dharma functions not as a hindrance but as a help to the attainment of the Transcendental Path. Both therefore insist upon a combination of Doctrine and Method, upon a simultaneous observance of the Absolute Truth and the relative truth. So far as the goal of the spiritual life is concerned, the only difference between the Mahayana and the Original Teaching lies in their opposite points of departure, and even this difference is due as much to the nature of the circumstances under which the Mahayana protest against Hinayana individualism was originally made as to the Mahayana's own distinctive character.

Language being mundane, and all mundane things being subject to a gravitational pull, it is not to be supposed that the conceptual formulations of the Mahayana are any more immune from misinterpretation than those of the Original Teaching. Should the unreality of the self be forgotten, the Arahant Ideal degenerates into spiritual individualism; similarly, as soon as the unreality of others is lost sight of, the Bodhisattva Ideal disintegrates into mere profane humanitarian sentiment. Divorced from Doctrine, and thus bereft of transcendental content and orientation, Method in both cases collapses into a mere conventional religiosity which strengthens rather than weakens one's attachment to the illusion of "self" and "others."

On the whole, however, though both are equally liable to misinterpretation, the Bodhisattva Ideal is to be preferred to that of the Arahant. Besides being a more positive formulation of the transcendental life, it differs from the Hinayana and agrees with the Original Teaching in emphasizing that, as the *Satipaṭṭhāna* and the *Saddharma Puṇḍarīka* both teach, there is in reality but one Way to Nirvana. As understood by the Hinayana, neither the Sravakayana nor the Pratyekabuddhayana can lead to Enlightenment. For, since there is in reality no individuality, there can be in the absolute sense no such thing as individual emancipation. The choice between what *The Voice of the Silence* calls "the Open Path," the Path of the Arahant, and "the Secret Path," the Path of the Bodhisattva, represents not an opportunity of choosing between two real alternatives but simply the temptation of thinking that Nirvana, or for the matter of that any transcendental attainment, can be in reality a personal gain. For those who, succumbing to the temptation, resolve to pursue

Nirvana can only be for all
no boundaries to self in that state

"the Open Path" of individual enlightenment further spiritual progress is in fact barred. Later Mahayana texts therefore treat the Arahant, the Pratyekabuddha and the Bodhisattva ideals as pertaining to the successive stages of the One Path. Pseudo-spiritual individualism can conduct us only part of the way. Sooner or later, should we really wish to advance, a different "choice" must be made.

Compassion speaks and saith: "Can there be bliss when all that lives must suffer? Shalt thou be saved and hear the whole world cry?"[1]

From the Mahayana point of view the doctrine of the two Paths is not designed to assert that two such paths actually exist, much less still that the attainment of individual enlightenment is really possible, but simply to exhibit the kind of compassion the Bodhisattva should possess. The Open Path is a spiritual *cul-de-sac.* Once again, remembering that the Bodhisattva represents not a doctrine but an ideal, one should take not the letter but the spirit of the Teaching.

III. The Path of the Bodhisattva: Preliminary Devotional Practices

Strictly speaking, the Path of the Bodhisattva consists primarily in the practice of the Six (or Ten) Perfections (*pāramitās*), the successful accomplishment of which carries him through ten successive stages (*bhūmis*) of spiritual attainment. So great, however, is the discrepancy between our ability to understand a spiritual teaching and our power to practise it, that most of those who give theoretical assent to the superiority of the Secret Path are unprepared for the practice even of the first *pāramitā.* Between the life of worldly or of "spiritual" individualism, on the one hand, and the Transcendental Path of the Bodhisattva on the other, the Mahayana therefore interpolates a number of observances, the purpose of which is to prepare the mind of the Bodhisattva—or rather, of the Bodhisattva-to-be—for the practice of the Six or Ten Perfections. Taking the Bodhisattva Path in its very widest sense, we find that, including these observances, it can be divided into three great stages (not to be confused with the ten *bhūmis* already mentioned, which correspond to the

---

[1] *The Voice of the Silence,* p. 78.

pāramitās). These stages are: (1) The preliminary devotional practices known collectively as *anuttara-pūjā* or Supreme Worship; (2) the rising of the Thought of Enlightenment (*bodhicitta-utpāda*), the making of a great Vow (*praṇidhāna*), and the receiving of an Assurance of Enlightenment (*vyākaraṇa*) from a living Buddha; (3) the four *caryās* or courses of conduct, the third and most important of which is the Practice of the Perfections (*pāramitā-caryā*). Before attempting to describe the Six or Ten Perfections, that is to say, the Bodhisattva Path proper, it will be our duty to give a brief account of the two preceding stages, that is to say, the stage of Supreme Worship and the stage of producing the Thought of Enlightenment.

By Supreme Worship is meant not only the adoption of a reverential attitude of mind, but the celebration by the aspirant to Bodhisattvahood of a sort of daily office. Our chief literary source for the details of this practice is the second chapter of Santideva's sublime canticle the *Bodhicaryāvatāra,* a work of the seventh century. The practice itself, however, was an ancient one. In fact, like many other observances, it was part of the enormous body of doctrines and methods which the Mahayana had inherited from the Hinayana and assimilated to its own tradition. Flowers, lights and incense had been offered to the Buddha even during His lifetime; sins had been confessed to Him; Brahma Sahampatti had implored Him to turn the Wheel of the Dharma. On the basis of occurrences of this kind the Hinayana framed a simple daily office which is still recited, in its Pali form, by both monks and laymen in Theravada lands. Some of the formulæ used are as old as Buddhism itself. The use of the term *anuttara,* unsurpassed or supreme, for the Mahayana office, was perhaps intended to suggest a comparison with its more rudimentary Hinayana original. As described by Santideva, Supreme Worship comprises: (1) Obeisance (*vandanā*) and worship (*pūjā*); (2) going for refuge (*śaraṇā-gamana*); (3) confession of sins (*pāpa-deśanā*); (4) rejoicing in merit (*puṇyānumodanā*); (5) prayer (*adhyeṣaṇā*) and supplication (*yācanā*); and (6) transference of merits (*pariṇāmanā*) and self-surrender (*atma-bhāvādi-parityāgaḥ*).

(1) Like his Theravadin counterpart, the Bodhisattva generally recites his daily office before a Buddha-image of clay, wood, stone or metal, or even of jewels. This image is installed on the

altar of a temple or shrine, which may be either public or private. Generally speaking the tendency of the Mahayana has been to encourage every serious-minded monk and layman (all of whom are potential Bodhisattvas) to maintain a miniature personal shrine in a cabinet or on a shelf in either his own apartment or in the best room of the house. On entering the shrine the Bodhisattva-to-be makes his obeisance in such a manner that toes, elbows and head touch the ground simultaneously. A more strenuous form of obeisance is that in which the breast also touches the ground, so that the body of the devotee lies prostrate at the feet of the Enlightened One. This observance has an extremely wholesome effect. Besides crushing, or at least badly bruising, the natural pride of the devotee, it renders his mind receptive to spiritual influences. In all branches of Buddhism, therefore, making obeisance has become an integral part, not only of religious but even of social custom. When visiting a temple, a stupa or a Bodhi-tree the devotee, instead of gaping at them like a tourist, should pay his respects in the traditional manner. Books on Buddhism, since they represent the Dharma, the second of the Three Jewels, should be similarly honoured. On being handed a volume of the Scriptures, or a canonical text, the devotee should immediately place it upon his head. Such a work ought never to be carried under the arm, or allowed to touch the floor, or be laid on the table either face downwards or underneath books of a non-religious character. Corresponding precautions should also be taken with regard to pictures of the Lord Buddha. Laymen are required to make obeisance to all members of the Sangha, representing a third of the Three Jewels, as well as to mother and father, secular teachers and elders. With the exception of their own spiritual teachers, who may be either monks or laymen, members of the Sangha honour only those who are senior to them in respect of monastic ordination.

By means of observances of this kind, which in a traditional Buddhist society are performed in a perfectly natural manner, does the Mahayana endeavour to permeate the daily life of the devotee with a sense of reverence for sacred things, and therethrough with faith in the transcendental realities they represent, which is not only the starting-point but the permanent basis of his "career." In the Hinayana, however, the term *vandanā* covers not only obeisance but also recitation of the praises of the Buddha, the Dharma and the Sangha of the three times, that is to say, of past, present and future. This wider connotation is reflected in the Mahayana practice of reciting, either at this stage of the office or later, hymns of praise to various Buddhas and Bodhisattvas, many of which are extremely beautiful.

By the term *pūjā,* which originally meant only respect, is to be understood the making of offerings. These offerings are of two kinds, material and mental. Of the material offerings the most important are lights, incense, a piece of silk, various eatables, and a white conch-shell, each representing—though the symbols are by no means constant—one of the five faculties of sense. Flowers, fruits, water, uncooked grains and even money are also offered. Though in some branches of the Mahayana tradition the preparation of material offerings had perhaps become an unnecessarily long, elaborate, and even costly business, the principle behind this kind of *pūjā* is quite clear: the devotee consecrates his five senses to the attainment of Enlightenment. In the second kind of *pūjā* he goes a step farther and imagines himself as offering to the Buddha all manner of rare and precious things until, in the end, he offers Him the entire universe. In some branches of the Mahayana a symbolic representation of the universe, including the realms of the gods, is actually placed on the altar. By making such material and mental offerings the devotee expresses, and thus strengthens, his attitude of devotion towards the Buddha. Theravadin *pūjā* is much simpler: offering lights, flowers and incense, the devotee reflects that the Buddha is the Light of the Three Worlds, that the body is transitory, and that the perfume of virtue is most excellent. All other offerings are made with the request that the Buddha accept them out of compassion for the devotee.

(2) Going for refuge (*śaraṇā-gamana*) means, of course, going for refuge to the Buddha, the Dharma and the Sangha. While even a non-Buddhist can, in a sense, respect and honour the Triple Gem, to take refuge in Them is the prerogative of the professing and practising Buddhist alone. Formal refuge, which is held to constitute one a member of the Buddhist community, can be taken simply by repeating after any ordained monk the refuge-formulæ and the five precepts. But effective refuge, of which

the formal refuge is at once the expression and the symbol, can be taken only by one who has an understanding of the true nature of the Triple Gem. The deeper this understanding goes, the more effective will be his refuge. Taking refuge in the Triple Gem is not, therefore, an act to be done once and for all time, but something which grows with one's understanding of Buddhism. The refuge is complete when one's understanding of Buddhism is complete, that is to say, when one attains Enlightenment. Then, paradoxically enough, there is no going for refuge: the Enlightened One is His own refuge. Perhaps it is because of its awareness that going for refuge is a living, growing experience that the Mahayana has made it an integral part of the would-be Bodhisattva's daily office.

Though the minimum degree of understanding that would enable one to take effective refuge in the Triple Gem is naturally difficult to estimate, we may at least assert with confidence that the conviction that the Buddha has attained the Transcendental, that the Dharma is the means to the Transcendental, and that the members of the Sangha, by which is meant in this context the Arya Sangha, have gained the Transcendental Path, are indispensable elements of such refuge. One who denies, or even seriously doubts, the existence of such a state as Nirvana, or the possibility or desirability of its attainment, is naturally precluded from taking refuge in any of Them. The same may be said of those whose conception of the Triple Gem is positively erroneous. None can truly take refuge in the Buddha who holds Him to have been an *avatāra* of Vishnu, or in the Dharma who insists upon maintaining that the Buddha believed in the existence of a Creator God and an unchanging immortal ego-entity or soul (*attā*). Understanding the Triple Gem means understanding Them in accordance with tradition. One has not to take refuge in one's personal opinions.

The Mahayana having a deeper understanding of the Triple Gem than the Hinayana, the significance which it attaches to the act of taking refuge is naturally more profound. For the Mahayanist, taking refuge in the Buddha means taking refuge, not in His *Nirmāṇakāya* but in His *Dharmakāya*. Similarly, refuge in the Sangha means, not refuge in the Stream-Entrant, the Once-Returner, the Non-Returner and the Arahant, who for the Mahayana typify spiritual individualism, but in the Assembly of Bodhisattvas. It should be borne in mind, though, that such differences are due mainly to the Mahayana's attempt to restore the spirit of the Original Teaching. That this attempt necessitated at times the formal repudiation of certain doctrinal categories of the Original Teaching, is due to the fact that, as explained at length in Chapter II, those categories had been deprived by the Hinayana literalists of much of their significance. Perhaps the only real change to have been made consists in the addition, by the Tibetan branches of the Mahayana, of a fourth refuge, in the Lama or Guru.[1] Such doctrinal differences notwithstanding, all schools of Buddhism, whether of the Great or of the Little Vehicle, agree in recognizing the decisive importance in the Buddhist life of the act of taking refuge. Man being composed of body, speech and mind, the act of taking formal refuge, like that of making obeisance, is threefold, each of the refuge-formulæ being repeated thrice. In practically all Buddhist lands, taking the Three Refuges and Five Precepts takes precedence of all other religious acts. In the absence of this observance, no Buddhist function, whether public or private, can be considered complete. The Refuges are generally taken from a *bhikṣu,* after whom the devotee is made to repeat the refuge-formulæ. In the absence of a *bhikṣu,* a Buddhist assembly may be "led" in the taking of the Three Refuges by any senior lay devotee. A would-be Bodhisattva who, without being himself a *bhikṣu,* takes the Refuges as part of his daily office, may be considered as taking them directly from the Buddha.

(3) Confession of sins (*pāpa-deśanā*) is another observance which dates from the early days of Buddhism. In the *Vinaya Piṭaka* confession, in the technical sense of an avowal of one's fault before a brother monk, is the penalty attaching to two whole classes of offences, the so-called *Pāṭidesanīya* and *paccittīya*: the monk hearing the confession admonishes the culprit and asks him not to repeat the offence, and there the matter ends. Confessions of this kind are generally mutual, senior confessing to junior and junior to senior. In Theravadin lands monks who have been spending their "rainy season retreat" at the same monastery, or who for any other reason have been living togeth-

---

[1] The Lama is the first of the "esoteric" refuges, the other two being the Yidam and the *Ḍākiṇī.*

er, still honour the ancient custom of begging each other's pardon for any fault of which they might have been guilty during this period. Disciples taking leave of their masters recite a Pali stanza asking forgiveness for whatever sins they might have committed by means of body, speech or mind. Similar stanzas, this time addressed to the Buddha, are generally included in the Theravadin office as recited by both monks and laymen. In the face of these facts one can hardly assert, as some have done, that confession of sins is an observance unknown to the Hinayana. At the same time, one is constrained to admit that in modern Theravadin practice the confession of sins, like so many other observances, has contracted into an icy formalism from which even the faintest spark of genuine feeling has been excluded.[1] Faults are confessed, if they are confessed at all, with the knowledge that they will be committed again immediately afterwards. In practice this hardly differs from Roman Catholicism, though doctrinally the difference is immense, for the Theravadins, adhering to the iron law of karma in all its rigidity, have never suggested that the confession of one's sins was a means of escaping their natural consequences. What the Hinayana treats as a formality becomes in the Mahayana, however, a profound spiritual experience—a cry uttered from the very depths of a heart on fire with remorse. As Santideva passionately exclaims,

> *Whatsoever be the sin that I, poor brute, in my beginningless round of past births or in this birth have in my madness done or made others do or approved for my own undoing, I confess the transgression thereof, and am stricken with remorse. Whatsoever wrong I have done by sin against the Three Gems or father or mother or other elders by deed, word, or thought, whatever dire offence has been wrought by me, a sinner foul with many a stain, O Masters, I confess all. How may I escape from it? Speedily save me, lest death come too soon upon me ere my sins have faded away.*[2]

Perhaps only in certain forms of Protestant Christianity do we find a conviction of sin as intense as that which overwhelms the Buddhist poet. But the sin of which Santideva convicts himself is not, of course, original sin, but his own acts in this and other

---

[1] *Kamalāñjali,* a Pali devotional poem by the late WIDURAPOLA PIYATISSA MAHA NAYAKA THERA of Ceylon, is an outstanding exception.

[2] *The Path of Light.* By A.D. BARNETT (John Murray, London, 1947), pp. 41-42.

lives. Moreover, unlike the followers of certain evangelical sects, the Mahayana devotee does not confess his sins in front of an admiring audience, neither does he lay claim to the honour of being considered the greatest sinner who ever lived. He confesses to the Buddhas and Bodhisattvas, and the purpose of the confession is to make him aware of the terrible retribution which, under the law of karma, will inevitably overtake him in the next world. This awareness stimulates his spiritual endeavours and goads him into seeking the help of the members of the Transcendental Hierarchy. Though Buddhism has never encouraged a morbid preoccupation with sin, it certainly does insist that clear awareness of the unwholesome contents of one's own mind, a feeling of contrition for them, and a resolve to eliminate them, are indispensable preliminaries of the spiritual life. Confession of sins, as understood by the Mahayana, is the verbal expression of this attitude. Besides its psychological utility as a means of helping the devotee to

Cleanse the stuffed bosom of the perilous stuff
That weighs upon the heart,

the practice of *pāpa-deśanā* is in essence yet another of the methods whereby the Mahayana endeavours to orient his consciousness in the direction of Enlightenment.

(4) Rejoicing in merits (*puṇyānumodanā*) is in spirit very similar to *muditā-bhāvanā*, the third of the four *brahma-vihāras* described in Chapter I, Section XVII. But whereas *muditā* consists in rejoicing in the worldly prosperity and good fortune of others, *puṇyānumodanā* is the act of rejoicing in their spiritual attainments. Moreover, while clearly the first practice is prescribed as an antidote to jealousy, it is no less clear that the purpose of the second practice cannot be so explained. Only a person of very peculiar psychological constitution could ever feel jealous of the actual holiness of another.[1] Coming as *puṇyānumodanā* does immediately after *pāpa-deśanā*, this practice is rather designed to counteract any feeling of depression or despair into which the spectacle of the enormity of his offences might have plunged the devotee. Recollection of the good deeds of others, and of the exalted attainments of the Arahants, Bodhisattvas and Buddhas,

[1] *Cf.* Browning's "*A Soliloquy of the Spanish Cloister.*"

would serve to confirm his shaken, if not shattered, faith in the possibility of living a spiritual life here on earth. He would be reminded that however deep he might be sunk in the mire of worldly existence, the voices of Compassion were calling him, the arms of Compassion were outstretched towards him, and that with Their help he could eventually extricate himself and reach the Farther Shore. As the sight of the dazzling snow-peaks of the Himalaya encourages the mountaineer as he sets out from his base camp, or as the vision of the golden roofs of the Potala, gleaming through the mists afar off, inspires and strengthens the weary pilgrim to the Holy City of Lhasa, so does the contemplation of the monolithic splendour of the Buddhas and Their Sons uplift the heart of the Mahayana devotee. The way in which *puṇyānumodanā* is made to succeed *pāpa-deśanā* may incidentally be cited as a good example of the extremely balanced methods employed by the Great Vehicle for the spiritual welfare of its adherents.

(5) By prayer (*adhyeṣaṇā*) and supplication (*yācanā*) is meant not a petition for material blessings, or even for spiritual gifts if these are to be enjoyed by the petitioner alone, but the making of that same request with which, in the fifth week after His Supreme Victory, Brahma Sahampatti knelt at the feet of the Enlightened One—the request that for the benefit of all sentient beings He turn the Wheel of the Dharma. Taking a hint from an ancient tradition, mentioned in the *Mahāparinibbāṇa Sūtta's* account of the "last" days of the Buddha, that had He been so requested the Lord could have remained on earth until the end of the kalpa, the Mahayana devotee according to Santideva also implores the Enlightened Ones not to disappear into Parinirvana "lest the world become blind." From this observance we are not to conclude, however, that without such prayer and supplication either the Sakyamuni or any other Buddha in the universe would remain inactive. Compassion, the dynamic aspect of Wisdom, is spontaneous, springing up in all its fullness the instant Enlightenment is attained. Brahma Sahampatti's appeal was not the cause of the Buddha's compassion so much as the objective occasion for its descent into the world-system over which that deity was regarded as presiding. The Buddhas do not need to be reminded of Their duty. Prayer

and supplication are in reality a means of strengthening the devotee's own desire for the universal dissemination of the Means to Enlightenment. Obviously at this stage, when he is still in the midst of the preliminary devotional practices, it would be ridiculous for the devotee to express his own intention of preaching the Dharma to the universe. His ardent desire that to all sentient beings should be given an opportunity of hearing the Truth therefore takes the form of an appeal to the Enlightened Ones not to withdraw into the absolute quiescence of a purely transcendental state of individual emancipation but to remain out of compassion the everlastingly active saviours of mankind.

The observance is in fact from one point of view an affirmation of the Mahayana conception of Nirvana against that of the Hinayana. It may also be regarded as a reminder of what one who is unable personally to preach the Dharma may still do in the way of arranging for the publication of the Scriptures, the distribution of free Buddhist literature, and the delivery of lectures and discourses by those members of the Sangha who, even if they are not yet Buddhas, have at least advanced a few degrees farther along the Path than he has. Reduced to their simplest terms, *adhyeṣaṇā* and *yācanā* are enthusiasm for the propagation of the Dharma.

(6) With the transference (*pariṇāmanā*) of merits and self-surrender (*atmabhāvādi-parityāgaḥ*) is reached the climax of the preliminary devotional practices. By means of the five preceding observances the devotee has accumulated a certain amount of what is technically known as *puṇya*. Every willed act, bodily, vocal or mental, is the product of a certain result, the *vipāka*. In the case of acts proceeding from greed, anger and delusion, the result is painful; in the case of acts proceeding from contrary states of mind, pleasant. Neither the reward following "good" acts nor the retribution which overtakes "bad" ones is necessarily experienced at once. *Puṇya,* which is a popular rather than a philosophical conception, represents as it were the spiritual credits laid to the account of a good action until such time as karmic and other factors permit it to be "cashed" in the form of happiness either here on earth or in one of the celestial realms. In some Buddhist circles this conception tended to reduce the spiritual life to a species of bookkeeping,

the purpose of which was to ensure that, at the time of death, the devotee had to his credit a quantity of *puṇya* sufficient to purchase a happy rebirth.

Such crudely literal conceptions of *puṇya* were not uncommon in Ancient India. We read of a Jain ascetic who, upon deciding to return to lay life, actually sold the *puṇya* he had accumulated as a result of his austerities and with the proceeds set himself up in business. The Mahayanists were not slow in utilizing the very literalness of the conception as the means of its own undoing. *Puṇya* was, they agreed, a species of personal property; it could accumulate; it could balance expenditure in the form of sin; it could be sold. Also, like all personal property, it could be *given* away. The *puṇya* accruing from any good deed, such as building a temple or giving alms to the Sangha, could by an act of will be transferred to the account of any other person or group of persons. This dual conception of *puṇya,* individualistic yet non-individualistic, eventually gained wide currency and today the transfer (*pariṇāmanā*) of merits is a popular observance not only in Mahayana but even in Hinayana lands. But whereas in the latter it is generally treated as a means of showing affection for one's deceased relatives, in the former it is regarded as an adumbration on the mundane level of the loftiest spiritual ideal. In bringing his daily office to a conclusion by an act of altruism by which all the merits accruing from its performance are transferred to other beings, the Mahayana devotee in fact foreshadows that supreme act of transcendental altruism—the final renunciation of individual emancipation—with which he will eventually bring to a triumphant conclusion his career as a Bodhisattva.

Renunciation of "mine" is not possible, however, without renunciation of "me." The devotee is required to give up not only his possessions but himself. Together with the transfer of merits (*pariṇāmanā*) must go self-surrender (*atmabhāvādi-parityāgah*). The spirit which inspires the devotee as he concludes the preliminary devotional practices which will prepare him for the second great stage, the stage of taking the Thought of Enlightenment, has been voiced by Santideva in a passage of matchless beauty:—

Whatever Good I have acquired by doing all this, may I (by that Merit) appease and assuage all the pains and sorrows of all living beings!

May I be like unto a healing drug for the sick! May I be the physician for them, and also tend them till they are whole again!

May I allay the pain of hunger and thirst by showers of food and drink! And may I myself be food and drink (for the hungry and the thirsty) during the intermediate æon of famine!

May I be an inexhaustible treasure for poor creatures! May I be foremost in rendering service to them with manifold and various articles and requisites!

I renounce my bodies, my pleasures and all my Merit in the past, present and future, so that all beings may attain the Good: I have no desire (for all those things).

To give up everything, that is nirvāṇa. *If I must give up everything, then it is best to bestow it upon the living beings.*

I have devoted this body to the welfare of all creatures. They may revile me all the time or bespatter me with mud; they may play with my body and mock me and make sport of me; yea, they may even slay me. I have given my body to them: why should I think of all that?

They may make me do such things as bring happiness to them. May no one ever suffer any evil through me!

If they have any thoughts of anger or of friendliness towards me, may those very thoughts be the means of accomplishing all that they desire!

Those persons who revile me, or do me harm, or scoff at me, may they all attain Enlightenment!

May I be the protector of the helpless! May I be the guide of wayfarers! May I be like unto a boat, a bridge and a causeway for all who wish to cross (a stream)! May I be a lamp for all who need a lamp! May I be a bed for all who lack a bed! May I be a slave to all who want a slave! May I be for all creatures a cintāmaṇi *(the philosopher's stone) and a* bhadraghaṭa *(a vessel from which a lottery is drawn, a pot of fortune), even like unto an efficacious rite of worship and a potent medicinal herb! May I be for them a* Kalpa-vṛkṣa *(the wish-fulfilling tree) and a* kāma-dhenu *(the cow yielding all desires)!*

(Bodhicaryāvatāra, *III. 6-19. Har Dayal's translation)*[1]

IV. The Thought of Enlightenment

Attainment of Supreme Buddhahood apart, the Rising of the Thought of Enlightenment (*bodhi-citta-utpāda*) is the most important event that can occur in the life of a human being. As by the discovery of a priceless jewel a poor man becomes immensely rich, so with the Rising of the Thought of Enlightenment the devotee is transformed into a Bodhisattva. The Path of the Bodhisattva being for the Mahayana the supreme archetype of all spiritual paths whatever, the Rising of the Thought of Enlightenment, by means of which that Path is entered upon,

[1] *The Bodhisattva Doctrine in Buddhist Sanskrit Literature,* pp. 57-58.

may be regarded as corresponding to what on a lower level of experience appears as the phenomenon of religious conversion. Hence on the day on which this Thought arises in his mind the devotee rejoices that his birth has become fruitful, his human life a blessing; that he has been born into the race of the Enlightened Ones and is now Their son.

Bodhi in the present context means not *śrāvaka-bodhi* or *pratyeka-bodhi,* the principal objectives of the Hinayana, but *samyak-sambodhi* or Supreme Enlightenment, the one unique goal both of the Mahayana and the Original Teaching. The term *citta,* being derived from the root *cit,* meaning "to perceive, to form an idea in the mind, etc.," should be interpreted as "thought, idea." The compound *bodhi-citta* therefore means the thought or idea of Supreme Enlightenment. Its denotation is not metaphysical but psychological. Some have, however, endeavoured to interpret the *bodhi-citta* metaphysically as that reflection of Enlightenment which exists in the heart of every sentient being, thus identifying the *bodhi-citta* with *bodhi* itself. Though the existence of such a reflection, the *Tathāgata-dhātu* or Element of Buddhahood, is not to be denied, this does not mean that the *Tathāgata-dhātu* is to be confused with the *bodhi-citta.* Both are reflections of Enlightenment, but whereas the *Tathāgata-dhātu* is its reflection in the ontological, the *bodhi-citta* is its reflection in the epistemological, order.

Despite the psychological denotation of *bodhi-citta,* the Rising of the Thought of Enlightenment is much more than the act of forming in the mind a conception of the state of Supreme Enlightenment. The reader has already encountered the word Enlightenment some scores of times; he has understood it; he has even assented to the ideal it represents; but he has not taken the Thought of Enlightenment and he is not a Bodhisattva. In other words, the Thought of Enlightenment though a thought is not an ordinary thought, and the taking of the Thought of Enlightenment not merely an ordinary act of conception. As a spark leaps up when two electrically charged terminals are brought in contact, so the Thought of Enlightenment arises not from theoretical considerations but from the conjunction in the spiritual life of the devotee of two quite different, seemingly divergent, trends of thought and emotion. The art of producing the Thought of Enlightenment consists in so stimulating these two trends that the mounting tension between them ultimately causes them to coalesce at a higher level of spiritual awareness. The product of this coalescence, the synthesis which emerges from the conflict of thesis and antithesis, in experience, is the Thought of Enlightenment.

The first trend corresponds to the ordinary dualistic conception of the religious life as the abandonment of the mundane and the attainment of the Transcendental by one person, or in other words to the Path of the Disciple or the Path of the Private Buddha. It is to be stimulated by various reflections which Har Dayal collates as follows from a number of scriptures:—

He [the devotee] should reflect that birth as a human being is a very rare privilege. He may be born as an animal, a preta *or a denizen of purgatory many times, and there is no chance of becoming a* bodhisattva *in those existences. Even if he has escaped those three calamities, it is extremely difficult to find the five or six other favourable conditions that are indispensable for his initiation as a* bodhisattva. *He may be born as one of the long-lived* devas, *who cannot aspire to* bodhi, *though they are very happy. He may be born among foreigners or in a barbarous country. He may be defective in his faculties and organs. He may be misled by false doctrines. And lastly, he may find himself on earth during a period when no Buddha has lived and taught, for the perfect Buddhas are very rare. He should consider himself fortunate in being free from these eight or nine difficulties and disqualifications, and, above all, in being born as a human being at all, for human life is a blessing that perhaps falls to one's lot only once in billions of years. He should never forget the famous simile of the blind turtle, which explains that the chance of being born as a human being is infinitesimally small. Buddha himself has spoken thus: "Suppose a man should throw into the ocean a yoke with a single aperture in it. It is blown west by an easterly wind or east by a westerly wind, again it is carried north by a southern wind or south by a northerly wind. Now suppose there were a blind turtle in that ocean, and he came to the surface once in a hundred years. What think you, Monks? Would that blind turtle get his neck into that single aperture of the yoke? . . . Verily, that turtle would more quickly and easily perform that feat than a fool in his misery can be born as a human being once again." So difficult it is to enjoy the blessing of life as a man or a woman under fortunate and favourable circumstances (*kṣaṇa-sampad*)! Further, an ordinary worldly person should realize that his life and the external world are painful, impermanent and unsubstantial. He should think of death and the inevitable retribution after death. Death and dissolution are everywhere around us. Nothing endures. The clouds, that strike terror into men's hearts with thunder, lightning and rain, melt away. The mighty rivers, that uproot the trees on their banks in the rainy season, shrink again to the size of small and shallow streams. The cloud-compelling winds, that smite the mountains and the oceans, abate their fury and die away. The beauty of the woodland too is evanescent. All happiness ends in sorrow, and life ends in death. All creatures begin their journey towards death from the very moment of their conception in the* *womb. Powerful monarchs, skilled archers, clever magicians, haughty* devas, *furious elephants, ferocious lions and tigers, venomous serpents and malignant demons—all these can quell, subdue and slay their enemies, but even they are powerless against death, the fierce and irresistible foe of all living beings. Realizing the peril of death and suffering after death, a wise man should feel fear and trepidation (*samvega*) and resolve to become a bodhisattva.*[1]

In short the devotee intensifies his aspiration to the Transcendental by means of systematic reflection on the unsatisfactoriness of the mundane.

The second trend of thought and emotion corresponds to the humanitarian sentiment in general, and to the feeling of pity in particular. It is to be stimulated by contemplating the now tragic, now sordid, spectacle of the sins and sufferings of ordinary infatuated men and women:—

*They are foolish wordlings [the devotee reflects], deluded by ignorance. They are attached to sense-pleasures and enslaved by egotism, pride, false opinions, lust, hate, folly, doubt, craving and evil imaginations. They are without refuge and protection and have no haven of rest. They are blind, and there is no one to guide them. They are travelling through this jungle of mundane existence and towards the precipice of the three states of woe. They do not love virtue and duty, and are ungrateful to their parents and spiritual teachers. They are addicted to violence, strife, falsehood and cunning. Their sins are many, and they suffer from dire diseases and famines. The true religion is rejected, and false creeds arise and flourish. The world is groaning under the five dreaded calamities of degeneracy (*kaṣāya*). The duration of life is decreasing. The living beings are degenerate, their sins and passions increase, and they hold wrong views. The great æon itself is nearing its end.*[2]

Here the devotee reflects on the evils of mundane existence not with a view to developing aversion but in order to intensify pity. Formerly he was concerned with suffering only to the extent that it affected, or might affect, him personally; now he is concerned with it in so far as it affects all sentient beings. Whereas the first kind of reflection sets up a movement of repulsion from the mundane and attraction towards the Transcendental, the second sets up its contrary, a movement of repulsion from the Transcendental, conceived as merely transcendental, and of attraction towards—not the mundane itself, but—the sentient beings who are subject to birth, old age, disease and death in the mundane: one is intellectual and egoistic,

[1] *Ibid.*, pp. 59-60.
[2] *Ibid.*, pp. 60-61.

In the Dharmakaya — opposing desire for the transcendental (repulsion) and compassion — inseparable

in the line of Wisdom; the other emotional and altruistic, in the line of Compassion. The two trends being absolute contraries, the devotee is pulled now in this direction, now in that; or rather, he is wrenched in both directions simultaneously. But in the *Dharmakāya*, Wisdom and Compassion, far from being contraries, are inseparable, the static and dynamic aspects of one Supreme Reality. That thought in which the devotee, rising for an instant to the level of the *Dharmakāya,* for the first time brings together, not by way of merely external juxtaposition, but by the realization of their essential non-duality, the trend of Wisdom and the trend of Compassion, is termed the Thought of Enlightenment. But though the Thought of Enlightenment is produced by the fusion of these two trends, so greatly does Wisdom and Compassion as one reality differ from Wisdom and Compassion as independent realities, that between the Thought of Enlightenment and its supposed components there seems to be an absolute discontinuity. Santideva therefore compares the production of the Thought of Enlightenment to the finding of a jewel on a dunghill by a blind man! Yet when he desires to give expression to the Thought of Enlightenment, the devotee—or Bodhisattva, as he may now be called—cannot do otherwise than treat it as continuous with Wisdom and Compassion and speak of it as though it were simply a combination or conjunction of these two trends. We therefore find Santideva declaring:—

As the Buddhas of yore accepted the Thought of bodhi *and regularly followed the discipline of the* bodhisattvas, *even so I too produce (in my mind) this Thought of* bodhi *for the good of the world, and I will follow that discipline in due order.*[1]

Or, in the words of the *Bodhisattvabhūmi:—*

O may I attain supreme and perfect Enlightenment, promote the good of all beings, and establish them in the final and complete nirvāṇa *and in the Buddha-Knowledge.*[2]

From now onwards the Bodhisattva aims at a Goal in which Wisdom and Compassion are not separate realities, and in which the attainment of Enlightenment and the promotion of the welfare of all sentient beings are no longer irreconcilable ideals. He begins to live simultaneously in the Transcendental and the mundane.

---

[1] *Bodhicaryāvatāra*, III, 22, 23.
[2] *Bodhisattvabhūmi*, Fol. 6A, 2.2 to 3.1.

ambitious creature

Between the taking of the Thought of Enlightenment and the attainment of Supreme Buddhahood lie millions of years of unremitting exertion. In order to strengthen his resolve and preclude the possibility of relapse the Bodhisattva makes as it were a public announcement of his having taken the Thought of Enlightenment in the form of a number of Great Vows (*mahā-praṇidhāna*). Such were the forty-eight vows which, as we saw in Chapter III, Section VI, the Bodhisattva Dharmākara, who is now dwelling in the Happy Land as the Buddha Amitabha, made in former ages at the feet of the Tathāgata Lokeśvararāja. But the Bodhisattva's vows are not usually represented as being so numerous and so elaborate. According to the *Daśabhūmika Sūtra* the Bodhisattva makes ten great *praṇidhānas,* which have been summarized as follows:—

(1) To provide for the worship of all the Buddhas without exception.
(2) To maintain the religious Discipline that has been taught by all the Buddhas and to preserve the teaching of the Buddhas.
(3) To see all the incidents in the earthly career of a Buddha.
(4) To realize the Thought of Enlightenment, to practise the duties of a bodhisattva, *to acquire all the* pāramitās *and purify all the stages of his career.*
(5) To mature all beings and establish them in the knowledge of the Buddha, viz., *all the four classes of beings who are in the six states of existence.*
(6) To perceive the whole Universe.
(7) To purify and cleanse all the Buddha-fields.
(8) To enter on the Great Way and to produce a common thought and purpose in all bodhisattvas.
(9) To make all actions of the body, speech and mind fruitful and successful.
(10) To attain the supreme and perfect Enlightenment and to preach the Doctrine.[1]

In other works the number has been reduced still farther to four, and it is in this succinct form, perhaps, that the Bodhisattva's vows are best known and most often recited in the Far Eastern Buddhist world. These are the Great Vows:—

(1) To save all beings (from difficulties);
(2) To destroy all evil passions;
(3) To learn the Truth and teach others;
(4) To lead all beings towards Buddhahood.

Like the Thought of Enlightenment itself, however, the

[1] *Ibid.,* p. 66.

Bodhisattva's Vow is in reality simply twofold: To attain Supreme Enlightenment and to deliver all sentient beings. What distinguishes the Thought from the Vow is the fact that the former is a private and personal experience, the latter a public declaration. After making his Great Vow the Bodhisattva belongs to the entire universe; the Vow itself possesses universal significance; it is in fact a cosmic force. This difference between the Thought of Enlightenment and the Vow is marked by the old tradition that, as in the case of Dharmākara, the Bodhisattva must make his Vow in front of a living Buddha and receive from Him a prediction (*vyākaraṇa*) concerning his attainment of Enlightenment. This prediction, which in some scriptures is extremely prolix, reveals the number of *kalpas* which will elapse before his attainment of Supreme Buddhahood, the name by which he will then be known, the name and situation of his Buddha-country, the duration of his Teaching, and other details of interest to the Bodhisattva. In the pages of Santideva, however, the prediction of Enlightenment is of no importance, and in modern Mahayana practice it is generally considered sufficient for the novice Bodhisattva to make his Vow in the presence of his own spiritual master, who according to some schools is to be looked upon as the *Dharmakāya* Itself in human form, and in the presence of all the Buddhas of the universe, every one of Whom includes in His field of knowledge not only His own Buddha-field but the entire cosmos. The conception of *vyākaraṇa* as found in earlier Mahayana literature is perhaps a survival of the Hinayana view that the Bodhisattva Ideal is not universally applicable. In the Mahayana this conception is simply a means of emphasizing the cosmic significance not only of the Vow but of every step in the Bodhisattva's career from the taking of the Thought of Enlightenment to the attainment of Supreme Buddhahood.

V. The Six Perfections

The four *caryās* or courses of conduct which the Bodhisattva has now to follow are (1) *bodhipakṣya-caryā* or practice of the constituents of Enlightenment; (2) *abhijñā-caryā*, or practice of the knowledges; (3) *pāramitā-caryā* or practice of the Perfections; and (4) *sattvaparipāka-caryā*, or practice of "maturing" living beings, by which is meant preaching and teaching. Before attempting to describe the practice of the Perfections, wherein the Path of the Bodhisattva principally consists, the constituents of Enlightenment must at least be enumerated. To the remaining *caryās,* (2) and (4), which have been dealt with in Sections XVI and VI respectively of Chapter I, no further reference need be made.

In the *bodhipakṣya-dharmāḥ,* the thirty-seven principles conducive to Enlightenment, are included almost all the important practices of the Original Teaching. They are generally said to comprise the four Foundations of Mindfulness (*smṛti-upasthānāni*), the four Right Efforts (*samyak-prahāṇāni*), the four Bases of Psychic Power (*ṛddhipādāḥ*), the five Spiritual Faculties (*indriyāṇi*), the five Spiritual Powers (*balāni*), the seven Factors of Enlightenment (*bodhi-aṅgāni*), and the Noble Eightfold Path (*āryāṣṭāṅga-mārgaḥ*). An account of practically every group of practices has been given in Chapter I. They reappear at this stage of the Bodhisattva's career only to bear witness to the fact that in the realm of Method, no less than in the field of Doctrine, the Hinyana is included in the Mahayana, and that the very practices which are sufficient to make an Arahant or a Pratyekabuddha, in the strictly Hinayanic sense of these terms, can do no more than prepare one for the practice of the Six Perfections constituting the Path of the Bodhisattva. At the same time, however, so confusing is the interplay between the literal and symbolical interpretations of the same terms that, as we shall now see, the Path of the Bodhisattva is described as consisting of practices apparently drawn from the Original Teaching. Once again must we insist that what on the whole divides the Hinayana and the Mahayana is not differences of doctrine, though such differences do exist, so much as differences in the evaluation of doctrines and doctrinal terms, one *yāna* regarding them as true in the literal sense, the other treating them as merely symbols for what is unthinkable and inexpressible.

The Six Perfections are (1) the Perfection of Giving (*dāna-pāramitā*), (2) the Perfection of Morality (*śīla-pāramitā*), (3) the Perfection of Patience (*kṣānti-pāramitā*), (4) the Perfection of Vigour (*vīrya-pāramitā*), (5) the Perfection of Meditation (*dhyāna-pāramitā*), and (6) the Perfection of Wisdom (*prajñā-pāramitā*). Now in the Original Teaching not one but two paths are prescribed, a path for the monk and a path for the lay disciple. The first is the Theefold Path of Morality (*śīla*), Meditation (*samādhi*) and Wisdom (*paññā*): this has been described in detail in Chapter I; the second is the Threefold Path of Giving (*dāna*), Morality (*śīla*), and Meditation (*bhāvanā*). Combining these two series of terms (for the Bodhisattva may be either a monk or a layman) we get a path consisting not of three but of four stages: Giving, Morality, Meditation and Wisdom. Only the Perfection of Patience and the Perfection of Vigour remain unaccounted for. Without Vigour, which is also one of the Five Spiritual Faculties, it is hardly possible for the Bodhisattva to bring to a successful conclusion a career lasting for millions of years. Without Patience he could scarcely endure all the trials and torments that inevitably befall him as he pursues the long road that leads through repeated births and deaths to Supreme Buddhahood. Vigour and Patience, which as active and passive qualities perfectly balance each other, are therefore interpolated in the middle of the four existing stages, thus making up the Six Perfections of Giving, Morality, Patience, Vigour, Meditation and Wisdom. In essence, therefore, the Bodhisattva Path coincides with the Threefold Way, of which it is simply an amplified restatement. A similar correlation can be established between the Six *Pāramitās* and the Eightfold Path. As shown in the following table the eight steps from Right Understanding to Right Meditation can all be distributed among the three stages of Morality, Meditation and Wisdom.

Right Understanding Right Aspiration	Wisdom
Right Speech Right Action Right Means of Livelihood	Morality
Right Exertion Right Mindfulness Right Concentration	Meditation

In the scheme of the Noble Eightfold Path the factors pertaining to Wisdom precede those pertaining to Morality and Meditation. The discrepancy is only apparent and due to the fact that the term Wisdom denotes, according to the context, not only the transcendental but also the mundane faculty of that name. Thus while as an intellectual understanding of the Doctrine Wisdom precedes Morality and Meditation, as an intuitive realization of that same Doctrine it succeeds them. In the latter case Wisdom, since it arises in dependence on the concentrated mind, is regarded as a subdivision of Meditation. If the Eightfold Path is in correlation with the Threefold Way, and if the Path of the Six Perfections is an expanded version of the Threefold Way, obviously the Eightfold Path and the Path of the Six Perfections are themselves in correlation. These facts alone are sufficient proof of our assertion that the Bodhisattva Ideal and the Bodhisattva Path represent under the aspect of Method not only the Mahayana but the whole Buddhist tradition and that they therefore constitute a unifying and consolidating factor of the very first importance.

Each of the Six Perfections has been dealt with at enormous length and with a staggering wealth of detail in numerous Mahayana texts. But it cannot be denied that the Perfection of Wisdom has been accorded a degree of attention that seems to reduce the rest of the *Pāramitās* to a position almost of insignificance. We have only to remember the extent of the *Prajñāpāramitā* class of literature, which, as its name indicates, is devoted to the elucidation of the sixth and last of the Perfections. Some texts go so far as to assert that as the Six Perfections comprehend all other spiritual practices whatsoever, so the Perfections themselves are all included in the Perfection of Wisdom. This emphasis on the paramountcy of Wisdom indicates the fact that in the practice of the Perfections right motive is of decisive importance. According to the *Laṅkāvatāra Sūtra* there are in each Perfection three degrees: ordinary, extraordinary, and superlative. When practised by worldly people for the sake of gaining happiness here or hereafter a Perfection is said to be ordinary; when cultivated by the Hinayanists for the sake of attaining individual Nirvana it is extraordinary; but when developed by the Bodhisattvas not for their own sake alone but for the sake of the welfare and liberation of all sentient beings it is superlative. In the same manner does the *Pañcaviṁśatisāhasrikā* distinguish between the mundane practice of a Perfection and the Transcendental, the one associated with, the other free from, the delusion of individual selfhood.

Hence it is possible for us to simplify our account of the

Bodhisattva Path by dwelling not on the details of the practice of each *Pāramitā* but on its spirit. As doctrinal terms the Six Perfections are common to both *yānas* and all schools of Buddhism. But it is the presence of the Bodhisattva spirit which enable them to be not dead dogmas or mechanical exercises but dynamic Transcendental realities. In the last analysis, any action performed with *Prajñā* can be considered a *Pāramitā*. This does not mean, though, that the practice of the Six Perfections can be dispensed with. To draw such a conclusion would be to have a one-sided conception of *Prajñā*. Once again the Path to Supreme Enlightenment is seen to lie in the simultaneous practice of the relative truth and the absolute Truth.

(1) *Dāna* or Giving, the first of the Six Perfections, may be dealt with from four different points of view. We may consider (a) to *whom* a gift is given, (b) *what* is given, (c) *how* it is given, and (d) *why* or with what motive it is given. This classification will enable us to extract from the voluminous literature of the subject some of its more important conclusions.

(a) Though sentient beings in general are the objects of the Bodhisattva's generosity, three classes of recipients are specially mentioned. These are (i) his own friends and relatives; (ii) the poor, the sick, the afflicted, and the helpless; and (iii) the members of the Sangha.

(i) The Mahayanist would agree that "charity begins at home." But his emphasis would be on the verb. As the practice of *mettā-bhāvanā* also indicates, Buddhism does not require the suppression of the natural affections so much as their universalization. That same feeling which, when directed to one person only, is a source of bondage and suffering, becomes, as soon as it is radiated towards all, one of the conditions making for liberation and bliss. Though for a lay Bodhisattva his own kith and kin are among the first objects of generosity, by no means are they the last. As he recollects that all living things have, in one birth or another, been his own mother and father, his own wives and children, his generosity becomes an ever-expanding circle that seeks to include all. A Bodhisattva who is a monk feels for his lay supporters the same affection as for his mother and father; his pupils he loves as though they were his own sons. He treats all sentient beings as his friends.

(ii) The poor, the sick, the afflicted and the helpless have been recipients of charity in most civilized communities and under all higher religions, so that abstracted from the all-important question of motive there is little that is distinctively Buddhist to distinguish this aspect of Giving. Perhaps its most remarkable feature is that, in sharp contradistinction to the Semitic faiths, Buddhism understands by such *dāna* the service not of human beings alone but also of animals. Asoka established hospitals for man and beast; and institutions for the care of sick or infirm dogs, horses, cows and other four-footed creatures are still found in Buddhist lands. The ransoming and setting free of birds and turtles is an integral part of Chinese Buddhist festivals. Travellers are unanimous that, in the words of Sir Francis Younghusband, "It is a joy to travel in a Buddhist country and see how tame the wild animals are." Into these idyllic scenes the aggressive materialism of the West makes terrible inroads. One of the saddest sights the author has ever seen is a Roman Catholic missionary priest taking a jeep-load of Buddhist boys, all armed with rifles, for a day's "sport" in the woods. One trembles at the shocking indifference of the parents of these boys—and there are millions like them all over Asia—who unthinkingly deliver their children for "education" into the hands of the enemies of Buddhism.

(iii) The term by which the texts denote the third class of recipients of *dāna* is *śramaṇa-brāhmaṇa*. At the time of the Buddha this compound meant the two great classes of religious foundations, one accepting, the other denying, the authority of the Vedas. Historically Buddhism belongs to the second class, and the Scriptures represent non-Buddhists as speaking of the Buddha not as Bhagavan but simply as Sramana Gautama: conversion is always marked by a corresponding change from the less respectful to the more respectful mode of address. In the Original Teaching *śramaṇa-brāhmaṇa* seems to have been a collective designation for all who were following the Threefold Path of Morality, Meditation and Wisdom, irrespective of whether they were formally members of the Sangha or not. As the whole of the *Brāhmaṇa Vagga*, the concluding chapter of the *Dhammapada*, however, makes clear, by *brāhmaṇa* is *not* meant one who is merely a member of the Brahmin caste. *Śramaṇa* and *brāhmaṇa* are in fact essentially synonymous terms. The former merely superimposes upon the spiritual ideal the aspect of formal monasticism. The Buddhist is enjoined to support *all* who are leading a life which, by Buddhist standards, is one of genuine holiness. But this does not mean that the Buddhist should support or help those who, like the Christian missionaries, are deliberately disseminating false doctrines and endeavouring to destroy the Dharma—however unexceptionable their personal lives may be. A Buddhist who either directly or indirectly assisted the organization to which belonged the priest mentioned in the previous paragraph would be a traitor to his tradition. Buddhists are taught tolerance, and practise it more sincerely than the followers of any other religion; but tolerance does not mean indifference any more than the good neighbourliness enjoined upon the householder means that he should allow burglars to break into his house and steal. In the present context, therefore, *śramaṇa-brāhmaṇa* means primarily the members of the Sangha. The lay Bodhisattva will be an ideal *dāyaka,* faithfully serving and supporting the *bhikṣus* and helping them not only with material requisites but also, if he is in a position to do so, with spiritual advice.

(b) *What* can be given away is potentially co-extensive with what can be possessed. The objects which the Bodhisattva gives away are multitudinous. They may be classified under the following headings: (i) material things; (ii) fearlessness; (iii) education; (iv) life and limbs; (v) merits; and (vi) the Dharma.

(i) Of the giving of material things, which occupy the lowest place in the hierarchy of gifts, a *sūtra* preserved in Chinese translation speaks in the following glowing terms:—

> *It means . . . transcending the boundaries of heaven and earth with a charity as wide as a river and as large as the sea; performing acts of generosity to all living beings; feeding the hungry; giving drink to the thirsty; clothing those who are cold; refreshing those overcome by the heat; being ready to help the sick; whether it be carriages, horses, boats, equipment, or any kind of precious material or famous jewel, or beloved or son or kingdom—whatever it may be that you are asked to give, it means giving at once.*[1]

That the giving of material things is not to be interpreted in terms of superficial humanitarianism according to which religion is summed up in the distribution of free buns and blankets, is evinced by an important passage from another *sūtra*:—

---

[1] Quoted by HENRI DE LUBAC, S.J. *Aspects of Buddhism* (Sheed and Ward, London and New York. 1953).

What is a bad means (anupaya)*? When by the practice of the perfections the Bodhisattvas help others, but are content to supply them with merely material aid, without raising them from their misery or introducing them into beatitude, then they are using a bad means.*

Why? Because material help is not sufficient. Whether a dunghill be large or small, it cannot possibly be made to smell sweet by any means whatsoever. In the same way, living beings are unhappy because of their acts, because of their nature; it is impossible to make them happy by supplying them with merely material aids. The best way of helping them is to establish them in goodness.[1]

The Bodhisattva is far from thinking that the prospect of riches in heaven is an adequate substitute for poverty and degradation on earth; but he would be the last person to suggest that motor cars and refrigerators can take the place of Enlightenment. Following the Middle Path, he strives for both the spiritual *and* the material amelioration of human life and practises *dāna* in *all* its forms.

(ii) The giving of fearlessness (*abhaya*) is a uniquely Buddhist conception. More than any other religion does Buddhism realize the havoc which may be wrought in the mind by fear, worry and anxiety, and the consequent importance of developing fearlessness as an integral part of the spiritual life. In the Scriptures the Buddha Himself is invariably depicted as devoid of even the faintest trace of fear: His confidence is unshakable. This mental quality is possessed in a pre-eminent degree by the Bodhisattva, who develops it not merely for his own benefit but in order to impart it to other beings. Like happiness, fearlessness in the highest sense of the term is unattainable by material means; fear being essentially fear for oneself can be overcome only with the elimination of the ego-sense. Absolute fearlessness is synonymous with Enlightenment and the giving of fearlessness equivalent, ultimately, to the conferring of Enlightenment. In the present context, however, the giving of fearlessness means that the Bodhisattva attempts to relieve people of anxiety with regard to person, property and livelihood either by providing material safeguards or psychotherapeutic treatment, or simply by means of his own radiant presence and confidence-inspiring behaviour. Among the immense Buddhist repertoire of spiritual exercises are many which especially aim at the conquest of fear. Midnight visits to graveyards and other fearsome places, concentration on

---

[1] *Ibid.*, p. 24.

the various stages of decomposition in a corpse, meditation on death, are all practices in which fear, stimulated to the point at which it invades the conscious mind, can be faced and overcome. The enemy must be dragged out into the open before it can be slain. Though the Bodhisattva's efforts are for the moment directed mainly to the creation of a feeling of confidence and security in the minds of men and animals he does not forget that the deathblow of fear can be struck only with the Excalibur of non-ego.

(iii) The giving of education (*śikṣā*) is included in *dāna* principally for two reasons. Firstly, education enables an individual to exercise his rights and perform his duties as a citizen and a member of society; secondly, only when he has reached a certain level of general culture is it possible for a man to understand the doctrines which constitute the theoretical basis for the actual practice of the Teaching. Theories of education of course vary from age to age. The traditional Buddhist disciplines—still upheld in Tibet and Mongolia—comprise philosophy, logic, grammar and medicine, together with the various arts, crafts and sciences. But there is nothing in the Buddhist conception of education that obliges us to debar from the curriculum of Buddhist studies, say at monastic schools and colleges, the main elements of modern knowledge. Care should only be taken to preserve intact its traditional hierarchical structure, wherein the rank assigned to each branch of knowledge is directly related to the part it plays in the attainment of Wisdom. The acquisition of knowledge by methods which, like vivisection—to take an extreme case—violate a principle of ethics, on whatsoever plea, can find no place in a truly Buddhist scheme of education. Moreover, no Buddhist should help in the advancement of scientific researches the results of which are likely to be utilized for the destruction of life. The Bodhisattva gives only that education which is not incompatible with effective taking of the Threefold Refuge and following the Path.

(iv) The giving away of his life and limbs by the Bodhisattva is the theme of numerous *Jātakas*, many of which have become a permanent part of the literature and folklore of Buddhist lands. The King of the Sivis, who gave away his eyes, Jīmūtavāhana, who allowed himself to be sacrificed to the *garuḍa* in the place of a *nāga* boy, and of course the anonymous hero who offered his body to feed the starving tigress, live in the popular Buddhist imagination far more vividly than any historical figures. "More than the seas He gave His blood, more than the stars His eyes," exclaims an ancient Sinhalese poem, referring to the Great Being Who in His last earthly life was known as Gautama Buddha.

It should not be thought, however, that the Bodhisattva is required merely to sacrifice his life at the first opportunity. According to the consensus of responsible Mahayana opinion, the body of the Bodhisattva does not belong to himself but to all beings; it is a sacred trust; consequently he has the right to sacrifice it only when the person for whom the sacrifice is made is able to render to sentient beings a service greater than his own. As was pointed out at the beginning of this chapter, the Bodhisattva Ideal is to be interpreted not literally but symbolically. Instead of trying to draw logical conclusions from the *Jātakas* we should imbibe their spirit. The story of the starving tigress does not mean that the Bodhisattva should make it an invariable rule to sacrifice his own life in order to preserve the lives of animals. It means that he should develop Compassion to such a pitch that he has no thought for himself. Whether he actually sacrifices his life for others in a given situation is for Wisdom to determine. The fact that the giving of life and limbs makes its appearance here as one of the recognized forms of *dāna* shows that the Mahayana does not exclude the possibility of the Bodhisattva being called upon to sacrifice himself in a quite literal sense, and therefore requires him to be fully prepared even for this eventuality.

(v) The practice of making a gift of one's merits, technically known as their "transference" (*pariṇāmanā*), was discussed in Section III of this Chapter. Little therefore need be said about it here. Between the transference of merits included in the list of preliminary devotional practices and the transference of merits which forms part of the Perfection of Giving there is in fact only one difference, though this is of fundamental importance. Whereas formerly the transference was effected in dissociation from *Prajñā,* so that the aspirant to Bodhisattvahood thought of himself as in reality giving something away and of others as in reality receiving it, now the same gift is made in association with *Prajñā,* and the Bodhisattva, as the aspirant has become, makes it with a mind absolutely free from all thought of self and others. Like the previous forms of Giving, the transference of merits now flows spontaneously from the depths of the Bodhisattva's realization of the truth of non-duality.

(vi) Their doctrinal differences notwithstanding, the schools of Buddhism are unanimous that *Dharma-dāna*, the Gift of the Doctrine, is the highest form of Giving. It is this fact which makes Buddhism a missionary religion in the true sense of the term. Being as it were in possession of the Means to Enlightenment, the Bodhisattva out of compassion desires to share it with all sentient beings. Hence in the same way that Wisdom gives birth to Compassion (for though the two are metaphysically identical one is logically prior to the other), Compassion in its turn is productive of various methods, technically known as *Upāya* or Devices, by means of which the Bodhisattva enables beings to participate in his own transcendental experience. One of the most important of these devices is the communication at the intellectual level, through the medium of the spoken or the written word, of those conceptual formulations which are the theoretical basis for the practice of the Doctrine. It is this communication which is known as *Dharma-dāna.* The forms which it is possible for this mode of Giving to assume are of course very numerous: most of them are too well known to be enumerated.

Perhaps the only aspect of *Dharma-dāna* to which special attention need be drawn is its dual function as both promulgation of Truth and refutation of error. Mañjuśrī, the Bodhisattva who as the embodiment of Wisdom presides over the propagation of the Dharma, is iconographically represented not only as bearing in his left hand a lotus blossom upon whose open petals rests a book, the Scriptures of Perfect Wisdom, but also as wielding with his right hand a flaming sword. While the first symbolizes the establishment of Truth the second symbolizes the destruction of untruth, that is to say, of those doctrines which do not constitute a basis for the attainment of the Transcendental Path. The two functions are inseparable. The Bodhisattva can no more preach the Dharma without refuting such wrong views as belief in a creator God and an unchanging individual self than it is possible for the sun to rise without dispelling the darkness. If the Bodhisattva happens to be a *bhikṣu* the performance of this dual function will be, from the social point of view, his principal duty. Even if he is a layman he will by no means neglect it. In neither case will there be any compromise with false teachings.

(c) *How* or in what manner the Bodhisattva gives may be gathered in short from the exhortations contained in the following collation of texts:—

*He should always be very courteous to the suppliants, and receive them with every mark of respect and deference (*satkṛtya*). He should also be happy and joyful, when he gives away anything. This condition is important and essential. The donor should be even happier than the recipient of the gift. A* bodhisattva *should not repent of his generosity after bestowing gifts on others. He should not talk of his charitable deeds. He should give quickly (*tvaritam*) and with a humble heart. He should make no distinction between friends and enemies, but should give to all alike. He should give to the deserving and the undeserving, the wicked and the righteous, everywhere and at all times. But he should not lose the sense of proportion in his charity.*[1]

As emphasized above, though the Bodhisattva is prepared to sacrifice even his own life for the sake of sentient beings, he will actually make such a sacrifice only if it is really needed. Moreover, in the giving of material things he exercises discretion. He does not, for example, supply anybody with the means of indulging in lust and cruelty, or in fact with anything which might be used in contravention of the Precepts. Again, whatever the Bodhisattva gives away has been acquired by honest means, and is both legally and morally his. He is no Robin Hood who plunders the rich to provide for the poor. Much less still is he one of those financial wizards who think that *dāna* can be given by creating mammoth charitable trusts out of the ill-gotten gains of a career of legalized robbery and exploitation.

(d) *Why* or with what motive the Bodhisattva practises the Perfection of Giving has already been partly disclosed. He practises it not for the sake of acquiring merits, or for the sake of gaining individual emancipation, but simply and solely for the sake of bringing Enlightenment to all sentient beings. If his practice is dissociated from *Prajñā,* it is said to be mundane, if associated with *Prajñā,* transcendental. It is in the practice of the Transcendental Perfection of Giving that *dāna-pāramitā* essentially consists. The difference between transcendental and

[1] *The Bodhisattva Doctrine in Buddhist Sanskrit Literature,* pp. 175-76.

mundane Giving has been made clear in the following passage from one of the scriptures of Perfect Wisdom:—

Sariputra: "What is the worldly, and what is the supramundane perfection of giving?"

Subhuti: "The worldly perfection of giving consists in this: The Bodhisattva gives liberally to all those who ask, all the while thinking in terms of real things. It occurs to him: 'I give, that one receives, this is the gift. I renounce all my possessions without stint. I act as one who knows the Buddha. I practise the perfection of giving. I, having made this gift into the common property of all beings, dedicate it to supreme enlightenment, and that without apprehending anything. By means of this gift and its fruit may all beings in this very life be at their ease, and may they one day enter Nirvana!' Tied by three ties he gives a gift. Which three? A perception of self, a perception of others, a perception of the gift.

"The supramundane perfection of giving, on the other hand, consists in the threefold purity. What is the threefold purity? Here a Bodhisattva gives a gift, and he does not apprehend a self, nor a recipient, nor a gift; also no reward of his giving. He surrenders that gift to all beings, but he apprehends neither beings nor self. He dedicates that gift to supreme enlightenment, but he does not apprehend any enlightenment. This is called the supramundane perfection of giving."

*(*Pañcaviṁśatisāhasrikā, *263-64. Conze's translation)*[1]

These profound words of Subhuti illustrate the fact that except in association with *Prajñā* not only Giving, but also Morality, Patience, Vigour and Meditation are not really Perfections, or at least, not Perfections in the highest sense of the term. As Subhuti's interlocutor, Sāriputra, himself points out in another section of the same great corpus of texts, Giving and the rest are like a company of blind men who cannot, without a leader, go along a path and arrive at a village, town or city. Only when laid hold of by the Perfection of Wisdom are they termed "perfections," "for then these five perfections acquire an organ of vision which allows them to ascend the path to all-knowledge."[2] The essence of each Perfection consists not in the distinctive practices it denotes but rather in the spirit in which these practices are carried out. This spirit is identical with *Prajñā.* The first five Perfections are really different modalities or different applications of the Perfection of Wisdom. The Perfection of Wisdom comprehends and includes them all.

For this reason we shall be able to deal with the remaining Perfections somewhat more briefly than we have dealt with the

---

[1] *Buddhist Texts,* pp. 136-37.

[2] *Selected Sayings,* p. 63.

Perfection of Giving. With the sole exception of the Perfection of Patience, they have been more or less adequately discussed in our earlier chapters. Instead of describing the mundane practice of the Perfections, thus going over ground already covered, we shall tend to confine ourselves to the transcendental practice. This procedure will enable us to drive home with the hammer-blows of repetition the supremely important fact that the Perfections are Perfections in the true sense of the term only when conjoined with Wisdom.

(2) By *śīla* or Morality, the second of the Six Perfections, is of course meant the observance of the rules of conduct, of which there are five for the laity and 250 (according to the Mahayana[1]) for members of the Sangha. All that was said on the subject in Chapter I, Section XVI, should be understood as repeated here. Some Mahayana texts speak of the Mundane Perfection of Morality in terms of the Ten Ways of Wholesome Action, that is to say, abstention from taking life, from taking what is not given, from sexual misconduct, from indulgence in intoxicants, from false, malicious, harsh and senseless speech, from covetousness, from ill will, and from wrong views. A Bodhisattva not only himself observes these ten wholesome ways of action but instigates others to observe them too. But whether the Bodhisattva observes a greater or a lesser number of precepts, such observance does not by itself constitute practice of the Perfection of Morality.

As we have more than once had occasion to point out in this work, both the "classical" Hinayana and the modern Theravadin observance of *śīla,* especially in the conventional monastic sense, is accompanied by so strong, not to say violent, an assertion of separate selfhood as to be not a help but a definite hindrance on the Path to Enlightenment. The transcendental practice of the Perfection of Morality, to which the Mahayana in general, and the Bodhisattva in particular, is committed, contrary to Hinayana misrepresentations, does *not* mean that ethical behaviour is of no importance. It means that egolessness being the supreme spiritual value the importance of ethical acts is in the last analysis to be determined by the extent to which they conduce to the

[1] Strictly speaking, according to the Sarvastivadin tradition which the Mahayana incorporated.

attainment of egolessness. From the transcendental viewpoint, conventionally moral actions become, when performed in an egoistic manner, immoral. Like the mundane practice of Giving, the mundane practice of Morality can tie the Bodhisattva in three ways. By a perception of self, by a perception of others, and by a perception of the moral action. In the first case he does good with the false view that he, the doer, is in reality a separate unchanging self. In the second, he imagines that the beings for whose sake he abstains from killing and stealing and practises the other-regarding virtues have like himself an absolute existence. In the third, he thinks of the moral observance itself as a species of property, and of the act of observance as a kind of acquisition. The moral life is interpreted in terms of the accumulation of moral property, the possession of which entitles the fortunate owner to indulge in the gratifying reflection that he is not as other men. This attitude of moral superiority is, as already noticed, distressingly common among certain contemporary Theravadins, many of whom take not only pride but even pleasure in contrasting their own flawless morality with the supposed "degeneracy" of their Mahayana brethren.

Leaving such "Theravadins" to the enjoyment of their superiority, we find that the three ties of self, others and moral observance give us, in their converse, a criterion by which to distinguish the mundane practice of Morality from the transcendental. Morality becomes conjoined with Wisdom, or in other words becomes truly the Perfection of Morality, when in the performance of a given moral act the Bodhisattva has no thought of himself as doer or of others as objects of the act, and when he does not consider himself as being by virtue of his performance of the act superior or inferior or even equal to others. This means (to reduce the principle to its simplest and most easily understood terms) that to however great an extent the Bodhisattva practises the Perfection of Morality he will never think of himself as virtuous. He will mix with thieves and prostitutes with the same sublime unself-consciousness with which he consorts with saints. He will wear his righteousness as lightly as a flower. He will never make of it a whip for the backs of the unrighteous. Yet despite his absolute freedom from moral egotism he will not deviate by even so much as a hair's breadth from the observance of the Ten Ways of Wholesome Action. He practises the Perfection of Morality by holding Morality and Wisdom in absolute equilibrium.

(3) *Kṣānti-pāramitā,* or the Perfection of Patience, is a composite virtue. In it are blended not only patience and forbearance, the literal meanings of the term, but also love, humility, endurance, and an absence of anger and of desire for retaliation and revenge. Around this sublime conception have been woven some of the most beautiful stories and teachings in Buddhist literature, and it is to these stories and teachings, rather than to any abstract doctrinal analysis, that we must turn for an understanding of the spirit by which the practice of the Perfection of Patience should be animated. In the justly famous Parable of the Saw, which belongs to one of the earliest strata of the Pali *Tipiṭaka,* the Buddha says:—

> *"Brethren, there are these five ways of speech which other man may use to you:—speech seasonable or unseasonable: speech true or false: speech gentle or bitter: speech conducive to profit or to loss: speech kindly or resentful.*
>
> *"When men speak evil of ye, thus must ye train yourselves: 'Our heart shall be unwavering, no evil word will we send forth, but compassionate of others' welfare will we abide, of kindly heart without resentment: and that man who thus speaks will we suffuse with thoughts accompanied by love, and so abide: and, making that our standpoint, we will suffuse the whole world with loving thoughts, far-reaching, wide-spreading, boundless, free from hate, free from ill-will, and so abide.' Thus, brethren, must ye train yourselves.*
>
> *"Moreover, brethren, though robbers, who are highwaymen, should with a two-handed saw carve you in pieces limb by limb, yet if the mind of any one of you should be offended thereat, such an one is no follower of my gospel."*
>
> (Majjhima-Nikāya, *I, 128-29. Woodward's translation)*[1]

Kṣānti is much more than mere stoical endurance of suffering. The Bodhisattva under torture does not grit his teeth: he smiles. This fact is brought out much more clearly, and its explanation from the doctrinal point of view supplied, in a passage from the *Prajñāpāramitā* wherein the transcendental practice of Patience is expounded with reference to the story of the sage Kṣāntivādin, or "Preacher of Patience," who was Gautama the Buddha Himself in a previous birth. Kṣāntivādin had enraged the King of Kalinga by preaching to the royal seraglio a sermon on Patience, and the king had caused him to suffer barbarous

[1] *Some Sayings of the Buddha,* pp. 97-98.

mutilation. The *Vajracchedikā* represents the Buddha as commenting on this episode and saying:—

"A Tathagata's perfection of Patience is really no perfection. Because, Subhuṭi, when the King of Kalinga cut my flesh from every limb, at that time I had no notion of a self, or of a being, or of a soul, or of a person, nor had I any notion or non-notion. And why? If, Subhuti, at that time I had had a notion of self, I would also have had a notion of ill-will at that time. If I had had a notion of a being, of a soul, of a person, then I also would have had a notion of ill-will at that time. And why? By my superknowledge I know the past, five hundred births, and how I have been the Rishi, "Preacher of Patience." Then also I have had no notion of a self, or a being, or a soul, or a person. Therefore, then, Subhuti, a Bodhisattva, a great being should, after he has got rid of all notions, raise his thought to the supreme enlightenment. Unsupported by form a thought should be produced, unsupported by sounds, smells, tastes, touchables or mind-objects a thought should be produced, unsupported by dharma a thought should be produced, unsupported by no-dharma a thought should be produced, unsupported by anything a thought should be produced. And why? What is supported has no support."[1]

The last tremendous sentences are of the utmost importance. In them the worldling's and the Hinayanist's conception of Patience are clearly distinguished from each other, and both from that of the Mahayanists. The worldling's conception is stoical. He thinks that forms, sounds, smells, etc., are realities and constitutive of realities, whether beings or things. With the thought that his sufferings are inflicted by real beings and things he endures them as best he can and suppresses his anger. Such a practice of *kṣānti* is said to be supported by form (*rūpa*), and the rest of the six *āyatanas*. The Hinayanist, analysing beings and things into their constituent *dharmas* or psychosomatic phenomena, practises *kṣānti* by realizing the foolishness of becoming angry with collocations of material and mental states. There is no doubt that by this method the grosser forms of anger and impatience can not only be controlled but even permanently eradicated. Unfortunately, the Hinayanists developed the habit of thinking of the *dharmas* themselves as realities, so that it became impossible for them to eliminate the subtler forms of anger. Hence their practice of *kṣānti* is said to be supported by *dharma*.

The Bodhisattva's practice is supported not even by no-dharma. As we saw in Chapter II, in order to counteract the excessive literalism of the Hinayana, which had crystallized in the concep-

---

[1] *Selected Sayings*, pp. 67-68.

tion of *pudgalanairātmya*, the Mahayana put forward the doctrine of *sarvadharmanairātmya*, according to which not only the so-called person but also his constituent *dharmas* were *śūnya*. Had the Mahayanists thought of *Śūnyatā* itself as possessing some kind of self-existence, and of the Bodhisattva as therefore practising the Perfection of Patience with no-dharma as his support, they would only have been repeating the mistake of the Hinayanists at a higher and subtler level. Consequently the Lord emphasizes that in his practice of Patience the Bodhisattva should be unsupported by no-dharma. Further explanation can be given only by having recourse to paradox. If what is supported has no support, only that which has no support is truly supported. For this reason the transcendental practice of Patience is, in the last resort, what is termed *anutpattika-dharma-kṣāntiḥ*, or acquiesence in the truth that all phenomena are in reality illusory, non-existent, unproduced and undifferentiated. According to the *Daśabhūmika* the Bodhisattva practises the Perfection of Patience in this exalted sense only from the eighth stage of his career.

(4) *Vīrya* or Vigour, the next of the Six Perfections, is another term with a very wide denotation. Besides the purely motor and volitional aspects of the Bodhisattva Ideal, which are obviously of the first importance, it covers the characteristically Buddhist virtues of vigilance or heedfulness (*apramāda*)—the theme of the celebrated second canto of the *Dhammapada*—and steadfastness or fortitude (*dhṛti*). From the Pali *Dhammasangaṇi*, Section 13, comes the following plethora of synonyms, which are common to the scholastic heritage of all schools:—

> *The striving and onward effort, the exertion and endeavour, the zeal and ardour, the vigour and fortitude, the state of unfaltering effort, the state of sustained desire, the state of not putting down the yoke and the burden, energy, right endeavour, this is* viriya.

According to Santideva and others Vigour is simply "energy in pursuit of the Good." This more succinct statement, which is a definition in the logical sense, has the merit of defining the Perfection of Vigour in terms of its ultimate objective. But what is "the Good"? According to the Hinayana it is individual enlightenment, the attainment of the Arahant; according to the Mahayana, it is Supreme Buddhahood for the sake of all sentient beings. As the ascent of Everest requires far more strength and resourcefulness than the scaling of one of its foothills, so the Mahayana objective, being infinitely greater than that of the Hinayana, naturally demands for its attainment an infinitely greater output of energy. Though the Sravaka, too, is one who stirs up energy, his comparatively limited exertions can no more be compared to the cosmic scale on which the Bodhisattva operates than the tiny trickle of a garden waterfall can be compared to the thundering cataracts of the Niagara.

At the same time, however, between Vigour as practised by the Sravaka and Vigour as practised by the Bodhisattva, there is still a difference not of kind but only of degree. Hinayana texts generally speak of Vigour in terms of the suppression and prevention of unwholesome, and the development and cultivation of wholesome, mental states. Those of the Mahayana speak of it, more broadly, as the energetic practice of the Perfections, which are thus no less dependent upon Vigour than upon Wisdom. Indeed, more so. For whereas only the transcendental practice of the Perfections depends upon Wisdom, both the mundane and the transcendental practice depend upon Vigour. Hence Santideva is not wrong in declaring "In Vigour lies Enlightenment." But whether, with the Hinayanists, we think of Vigour principally in terms of Meditation, or, with the Mahayanists, in terms of all the remaining five Perfections, the practice of Vigour is still mundane.

The Sravaka takes as his objective liberation of self; the Bodhisattva, liberation of others. Neither self nor others, however, exist in the absolute sense. We can rise to the transcendental practice of Vigour only by means of Wisdom, according to which self and others, beings and things, are all in the ultimate sense unreal. The Perfection of Vigour in the highest sense consists not in making a self-conscious effort for the attainment of a definite objective, however intense and prolonged that effort might be, but rather in releasing, through the realization of *Śūnyatā,* the "object" of *Prajñā,* an uninterrupted stream of impersonal energy with no definite direction and no logically definable goal. By practising the Perfection of Vigour in conjunction with the Perfection of Wisdom the Bodhisattva becomes a kind of cosmic force and participates in the universal transcendental activity of the *Dharmakāya.* Reduced to everyday terms, this means that however great, from the relative point of view, the Bodhisattva's exertions may be, he never thinks of himself as making any exertions. Hence in all his undertakings he acts without haste and without delay, neither exhilarated by success nor depressed by failure; under all circumstances he is serene, cheerful and optimistic. His energy is unflagging. After even the most heroic exertions he feels no fatigue, no desire for rest. To him exertion and rest are one. So great a joy does he find in the practice of the Perfection of Vigour that, in the beautiful words of Santideva,

When one work is brought to an end, he will plunge into another, as the elephant, vexed by the heat of midday, plunges straightway into the lake that he finds.[1]

Next to Wisdom and Compassion, Vigour is the most prominent of all the characteristics of the Bodhisattva.

(5) *Dhyāna-pāramitā,* or the Perfection of Concentration, differs hardly at all from the corresponding practices of the Original Teaching. Mahayana *sūtras* and *śāstras* describe the Bodhisattva as resorting to jungle, cave or cemetery, and passing through the various stages of Meditation, from mindfulness and self-possession to attainment of the superconscious states and development of the supernormal powers, in exactly the same manner and by means of exactly the same methods as were described in Chapter I, Section XVII, when *samādhi* was dealt with as the second stage of the Threefold Way. A number of Mahayana texts do indeed represent the Bodhisattva as master of hundreds and even thousands of different *samādhis*; the *Laṅkāvatāra* goes to the extent of speaking of "*samādhis* innumerable." But most of these are to all appearances only various states of transcendental consciousness as it were suffused with different emotional hues, and the three "Doors to Emancipation" (*vimokṣa-mukhāni*)—that is to say the *samādhis* of Aimlessness, Signlessness and Emptiness—which as the destroyers of the three unwholesome roots of greed, hatred and delusion occupy so prominent a place in the Original Teaching, are still regarded as being of all *samādhis* the most important.

Perhaps the only difference between Meditation as part of the Threefold Way and Meditation as one of the Perfections lies in the fact that the Bodhisattva has at his disposal all the peculiarly Tantric methods of inducing one-pointedness of mind. It

[1] *The Path of Light,* p. 80.

should not be forgotten, however, that such a difference exists only so far as literary records are concerned. As pointed out in Chapter III, Section XI, the Tantric tradition was transmitted orally for hundreds of years. Some of the methods now regarded as Tantric may have formed part of the Original Teaching. Hence even the difference of which we have spoken perhaps does not really exist. The only points that need be made in connection with the Perfection of Concentration concern (a) the extent to which Meditation can be practised by the layman, (b) the Bodhisattva's utilization of his psychic powers, and (c) the nature of the transcendental practice of this *Pāramitā.*

(a) In its reaction against Hinayana literalism the Mahayana had declared that the Bodhisattva could be either a monk or a layman. But though it reacted against attachment to the merely formal aspects of monasticism it certainly did not reject its spirit. That a Bodhisattva could be a layman did not necessarily mean that a layman could be a Bodhisattva. Without celibacy, for example, Enlightenment is unattainable. Even the married Bodhisattva is required to abstain from sexual intercourse. As Har Dayal, citing the *Aṣṭasāhasrikā,* puts it, "His marriage is a 'pious fraud' for the conversion of others. He does not really enjoy sensual pleasure: he remains a celibate."[1] Whereas the Hinayana monk only too often conceals beneath the garb of formal monasticism a very real worldliness the Mahayana layman occasionally keeps up, despite an appearance of worldliness, a genuine devotion to the practice of the Bodhisattva Ideal. In the case of *dhyāna-pāramitā,* however, the lay Bodhisattva's arrangements for leading a double life would seem to break down. The Mahayana *sūtras,* in agreement with the conclusion reached by all schools of Buddhism, are unanimous that for the successful or even safe practice of Meditation the Bodhisattva must retire to a solitary place. The *Bodhisattvabhūmi,* while it speaks of the first four *Pāramitās* as being practised by both monks and laymen, in the case of the Perfection of Meditation speaks of monks only.

Are we to infer from this that from the fifth *pāramitā* onwards it is impossible for the Bodhisattva to conform to the conventions of social life? We do not think that so sweeping a conclusion is justified. Yet at the same time the conditions for the

[1] *The Bodhisattva Doctrine in Buddhist Sanskrit Literature,* p. 222.

practice of *dhyāna,* among which are renunciation and solitude, being based not upon conventions but upon realities are inescapable. We therefore conclude that whether the Bodhisattva be living as monk or as layman, at least for the period of his practice of *dhyāna* literal retirement from the world is indispensable. Once the Bodhisattva has the power of entering into *samādhi* at will it makes little difference to him whether he lives in the forest or the city; but for the development of that power seclusion is essential.

The period of solitary practice required for the attainment of a certain level of superconsciousness is naturally not the same for all. In some cases it may be months, in others years, in yet others a whole lifetime. But whatever the period required, and whatever the stage at which the development of the Perfection of Meditation ceases to be incompatible with life as an ordinary member of society, the Bodhisattva should at all times beware of self-deception. Even greater than the sin of worldly monasticism is the conscious or unconscious use of the Bodhisattva Ideal as an excuse for a weak and cowardly life of self-indulgence and sensuality. The lay Bodhisattva should never forget that

Lilies that fester smell far worse than weeds.

(b) In Chapter I, Section XVII, we saw that the fourth *jhāna* (Skt. *dhyāna*) could be used as a basis for the development of the five mundane *abhiññā* (Skt. *abhijñā*), that is to say, psychic powers such as the creation of a mind-formed body, clairaudience, telepathy, recollection of previous births, and clairvoyance. According to the Hinayana, these powers being mundane were not conducive to Enlightenment and therefore should not be cultivated deliberately. The Mahayana, while agreeing that the powers referred to were mundane, nevertheless insisted that since they could be employed in the service of sentient beings, as well as for the protection and propagation of the Dharma, the Bodhisattva ought to master as many of them as possible. Far more important, as well as more distinctively Mahayanic, is the doctrine that through the practice of Meditation the Bodhisattva can create not merely a mind-formed body but the transcendental body in which he descends for the "attainment" of Supreme Enlightenment from the Tuṣita heaven to the earth, and in which after his apparent withdrawal from the world at the time of his Parinirvana he continues to live and work for the good of the entire cosmos. The transcendental body is the *Nirmāṇakāya* described in Chapter III, Section VI, and the "Diamond Body" (*vajrakāya*) mentioned in Chapter III, Section XI.

(c) The nature of the transcendental practice of the Perfection of Concentration is made clear with commendable brevity by a passage from the Perfection of Wisdom "in 25,000 Lines":—

If a Bodhisattva, although he enters the trances, the Unlimited, the formless attainments, does not gain rebirth through them, does not even relish them, that is his perfection of concentration.[1]

As explained in Chapter I, Section XVII, Buddhism divides the Samsara, or totality of phenomenal existence, into three principal planes, each with numerous subdivisions. Corresponding to each sub-plane is a certain state of consciousness or superconsciousness. Access to a higher "world" can be gained by attaining, through the practice of concentration, to the corresponding *dhyāna*. If during one's lifetime one has succeeded in attaining, for example, the second *dhyāna*, one may, after death, be reborn among the *parīttābhāḥ* or the *apramāṇābhāḥ*, or the *ābhāsvarāḥ* gods. But this the Bodhisattva does not desire. Though from the mundane point of view the worlds of the gods are superior to the world of men they are merely passive states of enjoyment wherein—so great is the bliss—no farther progress towards Enlightenment can be made. In order to ensure rebirth as a human being, for whom alone real spiritual progress is possible, the Bodhisattva has to develop the successive stages of *dhyāna* without allowing them to frustrate his intention of being reborn as a man. This he does by cultivating a feeling of disgust and aversion for the *dhyānas*. He reflects that, like all compounded things, even the most exalted of the superconscious states are inherently painful, transitory and unsubstantial. Taking in this way the *dhyānas* themselves as a support for the development of *Prajñā* constitutes the transcendental practice of the Perfection of Concentration.

(6) *Prajñā* or Wisdom, the last and most important of the *pāramitās*, has already formed the subject-matter of Chapter III, Section IV, when the Mādhyamika School was introduced with a

---

[1] *Selected Sayings*, p. 68.

brief exposition of the teaching of its basic *sūtras,* the Scriptures of Perfect Wisdom. Rather than burden the conclusion of this section with a lengthy repetition, we shall simply place before the reader the *sūtra* known as "The Heart of Perfect Wisdom." Dr. Conze rightly calls it "one of the finest and most profound spiritual documents of humanity." In it is described, as far as it is possible for so exalted an experience to be indicated by words, how the Bodhisattva courses in the transcendental practice of Wisdom, which is not only the chief but, strictly speaking, the only Perfection.

"Homage to the Perfection of Wisdom, the lovely, the holy! Avalokita the holy Lord and Bodhisattva, was moving in the deep course of the wisdom which has gone beyond. He looked down from on high; he beheld but five heaps; and he saw that in their own being they were empty. Here, O Sariputra, form is emptiness and the very emptiness is form; emptiness does not differ from form, nor does form differ from emptiness; whatever is form, that is emptiness, whatever is emptiness, that is form. The same is true of feelings, perceptions, impulses and consciousness. Here, O Sariputra, all dharmas are marked with emptiness, they are neither produced nor stopped, neither defiled nor immaculate, neither deficient nor complete. Therefore, O Sariputra, where there is emptiness there is neither form, nor feeling, nor perception, nor impulse, nor consciousness; nor form, nor sound, nor smell, nor taste, nor touchable, nor object of mind; no sight-organ element, and so forth, until we come to: no mind-consciousness element; there is no ignorance, nor extinction of ignorance, and so forth, until we come to: there is no decay and death, no extinction of decay and death; there is no suffering, nor origination, nor stopping, nor path; there is no cognition, no attainment and no non-attainment.

"Therefore, O Sariputra, owing to a Bodhisattva's indifference to any kind of personal attainment, and through his having relied on the perfection of wisdom, he dwells without thought-coverings. In the absence of thought-coverings he has not been made to tremble, he has overcome what can upset, in the end sustained by Nirvana. All those who appear as Buddhas in the three periods of time,—they all fully awake to the utmost, right and perfect enlightenment because they have relied on the perfection of wisdom. Therefore one should know the Prajñāpāramitā *as the great spell, the spell of great knowledge, the utmost spell, the unequalled spell, allayer of all suffering, in truth,—for what could go wrong. By the* Prajñāpāramitā *has this spell been delivered. It runs like this: Gone, gone, gone beyond, gone altogether beyond, O what an awakening, all hail!"*

(Prajñāpāramitāhṛdaya-Sūtra. *Conze's translation*)[1]

VI. The Ten Perfections and the Ten Stages

At the beginning of the last section we saw that the Path of the Six Perfections was simply an amplified restatement of the

---

[1] *Buddhist Texts,* pp. 152-53; *Selected Sayings,* pp. 74-75.

Threefold Path of Morality, Meditation and Wisdom, both of which were found to be in correlation with the successive steps of the Noble Eightfold Way. These facts, besides demonstrating the fundamental identity, as regards Method, of the Mahayana and the Original Teaching, vindicate the right of the Bodhisattva Ideal to be accepted as embodying the practical aspect of the entire Buddhist tradition and as being, therefore, a unifying factor among its various schools.

The question that now confronts us concerns the extent to which it is possible to correlate with the Six or Ten *Pāramitās,* and therethrough with the Threefold Path and Eightfold Way, the various stages (*bhūmi*) of attainment which the Mahayana texts represent the Bodhisattva as traversing. Systematizing and to some extent elaborating the Original Teaching, Hinayana scholasticism—which the Mahayana of course inherited and incorporated in its own tradition—declared that the stages of spiritual, or strictly speaking transcendental, progress were four in number—the respective "Paths" of the Stream-Entrant (*srotāpatti*), the Once-Returner (*sakridāgami*), the Non-Returner (*Anāgāmi*) and the Arahant. With these four stages were correlated the Threefold Way. According to both Theravadin and Sarvastivadin tradition, by practising Morality in its perfection (*adhisīla*) one could attain to the Paths of the Stream-Entrant and the Once-Returner, by practising Meditation (*adhicitta*) to the Path of the Non-Returner, and by practising Wisdom (*adhiprajñā*) to the Path of the Arahant. Comparing this scheme with the Eleven Abodes (*vihāras*) of the *Bodhisattvabhūmi-śāstra* and the Ten Stages of the *Daśabhūmika-sūtra,* the principal Mahayana authorities on the stages of the Bodhisattva's career, we find that *vihāras* 4-8 and *bhūmis* 2-6 both correspond with the Threefold Path and both, therefore, not only with each other but with the Four Transcendental Paths of the Hinayana. These correspondences may be set forth as follows:—

Adhiśīla		
Srotāpatti	*(4) Adhiśīla-vihāra*	*(2) Vimala-bhūmi*
Sakridāgāmin		
Adhicitta		
Anāgāmin	*(5) Adhicitta-vihāra*	*(3) Prabhākari-bhūmi*

Adhiprajñā			
Arahant	*(6) Adhiprajñā-vihāra*	*I*	*(4) Arciṣmati-bhūmī*
	(7) "	*II*	*(5) Sudurjaya-bhūmī*
	(8) "	*III*	*(6) Abhimukhī-bhūmi*

Into this complicated scheme the Six *Pāramitās* too, can be brought, at least partially. For, as we have seen, they are in essential correspondence with the Threefold Path. The Perfection of Patience and the Perfection of Vigour, being a later interpolation are, however, supernumerary. The direct correlation of the Six *Pāramitās* with the first six *bhūmis* (the Perfection of Giving corresponding to *pramudita*, the first *bhūmi*), so that one perfection was practised at each Stage, would amount to a repudiation of the correlation with Morality, Meditation and Wisdom, as well as of that with the Four Stages of the Transcendental Path. This would mean the complete dislocation of the scheme tabulated above. But it is exactly this that the *Daśabhūmika* does. In fact it does something bolder still. Taking over the four additional *pāramitās* which had been merely mentioned in earlier works, and increasing the Stages to the number recognized by the *Mahāvastu* and the *Śatasāhasrikā*, it establishes a scheme of its own, the most striking feature of which is a parallelism between the Ten Perfections and the Ten Stages, the practice of one *pāramitā* predominating in each *bhūmi*. On the basis of this parallelism it erects a magnificent architectonic system in which it manages to include all the important doctrinal categories, both Mahayanic and Hinayanic. Scholars see in this departure the influence of the decimal system, which seems to have been invented at about the same time as the composition of the great Mahayana *sūtras*. The explanation may hold good in the case of the Ten Perfections. But for the origin of the scheme of Ten Stages there seems to be a profounder reason.

As we have repeatedly insisted, the difference between the Mahayana and the Hinayana is at bottom one of attitude. All the great doctrinal categories are common to both, but whereas to the Hinayana they are true in the absolute sense, to the Mahayana they are true only relatively. From the Mahayana point of view, therefore, each of these categories has a double significance, one Hinayanic, the other Mahayanic. The more the two great traditions diverged from each other the less in common there was between their respective usages of the same terms. *Prajñā* as the Wisdom of the Arahant was quite a different thing from *Prajñā* as the Wisdom of the Bodhisattva. The term Arahant itself, originally synonymous in spiritual essence with the term Buddha, owing to the narrowly individualistic manner in which it was understood by the Hinayanists, came to be looked upon by the Mahayanists as representing an ideal infinitely inferior to that of the Bodhisattva.

Rather than discard the Hinayana and its categories altogether, thus interrupting the continuity of tradition, the Mahayana solved the problem by first more or less duplicating the Stages of the Path and then by placing the two sets of terms thus obtained as it were end to end to form one continuous series. The first set of terms, corresponding to *bhūmis* 1-6 of the *Daśabhūmika,* were Hinayanic, and carried the aspirant as far as Arahantship; the second was Mahayanic, and carried him to Supreme Buddhahood. According to this revised scheme, the Sixth *Pāramitā* no longer stood for Wisdom in the Mahayanic sense—which was promoted to the Tenth Stage and termed *jñāna*—but simply the Wisdom of the Arahant. Owing to the simplicity and grandeur of its general conception, as well as the skill with which it incorporated all the prodigious wealth of Buddhist tradition, the *Daśabhūmika's* account of the Ten Stages of the Bodhisattva's career has won recognition as the best and most authoritative account of this vitally important subject. With an enumeration of these Ten Stages we shall therefore bring to a close our account of the Bodhisattva Ideal.

But first we must briefly describe the four additional *pāramitās* which, though originally a very unremarkable group, are in the *Daśabhūmika* among the twenty great categories which, like the columns of a Doric temple, majestically uphold the ponderous doctrinal and methodological superstructure.

The four additional *pāramitās* are (1) *upāya-kauśalya,* (2) *praṇidhāna,* (3) *bala* and (4) *jñāna.*

(1) *Upāya-kauśalya-pāramitā,* or the Perfection of Skilful Means, is explained by Har Dayal as "skilfulness or wisdom in the choice or adoption of the means or expedients for converting others or helping them."[1] Though it is not until the Fifth Stage that he

[1] *The Bodhisattva Doctrine in Buddhist Sanskrit Literature,* p. 248.

becomes a fully qualified preacher, the inclusion of *Dharma-dāna* in the Perfection of Giving shows that from the very outset of his career the Bodhisattva cultivates the practice of sharing with others whatever truth he acquires. Wisdom and Compassion being inseparable, the systole and diastole of the Bodhisattva's heart, it is no more possible for him to receive without giving, whether on the material, the intellectual or the transcendental plane, than it is possible for the physical heart to contract without expanding, or for the lungs to go on breathing in without ever breathing out. In the Tantra *upāya* is, in fact, the technical term for Compassion. A number of Mahayana *sūtras* and *śāstras* enumerate at length the moral, intellectual and spiritual qualities which as an ideal preacher of the Dharma the Bodhisattva is expected to possess. In a far more literal sense than was intended by the Apostle to the Gentiles, be is expected to be "all things to all men." Japanese Buddhist tradition frequently represents Fugen Bosatsu (the Bodhisattva Samantabhadra) as assuming the form of a beautiful young courtezan in order to preach to those addicted to carnal pleasure. Not all preachers are expected to go to such lengths. Some of the more important requisities for successful propaganda are classified as (a) the four "Elements of Conversion" (*sangraha-vastus*); (b) the four "Analytical Knowledges" (*pratisaṁvids*); and (c) the "Magical Formulæ" (*dhāraṇīs*).

(a) The "Elements of Conversion" are (i) Giving (*dāna*), which has already been discussed; (ii) Loving Speech (*priya-vāditā*); (iii) Doing Good (*artha-caryā* or *artha-kriyā*), in the technical sense of exhorting and encouraging others to lead the holy life; and (iv) Exemplification (*samānārthāta*), or the practice of the virtues we recommend to our neighbours.

(b) The "Analytical Knowledges" are (i) the Analytical Knowledge of Phenomena (*dharma-pratisaṁvid*), in both their appearance and their reality: according to the *Daśabhūmika* this includes knowledge that the various Ways (of the Buddhist tradition) meet together in the One Way; (ii) the Analytical Knowledge of Meaning (*artha-pratisaṁvid*) by which is meant knowledge of the characteristics of phenomena, and of the various categories of the Doctrine; (iii) the Analytical Knowledge of Etymology (*nirukti-pratisaṁvid*), which besides denoting knowledge of etymology connotes a thorough acquaintance with such subjects as linguistics, public speaking and literary composition: this enables the Bodhisattva to avoid confusing the spirit and the letter of the Teaching, as well as to give with complete impartiality instruction in all the *yānas*; and (iv) the Analytical Knowledge of Courage, by which is meant "courage and boldness in speech, ready address."

(c) The "Magical Formulæ" are strings of syllables, often without meaning, the constant repetition of which sets up powerful protective vibrations that safeguard the preacher from harm at the hands of enemies and non-human beings. Such *dhāraṇīs* are generally taught to the Bodhisattva by benevolent deities who undertake to protect him from danger.

(2) *Praṇidhāna* or Vow has already been discussed in Section IV. Its elevation to the status of an independent *pāramitā* is indicative of the immense importance which it gradually assumed in the eyes of the Mahayanists.

(3) *Bala-pāramitā,* the Perfection of Strength or Power, is twofold, consisting of both a group of five and a group of ten powers. The Five Powers are simply the Five Spiritual Faculties in their dynamic aspect. The Ten Powers of which there are two different lists, not having been described in detail are of merely theoretical interest. Nowhere is the necessity of making up by some means or other the full complement of ten Perfections more nakedly apparent than in the case of this *pāramitā.*

(4) *Jñāna-pāramitā,* or the Perfection of Knowledge, the fourth and last of the additional Perfections, differs from the Perfection of Wisdom only in name and need not be separately discussed.

To give a brief and intelligible, yet at the same time faithful, description of the Ten Stages of the Bodhisattva's career, is, if possible at all, possible only for one who is upheld by the sustaining power of All the Buddhas. Not only do the *Daśabhūmika* and other *sūtras* describe each of the *bhūmis* in bewildering, dazzling detail, but they lavish upon each one the same superlatives, the same incredible superabundance of spiritual qualities, so that the reader is sometimes at a loss how to distinguish one from another. There are stars which, owing to their immense distance from the earth, appear to the naked eye to be no bigger than those stars which, though thousands of times smaller, are much closer to us. So it is with the *bhūmis.* Language is incapable of effectively distinguishing between them. Though we may speak of a fourth, a fifth, and a sixth dimension we are really multiplying words without meaning, for we can form no conception at all of such dimensions. In the same way, though we may reproduce the traditional descriptions of the *bhūmis* they will not mean anything to us, for there is nothing analogous to them in our experience. They are concerned essentially with the Transcendental. Hence we shall do no more than enumerate the principal doctrinal and methodological categories associated, according to the *Daśabhūmika,* with each of the Ten Stages. Those whose intellectual curiosity is unsatisfied by our own meagre account may consult Nalinaksha Dutt's *Aspects of Mahayana Buddhism and its Relation to Hinayana* and Har Dayal's *The Bodhisattva Doctrine in Buddhist Sanskrit Literature* for further information.

(1) *Pramudita,* or the Joyful, is entered upon immediately after the Production of the Thought of Enlightenment. As he thinks of the Supremely Enlightened Ones and of the Bodhisattva's career, and realizes that he is not only free from the fear of evil rebirths but assured of attaining Buddhahood for the sake of all sentient beings, the heart of the newly arisen Bodhisattva is flooded with an overwhelming joy. He develops, among other noble qualities, the Seven Factors of Enlightenment and makes his Ten Great Vows. In this *bhūmi* he especially devotes himself to the practice of Giving, which is both the first Perfection and the first of the Means of Conversion.

(2) *Vimala,* or the Immaculate, is attained by perfect purity of conduct. In this *bhūmi* the Bodhisattva scrupulously observes the Ten Ways of Wholesome Action and exhorts others to observe them likewise. Without neglecting the other Perfections, he pays special attention to the Perfection of Morality, and practises the second Means of Conversion, Loving Speech.

(3) *Prabhākarī,* or the Illuminating, indicates that in this stage the natural radiance of the Bodhisattva's mind shines forth unclouded by adventitious defilements. Realizing that his body is on fire with lust, hatred and delusion, he develops disgust and aversion for worldly things. Longing more intensely than ever for Supreme Enlightenment, he devotes himself day and night to the study of the Scriptures and the practice of Meditation. He experiences the four *dhyānas,* the four "formless attainments," the four *brahma-vihāras* and the six *abhijñās.* Though the text

describes him as specializing in the practice of the Perfection of Patience, it is obvious that in this *bhūmi* the Bodhisattva is more concerned with the Perfection of Meditation. The discrepancy obviously is due to the lingering influence of the categories of the Threefold Path. At this stage the Bodhisattva practises the third Means of Conversion, Doing Good.

(4) *Arciṣmatī,* the Blazing, is so called because in this *bhūmi* the Bodhisattva burns up the twin "coverings" (*āvaraṇa*) of defilement and ignorance by means of the rays of the *bodhipakṣya dharmas,* the thirty-seven principles conducive to Enlightenment. He enters into the Light of the Doctrine (*dharmāloka*) by obtaining insight into the realm of sentient being (*sattvadhātu*), of the worlds (*lokadhātu*), of the universe (*dharmadhātu*), of space (*ākāśadhātu*), of consciousness (*vijñānadhātu*), of desires (*kāmadhātu*), of forms (*rūpadhātu*), of formlessness (*ārūpyadhātu*), of noble intention and aspiration (*udārādhyāśayādhimuktidhātu*), and of magnanimous intention and aspiration (*māhātmyādhyāśayādhimuktidhātu*). It is noteworthy that despite his having already attained to great spiritual heights in the previous *bhūmis,* it is only at this Stage that the Bodhisattva is able to rid himself of wrong ideas based on the notion of a permanent *ātman.* Concentrating on the development of the Perfection of Vigour, the Bodhisattva in this *bhūmi* radiates energy as the sun radiates heat and light. He also practises Exemplification, the fourth Means of Conversion.

(5) *Sudurjayā,* or the Very Difficult to Conquer, refers to the Bodhisattva rather than to the stage itself: Mara is now hardly able to overcome him. He develops purity and equanimity (*cittāśaya-viśuddhisamatā*) with regard to: the *dharmas* of the past, present and future Buddhas; Morality; Meditation; removal of wrong views and doubts; knowledge of the right and the wrong path; practice of the principles conducive to Enlightenment; and the "maturing" of all beings. By this means he is able to understand not only the Four Truths, but also the various other aspects of Truth, from the relative truth and the Absolute Truth up to the Truth of the Origin of the Tathāgata-Knowledge. This in turn enables him to realize the emptiness of phenomena and the futility of a life of worldliness; he pities those who are the slaves of lust and pride. In this Stage he especially cultivates the Perfection of Meditation, practises all four Means of Conver-

sion, acquires a knowledge of all the arts and sciences, and receives from the devas various *dhāraṇīs* for his protection when preaching the Doctrine.

(6) *Abhimukhī*, or the Face-to-Face, is so called because in it the Bodhisattva stands as it were face to face with Reality. He realizes the absolute sameness of all phenomena in ten different ways, namely, in respect of their being all alike "signless" (*animitta*), devoid of characteristics (*alakṣaṇa*), unoriginated (*ajāta*), detached (*vivikta*), pure from the very beginning (*ādiviśuddha*), inexpressible (*niṣprapañca*), neither accepted nor rejected (*anāyūhaniryūha*), similar to a dream, an optical illusion, the reflection of the moon in water, and an echo (*māyāsvapnapratibhāsapratiśrutkopama*), and the identity (literally non-duality) of existence and non-existence (*bhāvābhāvādvaya*). Through his tenfold comprehension of the formula of Conditioned Co-production, which exhibits the seeds of defilement as originating in our own consciousness, he realizes that the tree of suffering grows without there being any doer or feeler, and that the three worlds are in reality nothing but absolute Mind (*cittamātra*). He apprehends Reality under its three modes, the Signless, the Wishless, and Emptiness, and obtains the corresponding Emancipations. In this *bhūmi*, in which the Bodhisattva is represented as having gained in addition to the attributes of a Bodhisattva all the qualities of an Arahant, he particularly practises the Perfection of Wisdom. But where the Hinayana ends the Mahayana begins.

(7) *Dūraṅgamā*, or the Far-Going, is so called because commencing from this *bhūmi* the Bodhisattva, transcending the Hinayana, moves in the direction of Supreme Enlightenment, the goal of the One Way of the Mahayana. From this point onwards all attempts to describe the Stages through which he passes must inevitably result in positive misrepresentation. Attaining Emancipation without entering personal Nirvana, as he does in this Stage, the Bodhisattva's progress is no longer that of an individual. He is now an impersonal cosmic force, and his activities are part of the omnipresent transcendental activities of the *Dharmakāya*. That we perceive him functioning as an individual being is due simply to our mental defilements. According to the statement of the *sūtras*, which are of course not meant to be taken literally, "the Bodhisattva" embarks upon the distinctively

Mahayanic Path with the help of the ten kinds of Knowledge of Skilful Means (*upāyaprajñājñāna*). Not even for a moment does he remain dissociated from activities pertaining to the Path and activities pertaining to Knowledge. He fulfils the Ten Perfections, the four Means of Conversion, the four Resolutions, and thirty-seven principles conducive to Enlightenment. Walking upon the ten paths of wholesome action of a Supreme Buddha, he performs spontaneously the functions connected with the various arts and sciences mastered in the fifth Stage, and becomes the teacher of the 3,000 worlds. In accordance with his Great Vow he appears in the various planes of mundane existence in order to help and deliver sentient beings. Though generally appearing in all his true spiritual glory, so great is his compassion that he does not hesitate to assume, if necessary, the form of a Sravaka, a Pratyekabuddha, or even an evil-doer or a follower of a non-Buddhist teacher. In this *bhūmi* the Perfection of Skilful Means is the object of special cultivation.

(8) *Acalā,* or the Immovable, is the *bhūmi* in which the Bodhisattva, undisturbed by the twin concepts of causation and no-causation, develops the *kṣānti* known as *anutpattika-dharma-kṣāntiḥ,* or acquiescence in the unoriginatedness of phenomena. The Buddhas, by reminding him of his Great Vow, once and for all prevent him from relapsing into personal Nirvana, and encourage him to acquire like Them an immeasurable body, worlds, effulgence, purity of voice and limbs, insight into the ten worlds, Buddha-field, beings, and variety of *dharmas* of the ten directions, all of which are indispensable to Supreme Enlightenment. He knows in detail the evolution and involution of the universe, the composition of its elements and the nature of its beings. He is now in possession of all the qualities of a Buddha, in consequence of which the possibility of retrogression is permanently precluded. So important is this *bhūmi,* in which the Perfection of Vows receives the greatest attention, that it is termed the Stage of Perfection, Birth and Finality.

(9) *Sādhumatī,* or Good Thoughts, is so called because in this Stage the Bodhisattva possesses good thoughts on account of the Analytical Knowledge he has acquired. He knows truly the distinctive characteristics of all *dharmas*; he knows the duties of the Sravakas, Pratyekabuddhas, Bodhisattvas and Buddhas; he knows thoroughly all the thoughts and desires of men, in their

minutest particulars, and is able to preach to them in accordance with their respective temperaments. In this *bhūmi* he dwells continually in the sight of the Buddhas and practises the Perfection of Strength.

(10) *Dharmamegha,* the Cloud of the Doctrine, according to one authority is thus called because it is pervaded by various *samādhis* and *dhāraṇīs* as the sky with clouds. As the result of these *samādhis* there appears a magnificent jewel-adorned lotus of infinite size and radiance on which the Bodhisattva, with a no less glorious body, appears seated in the Samadhi of the Consecration of Omniscience. He is surrounded by countless Bodhisattvas belonging to the nine Stages, all of whom have their eyes steadfastly fixed upon him. The rays of light issuing from his body make happy all sentient beings. While he is thus seated on the jewel-lotus rays come forth from All the Buddhas and consecrate him as a *Tathāgata* possessed of Omniscience. This stage is therefore called the Stage of Consecration. The Bodhisattva, now a Supreme Buddha, has reached the "endless end" of his career. Having practised in this Stage the Perfection of Knowledge, he performs feats of supernormal power and emanates the countless Transcendental Forms through which, in fulfilment of His Great Original Vow, He will henceforth work for the emancipation of all sentient beings.

Select Bibliography of Translations, Surveys and Studies

Not all of the books in this section are free from the drawbacks described in Chapter I, Section II. But they are the best available, and the student who utilizes them as a whole, in the light of the principles we have formulated and endeavoured to apply, will not go far astray. Though an attempt has been made to distribute them under our chapter headings there has, inevitably, been much overlapping. Moreover, the emphasis of the *Survey* being on matters doctrinal and spiritual, works dealing with Buddhist art, history, biography, jurisprudence, etc., have been omitted. The dates of publication given below are the latest edition known to me.

GENERAL

Texts

Buddhist Texts Through the Ages. Edited by Edward Conze. New York: Harper & Row, 1954.

The Teachings of the Compassionate Buddha. Edited by E. A. Burtt. New York: Mentor, 1955.

A Buddhist Bible. Edited by D. Goddard. Boston: Beacon Press, 1970.

The Buddhist Experience: Sources and Interpretations. Stephan Beyer. Belmont, Calif.: Dickenson Publishing Co., Inc., 1974.

Surveys

Buddhism: Its Essence and Development. Edward Conze. New York: Harper & Row, 1963.

The Path of the Buddha. Edited by K. W. Morgan. New York: Ronald Press, 1956.

The Three Jewels. Bhikshu Sangharakshita (Sthavira). London: Windhorse Publications, 1977.

Studies

Buddhism: A Non-Theistic Religion. Helmuth von Glasenapp. London: Allen & Unwin, 1970.

CHAPTER I

Texts

Buddhism in Translations. Translated by Henry Clark Warren. New York: Atheneum, 1963.

Some Sayings of the Buddha. Translated by F. L. Woodward. London: Oxford University Press, 1973.

Early Buddhist Scriptures. Translated by E. J. Thomas. London: Kegan Paul, 1935.

Dialogues of the Buddha. Translated by T. W. Rhys Davids. 3 vols. London: The Pali Text Society, 1971-1973.

The Collection of the Middle Length Sayings. (*Majjhima-Nikāya*). Translated by I. B. Horner. 3 vols. London: Luzac & Co., Ltd., 1967.

Woven Cadences of Early Buddhists. (*Sutta-Nipāta*). Translated by E. M. Hare. London: Oxford University Press, 1947.

The Minor Anthologies of the Pāli Canon, Part II. "Udāna: Verses of Uplift and Itivuttaka: As It Was Said." Translated by F. L. Woodward. London: Geoffrey Cumberlege, 1948.

The Dhammapada. Translated by N. K. Bhagwat. Bombay: The Buddha Society, 1935.

The Mahāvastu. Translated by J. J. Jones. 3 vols. London: Luzac & Co., Ltd., 1949, 1952, 1956.

The Questions of King Milinda. Translated by T. W. Rhys Davids. 2 vols. New York: Dover Publications, 1963.

Buddhist Meditation. Translated by Edward Conze. New York: Harper & Row, 1956.

Buddhist Monastic Discipline: The Sanskrit Prātimokṣa Sūtras of the Mahāsāmghikas and Mūlusarvāstivādins. Charles S. Prebish. University Park, Pa. and London: The Pennsylvania State University Press, 1975.

Studies

Sarvāstivāda Literature. A. C. Banerjee. Calcutta: D. Banerjee, 1957.

The Doctrine of Awakening. J. Evola. London: Luzac & Co., Ltd., 1951.

Buddhist Meditation in Theory and Practice. P. Vajirañāṇa Mahā Thera. Kuala Lumpur: Buddhist Missionary Society, 1975.

The Heart of Buddhist Meditation. Nyānaponika Thera. New York: Samuel Weiser, 1972.

CHAPTER II

Texts

HINAYANA

The Path of Purification. (*Visuddhimagga*). Bhadantācariya Buddhaghosa. Translated by Bhikkhu Ñānamoli. 2 vols. Boulder and London: Shambhala Publications, 1976.

The Abhidhamma Philosophy. J. Kashyap. Sarnath, India: Maha Bodhi Society of India, 1942.

MAHAYANA

Most of the following texts are especially connected with one or another of the main Mahayana schools, but since each and every text is revered by all schools they have been listed under this chapter rather than under the next.

Buddhist Mahāyāna Sūtras. Translated by E. B. Cowell, F. M. Muller, and J. Takakusu. The Sacred Books of the East, vol. 49. Oxford: Clarendon Press, 1894.

Manual of Zen Buddhism. D. T. Suzuki. London: Rider & Co., 1956.

Chinese Buddhist Verse. Translated by R. Robinson. London: John Murray, 1954.

Scripture of the Lotus Blossom of the Fine Dharma. Translated by Leon Hurvitz. (Translated from the Chinese of Kumārajīva.) New York: Columbia University Press, 1976.

The Lotus of the Wonderful Law. W. E. Soothill. Oxford, 1930.

Selected Sayings from the Perfection of Wisdom. Translated by Edward Conze. Boulder: Prajñā Press, 1978.

The Perfection of Wisdom in Eight Thousand Lines and Its Verse Summary. Translated by Edward Conze. Bolinas, Calif.: Four Seasons Foundation, 1973.

Buddhist Wisdom Books. Translated and explained by Edward Conze. (Containing the *Diamond Sutra* and the *Heart Sutra*). New York: Harper & Row, 1975.

The Holy Teaching of Vimalakīrti: A Mahāyāna Scripture. Translated by Robert A. F. Thurman. University Park, Pa. and London: The Pennsylvania State University Press, 1976.

The Lion's Roar of Queen Śrīmālā: A Buddhist Scripture on the Tathāgatagarbha Theory. Translated with an introduction and notes by Alex Wayman and Hideko Wayman. New York: Columbia University Press, 1974.

The Sūtra of Golden Light. (*Suvarṇabhāsottamasūtra*). Translated by R. E. Emmerick. London: Luzac & Co., Ltd., 1970.

The Laṅkāvatāra Sūtra. Translated by D. T. Suzuki. Boulder: Prajñā Press, 1979.

The Śūraṅgama Sūtra. (*Leng Yen Ching*). Translated by Upasaka Lu K'uan Yü (Charles Luk). London: Rider & Co., 1973.

The Precious Garland and the Song of the Four Mindfulnesses. Nāgārjuna and the Seventh Dalai Lama. Translated and edited by Jeffrey Hopkins and Lati Rinpoche. London: Allen & Unwin, 1975.

Mahāyānaviṃśaka of Nāgārjuna. Translated and edited by V. Bhattacharya. Calcutta, 1931.

Studies

COMPARATIVE

Aspects of Mahāyāna Buddhism in Its Relation to Hīnayāna. N. Dutt. London: Luzac & Co., Ltd., 1930.

Philosophy and Psychology in the Abhidharma. Herbert V. Guenther. Boulder and London: Shambhala Publications, 1975.

HINAYANA

The Central Conception of Buddhism and the Meaning of the Word "Dharma". T. Stcherbatsky. Calcutta: Susil Gupta, 1961.

Guide Through the Abhidhamma-Pitaka. Nyānatiloka. Colombo, Ceylon: Buddha-Sahitya-Sabha, 1938.

Abhidhamma Studies. Nyānapoṇika Thera. Colombo, Ceylon: Frewin & Co., 1949.

The Psychological Attitude of Early Buddhist Philosophy. Lama A. Govinda. New York: Samuel Weiser, 1961.

The Four Essential Doctrines of Buddhism. C.L.A. de Silva. Colombo, Ceylon, 1948.

Early Buddhist Monachism. Sukumar Dutt. Bombay: Asia Publishing House, 1960.

MAHAYANA

An Introduction to Mahāyāna Buddhism. W. M. McGovern, Varanasi, India: Sahitya Ratan Mala Karyalaya, 1968.

On Indian Mahāyāna Buddhism. D. T. Suzuki. Edited with an introduction by Edward Conze. New York: Harper & Row, 1968.

CHAPTER III

General

[The following two works deal mainly with Mahayana schools.]

Systems of Buddhistic Thought. Y. Sogen. Calcutta: University of Calcutta, 1912.

The Essentials of Buddhist Philosophy. J. Takakusu. Bombay: Asia Publishing House, 1956.

Buddhist Though in India: Three Phases of Buddhist Philosophy. Edward Conze. Ann Arbor: University of Michigan Press, Ann Arbor Paperbacks, 1967.

Individual Schools

THE NEW WISDOM SCHOOL

Nāgārjuna: A Translation of His Mūlamadhyamakakārikā with an Introductory Essay. Translated by Kenneth K. Inada. Tokyo: The Hokuseido Press, 1970.

Emptiness: A Study in Religious Meaning. Frederick J. Streng. Nashville and New York: Abingdon Press, 1967.

Nāgārjuna's Philosophy: As Presented in the Mahāprajñāpāramitā-Śāstra. K. Venkata Ramanan. London: Books from India, Ltd., 1976.

The Central Philosophy of Buddhism. T.R.V. Murti. London: Allen & Unwin, 1955.

Early Mādhyamika in India and China. Richard H. Robinson. Madison, Milwaukee, and London: The University of Wisconsin Press, 1967.

THE BUDDHISM OF FAITH AND DEVOTION

Śatapañcāśatkastotra of Matṛceta. Translated and edited by D.R. Shackleton-Bailey. Cambridge, 1951.

Amitābha: The Life of Naturalness. K. Kanamatsu. Higashi Honganji, Kyoto: Otani Publishing Co., 1949.

Shin Buddhism. D.T. Suzuki. New York: Harper & Row, 1970.

BUDDHIST IDEALISM

Ch'eng Wei-Shih Lun: The Doctrine of Mere-Consciousness. Hsüan Tsang. Translated by Wei Tat. Hong Kong: The Ch'eng Wei-Shih Lun Publication Committee, 1973.

The Trisvabhāvanirdeśa of Vasubandhu. Translated and edited by S. Mukhopadhyaya. India: Visvabharati, 1939.

Mind in Buddhist Psychology. Translated by Herbert V. Guenther and Leslie S. Kawamura. Emeryville, Calif.: Dharma Publishing, 1975.

The Awakening of Faith. Attributed to Aśvaghosha. Translated with commentary by Yoshito S. Hakeda. New York: Columbia University Press, 1967.

Hua-yen Buddhism: The Jewel Net of Indra. Francis H. Cook. University Park, Pa. and London: The Pennsylvania State University Press, 1977.

The Buddhist Teaching of Totality: The Philosophy of Hua Yen Buddhism. Garma C. C. Chang. University Park, Pa. and London: The Pennsylvania State University Press, 1971.

The Platform Scripture. Translated with an introduction and notes by Wing-Tsit Chan. New York: St. John's University Press, 1963.

The Blue Cliff Record. (*Pi Yen Lu*). Translated by Thomas and J. C. Cleary. 3 vols. Boulder and London: Shambhala Publications, 1977.

A First Zen Reader. Compiled and translated by Trevor Leggett. Rutland, Vt. and Tokyo: Charles E. Tuttle Co., 1963.

The Tiger's Cave: Translations of Japanese Zen Texts. London: Routledge & Kegan Paul, 1977.

A Primer of Sōtō Zen. (*Shōbōgenzō Zuimonki*). Dōgen. Translated by Reihō Masunaga. Honolulu: University of Hawaii Press, 1972.

The Zen Master Hakuin: Selected Writings. Translated by Phillip Yampolsky. New York: Columbia University Press, 1971.

THE TANTRA OR MAGICAL BUDDHISM

The Hevajra Tantra: A Critical Study. Translated and edited with a commentary by D. L. Snellgrove. "Part I: Introduction and Translation" (one of two volumes). London: Oxford University Press, 1959.

The Royal Song of Saraha: A Study in the History of Buddhist Thought. Translated and annotated by Herbert V. Guenther. Boulder & London: Shambhala Publications, 1973.

An Introduction to Tantric Buddhism. Shashi Bhushan Dasgupta. Boulder and London: Shambhala Publications, 1974.

The Buddhist Tantras: Light on Indo-Tibetan Esoterism. Alex Wayman. New York: Samuel Weiser, 1973.

Buddhist Himalaya. David L. Snellgrove. Oxford: Ernest Cassirer, 1957.

The Hundred Thousand Songs of Milarepa. Translated and annotated by Garma C. C. Chang. 2 vols. Boulder and London: Shambhala Publications, 1977.

Mkhas Grub Rje's Fundamentals of the Buddhist Tantras. Translated by Ferdinand D. Lessing and Alex Wayman. The Hague and Paris: Mouton, 1968.

Kūkai: Major Works. Translated with an account of his life and a study of his thought by Yoshito S. Hakeda. New York: Columbia University Press, 1972.

CHAPTER IV

Texts

Jātaka Tales. Translated by H. T. Francis and E. J. Thomas, Cambridge, 1916.

The Perfect Generosity of Prince Vessantara: A Buddhist Epic. Translated by Margaret Cone and Richard F. Gombrich. (Illustrated by unpublished paintings from the Sinhalese temples.) Oxford: Clarendon Press, 1977.

Entering the Path of Enlightenment. (*Bodhicaryāvatāra*). Śāntideva. Translated with a guide by Marion L. Matics. London: Allen & Unwin, 1971.

The Path of Light. (*Bodhicaryāvatāra*). Śāntideva. Translated by L. Barnett. London: John Murray, 1947.

Śikṣā-Samuccaya: A Compendium of Buddhist Doctrine. Compiled by Śāntideva. Translated by Cecil Bendall and W.H.D. Rouse. Delhi: Motilal Banarsidass, 1971.

The Jewel Ornament of Liberation. sGam.po.pa. Translated and annotated by Herbert V. Guenther. Boulder and London: Shambhala Publications, 1971.

Studies

The Bodhisattva Doctrine in Buddhist Sanskrit Literature. Har Dayal. London: Kegan Paul, 1932.

INDEX

[The terms Buddha, Dharma, Sangha and their equivalents, as well as subjects dealt with in special subdivisions, have with a very few exceptions not been indexed. Where both the Sanskrit and the Pali forms of a word have been used the latter follows the former in brackets. Words appearing in the text without diacritical marks have occasionally been equipped with them in the Index.]

A

B

N

R

T

U

DEC 16 1992